CONTENTS

Football Club United Of Manchester was officially formed in June 2005, but the seeds had been sown during the previous months as American businessman Malcolm Glazer and his family were signalling their intention to complete a takeover of Manchester United. They had been gradually buying up shares since 2003, but when details emerged in October 2004 of their intention to launch a full bid, the nature of the terms of the takeover were unacceptable to many United supporters.

As the Glazers increased their stake in February 2005, an article proposing the formation of a breakaway club was published in the influential fanzine *Red Issue*, penned by the magazine's editor John-Paul O'Neill. He admitted that the article was only intended as a propaganda piece, one of many options that could be used to fight the takeover attempt. But when Glazer bought the stake of the highest shareholders the Coolmore racing conglomerate on 12th May, it took his holding over the 30% threshold required to launch a formal takeover bid.

The next evening, at the annual *Red Issue* curry night, the focus was on organising fan opposition to the takeover. Calls to boycott matches and sponsors were made, ahead of a fans meeting quickly organised by the fanzines and IMUSA at Manchester's Central Methodist Hall on 19th May. AFC Wimbledon's Kris Stewart spoke of the virtues of fan-owned clubs, as he also did at a larger rally at the Apollo on Bank Holiday Monday 30th May. The number of pledges to support a new club fell just short of the aspired level, but Stewart encouraged the organisers to have faith in their convictions.

With the help of Luc Zentar, Russ Delaney, Mike Adams and Jules Spencer, O'Neill had already moved to register a limited company and enquired with the Northern Premier League and North West Counties Football League. Joining them on the Steering Committee were Pete Munday, Tony Pritchard, Vasco Wackrill, Tony Jordan, Martin Morris, Rob Brady, Adam Brown, Andy Walsh, Andrew Howse, Phil Bedford and Phil Sheeran.

Between them the group spent the next few hectic weeks working on a number of crucial tasks. These included the preparation of a business plan; writing the club's constitution; corresponding with the Football Association and affiliating to the local Manchester FA; dealing with copyright registration; setting up a website for information and to receive pledges; organising designs for the club's badge and kits; finding a manager for the new team, as well as a ground to play at.

With the club's name still not decided, the committee whittled down the suggestions and put the options to an online vote. The choices were FC United Of Manchester, FC Manchester Central, AFC Manchester 1878 and Newton Heath United, the latter added shortly before voting commenced on 9th June. The polls closed at 5pm on 13th June, with the winning name gaining 44.7% of the response. The following day, the club was registered with the FA as a formal application was made to join the NWCFL, and FC United became a viable entity when accepted at the league's AGM in Kendal on 18th June.

At the start of that week, two candidates had been interviewed for the role of the team's manager. The committee's choice was 34-year-old ex-professional and non-league veteran Karl Marginson, who had recently retired from playing and was making his way into coaching. His appointment was announced at the Midland Hotel on 22nd June, during a press conference held to launch the club to the world. Marginson immediately began to work alongside members of the steering group to source training facilities and organise friendly matches, and persuaded former playing colleagues Phil Power and Darren Lyons to work with him. They ran the rule over 200 players at an open trials day held at the Armitage Centre in Fallowfield on 26th June, from which they invited 17 to join those Margy had already recruited at the first training session at Parrs Wood High School two days later.

Finding a ground for the team's home games was one of the biggest issues. An offer to share was made by Leigh RMI, but their location was considered too far from central Manchester. However, an outline agreement was made in order to satisfy the league entry requirements, and in return Leigh would host FC's first ever game. The preferred option, and the frontrunner for several weeks, was Droylsden, but news emerged late in June that their lease did not permit a groundshare.

The club was ratified as an Industrial & Provident Society at the inaugural EGM at the Methodist Hall on Tuesday 5th July. Delaney, Spencer, Munday, Pritchard, Morris, Wackrill, Brown, Walsh, Bedford and Sheeran were joined by Scott Fletcher and Joe Tully as the 11 successful candidates from 23 applicants to form the club's first board. A vote to decide the club's crest was also held, and Tempest were announced as the kit supplier.

Ten days later, an agreement to play at Bury's Gigg Lane finally announced, the day before the team took to the field for the first time in a friendly at Leigh's Hilton Park. A crowd of 2,552 witnessed a 0-0 draw which was followed by a joyous pitch invasion. Defeats at Wimbledon and Stalybridge Celtic left us still awaiting the club's first goal, but that duly arrived in the final warm-up game at Flixton when Steve Torpey's long-range dipper hit the back of the net to set up a 5-2 win.

FC United Of Manchester's first ever game was the friendly at Leigh RMI on 16th July 2005

FC United of Manchester's squad line-up ahead of the club's first ever game at Leigh RMI on 16th July 2005:
Back: Phil Power, Rob Trees, Kevin Elvin, Craig Fleury, Rob Nugent, Joz Mitten, Billy McCartney, Barrie George, Matt Weston, Scott Holt, Ryan Gilligan, Darren Lyons, Karl Marginson
Front: Matt Haley, Ryan Hevicon, Paul Mitten, Mark Rawlinson, Gareth Ormes, Tony Coyne, Steve Torpey, Luke Byrne, Adie Orr

This Badge Is Your Badge

Three designs for FC United's crest were put to the vote at the club's first Extraordinary General Meeting on 5th July 2005:

The winning badge, which gained over 50% of the vote, was designed by Matt Wilkinson, who also produced several other ideas for the club's crest. There was also an alternative version of Rick Healey's submission:

The full and detailed account of FC United's formation, and the events leading up to it in the summer of 2005 was told by **John-Paul O'Neill** in his book *Red Rebels* (published by Yellow Jersey in 2017)

2005/06: Inaugural season, North West Counties Football League Division Two

On 13th August 2005, Mark Rawlinson led the FC United team out away at Leek CSOB for the first competitive game in the North West Counties Football League Division Two, although the start of the game experienced some difficulties. Kick-off was delayed to cope with the crowd of 2,590, the opening exchanges were played out in a torrential downpour, and the hosts shocked FC by taking a 14th minute lead. In the 20th minute Steve Spencer levelled the score with United's first ever competitive goal before Joz Mitten put them ahead.

Spencer restored the advantage after a Leek equaliser, and further goals from Steve Torpey and Adie Orr earned a 5-2 win.

FC United's first home match at our adoptive home of Gigg Lane saw David Chadwick make his debut as captain as Padiham were beaten 3-2 thanks to a double from Rory Patterson and another from Orr, whilst the first night match saw a comprehensive 7-1 triumph over Eccleshall. The first points were dropped in a feisty encounter away to Winsford United, who were one of the division's strongest sides, but the team bounced back with consecutive wins over Ashton Town, Blackpool Mechanics and Castleton Gabriels.

Steve Torpey salutes his goal at Leek CSOB in FC United's first competitive fixture

OFFICIAL MATCHDAY PROGRAMME
VOLUME 1 · ISSUE ONE · £2.00

FC UNITED OF MANCHESTER
vs Padiham FC
Moore and Co Construction Solicitors Division 2
GIGG LANE, BURY · SATURDAY AUGUST 20 2005 · KICK OFF 3.00PM

INSIDE »»
GIGG LANE > MARGINSON > STEVE TORPEY
> FRIENDLIES > AWAY MATCH TRAVEL

OFFICIAL MATCH SPONSOR

An already iconic image of Joz Mitten raising his boots after the friendly at Leigh adorned FC's first home matchday programme

FC United fans pack out the Manchester Road End at Gigg Lane for the club's first home game against Padiham on 20th August 2005

Norton United hit two late goals at Gigg Lane to inflict FC's first competitive defeat in late September, though the Reds bounced back with four memorable victories as crowds began to rise above 3,000. A superb Simon Carden winner against Oldham Town preceded thrashings of Daisy Hill and Nelson in the league and Cheadle Town in the League Cup, during which Adie Orr became the first player to score a hat-trick for the club.

As we entered November, United had their first experience of two consecutive games without victory, failing to score for the first time in a 0-0 draw at Eccleshall and then exiting the League Cup away to Colne. Victories at Darwen and home to New Mills preceded a 3-3 draw away to Cheadle Town, but the month will mainly be remembered for the loss of two heroes. Steering group and board member Russell Delaney, whose determination despite illness played a huge part in ensuring that FC United was born, finally lost his long battle against lung disease just days before the passing of United legend George Best. Both received their own minutes of applause.

David Chadwick is engulfed by team-mates after his last-minute header earns a draw with Cheadle Town

The build-up to Christmas rewarded the team with progress in the Division Two trophy with another big win over New Mills, as well as record scoring feats as Simon Carden hit five goals

Joz Mitten celebrates with Josh Howard and Tony Coyne after his second goal in the club's record 10-2 win over Castleton Gabriels

in a 10-2 league defeat of Castleton Gabriels. He recorded his 16th in 12 games the following week at Holker Old Boys as the Reds held a 13-point lead at the top of the table.

The festive period threw up two tough fixtures, with a trip to third-placed Flixton on Boxing Day resulting in a 1-1 draw, followed by the visit of second-placed Winsford United on 2nd January. An amazing crowd of 4,328 were silenced by the visitors taking the lead early in the second half before Carden equalised after good work from debutant Leon Mike. With seven minutes remaining, substitute Patterson crashed home the winner to cue scenes of delirium in the stands.

The grip on the leadership was tightened during the rest of the month with victories over Darwen (when Josh Howard scored with an outrageous effort from near the touchline), Nelson and Ashton Town, but was tempered by the loss of Chadwick and Carden with injuries.

In February, our run in the Division Two Trophy was ended in the last minute of extra-time by a Nelson winner, but the team were immediately back to winning ways away to Daisy Hill. The following week came the much-anticipated trip to face Blackpool Mechanics at Bloomfield Road, with the majority of the 4,000 travelling supporters making a weekend of it, and they weren't disappointed with the 4-2 victory. The next league game saw a home match being played away from Gigg Lane for the first time, as Altrincham's Moss Lane hosted the 4-1 win over Holker Old Boys. The visitors' goal was scored by Dave Swarbrick, who joined FC United just a week later.

FC United players go wild in front of the MRE after Simon Carden's equaliser in the clash with title rivals Winsford United

A lone FC United fan toasts Rory Patterson's successful penalty against Great Harwood Town on a freezing February evening in Accrington. Reds photographer Thomas McEldowney won the BBC's prestigious Sport Photographer of the Year for this wonderfully iconic image

FC players celebrate after skipper David Chadwick's volley put the Reds ahead in the memorable trip to face Blackpool Mechanics

"It'll be off" had become a popular phrase amongst FC fans early in the year as several matches fell victim to the weather. In late January, the away game against Great Harwood Town was called off little more than an hour before kick-off, and was eventually played on a freezing Monday night a month later, resulting in a 1-1 draw. Following further postponements, the Reds resumed with a disappointing 1-2 reverse at home to challengers Flixton in mid-March. This prompted a minor shake-up of the team by the manager, and he was rewarded with wins over Leek CSOB, Oldham Town and New Mills.

By the start of April, FC held such a commanding lead at the top of the league table that fans were starting to work out when promotion could be confirmed. This appeared to be delayed by a 1-1 draw with Cheadle at home and then an equaliser by our first conquerors Norton United in the away game at Vale Park. However the Reds rallied again with two late goals to emerge 3-1 winners on a day that had experienced four seasons of weather during the match.

United now had four games remaining, and remarkably two of those were against Chadderton, a team we had not yet played home or away due to a series of postponements and rearrangements. When we eventually met them, a midweek crowd of just under 3,000 were ecstatic as they witnessed a 4-0 victory which confirmed that FC United had been promoted to Division One. Three days later, United were crowned as champions, despite only playing a friendly at Clitheroe, as closest rivals Flixton and Nelson had both dropped points.

The celebrations carried on for the last three games, with away wins over Chadderton and Padiham (both matches held at Oldham Athletic's Boundary Park) sandwiching the last home game against Great Harwood Town. Despite the 0-1 defeat on the day, an incredible league record crowd of 6,023 saw the players lift the trophy before embarking on an unforgettable open-top bus journey from the ground to the Swan & Cemetery pub on Manchester Road.

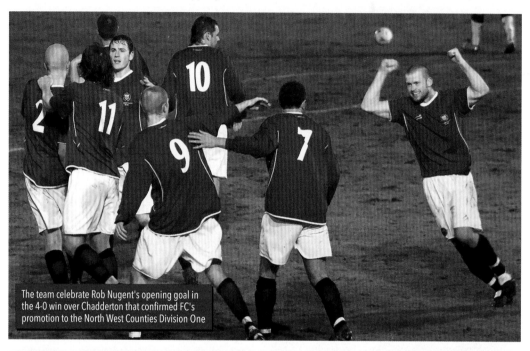

The team celebrate Rob Nugent's opening goal in the 4-0 win over Chadderton that confirmed FC's promotion to the North West Counties Division One

Rob Nugent shortly after a friendly at Clitheroe upon hearing confirmation that FC United have won the North West Counties Division Two title

6,023 fans packed Gigg Lane at the last home game against Great Harwood Town to see FC United pick up the Second Division title trophy, and the celebrations continued with a memorable open-top bus ride along Manchester Road to the Swan & Cemetery pub

NORTH WEST COUNTIES FOOTBALL LEAGUE DIVISON TWO CHAMPIONS 2005/06

27 wins in 36 league games, well over 100 goals scored, a home crowd averaging over 3,000 and a total of over 100,000 people through the gates were headline statistics that told only a small part of the story of a quite phenomenal first season. For every FC United Of Manchester follower, the pride and enjoyment was brought back to football. The club even had an end of season European away trip to Germany to face FC Lokomotiv Leipzig, where fans were treated to an entertaining 4-4 draw.

2006/07: North West Counties Football League Division One

After a highly successful first campaign, the FC United squad returned to embark on a challenging pre-season programme with several quality additions to their number. Rhodri Giggs and Stuart Rudd, who was the North West Counties League's all-time leading goalscorer, added another dimension to the attack and the defence was strengthened by goalkeeper Sam Ashton and full-backs Matty Taylor and Alex Mortimer. Two of the Leigh RMI team from the first friendly a year earlier, Steve Smith and Liam Coyne, also joined the ranks.

However we said a sad farewell to first season heroes Steve Torpey (signed up by Halifax Town after scoring a superb goal against them in a friendly), Joz Mitten, Mark Rawlinson and Billy McCartney. Also leaving the squad were Tony Cullen and Chris Simms, but both stayed at the club to manage the new reserve and youth teams respectively.

The team immediately settled into life in the First Division by winning all of the first 12 matches, scoring 46 goals with Rudd leading the way with 15. At the other end the defence were just as impressive, conceding just a single penalty in the first eight games, and only five in total during the winning run. The 13th game proved unlucky however, as Salford City came from behind to score twice in the last two minutes of an edgy game at The Willows. The team bounced back by emerging victorious in the next six league games, with two of them by 8-0 scorelines and another by 7-0. There were two memorable and hard-fought victories in amongst them though – Simon Carden scoring twice late on in a 3-2 win at Newcastle Town that featured Rory Patterson taking over in goal; and a Rudd brace settling the eagerly-anticipated 'mini-derby' with Maine Road at Stalybridge.

Matty Taylor celebrates with jubilant Reds after Simon Carden's late winner completes a dramatic fightback at Newcastle Town

FC United players and staff celebrate the opening goal in the first 'mini-derby' against Maine Road at Bower Fold in Stalybridge

A mini-slump that yielded two points from three games began with a 0-3 home reverse against Atherton Collieries, courtesy of a hat-trick from young striker Anthony Pilkington, who promptly joined the professional ranks with Stockport County. A welcome distraction from the league came in the form of the club's venture into the FA Vase, where we had disposed of Brodsworth Miners Welfare, Padiham and Salford City in away ties before being handed a meaty home draw with Quorn.

The events of that afternoon will surely never be forgotten by all who witnessed them, as despite crashing out of the competition with a 2-3 defeat, the sense of pride in the performance of both players and supporters alike was worth more than any amount of trophies. Early in the second half with the score at 1-1, the referee inexplicably sent off first Liam Coyne and then Josh Howard. This fired up the crowd to raise the noise in support of the nine men, with the hope that we could take the game to a replay. Substitute Phil Power had other ideas, firing home with four minutes remaining to set up an unlikely victory, but this was snatched away by an equaliser in the last minute. In a compelling extra-time period, the depleted team refused to roll over, epitomised by a clearly injured Matty Taylor bravely putting his body on the line in defence yet still driving forward in search of a goal. Cruelly denied a replay by virtually the last kick in the 120th minute, the team left the pitch to a rapturous standing ovation.

Phil Power puts the nine men ahead with four minutes to play against Quorn in the FA Vase, but heartbreak for FC was just around the corner

The emotions of that day looked like they may have lingered over the Christmas period as FC found themselves 0-2 down with less than 20 minutes to play on Boxing Day against Ramsbottom United. At this point we had dropped to 2nd place in the league behind Salford, albeit with games in hand, but once again both team and crowd refused to give up. David Chadwick and Mortimer pulled the scores level before recent signing Nicky Platt fired home from the edge of the area with three minutes left to get the title chase back on track.

From then on the team never looked back, and won all but two of the final 20 games as they stormed to the title. The only dropped points were a draw at challengers Nantwich Town, and a remarkable 4-4 tie with Trafford after the league had been sewn up. Settling comfortably into the team in the New Year was winger Jerome Wright, signed from Maine Road to bring balance to the left hand side. A combination of postponements, cup-ties and fixture scheduling meant that he didn't play at Gigg Lane until late February, but his home debut proved to be memorable. The 3-2 win over nearest rivals Curzon Ashton saw substitute Gary Sampson twice equalise before Rudd hit a dramatic winner.

Hundreds of Reds travelled to Ramsbottom via steam train on the East Lancashire Railway and were rewarded with a 2-1 win that clinched promotion. The achievement was not straightforward on the day as FC found themselves a goal behind and a man down early on when Rudd was dismissed. However, Wright equalised with a smart lob and Platt kept his nerve to win the game with a penalty. The title was now in sight, and after thrashings of Maine Road and Colne, United became champions with a 7-1 hammering of Atherton LR at Gigg Lane. The goals continued to flow even with the title confirmed; Giggs claimed a hat-trick in a 4-2 victory over his former club Salford, and Patterson hit two trebles in successive matches. The league campaign was wrapped up with a 5-0 defeat of Formby that featured the long-awaited debut of Karl Marginson who came off the bench for the last 20 minutes.

Nicky Platt buries the penalty at Ramsbottom to seal FC United's second successive promotion

Dave Brown and Rory Patterson both scored in the 3-0 victory in the second 'mini-derby' against Maine Road

Rhodri Giggs celebrates hitting a hat-trick in the triumph over his former club Salford City in April

FC United celebrate winning the North West Counties Division One title against Atherton LR (above), and receive the trophy after the game with Formby (below)

NORTH WEST COUNTIES FOOTBALL LEAGUE DIVISON ONE CHAMPIONS 2006/07

The season wasn't over as FC still had the League Cup Final to contest. After comfortable victories over Nantwich, Colne and Silsden in the earlier rounds, FC had drawn 2-2 with Congleton Town in the semi-final first leg. The home leg was a see-saw encounter in which United fell behind twice and let a lead slip when down to ten men with Mortimer dismissed. The Reds came back superbly to win 4-3 thanks to another Rudd brace, a long-range screamer from Patterson and a bullet header from Rob Nugent.

The final itself pitted FC United against Curzon Ashton at their own Tameside Stadium, and was a nervy clash until Curzon took the lead on 67 minutes while the Reds were down to ten men as Platt was receiving stitches to a head wound. He returned to the fray and within two minutes had coolly equalised from the penalty spot after Howard had been felled. With ten minutes remaining Howard himself scored a goal that was fit to win any cup final, beating four men before slotting home to seal the club's first cup win and the second trophy of another magnificent season.

Rob Nugent salutes the MRE after his bullet header finally settles the epic League Cup semi-final encounter with Congleton Town

Captains David Chadwick and Dave Birch line up with the mascots and officials before FC United face Curzon Ashton in the League Cup Final

Josh Howard is pursued by jubilant FC United team-mates after his superb solo goal wins the League Cup Final against Curzon Ashton

NORTH WEST COUNTIES FOOTBALL LEAGUE CHALLENGE CUP WINNERS 2006/07

2007/08: Northern Premier League Division One North

As a result of a restructuring programme in the non-league pyramid, FC United were now competing in a newly-created division called the Northern Premier League First Division North (sponsored by Unibond). As the division contained 18 clubs, a somewhat confusing fixture schedule was devised in which the clubs were split into two groups, with each team playing the others in their group three times, as well as those in the opposite group twice, in order to reach a final total of 42 league games.

The Reds embarked on this season with virtually the same squad that had won the double at the close of the previous campaign, with only Gary Sampson and Rhodri

Giggs departing for pastures new. Joining the ranks were midfielders Chris Baguley and Dale Whitehead, plus striker Anthony Hargreaves.

The flying start to which we had become accustomed did not materialise this time as, lacking the firepower of the suspended Stuart Rudd, the team fell to an opening day defeat at Lancaster City. The striker returned for the first home game, but was dubiously sent off again as FC were beaten by the bruising Garforth Town in a frustrating encounter. The season was kick-started with a 6-0 thrashing of Bridlington Town, in which Rory Patterson netted four times, followed by a 2-1 victory at Rossendale United.

Rob Nugent is congratulated by Steve Spencer, Matty Taylor, Jerome Wright and Shaun Roscoe for scoring the club's first ever FA Cup goal in the preliminary round tie with Trafford

In early September the club played its first ever game in the FA Cup, and successfully overcame Trafford 5-2 in the preliminary round, but dreams of Wembley were dashed with an unlucky 1-2 defeat at Fleetwood Town in the next round. In between, the League Challenge Cup was also exited with an extra-time loss to Alsager Town. The ascent up the league table continued with wins over Harrogate Railway Athletic and Chorley, as well as a draw with Woodley Sports, but hit the buffers with a defeat at Skelmersdale United.

Hampered by several injuries at this stage, the situation worsened with the loss of both Rudd and new signing Adam Carden within the first 15 minutes of the FA Trophy tie at Bradford Park Avenue. Despite this, the Reds took a deserved lead through Patterson, but were pegged back by a questionable late equaliser before being comprehensively beaten in the replay. Within a few days the injury crisis deepened as midfield lynchpin Steve Spencer was forced to take a break from the game due to a back injury and skipper David Chadwick was ruled out until the new year. Having recently introduced young striker Cayne Hanley, Karl Marginson further reinforced the squad by adding midfielder Jamie Baguley (brother of Chris) and forwards Peter Thomson and Aaron Burns. The signing of Burns was significant in that he had only left Manchester United that summer after being top scorer in the reserves, but complicated regulations meant that he could only sign for clubs at our level until January, so he joined on a short-term agreement.

The new signings helped to inspire the team to a run of seven wins in eight games, beginning with a 2-1 home victory over Wakefield thanks to two stunning free-kicks from Chris Baguley. Burns made an immediate impact by netting twice on his debut at Clitheroe, and scored eight goals in his first seven games, including a fantastic hat-trick in a 5-1 defeat of Rossendale. FC progressed in the league's President's Cup with a 5-0 hammering of Bamber Bridge, but the highlight of the run was a 3-2 win at Droylsden in the Manchester Premier Cup that was more comprehensive than the scoreline suggests. Hanley, Patterson and a screamer from Burns put United 3-0 up before two late goals from the hosts, who at the time were plying their trade three levels above in the Conference.

The charge up the table was halted by four defeats in five games in November, which prompted the manager to call for a siege mentality to ride through the crisis. Despite having Patterson, Hanley, Thomson, Sam Ashton, Matty Taylor, Shaun Roscoe and Rob Nugent all sidelined at various points, the team responded with battling displays that yielded four points from matches with Rossendale and Radcliffe Borough.

Aaron Burns and Liam Foster salute FC fans at Droylsden after a superb win in the Manchester Premier Cup

Rory Patterson pounces to slot past Bradford Park Avenue keeper Jon Worsnop as he claims FC United's first ever goal in the FA Trophy in October 2007

The Christmas period of 2007 will be remembered by most at FC United of Manchester for events surrounding the game at Curzon Ashton. The club's board represented the rights of its supporters by asking them not to attend a game in protest of the league's decision to switch the kick-off time to accommodate it being televised. Whilst acknowledging the importance of television in football, the board took the action after the change was enforced without the agreement of the participating clubs.

Simon Carden slots past Curzon Ashton keeper David Carnell to give FC United the lead in the game that was boycotted by thousands of Reds

Rob Nugent beats Adam Jones to seal FC's 2-0 victory over the league leaders Curzon Ashton in front of the sparsely populated terraces

As a result a fantastically executed boycott by FC fans of arguably their biggest away game of the season took place on 29th December. Unfortunately for innocent party Curzon, their loss was Abbey Hey's gain as proud, principled Reds filled the Gorton outfit's Goredale Avenue to noisily support the club's reserves, a stark contrast to the deafening silence at the Tameside Stadium. The siege mentality was never more evident as the team repaid the non-support with a tremendous 2-0 victory over their table-topping hosts. The reserves put the cherry on the cake by delighting the crowd with a 3-1 win over their title rivals Club AZ to complete one of the proudest days in the club's history.

That was the start of a run that saw the team win nine and draw three of the next 12 league games, during which special mention should go to Rory Patterson, whose tally of 14 goals included five braces and a hat-trick off the bench on New Year's Day at home to Mossley. The returns from injury of Chadwick and Rudd helped to settle the side, and Josh Howard also reappeared after a long lay-off, although Ashton was out for several weeks with a hand injury. His replacement was Aaron Grundy, on loan from landlords Bury, who made a superb debut in the 3-0 win over fellow challengers Skelmersdale and went on to win the league's Goalkeeper of the Month award. Hanley and Burns both departed after New Year, but the squad was strengthened with the additions of left-sided defender Bradley Howard, battling midfielder James Holden and versatile forward Nick Robinson.

Two of the drawn games in the run were with promotion title rivals Bamber Bridge, the second thanks to a tremendous injury time equaliser from Chris Baguley. Another impressive victory was gained over Curzon by a 3-2 margin, and then

Newcastle Blue Star were sunk by the same score a week later with another injury-time strike, this time from Adam Carden with his first for the club. The following week brought a further last minute winner when a superb overhead kick by Rudd on the plastic pitch at Woodley Sports kept the title dream alive.

Distractions from the promotion race came in the two cup competitions in which FC United were still participating. The President's Cup saw Rossendale beaten for the fourth time this season, before the Reds were thrashed 1-5 at Nantwich Town. However, the victors were later disqualified for fielding an unregistered player, although he only played for the last 13 minutes when the scoring was already completed. Despite FC's support for Nantwich's appeal, the decision was upheld and the reinstated Reds went on to win the semi-final 3-1 at Goole. In the Manchester Premier Cup, FC defeated Flixton 4-1 in what was technically a home game but played at the opponent's Valley Road ground, before being knocked out at Radcliffe Borough.

That game at Stainton Park was the second of what turned out to be a gruelling 19 game schedule in just seven weeks that severely threatened to scupper the promotion bid. The fixture pile-up was caused by the cup progress added to a series of winter postponements, and produced a mixed bag of results. The weather was still causing problems too, delaying the second half of a home game with Lancaster, and the farcical conditions led to the visitors earning a 2-2 draw with a last-minute equaliser. Disappointing defeats at Ossett Albion and Wakefield were sandwiched by crucial 0-0 draws with both Skelmersdale and Bradford PA, before the Reds got back on track with four wins in a row, over Harrogate RA, Lancaster, Radcliffe and Newcastle BS.

Adam Carden wheels away after burying the injury-time winner against Newcastle Blue Star

FC United also met Radcliffe for a fifth time in the President's Cup Final, held at the Tameside Stadium. With less than 10 minutes remaining, most of the crowd were preparing for extra time with the scores at 0-0, until Rudd sent over a superb cross that was buried by an equally impressive header from Chris Baguley to put the Reds in front. It wasn't over though, as a minute later Liam Foster cleared off the line – one of about a dozen certain goals the young full-back saved during the campaign with similar interventions. But a famous victory was sealed in stoppage time when Rudd lashed the ball into the roof of the net to win the team's latest piece of silverware.

Hopes of the title and automatic promotion were extinguished the following week with a draw at home to Woodley, but second place was secured with a win at Garforth. This guaranteed home advantage for the play-offs, and in the semi-final United came out 3-2 winners over Bamber Bridge in a tense thriller. This set up a final at home to Skelmersdale, where the Reds made a nervy start and fell behind after just 10 minutes. However, the pendulum swung back in our favour just before half-time when the visiting captain Michael White was sent off for handball on the line, and Nicky Platt coolly dispatched the resulting penalty. Early in the second half FC were in front thanks to a towering back post header by Chadwick, before being awarded another penalty, but this one was missed by Platt. When a third spot-kick was given, Patterson took over and made no mistake, before substitute Chris Baguley made it 4-1 near the end to seal a third successive promotion for FC United of Manchester.

This had been an extremely challenging season for a variety of reasons, but the spirit shown by the team, staff and supporters in fighting against adversity was truly remarkable, making the double success of promotion and another cup win all the sweeter.

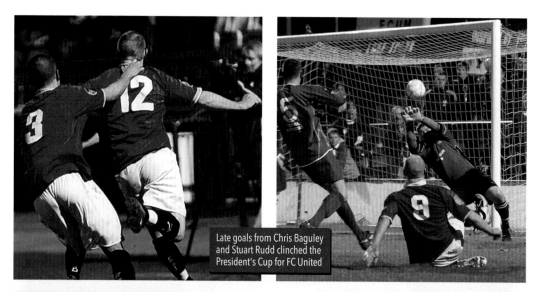

Late goals from Chris Baguley and Stuart Rudd clinched the President's Cup for FC United

FC United skipper David Chadwick lifts the President's Cup after the 2-0 victory over Radcliffe Borough at the Tameside Stadium

NORTHERN PREMIER LEAGUE DIVISION ONE
PRESIDENT'S CUP WINNERS 2007/08

Adam Carden gives FC the lead in the play-off semi-final against Bamber Bridge

David Chadwick's back post header puts the Reds ahead in the play-off final against Skelmersdale United

FC United won a third successive promotion after a 4-1 play-off final victory over Skelmersdale United

NORTHERN PREMIER LEAGUE DIVISION ONE NORTH PLAY-OFF FINAL WINNERS 2007/08

2008/09: Northern Premier League Premier Division

FC United's preparations for their first season in the Northern Premier League Premier Division took an early setback when the club's top scorers Rory Patterson and Stuart Rudd both signed for rivals Bradford Park Avenue on lucrative deals. In an eventful summer, the Reds also lost the services of stalwarts Josh Howard, Nicky Platt, Dave Swarbrick and Shaun Roscoe. Manager Karl Marginson reinforced the squad with the signings of former England Youth striker Kyle Wilson, the exciting attacker Carlos Roca, young winger Danny Williams, and midfielders Danny Self, Dave Neville and Tunji Moses.

The team had a mixed start at the new level, as an opening day 3-3 draw with Matlock Town preceded two wins and four defeats. Wilson made an explosive start by scoring eight of the team's 11 goals in the first month, the other goals being Jamie Baguley's winner at Buxton and two from Chris Baguley.

Ahead of the FA Cup tie at Nantwich Town in September, the manager added full-backs Danny Warrender and Simon Garner, who went straight into the team, and named another

addition, Alex Skidmore, on the bench. In an exciting 0-0 draw, Sam Ashton saved a penalty to earn a replay at Gigg Lane, which turned out to be far more eventful. The Reds found themselves 0-3 down within minutes of the second half, before Simon Carden pulled one back. The visitors regained their three-goal cushion thanks to a controversial penalty, but late goals from Self and Wilson brought FC back into the game at 3-4. Unfortunately United ran out of time to find an equaliser and crashed out of the cup at the first hurdle.

The Reds made an improvement with a run of six victories and just one defeat in nine games, which included impressive wins over Ossett Town, Frickley Athletic and Ilkeston Town. A memorable performance was at home to Witton Albion when FC were 3-0 up inside the first 12 minutes, with Kyle Wilson scoring the club's fastest goal after 14 seconds, before eventually triumphing 5-3. However it wasn't all good news as Williams suffered a broken leg at Whitby, just days after he had scored his first goal for the club. FC also made progress in the FA Trophy, defeating Radcliffe Borough through a last-minute Adam Turner header, and overcoming Worksop Town before eventually being eliminated by Boston United.

Kyle Wilson nets the fastest goal in FC United's history after just 14 seconds against Witton Albion

Kyle Wilson is congratulated after scoring the team's opening goal of the season, and his first goal for FC, on his debut against Matlock Town

The team celebrate Adam Turner's last-minute FA Trophy winner against Radcliffe Borough

Nick Robinson's last-minute equaliser completed FC's comeback in the amazing 5-5 draw with Cammell Laird

In November, Gigg Lane witnessed one of the most amazing games in the history of FC United when they hosted Cammell Laird. In a see-saw first-half, the lead changed hands three times, but the Reds found themselves trailing 2-5 with 20 minutes to play. The manager introduced substitutes Papis Dieyte, Chris Baguley and Nick Robinson, who all had a hand in inspiring an unlikely fightback. Roared on by a noisy Main Stand, Dieyte stirred the troops into action when he rattled a post, just before Wilson nodded home from a corner to reduce the deficit. With ten minutes remaining, Robinson sent over a superb cross that was matched by Baguley's header to leave FC just a goal behind. The game was in the final minute when Jerome Wright's low cross from the left was despatched at the back post by the outstretched boot of Robinson, who was swamped by his jubilant team-mates.

That was the first of a run of seven games that produced just one win, although in typical FC style those three points came in a magnificent 3-0 victory over table-topping Hednesford Town. The dropped points came in two defeats by Eastwood Town and a draw at Guiseley, but it should be noted that both of those teams were in the top four. A much-changed team with several teenagers suffered a League Challenge Cup exit at Woodley Sports, where the line-up was notable for featuring both the oldest and youngest players to start a game for the club in 42-year-old Darren Lyons and 17-year-old Sam Freakes respectively. The visit of third-placed Marine produced more late drama: after latest signing Tommy Turner's first goal for the club plus another strike from Chris Baguley, the Reds were tied at 2-2 with just over a minute to go, until Robinson came to the rescue again with a superb winner.

After a Boxing Day setback at Ashton United (yet another title challenger), FC's form improved in the New Year as they began to steadily climb the table. Comfortable wins over strugglers Worksop, Prescot Cables and Leigh Genesis went with an impressive win at Boston thanks to Wilson's late winner. Another fantastic late show was at home to Guiseley, when Wright and Tommy Turner both scored in the last two minutes to gain a 2-1 victory. Moses made his long-awaited debut after suspension, and the manager reinforced the ranks with the addition of defender Adam Tong, midfielder Neil Chappell and striker Tristram Whitman, after the departures of Chris Baguley, Liam Foster and Adam Turner.

However, the team still continued to suffer setbacks, such as the inexplicable defeats to relegation-threatened Witton and Leigh. Wilson, who was the top scorer in the entire country with 24 goals, was ruled out for the rest of the season after picking up a knee injury. Carl Lomax was brought in to replace Wilson, and was followed soon after by Phil Marsh, whose hat-trick for Leigh had sunk the Reds. Marsh's debut in a draw at Hednesford was significant, as he became the first player to represent both Manchester United and FC United of Manchester in first-team matches. The squad was further strengthened a few days later with the return of Nicky Platt after a spell with Stalybridge Celtic.

Tommy Turner's last-minute header won the game at home to Guiseley. FC had been a goal behind just 60 seconds earlier

Tunji Moses buries a thundering header in the 4-0 demolition of North Ferriby United in April, the sixth win in seven matches that took the Reds to the brink of the promotion play-off places

Danny Williams squeezed home the last-gasp winner at Ilkeston Town to send the travelling Reds into raptures

With only 10 games remaining, FC United were in ninth position in the table, having played more games than the teams above, and looked resigned to a mid-table finish. However, the team put together a storming run of six wins and a draw, which included 4-0 demolitions of both North Ferriby United and Ashton United, the latter thanks to Roca's tremendous hat-trick. The momentum was halted with a 0-0 draw with Nantwich, and the penultimate match at second-placed Ilkeston was heading the same way until substitute Williams bagged a dramatic injury-time winner to catapult the Reds into a play-off spot.

This set up a thrilling finish to the league season as the three teams vying for the final play-off place – FC United, Bradford PA and Kendal Town – all had 71 points. FC had a slightly better goal difference, but an added twist was that Bradford were the visitors to Gigg Lane, whereas Kendal were playing Buxton. Spurred on by the season's biggest crowd of 3,718, the Reds took an 8th minute lead through Tong, and held the advantage until an equaliser five minutes from time. At this point, Kendal were level and so had the scores remained thus then FC would have qualified. However in the final minutes news came through that Kendal had grabbed a late winner to nick the final spot at the death. A fourth successive promotion was therefore not to be, however the Reds could take heart that they could more than hold their own in this division, and the curtain came down with the feeling that the club was well-equipped for a challenge next term. They would have to do it without the services of the season's big success, however, as top scorer Kyle Wilson was offered a return to the professional ranks with Macclesfield Town upon his return from injury.

Adam Tong's early strike against Bradford PA looked to secure a play-off spot, but FC were denied by Kendal Town's late goal elsewhere

2009/10: Northern Premier League Premier Division

After an interesting pre-season build-up that included a trip to South Korea to play Bucheon FC 1995 in front of 23,000 supporters, FC United began their second campaign in the UniBond Premier Division with the majority of the squad that narrowly missed out on a play-off spot.

Kyle Wilson had been snapped up by League Two side Macclesfield Town, Jamie Baguley joined Leigh and Nicky Platt took an opportunity to play in Australia. Taking their places were big striker Ben Deegan, midfielder Jake Cottrell and left-sided Ben Morris, while teenage forward Jamie Mack was given the chance to stake a claim.

The Reds got off to a poor start, picking up just a single point in the first three games, before finding their feet with a 3-0 win over Marine in which Deegan and Mack both opened their accounts. After winning the next two, there came a further slump that yielded one point from four games, a run that looked set to continue into October when the Reds found themselves 1-3 down at home to Stocksbridge Park Steels. However, the lads dug deep and produced a stirring fightback that was capped by an injury-time winner from Carlos Roca. The belief was back, and a few days later Nantwich Town were destroyed 4-0, thanks to a tremendous hat-trick by Phil Marsh, plus another from Mack.

The FA Cup proved to be a welcome distraction, and having already disposed of Sheffield FC and North Ferriby United in away ties, confidence was high going into a home encounter with high-flying Conference North side Stalybridge Celtic. FC United took a deserved 2-0 lead through Roca and Marsh before Celtic pulled one back, but skipper David Chadwick restored the advantage early in the second half. However, the visitors came back to level at 3-3 to take the tie to a replay at their Bower Fold ground. Despite being the underdogs, FC produced a fantastic performance to progress 1-0 thanks to a tremendous long-range swerving effort from Jerome Wright. This set up a final qualifying round tie away at Conference club Northwich Victoria, where the Reds were finally eliminated in a closer encounter than the 0-3 scoreline would suggest.

Carlos Roca's injury-time winner claimed all three points at home to Stocksbridge Park Steels after the Reds had earlier trailed 1-3

Jerome Wright races away to celebrate his long-range swerving screamer that won the tense FA Cup replay at Stalybridge Celtic

Ben Deegan roars in delight after scoring the only goal of the FA Cup tie away at North Ferriby United

Tunji Moses rushes to congratulate Phil Marsh for putting the blue-shirted Reds ahead in the FA Trophy win at Ashton United in October

The team also had a decent run in the FA Trophy in the autumn, winning 3-1 at Ashton United before throwing away a 2-0 lead gained by new signing Joe Yoffe to draw 3-3 at Lancaster City. The visitors proved hard to break down in the replay, but were eventually overcome 1-0 through an extra-time Deegan winner. Conference North side Harrogate Town were the visitors in the next round, and looked a class apart in the first hour as they took a deserved three-goal lead. However, from then on the Reds were a different team and deserved something from the game, but two goals from Simon Carden were ultimately not enough to complete a comeback. Further hopes of cup success were ended with a defeat at Kendal in the League Challenge Cup, leaving United to concentrate solely on the league.

Just four points were picked up in a disappointing run before Christmas which left FC in the bottom three, albeit with several games in hand on the teams above due to the cup exploits. Optimism was provided by the form of Jake Cottrell, who had earned a regular place, as well as the introduction of teenage defender Nick Swirad and Guadeloupe international full-back Ludovic Quistin. However, the team was unable to get a run of games together as a succession of postponements due to weather conditions left them without a game for six weeks.

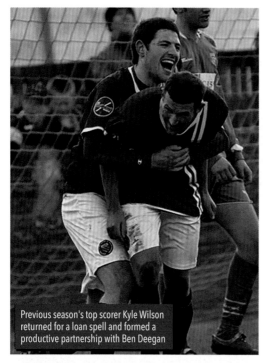

Previous season's top scorer Kyle Wilson returned for a loan spell and formed a productive partnership with Ben Deegan

By the time the team eventually played a game in 2010, Karl Marginson had been forced to reshape his squad. Simon Garner, Dave Neville and Danny Williams had all left the club, while Danny Warrender and Tunji Moses were both sidelined for the rest of the season. Following them soon after was Adam Tong, who moved to Australia. Reinforcements arrived in the shape of right-back Kyle Jacobs, the creative Adriano Rigoglioso, and the returns of James Holden and Kyle Wilson, the latter on a month's loan from Macclesfield. The new arrivals sparked a revival in fortunes, and after drawing the first two games the next six produced five wins and a draw. Wilson reminded us of what we were missing with a hat-trick in a 6-1 win at Nantwich, and his presence brought out the best in Deegan, who hit five goals alongside him.

With the upturn in fortunes, thoughts began to turn towards a push for the play-offs, but that was as good as it got as the campaign petered out from that point. The worst run in the club's history to date garnered nine defeats and two draws from 12 games, the sole win being a 2-0 home victory over Hucknall Town. Confidence was low as heavy losses were suffered at the hands of Buxton, Bradford Park Avenue, Kendal and Boston United, but the lowest point was arguably the 1-2 reverse at home to rock-bottom Durham City, who had lost every single one of their 28 games up to that point.

The lack of a settled squad was also proving to be a problem in the latter stages of the season, with the composition seemingly under constant changes. Wilson's loan had ended and Rigoglioso had already moved on, while defenders Mark Ayres and Adam Karim, midfielder Angelos Tsiaklis and winger Chris Ovington were added. Opportunities were also given to several more players who had impressed in the youth team, such as goalkeeper Grant Shenton, midfielders Stefanos Ioannou and Cedric Krou and striker Gage Eme. A debut was also given to Scott Cheetham, who became the youngest player to feature in a league match for the club when he entered the fray at Burscough in April.

David Chadwick continued to lead by example, bagging vital goals against Marine and North Ferriby United

The long wait for a win was finally ended seven minutes from time in the last game of the season, when Rob Nugent's perfectly weighted 40-yard pass set up Jerome Wright for the only goal of a 1-0 victory over Matlock Town. The three points and clean sheet were a fitting send off for Nugent, the club's longest serving player, who had announced his decision to retire due to a niggling back injury. United eventually finished in a disappointing 13th place in the table, meaning the season will be remembered as a transitional one on the pitch. However, the announcement late in the campaign that the club had reached agreement with Manchester City Council to build our own ground at Ten Acres Lane in Newton Heath left the supporters eagerly looking towards a very bright future.

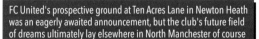

FC United's prospective ground at Ten Acres Lane in Newton Heath was an eagerly awaited announcement, but the club's future field of dreams ultimately lay elsewhere in North Manchester of course

Rob Nugent was FC United's longest-serving player, and the only survivor of the club's first game, when he helped the Reds to win the last game of his football career in April 2010

2010/11: Northern Premier League Premier Division

After the trials and tribulations of the previous season, it was no surprise that Karl Marginson significantly refreshed his squad in the summer of 2010. After the worst goal return since the club's formation, he wasted no time in snapping up Curzon Ashton's prolific forward Michael Norton, a player well known to the club's supporters after scoring more than 200 goals over the previous five years.

The return of favourite Steve Torpey also added to the firepower, as did massively experienced veteran Colin Little. Nicky Platt also returned after his season in Australia to provide midfield competition with the versatile Richard Battersby. With the retirement of Rob Nugent and the ongoing injury problems of skipper David Chadwick, central defensive reinforcements were recruited in the form of Martin Parker, Scott McManus and the experienced Karl Munroe. Left-back Lee Neville signed

after a previous short spell the year before, and goalkeeper Zach Hibbert was brought in to provide cover for Sam Ashton.

The reshaped team got the campaign off to a flyer by winning their first three games, scoring eight goals and conceding just one. Norton started as he meant to go on with a brace on the opening day at Marine, a feat that was matched by Little with two magnificent strikes on his own debut off the bench against Retford United. However, a narrow defeat at Ashton United was followed by three consecutive heavy losses to Matlock Town, Bradford Park Avenue and Stocksbridge Park Steels. In truth, the team's performances did not warrant the scorelines, which were mainly down to individual mistakes and bad luck in front of goal. This prompted the manager to temporarily alter the shape of the team to tighten things up, but after a disappointing reverse at Mickleover Sports he reverted to setting the team up in a more attacking fashion. The change worked as Ossett Town were put to the sword in a 4-1 victory, and then the same opponents were defeated 3-0 in the next league game three weeks later.

FC topped the table with nine points from the first three games, which featured a 40-yard strike by Jake Cottrell against Retford United

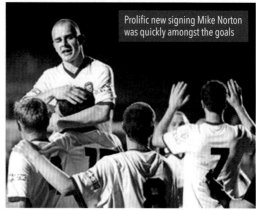

Prolific new signing Mike Norton was quickly amongst the goals

James Holden begins United's FA Cup run by slotting past stranded Radcliffe Borough keeper Nick Culkin

In between, the renewed confidence was also paying dividends as the team enjoyed successful runs in both FA competitions. In the FA Trophy they defeated Newcastle Town 5-0 with help from Ben Deegan's first hat-trick for the club, as well as a double from Norton. They followed this with a 2-1 win over Colwyn Bay, before ultimately falling 1-2 at home to Hinckley United. It was in the FA Cup, though, that FC United reached new heights. The run began with a 3-0 defeat of Radcliffe Borough thanks to another Norton brace and James Holden's first goal for the club. In the next round, Gainsborough Trinity were beaten 2-1 by two goals from Glyn Hurst, who had joined the squad after Little left due to work commitments.

At Norton & Stockton Ancients in the next round, Hurst scored again to add to a Deegan strike and Mike Norton's first hat-trick for the club as the Reds recorded a 5-2 victory to earn a home tie with Conference Premier side Barrow in the final qualifying round. The crowd of 3,263 were treated to a fantastic display by FC as they played the visitors off the park, but for the most part were frustrated by some acrobatic saves and Norton striking the woodwork. However, the team remained calm and were rewarded for their patience in the 78th minute when good work from Norton and Chris Ovington set up Carlos Roca who gleefully swept the ball home to send the home faithful into raptures.

Jerome Wright is carried from the field by jubilant Reds after the FA Cup win away at Norton & Stockton Ancients

FC United players and fans went wild after Carlos Roca's late goal beat Barrow to send the Reds into the FA Cup 1st Round

For their first ever game in the first round proper of the FA Cup, FC United of Manchester were drawn away to local League One side Rochdale, who were four divisions and 97 places higher in the football pyramid. After much deliberation, the club agreed to the tie being televised live on ESPN, and so the game was scheduled for the evening of Friday 5th November. The manager was given a selection headache as the ever-present Lee Neville had broken his ankle the week before, so Richard Battersby was drafted in for his first game in a month to play as makeshift left-back.

In front of a crowd of 7,048 at Spotland, plus the watching TV audience, FC weathered an expected early storm from the hosts before shocking all but their own devoted followers by taking the lead just before half-time. Jerome Wright played a perfectly weighted pass into the stride of the breaking Nicky Platt, who calmly chipped the advancing keeper to the noisy delight of the travelling masses. The decibel levels were raised even higher four minutes after the interval when an excellent

turn on the left from Deegan created an opening for Platt. He calmly laid the ball off to the onrushing Jake Cottrell, who hit a thunderous first-time shot that arrowed straight into the top corner to put the Reds 2-0 up.

Determined not to go out without a fight, Rochdale soon pulled a goal back, and this spurred them on to become more of an attacking threat. Several chances followed as FC defended resolutely, with Battersby's goal-line clearance preventing a certain equaliser. Inevitably Dale drew level with 12 minutes remaining, at which point it seemed that most in the ground would be happy to settle for a well-deserved replay. The Reds had other ideas, though, and deep into injury time Wright fed the ball forward to Norton, who capitalised on a defensive mix-up to nick the ball from the keeper and stroke it into the empty net to make it 3-2. Pandemonium ensued amongst the United fans, and as the final whistle sounded seconds later thousands poured on to the pitch to celebrate with their red shirted heroes.

Goals either side of the break from Nicky Platt and Jake Cottrell put FC 2-0 up at Rochdale in the FA Cup

Mike Norton rolls the ball into the empty net deep into stoppage time for the winning goal at Rochdale

Mike Norton is swamped by his team-mates after his last-gasp winner in the FA Cup at Rochdale

The second round draw gave FC United a trip to League One leaders Brighton & Hove Albion, who were the highest ranked team in the competition, but they proved once more that they cared little for reputations as they pulled off another shock result. History repeated itself as Platt once again put the Reds in front just before half-time after good work from Roca and Norton. Albion had been threatening from the off, but the goal gave the Reds added confidence and they began the second half brightly, until being dealt a blow when McManus was dismissed for violent conduct. Despite the hosts piling on the pressure with the extra man advantage, FC almost doubled the lead but Munroe's powerful header produced a good save from the keeper. Sadly with seven minutes to go

the Reds could hold on no longer as Sandaza poked home the equaliser, to set up a tense finale. In the six minutes of added time, Munroe was again in the thick of the action as he brilliantly headed a goal-bound effort off the line, before the referee awarded a penalty against him for a robust shoulder charge. It looked like the Reds would be eliminated in the cruellest fashion, but Bennett's spot-kick was magnificently saved by Ashton to earn his team a replay and a conditional place in the third-round draw.

The manager was once again forced to shuffle his pack for the replay as Wright and McManus were ruled out through suspension, and handed starts to Parker and Ludovic Quistin, his first of the season after injury. In front of 6,731 supporters, our highest ever crowd at Gigg Lane, the visitors took the lead midway through the first half, and then doubled their advantage against the run of play on the stroke of half-time. FC were awarded a penalty in the 68th minute but the opportunity to get back in the match went begging as Cottrell's effort struck the post, the sixth consecutive spot-kick missed by the Reds. Again the team increased their efforts, but they were to be in vain as Albion put some gloss on the scoreline with two further goals in the final five minutes to signal an end to United's involvement in that season's FA Cup.

Nicky Platt struck again to give FC the lead at Brighton, before Sam Ashton secured a replay with a last-minute penalty save

That, plus an earlier defeat at Ashton United in the League Challenge Cup, had left FC United to concentrate on the league, but on New Year's Day they found themselves in the relegation spaces having not picked up a point since the clocks went back. In reality this was somewhat of a false position, as they had only played four league games in that time with postponements due to the cup runs and weather conditions. Also, the four defeats were to the top three teams – Northwich Victoria, Colwyn Bay and FC Halifax Town (twice). The Reds eventually got back to winning ways on 3rd January with a 2-1 defeat of Ashton United, the first of four successive wins which also included a long-awaited victory over Bradford PA. There followed comfortable demolitions of Hucknall Town and Retford, the latter notable for Sam Ashton scoring with a long punt from his own area, while recent signing Matthew Wolfenden was also among the goals.

After two unfortunate losses to Kendal Town and Colwyn Bay, Hucknall were beaten again to begin an incident-packed run of 16 games that yielded 12 wins and four draws to propel United into the play-off places. Some matches produced comfortable victories, such as home wins over Whitby Town and Burscough, and a tremendous 4-1 win at Nantwich Town thanks to Wolfenden's hat-trick, whereas other points were gained the hard way. At home to Chasetown, the Reds found themselves a goal and a man down after Battersby's harsh dismissal just before the break, but the ten men responded with a tremendous performance to eventually triumph 4-2. Late goals from Norton earned a point at rivals Buxton and a win at Whitby, a great return from two difficult away trips.

During this superb run, FC United were dealt a massive blow when the council announced that our prospective new home at Ten Acres Lane in Newton Heath was no longer a viable option due to government funding cuts. The setback meant that we would not be in our own ground the following year, as was initially hoped, but as a compromise the club was offered an alternative, larger site at Broadhurst Park in Moston.

Back on the pitch, the drama intensified in April as each game produced crucial incidents, beginning with a last minute penalty despatched by Wright that gave FC three points at Worksop Town. The visit of Northwich was fairly uneventful until Ashton was sent off for violent conduct, the referee also awarding a penalty. With no substitute keeper on the bench,

Ben Deegan was brought on to go in goal, and he amazingly saved the spot-kick with his first touch. He later turned provider when his goal-kick fell to Norton, who raced clear and smashed the ball home, and the 1-0 lead was preserved with further saves from the stand-in. Another red card and conceded penalty, this time by Munroe, meant United had to come from behind to beat Frickley Athletic 4-1, a win that was capped with Deegan's first league goal of the season in a memorable few days for the big man.

The unbeaten run came to an end amidst even more controversy at Chasetown, as FC were reduced to nine men with the harsh dismissals of both Norton and Wright. It was back to winning ways as Deegan emerged from the bench to bag the winner against Marine, and he stepped up to make his first start of 2011 in the penultimate game at Matlock. However, it was not in his preferred position up front – after his heroics against Northwich, he was pressed into emergency action in goal with Ashton suspended and deputy Grant Shenton attending his brother's wedding, and he did remarkably well in a 2-1 win. Shenton returned for the last game at home to Kendal, and saved a controversial last-minute penalty with the scores level. However, the rebound was smashed home by former FC winger Danny Williams to condemn the Reds to defeat and a fourth-placed finish.

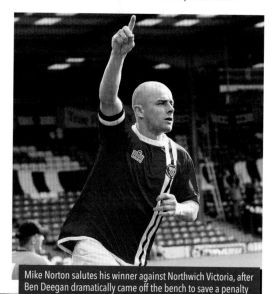

Mike Norton salutes his winner against Northwich Victoria, after Ben Deegan dramatically came off the bench to save a penalty

The final standings resulted in a trip to face old foes Bradford PA in the play-off semi-final, where over 2,000 FC fans were there to roar the team on, generating an atmosphere that the home side admitted they found intimidating. An early Wolfenden goal put United in control, and the lead was increased by Wright just after the interval, with the score remaining at 2-0 after the hosts were reduced to ten men. This set up a final at Colwyn Bay for a place in the Conference North, but the Reds had to do it without the services of their main goal providers, Norton and Wright, who were serving their suspensions. Their absence was a crucial factor, as FC went down 0-1 to a counter-attacking goal after being unable to convert a number of opportunities. Roca, Platt, Deegan and Chadwick were all inches away from scoring, as was teenage midfielder Matt Tierney who had shown a maturity that belied his tender years in the dramatic end to an unforgettable season.

Matthew Wolfenden and Jerome Wright hit the goals as FC won 2-0 in the play-off semi-final at Bradford Park Avenue

Scores of ticketless Reds watched FC's narrow defeat in the play-off final from a hill at Colwyn Bay

2011/12: Northern Premier League Premier Division

Having come so close to another promotion in the spring, Karl Marginson was determined to keep the majority of the squad together and only strengthen where necessary in 2011. In came goalkeeper James Spencer, defenders Adam Jones, Dean Stott and Paul Armstrong, plus midfielders Michael Carr, Daniel Grimshaw and Adam Edwards. Two of the mainstays of the previous campaign, Jerome Wright and Scott McManus, had already moved on before pre-season training began, and were followed by Sam Ashton, Simon Carden and Martin Parker once the likely first choice selection was determined.

Marginson was laid low for a few weeks with a kidney infection, but under the stewardship of Roy Soule the Reds started the season in determined fashion with a goal from Matthew Wolfenden in the first minute of the opening game at Stafford Rangers. Stott doubled the lead on the stroke of half time to ensure a winning start to FC's campaign, which they followed up in midweek with a thrilling 6-3 home victory over North Ferriby United. After a couple of disappointing 1-2 defeats at the hands of Chasetown and Chester, United ended August amongst the goals with a 4-0 win at Buxton and a satisfying 5-2 victory over promotion rivals Bradford Park Avenue.

A series of injuries in September disrupted the momentum and saw the team pick up just one point from four games. One of those was the match at Chorley that had been made all-ticket, with a reduced away allocation, and moved to an earlier kick-off without consultation with FC United. Echoing the stance taken four years previously at Curzon Ashton, the club's board and supporters decided not to attend the fixture in protest at the draconian measures.

The Reds were first off the mark in the entire league when Matthew Wolfenden struck within a minute of the kick-off in the season's opening game away at Stafford Rangers

Defenders Lee Neville and Adam Jones both scored with headers in the big win over Bradford Park Avenue in August

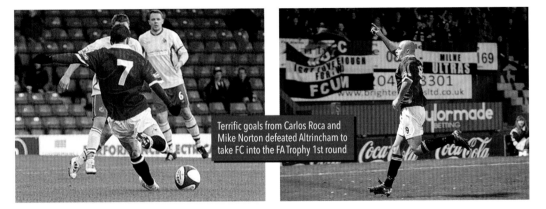

Terrific goals from Carlos Roca and Mike Norton defeated Altrincham to take FC into the FA Trophy 1st round

The Reds returned to winning ways by disposing of Woodley Sports in the FA Cup after a replay, which provided the impetus to gain ten points from the next four league games. Dreams of a cup run to emulate the heroics of the previous season were dashed by a disappointing home defeat to Lancaster City, whilst the Manchester Premier Cup was also exited at Mossley where Jones played the entire game in goal. In between, Chester extended their lead at the top of the table by grabbing a last-minute winner at Gigg Lane after Jones was dismissed.

Nine points were gained from three games in mid-November, which came in the middle of the club's longest run up to that date in the FA Trophy. After disposing of Frickley Athletic and Durham City, United were drawn at home to local rivals Altrincham of the Conference North, and the team showed once again that they could more than match sides from higher up the pyramid. A beauty from Carlos Roca put the Reds ahead, but they were pegged back when Jack Redshaw equalised with a free header. Unperturbed, FC put immense pressure on the visitors' goal and were rewarded when Mike Norton headed a superb winner from a wonderful cross by recent signing Astley Mulholland. Also joining in mid-season were winger Stephen Johnson and giant defender Greg Stones, whilst club legends David Chadwick, Steve Torpey and Ben Deegan moved on to

pastures new along with Carr, Edwards and James Holden.

FC once again faced opposition from the league above in the first round of the FA Trophy when they were handed a trip to Guiseley. Despite being the better team for much of the game and hitting the woodwork twice, the Reds were defeated 0-2 as the hosts converted two late goals against the run of play. A last chance for cup success was in the League Challenge Cup, where FC made progress with victories at Burscough and Chorley, before being eliminated at Frickley.

Three difficult games, away to Nantwich Town and Northwich Victoria and at home to Chorley, yielded two points in the run-up to Christmas, before two impressive victories over the holiday period. Ashton United were defeated 2-1 on Boxing Day, before a convincing display at Bradford PA brought a repeat of the early-season 5-2 scoreline. Having climbed to just a point below the play-off places progress was stalled by a home defeat to Stafford and a goalless draw at North Ferriby, but a tremendous run of eight wins and two draws from the next 11 matches put the Reds back on track. Key moments during this sequence were late goals at Frickley and Marine, two priceless wins over promotion rivals Hednesford Town, and Wolfenden's hat-trick to defeat Stocksbridge Park Steels.

James Spencer's superb save was the last action of the game as FC won 2-1 at rivals Hednesford Town to claim a vital victory

Matthew Wolfenden's 20th goal of the season in the last league game against Northwich Victoria helped to confirm United's place in the play-offs

Mike Norton celebrates with his team-mates in front of the FC fans after his wonderful chip broke the deadlock in the play-off semi-final at Chorley

However, just as the Reds were looking certainties for the play-offs, they hit a run of disappointing results in April with three narrow defeats preceding a home draw with already-relegated Burscough. A final day 4-1 thrashing of second-placed Northwich ultimately proved crucial as, despite finishing sixth, FC United were awarded the final play-off spot at the expense of the visitors. Northwich were found guilty of failing to comply with League rules relating to financial matters, and an FA decision relegated them to the tier below.

Despite qualifying for the play-offs by default, United were determined not to let the opportunity pass when they once again travelled to Chorley for the semi-final, and they did not disappoint by triumphing 2-0 thanks to superb strikes from Norton and Mulholland. This earned the Reds a place in the final, where they would cross the Pennines to face old rivals Bradford Park Avenue, who were out for revenge after the two 5-2 drubbings and the defeat in the previous year's semi-final.

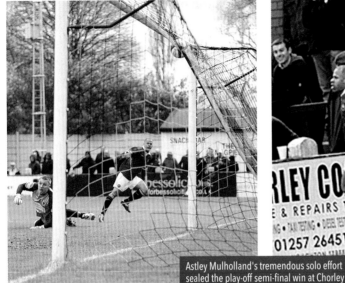

Astley Mulholland's tremendous solo effort sealed the play-off semi-final win at Chorley

Confusion surrounding arrangements for the game dominated the week, and the ultimate late decision to move the game to Sunday undoubtedly affected the number of FC United fans that were able to buy tickets. On the pitch, the team's preparations were hit by the loss of ever-present goalkeeper Spencer, who had injured a finger on the eve of the game. Drafted in to make his debut against his former club was deadline day signing Jon Worsnop, who acquitted himself well in a closely fought contest. With neither side able to break the deadlock within the 90 minutes, the game went into extra-time, when FC United were dealt a cruel blow. With the match looking destined for a penalty shoot-out, a ball across the six-yard box in the very last minute eluded Worsnop and was bundled home by Bradford substitute Tom Greaves, leaving United no time to reply.

It was another sad ending to the season but looking back, it was one with plenty of positives, both on and off the pitch, to demonstrate a club that was continuing to flourish. During the season several initiatives such as Big Coat Day, People United Day and Youth United Day were held which led to the Reds being named as the Football Foundation Community Club of the Year. It also marked the establishment of the women's football team and the target £1.6 million was raised to build FC United of Manchester's new stadium and community sports facility at Broadhurst Park in Moston.

Heartbreak is ahead as FC United prepare for extra-time in the play-off final at Bradford Park Avenue

2012/13: Northern Premier League Premier Division

After the heartbreaking end to the previous season, FC United of Manchester could feel confident about mounting a concerted push for promotion from the Northern Premier League at the fifth time of asking. As they were obviously one of the strongest teams in the league, manager Karl Marginson kept squad changes to a minimum with only five new arrivals.

Jerome Wright and Rhodri Giggs made welcome returns to the fold, and were joined by defender Charlie Anderson, midfielder Dave Birch and striker Chris Amadi. Meanwhile, Astley Mulholland, Richard Battersby and Greg Stones all moved on to pastures new during the summer.

The team made an explosive start to the campaign by winning the first three matches against the Towns of Grantham, Whitby and Matlock, scoring 11 goals in the process. Draws with Witton Albion and Hednesford Town were followed by another win over Whitby which gave FC 14 points from 18 available.

The first defeat of the season came at the hands of Nantwich Town, who snatched two late goals, and the Reds then surrendered another lead in a 1-1 draw at Stafford Rangers.

Most of September and October was spent on cup duty, and produced another good run in the FA Cup, disposing of three old rivals along the way. The Reds began by putting five goals past Cammell Laird, this time without reply, before a fantastic hat-trick from Nicky Platt earned progress at Salford City. United gave the fans a nervy finish, though, as the hosts pulled two goals back in the final two minutes and James Spencer was sent off to leave Michael Norton to finish the game in goal. Kendal Town were eliminated in the next round, which set up a final qualifying round home tie with Conference side Hereford United. FC once again proved that they can be a match for teams from a higher level, as despite being on the wrong end of the 0-2 scoreline, the Reds were extremely unlucky on the balance of play.

The FA Trophy also provided degrees of excitement, beginning with the home tie with Mossley when FC were trailing 0-3 with 17 minutes to go. Two strikes from Amadi and an equaliser by Wright earned a replay, where the Reds triumphed 3-1 in a match that will be remembered for a stunning first goal for the club from Birch. The next round provided a trip to Stamford, where this time FC were on the wrong end of an upset as the team from the level below emerged victorious. After leading through Norton's early strike, United conceded twice in the second half, and finished another game with an outfield player in goal – this time Birch, after Spencer was substituted due to concussion. Hopes of lifting the Manchester Premier Cup were also dashed with a 2-3 defeat in another visit to Mossley, with Amadi bagging another brace against the hosts.

Only two league games were played amongst the cup commitments – a lacklustre 2-4 defeat at AFC Fylde, and a creditable 1-1 draw at table toppers North Ferriby United. The team returned to winning ways with a 2-1 victory at Ashton United, thanks to an early Matthew Wolfenden brace, and a

Nicky Platt's treble won the FA Cup tie at Salford City

comfortable 4-1 stroll at home to Eastwood Town. However, the momentum was halted by a draw at Ilkeston and two home defeats to Rushall Olympic and Marine. At this stage the make-up of the squad was changed a little as Anderson, Amadi, Stephen Johnson and Daniel Grimshaw all departed, while defenders Mathew Carr and Louis Horne, midfielder Lewis Chalmers, wingers Phil McGrath and Adam Dawson, and striker Tom Fisher all had brief spells with the club. Forward Greg Daniels also joined and began to make an impact.

The belief returned in the run-up to Christmas as FC recorded three wins from four games, with the only setback being an unlucky defeat at Hednesford. Matthew Tierney's late thunderbolt won the points at Chorley, and Wolfenden's even later winner saw off Grantham at home. In between, the Reds also won at Blyth Spartans in a game marred by an unfortunate facial injury suffered by Platt. The Boxing Day game at home to Witton was abandoned after ten minutes due to a waterlogged pitch, and the ground had not recovered to stage the scheduled match with Ilkeston three days later.

The lack of festive fixtures did not dampen confidence into the New Year as the team won all seven league games in the first two months to put themselves right back in the mix for automatic promotion. Attacking reinforcements arrived in the shape of the returning Mulholland, as well as forward Tom Greaves, the man who had broken our hearts the previous May. Greaves immediately settled in by scoring a spectacular long-range volley on his debut against Stafford, bagged another at Frickley Athletic, and then scored all three at Marine. Impressive wins were also gained at Nantwich and Buxton, while at home another Wolfenden brace saw off Fylde and a late thundering header from Adam Jones defeated Ilkeston.

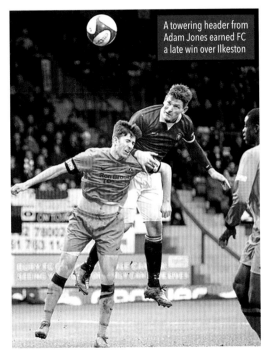

A towering header from Adam Jones earned FC a late win over Ilkeston

Rhodri Giggs and Matthew Wolfenden combined for the last-gasp winning goal at home to Grantham Town

Matthew Wolfenden's brace completed a great team performance as FC recovered from a goal down to beat AFC Fylde 2-1

The League Challenge Cup campaign also began and ended during this spell, with FC initially progressing with another 2-1 win at Ashton before then being eliminated by losing 3-4 in a see-saw game at Witton. That was not to be the end of the matter, however, as the hosts were later found to have fielded a cup-tied player, but that fact was not discovered until Witton were due to kick-off in the next round against Curzon Ashton. Witton won this game after the League advised that it should go ahead, but then Curzon were reinstated due to an error in a match in which they had no involvement. Despite FC United's appeals to the League that we should be reinstated to play Curzon, and believing we had a very strong case on a number of grounds based on many precedents, the League refused to let us back in. The cup games afforded the chance to hand debuts to youth team captain Lewis Lacy, as well as two recent signings – full-back Travis Gray and striker Matt Walwyn – and they all played their part in the latter stages of the season.

March began with the visit of leaders North Ferriby, with FC knowing that a win would put serious pressure on the guests due to our games in hand. The away side took the lead with a penalty before Greaves equalised, and they managed to hold on for a 1-1 draw despite a bombardment from the Reds. Another draw followed in midweek, this time 2-2 at Matlock where Jones scored twice, before the unbeaten run fell at home to Chorley. Two further defeats, at Worksop and home to Buxton, gave United a mountain to climb just three weeks since top spot was well within sight.

On 23rd March, snow had wreaked havoc with most of the country's football fixtures, meaning that only one game in the entire Northern Premier League went ahead. That game was at Gigg Lane after an army of FC United volunteers helped to clear the pitch to allow the game with Blyth to take place. With the team still looking short of confidence, the sterling work looked initially to be in vain as the visitors took an early lead, which they still held with less than ten minutes remaining. The fans were eventually rewarded as strikes from Norton and Greaves won the game to get the promotion bid back on track. Midfielder Sam Fitzgerald had made an impressive debut in the game, and he was joined in the squad by Sergio Rodríguez and Ollie Banks, who proved an astute signing for the run-in.

After Blyth, United were blessed with a run of fixtures that included most of the bottom teams, and they duly recorded easy victories over Kendal Town (twice) and Stocksbridge Park Steels (also twice). However, they still contrived to draw 2-2 at rock-bottom Eastwood, which would have been worse had it not been for a last-minute equaliser from Greaves, and also disappointed in a 0-1 home defeat to Witton which saw the visitors leapfrog them in the standings. With the chance of winning the league now all but gone, the players had to make sure that they qualified for the play-offs, which was by no means a foregone conclusion with several teams still in contention. They responded magnificently, though, winning all of the last five games to finish in third place, their highest ever league finish with a points total to match. However there was a downside when skipper Jones sustained a serious Achilles injury at home to Worksop, which led to the team finishing the league campaign with two teenage centre-backs: Lacy and the on-loan Kevin Masirika.

Tom Greaves forces home the late winner two minutes after Mike Norton had equalised against Blyth Spartans to reward the volunteers who cleared the pitch of snow

Relief for the Reds as Matthew Wolfenden got the only goal with a second half strike at home to Worksop Town

Matthew Wolfenden's spectacular 40-yard strike and another solo goal from Astley Mulholland set FC up for victory over Witton Albion in the play-off semi-final

The reward for third place was a home tie in the play-off semi-final against Witton Albion, who had gained the upper hand over United in the head-to-head meetings this season. The Reds did not let that affect them, though, and came racing out of the blocks, taking an early lead with a spectacular 40-yard strike from Wolfenden. They suffered another injury blow when Lacy had to be stretchered off following a hefty challenge, but extended the lead before half-time when Mulholland raced clear and provided a calm finish. The visitors pulled one back from the spot early in the second half, but Dean Stott calmed FC nerves by converting a penalty of his own to seal a 3-1 win and send his team into another final.

For the third year running, FC United faced a promotion play-off final as an away team, this time travelling to the home of Hednesford, who had finished ten points ahead and only lost the title to North Ferriby on goal difference. The injury to Lacy forced the manager into just one change, with Masirika partnering Stott in the centre of defence. The Reds were stunned as poor defending led to the hosts taking the lead within two minutes, and they added a similar goal on the half-hour to leave FC in all kinds of trouble. Marginson decided to

make adjustments before the break, and his team came out firing for the second half, getting their reward when Norton powered a header home. United piled on the pressure as Banks went agonisingly close with a free-kick and Wolfenden struck the woodwork, but the hosts held on to the lead to consign FC to a third successive play-off final defeat.

Mike Norton's header reduces FC United's arrears in the promotion play-off final at Hednesford Town

2013/14: Northern Premier League Premier Division

Having finished third behind the two promoted teams the previous season, FC United entered the 2013/14 campaign feeling confident that they were the best side in the Northern Premier League. The pre-season friendlies produced a mixed bag of results, but Karl Marginson was pleased with how the team performed and how his new arrivals had settled in. The summer had seen crowd favourites Kyle Jacobs, Jake Cottrell, Carlos Roca and Matt Tierney moving on, and the manager knew he would also be without Adam Jones and Lewis Lacy for the first few months due to their injuries sustained in the spring. Into the squad came full-backs Liam Brownhill and Cavell Coo, centre-backs Charlie Raglan, Tom Davies and Andy Pearson, plus midfielder Chris Worsley.

Matt Walwyn hit five goals as a substitute in three games as FC topped the league at the end of August

The Reds again beat Witton Albion 3-1 at home in a tense encounter

The first two matches of the league season mirrored the pre-season games in that the team performed well but gained just a single point and failed to score. A tight opener at Worksop Town looked to be heading for stalemate until two late defensive howlers gifted a victory to the home side, which was compounded by Dean Stott's saved penalty. In midweek, a thoroughly entertaining game at home to AFC Fylde ended goalless. The Reds finally got off the mark in style with a 6-0 hammering of Stamford when Tom Greaves bagged a hat-trick and Matt Walwyn came off the bench to notch two late strikes. A see-saw game at Trafford saw United lead through Astley Mulholland and then fall behind early in the second half, before substitutes Walwyn and Greaves hammered late goals to earn victory. Walwyn was at it again by scoring twice as a sub in the 5-1 win at Grantham Town that put the Reds on top of the table, which was consolidated by winning a bruising encounter against Witton Albion.

That win came at a price, however, as an injury to star midfielder Ollie Banks kept him out of the disappointing home defeat to Rushall Olympic. Banks was back for the 2-1 win at Frickley Athletic, but this was his last game for the club as he jumped at an opportunity to return to the professional ranks by signing for Chesterfield in League Two. His place in the squad was taken by Callum Byrne, but during his settling-in period the team was hit by injuries to Raglan, Davies, Worsley and Jerome Wright, and struggled in a run that brought just two wins in twelve outings. Maximum points gained from Marine and Stocksbridge Park Steels, and hard fought draws at Nantwich Town, King's Lynn Town and Rushall, were offset by disappointing defeats to Stafford Rangers, Whitby Town and Skelmersdale United in the league.

Three competitions were unluckily exited in this sequence – the FA Cup due to a 0-1 defeat to Chorley, the Manchester Premier Cup on penalties at New Mills after a 3-3 draw, and the FA Trophy with a 1-2 loss at Witton where FC were reduced to nine men. This tie was a long-running saga that began with a 2-2 draw in Northwich where the hosts equalised with a controversial last-minute penalty. The replay scheduled for Gigg Lane was postponed twice, and then switched to Radcliffe Borough's Stainton Park, but this was abandoned after 75 minutes due to a thunderstorm with the score again at 2-2. After the second abandonment in less than a year against the same opponents, FC forfeited home advantage for the tie that was eventually settled at the fifth attempt, and which was the ninth game to have kicked off between the two clubs in just over fourteen months.

Despite the results, the performances had been improving, and Michael Norton was back among the goals after a disrupted start to his campaign. A much needed 2-1 win over Ramsbottom United came in the League Challenge Cup, and spurred the Reds into climbing the table from their position in 13th place. A good pre-Christmas run of 17 points from seven games put FC into the play-off positions, with a 1-1 draw at Matlock Town and a thrilling 4-4 draw with Worksop being the only dropped points. Impressive home wins were gained over Frickley Athletic, Blyth Spartans and Barwell, while maximum points were gained on the road at Droylsden, with another Greaves treble, and a 2-0 win in an eventful encounter at AFC Fylde which saw Norton play the second half in goal after a season-ending injury to the unfortunate James Spencer.

With Jon Worsnop having accepted the offer of a contract with Conference outfit Alfreton Town, Marginson was suddenly left without a goalkeeper. He enlisted the on-loan help of Huddersfield Town's young stopper Ed Wilczynski, who kept goal for three games over the festive period – the 2-0 wins over Barwell and at Buxton that bookended a 1-2 defeat at Ashton United. A permanent no.1 in the shape of David Carnell was signed, joining fellow recent arrivals Joe Fox and Nelson Mota in a squad that had seen Pearson and Coo both depart.

Carnell had to wait until his fourth league outing to sample a win, as a 2-3 defeat at Whitby was sandwiched by a 3-3 draw at Ilkeston and a 1-1 draw with Trafford in terrible weather conditions. He did emerge victorious in a 2-1 League Cup win at Ossett Town in which Rhodri Giggs scored before receiving

Mike Norton played the second half in goal at Fylde and kept a clean sheet in a vital 2-0 victory

his marching orders. The Reds had reached this stage by defeating Ashton United 2-0 in the previous round, before eventually falling 1-2 at Carlton Town.

The dropped league points in January saw FC fall back to 10th position, before everything fell into place on a wet and windy day at Marine. With Jones and Wright now back from long-term injuries, the manager decided to alter the team's formation to 3-5-2 to accommodate them, which also allowed him to field both Norton and Greaves in the line-up. The change proved to be a masterstroke, as the 2-0 win was just the first of a club-equalling 12 consecutive victories that propelled them to the top of the table. The goals began to flow as Ilkeston, Droylsden and Stocksbridge were all beaten by a 4-1 scoreline, Stafford were thrashed 4-0 and a 5-2 win was recorded at Witton. The Reds also won closer encounters against Nantwich, King's Lynn, Matlock and Blyth.

Tom Davies opens the scoring at Marine to begin a terrific run of 12 consecutive victories

An injury-time volley from Tom Greaves won the clash at major rivals Chorley

The best two results in the run both came away to fellow title challengers. When United visited leaders Chorley we were 12 points behind them, but with a game in hand and the knowledge that we still had to play them at home. The hosts seemed content for a goalless draw to dent our promotion bid, but FC showed their opponents that it wasn't over yet when a Greaves volley three minutes into added time gained a last-gasp win. Skelmersdale had led the table for much of the season before recently losing some ground, but they were still well-equipped to keep the race wide open. The Reds were undaunted by the task, and took a deserved first-half lead when Wright's speculative effort was spilled into his own net by former FC goalkeeper Zach Hibbert. A tremendous Greaves header extended the advantage before the hosts pulled one back, only for Brownhill to seal the 3-1 win soon after.

Two of the season's star performers had been attracting interest from professional clubs, and within a few days of each other it was announced that Tom Davies had signed a contract to play for Fleetwood Town the following season, and Charlie Raglan would be joining Ollie Banks at Chesterfield in the summer. Whilst naturally disappointed to lose their talents, the club were proud to provide a route for players to achieve their ambitions. Chesterfield returned the favour by sending young forward Jacob Hazel to FC on loan for the rest of the season, and he joined fellow striker Connor Bower and goalkeepers Nick Culkin and Andy Robertson in the squad.

The dozen wins set up the match of the season between the top two, with visitors Chorley three points ahead of FC having played a game more, but with a superior goal difference that was unlikely to be overhauled in the remaining games. United were desperate to win and the feeling was that the visitors would be content with a draw, but they found themselves two goals ahead thanks to defensive errors, one of which led to a controversial penalty. The crowd of 4,152 were treated to a pulsating encounter as FC bombarded the visitors, who to their credit held firm until Raglan's fierce volley rippled the net with seven minutes to go. Three minutes later the scores were level when Greaves kept his cool to fire into the far corner, but Chorley repelled all further attacks to hold onto their point.

The unbeaten run finally came to an end with a 1-2 defeat at home to Buxton, but the team picked themselves up to take the title race down to the very last day. After a nervy first half, Grantham were eventually beaten 3-0, and then United twice came from behind to get a 3-2 win at Stamford which was sealed by Norton's superb late winner. On Easter Monday, Ashton United came to Gigg Lane looking to consolidate their own play-off spot, and raced into an early two-goal lead. With the title slipping away, the manager changed formation before half-time, and the move reaped rewards in the second period as Greaves and Norton drew the Reds level. With Chorley winning their game, a draw would not be enough to keep FC in the hunt, but Ashton were managing to hold on despite constant threats to their goal. The scores were still level as the game entered stoppage time, until Greg Daniels headed a dramatic winner to keep FC one point behind Chorley going into the last match of the season.

Matthew Wolfenden's winner at Blyth Spartans made it 12 consecutive victories as the Reds chased promotion

Charlie Raglan's ferocious volley got FC back in the game at home to Chorley

Greg Daniels nodded the stoppage-time winner as FC came from two goals down to beat Ashton United and take the title race to the final day

A large vocal following accompanied the Reds down to Barwell for the final match of the league campaign with the hopes of roaring their heroes to the title, but they knew that only a United win coupled with Chorley dropping points at Buxton would secure top spot. The team did their bit by racing to a two-goal lead thanks to Davies and Norton, before Byrne's lovely lob sealed the 3-0 victory, but by then news had reached the ranks that Chorley had edged ahead, and they did not relinquish the advantage and deservedly gained the automatic promotion spot.

FC's second-placed finish gave us a home semi-final with Ashton United, where after a nervy first half the Reds took the lead with a penalty from Wright. However, in the last 25 minutes Greaves, Norton and Wright – the main providers of goals – were all withdrawn due to injury. In that situation, most other teams would introduce defensive reinforcements to protect the advantage, but the Reds felt that the safest way to progress would be to bag a second. Mulholland rattling the crossbar was the closest they came, and they paid the ultimate price when Ashton's Dale Johnson equalised from a counter-attack in stoppage time to force the game into an extra half hour. The noise levels from the terraces became higher, spurring the players on, but despite several chances the lack of the team's most clinical finishers was showing and a penalty shoot-out looked inevitable. But the visitors won a corner with

Despite winning at Barwell on the final day, the title narrowly eluded the Reds

120 minutes on the clock, which was scrambled home at the back post to crush our promotion hopes for another year.

That was pretty much the last kick of FC United's tenure at Gigg Lane, and whilst the heartache of a fourth successive play-off defeat was clear, all at the club could be proud of the achievements this season, both on and off the pitch. The team finished in their highest ever league position, and also racked up their highest points tally in the Northern Premier League. There was also the not-so-insignificant matter of building work beginning at Broadhurst Park to re-affirm the pride that all FC United supporters feel in owning their own football club.

Jerome Wright gives FC the lead from the spot in the play-off semi-final against Ashton United but the Reds fell to injury-time goals in both normal and extra-time

2014/15: Northern Premier League Premier Division

With the heartbreak of another play-off defeat still fresh in our minds, FC United regrouped for the 2014/15 campaign determined not to suffer the same way again, with automatic promotion by winning the league very much the priority. Joining Tom Davies and Charlie Raglan in leaving the club was former skipper Adam Jones, whilst Rhodri Giggs retired from playing duties to manage the reserve team and Chris Worsley was expected to miss the season after his injury the previous campaign. Needing some new centre-backs, manager Karl Marginson signed James Knowles from Bradford Park Avenue, and also persuaded two former players to return in the shape of Andy Pearson and Shaun Connor. Adding to the attacking talents was the exciting Craig Lindfield who boasted plenty of Football League experience, and midfielder John Pritchard.

The team gelled well during the pre-season programme, but made a slow start in the league by drawing each of the first four games – away at Barwell and Trafford, and home to Buxton and Belper Town at the club's new temporary base of Bower Fold in Stalybridge. The first win came at home to Ramsbottom United at the end of August, by which time extra defensive reinforcements had been drafted in. Chris Lynch and Luke Ashworth were enrolled after a bad injury to Connor

After drawing each of the first four league games, FC finally picked up a win against Ramsbottom United at Bower Fold

and a suspension for Pearson. They were just two of a number of early-season changes the manager made to the squad, as he allowed Lee Neville, Astley Mulholland and Nelson Mota to find new clubs. Into the set-up came teenage midfielder Tom Brown and former Premier League star Andy Welsh, with a brief return for former winger Stephen Johnson.

A Joe Fox volley, his first strike for the club, earned a priceless win at Blyth Spartans before the Reds uncharacteristically recorded two consecutive goalless draws, at Marine and home to Matlock Town. The FA Cup campaign began and ended at home within a fortnight, as a Tom Greaves brace helped defeat Prescot Cables before Lancaster City knocked FC out for the second time in four seasons when they bagged a late winner against the run of play. In between, the unbeaten league record fell with a 1-4 defeat at Frickley Athletic before the team made amends when Matthew Wolfenden's double inspired a 3-1 win over Grantham Town.

October began well when Welsh's goal inspired a league win over Whitby Town, before a much-changed team exited the Manchester Premier Cup at Radcliffe Borough on penalties after a 1-1 draw. 18-year-old Michael Brewster scored FC's goal on his debut (he would later sign for St Mirren) while fellow debutant, keeper Nick Culkin (36), became only the second player to represent both Manchester United and FC United of Manchester at first-team level. The Reds fell behind at Nantwich Town, before substitutes Greaves and Brown turned the game around to record a third league win on the trot. The rest of the month produced a mixed bag of results, with disappointing defeats at home to Skelmersdale United and at Ilkeston alongside two further goalless draws – at Matlock and home to Blyth, when Michael Norton suffered a serious injury. The only highlight was a hard-earned home win over Rushall Olympic when recent signing Matty Kay struck on his home debut before Scott Cheetham was sent off as the Reds held on.

The league results in November were also varied, although the performances were steadily improving. United dug deep to gain a point at Buxton after Wolfenden was harshly dismissed, but he made amends days later by scoring twice in the first five minutes to set FC on the way to a 4-0 victory over Witton Albion. A late Greaves winner saw off Frickley in a five-goal thriller that saw a first goal and a red card for Lindfield, who was now having a major influence after a two-month lay-off. Then came an unlucky 1-2 loss at Stourbridge, which turned out to be an experience the team would not relive for a while.

November was also a busy month on the cup front, seeing the beginning of a memorable campaign whilst another was exited at the first hurdle. In the League Challenge Cup, United were again eliminated on penalties at Curzon Ashton after a 0-0 draw, but it was the FA Trophy that really helped to bring the season to life and reinforce the belief and spirit within the squad. Goals from Jerome Wright and Matt Walwyn defeated Padiham 2-0, and Wolfenden's double earned progress by the same score against Buxton. After the team fell behind against the run of play at Barwell, Callum Byrne's deserved equaliser set up what turned out to be a very eventful replay. Both teams were reduced to ten men in the first half, with Lynch's dismissal also gifting Barwell a penalty, which was converted by their goalkeeper. The visitors then doubled their lead early in the second half, which remained until Byrne's terrific strike reduced the deficit with 13 minutes remaining. United were still trailing deep into added time before a comical own goal from Connor Gudger levelled the scores, and in the 95th minute the goalkeeper could only parry a dipping shot from Brown, allowing Walwyn to rifle home a dramatic winner.

The club's first appearance in the FA Trophy's first round saw us handed a home draw with Conference North side Harrogate Town, and FC recorded a thoroughly impressive but comfortable 4-0 win. Captain Dean Stott scored a first-half brace, the first of which was an astonishing effort from near

Jerome Wright opened the scoring against Padiham to begin the FA Trophy run

the halfway line, and further goals from Wolfenden and Greg Daniels sealed the victory. A series of postponements meant that the team played no league matches for over a month, leaving them halfway down the table but with games in hand on most of the title challengers. A now-customary second half of the season charge up the table would be required, and the team began that in style by winning all four matches over the festive period. New landlords Curzon Ashton, sitting in second place, were soundly beaten 4-0, but United suffered a huge blow when Knowles was stretchered off with a broken leg that ended his season. The long trip to King's Lynn Town produced a 2-1 victory that was sealed by Lewis Lacy's first FC goal, then lowly Trafford were beaten 3-0 before the Reds triumphed 2-0 in the visit to another title challenger, Ashton United.

FC were trailing to Barwell in the FA Trophy deep into added time, but a terrific last-gasp winner by Matt Walwyn completed a remarkable turnaround

The goalscoring exploits of Greaves, Wolfenden and Lindfield had been crucial in recent matches, and they carried their excellent form through the memorable matches of the first weeks of 2015. Returning to FA Trophy duty, FC were drawn away to old rivals Chorley in the second round, and the hosts' psychological advantage after pipping United to the title last season looked to have gained them the upper hand as they found themselves two goals up at the break. However, a superb brace from Greaves and a cool finish from Wolfenden turned the tie on its head with eight minutes to go, only for the home side to bag an equaliser shortly afterwards. Luckily for FC, in the replay Greaves carried on where he left off by scoring the only goal with an unstoppable shot.

The manager added to the ranks by signing exciting striker Shelton Payne from Trafford, and he was soon joined by midfielder Rory Fallon and defender Nia Bayunu from the same club. Payne made his debut when FC made a brief return to league action, and to Bower Fold, for the game with Nantwich, which only went ahead due to the efforts of more than 100 supporters who helped to clear snow from the pitch. In a similar situation to the previous time this had happened, against Blyth two years previously, it initially looked as though the endeavours would be in vain as the visitors took an early lead, which they held until the 70th minute when Greaves,

just on as a substitute, equalised with his first touch. It seemed that the Reds would have to settle for a point in difficult conditions until Payne's low cross deep into injury time was bundled home by Lindfield to earn the win that rewarded the hard work of the volunteers.

The third round of the FA Trophy gave FC a home tie with AFC Fylde, the other club that were promoted at our expense last season, but yet again United saw to it that higher-ranked opposition were blown away with a wonderful 3-1 victory. Lindfield was the inspiration with a fantastic early brace, and Wright's penalty extended the lead before the visitors pulled a goal back. FC were the lowest-ranked club in the draw for the quarter-finals, and the reward was a trip to Torquay United, who had been a Football League side the previous season. In a much-anticipated encounter, almost 1,400 Reds travelled down to Devon to roar on their team, and both players and fans would be proud of each other with their respective performances. The fans were making all the noise in the stands, and the team were not undaunted on the pitch and took the game to their hosts. Sadly, the home side claimed a late winner on the counter-attack, and despite Walwyn almost coming to the rescue again when his header hit the bar, the club's tremendous and unforgettable run in the competition was over for this season.

Craig Lindfield's early double set up a fantastic win over AFC Fylde to send United into the FA Trophy quarter-finals

Matt Walwyn's late header crashes back off the bar as FC's memorable FA Trophy run comes to an end at Torquay United

Greg Daniels hit the winner against Halesowen Town to send the Reds to the top of the table for the first time

The Trophy run, and the concurrent league wins, had helped to raise the spirit within the squad to unprecedented levels, and now all sights were set on harnessing that to achieve that much-desired promotion. When they returned to league action, FC were sitting in eighth position in the standings, some 14 points off the top but with nine games in hand over the leaders, and also having played several fewer games than any of the other teams above. Facing a schedule of 20 games in 11 weeks, the squad embraced the task and won each of the six games in February to take the winning streak to 11 consecutive victories. Lindfield got the ball rolling with a superb strike at home to Barwell before Greaves sealed the win with a quick-fire double. Relegation-threatened Marine were set to pull off a shock when they raced into a two-goal lead before the Reds hit back to win 5-2, and another Greaves brace inspired a tremendous 3-0 win over Ashton United that enabled FC to leapfrog the visitors into second place. Another

two from Greaves and a screamer from Payne earned a 3-1 win at Belper after United had fallen behind early on, before a winner from Daniels in a tight encounter with Halesowen Town saw the Reds hit top spot for the first time.

Daniels and Lynch scored to earn a 2-1 win at Grantham, before the winning run was halted with a 1-1 draw at Rushall Olympic. After a victory over King's Lynn, Greaves rescued a precious point in an entertaining 2-2 draw with fellow challengers Ilkeston, before Lindfield's header gained another narrow win in tricky conditions at Halesowen. The visit of Workington saw FC take on the team with the greatest potential to overhaul the lead, so Lacy's early winner earned the crucial, but deserved, three points. A couple of dubious refereeing decisions arguably contributed to a 1-1 draw at Stamford, but the Reds responded with two wins on the road, at Whitby and Ramsbottom.

Lewis Lacy's strike settled the crucial encounter with closest title challengers Workington

United could almost taste promotion when Lindfield opened the scoring in the home game with landlords Curzon, but the 'away' side bagged an equaliser in the second half which began a nervy run-in for the Reds. Two more points were dropped in a goalless draw at lowly Witton, before FC tasted a league defeat for the first time in five months at Skelmersdale. When Stamford, sitting in the relegation spots, took an early lead in the return to Bower Fold, the fans could be forgiven for feeling a little concerned. The players, however, did not panic, and clinical finishes from Greaves, Lindfield and Payne turned the deficit into a confidence-boosting 3-1 victory.

FC now had just two matches remaining, and knew that they ideally needed to win the final home game with Stourbridge, because if they dropped points the last game was a trip to Workington in what would be a last-day title decider. United's vastly superior goal difference would give them a massive advantage in the event of a draw with the Midlanders, but a defeat would mean that Workington could claim the title with a win. This didn't bear thinking about, and so the season's largest home crowd of 3,588 was in attendance to roar their lads home. After a somewhat cagey first half, the noise levels increased as the team took to the field for the second period, and they responded with a fantastic performance, pouring forward at every opportunity. The persistence paid off in the 69th minute when a tremendous crossfield ball from Liam Brownhill picked out Lindfield, whose cross was headed home by the leaping Daniels to send the Reds into raptures. Minutes later, a free-kick for the visitors pierced the wall, but David Carnell saved well to preserve his 25th clean sheet of a terrific season, and the most important as soon after the whistle blew and FC United of Manchester were finally crowned as the Northern Premier League champions and earned promotion to the newly-named National League North.

Greg Daniels heads home against Stourbridge to win the 2015 Northern Premier League title for FC United

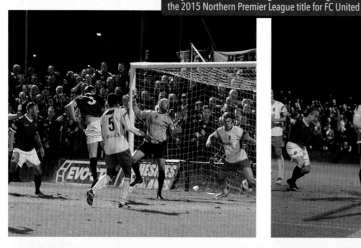

NORTHERN PREMIER LEAGUE
PREMIER DIVISION CHAMPIONS 2014/15

Captain Dean Stott lifts the Northern Premier League championship trophy

While the result of the remaining trip to Workington was irrelevant to FC, the hosts needed to win to cement their place in 2nd spot, and they duly achieved that with a narrow victory. For United, the competitive season was over, but there were still two significant fixtures planned for May, when we would finally play at our new home of Broadhurst Park after ten years of hard work, determination and belief. The opening event was a wonderful occasion as the current first team took on a team of FC United Old Boys. Greaves had the honour of scoring the ground's first goal, and Daniels added two more before strikes from Tunji Moses and Nicky Platt ensured that the match finished 3-2. On 29th May, 4,232 people created a fantastic atmosphere at the showpiece friendly with an SL Benfica XI for the ground's official opening, which the visitors won with a late strike from Diogo Gonçalves.

FC United line up before the showpiece friendly with Benfica that marked the official opening of Broadhurst Park

2015/16: National League North

FC United embarked on their first season in the National League North with much the same squad that had won promotion in the spring. Joe Fox, Matty Kay and Shelton Payne had moved on to pastures new, whilst Lewis Lacy ventured to play in the USA on a scholarship. Joining the club in pre-season were Adam Thurston, Sean Cooke and Cameron Murray, all of whom had experience of playing at a higher level. The squad was further strengthened the week before the season began with the addition of exciting forward Sam Madeley.

The first game in the new division was a trip to Cheltenham to face Gloucester City, but FC slipped to a narrow 0-1 defeat on a frustrating afternoon. The first league game at Broadhurst Park saw the Reds lose 1-2 to Stockport County, but not before Rory Fallon had delighted the home crowd by firing United ahead with the first competitive goal at the ground. Luke Ashworth's equaliser against Tamworth earned a first point in Moston, but the team then slumped to a 0-3 defeat with a terrible display at Chorley, with Jerome Wright sent off for the second game running. Despite conceding an early goal at home to Brackley Town, FC finally earned their first win of the season with goals from Matthew Wolfenden, Sam Madeley and Tom Greaves.

Sam Madeley's spectacular volley began the superb late comeback in the 3-3 draw with Curzon Ashton

Tom Greaves sealed FC United's first win at Broadhurst Park and the first in National League North against Brackley Town

That was the beginning of a good run that produced 13 points from five games and saw the Reds shoot up to eighth in the table. Comfortable wins at Hednesford Town and Lowestoft Town were followed by a late Wolfenden winner at home to Corby Town, with the only dropped points coming in a 3-3 home draw with Curzon Ashton. Despite trailing 1-3 with three minutes remaining, a spectacular strike from Madeley was quickly followed by an equaliser from Fallon to snatch a point and prompt Broadhurst Park's first proper 'goon'.

Unfortunately the league results then took a drastic downturn, starting with a 0-4 defeat at AFC Fylde as the home side ruthlessly exploited the dismissal of goalkeeper Dave Carnell. Four days later, Nia Bayunu was shown the team's fourth red card of the season and Stalybridge Celtic took the points by converting the resultant penalty. Further losses to Worcester City, North Ferriby United, Boston United, AFC Telford United and Gainsborough Trinity meant an unwanted club record of seven consecutive league defeats and left the team hovering around the relegation places by mid-November.

Broadhurst Park's first FA Cup match saw the Reds beat Witton Albion 3-1

Luke Ashworth headed a late consolation as FC were knocked out of the FA Cup in the first round by League One Chesterfield

The FA Cup provided a welcome autumn distraction, with the Reds emerging victorious over old rivals Witton Albion in Moston's first game in the competition. Another old foe, Buxton, were defeated after a replay before the team disposed of Midland League side Sporting Khalsa to progress to the first round for only the second time in the club's history. FC were rewarded with a home draw against League One club Chesterfield, but the controversial scheduling of the match on a Monday night for live TV coverage saw hundreds of supporters boycotting the first half, and then continuing the passionate protest inside the ground for the second period.

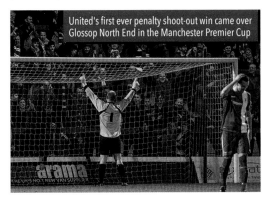

United's first ever penalty shoot-out win came over Glossop North End in the Manchester Premier Cup

Tom Greaves headed FC's winner at Stockport County

On the pitch, the visitors bagged two early goals on their way to a comfortable victory that saw them introduce former FC favourites Ollie Banks and Charlie Raglan from the bench. Banks hit his side's fourth goal before Ashworth headed a late consolation for United.

On an eventful day in late October, the club announced the return of record goalscorer Rory Patterson after seven years away, before knocking Glossop North End out of the Manchester Premier Cup. Michael Norton scored his first goal at Broadhurst, but the game ended 2-2 and so was decided on penalties. Veteran goalkeeper Nick Culkin helped United to a commanding position before former Red Martin Parker hit the post to ensure FC won a penalty shoot-out for the first time. In the next round, the team were eliminated by the odd goal in seven in an entertaining encounter with Stalybridge. A few days later, United were unable to repeat their tremendous FA Trophy run of the previous campaign and fell at the first hurdle to Telford.

With the team near the bottom of the table and out of all cups, Karl Marginson took steps to rejuvenate the squad. Leaving the club were Michael Norton, Dave Birch, Nia Bayunu, Callum Byrne, Scott Cheetham, Sean Cooke, James Knowles, Chris Lynch and Cameron Murray, with Patterson returning to Derry City soon after. In their places came midfielders Sam Sheridan, Harry Winter and Scott Kay, defender Tom Smyth, plus the attack-minded George Thomson on loan from Chester. The additions contributed to an upturn in results, starting with an unexpected 2-2 draw at league leaders Nuneaton Town where only a disputed injury-time penalty earned the hosts a point. After a tremendous win at Stockport, Nuneaton were beaten 3-2 at Broadhurst as the new line-up was beginning to gel.

Broadhurst Park

M40 0FJ

FOOTBALL CLUB UNITED OF MANCHESTER

Sam Madeley's winner completed the amazing comeback against Harrogate Town after the Reds were three down

Three home games over the festive period brought a defeat to Gloucester, a draw with Hednesford and a win over Bradford Park Avenue, and similar inconsistency would continue to haunt the team until March. A last-gasp Tamworth equaliser denied them a hard-earned win after Smyth's sending-off, but an abject performance resulted in a deserved 0-4 thrashing at Brackley. Further defensive reinforcements were added with the return of Lewis Lacy and the signings of Chris Chantler and Tom Eckersley, and both Chantler and Lacy scored to help the Reds to the highest win of the season when Lowestoft were soundly beaten 6-1. The following week, Harrogate Town raced into a three-goal lead after 36 minutes before goals from Thomson, Sheridan, Greaves and Madeley turned the game around for a sensational 4-3 victory.

Those results, plus the permanent signing of Thomson, provided renewed confidence that the team would be good enough to prosper in this division, but a wretched run of results in February kept the fear of relegation looming. An extraordinary sequence of events contributed to a 1-5 defeat at Telford as Carnell was injured and replaced in goal by Madeley, who conceded an unfortunate own goal and was then harshly dismissed. He in turn was replaced by Ashworth, who was powerless to prevent the subsequent penalty and three further strikes. Ashworth himself was sent off in a 1-3 defeat by Alfreton Town, which was closely followed by a similar result at Bradford and then the club's record defeat at the time when Harrogate gained revenge with a 0-5 drubbing. Despite performing admirably, it had certainly been a baptism of fire for stand-in teenage goalkeeper Dylan Forth.

Carnell was back for the visit of high-flying North Ferriby, but the Reds conceded an early soft penalty to once again give themselves a mountain to climb. However, a Wolfenden brace looked to have sealed the points until the visitors equalised in the last minute. Undeterred, FC attacked again and Craig Lindfield hit the winner deep into injury-time to seal a priceless 3-2 victory. That was the winger's last kick for the club for the

time being as he and Liam Brownhill joined Ashton United on loan, and Dean Stott also left the squad with a move to Colne. To replace them, the manager added the vastly experienced defender Dale Tonge and classy striker Dale Johnson.

Craig Lindfield came on to grab the last-gasp winner over North Ferriby United

Broadhurst Park's biggest crowd of the season saw new signing Dale Johnson seal the terrific victory over Chorley

After a hard-fought point gained at Worcester and a narrow defeat to promotion-chasing Fylde, the new boys helped to make a difference in a tremendous win at runaway league leaders Solihull Moors. The returning Jerome Wright scored his first goal at this level in the opening minute, and Thomson struck the winner just two minutes after the hosts had equalised. Thomson hit another winner at Alfreton, before another wonderful performance saw Chorley defeated 2-0 in Moston thanks to Wright's penalty and Johnson's first goal for the club in front of 4,150 supporters. For the first time in the season the team had won three consecutive matches, and the climb to 12th place in the table had helped to ease the relegation fears.

However, despite demotion now being decidedly unlikely, FC would still not be mathematically safe for another three weeks. After a goalless draw at Curzon, home defeats by Boston and Stalybridge came either side of a win at Corby before the Reds were finally assured of keeping their place in the National League North for another term. The campaign ended on a high with a win at Gainsborough, followed by a late comeback when a Greaves brace earned a 2-2 draw at home to champions Solihull. At the end of a somewhat transitional season, the revamped team finished in a creditable 13th position in the table, and could look to the results of the final 12 games to provide inspiration that they could compete well in the division.

Tom Greaves hit a late brace as FC came from two down to draw with champions Solihull Moors on an eventful last day of the campaign

2016/17: National League North

The summer of 2016 was quite eventful off the field at FC United, with an almost completely new board being voted in and taking up their posts during the close season. In contrast, for the first time in the club's history each of the starting XI on the pitch for the team's opening league game had been with the squad the previous season. Leaving the ranks over the summer were Greg Daniels, Adam Thurston, Matt Walwyn and Dylan Forth, and their places were taken by a group of exciting youngsters with great potential. Defenders Zac Corbett and Jake Williams, midfielders Nathan Lowe, Kieran Glynn and Kisimba Kisimba, plus strikers Jason Gilchrist and Harry Pratt had all impressed in pre-season and were given a chance by Karl Marginson to stake their claims.

The league campaign began with a trip to old foes Chorley, and supporters would have been worried about the lack of experience added to the squad when FC fell behind to an early goal. However, two strikes from George Thomson and another by Jerome Wright saw the Reds twice take the lead before the hosts made it 3-3 with five minutes remaining. The equaliser was particularly frustrating for goalkeeper Dave Carnell,

Matthew Wolfenden put United ahead in a superb 2-0 win over Stockport County at Broadhurst Park

who had just made a great save from a penalty only for the home side to score from the resulting corner. A point was also gained with a goalless draw in the first home game against AFC Telford United, before local rivals Stockport County came to Broadhurst for a Friday night game boasting a 100% record from their opening fixtures. Undaunted, FC put in a great performance and went ahead when Matthew Wolfenden's superb first time strike broke the deadlock just after the half hour mark. The win was sealed with four minutes to play when Lowe's first touch saw the ball hit the back of the net just 40 seconds after he had entered the field as a substitute. Dale Johnson had actually got the final touch that took it past the keeper, but no matter who got the credit for the goal, the whole team deserved the plaudits on the night.

They were unable to build on the unbeaten start, however, and the remaining four matches in August yielded just one point. That came courtesy of Johnson's strike at home to Worcester City which separated narrow defeats to Salford City and Brackley Town. The month closed with an agonising home loss to Darlington 1883, in which FC had fought back from two goals down only to fall behind again with ten minutes remaining when a cruel deflection left debutant goalkeeper Ashley Frith helpless. Gilchrist had scored his first goal for the club with a superb long-range chip, and he followed that up by adding to a Tom Greaves double to claim the winning goal at Boston United. September produced a further two defeats, to high-flyers Harrogate Town and AFC Fylde, and two draws with Tamworth and Curzon Ashton. The squad was bolstered during the month by two loan signings from Rochdale: goalkeeper Johny Diba Musangu and attacker James Hooper, who scored the equaliser at Tamworth.

The club's participation in the FA Cup began with a 2nd Qualifying Round trip to former Northern Premier League rivals Ossett Town, and they returned with a 7-1 victory to record the team's biggest win for over three years. The unlikely hero of the day was centre-back Luke Ashworth, who became the first United defender to score a hat-trick. The reward was

The Reds threw away a three-goal lead over Alfreton Town, but Luke Ashworth spared the blushes with a late winner

Jerome Wright's late equaliser and an injury-time winner from Harry Winter earned three points for FC at Gainsborough Trinity

a home tie with Harrogate, in which FC looked comfortable leading 3-1 with 12 minutes to go. But the visitors hit two late goals, with the equaliser in the sixth minute of stoppage time, to earn a replay where the Reds fell to a 0-2 defeat.

The lads looked to have recovered when they stormed into a three-goal lead at home to Alfreton Town, only to allow the visitors to draw level in the second half. Thankfully, the Reds responded well and Ashworth fired home the winner in the 82nd minute. He was on the mark again a fortnight later when FC upset the odds with a 2-0 win at title contenders Kidderminster Harriers, but these were the only points gained in a five-match spell. Losses on the road at Telford and FC Halifax Town preceded disappointing home defeats to Gloucester City and bottom placed Bradford Park Avenue, and left United slipping down the table themselves.

They were back to winning ways on the short trip to Stalybridge Celtic, where Marginson was faced with a selection dilemma due to Ashworth's suspension and Tom Eckersley leaving the club. He pulled Scott Kay back into defence alongside 17-year-old Sam Baird, who had recently captained the FA Youth Cup team. The youngster was voted man of the match in the 4-2 victory, and kept his place for the midweek Manchester Premier Cup tie at Abbey Hey. He was joined by fellow teenagers Kisimba, Pratt, Michael Jones and Chris Hill as a hat-trick from Tom Greaves saw United through to the semi-final. Greaves had also scored twice in the previous round, to add to George Thomson's treble, when FC eased past Chadderton with a 6-0 win. Also joining the squad in the autumn was former Workington striker Gareth Arnison.

A comfortable 3-0 home triumph over Nuneaton Town was followed by a 2-1 win at Gainsborough Trinity, where very late goals from Wright and Harry Winter completed the comeback for the fourth straight victory. This run came to an abrupt end in the FA Trophy at home to Nuneaton, who gained a quick revenge with a 1-5 thrashing. Two 1-1 home draws over the festive period, with Boston and Altrincham, came either side of a 3-0 win at Moss Lane, where 41-year-old Brazilian goalkeeper Adriano Basso became the club's oldest debutant.

The Christmas period once again demonstrated the special nature of FC United, as an initiative led by Community Manager Andy Cheshire provided food and comforts to the homeless of Manchester. Volunteers including players and staff helped to feed people in the city centre, and the club opened the ground on Christmas Day to offer food, shower facilities, warm clothing and entertainment.

The league results in the first seven matches of 2017 were not kind to the Reds, with four draws and three defeats, although those losses came at the hands of league leaders Fylde and fellow promotion chasers Salford and Stockport. Basso's penalty save earned a point at Worcester before the Reds were unluckily denied all three when Gilchrist had a late goal ruled out in the 2-2 home draw with Harrogate. They also cursed their luck at home to Chorley; goals from Gilchrist, Wolfenden and Lowe had given FC a commanding three-goal half-time lead, but the visitors clawed two back early in the second half. United hung on until Basso was sent off in injury time, and his replacement Sam Sheridan was powerless to prevent a 96th minute equaliser from Scott Leather, who coincidentally had also made it 3-3 in the late stages on the opening day.

The club had taken the opportunity of a free Saturday on 4th February to organise an international friendly match at Broadhurst Park to generate much needed revenue, with fellow supporter-owned club SV Austria Salzburg providing the opposition. Further events around the game, which included a beer festival, made the weekend a success as the Reds ran out 3-0 winners in the main attraction. They followed this by beating West Didsbury & Chorlton 7-1 in the Manchester Premier Cup semi-final, to reach the final for the first time. Gilchrist scored a first-half hat-trick, with Wolfenden adding his own treble after coming on as a substitute at half-time.

A turning point with regards to league results came at Gloucester City on 25th February. The Reds trailed 0-2 at half-time before Lowe's sublime chip got them back into the game.

Nathan Lowe hit a stunning late winner at Gloucester City from inside his own half

FC thought the chance of a point had gone when Wright's penalty was saved, but substitute Greaves hit the equaliser with four minutes left. Less than a minute later Lowe spotted the home keeper off his line and hit an audacious lob from inside his own half to snatch a dramatic win. United beat Kidderminster 1-0 at home the following week to claim the double over the third-placed side, and were victors by the same score at home to Tamworth. With the game goalless deep into injury time, Lowe struck again with another spectacular long range effort with virtually the last kick of the game to seal a third successive victory.

Changes to the squad around this time included the additions of defender Jordan Fagbola, midfielder Greg Wilkinson and forward Tomi Adeloye, although Harry Winter left to join Stockport soon after captaining the Reds against them. A defeat at Alfreton was followed by another at home to Halifax before a much changed team snatched another late comeback win at Curzon Ashton. Lowe capped off a great few weeks with a wonderful equaliser before Wolfenden's close range finish claimed the points with just two minutes remaining. April began with two disappointing draws: 2-2 at home to Stalybridge and 0-0 at Bradford, where Huddersfield Town's loanee goalkeeper Ryan Schofield made his debut to become the youngest player to start a league game for FC United.

George Thomson broke away to slot home the winning goal as FC did the double over title candidates Kidderminster Harriers

Academy Student of the Year, Lewis Unwin, with the Nobby Stiles Shield

With the Reds assured of their place in the division for next season, it was little surprise that they lost their next two fixtures to Brackley and Darlington, who were both chasing a place in the play-offs. They recovered to complete the National League North fixtures with their two biggest victories of the league campaign, 4-1 at Nuneaton and then 5-1 at home to Gainsborough. Wolfenden's double in the last game took his career total to 94 goals for FC United, the second highest in the club's history at the time. This was witnessed by the highest crowd of the season at 4,064, which was boosted by many local residents who were offered free admission. Before the game the club's Academy Student of the Year, Lewis Unwin, was presented with the inaugural Nobby Stiles Shield by the family and friends of the North Manchester football legend.

The season ended in May at Oldham Athletic's Boundary Park, where the Reds faced Stalybridge in the Manchester Premier Cup Final. FC took an early lead in the 3rd minute when Jake Williams netted his first goal for the club with a mis-hit cross that deceived the goalkeeper and nestled into the back of the net. He may not have meant it, but neither he nor the United fans cared one bit as they had one hand on the trophy. Both sides had chances to score, with FC missing several and Celtic going close to an equaliser on numerous occasions, but the Reds defence held firm to claim the trophy for the first time in the club's history. Captain Jerome Wright lifted the trophy and collected his fourth medal on his 400th appearance for FC.

A 3rd minute cross from full-back Jake Williams from out by the right touchline deceived the Stalybridge Celtic goalkeeper to give FC United an early lead in the Manchester Premier Cup Final

MANCHESTER FOOTBALL ASSOCIATION PREMIER CUP WINNERS 2016/17

Captain Jerome Wright lifts the Manchester Premier Cup after United's 1-0 victory over Stalybridge Celtic in the final

An unexpected 2-0 win at York City was a rare highlight during FC United's poor start to the 2017/18 campaign

2017/18: National League North

Despite ending the previous season with silverware, Karl Marginson drastically overhauled his FC United squad during the summer of 2017. Among the players leaving the club were stalwarts Jerome Wright, Matthew Wolfenden, Dave Carnell, Luke Ashworth, Sam Sheridan, George Thomson, Chris Chantler and Dale Tonge. Goalkeeper Lloyd Allinson, defenders Joel Senior, Matty Hughes, Danny Wisdom and Danny Brady, midfielders Richie Baker and Callum Nicholas, wingers Joel Logan and Jason St Juste plus forward Connor McCarthy took their places in the squad. They were joined by the returning Craig Lindfield and Lewis Lacy as the recruits made a promising start to the pre-season campaign, but this turned to inconsistency that was carried into the new term.

The team made the worst start to a league campaign in the club's history so far, picking up just one point in the first five games and dropping points from drawing or winning positions in four of those. The first three games were odd-goal defeats, away at Brackley Town and to both Spennymoor Town and Kidderminster Harriers at home, during which only Wisdom and Jason Gilchrist had scored for the Reds. Bolstered by the additions of midfielder Michael Connor and forward James Hooper, FC looked to have kick-started the campaign with a good display away at Southport. They led 3-1 with just three minutes remaining, but the hosts struck twice in the final moments to level the game at 3-3. A terrible 0-3 defeat at Bradford Park Avenue then left United rooted firmly to the bottom of the National League North table.

The Reds finally got their first win at home to Boston United, who had two men sent off early in the second half of the 2-1 victory. Two days later United faced a daunting trip to York City, where for much of the game they had to defend well as the hosts dominated. However another red card for the opponents allowed FC to take advantage and Tom Greaves slotted home when ten minutes to go. Gilchrist added a terrific second to seal the points and take the Reds up to 16th in the table.

Unfortunately FC were unable to build on this momentum and proceeded to slip to four straight defeats in the first half of September. Leamington and Blyth Spartans both left Broadhurst Park with the points, before United suffered a first-ever loss to Curzon Ashton. The Reds were given a glimmer of hope during the tough midweek trip to Darlington when the hosts were a man down at half-time, but FC self-destructed with two of their own sent off. Hughes and Connor both saw red and the home side capitalised to propel United back into the bottom two. In the meantime the club had accepted an offer from Southport for Nathan Lowe, who signed a professional contract with the full-time outfit.

United were given some welcome respite from their league woes with an away tie at Northern Counties East side Handsworth Parramore in the FA Cup 2nd qualifying round. Impressive recent midfield signing Steve Irwin gave FC the lead from the penalty spot, but the hosts grabbed a last-minute equaliser to earn a replay. The Reds made no mistake back in Moston, where goals from Connor, Gilchrist, Logan and a McCarthy hat-trick saw FC progress with a 6-2 win. United then earned a deserved 3-1 victory at home to Tamworth, when Gilchrist hit a goal-of-the-season contender by hammering the ball into the top corner from a position wide on the right.

In-form striker Jason Gilchrist scored with an outstanding shot from out by the right touchline in the 3-1 victory over Tamworth

The next round of the FA Cup gave United a short trip to Stockport County, but they looked to be crashing out of the competition when they found themselves 0-3 down in a disastrous first half. Marginson made a triple substitution at the break, and got an early response when Gilchrist pulled one back. One of the replacements was Greaves, who earlier in the week had been sent out to play for Ramsbottom United on a dual-registration basis. He celebrated his recall by further reducing the deficit in the 72nd minute, before being bundled over in the box with six minutes left. Irwin stepped up to bury another penalty and complete the unlikely comeback.

Those efforts looked to have been in vain back at Broadhurst for the replay when the Reds were reduced to nine men before the break, with Hughes and Connor the guilty men again. However, FC grabbed an unlikely lead three minutes into the second half when Greaves forced the ball home from close range. A shocked County had the vast majority of possession,

but struggled to break through a resolute United rearguard. When they did create chances they were still unable to beat a colossal Allinson as FC held on for a famous victory.

Marginson had added to the squad with forwards Tim Kinsella and Sefton Gonzales and wide men Tom Walker and Kallum Mantack, the latter on a month's loan from Oldham Athletic. Walker opened the scoring on his debut at bottom club North Ferriby United, where FC again dropped points with a late equaliser. The Reds also looked to have earned another FA Cup replay at AFC Telford United, but two strikes deep in injury time sent FC crashing out of the competition at the 4th qualifying round. Back on league duty, a dismal 0-1 defeat at Chorley the following week left United second bottom with just 11 points from 14 games, and would signal a historic change at the club.

On 24th October 2017, FC United announced that Karl Marginson would be leaving his post as manager by mutual agreement with immediate effect after more than 12 years in charge, during which the club won four promotions and three cup finals. Tom Greaves was put in temporary charge of the first team, becoming a caretaker player-manager until a permanent appointment could be made.

Also leaving the club along with Marginson were his trusted deputies Darren Lyons, Garry Vaughan and Nick Culkin. Greaves enlisted the help of Academy Coaches Jack Doyle and Tom Conroy plus Women's Team Manager Luke Podmore to join his staff alongside Goalkeeping Coach Paul Chapman.

Tom Greaves pounced as FC dumped Stockport County out of the FA Cup despite playing over half of the match with just nine men

Tom Greaves with his first FC United squad

The team made a good start to life under Greaves with a 2-1 win over Nuneaton Town. Goals from Gilchrist and Jordan Fagbola brought some optimism back to the Broadhurst terraces. They were brought back down to earth the following week with a 1-4 defeat at Stockport, who gained revenge for the FA Cup shock. Greaves selected four teenagers to start the midweek Manchester Premier Cup tie at league leaders Salford City, and his faith was rewarded with a 3-0 win. Gilchrist's brace and another from Kieran Glynn, recalled from a spell at Padiham, allowed Greaves the luxury of introducing Tyrell Palmer, a recruit from partner club Moston United, for his debut.

The galvanised Reds then picked up maximum points from two home games in mid-November, on both occasions coming from behind to earn the victories. Telford took an early lead, but Greaves led by example to level before Gilchrist took over. He put FC ahead after a wonderful piece of skill, before applying the gloss with an outrageous effort from over 40 yards to complete a 3-1 win. A few days later, Alfreton Town were two up at the break before Glynn's overhead kick pulled one back. Gilchrist coolly converted a penalty to equalise with three minutes left, and the Reds then pressed for the winner. They got their rewards in the 90th minute when Logan's cross was diverted over the line by visiting defender Tom Platt.

FC travelled to Gainsborough Trinity without prolific top scorer Jason Gilchrist, after he also joined Southport on a professional deal. His loss took the wind from the sails as the team fell to a 0-1 defeat, and then exited the FA Trophy by the same score at Northern Premier League side Marine. In between, the club appointed Greaves as Manager on a permanent basis.

Tom Greaves, Tom Conroy and Jack Doyle celebrate winning their first game in charge

Joel Logan is congratulated by United team-mates after his cross produced the last-minute winner over Alfreton Town

Jason Gilchrist celebrates his amazing long-range goal against Telford. He soon joined Southport and ended the season as top scorer for both clubs

Tom Greaves equals, and then breaks FC United's goalscoring record late on in the 3-2 win over Harrogate Town

FC trailed 0-1 at half-time to second-placed Harrogate Town in Moston on 2nd December, but produced a terrific second half display on a memorable occasion. Lindfield levelled from Walker's corner just after the break, and it was from another of his corners that FC took the lead with seven minutes to go when Greaves nodded home to claim his 99th goal for the club and equal Rory Patterson's long-standing record. The ground erupted in the last minute when Greaves converted McCarthy's cross to hammer home his 100th goal for the Reds and seal a magnificent win, although with the last kick of the game the visitors did pull one back from the penalty spot.

That began a month of remarkable results for United. Another inch-perfect spot-kick from Irwin earned a 1-1 draw with Brackley, who had leapfrogged Harrogate into second. It seemed like the long pre-Christmas journey to high-flying Spennymoor had taken its toll when FC were 1-4 down early in the second half, but a brace from McCarthy either side of Lindfield's strike completed an amazing 4-4 draw.

Table-topping Salford came to Moston on Boxing Day and twice went ahead as FC trailed 1-2 at the break. But after a red card for the visitors just into the second half, United took control and got a deserved equaliser with 16 minutes to play. Walker's cross was only partially cleared to the edge of the box, where Zac Corbett hammered home an unstoppable shot for his first goal for the club. Walker was having a field day

Tom Greaves headed the Boxing Day winner over Salford City at Broadhurst Park. Craig Lindfield and Zac Corbett earned a 2-2 draw in the return fixture

down the left side, and with nine minutes to go his chipped cross was nodded home by Greaves to complete a 3-2 win. FC travelled to Salford for the return match on New Year's Day, and again twice fell behind. Lindfield had curled home a wonderful first equaliser before Corbett made it 2-2 for the second time in a week to earn a share of the spoils.

So United had, unexpectedly, picked up nine points from five games against teams in the top five of the table over the previous month, and they carried this form into January. Another Greaves goal earned a 1-0 home win over a Southport side containing four ex-Reds, and the boss was at it again with the equaliser at promotion-chasing Blyth. The great run came to a shuddering halt at Kidderminster, where Corbett was dismissed as the hosts hit four second-half goals without reply. The Reds recovered well as their superb home form continued with a 2-0 win over Curzon, the 11th game without defeat at Broadhurst, despite Glynn's red card.

Tom Walker's displays had impressed Salford, and their offer of a full-time contract was too good to refuse for the promising youngster. With the squad short of midfield options, Greaves brought in the experienced Danny Racchi to join other recent recruits Sam Tattum, Adam Gilchrist and Jamal Crawford. After Wisdom was ruled out with a season-ending injury they were joined by Luke Higham on loan from Fleetwood Town, and all were involved as Gilchrist's early winner saw off Hyde United in the Manchester Premier Cup semi-final. However, this was the only goal scored by FC in six matches, as they gained just one league point from a 0-0 draw with Chorley. Narrow defeats to Nuneaton, Stockport and Telford were followed by the club's record hammering at the time, 0-6 at Harrogate where ex-Red George Thomson hit a hat-trick. This disastrous run plunged United back into the relegation mix.

Two young players, Jeff King from Bolton Wanderers and Gerard Garner from Fleetwood, were brought in on loan to help the goal-shy attack, and they both played their part in ending the famine in spectacular style. The Reds were three down early on at Boston, but despite Lindfield and King reducing the deficit they still trailed 2-4 with just two minutes left. Garner then got FC's third before Lindfield's stoppage time header made it 4-4 to end the losing streak. United took the momentum back to Moston, where Lindfield's cheeky flick was the only goal of the game against fellow strugglers Gainsborough. The fears were further eased with a 4-0 home win over Bradford Park Avenue, although the result largely hinged on two red cards for the visitors shortly before half-time. King took advantage by hitting home two free-kicks and a penalty for a hat-trick in his last game for the club, with fellow loanee Garner grabbing the other.

United were looking to avoid defeat from two crucial trips to the Midlands to face other relegation threatened sides, but fell to a disappointing 0-1 loss in the first at Leamington. When Hughes was harshly dismissed in the closing stages at Tamworth, FC would probably have been happy with the game ending scoreless. However, an innocuous shot from Lindfield was inexplicably spilled into his own net by the home keeper with just five minutes remaining, and then Garner made it 2-0 with almost the last kick of the game to give the Reds just their second away league victory of the campaign.

A 1-2 home defeat to Darlington meant that FC were still not safe, but their place in the National League North for next season was finally confirmed by McCarthy's winner as United completed the double over York. The league season petered out with two forgettable defeats to Alfreton and North Ferriby, although special mention must be given to Danny Racchi, Sam Tattum and Adam Gilchrist who all played the final games without payment to help the club's financial situation. Greaves also gave debuts to teenagers Elliot Simões and Steven Affleck, both graduates of the club's academy teams.

Craig Lindfield's injury-time equaliser completed FC's comeback in the amazing 4-4 draw at Boston United

A 1-0 win over York City at Broadhurst Park ensured that United would remain in the National League North or another season

Before the curtain came down on the league season, the club once again contested the final of the Manchester Premier Cup. At the Ewen Fields home of Hyde United, opponents Trafford twice took the lead but the Reds found equalisers from unlikely sources. Captain Scott Kay's tremendous header was the first leveller before Joel Senior's first goal for FC made it 2-2. That was the final score, and so the destination of the trophy was decided by a penalty shoot-out. Senior's kick was saved, but Greaves, Kay and Glynn all converted and player-of-the-year Allinson produced a fantastic save to put the pressure on Trafford. They put their next two efforts over the bar to send the cup to Broadhurst Park for the second year running.

Equalisers from Scott Kay and Joel Senior took the Manchester Premier Cup Final to penalties, where Lloyd Allinson helped FC United to defeat Trafford

MANCHESTER FOOTBALL ASSOCIATION PREMIER CUP WINNERS 2017/18

Tom Greaves and his young squad after FC overcame Trafford in the Manchester Premier Cup final

2018/19: National League North

With Tom Greaves given the FC United manager's job on a permanent basis, he set about reshaping his squad during the summer of 2018. Leaving the club were Jordan Fagbola, Matty Hughes, Zac Corbett, Kieran Glynn and Craig Lindfield. Defenders Steve O'Halloran and Chris Lynch, midfielder Brad Barnes and forwards Kurt Willoughby, Liam Dickinson, Jack Banister and Brodie Litchfield joined the returning Harry Winter and Luke Ashworth for the pre-season campaign. The squad posted an impressive sequence of results in the friendlies, but the preparations were thrown into disarray a week before the league season began when Lloyd Allinson's self-inflicted hand injury left the club without a goalkeeper.

England youth stopper Billy Crellin was drafted in on loan from Fleetwood Town, but the team was further hampered just two seconds into the opening game at Stockport County when key signing Barnes twisted a knee challenging for the ball and was carried off shortly afterwards. Willoughby claimed a debut goal, but it was a mere consolation in a 1-5 thrashing. The striker scored again as the Reds led Ashton United 3-1 at half-time in the first home game, only to eventually contrive to lose 3-4, before being soundly beaten by Boston United. Scott Kay was persuaded to return to bolster the midfield as FC finally got off the mark with a tremendous 2-1 win at Altrincham, thanks to Dickinson's header and a superb solo strike from Willoughby, but the team failed to gain any momentum as they lost 0-2 to both Leamington and Spennymoor Town to record another terrible start to a league campaign.

On 28th August 2018, Tom Greaves resigned as FC United's manager, with under-21s coach and former captain David Chadwick taking over as caretaker manager whilst the club searched for a new permanent boss.

Chadwick's stint began with a 2-2 draw at home to Bradford Park Avenue, when the Reds recovered from a two-goal deficit to earn a share of the points with goals from Litchfield and

Former skipper David Chadwick stepped up to steady the ship as caretaker manager in August

Willoughby's injury-time penalty. Danny Racchi had already left the club, and he was followed over the next few weeks by Ashworth, Dickinson, Kay and Sam Baird, who joined Droylsden on a long-term loan. Crellin was recalled by Fleetwood and was replaced initially by the return of Dave Carnell. Chadwick filled the gaps by recruiting winger Michael Donohue, left-back Lewis Thompson, forward Lewis Mansell and centre-back Billy Priestley on loan deals, and also added youngsters Theo Brierley and Cole Lonsdale during September.

The team gained two further creditable draws with Southport and Chester, but then fell to extremely disappointing defeats at fellow strugglers Guiseley and Nuneaton Borough. They managed to progress in the FA Cup with a 2-0 win over Colne, but were sent crashing out at the next stage by Witton Albion, finishing the calamitous 1-2 defeat with just eight men after Willoughby, Winter and 18-year-old winger Elliot Simões were sent off. The teenager made amends with both goals in the 2-0 win at Glossop North End in the Manchester Premier Cup, when he was joined in the line-up by fellow academy player Jan Palinkas. Brierley's superb volley put United ahead at home to Darlington, but the visitors hit back to win as the Reds suffered two further red cards for Sam Tattum and Mansell.

An extremely young line-up secured a memorable away win at high-flying Kidderminster Harriers in October

On 18th October 2018, FC United announced the appointment of Neil Reynolds as the club's new manager. He joined after a successful spell in charge at Bamber Bridge, and brought Mike Faulkner and Jamie Milligan with him as part of the backroom staff, whilst retaining the services of Dave Chadwick.

Before Reynolds officially took over on 22nd October, the team faced a daunting trip to second-placed Kidderminster Harriers. Chadwick was absent due to family commitments, but picked the team with coaches Jack Doyle and Tom Conroy who were in charge for the day. With the squad shorn of several key players due to injury and suspension, they handed league debuts to Lonsdale and midfielder Liam Healey, who were both amongst five teenagers in the starting line-up with a further three on the bench. Simões led the line, whilst the team was boosted by the return of Allinson after a 15-match absence. Despite falling behind to an early goal, the blue-shirted Reds hit back with two goals from Banister to claim only their second win of the season with a memorable 2-1 victory.

Reynolds promptly reinforced the team, bringing in his trusted captain Michael Potts and fellow midfielder Josh Wallen, and they made an immediate impact. Potts scored the first goal of the new regime with a precise long-range curler against Brackley Town, and Wallen's header put FC ahead against Alfreton Town, although on both occasions the opponents hit back to equalise in 1-1 draws. The new reign's first win came in a great performance at Blyth Spartans with Willoughby and debutant Tom Peers on the mark in a 3-0 success, and both front men struck again a week later in a 3-1 victory at Hereford.

The Reds also progressed in the Manchester Premier Cup with a 2-0 win at Mossley, where Ryan White became the third of Reynolds' signings to score on his debut. Later in the game David Chadwick came on as a substitute for his first appearance for the club since 2011, at the age of 41 – he replaced the 38-year-old Milligan. However, FC were later removed from the competition after it emerged that Simões had been playing without the required international clearance.

Back on league duty, Peers scored for the third game running to equalise at home to AFC Telford United, only for the visitors to grab a controversial winner. In the FA Trophy, the Reds produced a great first half display to deservedly lead Hereford at the break, but collapsed in the second half to exit the competition with a 1-3 defeat. The team had been weakened before the game when the excellent Thompson was recalled by parent club Blackburn Rovers, so Reynolds plugged the gap by signing Caleb Richards on loan from Norwich City. Despite another decent performance, United returned empty-handed from a trip to York City, before ending the long wait for a first home league win when goals from Wallen and Willoughby secured a 2-0 triumph over Curzon Ashton on 8th December.

Neil Reynolds became FC United manager in October, with new captain Mike Potts scoring the first goal of his reign against Brackley Town

November brought impressive victories at Blyth and Hereford, before Kurt Willoughby sealed a first home league win in December against Curzon Ashton

With a blank weekend, the club organised a fund-raising friendly with local North West Counties side Chadderton, when new signing Chris Sharp impressed with a clinical hat-trick in a 6-0 win. United showed their resilience by twice equalising at Leamington to claim a hard earned point, but twice ran out of steam in the second half to be outmanoeuvred by high-flying Chorley in the festive bank holiday fixtures. In between, a goal from Potts had put the Reds in control at home to Spennymoor, but a red card for Peers turned the game and three late goals for the visitors left FC on the wrong end of a 1-3 scoreline.

United remained in the drop zone after another home defeat to Chester in early January, and Reynolds took the extremely difficult decision to release Jamie Milligan from his coaching role in order to generate more funds for on-field reinforcements. Despite the news, Milligan still travelled with the team for the next match as they bounced back with a terrific 3-2 win at promotion-chasing Bradford PA. With a defence containing new signing Danny Morton and teenage loanees Zehn Mohammed and Billy Sass-Davies, the Reds came from behind to claim the points thanks to classy strikes from Sharp, Banister and Willoughby. That was the last game for Simões, whose exciting displays had attracted the attention of higher-ranked clubs, and he was signed by Championship side Barnsley for an undisclosed fee. Reynolds also lost captain Potts, who required a hernia operation, but welcomed back Winter after a spell at Trafford regaining fitness after injury.

Unfortunately the Bradford victory proved to be another false dawn as the team then fell to four straight single-goal defeats. Ashton United grabbed a late winner in a vital relegation clash, before FC lost 1-2 after taking early leads against both

Jack Banister's long-range screamer was the highlight of the tremendous win at Bradford Park Avenue in January

Stockport and Boston. The Reds also lost by the same score to Altrincham, when two cruel deflections left loan signing Dale Whitham's precise headed equaliser in vain. That game also saw debuts for Moston-raised striker Louis Myers, Scottish defender Bob Harris, and goalkeeper Andy Fisher, signed on loan from Blackburn to cover for Allinson's loss of confidence.

The Reds were trailing to relegation rivals Guiseley at Broadhurst Park before late goals from Willoughby and Peers earned a 3-3 draw, and another injury-time equaliser from Willoughby gained a point in a 2-2 home draw against Hereford a fortnight later. In between, United were perhaps unlucky not to claim a win in a hard-fought stalemate at Southport, but those points provided the springboard for another great away win at a promotion-chasing side. Winger Dominic McHale became the fifth goalscoring debutant of the season when he put FC ahead at Telford, before Willoughby and Peers sealed a 3-1 victory.

March brought another victory away at a promotion chasing side, this time a terrific triumph at AFC Telford United

United live to fight another day as Sam Baird's bullet header won the points at Alfreton Town

With confidence climbing, United were then frustrated by the weather when the home fixture with York in mid-March was postponed due to a waterlogged pitch after an early afternoon deluge of rain. The enforced break stalled the momentum as the team failed to capitalise on Willoughby's early goal and fell to a 1-3 defeat at Curzon. A superb brace from Whitham and another from Willoughby put the Reds into a commanding position in the rearranged game against York, only for them to allow the ten men of the visitors to fight back for a 3-3 draw. With six games to go United were now five points from safety, but with rock-bottom Nuneaton the next visitors to Broadhurst they held high hopes of clawing back some of the deficit. However, what transpired was one of the worst performances in the club's history as they lost 0-4 to the basement side.

Reynolds began April by making immediate changes to the squad. Whitham was recalled by Chorley, and following him out of Broadhurst were McHale, Morton and Harris. Despite not yet being fully fit, Potts made himself available for the trip to Darlington and led out a team containing debutants Jack Grimshaw, Will Ozono and Mark West from the under-21 side, alongside two other teenagers in Palinkas and Mohammed. Despite the 0-2 defeat, they all kept their places in the squad

for the home defeat to Kidderminster, when they were also joined by Northern Ireland youth international Salou Jallow.

With Lynch unavailable and Palinkas injured, Reynolds was forced into a rethink for the trip to Alfreton, where a defeat would consign the team to the drop. He recalled Baird from Droylsden in the morning, and asked Peers and Banister to play unfamiliar roles as wing-backs. Against all the odds, the changes worked as the team pulled off a memorable 3-2 win. Myers scored his first goal for the club with a thumping header, and Willoughby grabbed his 21st of the season before Baird's bullet header claimed the points with 12 minutes left.

The Reds still needed to win the final two games and hope other results fell favourably, but despite Banister's late equaliser, relegation to the Northern Premier League was sadly confirmed when Blyth scored a winner shortly afterwards. That result also meant that FC had won just one home league game all season, and with 57 players having been selected by three different managers the drop ultimately came as no surprise. The season ended with a 0-1 loss at Brackley, before Reynolds immediately went to work on building his own competitive playing squad for the next campaign.

The FC United squad reflect afer the club's first relegation was confirmed following the home defeat to Blyth Spartans

2019/20: Northern Premier League Premier Division

As soon as the curtain had fallen on the disastrous 2018/19 term, Neil Reynolds began re-shaping his squad in preparation for his first full campaign at the club. The majority of the pre-season squad were announced before the end of May, with just four players – Mike Potts, Mike Donohue, Louis Myers and Chris Sharp – retained. They were joined by goalkeeper Paddy Wharton; defenders Aaron Morris, Curtis Jones, Chris Doyle, Adam Dodd, James Joyce and Tom Dean; midfielders Luke Griffiths, Jack Lenehan, Craig Carney and Rhain Hellawell; plus attackers Paul Ennis, Regan Linney and Nialle Rodney.

An encouraging set of summer friendly results raised excitement amongst supporters ahead of the new campaign kicking off back in the Northern Premier League. However, for the third season running the team proceeded to lose their first three competitive fixtures, although of the single-goal defeats to Grantham Town, Hyde United and Scarborough Athletic only the last was a deserved loss on the balance of play. The Reds fell behind again when club legend Matthew Wolfenden put Radcliffe ahead on August Bank Holiday Monday, but Linney soon equalised with his third goal in four games to earn FC's first point of the season.

Then came the signing that would make all the difference, when Reynolds was alerted to a chance sighting of former FC reserve team striker Tunde Owolabi, who had scored 26 times for Radcliffe the previous term. The boss moved quickly to snap him up, and Owolabi became an instant hero when he put United ahead within five minutes of his debut against Morpeth Town. He added another before half-time, with Ennis also bagging a brace as the Reds gained their first win of the campaign with a 4-2 margin.

September brought two hard-fought goalless draws on the road at Lancaster City and Stafford Rangers, either side of progression in the FA Cup thanks to a late header from Morris in a replay at Atherton Collieries. The Reds fell at the next hurdle at home to Warrington Town, but gained revenge away in the league just three days later when new signing Jordan Buckley headed the only goal of the game. Midfielders Alex Curran and Alex Babos also arrived on loan, and all three new boys helped to see the month out with a 1-0 home win over Bamber Bridge with Owolabi grabbing the winner.

Despite a decent display FC fell to fully professional league leaders South Shields, before coming back to win in injury time at Stalybridge Celtic thanks to Owolabi and two from substitute Ennis. Experienced goalkeeper Cameron Belford had signed on loan from Nuneaton Borough as cover, and stepped in for the injured Wharton as United progressed in the Manchester Premier Cup with a shoot-out win at Radcliffe.

Tunde Owolabi scores the first of his 34 goals just five minutes into his debut at home to Morpeth Town

New boy Jordan Buckley headed the only goal on his debut to earn three vital points at Warrington Town

Tunde Owolabi bags his fourth goal in the 7-0 thrashing of Buxton at Broadhurst Park

Paul Ennis claimed the winner at Stalybridge Celtic with a dramatic injury time free-kick

United bounced back with a league win at Atherton, which witnessed terrific strikes from Potts and Linney, and also won on their third trip to Radcliffe, this time in the FA Trophy. With the team now looking settled, Reynolds allowed Joyce, Dean, Carney, Hellawell, Rodney and Sharp to seek regular football at other clubs, whilst Babos returned to Derby County at the conclusion of his month's loan. Ashley Young and Ben Kerr joined the squad to provide cover in defence and midfield.

November draws with Gainsborough Trinity at home and at Witton Albion felt like vital points were dropped, but progress was made in three cup competitions. The Reds gained revenge over Basford in the FA Trophy before going on to win at Runcorn Linnets, and also eliminated Hyde United from the Manchester Premier Cup when Owolabi broke a club record by scoring in his seventh consecutive match. Belford was the hero of the League Challenge Cup tie with Glossop North End, saving four penalties in an epic shoot-out to send FC through.

Back on league duty, Owolabi struck four times in a 7-0 victory over Buxton in the most comprehensive display seen since the move to Broadhurst Park. The striker also put the Reds ahead against the league's other big spenders Basford United, but the visitors came back to win with the help of a freak long-range header that deceived Belford.

Another Ennis double gave the Reds an early commanding lead at home to high-flying Lancaster, only for the visitors to equalise with two late goals. Undeterred, FC continued to plough forward and were rewarded when Doyle nodded a stoppage time winner to send Broadhurst into delirium.

Chris Doyle heads past Sam Ashton to score another stoppage time winner against promotion rivals Lancaster City

A stunning hat-trick from Owolabi was the highlight of December's 5-2 win over Matlock Town, and the marksman went on to bag doubles in the next two games to help overcome National League North side Kettering Town in the FA Trophy and avenge the opening day league defeat to Grantham. The club once again opened the doors of Broadhurst Park to provide the now annual Christmas Comforts to provide meals, entertainment and vital services to homeless and vulnerable people in the local community. Back on the pitch, the team closed the decade with another injury-time winner when Donohue's free kick won the points at Ashton United and sent FC into third place in the league table.

The Reds overturned a half-time deficit to beat Radcliffe in an eventful New Year's Day encounter, before doubles from Linney and Owolabi in a 5-1 win at Hyde United made it eight victories on the trot for the free-scoring side. Exciting winger Finlay Sinclair-Smith had been added to the squad, and was soon joined by defender Lewis Lacy who returned for a fourth spell at the club. Teenage defender Jorge Sikora had featured on loan from Bradford City, and big striker Kyle Hawley also came in for a temporary spell from Morecambe. Outgoing were Buckley, Young, Myers and Wharton, who moved on after finding regular opportunities hard to come by.

In the 2nd round of the FA Trophy, FC were drawn away at National League leaders Barrow, where the best non-league side in the country emphatically ended the long unbeaten run by inflicting the club's heaviest defeat. Despite going down 0-7 and having Doyle sent off, the players and staff were moved by the reaction of the United supporters present, who sang louder and louder as the game went on in atrocious conditions. Hawley marked his debut with a late winner within five minutes of emerging from the bench at Whitby Town, and FC also left it late to claim a point at Buxton thanks to an injury-time screamer from Ennis. However, the game was marred by a shocking injury to Curran that brought a premature end to his campaign, and Jones also hobbled off to spend a month on the sidelines.

Reynolds again turned to the loan market for reinforcements, introducing tall defender Matty Elsdon and attacking midfielders Morgan Homson-Smith and Daniel Trickett-Smith during February. The Reds again reached the Manchester Premier Cup Final by beating Irlam at home, but had been eliminated by a stoppage time winner from Sheffield, the world's oldest football club, in the League Challenge Cup. Homson-Smith was quick to make an impact, scoring on his debut in a 3-3 draw with Mickleover Sports and hitting a superb late winner over Stafford, either side of a 1-1 draw at Basford. The 14-game unbeaten league run came to an end with a 0-3 defeat at the manager's former club Bamber Bridge, where Larnell Cole became only the third player, after Phil Marsh and Nick Culkin, to appear in the first team for both Manchester United and FC United Of Manchester.

Mike Potts equalised before Tunde Owolabi beat keeper Ollie Martin to make sure of the points in the crunch clash with rivals Radcliffe

Curtis Jones celebrates his injury time leveller at home to Warrington Town

FC responded with a hard-fought win at promotion rivals Nantwich Town, where Morris headed the only goal of the game, before a thrilling encounter at home to fellow challengers Warrington. United went two up, only for ex-Red Buckley to help the visitors to take the lead twice, before a precise header from Jones made it 4-4 deep into injury-time. Owolabi hit another superb hat-trick in a 4-0 win at Mickleover a week later, before bagging a further treble in a 3-5 defeat at leaders South Shields in mid-March.

That loss looked to guarantee the title to the hosts, only for the league season to be suspended two days later due to the COVID-19 pandemic, with the Reds in 2nd place in the table. The campaign was officially abandoned on 26th March, with all results expunged, and no promotion or relegation in place. There became far greater things to worry about than football, but despite the results ultimately counting for nothing, it had been the most enjoyable season since FC moved to Moston.

2020/21: Northern Premier League Premier Division

With restrictions still in force due to the coronavirus pandemic, FC United's Northern Premier League campaign began a month later than usual, in mid-September. To little surprise, last term's top scorer Tunde Owolabi had been snapped up by a professional club, Hamilton Academical of the Scottish Premiership, and so Neil Reynolds attempted to fill his void by signing forwards Dan Cockerline and Michael Fowler, the latter on a season-long loan from Fleetwood Town. Morgan Homson-Smith signed permanently for the Reds after his impressive loan spell, new goalkeeper Dan Lavercombe claimed the no.1 jersey, and young defenders Tom Stead and Kain Dean added cover for the backline. They would be joined by wide men Morgan Penfold and Tre Pemberton, midfielder Jordan Simpson and defenders Joe White and Calum Woods after the season got underway.

Amidst the backdrop of attendances capped at 600 spectators, FC once again had a consistent, if unspectacular opening to the season. However, whereas the previous three years had produced losing starts, United began 2020/21 by drawing the first three games, at home to Nantwich Town and Scarborough Athletic, and away at Hyde United. The team's first two victories both came in the FA Cup, with a 6-2 home win over Pontefract Collieries followed by a terrific 2-1 triumph at Curzon Ashton, and the Reds also progressed through a further round without playing after opponents Alfreton Town were forced to withdraw due to a positive COVID-19 test at the club.

The Reds came from behind to win a league game at the fourth attempt when headers from Cockerline and Fowler sealed a 2-1 home victory over Stafford Rangers, before Cockerline struck again in a 1-1 draw with Lancaster City. With just a minute to play in the FA Cup 4th qualifying round, FC and Guiseley were level with a goal apiece, but Finlay Sinclair-Smith stepped up to fire United into the 1st round proper for the third time in the club's history. The team then suffered their first loss of the season at South Shields in midweek, and also departed the FA Trophy when Marske United scored a stunning stoppage-time winner at Broadhurst Park.

FC picked up their second league win with arguably the best performance of the term when Sinclair-Smith's double and one from Curtis Jones defeated Warrington Town 3-1. As the nation entered another lockdown, the club's biggest match for five years was somewhat anti-climactic with no spectators allowed in Broadhurst Park as United hosted Doncaster Rovers in the FA Cup 1st round. The League One visitors produced an exhibition of professionalism before a live TV audience, and although Regan Linney gave FC some hope with a composed solo effort, the Reds exited the competition with a 1-5 defeat.

The league season was suspended from that weekend, and a proposed Boxing Day restart failed to materialise before a second consecutive campaign was officially curtailed on 24th February 2021.

Aaron Morris completed the scoring as the Reds began the FA Cup run with a 6-2 home win over Pontefract Collieries

Goals from Dan Cockerline and Michael Fowler earned United's first league win of the season against Stafford Rangers

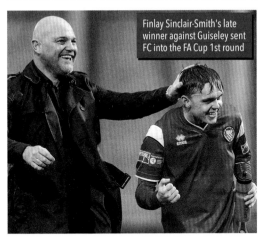
Finlay Sinclair-Smith's late winner against Guiseley sent FC into the FA Cup 1st round

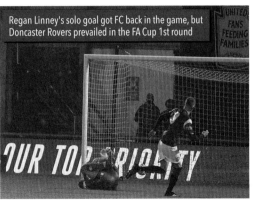
Regan Linney's solo goal got FC back in the game, but Doncaster Rovers prevailed in the FA Cup 1st round

2021/22: Northern Premier League Premier Division

As restrictions became relaxed, the Northern Premier League began the season at the third attempt in the summer of 2021. FC United boss Neil Reynolds had lost the services of two of his most influential players, Luke Griffiths and Chris Doyle, but bolstered his squad with some exciting new recruits. He added young defenders Drew Baker and Matty Rain, vastly experienced midfielder Jonathan Smith and forwards Ali Waddecar and Cedric Main, while also promoting the impressive youth team skipper Jack Bennett. They would soon be joined by on-loan striker Jamie Cooke and goalkeeper Lewis King, who began a second spell at FC to cover when Dan Lavercombe fell ill with food poisoning.

Despite dominating possession, United's long wait for an opening day victory continued as they lost 0-2 at Warrington Town, where old boy Jordan Buckley grabbed both goals. The Reds opened their account with strikes from Smith, Jordan Simpson and Paul Ennis for an impressive 3-0 win over Morpeth Town, before gaining creditable 1-1 draws with Buxton and at South Shields, the two sides who would fight it out for the title. FC were denied a third consecutive draw when Main's late penalty was saved to condemn his side to a 1-2 defeat at Hyde United, before goals from Cooke, Rain and a screamer from Adam Dodd secured a comfortable 3-0 Bank Holiday win over Radcliffe at Broadhurst.

An early double from Main put the Reds in a commanding position at Bootle in the FA Cup in early September, but the hosts fought back to force a replay with an injury-time leveller. United were on the brink of elimination in the last minute back in Moston three days later, but an equaliser from Rain and a winner from Regan Linney secured a dramatic 3-2 victory. The reward was a trip to National League North side Blyth Spartans, where Main's equaliser earned a 1-1 draw and another Broadhurst Park replay. Unfortunately, FC were unable to recreate the spirit of the previous round and went out with

a 0-2 defeat. The month's league results were typical of the team's inconsistency, with disappointing defeats to Stafford Rangers and Stalybridge Celtic both followed by impressive home wins over promotion challengers. New loan striker Bradley Holmes grabbed the only goal on his debut against Bamber Bridge, and he also scored in the fantastic 6-0 victory over Scarborough Athletic.

The pattern continued in early October, when United fell to a last-gasp 0-1 defeat at high-flying Matlock Town, before a thumping goal from skipper Michael Potts earned the first away win of the season, 1-0 at Basford United. There then followed three straight losses in which the team failed to score, which prompted Reynolds to freshen up his squad. He swooped to re-sign Griffiths, and also dipped into the loan market again for forwards Sam Burns and Cian Hayes, whilst Main was among those to depart. The changes had the desired effect as the team chalked up their first Saturday win of the campaign at Witton Albion, although they made life difficult for themselves in the process. Seemingly coasting when Baker and Hayes put them two goals up, FC allowed the hosts back to level before a last minute own goal secured a 3-2 victory.

The first of Regan Linney's 20 goals in 2021/22 was a dramatic last gasp FA Cup winner against Bootle

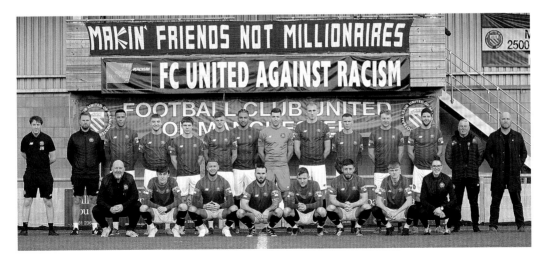

That set the Reds up nicely for their first game in the season's most exciting competition, the brand new FENIX Trophy. FC were honoured to be included amongst the clubs invited to participate in the inaugural campaign, which featured eight carefully chosen non-professional sides from seven European countries. United were drawn in Group B alongside AKS Zły from Warsaw, Brera from Milan and DWS from Amsterdam, although the Dutch club would later withdraw from the group stage due to travel restrictions. Our first trip was to Poland, where Holmes scored FC's first competitive European goal. He went on to grab a hat-trick, with further strikes from Ennis, Burns and Dodd completing a 6-1 win.

Burns and Ennis scored again to ensure progress in the FA Trophy with a 2-0 victory at Runcorn Linnets, before the Reds made it four wins on the trot by defeating Gainsborough Trinity 3-2 in Moston in early November. They then came crashing down again with three straight losses on the road: narrow league defeats at Whitby Town and Atherton Collieries either side of a 2-3 FA Trophy elimination at the hands of Marske United for the second year running. The month ended on a

high though when goals from Aaron Morris and Hayes earned a 2-0 triumph over Mickleover. Burns, Hayes and Holmes were all recalled by their parent clubs in the run-up to Christmas, but new additions included forwards Joe Duckworth and Jayden Major, midfielder Harry Wilson and defenders Andy White and Andy Halls, the last three on further loan deals.

After the scheduled home game with Whitby Town in early December was postponed due to a waterlogged pitch, the Reds recorded two tremendous away victories. Waddecar ended his long wait for his first FC goal by striking twice in quick succession to earn a 2-0 win at Stafford, before Curtis Jones and Duckworth ensured United came from behind to beat league leaders Buxton 2-1. The Reds ended the year by playing at home against Ashton United in their yellow and green change kit to support the homeless charity Shelter's No Home Kit campaign. With Lavercombe unavailable due to a positive covid test, Reynolds signed young goalkeeper George McMahon as emergency cover for the thrilling 4-3 win. An Ennis penalty, a Duckworth double and a sublime solo run and chip by Michael Donohue sealed a fourth consecutive win.

A wonderful solo goal from Michael Donohue helped FC to an exciting 4-3 win over Ashton United

Duckworth struck again to put United two up at Radcliffe on New Year's Day, but the hosts turned the game around with three goals in 14 minutes late in the second half before Linney grabbed his second to make it 3-3 with a minute to go. The momentum was halted when the home fixture with Warrington fell victim to the weather, but the Reds returned to gain a hard-earned point in a 0-0 draw at second placed Bamber Bridge. New loan striker Ewan Bange headed FC into an early lead on his debut at home to Stalybridge, but limped off with a hamstring injury just minutes later. An Ennis penalty secured a 2-1 win that extended the unbeaten run to seven games, but that was ended with a 3-4 home defeat to Whitby.

The Reds were trailing at Grantham Town, but late goals from Linney and Donohue ensured they returned to winning ways with a 2-1 victory. Morris's fifth goal of the season and a lovely strike from the latest loan striker, Josh Galloway, earned a 2-0 win over Witton, before Linney grabbed the only goal of a tight encounter with Lancaster City with a tremendous solo effort. That took FC to just outside the play-off places on goal difference, but their hopes were hindered by a 2-3 defeat at Gainsborough and an agonising loss to fifth-placed Warrington, who snatched the only goal of the game deep into added time. A 2-2 draw at fourth-placed Scarborough restored some confidence, but points were again dropped at home in injury time when title-chasing Matlock scored a penalty to equalise Waddecar's earlier opener.

With no league fixture scheduled on 5th March, FC took the opportunity to welcome AKS Zły to Moston for the return game in the FENIX Trophy. The visitors were well supported on a memorable occasion, but the Reds left no room for sentiment and racked up the club's record victory as a Linney hat-trick, doubles from Duckworth and Bange and further goals from Ennis, Galloway and Smith saw United win 10-0.

Back on league duty, FC fell to a lacklustre 0-2 defeat at Nantwich, before twice coming from behind to beat Basford 3-2 at home thanks to Griffiths and a Donohue brace. The Reds were twice behind at Mickleover too, but goals from Linney, Ennis and Jones secured a 3-3 draw. The manager had added further new faces in the form of the vastly experienced Chris Taylor, goalkeeper Ryan Hamer, returning defender Jorge Sikora, teenage loan midfielder Harry McGee and exciting attacker Josh Askew as the play-offs still remained a possibility.

Askew grabbed his first goal to set up a 2-0 home win over Atherton Collieries, before the team flew to Milan to face Brera in our third FENIX Trophy fixture on 6th April. In the magnificent and historic Arena Civica, the hosts took an early lead from the spot but the Reds came back to win 3-1, with both Ennis and Linney also scoring penalties in addition to a superb solo goal from Waddecar. Sadly the play-off hopes were extinguished by two 0-1 defeats, at Morpeth Town and at home to title-chasing South Shields. Another Linney treble earned a 3-0 win at Ashton United before the league campaign ended with a disappointing 0-2 home loss to Hyde that meant FC finished in ninth position in the table.

Jonathan Smith hit the final goal as FC United beat AKS Zły 10-0 in the FENIX Trophy to record the club's record victory

The season wasn't quite over as matches still remained in the FENIX Trophy, with FC welcoming Brera to Broadhurst Park on 4th May for the final group game. Superb strikes from Askew and Galloway earned a victory that was far more dominant than the 2-1 scoreline would suggest, ensuring that the Reds topped the group with a 100% record.

Hundreds of Reds fans then made the trip to the Italian coastal resort of Rimini for the final against Group A winners Prague Raptors on 11th June. Potts and Waddecar had both announced their intention to retire from football following the match, and they finished on a perfect high. Waddecar gave FC an early lead when he converted Duckworth's inviting cross at the near post. Five minutes before half-time, Duckworth got his reward for a fine individual performance by steering home a Linney centre to double the advantage. The Reds preserved the 2-0 lead throughout the second half to delight the travelling fans by lifting the first trophy of Reynolds' reign, and the first European trophy in FC United of Manchester's history.

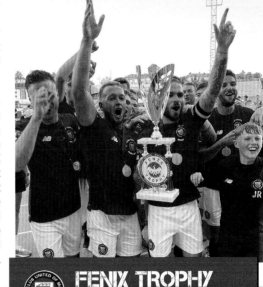

FENIX TROPHY WINNERS 2021/22

NORTH WEST COUNTIES FOOTBALL LEAGUE DIVISION TWO

Date	Opponents	Venue	Score	1	2	3	4	5	6	7	8	9	10	11
13.08	Leek CSOB	A	5-2	George B	Rawlinson	Ormes	Spencer S 2	Nugent	Elvin	Fleury*	Coyne T*	Mitten J 1*	Torpey 1	Patterson
20.08	Padiham	H	3-2	George B	Elvin	Ormes	Spencer S*	Chadwick	Nugent	Rawlinson*	Coyne T	Mitten J	Patterson 2	Orr 1*
24.08	Eccleshall	H	7-1	George B	Elvin	Ormes	Spencer S*	Chadwick	Nugent 1	Rawlinson 2	Coyne T*	Mitten J	Torpey 1*	Patterson
31.08	Winsford United	A	2-2	Priestley P	Rawlinson	Spencer S	Carden S	Chadwick	Nugent	Orr 1	Coyne T*	Mitten J*	Torpey 1	Patterson
03.09	Ashton Town	A	4-0	George B	Rawlinson	Elvin	Spencer S	Chadwick	Nugent	Gilligan	Carden S	Mitten J*	Torpey 1*	Patterson 1
10.09	Blackpool Mechanics	H	4-2	George B	Rawlinson	Elvin	Spencer S 1	Chadwick	Nugent 1	Orr*	Gilligan*	Mitten J 1*	Torpey	Patterson 1
17.09	Castleton Gabriels	A	3-0	George B	Elvin	Ormes	Spencer S	Chadwick	Nugent 1	Rawlinson	Gilligan 1*	Mitten J*	Patterson 1*	Orr
24.09	Norton United	H	1-2	George B	Rawlinson*	Ormes	Spencer S	McCartney	Nugent	Holt*	Carden S	Lyons*	Torpey	Patterson 1
05.10	Oldham Town	H	1-0	George B	Elvin*	Ormes	Spencer S*	Chadwick	McCartney	Rawlinson	Carden S 1	Patterson	Torpey	Orr
08.10	Daisy Hill	H	6-0	George B	Elvin*	Ormes	Spencer S*	Chadwick	McCartney	Lyons 1	Carden S 1*	Mitten J 1	Patterson 1	Orr 2
17.10	Cheadle Town (LCC:1)	A	5-1	George B	Elvin	Ormes	Spencer S*	Chadwick	McCartney	Lyons*	Carden S 1	Mitten J	Patterson 1*	Orr 3
22.10	Nelson	H	5-0	George B	Elvin*	Ormes	Spencer S 1	Chadwick	McCartney*	Lyons	Carden S 1	Mitten P 1*	Patterson	Orr 2
05.11	Eccleshall	A	0-0	George B	Cullen	Elvin	Rawlinson*	Chadwick	McCartney	Lyons	Carden S	Mitten J*	Patterson	Orr
13.11	Colne (LCC:2)	A	1-2	George B	Cullen*	Elvin	Gilligan	Chadwick	McCartney	Howard J	Carden S	Orr	Torpey 1	Patterson* ■
19.11	Darwen	A	2-1	George B	Cullen	Nugent	Spencer S	Chadwick	Brown D 1	Ahern*	Carden S 1	Mitten J*	Torpey*	Elvin
23.11	New Mills	H	6-1	George B	Cullen	Nugent	Spencer S	Chadwick 1	Brown D*	Ahern	Carden S 3*	Mitten J	Torpey	Orr 1*
26.11	Cheadle Town	A	3-3	George B	Cullen	Nugent	Spencer S	Chadwick 1	Brown D	Ahern*	Carden S 1	Mitten J*	Torpey 1	Orr
03.12	New Mills (D2T:2)	A	5-0	George B	Nugent	Elvin	Spencer S	Chadwick*	Brown D	Howard J	Carden S 1*	Mitten J*	Torpey 3	Orr*
10.12	Castleton Gabriels	H	10-2	George B	Nugent	Elvin	Spencer S*	Chadwick*	Brown D	Howard J 1	Carden S 5	Mitten J 2 ■	Torpey 1	Orr 1*
17.12	Holker Old Boys	A	2-0	George B	Nugent	Elvin	Spencer S	McCartney	Brown D	Howard J	Carden S 1	Patterson	Torpey	Orr 1
26.12	Flixton	A	1-1	George B	Nugent	Elvin	Spencer S	Chadwick	Brown D	Howard J	Carden S	Mitten J*	Torpey*	Orr 1
02.01	Winsford United	H	2-1	George B	Nugent	Elvin	Spencer S	McCartney	Brown D	Howard J	Carden S 1	Mike*	Torpey*	Orr*
07.01	Darwen	H	2-0	George B	Nugent	Elvin	Spencer S	McCartney	Brown D	Howard J 1	Carden S 1*	Patterson*	Torpey*	Orr
15.01	Nelson	A	3-1	George B	Nugent	Elvin	Spencer S	McCartney	Brown D	Howard J	Simms*	Mitten J 1*	Torpey 2	Orr*
21.01	Ashton Town	H	2-1	George B	Cullen	Elvin	Spencer S*	McCartney	Brown D	Howard J	Ahern	Mitten J*	Torpey 1*	Orr 1
04.02	Nelson (D2T:QF)	H	0-1 e	George B	Cullen	Elvin*	Spencer S*	McCartney	Brown D	Howard J	Ahern	Mike*	Torpey*	Orr
11.02	Daisy Hill	A	3-0	George B	Nugent	Ormes	Simms	McCartney	Chadwick 1	Howard J 1	Ahern	Band*	Mike*	Orr*
18.02	Blackpool Mechanics	A	4-2	George B	Nugent	Ormes	Simms	McCartney	Chadwick 1	Howard J*	Ahern 1	Band*	Torpey*	Patterson 2
25.02	Holker Old Boys	H[1]	4-1	George B	Nugent	Ormes*	Simms 1	Chadwick*	McCartney	Howard J 1	Power P	Ahern 1	Torpey*	Patterson 1
27.02	Great Harwood Town	A	1-1	George B	Nugent	Cullen	Simms*	Chadwick	McCartney	Howard J	Ahern	Orr*	Torpey	Patterson 1
15.03	Flixton	H	1-2	George B	Nugent	Ormes	Simms*	Chadwick 1	McCartney*	Howard J*	Ahern	Orr	Torpey	Patterson
18.03	Leek CSOB	H	8-1	Melville	Nugent	Cullen	Spencer S	Chadwick*	Brown D	Power P 2*	Ahern*	Swarbrick 1	Torpey 1	Patterson 3
22.03	Oldham Town	A	1-0	Melville	Nugent	Cullen	Spencer S	Chadwick 1	Brown D	Power P*	Ahern	Swarbrick*	Torpey*	Patterson
25.03	New Mills	A	2-0	Melville	Nugent	Cullen	Spencer S	Chadwick	Brown D	Swarbrick*	Ahern	Mitten J 1*	Torpey*	Patterson 1
01.04	Cheadle Town	H	1-1	Melville	Nugent	Cullen	Spencer S	Chadwick	Brown D	Swarbrick	Ahern	Mitten J*	Torpey*	Patterson*
09.04	Norton United	A	3-1 o	Melville	Nugent	Cullen	Spencer S	Chadwick*	Brown D	Howard J 1	Carden S	Swarbrick*	Torpey 1	Patterson*
12.04	Chadderton	H	4-0	Melville	Nugent 1	Cullen	Spencer S*	McCartney	Brown D	Howard J	Carden S*	Swarbrick	Torpey 1*	Patterson 1
19.04	Chadderton	A	3-2	George B	Collier*	Cullen	Ahern	McCartney	Orr 1	Lyons 1	O'Neill 1*	Mitten J	Simms	Mike*
22.04	Great Harwood Town	H	0-1	Melville	Nugent	Cullen	Spencer S	Chadwick	Brown D	Power P ■	Carden S*	Howard J*	Torpey*	Patterson
29.04	Padiham	A	2-1	George B	Nugent	Swarbrick	Spencer S*	Chadwick	Brown D*	Howard J*	Carden S 1	Ahern	Torpey 1	Orr

FOOTBALL CLUB UNITED OF MANCHESTER
CHAMPIONS 2005-2006

APPEARANCES & GOALS

Player	League		Cups		Totals	
Will **Ahern**	15 (+9)	**3**	1	0	16 (+9)	**3**
Simon **Band**	2	0	0	0	2	0
Dave **Brown**	18 (+5)	**1**	2	0	20 (+5)	**1**
Simon **Carden**	19 (+6)	**17**	3	**2**	22 (+6)	**19**
David **Chadwick**	27 (+1)	**6**	3	0	30 (+1)	**6**
Warren **Collier**	1	0	0	0	1	0
Tony **Coyne**	4 (+8)	0	0	0	4 (+8)	0
Tony **Cullen**	14 (+9)	0	2 (+1)	0	16 (+10)	0
Kevin **Elvin**	18 (+1)	0	4	0	22 (+1)	0
Craig **Fleury**	1	0	0	0	1	0
Barrie **George**	28	0	4	0	32	0
Ryan **Gilligan**	3 (+4)	**2**	1	0	4 (+4)	**2**
Matt **Haley**	0	0	0	0	0	0
Scott **Holt**	1 (+3)	**2**	0	0	1 (+3)	**2**
Josh **Howard**	16 (+2)	**5**	3	0	19 (+2)	**5**
Darren **Lyons**	5 (+8)	**3**	1 (+1)	0	6 (+9)	**3**
Karl **Marginson**	0	0	0	0	0	0
Billy **McCartney**	17 (+3)	0	3	0	20 (+3)	0
Phil **Melville**	7	0	0	0	7	0
Leon **Mike**	3 (+2)	0	1	0	4 (+2)	0
Joz **Mitten**	19 (+5)	**7**	2 (+2)	0	21 (+7)	**7**
Paul **Mitten**	1 (+2)	**1**	0 (+2)	0	1 (+4)	**1**
Rob **Nugent**	30 (+1)	**4**	1 (+1)	0	31 (+2)	**4**
Michael **O'Neill**	1	**1**	0	0	1	**1**
Gareth **Ormes**	12 (+1)	0	1	0	13 (+1)	0
Adie **Orr**	22 (+7)	**15**	4	**3**	26 (+7)	**18**
Rory **Patterson**	25 (+5)	**18**	2 (+1)	**1**	27 (+6)	**19**
Phil **Power**	4 (+7)	**2**	0 (+1)	**1**	4 (+8)	**3**
Phil **Priestley**	1	0	0	0	1	0
Mark **Rawlinson**	10 (+4)	**2**	0 (+1)	0	10 (+5)	**2**
Chris **Simms**	7 (+7)	**3**	0 (+1)	0	7 (+8)	**3**
Steve **Spencer**	29 (+1)	**4**	3	0	32 (+1)	**4**
Dave **Swarbrick**	7 (+2)	**1**	0	0	7 (+2)	**1**
Steve **Torpey**	29	**13**	3	**4**	32	**17**

Substitutes					Attendance
Lyons (7)	Ahern (8)	Orr (9) **1**			2,590
Gilligan (4)	Ahern (11)	Holt (7)			2,498
Gilligan (4) **1**	Carden S (8)	Orr (10) **2**			1,978
Gilligan (8)	Holt (9)	Haley			2,220
Cullen (11)	**Holt** (10) **2**	Power P (9)			1,424
Cullen (8)	Coyne T (9)	Power P (7)			2,226
Cullen (8)	McCartney (9)	Carden S (10)			2,473
Cullen (7)	Elvin (2)	Mitten J (9)			2,435
Cullen (4)	Nugent (2)	Coyne T (10)			3,110
Cullen (2)	Rawlinson (4)	Coyne T (8)			3,808
Cullen (7)	Rawlinson (4)	Mitten P (10)	Nugent	Melville	2,200
Cullen (2)	Rawlinson (9)	Brown D (6)			3,093
Nugent	Gilligan (4)	Power P (9)			2,011
Nugent	Lyons (2)	Mitten J (11)			2,762
Rawlinson (7)	Lyons (10)	Orr (9)			1,715
Rawlinson (8)	McCartney (6)	Patterson (11) **1**			2,297
Rawlinson	Mitten P (7)	Patterson (9)			3,373
Power P (11) **1**	Mitten P (8)	Patterson (9)			1,473
Coyne T (4)	Mitten P (5)	Patterson (11)			3,154
Coyne T (8)	Ahern (11)	Power P (9)			2,303
McCartney	Simms (9)	Patterson (10)			2,050
Ahern (10)	Simms (11)	**Patterson** (9) **1**			4,328
Ahern (10)	Simms (8)	Power P (9)			3,371
Ahern (11)	Cullen (9)	Coyne T (8)			2,011
Mike (9)	Simms (10)	Coyne T (4)			3,549
Nugent (3)	Simms (10)	Mitten J (9)			3,007
Brown D (9)	**Lyons** (11) **1**	Coyne T (10)			1,682
Brown D (10)	Lyons (7)	Power P (9)			4,300
Brown D (5)	Cullen (3)	Orr (10)			3,159
Brown D (4)	Lyons	Mike (9)			1,028
Spencer S (6)	Carden S (4)	Swarbrick (7)			1,924
Lyons (7)	**Simms** (5) **1**	Mitten J (8)			2,559
Lyons (9)	Carden S (10)	Mitten J (7)			1,767
Lyons (7)	Carden S (10)	Simms (9)			1,952
Howard J (11)	Carden S (10)	**Simms** (9) **1**			2,713
Ahern (5)	Mitten J (11)	Orr (9)			1,284
Ahern (4) **1**	Mitten J (10)	Orr (8)			2,788
Chadwick (2)	Howard J (8)	Power P (11)			2,352
Ahern (8)	Swarbrick (10)	Orr (9)			6,023
McCartney (6)	Ormes (4)	Lyons (7)			1,905

o Opposition Own Goal for FC United:

Tony **Kirk**	09/04/2006	FC's 3rd v Norton United (NWCFL2)	A 3-1

FC United goals listed first. All games League unless stated otherwise:
LCC North West Counties Football League Challenge Cup
D2T North West Counties Football League Division Two Trophy
H Played at Gigg Lane (Bury FC) **e** After Extra Time
H¹ Played at Moss Lane (Altrincham FC)
* Player Substituted (2) Substituted player's number Goalscorers in **bold**
■ Player Sent off (+1) Number of substitute appearances

	Team	Pld	W	D	L	F	A	GD	Pts
1	FC UNITED OF MANCHESTER ↑	36	27	6	3	111	35	+76	87
2	Flixton ↑	36	24	7	5	93	37	+56	79
3	Nelson ↑	36	23	5	8	82	53	+29	74
4	Winsford United	36	19	8	9	65	41	+24	65
5	Padiham	36	19	5	12	76	52	+24	62
6	Great Harwood Town	36	18	8	10	51	33	+18	62
7	Ashton Town	36	17	7	12	59	57	+2	58
8	Norton United	36	13	12	11	45	47	-2	51
9	Blackpool Mechanics	36	13	10	13	48	51	-3	49
10	Oldham Town	36	14	6	16	44	51	-7	48
11	Eccleshall	36	13	7	16	50	64	-14	46
12	New Mills	36	13	7	16	46	62	-16	46
13	Chadderton -3 points	36	13	8	15	51	62	-11	‡44
14	Cheadle Town -6 points	36	14	6	16	55	53	+2	‡42
15	Holker Old Boys	36	11	8	17	58	74	-16	41
16	Darwen	36	11	2	23	47	61	-14	35
17	Leek CSOB	36	7	7	22	51	82	-31	28
18	Daisy Hill	36	7	6	23	38	75	-37	27
19	Castleton Gabriels -8 points	36	2	3	31	38	122	-84	‡1

‡: Chadderton were deducted 3 points for fielding an ineligible player
‡: Cheadle Town were deducted 6 points for breaching league regulations
‡: Castleton Gabriels were deducted 8 points due to registration irregularities

NORTH WEST COUNTIES FOOTBALL LEAGUE DIVISION ONE

Date	Opponents	Venue	Score	1	2	3	4	5	6	7	8	9	10	11
12.08	St Helens Town	A	2-0	Ashton	Taylor Ma	Mortimer	Spencer S*	Chadwick	Nugent	Giggs*	Ahern	Rudd 1*	Swarbrick	Patterson
16.08	Nelson	H	6-0 o	Ashton	Taylor Ma*	Mortimer	Spencer S	Chadwick	Nugent	Giggs	Carden S	Rudd 1	Ahern*	Patterson 3*
19.08	Nantwich Town	H	2-0	Ashton	Taylor Ma	Mortimer	Spencer S	Chadwick	Nugent	Giggs	Carden S 1*	Rudd	Ahern*	Patterson 1
21.08	Glossop North End	A	4-1	Ashton	Taylor Ma	Mortimer	Spencer S*	Chadwick	Nugent	Giggs	Carden S 1*	Rudd 2	Ahern*	Patterson 1
26.08	Atherton Laburnum Rovers	A	7-0	Ashton	Taylor Ma	Mortimer 1	Spencer S*	Chadwick*	Nugent 1	Giggs*	Carden S 1	Rudd 3	Howard J 1	Patterson
30.08	Flixton	H	4-0	Ashton	Lomax M	Mortimer	Spencer S	Chadwick	Nugent 1	Giggs 2	Carden S*	Rudd*	Howard J 1	Patterson*
06.09	Congleton Town	H	3-0	Ashton	Taylor Ma	Mortimer	Spencer S	Chadwick	Nugent	Giggs*	Carden S*	Rudd 1	Howard J*	Patterson 1
09.09	Trafford	A	1-0	Ashton	Taylor Ma	Mortimer	Spencer S	Chadwick	Nugent	Giggs*	Carden S	Rudd	Howard J*	Patterson*
13.09	Abbey Hey	H	7-1 oo	Ashton	Lomax M	Mortimer	Coyne L	Chadwick*	Nugent	Howard J 2	Smith S*	Rudd 3*	Ahern	Orr
16.09	Silsden	H	4-2	Ashton	Taylor Ma	Mortimer	Spencer S*	Chadwick	Nugent	Howard J*	Carden S 1*	Rudd 1	Ahern	Patterson 2
18.09	Curzon Ashton	A	3-1 o	Ashton	Taylor Ma*	Mortimer	Spencer S	Chadwick	Nugent	Howard J*	Carden S 1	Rudd 1*	Ahern ■	Patterson
23.09	Brodsworth Miners Welfare (FAV:Q2)	A	3-1	Ashton	Taylor Ma	Mortimer	Spencer S*	Coyne L	Nugent	Giggs*	Ahern*	Rudd 1	Howard J 1	Patterson 1
30.09	Bacup Borough	H	3-0	Ashton	Taylor Ma	Mortimer	Spencer S	Chadwick	Coyne L 1	Giggs*	Ahern*	Rudd 2	Howard J*	Patterson
03.10	Salford City	A	1-2	Ashton	Taylor Ma	Mortimer	Spencer S	Chadwick	Nugent*	Howard J 1	Ahern	Rudd	Orr*	Patterson*
07.10	Padiham (FAV:1)	A	3-0	Ashton	Taylor Ma*	Mortimer	Spencer S	Chadwick	Nugent	Giggs	Carden S 2	Rudd	Howard J	Patterson*
11.10	St Helens Town	H	3-0	Ashton	Taylor Ma	Mortimer*	Spencer S*	Brown D 1	Coyne L	Giggs	Carden S 1*	Rudd 1	Howard J	Patterson
14.10	Squires Gate	H	8-0	Ashton	Taylor Ma	Mortimer	Spencer S	Brown D	Coyne L*	Giggs	Carden S*	Rudd 3	Howard J*	Patterson 4
21.10	Newcastle Town	A	3-2	Ashton*	Taylor Ma	Mortimer	Spencer S 1	Brown D	Nugent	Giggs*	Carden S 2	Rudd	Howard J	Patterson
28.10	Glossop North End	H	8-0	Ashton	Taylor Ma*	Mortimer	Platt 1	Chadwick 1	Nugent 1	Giggs 1	Carden S 1	Rudd	Phoenix 1*	Patterson 2
04.11	Maine Road	A	2-1	Ashton	Taylor Ma	Mortimer	Spencer S	Chadwick	Nugent*	Giggs	Carden S	Rudd 2	Howard J*	Patterson*
11.11	Nantwich Town (LCC:2)	A	3-0	Ashton	Taylor Ma	Mortimer*	Spencer S*	Chadwick 1	Brown D	Giggs 1	Carden S	Rudd 1	Howard J*	Platt
18.11	Salford City (FAV:2)	A	3-2	Ashton	Taylor Ma	Mortimer	Spencer S	Chadwick 1	Nugent	Giggs*	Carden S 1	Rudd 1	Howard J*	Platt
25.11	Stone Dominoes	H	7-0	Ashton	Lomax M*	Ormes	Ahern	Brown D	Coyne L	Sampson*	Platt*	Rudd 2	Allen 3	Patterson 2
29.11	Atherton Collieries	H	0-3	Ashton	Taylor Ma	Mortimer	Spencer S	Ormes*	Nugent	Giggs*	Carden S	Rudd	Platt*	Patterson
03.12	Congleton Town	A	1-1	Ashton	Ormes	Mortimer	Brown D*	Chadwick	Nugent	Sampson*	Carden S	Allen*	Howard J 1	Patterson
09.12	Quorn (FAV:3)	H	2-3 e	Ashton	Taylor Ma	Mortimer	Spencer S	Coyne L ■	Nugent	Giggs*	Carden S*	Rudd	Howard J ■	Patterson 1*
23.12	Flixton	A	1-1	Ashton	Taylor Ma*	Mortimer	Spencer S	Chadwick	Nugent	Platt	Carden S	Rudd	Swarbrick	Patterson 1*
26.12	Ramsbottom United	H	3-2	Ashton	Foster*	Mortimer 1	Spencer S	Chadwick 1	Nugent	Howard J	Platt 1	Rudd	Allen*	Giggs*
30.12	Newcastle Town	H	5-1	Ashton	Foster	Roscoe	Spencer S*	Chadwick*	Nugent	Swarbrick	Platt	Rudd 3	Mortimer*	Patterson 1
06.01	Atherton Collieries	A	3-0	Ashton	Foster	Roscoe	Spencer S	Chadwick	Nugent	Swarbrick 2	Platt*	Rudd 1*	Wright	Patterson*
27.01	Colne (LCC:3)	A	4-0	Ashton	Foster	Roscoe	Spencer S	Chadwick	Nugent 1	Giggs*	Sampson	Rudd 1*	Swarbrick*	Patterson 1
03.02	Bacup Borough	A	2-1	Ashton	Foster	Roscoe	Spencer S	Chadwick	Nugent*	Swarbrick*	Howard J*	Rudd 1	Wright	Patterson 1*
17.02	Silsden (LCC:QF)	A	3-0	Ashton	Foster	Roscoe	Spencer S*	Chadwick	Nugent	Swarbrick	Carden S 1	Rudd*	Howard J 1	Patterson 1*
21.02	Curzon Ashton	H	3-2	Ashton	Taylor Ma	Mortimer	Spencer S	Chadwick	Nugent	Swarbrick*	Carden S*	Rudd 1	Wright*	Patterson
24.02	Nantwich Town	A	1-1	Ashton	Taylor Ma	Mortimer	Platt	Chadwick	Nugent	Howard J*	Sampson	Rudd	Wright	Patterson 1
03.03	Colne	H	6-2	Ashton	Foster	Mortimer	Platt	Chadwick 1	Nugent*	Giggs 1	Sampson*	Rudd*	Wright 2	Patterson 1
10.03	Squires Gate	A	1-0	Ashton	Taylor Ma	Mortimer	Platt 1	Chadwick	Brown D	Giggs*	Sampson*	Rudd	Wright	Patterson
15.03	Congleton Town (LCC:SF1)	A	2-2	Ashton	Taylor Ma	Roscoe	Spencer S*	Chadwick	Nugent	Giggs 1	Platt*	Rudd*	Mortimer	Patterson
17.03	Abbey Hey	A	5-1	Ashton	Taylor Ma	Roscoe	Spencer S*	Chadwick	Nugent*	Howard J 2	Carden S 1*	Rudd 2	Wright	Patterson
21.03	Formby	A	3-1	Ashton	Taylor Ma	Mortimer	Platt	Chadwick	Nugent	Howard J	Carden S*	Rudd 1	Wright 1	Patterson ■
24.03	Stone Dominoes	A	4-0 o	Ogden	Taylor Ma*	Mortimer*	Platt*	Chadwick	Nugent	Howard J	Carden S	Rudd	Wright 1	Patterson 2
29.03	Silsden	A	3-1	Ashton	Foster	Roscoe	Spencer S	Chadwick	Brown D	Giggs*	Sampson	Rudd 1*	Wright	Patterson 2*
31.03	Congleton Town (LCC:SF2)	H	4-3	Ashton	Taylor Ma	Mortimer ■	Spencer S	Chadwick	Nugent 1	Giggs 1	Platt	Rudd 2*	Howard J*	Patterson 1
04.04	Nelson	A	8-0	Ashton	Taylor Ma*	Mortimer	Platt*	Chadwick*	Nugent 1	Howard J 1	Carden S 1	Giggs 2	Wright 1	Patterson
07.04	Ramsbottom United	A	2-1	Ashton	Taylor Ma	Mortimer	Platt 1	Brown D	Nugent	Giggs*	Carden S*	Rudd ■	Wright 1	Patterson
09.04	Maine Road	H	3-0	Ashton	Taylor Ma*	Mortimer	Platt	Brown D 1	Nugent 1	Giggs*	Carden S*	Rudd	Wright	Patterson 1
14.04	Colne	A	5-1	Ashton	Taylor Ma	Mortimer	Platt	Brown D	Nugent 2*	Howard J	Carden S	Rudd 1	Wright 1*	Giggs
18.04	Atherton Laburnum Rovers	H	7-1	Ashton	Taylor Ma	Mortimer	Platt 1	Brown D 1*	Nugent 1	Howard J	Carden S*	Rudd 1	Wright 1*	Giggs 1
21.04	Salford City	H	4-2	Ashton	Taylor Ma*	Roscoe	Platt 1	Chadwick	Nugent	Howard J*	Carden S	Rudd*	Wright	Giggs 3
25.04	Trafford	H	4-4	Ogden	Taylor Ma*	Wright	Spencer S	Chadwick	Nugent	Brown D	Sampson*	Rudd 1	Giggs*	Patterson 3
28.04	Formby	H	5-0 o	Ashton	Taylor Ma	Roscoe*	Platt*	Chadwick	Brown D	Lyons	Carden S*	Giggs 1	Wright	Patterson 3
03.05	Curzon Ashton (LCC:F)	N	2-1	Ashton	Taylor Ma	Mortimer	Spencer S	Chadwick	Nugent	Howard J 1*	Carden S	Giggs	Platt 1	Patterson

APPEARANCES & GOALS

Substitutes				Attendance
Coyne L (9)	Smith S (4)	Carden S (7) 1		1,723
Coyne L (2)	**Smith S (10) 1**	Swarbrick (11)		2,129
Howard J (10)	Smith S (8)	Swarbrick		2,736
Howard J (10)	Smith S (4)	Orr (8)		1,219
Coyne L (5)	Smith S (4)	Orr (7)		1,324
Phoenix (11)	Smith S (8)	Orr (9)		2,593
Phoenix (10) 1	Smith S (8)	Orr (7)		2,051
Phoenix (7)	Ahern (10)	Orr (11)		1,643
Spencer S (8)	Vaz Tê (5)	Ellis (9)		1,566
Giggs (7)	Smith S (4)	Orr (8)		3,381
Giggs (7)	Smith S (2)	Orr (9)		1,683
Lomax M	Smith S (7)	Lyons (4)	Ellis (8) Mike	1,251
Carden S (7)	Smith S (8)	Orr (10)		3,268
Carden S (11)	Smith S (6)	Giggs (10)		4,058
Lomax M (2)	Smith S	Phoenix (10)	Coyne L Orr (11)	1,371
Ormes (3)	Smith S (8)	Platt (4)		1,851
Shannon (8) 1	Phoenix (10)	Platt (6)		2,378
Chadwick	Phoenix (7)	Platt (1)	*Patterson in goal from 62 mins*	1,833
Brown D	Spencer S (2)	Allen (10)		3,257
Brown D (6)	Platt (11)	Phoenix (10)		3,181
Lomax M (3)	Sampson (4)	Allen (10)		1,240
Lomax M	Sampson (10)	Allen (7)	Phoenix Ogden	2,799
Chadwick (2)	Giggs (7)	Swarbrick (8)		3,020
Sampson (5)	Howard J (7)	Allen (10)		1,723
Spencer S (4)	Platt (7)	Power P (9)		1,106
Roscoe	Platt (7)	**Power P (8) 1**	Allen Ogden	1,858
Brown D (2)	Howard J (11)	Giggs		1,025
Brown D (2)	Swarbrick (10)	Patterson (11)		2,924
Brown D (5)	Carden S (4)	**Giggs (10) 1**		2,368
Brown D (9)	Howard J (8)	Giggs (11)		1,461
Brown D (9) 1	Howard J (7)	Phoenix (10)		1,470
Brown D (6)	Carden S (8)	Giggs (7)		1,504
Brown D (9)	Platt (4)	Giggs (11)		1,564
Roscoe (10)	**Sampson (8) 2**	Howard J (7)		2,493
Brown D	Harrop	Swarbrick (7)		1,436
Roscoe (6)	**Power P (9) 1**	Swarbrick (8)		2,456
Roscoe	Spencer S (7)	Carden S (8)		1,650
Brown D	Howard J (9)	Carden S (8)		1,062
Brown D (6)	Platt (4)	Giggs (8)		981
Power P	Sampson	**Giggs (8) 1**		671
Foster (2)	Sampson (4)	Giggs (3)		840
Lyons (7)	Power P (9)	Carden S (11)		1,140
Brown D	Sampson (10)	Carden S (9)		2,138
Brown D (5)	Lyons (2)	**Rudd (4) 1**		640
Turner A	Spencer S (7)	Sampson (8)		1,653
Howard J (7)	Spencer S (2)	Sampson (8)		3,605
Chadwick (6)	Spencer S (8)	**Power P (10) 1**		858
Chadwick (5) 1	Spencer S (10)	Power P (8)		2,249
Foster (2)	Spencer S (9)	Swarbrick (7)		2,594
Lyons (2)	Platt (8)	Swarbrick (10)		1,717
Spencer S (3)	Howard J (4)	Marginson (8)		3,847
Brown D	Sampson (7)	Swarbrick		3,210

Player	League		FAC & FAT		Other		Totals	
Will **Ahern**	10 (+1)	0	1	0	0	0	11 (+1)	0
Danny **Allen**	3 (+2)	3	0 (+1)	0	0 (+1)	0	3 (+4)	3
Sam **Ashton**	40	0	4	0	6	0	50	0
Dave **Brown**	13 (+8)	3	0	0	1 (+2)	1	14 (+10)	4
Simon **Carden**	27 (+7)	12	3	3	3 (+2)	1	33 (+9)	16
David **Chadwick**	33 (+3)	4	2	1	6	1	41 (+3)	6
Liam **Coyne**	5 (+3)	1	2	0	0	0	7 (+3)	1
Lee **Ellis**	0 (+1)	0	0 (+1)	0	0	0	0 (+2)	0
Liam **Foster**	6 (+2)	0	0	0	2	0	8 (+2)	0
Rhodri **Giggs**	27 (+10)	13	4	0	5 (+1)	2	36 (+11)	15
Kyle **Harrop**	0	0	0	0	0	0	0	0
Josh **Howard**	24 (+8)	9	4	1	4 (+2)	2	32 (+10)	12
Mike **Lomax**	3	0	0 (+1)	0	0 (+1)	0	3 (+2)	0
Darren **Lyons**	1 (+3)	0	0 (+1)	0	0	0	1 (+4)	0
Karl **Marginson**	0 (+1)	0	0	0	0	0	0 (+1)	0
Leon **Mike**	0	0	0	0	0	0	0	0
Alex **Mortimer**	34	2	4	0	4	0	42	2
Rob **Nugent**	35	8	4	0	5	2	44	10
John **Ogden**	2	0	0	0	0	0	2	0
Gareth **Ormes**	3 (+1)	0	0	0	0	0	3 (+1)	0
Adie **Orr**	2 (+8)	0	0 (+1)	0	0	0	2 (+9)	0
Rory **Patterson**	37 (+1)	33	3	2	5	4	45 (+1)	39
Jamie **Phoenix**	1 (+6)	2	0 (+1)	0	0 (+1)	0	1 (+8)	2
Nicky **Platt**	19 (+7)	6	1 (+1)	0	4 (+1)	1	24 (+9)	7
Phil **Power**	0 (+5)	2	0 (+1)	1	0	0	0 (+6)	3
Shaun **Roscoe**	7 (+2)	0	0	0	3	0	10 (+2)	0
Stuart **Rudd**	39 (+1)	37	4	3	5	4	48 (+1)	44
Gary **Sampson**	7 (+5)	2	0 (+1)	0	1 (+3)	0	8 (+9)	2
Danny **Shannon**	0 (+1)	1	0	0	0	0	0 (+1)	1
Steve **Smith**	2 (+12)	2	0 (+1)	0	0	0	2 (+13)	2
Steve **Spencer**	26 (+10)	1	4	0	6	0	36 (+10)	1
Dave **Swarbrick**	6 (+7)	2	0	0	2	0	8 (+7)	2
Matty **Taylor**	32	0	4	0	4	0	40	0
Adam **Turner**	0	0	0	0	0	0	0	0
Fernando **Vaz Tê**	0 (+1)	0	0	0	0	0	0 (+1)	0
Jerome **Wright**	18	8	0	0	0	0	18	8

o Opposition Own Goals for FC United:

Duncan **Bennett**	16/08/2006	FC's 1st v Nelson (NWCFL1)	H 6-0
Steve **Lester**	13/09/2006	FC's 2nd v Abbey Hey (NWCFL1)	H 7-1
Steve **Worthington**	13/09/2006	FC's 7th v Abbey Hey (NWCFL1)	H 7-1
Andrew **Watson**	18/09/2006	FC's 2nd v Curzon Ashton (NWCFL1)	A 3-1
Ashley **Flood**	24/03/2007	FC's 1st v Stone Dominoes (NWCFL1)	A 4-0
Chris **Pauls**	28/04/2007	FC's 3rd v Formby (NWCFL1)	H 5-0

	Team	Pld	W	D	L	F	A	GD	Pts
1	FC UNITED OF MANCHESTER ↑	42	36	4	2	157	36	+121	112
2	Curzon Ashton ↑	42	31	6	5	116	38	+78	99
3	Nantwich Town ↑	42	29	8	5	108	41	+67	95
4	Salford City	42	26	9	7	103	55	+48	87
5	Trafford	42	24	11	7	94	46	+48	83
6	Maine Road	42	22	7	13	79	58	+21	73
7	Atherton Collieries	42	19	13	10	72	55	+17	70
8	Ramsbottom United	42	19	7	16	78	63	+15	64
9	Glossop North End	42	19	6	17	71	71	0	63
10	Congleton Town	42	18	8	16	75	62	+13	62
11	Colne	42	16	13	13	75	70	+5	61
12	Newcastle Town	42	16	10	16	70	63	+7	58
13	Flixton	42	14	12	16	69	65	+4	54
14	Silsden	42	16	6	20	66	79	−13	54
15	Bacup Borough	42	11	13	18	50	65	−15	46
16	Atherton Laburnum Rovers	42	11	9	22	65	106	−41	42
17	Abbey Hey	42	10	10	22	44	83	−39	40
18	Squires Gate	42	10	8	24	56	97	−41	38
19	St Helens Town	42	10	6	26	47	92	−45	36
20	Nelson	42	7	7	28	39	110	−71	28
21	Formby	42	6	4	32	43	111	−68	22
22	Stone Dominoes ↓	42	2	3	37	36	147	−111	9

FC United goals listed first.   All games League unless stated otherwise:
FAV FA Vase   **LCC** North West Counties Football League Challenge Cup
H Played at Gigg Lane (Bury FC)   **e** After Extra Time
N Played at Tameside Stadium (Curzon Ashton FC)
* Player Substituted   (2) Substituted player's number   Goalscorers in **bold**
■ Player Sent off   (+1) Number of substitute appearances

NORTHERN PREMIER LEAGUE DIVISION ONE NORTH

Date	Opponents	Venue	Score	1	2	3	4	5	6	7	8	9	10	11
18.08	Lancaster City	A	1-2	Ashton	Spencer S	Mortimer*	Whitehead*	Chadwick	Nugent	Howard J	Platt	Hargreaves*	**Wright 1**	Patterson
22.08	Garforth Town	H	0-1	Ashton	Taylor Ma	Roscoe	Platt	Chadwick	Nugent	Swarbrick	Whitehead*	Rudd ■	Wright	Patterson*
25.08	Bridlington Town	H	6-0	Ashton	**Taylor Ma 1**	Roscoe	Spencer S*	Chadwick	Nugent	Swarbrick*	Carden S*	Rudd	Wright	**Patterson 4**
27.08	Rossendale United	A	2-1	Ashton	Taylor Ma	Mortimer	Spencer S*	Chadwick	Nugent	**Platt 1**	Carden S	**Rudd 1***	Wright	Hargreaves*
02.09	Trafford (FAC:P)	A	5-2	Ashton	Taylor Ma	Roscoe	Spencer S*	Chadwick	**Nugent 1**	**Howard J 1**	**Carden S 1**	Rudd	Wright	**Platt 1***
05.09	Alsager Town (LCC:1)	H¹	0-1 e	Ashton	Foster	Roscoe*	Baguley C	Brown D	Nugent	George L	Carden S	Hanley	Hargreaves	Swarbrick*
08.09	Harrogate Railway Athletic	H	2-0	Ashton	Taylor Ma	Roscoe	Spencer S*	Chadwick	Nugent	George L	**Carden S 1***	Platt*	Wright	**Patterson 1**
11.09	Clitheroe	A	1-1 a	*Ashton*	*Taylor Ma*	*Roscoe*	*Spencer S*	*Chadwick*	*Brown D*	*George L*	*Carden S*	*Platt*	*Wright*	*Patterson 1*
15.09	Fleetwood Town (FAC:Q1)	A	1-2	Ashton	Taylor Ma	Roscoe	Spencer S*	Chadwick	Nugent	George L*	Carden S	Platt	Wright	**Patterson 1**
22.09	Woodley Sports	H	1-1	Ashton	Taylor Ma	Roscoe	Spencer S	Chadwick*	Brown D	Carden A	Carden S*	Rudd*	Wright	**Patterson 1**
29.09	Chorley	A	3-0	Ashton	Taylor Ma	Roscoe	Platt	Chadwick	Spencer S	Carden A*	Baguley C*	**Rudd 1***	Wright	**Patterson 2**
02.10	Skelmersdale United	A	1-3	Ashton	Taylor Ma*	Roscoe	Platt*	Chadwick	Brown D*	Carden A	Baguley C	Rudd	Wright	**Patterson 1**
06.10	Bradford Park Avenue (FAT:P)	A	1-1	Ashton	Foster	Roscoe	Spencer S*	Chadwick	Nugent	Carden A*	Carden S	Rudd*	Wright	**Patterson 1**
10.10	Bradford Park Avenue (FAT:PR)	H¹	1-4	Ashton	Foster*	Roscoe*	Spencer S	Chadwick	Nugent	Swarbrick*	Carden S	**Hanley 1**	Wright	Patterson
13.10	Wakefield	H	2-1	Ashton	Foster	Roscoe	Platt*	Chadwick*	Nugent	Carden A	**Baguley C 2**	Hanley*	Wright	Patterson
16.10	Clitheroe	A	3-0	Ashton	Foster	Roscoe	Baguley C	Brown D*	Nugent*	Carden A	Carden S*	**Burns A 2**	Wright	**Patterson 1**
23.10	Droylsden (MPC:1)	A	3-2	Ashton	Foster	Roscoe	Platt	Brown D	Nugent	**Hanley 1***	Baguley C	**Burns A 1**	Wright	**Patterson 1***
27.10	Ossett Albion	H	3-1	Ashton	Foster	Roscoe	Platt	Brown D	Nugent	Hanley*	Baguley C	Burns A*	Wright	**Patterson 2**
31.10	Bamber Bridge (LPC:2)	H¹	5-0	Ashton	Foster	Roscoe	**Platt 1**	Bell	Whitehead	Baguley J*	**Baguley C 2***	Thomson P	**Burns A 1**	**Wright 1***
03.11	Bridlington Town	A	3-0	Ashton	Foster	Roscoe	Platt	Bell*	Nugent	Baguley J	Baguley C	**Burns A 1***	**Wright 1**	**Patterson 1**
10.11	Clitheroe	A	1-2	Ashton	Foster*	Roscoe	Platt*	Brown D	Nugent	Baguley J*	**Baguley C 1**	Burns A	Wright	Patterson
14.11	Rossendale United	H	5-1	Ashton	Taylor Ma	Roscoe*	Platt	Bell	Nugent	Hanley	**Baguley C 1**	**Burns A 3***	Wright	**Patterson 1**
17.11	Bamber Bridge	A	0-3	Ashton	Foster	Roscoe	Platt	Bell*	Nugent	Hanley*	Baguley C	Burns A	Wright	Patterson
24.11	Bradford Park Avenue	H	3-4	Priestley P	Taylor Ma	Roscoe	Platt*	**Turner A 1**	Jarrett	Baguley J*	**Baguley C 1**	Burns A	Wright	**Patterson 1**
27.11	Mossley	A	0-2	Priestley P	Taylor Ma	Roscoe	Baguley C*	Turner A ■	Jarrett	Baguley J*	Carden S*	Burns A	Wright	Patterson
01.12	Rossendale United	H¹	2-1	Priestley P	Taylor Ma	Roscoe	Baguley C*	Turner A	Nugent	Baguley J*	Carden S	Burns A	**Wright 1**	**Patterson 1***
26.12	Radcliffe Borough	A	1-1	Ashton	Taylor Ma*	Foster*	Platt	Bleau	Nugent	**Baguley C 1**	Carden S	Hanley*	Burns A	Baguley J
29.12	Curzon Ashton	A	2-0	Foster	Howard B	Platt	Bleau	**Nugent 1**	Baguley J*	Baguley C*	**Carden S 1***	Burns A	Wright	
01.01	Mossley	H	5-2	Foster	Howard B	**Platt 1**	Bleau	Nugent	Baguley J	Baguley C*	Carden S*	Burns A*	**Wright 1**	
12.01	Chorley	H	2-1	Foster	Howard B*	Platt	Bleau	Nugent	Baguley J	Baguley C*	Robinson		Wright	**Patterson 1**
23.01	Flixton (MPC:QF)	H²	4-1	Foster	**Howard B 1**	Holden*	Bleau	Turner A	Carden A	Carden S*	Robinson	Howard J*		**Patterson 1**
26.01	Rossendale United (LPC:3)	H	2-1	Foster	Howard B	Platt	Turner A	Nugent	Carden A*	Baguley C*	Carden S*		Wright	**Patterson 1**
16.02	Skelmersdale United	H	3-0	Grundy	Foster	Howard B	Platt	Chadwick	Nugent	Baguley J*	Carden S*	Rudd*	Wright	**Patterson 2**
23.02	Bamber Bridge	A	0-0	Grundy	Foster	Howard B*	Platt	Chadwick	Nugent	Baguley J*	Carden S	Rudd	Wright	**Patterson 1**
25.02	Nantwich Town (LPC:QF)	A	1-5 ‡	Grundy	Foster*	Howard B*	Platt	Bleau	Turner A	Carden A	Baguley C	Howard J	**Wright 1**	Patterson*
27.02	Clitheroe	H	3-0	Grundy	Foster*	Howard B	Baguley C	Chadwick	Nugent	Howard J*	**Carden S 1**	Rudd*	Wright	**Patterson 2**
01.03	Bamber Bridge	H	2-2	Grundy	Foster	Wright	Baguley J	Chadwick	Nugent	Howard J*	**Carden S 1**	Rudd	**Baguley C 1**	Patterson*
05.03	Curzon Ashton	H	3-2	Grundy	Foster*	Howard B	Platt	**Chadwick 1**	Nugent	Baguley J*	Carden S	Rudd	Wright	**Patterson 2**
08.03	Goole (LPC:SF)	A	3-1	Grundy	Carden A	Howard B*	Hampson	Chadwick	Bleau	Howard J	Baguley J	Wright	**Baguley C 2***	**Patterson 1***
15.03	Newcastle Blue Star	H	3-2	Grundy	Foster	Robinson*		Chadwick	Nugent	Baguley J*	Baguley C*	Rudd	Wright	**Patterson 2**
18.03	Radcliffe Borough (MPC:SF)	A	1-3	Grundy	Foster	Howard B	Robinson*	Bleau*	Nugent	Baguley J	**Baguley C 1**	Rudd	Wright	Patterson
22.03	Radcliffe Borough	H	2-2	Ashton	Foster	Howard B	Hampson*	Chadwick	Nugent	**Howard J 1***	**Carden S 1**	Rudd*	Wright	Patterson
24.03	Woodley Sports	A	2-1	Ashton	Foster	Roscoe	**Baguley J 1**	Chadwick	Nugent	Carden A*	Baguley C	Robinson	Wright	Patterson*
26.03	Chorley	H	3-0	Ashton	Foster	Howard B	Baguley J*	Chadwick	Nugent	Carden A*	Baguley C	**Rudd 1**	Wright	**Patterson 2***
29.03	Lancaster City	H	2-2	Ashton	Foster	Howard B	**Baguley J 1***	Chadwick	Nugent	**Carden A 1***	Baguley C	Robinson	Wright	Patterson
01.04	Skelmersdale United	A	0-0	Ashton	Foster	Howard B	Baguley J*	Chadwick	Nugent	Baguley C*	**Carden S 1**	Rudd	Wright	Patterson
03.04	Ossett Albion	A	1-3	Ashton	Foster*	Roscoe	Baguley J	Chadwick	Nugent	Baguley C*	**Carden S 1**	Rudd	Wright	Patterson
05.04	Wakefield	A	2-3	Ashton	Harrop	Howard B	Holden*	**Chadwick 1**	Nugent	Swarbrick*	Baguley J*	Robinson	Power P	Wright
07.04	Bradford Park Avenue	A	0-0	Ashton	Foster	Howard B	Platt	Chadwick	Nugent	Baguley J*	Carden S	Rudd*	Wright	Patterson
09.04	Harrogate Railway Athletic	A	3-1	Ashton	Foster*	Howard B	Platt	Chadwick	Roscoe	Baguley J*	**Baguley C 1**	**Rudd 2**	Wright*	Patterson
12.04	Lancaster City	H	5-2	Ashton	Foster	Howard B	Platt	Chadwick	**Nugent 2**	Baguley C	Carden S*	**Rudd 1**	Wright	**Patterson 2***
15.04	Radcliffe Borough	A	2-0	Ashton	Harrop	Roscoe	Howarth	Bleau	Nugent	Carden A	Rother	**Robinson 1***	**Baguley C 1***	Swarbrick*
17.04	Radcliffe Borough (LPC:F)	N	2-0	Ashton	Foster	Howard B	Platt	Chadwick	Nugent	Baguley J*	Carden S	**Rudd 1**	Wright	Patterson
19.04	Newcastle Blue Star	A	4-0	Foster	Roscoe	Platt	**Chadwick 1**	Howard B*	Baguley J*	Baguley C	Rudd*		**Wright 1**	**Patterson 1**
23.04	Woodley Sports	H¹	1-1	Ashton	Roscoe	Platt*	Chadwick*	Howard B	Carden A	Baguley C	Rudd		**Wright 1**	Patterson
26.04	Garforth Town	A	2-1	Ashton	Harrop	Roscoe	**Platt 1**	Howard B*	Nugent	Carden A	Baguley C*	Rudd*	Robinson	**Baguley J 1**
30.04	Bamber Bridge (PPO:SF)	H	3-2	Ashton	Foster	Roscoe*	Platt	Turner A	Nugent	**Carden A 1**	Carden S	Rudd*	**Wright 1**	**Patterson 1**
03.05	Skelmersdale United (PPO:F)	H	4-1	Ashton	Foster	Baguley J	**Platt 1**	**Chadwick 1***	Nugent	Carden A	Carden S	Rudd*	Wright	**Patterson 1***

a: Match abandoned after 57 minutes due to floodlight failure; appearances and goals are not counted in player totals. ‡: FC United were reinstated to the President's Cup after Nantwich Town fielded an ineligible player

APPEARANCES & GOALS

Substitutes					Attendance
Baguley C (3)	Carden S (4)	Swarbrick (9)			2,257
Baguley C (8)	Carden S (7)	Hargreaves (11)			2,216
Baguley C (7)	Platt (4)	**Hargreaves** (8) **1**			2,253
Baguley C (4)	Whitehead (9)	Swarbrick (11)			2,023
Baguley C (11)	**Hargreaves** (4) **1**	Swarbrick	Mortimer	Foster	2,238
Taylor Ma (3)	Harrop	Wright (11)			867
Brown D (4)	Hargreaves (8)	Hanley (9)			2,196
Hampson	Hargreaves	Hanley			952
Brown D (3)	Hargreaves (4)	Hanley (7)	Power P	Foster	3,112
Platt (5)	Hargreaves (8)	George L (9)			2,283
Power P (9)	Carden S (8)	George L (7)			1,736
Foster (2)	Carden S (4)	George L (6)			617
Baguley C (4)	Platt (7)	Coleman	Lomax M	Hanley (9)	1,310
Baguley C (7)	Platt (2)	Coleman (3)	Lomax M	Allen	951
Brown D (5)	Carden S (4)	Swarbrick (9)			1,955
Turner A (5)	Hanley (6)	Swarbrick (8)			834
Carden S (11)	Carden A	Swarbrick (7)	Bell	Lyons	1,048
Carden S	Baguley J (7)	**Thomson P** (9) **1**			2,160
Carden S (8)	Hanley (7)	Swarbrick (11)			585
Carden S (9)	Hanley (5)	Thomson P (11)			1,006
Carden S (4)	Hanley (2)	Thomson P (7)			1,245
Carden S (9)	Baguley J (3)	Thomson P			1,691
Foster	Baguley J (5)	Thomson P (7)			1,435
Foster	Carden S (4)	Thomson P (7)			2,283
Foster (7)	Platt (4)	Hanley (8)			889
Carden A (7)	Platt (4)	Hanley (11)			1,744
Carden A (9)	Holden (3)	Jarrett (2)			1,290
Carden A (7)	Holden (8)	Self (9)			297
Patterson (9) **3**	Holden (8)	Robinson (10)			2,017
Carden A (7)	Howard J (3)	**Carden S** (8) **1**			2,011
Baguley C (10) **1**	Baguley J	**Rudd** (8) **1**	Platt (4)	Chadwick	512
Howard J (8)	Baguley J (7)	**Rudd** (9) **1**			1,554
Carden A (7)	Baguley C (8)	**Robinson** (9) **1**			2,168
Carden A	Baguley C (3)	Robinson (7)			1,236
Nugent (2)	Baguley J (3)	Rudd (11)			873
Carden A (7)	Baguley J (2)	Robinson (9)			1,624
Carden A (7)	Hampson	Robinson (11)			3,348
Carden A (7)	Baguley C	Robinson (2)			1,879
Harrop (3)	Cosgrave (11)	Power P (10)			967
Carden A (8) **1**	Hampson (4)	Howard J (7)			2,048
Carden A	Hampson	Howard J (4)	Roscoe	Cosgrave (5)	837
Carden A (7)	Baguley J (4)	Robinson (9)			2,163
Howard B	Howard J (7)	**Rudd** (11) **1**			1,066
Hampson (4)	Holden (7)	Robinson (11)			1,645
Bleau	Holden (4)	Carden S (7)			1,859
Roscoe	Swarbrick (4)	Robinson (9)			674
Howard B	Swarbrick (7)	Robinson (2)			456
Carden S (8) **1**	Patterson (7)	Rudd (4)			1,378
Roscoe	Baguley C (9)	Robinson (7)			1,264
Harrop (2)	Swarbrick (7)	Robinson (10)			365
Carden A (11)	Swarbrick (10)	Robinson (8)			2,704
Collier (11)	Patterson (10)	Rudd (9)			743
Roscoe	Carden A (7)	**Baguley C** (8) **1**			1,753
Bleau (6)	Carden A (7)	**Robinson** (9) **1**			647
Harrop (2)	Baguley J (4)	Robinson (5)			1,558
Bleau (5)	Carden S (8)	Power P (9)			1,215
Baguley J (3)	Baguley C	Robinson (9)			1,820
Turner A (5)	**Baguley C** (11) **1**	Robinson (9)			3,258

Player	League		FAC & FAT		Other		Totals	
Danny **Allen**	0	0	0	0	0	0	0	0
Sam **Ashton**	33	0	4	0	9	0	46	0
Chris **Baguley**	30 (+7)	9	0 (+3)	0	7 (+3)	8	37 (+13)	17
Jamie **Baguley**	24 (+6)	3	0	0	5 (+3)	0	29 (+9)	3
Colin **Bell**	3	0	0	0	1	0	4	0
Micah **Bleau**	5 (+2)	0	0	0	4	0	9 (+2)	0
Dave **Brown**	5 (+2)	0	0 (+1)	0	2	0	7 (+3)	0
Aaron **Burns**	12	6	0	0	2	2	14	8
Adam **Carden**	11 (+12)	2	1	0	6 (+1)	1	18 (+13)	3
Simon **Carden**	20 (+13)	8	4	1	6 (+2)	0	30 (+15)	9
David **Chadwick**	27	3	4	0	3	1	34	4
Theo **Coleman**	0	0	0 (+1)	0	0	0	0 (+1)	0
Warren **Collier**	0 (+1)	0	0	0	0	0	0 (+1)	0
Martin **Cosgrave**	0	0	0	0	0	0	0 (+2)	0
Liam **Foster**	26 (+2)	0	2	0	10	0	38 (+2)	0
Liam **George**	1 (+3)	0	1	0	1	0	3 (+3)	0
Aaron **Grundy**	6	0	0	0	2	0	8	0
Matthew **Hampson**	1 (+2)	0	0	0	1	0	2 (+2)	0
Cayne **Hanley**	5 (+6)	0	1 (+2)	1	2 (+1)	1	8 (+9)	2
Anthony **Hargreaves**	2 (+4)	1	0 (+2)	1	1	0	3 (+6)	2
Kyle **Harrop**	3 (+2)	0	0	0	0 (+1)	0	3 (+3)	0
James **Holden**	1 (+5)	0	0	0	1	0	2 (+5)	0
Brad **Howard**	19	0	0	0	6	1	25	1
Josh **Howard**	4 (+3)	1	1	1	3 (+2)	0	8 (+5)	2
Rob **Howarth**	1	0	0	0	0	0	1	0
Danny **Jarrett**	2 (+1)	0	0	0	0	0	2 (+1)	0
Mike **Lomax**	0	0	0	0	0	0	0	0
Darren **Lyons**	0	0	0	0	0	0	0	0
Alex **Mortimer**	2	0	0	0	0	0	2	0
Rob **Nugent**	34	3	4	1	7 (+1)	0	45 (+1)	4
Rory **Patterson**	35 (+3)	33	3	2	9	6	47 (+3)	41
Nicky **Platt**	26 (+4)	3	2 (+2)	1	7 (+1)	2	35 (+7)	6
Phil **Power**	1 (+2)	0	0	0	0 (+1)	0	1 (+3)	0
Phil **Priestley**	3	0	0	0	0	0	3	0
Nick **Robinson**	7 (+15)	3	0	0	2 (+2)	0	9 (+17)	3
Shaun **Roscoe**	23	0	4	0	4	0	31	0
Jamie **Rother**	1	0	0	0	0	0	1	0
Stuart **Rudd**	22 (+3)	7	2	0	4 (+3)	3	28 (+6)	10
Danny **Self**	0 (+1)	0	0	0	0	0	0 (+1)	0
Steve **Spencer**	6	0	4	0	0	0	10	0
Dave **Swarbrick**	4 (+8)	0	1	0	1 (+2)	0	6 (+10)	0
Matty **Taylor**	13	1	2	0	0 (+1)	0	15 (+1)	1
Peter **Thomson**	0 (+5)	1	0	0	1	0	1 (+5)	1
Adam **Turner**	3 (+1)	1	0	0	4 (+1)	0	7 (+2)	1
Dale **Whitehead**	2 (+1)	0	0	0	1	0	3 (+1)	0
Jerome **Wright**	39	6	4	0	9 (+1)	3	52 (+1)	9

	Team	Pld	W	D	L	F	A	GD	Pts
1	Bradford Park Avenue ↑	42	25	7	10	91	43	+48	82
2	FC UNITED OF MANCHESTER ↑	42	24	9	9	91	49	+42	81
3	Skelmersdale United	42	23	9	10	94	46	+48	78
4	Curzon Ashton	42	23	9	10	78	48	+30	78
5	Bamber Bridge	42	22	8	12	70	54	+16	74
6	Ossett Albion	42	20	10	12	77	65	+12	70
7	Wakefield	42	19	7	16	58	49	+9	64
8	Newcastle Blue Star	42	17	12	13	71	58	+13	63
9	Rossendale United	42	16	11	15	66	74	−8	59
10	Garforth Town	42	16	8	18	61	62	−1	56
11	Lancaster City	42	15	9	18	54	70	−16	54
12	Harrogate Railway Athletic	42	13	12	17	51	58	−7	51
13	Clitheroe	42	13	11	18	63	77	−14	50
14	Chorley	42	10	12	20	56	80	−24	42
15	Mossley	42	12	6	24	60	100	−40	42
16	Radcliffe Borough	42	9	11	22	53	75	−22	38
17	Woodley Sports	42	7	13	22	38	65	−27	34
18	Bridlington Town ↓	42	8	8	26	42	99	−57	32

FC United goals listed first. | All games League unless stated otherwise:

FAC FA Cup	**FAT** FA Trophy	**MPC** Manchester FA Premier Cup
LPC Unibond League President's Cup	**PPO** Promotion Play-Offs
LCC Unibond League Challenge Cup	‡ Club reinstated to cup
H Played at Gigg Lane (Bury FC)	H² Played at Valley Road (Flixton FC)
H¹ Played at Stainton Park (Radcliffe Borough FC)	*a Match Abandoned*
N Played at Tameside Stadium (Curzon Ashton FC)	*e After Extra Time*
* Player Substituted	(2) Substituted player's number	Goalscorers in **bold**
■ Player Sent off	(+1) Number of substitute appearances

NORTHERN PREMIER LEAGUE PREMIER DIVISION

Date	Opponents	Venue	Score	1	2	3	4	5	6	7	8	9	10	11
16.08	Matlock Town	H	3-3	Ashton	Foster	Howard B	Whitehead*	Chadwick	Bleau*	Baguley J*	Carden S	**Wilson K 2**	Roca	Williams D
19.08	Cammell Laird	A	1-2	Ashton	Foster	Howard B	Whitehead*	Chadwick	Turner A	Roca*	Carden S	**Wilson K 1**	Robinson*	Williams D
23.08	Buxton	A	1-0	Ashton	Foster	Howard B	Whitehead*	Chadwick	Turner A	**Baguley J 1***	Carden S	Wilson K*	Baguley C	Williams D
25.08	Boston United	H	0-1	Ashton	Foster	Howard B	Baguley J*	Chadwick	Turner A	Roca	Carden S	Wilson K	Baguley C*	Williams D*
30.08	Whitby Town	H	3-1	Ashton	Foster*	Howard B	Whitehead	Chadwick	Turner A	Baguley J	Carden S	**Wilson K 3***	Wright*	Baguley C
01.09	Bradford Park Avenue	A	0-2	Ashton	Self*	Howard B	Whitehead	Chadwick	Wood	Roca*	Carden S*	Wilson K	Wright	Baguley C ■
09.09	Prescot Cables	A	3-4	Ashton	Self*	Howard B*	Whitehead	Chadwick	Wood	Carden A	Carden S	**Wilson K 2**	Wright	Roca*
13.09	Nantwich Town (FAC:Q1)	A	0-0	Ashton	Warrender	Garner S*	Baguley J*	Chadwick	Turner A	Carden A	Carden S	Wilson K	Wright	Roca*
17.09	Nantwich Town (FAC:Q1R)	H	3-4	Ashton	Warrender	Garner S*	Neville D	Chadwick	Turner A	Carden A*	**Carden S 1**	**Wilson K 1**	Wright	Williams D*
20.09	Worksop Town	H	0-0	Ashton	Warrender	Garner S	Neville D*	Chadwick*	Turner A	Roca	Carden S	Wilson K	Wright	Self*
23.09	Ossett Town	A	4-0	Ashton	Warrender	Garner S	Baguley C	Chadwick*	Turner A	Carden A*	Carden S	**Wilson K 2***	Wright	**Roca 2**
04.10	Witton Albion	H	5-3	Ashton	Warrender	Garner S	**Baguley C 2**	Chadwick*	Turner A	Carden A	Carden S*	**Wilson K 2**	**Wright 1**	Roca*
15.10	Kendal Town	H	1-3	Ashton	Warrender	Garner S ■	**Baguley C 1**	Chadwick	Turner A*	Carden A	Carden S*	Wilson K	Wright	Roca*
18.10	Radcliffe Borough (FAT:Q1)	H	1-0	Ashton	Warrender	Garner S	Baguley C*	Chadwick	**Turner A 1**	Carden A	Carden S	Wilson K	Wright	Roca*
22.10	Frickley Athletic	A	3-1	Ashton	Foster*	**Garner S 1**	Warrender	Chadwick	Turner A	Carden A	Carden S	**Wilson K 1***	Wright*	**Williams D** *
25.10	Whitby Town	A	0-0	Ashton	Foster	Garner S	Warrender	Chadwick	Turner A	Carden A	Neville D*	Wilson K	Wright	Williams D*
29.10	Ilkeston Town	H	3-1	Ashton	Foster	Skidmore	Warrender	Chadwick	Turner A	Carden A	Carden S*	**Wilson K 1**	Wright	**Roca 2***
01.11	Worksop Town (FAT:Q2)	A	3-0	Ashton	Foster	Skidmore	Warrender	**Chadwick 1***	Turner A	Carden A	Carden S*	**Wilson K 2**	Wright	Roca*
12.11	Cammell Laird	H	5-5	Ashton	Foster*	Skidmore*	Warrender	Nugent	Turner A	Carden A	**Carden S 1**	**Wilson K 2**	Wright	Roca*
16.11	Guiseley	A	2-2	Ashton	Warrender	Garner S	Dieyte*	Chadwick	Turner A	Carden A	Carden S	**Wilson K 1**	Wright	**Baguley C 1**
19.11	Eastwood Town	H	0-1	Ashton	Warrender	Garner S	Dieyte*	Chadwick	Turner A*	Carden A	Carden S	Wilson K	Wright	Baguley C*
26.11	Boston United (FAT:Q3)	H	1-3	Ashton	Warrender	Garner S*	**Dieyte 1**	Chadwick	Turner A*	Carden A	Carden S*	Wilson K	Wright	Roca
29.11	Hednesford Town	H	3-0	Ashton	Warrender	Garner S	Baguley C	Chadwick	Nugent	Carden A*	Carden S*	**Wilson K 2**	**Wright 1**	Turner T*
02.12	Woodley Sports (LCC:3)	A	0-3	Shenton	Lyons	Skidmore	Dieyte*	Turner A	Swirad	Baguley C*	Robinson	Roca	Turner T	Freakes*
06.12	Eastwood Town	A	2-4	Ashton	Turner A	Skidmore*	Dieyte*	Chadwick	Nugent	Carden A	**Carden S 1**	**Wilson K 1**	Baguley C	Turner T
20.12	Marine	H	3-2	Ashton	Foster*	**Baguley C 1***	Turner A	Nugent	Carden A	Carden S	Wilson K	Wright	**Turner T 1***	
26.12	Ashton United	A	1-2	Ashton	Warrender*	Garner S	Baguley C*	Chadwick	Nugent	Carden A	Carden S*	Wilson K	Wright	**Turner T 1**
03.01	Worksop Town	A	3-0	Ashton	Turner A	Garner S	Neville D*	Chadwick	Nugent	Carden A*	**Carden S 1***	Wilson K	Wright	**Turner T 2**
10.01	Boston United	A	1-0	Ashton	Warrender	Garner S	Neville D	Chadwick	Nugent	Carden A*	Carden S*	**Wilson K 1**	Wright	Turner T*
17.01	Prescot Cables	H	2-0	Ashton	Warrender*	Garner S	Neville D	Turner A	Nugent	Carden A	**Carden S 2***	Wilson K	Wright	Turner T*
24.01	Witton Albion	A	1-2	Ashton	Warrender	Garner S	Neville D	Chadwick	Nugent*	Carden A*	Carden S*	Wilson K	Wright	**Whitman 1**
27.01	Leigh Genesis	A	2-0	Ashton	Carden A	Garner S	Neville D*	Chadwick	Warrender	Roca	Carden S*	Wilson K	**Wright 1**	Whitman*
31.01	Guiseley	H	2-1	Ashton	Warrender	Garner S*	Neville D	Chadwick	Tong	Carden A	Carden S*	Wilson K*	**Wright 1**	**Turner T 1**
07.02	Nantwich Town	A	0-3	Ashton	Warrender	Garner S	Moses	Tong	Nugent	Carden A	Carden S*	Turner T*	Wright	Whitman*
14.02	Leigh Genesis	H	2-4	Ashton	Warrender	Garner S*	Moses*	Chadwick	Tong	Roca	**Chappell 1**	**Lomax C 1**	Wright	Williams D*
21.02	Kendal Town	A	2-1	Ashton	Warrender	Garner S	Neville D*	Chadwick	Tong	Chappell	**Carden S 1**	Lomax C	**Wright 1***	Roca*
28.02	Buxton	H	1-1	Ashton	Warrender	Garner S	Moses*	Chadwick	**Tong 1**	Chappell*	Carden S	Lomax C	Wright ■	Roca*
08.03	Matlock Town	A	1-2	Ashton	Carden A	Garner S	Moses	Tong	Nugent	Chappell*	Baguley J*	Lomax C*	Wright	**Roca 1**
14.03	Frickley Athletic	H	2-0	Ashton	**Warrender 1**	Garner S	Moses	Tong	Nugent	Carden A*	**Carden S 1**	Baguley J*	Lomax C*	Roca
17.03	North Ferriby United	A	2-0	Ashton	Warrender	Garner S	Moses*	Tong	Nugent	Carden A	**Carden S 1***	Baguley J*	Wright	**Roca 1**
21.03	Hednesford Town	A	2-2	Ashton	Warrender	**Garner S 1**	Moses	Tong	Nugent*	**Carden A 1**	Baguley J*	Marsh	Wright	Roca
25.03	Ashton United	H	4-0	Ashton	Warrender	Garner S	Moses	Tong	Nugent*	**Roca 3**	Carden S*	**Lomax C 1**	Wright*	Marsh
28.03	Marine	A	3-2	Ashton	Warrender	Garner S	Moses	Tong	Nugent	Roca*	**Carden S 1***	**Lomax C 2**	Wright	Marsh*
01.04	Ossett Town	H	3-2	Ashton	Carden A	Garner S	Moses*	**Tong 1**	Nugent	Roca	**Carden S 1**	Lomax C ■	Wright	**Marsh 1***
04.04	North Ferriby United	H	4-0	Ashton	Carden A	Garner S	**Moses 1**	Tong	Nugent*	**Roca 1**	**Carden S 1**	Lomax C	**Wright 1**	Marsh*
13.04	Nantwich Town	H	0-0	Ashton	Carden A	Garner S	Platt	Tong	Nugent	Roca*	Carden S*	Marsh	Wright	Moses*
18.04	Ilkeston Town	A	1-0	Ashton	Carden A	Garner S	Platt	Tong	Nugent	Roca	Carden S*	Marsh*	Wright	Moses*
25.04	Bradford Park Avenue	H	1-1	Ashton	Carden A	Garner S	Platt	**Tong 1**	Nugent	Roca*	Carden S*	Marsh*	Wright	Moses

APPEARANCES & GOALS

Substitutes				Attendance
Self	Harrop	Neville D (4)	Robinson (6)	**Baguley C** (7) **1**	2,344
Self	Howarth	Neville D (4)	Baguley J (7)	Baguley C (10)	569
Self (7)	Howarth	Neville D (4)	Robinson (9)	Roca	2,090
Self	Howarth	Neville D (10)	Robinson (4)	Wright (11)	2,825
Self (2)	Carden A	Neville D	Williams D (9)	Roca (10)	2,071
Howarth	Carden A (2)	Baguley J (8)	Williams D (7)	Robinson	1,077
Neville D	**Baguley C** (2) **1**	Baguley J (3)	Williams D (11)	Robinson	704
Neville D (3)	Baguley C (4)	Skidmore	Williams D (11)	Howarth	Self	Howard B	1,783
Nugent (3)	Wood	Skidmore	Edwards J	Howarth	Self (7) **1**	Roca (11)	1,012
Nugent (5)	Wood	Skidmore (4)	Edwards J	Howarth (11)	2,033
Nugent (5)	Neville D (9)	Skidmore	Self	Howarth (7)	544
Nugent (5)	Neville D (8)	Skidmore	Williams D (11)	Howarth	2,201
Nugent	Neville D	Skidmore (6)	Williams D (11)	Howarth (8)	1,801
Nugent	Foster (4)	Skidmore	Williams D (11)	Howarth	1,227
Nugent (2)	Neville D	Skidmore (9)	Robinson (10)	Roca	782
Nugent	Edwards J	Skidmore (8)	Robinson	Roca (11)	1,027
Nugent	Dieyte (8)	Baguley C (11)	Robinson	Neville D	1,550
Edwards J	Dieyte (8)	Baguley C (11)	Robinson (5)	Neville D	599
Edwards J	Dieyte (11)	**Baguley C** (2) **1**	**Robinson** (3) **1**		1,714
Foster	Nugent	Skidmore	Robinson (4)	Roca	1,283
Foster	Nugent (6)	Skidmore	Robinson (11)	Roca (4)	1,636
Foster	Nugent (6)	Skidmore	Robinson (3)	Baguley C (8)	936
Foster	Dieyte (8)	Skidmore	Robinson (11)	Roca (7)	1,946
Connor S (7)	Edwards J	Buckley (11)	Reeves	Mack (4)	366
Swirad	Edwards J	Williams D	Robinson (3)	Roca (4)	820
Skidmore	Dieyte	Neville D (4)	**Robinson** (11) **1**	Roca (2)	2,122
Foster	Chappell (8)	Neville D	Robinson (4)	Roca (2)	1,561
Baguley J (7)	Chappell (4)	Dieyte (8)	Robinson	Roca	443
Turner A	Chappell (8)	Dieyte	Whitman (7)	Roca (11)	1,625
Moses (2)	Chappell	Dieyte	Whitman (11)	Roca (8)	2,045
Turner A (6)	Chappell (8)	Dieyte	Turner T	Roca (7)	1,030
Moses (8)	Chappell	Dieyte	Turner T (11)	**Baguley J** (4) **1**	1,302
Moses	Chappell	Roca (8)	Whitman (9)	Baguley J (3)	1,986
Chadwick (11)	Chappell	Dieyte	Williams D (8)	Baguley J (9)	1,547
Nugent	Carden A (4)	Turner T (11)	Whitman	Baguley J (3)	1,850
Swirad	Moses (4)	Williams D (11)	Whitman	Baguley J (10)	1,010
Nugent	Carden A (7)	Williams D (11)	Whitman	Baguley J (4)	2,158
Whitman (8)	Dieyte (7)	Williams D (9)			1,038
Chadwick	Dieyte	Williams D (7)	Chappell (9)	Stopforth (10)	1,849
Swirad	Dieyte (4)	Williams D	Chappell (8)	Stopforth (9)	376
Chadwick (6)	Dieyte	Williams D	Chappell	Lomax C (8)	1,077
Chadwick (6)	Dieyte	Williams D (10)	Chappell	Platt (8)	1,714
Chadwick	Carden A (7)	Williams D (8)	Chappell	Platt (11)	1,146
Chadwick	Neville D	Williams D (11)	Baguley J	Platt (4)	1,665
Chadwick (6)	Neville D	Williams D (11)	Baguley J	Platt (8)	3,120
Chadwick (11)	Neville D (8)	Williams D	Baguley J (7)	Dieyte	2,840
Chadwick (9)	Neville D	**Williams D** (11) **1**	Baguley J (8)	Wilson K	1,313
Chadwick (8)	Neville D	Williams	Baguley J (7)	Lomax C (9)	3,719

Player	League		FAC & FAT		Other		Totals	
Sam Ashton	42	0	5	0	0	0	47	0
Chris **Baguley**	13 (+5)	**8**	1 (+3)	0	1	0	15 (+8)	**8**
Jamie **Baguley**	8 (+13)	**2**	1	0	0	0	9 (+13)	**2**
Micah **Bleau**	1	0	0	0	0	0	1	0
John **Buckley**	0	0	0	0	0 (+1)	0	0 (+1)	0
Adam **Carden**	30 (+4)	**1**	5	0	0	0	35 (+4)	**1**
Simon **Carden**	38	**11**	5	1	0	0	43	**12**
David **Chadwick**	27 (+7)	0	5	1	0	0	32 (+7)	**1**
Neil **Chappell**	4 (+6)	**1**	0	0	0	0	4 (+6)	**1**
Shaun **Connor**	0	0	0	0	0 (+1)	0	0 (+1)	0
Papis **Dieyte**	3 (+6)	0	1 (+1)	**1**	1	0	5 (+7)	**1**
Jake Edwards	0	0	0	0	0	0	0	0
Liam **Foster**	10	0	1 (+1)	0	0	0	11 (+1)	0
Sam **Freakes**	0	0	0	0	1	0	1	0
Simon **Garner**	32	**2**	4	0	0	0	36	**2**
Kyle **Harrop**	0	0	0	0	0	0	0	0
Brad **Howard**	7	0	0	0	0	0	7	0
Rob **Howarth**	0 (+3)	0	0	0	0	0	0 (+3)	0
Carl **Lomax**	9 (+2)	**4**	0	0	0	0	9 (+2)	**4**
Darren **Lyons**	0	0	0	0	1	0	1	0
Jamie **Mack**	0	0	0	0	0 (+1)	0	0 (+1)	0
Phil **Marsh**	8	**1**	0	0	0	0	8	**1**
Tunji **Moses**	14 (+3)	**1**	0	0	0	0	14 (+3)	**1**
Dave **Neville**	9 (+8)	0	1 (+1)	0	0	0	10 (+9)	0
Rob **Nugent**	21 (+5)	0	0 (+2)	0	0	0	21 (+7)	0
Nicky **Platt**	3 (+4)	0	0	0	0	0	3 (+4)	0
Mark **Reeves**	0	0	0	0	0	0	0	0
Nick **Robinson**	1 (+11)	**2**	0 (+2)	0	1	0	2 (+13)	**2**
Carlos **Roca**	26 (+11)	**10**	4 (+1)	0	1	0	31 (+12)	**10**
Danny **Self**	3 (+2)	0	0 (+1)	**1**	0	0	3 (+3)	**1**
Grant Shenton	0	0	0	0	1	0	1	0
Alex **Skidmore**	3 (+4)	0	1	0	1	0	5 (+4)	0
Gary **Stopforth**	0 (+2)	0	0	0	0	0	0 (+2)	0
Nick **Swirad**	0	0	0	0	1	0	1	0
Adam **Tong**	16	**3**	0	0	0	0	16	**3**
Adam **Turner**	18 (+1)	0	5	1	1	0	24 (+1)	**1**
Tommy **Turner**	9 (+2)	**5**	0	0	1	0	10 (+2)	**5**
Danny **Warrender**	26	**1**	5	0	0	0	31	**1**
Dale **Whitehead**	6	0	0	0	0	0	6	0
Tristram **Whitman**	3 (+4)	**1**	0	0	0	0	3 (+4)	**1**
Danny **Williams**	7 (+15)	**2**	1 (+2)	0	0	0	8 (+17)	**2**
Kyle **Wilson**	27	**21**	5	3	0	0	32	**24**
Jacob **Wood**	2	0	0	0	0	0	2	0
Jerome **Wright**	36 (+1)	**6**	5	0	0	0	41 (+1)	**6**

	Team	Pld	W	D	L	F	A	GD	Pts
1	Eastwood Town ↑	42	25	12	5	82	37	+45	87
2	Ilkeston Town ↑	42	23	13	6	59	34	+25	82
3	Nantwich Town	42	22	10	10	83	41	+42	76
4	Guiseley	42	22	10	10	98	60	+38	76
5	Kendal Town	42	21	11	10	85	63	+22	74
6	**FC UNITED OF MANCHESTER**	42	21	9	12	82	58	+24	72
7	Bradford Park Avenue	42	20	12	10	74	52	+22	72
8	Hednesford Town	42	21	6	15	78	52	+26	69
9	Ashton United	42	16	10	16	71	75	−4	58
10	North Ferriby United	42	16	6	20	67	65	+2	54
11	Frickley Athletic	42	13	15	14	50	58	−8	54
12	Ossett Town	42	15	8	19	71	74	−3	53
13	Marine	42	15	6	21	54	75	−21	51
14	Buxton	42	13	10	19	56	58	−2	49
15	Matlock Town	42	13	13	17	65	74	−9	49
16	Boston United	42	12	13	17	38	52	−14	49
17	Worksop Town	42	12	12	18	48	87	−39	48
18	Cammell Laird ‡↓	42	12	11	19	58	70	−12	47
19	Whitby Town	42	12	10	20	58	71	−13	46
20	Witton Albion ↓	42	12	6	24	53	73	−20	42
21	Leigh Genesis ↓	42	11	7	24	42	88	−46	40
22	Prescot Cables ↓	42	5	12	25	52	107	−55	27

FC United goals listed first. All games League unless stated otherwise:
FAC FA Cup   **FAT** FA Trophy   **LCC** Unibond League Challenge Cup
H Played at Gigg Lane (Bury FC)
* Player Substituted   (2) Substituted player's number   Goalscorers in **bold**
■ Player Sent off   (+1) Number of substitute appearances

‡: Cammell Laird were relegated to Division One South due to ground grading issues, earning Whitby Town a reprieve

NORTHERN PREMIER LEAGUE PREMIER DIVISION

Date	Opponents	Venue	Score	1	2	3	4	5	6	7	8	9	10	11
15.08	Boston United	H	1-2	Ashton	Warrender	Garner S*	Moses	Tong 1	Nugent	Carden A	Carden S	Lomax C*	Wright	Williams D*
17.08	Bradford Park Avenue	A	2-3	Ashton	Warrender	Garner S	Moses	Tong	Nugent	Carden A*	Carden S 2	Deegan	Wright*	Cottrell*
22.08	Retford United	A	1-1	Ashton	Carden A	Garner S*	Warrender	Tong 1	Nugent	Roca	Carden S	Deegan	Wright	Marsh*
26.08	Marine	H	3-0	Ashton	Carden A	Garner S	Warrender	Tong	Nugent 1*	Roca*	Carden S	Deegan 1	Wright*	Marsh
29.08	Burscough	H	2-0	Ashton	Carden A	Garner S	Warrender	Chadwick	Tong	Roca*	Carden S*	Deegan	Wright 1*	Marsh 1
31.08	Ossett Town	A	2-1	Ashton	Carden A	Garner S	Warrender	Chadwick 1	Nugent	Roca*	Carden S*	Deegan 1	Wright*	Marsh
05.09	Kendal Town	A	0-1	Ashton	Carden A*	Garner S	Warrender	Chadwick	Nugent	Roca*	Carden S	Deegan	Wright*	Marsh
09.09	Whitby Town	H	1-1	Ashton	Warrender*	Garner S	Moses	Chadwick	Tong	Carden A	Carden S*	Deegan	Marsh	Williams D*
12.09	Sheffield FC (FAC:Q1)	A	3-1	Ashton	Warrender	Garner S	Moses*	Chadwick	Tong*	Carden A	Carden S*	Deegan 1	Wright	Roca 2
19.09	Guiseley	H	1-2	Ashton	Warrender	Garner S*	Moses*	Chadwick	Tong	Carden A	Carden S*	Deegan	Wright 1	Roca
23.09	Worksop Town	A	1-3	Ashton	Carden A	Garner S*	Warrender	Chadwick	Nugent ■	Roca	Moses	Deegan	Marsh*	Morris B*
26.09	North Ferriby United (FAC:Q2)	A	1-0	Ashton	Warrender	Garner S	Moses	Chadwick	Tong	Carden A	Carden S*	Deegan 1	Wright*	Roca*
03.10	Stocksbridge Park Steels	H	4-3	Ashton	Warrender*	Garner S	Moses	Chadwick	Tong	Carden A	Carden S*	Deegan 1	Wright 1	Roca 2
07.10	Nantwich Town	H¹	4-0	Ashton	Carden A	Garner S	Moses	Chadwick	Tong	Roca*	Cottrell	Deegan	Wright*	Marsh 3*
11.10	Stalybridge Celtic (FAC:Q3)	H	3-3	Ashton	Carden A	Garner S	Moses*	Chadwick 1	Tong*	Roca 1	Cottrell	Deegan	Wright	Marsh 1
13.10	Stalybridge Celtic (FAC:Q3R)	A	1-0	Ashton	Carden A ■	Garner S	Moses*	Chadwick*	Tong	Roca*	Cottrell	Deegan	Wright 1	Marsh*
17.10	Ashton United (FAT:Q1)	A	3-1	Ashton	Carden A	Garner S	Moses*	Tong 1	Nugent	Roca 1*	Cottrell	Deegan	Wright*	Marsh 1
24.10	Northwich Victoria (FAC:Q4)	A	0-3	Ashton	Carden A	Garner S*	Moses*	Chadwick	Tong	Roca	Cottrell	Deegan*	Wright	Marsh
27.10	North Ferriby United	A	0-1	Ashton	Quistin*	Garner S	Neville D ■	Chadwick	Tong	Roca*	Cottrell	Deegan*	Wright	Marsh
31.10	Lancaster City (FAT:Q2)	A	3-3	Ashton	Garner S	Quistin	Moses	Tong	Nugent*	Roca 1*	Cottrell	Yoffe 2	Wright	Marsh*
04.11	Lancaster City (FAT:Q2R)	H	1-0 e	Ashton	Quistin	Garner S	Swirad	Tong	Roca	Carden	Cottrell	Yoffe*	Wright	Marsh*
07.11	Buxton	H	0-1	Ashton	Quistin	Garner S*	Cottrell	Swirad	Tong	Roca	Carden S*	Yoffe	Wright	Marsh*
14.11	Hucknall Town	A	3-2	Ashton	Carden A	Quistin	Cottrell 1*	Tong	Swirad	Moses*	Carden S	Deegan*	Wright	Marsh 2
21.11	Harrogate Town (FAT:Q3)	H	2-3	Ashton	Carden A	Quistin	Moses	Tong	Swirad*	Roca	Carden S 2	Deegan*	Wright	Marsh*
05.12	Whitby Town	A	2-2 o	Ashton	Warrender	Garner S	Cottrell	Tong	Swirad	Roca*	Carden S	Ibrahim*	Yoffe 1	Quistin
08.12	Kendal Town (LCC:3)	A	1-2 ‡	Ashton	Warrender*	Quistin	Neville D	Tong 1	Swirad	Cottrell	Garner S	Deegan*	Yoffe	Marsh*
12.12	Retford United	H	2-4	Ashton	Quistin	Garner S	Neville D*	Tong	Swirad*	Roca 1	Carden S 1	Cottrell	Yoffe	Marsh
23.01	Stocksbridge Park Steels	A	1-1	Ashton	Jacobs	Quistin	Cottrell	Tong	Nugent	Roca 1*	Carden S	Yoffe*	Wright	Marsh
27.01	Frickley Athletic	H	0-0	Ashton	Jacobs*	Quistin	Cottrell	Tong	Nugent	Rigoglioso ■	Carden S	Wilson K*	Wright	Marsh*
30.01	Durham City	A	2-1	Ashton	Jacobs	Quistin	Cottrell	Chadwick	Nugent	Yoffe 1*	Rigoglioso	Wilson K*	Wright	Marsh 1
06.02	Nantwich Town	A	6-1	Ashton	Jacobs	Quistin ■	Cottrell	Chadwick	Tong	Deegan 1*	Carden S 1	Wilson K 3*	Wright 1	Marsh*
13.02	Worksop Town	H	2-0	Ashton	Jacobs	Quistin	Cottrell	Chadwick	Tong	Deegan*	Carden S 2*	Wilson K	Wright*	Marsh
20.02	Frickley Athletic	A	2-0	Ashton	Jacobs	Quistin	Holden	Chadwick	Tong*	Roca*	Carden S	Wilson K 1	Wright	Deegan 1*
27.02	North Ferriby United	H	3-3	Ashton	Quistin	Cottrell	Holden*	Chadwick 1	Nugent ■	Roca	Carden S	Wilson K*	Wright	Deegan 2
03.03	Ossett Town	H	2-1	Ashton	Marsh	Quistin	Cottrell	Chadwick	Ayres	Roca*	Carden S	Wilson K*	Wright 1	Deegan 1
06.03	Buxton	A	0-3	Ashton	Jacobs	Quistin	Cottrell	Chadwick	Ayres*	Roca*	Carden S	Yoffe*	Marsh	Deegan
13.03	Durham City	H	1-2	Ashton	Marsh	Quistin	Cottrell	Chadwick	Jacobs*	Roca 1	Carden S	Rigoglioso*	Wright	Deegan
16.03	Matlock Town	A	3-4	Ashton	Holden*	Quistin	Cottrell	Chadwick 1	Swirad*	Roca	Carden S	Deegan	Wright 1	Marsh 1
20.03	Hucknall Town	H	2-0	Ashton	Holden	Quistin	Cottrell	Chadwick 1	Swirad*	Roca 1*	Carden S*	Marsh*	Wright	Deegan
24.03	Bradford Park Avenue	H	1-5	Ashton	Holden	Quistin	Cottrell	Nugent*	Swirad	Roca*	Carden S*	Marsh 1	Wright	Deegan ■
27.03	Guiseley	A	0-2	Ashton	Holden	Quistin	Cottrell*	Nugent	Swirad	Ovington*	Carden S	Marsh*	Wright	Deegan ■
02.04	Marine	A	1-1	Ashton	Holden	Quistin	Tsiaklis	Chadwick 1	Swirad	Ovington*	Krou	Marsh	Wright*	Roca*
05.04	Ashton United	A	2-2	Ashton	Holden	Quistin	Tsiaklis	Nugent*	Swirad*	Ovington	Krou*	Marsh	Wright	Roca 2
07.04	Kendal Town	H	1-4	Ashton	Holden	Quistin	Tsiaklis	Chadwick	Swirad*	Ovington	Carden S	Marsh*	Wright*	Roca*
10.04	Burscough	A	0-1	Shenton	Holden	Quistin	Tsiaklis*	Chadwick	Jacobs	Roca	Carden S	Mack*	Wright	Yoffe*
17.04	Boston United	A	1-4	Shenton	Jacobs	Quistin	Krou	Chadwick	Ayres*	Roca*	Carden S	Marsh	Wright 1	Morris B*
21.04	Ashton United	H	2-3	Shenton	Jacobs	Morris B*	Cottrell	Nugent	Swirad*	Deegan 1	Carden S	Marsh 1	Wright	Ovington*
24.04	Matlock Town	H	1-0	Ashton	Jacobs	Quistin	Cottrell	Ayres*	Nugent	Roca	Carden S	Ovington*	Wright 1	Deegan*

‡: FC United were initially drawn to play Kendal Town at home in the League Challenge Cup on 25th November, but due to the unavailability of Gigg Lane the fixture was reversed and played as an away game.

APPEARANCES & GOALS

Substitutes							Attendance
Morris B	Cottrell (3)	Roca (11)	Deegan (9)	Mack			2,482
Morris B	Lomax C (10)	Roca (11)	Williams D	Mack (7)			1,150
Morris B (11)	Chadwick	Cottrell	Williams D (3)	Mack			613
Morris B	Chadwick (6)	Cottrell	Williams D (10)	**Mack (7) 1**			1,884
Morris B (10)	Nugent	Cottrell (8)	Williams D (7)	Mack			1,879
Morris B (7)	Tong	Cottrell (8)	Williams D (10)	Mack			823
Morris B	Moses (2)	Cottrell (7)	Williams D (10)	Mack			1,117
Morris B	Nugent	Cottrell (8)	**Wright (11) 1**	Roca (2)			1,716
Morris B	Nugent (6)	Cottrell (4)	Williams	Marsh (8)	Mack	Shenton	1,208
Morris B (3)	Nugent	Cottrell (4)	Williams D	Marsh (8)			2,106
Tong (3) 1	Shenton	Cottrell (10)	Williams D (11)	Mack			345
Morris B	Nugent (10)	Cottrell (8)	Williams D	Marsh (11)	Mack	Shenton	838
Morris B	Nugent	Cottrell (8)	Williams D	Marsh (2)			1,888
Morris B	Neville D (10)	Carden S	Ibrahim (7)	**Mack (11) 1**			1,650
Morris B	Nugent (6)	Carden S (7)	Ibrahim	Mack	Warrender	Shenton	2,819
Morris B	Nugent (5)	Carden S (4)	Ibrahim	Mack (11)	Warrender	Shenton	1,923
Neville D (4)	Yoffe (10)	Carden S (7)	Ibrahim	Mack			729
Nugent	Yoffe (3)	Carden S (4)	Ibrahim (9)	Mack	Swirad	Shenton	2,615
Nugent	Yoffe (2)	Carden S (9)	Ibrahim	Moses (7)			412
Neville D (6)	Deegan (11)	Carden S	Ibrahim	Mack (7)			743
Neville D	**Deegan (11) 1**	Carden S (4)	Ibrahim	Mack (9)			798
Neville D (3)	Nugent	Carden A (8)	Ibrahim	Mack (11)			2,147
Warrender	Garner S (7)	Roca	Yoffe (4)	Mack (9)			573
Warrender (6)	Nugent (11)	Neville D	Yoffe (9)	Mack			1,166
Shenton	Nugent	Neville D	Deegan (9)	Marsh (7)			636
Shenton	Nugent (11)	Ibrahim (9)	Carden S (2)				181
Moses	Nugent (6)	Ibrahim	Deegan (4)	Mack			1,920
Chadwick	Swirad	Holden	Deegan (7)	Rigoglioso (9)			761
Chadwick (2)	Roca	Holden	Deegan (11)	Yoffe (9)			1,468
Tong	Roca (7)*	Holden (S)	Deegan (9)	Carden S			606
Rigoglioso (7)	Roca	Holden (11)	Yoffe (9)				1,171
Nugent	Roca (10)	Holden (8)	Yoffe (7)	Jones W			2,137
Nugent	Ayres (6)	Marsh (11)	Yoffe (7)	Jones W			701
Karim	Tsiaklis	Marsh (4)	Yoffe (9)	Shenton			2,021
Karim	Tsiaklis (9)	Nugent	Yoffe (7)	Rigoglioso			1,681
Karim (6)	Tsiaklis (7)	Nugent	Holden	Rigoglioso (9)			1,232
Karim	Ayres (6)	Yoffe (9)	Holden	Shenton			2,164
Ioannou (2)	Tsiaklis	Krou (6)	Mack	Shenton			562
Jacobs	Nugent	Krou (8)	Eme (9)	Ovington (7)			2,016
Jacobs	Tsiaklis (7)	Mack (5)	Eme (8)	Shenton			1,891
Jacobs	Tsiaklis (4)	Yoffe	Eme (9)	Roca (7)			841
Morris B (10)	Ayres	Yoffe (11)	Eme (7)	Mack			1,093
Morris B	Chadwick (5)	Yoffe	Jacobs (6)	Carden S (8)			707
Morris B	Krou	Yoffe (11)	Jacobs (6)	**Mack (9) 1**			1,585
Morris B	Krou (4)	Marsh	Cheetham (11)	Ovington (9)			675
Holden (11)	Tsiaklis	Yoffe (6)	Eme	Ovington (7)			2,533
Holden	Ayres (6)	Yoffe (3)	Roca (11)	Mack			1,624
Holden	Swirad (5)	Yoffe	Ioannou (9)	Marsh (11)			2,871

Player	League		FAC & FAT		Other		Totals	
Sam Ashton	35	0	9	0	1	0	45	0
Mark Ayres	4 (+3)	0	0	0	0	0	4 (+3)	0
Adam Carden	3 (+1)	0	7	0	0	0	10 (+1)	0
Simon Carden	32 (+2)	6	3 (+4)	2	0 (+1)	0	35 (+7)	8
David Chadwick	23 (+3)	5	5	1	0	0	28 (+3)	6
Scott Cheetham	0 (+1)	0	0	0	0	0	0 (+1)	0
Jake Cottrell	23 (+8)	1	6 (+2)	0	1	0	30 (+10)	1
Ben Deegan	26 (+6)	9	7 (+2)	3	1	0	34 (+8)	12
Gage Eme	0 (+4)	0	0	0	0	0	0 (+4)	0
Simon Garner	16 (+1)	0	8	0	1	0	25 (+1)	0
James Holden	10 (+4)	0	0	0	0	0	10 (+4)	0
Abdirashid Ibrahim	1 (+1)	0	0 (+1)	0	0 (+1)	0	1 (+3)	0
Stephanos Ioannou	0 (+2)	0	0	0	0	0	0 (+2)	0
Kyle Jacobs	12 (+2)	0	0	0	0	0	12 (+2)	0
Will Jones	0	0	0	0	0	0	0	0
Adam Karim	0 (+1)	0	0	0	0	0	0 (+1)	0
Cédric Krou	3 (+3)	0	0	0	0	0	3 (+3)	0
Carl Lomax	1 (+1)	0	0	0	0	0	1 (+1)	0
Jamie Mack	1 (+7)	3	0 (+3)	0	0	0	1 (+10)	3
Phil Marsh	29 (+6)	10	7 (+2)	2	1	0	37 (+8)	12
Ben Morris	3 (+5)	0	0	0	0	0	3 (+5)	0
Tunji Moses	8 (+2)	0	9	0	0	0	17 (+2)	0
Dave Neville	2 (+2)	0	0 (+2)	0	1	0	3 (+4)	0
Rob Nugent	16 (+1)	1	2 (+5)	0	0 (+1)	0	18 (+7)	1
Chris Ovington	6 (+3)	0	0	0	0	0	6 (+3)	0
Ludovic Quistin	24	0	3	0	1	0	28	0
Adriano Rigoglioso	3 (+3)	0	0	0	0	0	3 (+3)	0
Carlos Roca	28 (+7)	8	9	5	0	0	37 (+7)	13
Grant Shenton	3	0	0	0	0	0	3	0
Nick Swirad	12 (+1)	0	2	0	1	0	15 (+1)	0
Adam Tong	19 (+1)	3	9	1	1	1	29 (+1)	5
Angelos Tsiaklis	4 (+4)	0	0	0	0	0	4 (+4)	0
Danny Warrender	12	0	2 (+1)	0	1	0	15 (+1)	0
Danny Williams	2 (+6)	0	0	0	0	0	2 (+6)	0
Kyle Wilson	7	4	0	0	0	0	7	4
Jerome Wright	33 (+1)	9	9	1	0	0	42 (+1)	10
Joe Yoffe	7 (+13)	2	2 (+3)	2	1	0	10 (+16)	4

o Opposition Own Goal for FC United:
Andy Leeson — 05/12/2009 — FC's 1st v Whitby Town (NPLP) — A 2-2

FC United goals listed first. All games League unless stated otherwise:
FAC FA Cup | **FAT** FA Trophy | **LCC** Unibond League Challenge Cup
H Played at Gigg Lane (Bury FC) | ‡ Fixture reversed
H1 Played at Ewen Fields (Hyde United FC) | **e** After Extra Time
***** Player Substituted | (2) Substituted player's number | Goalscorers in **bold**
■ Player Sent off | (+1) Number of substitute appearances

	Team	Pld	W	D	L	F	A	GD	Pts
1	Guiseley ↑	38	25	4	9	73	41	+32	79
2	Bradford Park Avenue	38	24	6	8	94	51	+43	78
3	Boston United ↑	38	23	8	7	90	34	+56	77
4	North Ferriby United	38	22	9	7	70	38	+32	75
5	Kendal Town	38	21	8	9	75	47	+28	71
6	Retford United	38	18	11	9	73	46	+27	65
7	Matlock Town	38	17	9	12	72	49	+23	60
8	Buxton	38	16	12	10	66	43	+23	60
9	Marine	38	17	6	15	60	55	+5	57
10	Nantwich Town	38	16	6	16	64	69	−5	54
11	Stocksbridge Park Steels	38	15	7	16	80	68	+12	52
12	Ashton United	38	15	6	17	48	63	−15	51
13	FC UNITED OF MANCHESTER	38	13	8	17	62	65	−3	47
14	Whitby Town	38	12	10	16	56	62	−6	46
15	Frickley Athletic	38	12	9	17	50	66	−16	45
16	Burscough	38	13	5	20	55	65	−10	44
17	Hucknall Town	38	12	8	18	65	81	−16	44
18	Worksop Town	38	7	9	22	45	68	−23	30
19	Ossett Town	38	6	7	25	46	92	−46	25
20	Durham City -6 points ↓	38	2	0	36	27	168	−141	‡ 0

‡: Durham City deducted 6 points for fielding a suspended player under a false name
Newcastle Blue Star resigned from the league prior to the season's start
King's Lynn folded in December and their record was expunged (they did not play FC)

NORTHERN PREMIER LEAGUE PREMIER DIVISION

Date	Opponents	Venue	Score	1	2	3	4	5	6	7	8	9	10	11
22.08	Marine	A	2-0	Ashton	Jacobs	Neville L	Battersby*	Parker	McManus	Ovington*	Cottrell	**Norton 2**	Wright	Deegan*
25.08	Nantwich Town	H	1-0	Ashton	Jacobs	Neville L	Battersby*	Parker	McManus	Ovington*	Cottrell	Norton	**Wright 1**	Deegan*
28.08	Retford United	H	5-1	Ashton	Jacobs*	Neville L	Battersby*	**Parker 1**	McManus	Ovington*	**Cottrell 1**	Norton	Wright	**Roca 1**
30.08	Ashton United	A	0-1	Hibbert	Jacobs	Neville L	Platt	Parker	McManus	Roca*	Carden S*	Norton	Wright	Cottrell
05.09	Matlock Town	H†	1-5	Hibbert	Jacobs	Neville L	Cottrell	Parker	McManus	Roca*	Platt	**Norton 1**	Wright ■	Little*
08.09	Bradford Park Avenue	A	1-4	Ashton	Jacobs	Neville L	Cottrell	Parker	McManus	Roca*	Battersby	Norton	Wright*	**Ovington 1***
11.09	Radcliffe Borough (FAC:Q1)	H	3-0	Hibbert	Jacobs	Neville L	Battersby	Parker*	McManus	Ovington*	**Holden 1***	**Norton 2**	Wright	Cottrell
18.09	Stocksbridge Park Steels	H†	1-4	Ashton	Jacobs*	Neville L	Battersby	Parker	McManus*	Roca*	Cottrell	Norton	Wright	Deegan
21.09	Burscough	A	2-0 o	Hibbert	Jacobs	Neville L	Platt	Munroe	McManus	Battersby*	Carden S	**Norton 1**	Hurst*	Holden*
25.09	Gainsborough Trinity (FAC:Q2)	H	2-1	Hibbert	Jacobs	Neville L	Platt	Munroe	McManus	Battersby	Carden S*	Norton	**Hurst 2***	Holden
29.09	Buxton	H	1-2	Ashton	Jacobs	Neville L	Platt	Munroe	McManus	Battersby*	Carden S*	Norton	**Hurst 1**	Holden*
02.10	Mickleover Sports	A	0-2	Hibbert	Jacobs	Neville L	Platt	Munroe	McManus	Battersby*	Carden S*	Norton	Hurst	Holden*
06.10	Ossett Town	H†	4-1	Ashton	Jacobs	Neville L	Battersby*	Munroe	McManus	**Roca 2**	Cottrell	**Norton 1**	**Wright 1***	Hurst*
09.10	Norton & Stockton Ancients (FAC:Q3)	A	5-2	Ashton	Jacobs	Neville L*	Platt	Parker	McManus	Roca*	Cottrell	**Norton 3**	Wright	**Hurst 1***
16.10	Newcastle Town (FAT:Q1)	H	5-0	Ashton	Jacobs	Neville L	Holden	Parker*	McManus	Roca*	Cottrell*	**Norton 2**	Wright	**Deegan 3**
24.10	Barrow (FAC:Q4)	H	1-0	Ashton	Jacobs	Neville L	Holden	Munroe	McManus	**Roca 1***	Cottrell	Norton	Wright	Deegan*
26.10	Ossett Town	A	3-0	Ashton	Jacobs	Neville L	Platt	Ayres	McManus	Roca*	**Carden S 1***	Norton	**Wright 2**	Cottrell*
30.10	Colwyn Bay (FAT:Q2)	H	2-1	Ashton	Jacobs	Neville L*	Platt	Ayres	McManus	**Ovington 1***	Cottrell	Norton	**Wright 1**	Wolfenden*
05.11	Rochdale (FAC:1)	A	3-2	Ashton	Jacobs	Battersby*	**Platt 1**	Munroe	McManus	Roca*	**Cottrell 1**	**Norton 1**	Wright	Deegan*
13.11	Northwich Victoria	A	0-1	Ashton	Jacobs*	Battersby	Platt	Munroe	McManus	Roca	Cottrell	Hurst*	Wright*	Deegan*
16.11	Colwyn Bay	A	1-3	Ashton	Battersby	Parker*	Platt	Munroe	McManus	Roca*	Cottrell	**Norton 1***	Wright	Hurst
20.11	Hinckley United (FAT:Q3)	H	1-2	Ashton	Battersby	Ovington*	Platt	Munroe	McManus	Roca*	Cottrell	Norton	**Wright 1**	Hurst*
22.11	Ashton United (LCC:3)	A	1-3	Shenton	Holden	Fitton*	**Tierney 1**	Chadwick	Ayres	Ovington	Carden S	Deegan*	Wolfenden	Cheetham*
27.11	Brighton & Hove Albion (FAC:2)	A	1-1	Ashton	Jacobs*	Ovington*	**Platt 1**	Munroe	McManus ■	Roca	Cottrell	Norton	Wright	Deegan*
08.12	Brighton & Hove Albion (FAC:2R)	H	0-4	Ashton	Jacobs*	Quistin*	Platt	Munroe	Parker	Roca	Cottrell	Norton	Ovington*	Deegan
11.12	FC Halifax Town	H	0-1	Ashton	Jacobs	Quistin	Platt	Munroe	Parker	Roca	Cottrell	Norton	Wright	Wolfenden
01.01	FC Halifax Town	A	1-4	Ashton	Jacobs*	Quistin*	Platt	Chadwick	Parker	Wolfenden	Carden S*	Norton	**Wright 1**	Battersby
03.01	Ashton United	H	2-1	Ashton	Battersby*	Quistin*	Platt	Chadwick	Parker	**Wolfenden 1**	Cottrell	**Norton 1***	Wright	Holden
08.01	Bradford Park Avenue	H	2-0	Ashton	Battersby	Neville L	Holden	Munroe	Parker	Wolfenden*	Carden S	Norton	**Wright 1**	Cottrell
15.01	Retford United	A	4-0	**Ashton 1**	Battersby	Neville L	Holden*	Parker	McManus	**Wolfenden 1***	Carden S	Norton*	**Wright 1**	**Cottrell 1**
22.01	Hucknall Town	H	4-1	Ashton	Holden*	Neville L	Platt	Parker*	McManus	**Wolfenden 1**	Carden S*	**Norton 1**	**Wright 1**	**Cottrell 1**
25.01	Kendal Town	A	2-3	Ashton	Quistin*	Neville L	Platt	Munroe	McManus	Wolfenden	**Carden S 1***	Norton	**Wright 1**	Cottrell
02.02	Colwyn Bay	H	0-1	Ashton	Munroe*	Neville L	Platt*	Parker	McManus	Wolfenden	Carden S*	Norton	Wright	Cottrell
05.02	Hucknall Town	A	2-1	Ashton	Holden*	Neville L	Tierney ■	Parker	McManus	Wolfenden	**Carden S 1***	**Norton 1**	Wright	Cottrell
08.02	Frickley Athletic	A	0-0	Ashton	Holden	Neville L	Platt*	Parker*	McManus ■	Wolfenden	Carden S	Norton	Wright	Cottrell
12.02	Whitby Town	H	4-0 o	Ashton	Battersby*	Neville L	Tierney	Chadwick	McManus*	**Wolfenden 1**	**Holden 1**	**Norton 1**	Wright	Cottrell
16.02	Chasetown	H†	4-2	Ashton	Battersby ■	Neville L	Tierney*	Chadwick	McManus	**Wolfenden 1**	Holden	**Norton 2***	Wright	**Cottrell 1***
19.02	Burscough	H	3-1	Ashton	Battersby	Neville L	Holden*	Chadwick	McManus	Wolfenden	Carden S*	**Norton 1**	**Wright 1**	Cottrell*
26.02	Stocksbridge Park Steels	A	2-1	Ashton	Battersby	Neville L	Holden*	Chadwick	Munroe	Roca*	Carden S	Norton	Wright*	**Wolfenden 2**
01.03	Nantwich Town	A	4-1	Ashton	Battersby*	Neville L	Platt	Chadwick	Munroe	**Roca 1**	Carden S*	Norton	**Wolfenden 3***	Cottrell
05.03	Mickleover Sports	H	0-0	Ashton	Holden	Neville L	Tierney*	Chadwick	McManus	Roca	Platt*	Norton	Wolfenden	Cottrell
12.03	Worksop Town	H	2-1 o	Ashton	Battersby	Neville L	Tierney	Chadwick	McManus	Roca*	Platt	**Norton 1***	Wolfenden*	Cottrell
15.03	North Ferriby United	A	1-1 o	Ashton	Battersby	Neville L	Platt*	Chadwick	McManus	Wolfenden*	Carden S*	Norton	Wright	Cottrell
19.03	Buxton	A	2-2	Ashton	Battersby*	Neville L	Holden*	Chadwick	McManus	Wolfenden	Carden S*	**Norton 2**	Wright	Cottrell
23.03	Whitby Town	A	1-0	Ashton	Jacobs	Neville L	Holden*	Chadwick	McManus	Wolfenden*	Carden S*	**Norton 1**	Wright	Cottrell
26.03	North Ferriby United	H	2-0	Ashton	Jacobs	Neville L	Platt*	Chadwick	McManus	Roca*	Carden S*	**Norton 2**	Wright	Cottrell
02.04	Worksop Town	A	2-1	Ashton	Jacobs	Neville L	Platt	Chadwick	McManus*	Roca*	Carden S*	**Norton 1**	**Wright 1**	Cottrell
09.04	Northwich Victoria	H	1-0	Ashton ■	Jacobs	Neville L	Platt	Chadwick	McManus	Roca*	Carden S*	**Norton 1**	Wright*	Cottrell
13.04	Frickley Athletic	H†	4-1	Ashton	Battersby	Neville L	Platt	Munroe ■	**McManus 1**	Wolfenden*	Carden S*	**Norton 1***	**Wright 1**	Cottrell
16.04	Chasetown	A	0-2	Ashton	Jacobs	Neville L	Platt*	Chadwick	McManus	Wolfenden*	Carden S*	Norton ■	Wright ■	Cottrell
20.04	Marine	H†	2-1	Ashton	Jacobs	Neville L	Platt*	Chadwick	McManus	Wolfenden	Tierney*	**Norton 1**	Wright	Cottrell
23.04	Matlock Town	A	2-1	Deegan	Jacobs	Neville L	Tierney*	Munroe	McManus	**Wolfenden 1***	Battersby	Norton	**Wright 1**	Cottrell*
25.04	Kendal Town	H	1-2	Shenton	Jacobs*	Neville L	Battersby	Munroe	McManus	Roca*	Carden S	**Norton 1**	Wright	Holden*
28.04	Bradford Park Avenue (PPO:SF)	A	2-0	Shenton	Jacobs	Neville L	Battersby*	Chadwick	McManus	**Wolfenden 1***	Tierney*	Norton	**Wright 1**	Little
02.05	Colwyn Bay (PPO:F)	A	0-1	Ashton	Jacobs	Neville L	Platt*	Chadwick	McManus	Roca*	Tierney*	Deegan	Wolfenden	Cottrell

APPEARANCES & GOALS

Substitutes							Attendance
Chadwick	Ayres	Holden (11)	Carden S (4)	Roca (7)			933
Platt (4)	Ayres	Holden	Carden S (11)	Roca (7)			1,866
Platt (4)	Ayres (2)	Holden	Carden S	**Little (7) 2**			1,785
Munroe	Ayres	Holden	Torpey (8)	Little (7)			1,069
Ovington (11)	Ayres	Holden (S)	Torpey (7)*	Carden S			1,801
Munroe	Ayres	Holden (7)	Platt (11)	Carden S (10)			990
Munroe (5)	Ayres	Deegan (8)	Platt	Carden S	Cheetham	Roca (7)	1,144
Holden	**Hurst (7) 1**	Ovington (6)	Platt (2)	Carden S			1,793
Parker	Cottrell (7)	Ovington	Roca (11)	Deegan (10)			468
Parker	Cottrell (8)	Ovington	Roca	Deegan (10)	Ashton		1,037
Parker	Cottrell (7)	Ovington	Roca (11)	Deegan (8)			1,761
Parker	Cottrell (8)	Wright (7)	Roca (11)	Deegan			1,074
Parker	Holden (4)	Platt (10)	Carden S	Deegan (11)			1,333
Ovington	Holden (3)	Hibbert	Carden S (7)	**Deegan (11) 1**			1,526
Ovington (7)	Platt	Munroe (5)	Carden S (8)	Hurst			1,035
Ovington (S)	Platt (7)	Chadwick	Carden S	Hurst (11)*	Cheetham	Hibbert	3,263
Ovington (7)	Holden (8)	Chadwick (11)	Hibbert				387
Parker	Holden (3)	Chadwick (11)	Carden S	Roca (7)			1,259
Parker	Holden (3)	Ayres	Carden S (11)	Ovington (7)	Hurst	Hibbert	7,048
Parker	Holden (2)	Wolfenden	Carden S (9)	Ovington (11)			1,663
Ayres (3)	Holden	Wolfenden (9)	Carden S	Ovington (7)			1,003
Ayres	Holden (3)	Wolfenden (11)	Carden S	Tierney (7)			1,249
Haslam (3)	Burke J (11)	Reeve (9)					332
Parker (11)	Holden (2)	Tierney	Carden S	Wolfenden (3)	Ayres	Hibbert	5,362
Battersby (2)	Holden	Tierney	Carden S (3)	Wolfenden (10)	Ayres	Hibbert	6,731
Battersby	Holden	Neville L	Carden S	Ovington			2,805
Hibbert	Holden (2)	Neville L (3)	Moloney	Deegan (8)			4,023
Munroe	Carden S (2)	Neville L (3)	Moloney	Deegan (9)			2,062
McManus	Quistin	Ovington	**Roca (7) 1**	Deegan			1,962
Chadwick	Quistin	Platt (4)	Roca (7)	Deegan (9)			544
Munroe (2)	Quistin (5)	Ovington	Roca (8)	Deegan			1,883
Chadwick	Holden	Ovington	Roca (2)	Deegan (8)			508
Chadwick (8)	Holden (2)	Ovington	Roca (4)	Quistin			1,560
Munroe	Devenney	Ovington (8)	Roca	Platt (2)			432
Chadwick (5)	Devenney	Deegan (S)	Roca (4)*				487
Carden S	Devenney (2)	Deegan	Roca	Platt (6)			1,662
Carden S (4)	Devenney	Deegan (9)	Roca (11)	Platt			1,445
Munroe	Devenney (11)	Deegan	**Roca (8) 1**	Platt (4)			2,030
Jacobs	Devenney (7)	Deegan (10)	Haslam	Platt (4)			837
Dainty	Devenney (8)	Deegan	Haslam (10)	Holden (2)			616
Jacobs	Devenney	Deegan (4)	Carden S (8)	Reeve			2,155
Munroe	Holden	Deegan (9)	Carden S (10)	Wright (7)			1,886
Jacobs	Holden (4)	Deegan	Devenney (8)	Roca (7)			472
Jacobs (2)	Platt (8)	Deegan (4)	Devenney	Torpey			1,726
Munroe	Platt (7)	Deegan (4)	Devenney (8)				588
Munroe	Battersby (8)	Deegan (4)	Devenney	Torpey (7)			2,827
Munroe (6)	Battersby	Deegan (8)	Wolfenden (7)	Torpey			892
Holden	Battersby	Deegan (7)	Wolfenden (8)	Torpey (10)			2,250
Holden	Jacobs (8)	**Deegan (9) 1**	Roca	Torpey (7)	Deegan in goal from 60 mins		1,731
Holden (4)	Battersby	Deegan (8)	Roca	Torpey (7)			1,089
Holden	Carden S (8)	**Deegan (4) 1**	Roca	Torpey			1,848
Holden	Carden S (11)	Platt (4)	Roca (7)	Torpey			1,249
Tierney (11)	Wolfenden	Platt (2)	Deegan	Torpey (7)			2,839
Roca	Carden S (8)	Platt (4)	Deegan	Torpey (7)			2,785
Holden	Carden S (8)	Battersby	Parker (4)	Walcott (7)			2,000

Player	League		FAC & FAT		Other		Totals	
Sam Ashton	34	1	8	0	1	0	43	1
Mark Ayres	1 (+2)	0	1	0	1	0	3 (+2)	0
Richard Battersby	26 (+1)	0	4 (+1)	0	1	0	31 (+2)	0
Josh Burke	0	0	0	0	0 (+1)	0	0 (+1)	0
Simon Carden	25 (+10)	3	1 (+4)	0	1 (+2)	0	27 (+16)	3
David Chadwick	17 (+3)	0	0 (+1)	0	3		20 (+4)	0
Scott Cheetham	0	0	0	0	1	0	1	0
Jake Cottrell	36 (+3)	4	9 (+1)	1	2		47 (+4)	5
Jordan Dainty	0	0	0	0	0	0	0	0
Ben Deegan	5 (+20)	2	5 (+3)	4	2		12 (+23)	6
Oliver Devenney	0 (+6)	0	0	0	0	0	0 (+6)	0
Carl Fitton	0	0	0	0	1	0	1	0
Jake Haslam	0 (+1)	0	0	0	0 (+1)	0	0 (+2)	0
Zach Hibbert	6	0	2	0	0	0	8	0
James Holden	17 (+11)	1	4 (+5)	1	1		22 (+16)	2
Glynn Hurst	6 (+1)	2	3 (+1)	3	0	0	9 (+2)	5
Kyle Jacobs	23 (+2)	0	9	0	2		34 (+2)	0
Colin Little	1 (+2)	2	0	0	0	0	1 (+2)	2
Scott McManus	36	1	9	0	2		47	1
Dylan Moloney	0	0	0	0	0	0	0	0
Karl Munroe	15 (+2)	0	6 (+2)	0	0	0	21 (+4)	0
Lee Neville	37 (+2)	0	6	0	2		45 (+2)	0
Mike Norton	41	24	10	8	1		52	32
Chris Ovington	4 (+6)	1	5 (+3)	1	1		10 (+9)	2
Martin Parker	17	1	4 (+1)	0	0 (+1)	0	21 (+2)	1
Nicky Platt	25 (+14)	0	7 (+1)	2	1 (+1)	0	33 (+16)	2
Ludovic Quistin	4 (+1)	0	1	0	0	0	5 (+1)	0
Harrison Reeve	0	0	0	0	0 (+1)	0	0 (+1)	0
Carlos Roca	18 (+15)	6	7 (+2)	1	1		26 (+17)	7
Grant Shenton	1	0	0	0	2		3	0
Matthew Tierney	7 (+1)	0	0 (+1)	0	3	1	10 (+2)	1
Steve Torpey	0 (+7)	0	0	0	0 (+1)	0	0 (+8)	0
Jay Walcott	0	0	0	0	0 (+1)	0	0 (+1)	0
Matthew Wolfenden	24 (+3)	11	1 (+3)	0	3	1	28 (+6)	12
Jerome Wright	36 (+2)	13	8	2	1	1	45 (+2)	16

FC United goals listed first. All games League unless stated otherwise:
FAC FA Cup   FAT FA Trophy   LCC EvoStik League Challenge Cup
H Played at Gigg Lane (Bury FC)   PPO Promotion Play-Offs
H¹ Played at Bower Fold (Stalybridge Celtic FC)
* Player Substituted   (2) Substituted player's number   Goalscorers in **bold**
■ Player Sent off   (+1) Number of substitute appearances

	Team	Pld	W	D	L	F	A	GD	Pts
1	FC Halifax Town ↑	42	30	8	4	108	36	+72	98
2	Colwyn Bay ↑	42	24	7	11	67	56	+11	79
3	Bradford Park Avenue	42	23	8	11	84	55	+29	77
4	FC UNITED OF MANCHESTER	42	24	4	14	76	53	+23	76
5	North Ferriby United	42	22	7	13	78	51	+27	73
6	Buxton	42	20	10	12	71	52	+19	70
7	Kendal Town	42	21	5	16	80	77	+3	68
8	Marine	42	20	7	15	74	64	+10	67
9	Worksop Town -3 points	42	21	6	15	72	54	+18	‡66
10	Chasetown	42	20	6	16	76	59	+17	66
11	Matlock Town	42	20	6	16	74	59	+15	66
12	Northwich Victoria	42	18	9	15	66	55	+11	63
13	Stocksbridge Park Steels	42	17	6	19	75	75	0	57
14	Ashton United	42	16	5	21	57	62	-5	53
15	Mickleover Sports	42	15	7	20	70	76	-6	51
16	Whitby Town	42	14	9	19	58	77	-19	51
17	Nantwich Town	42	13	7	22	68	90	-22	46
18	Frickley Athletic	42	11	11	20	43	68	-25	44
19	Burscough	42	12	7	23	56	73	-17	43
20	Hucknall Town ↓	42	11	10	21	57	80	-23	43
21	Ossett Town ↓	42	9	5	28	45	103	-58	32
22	Retford United ↓	42	5	2	35	31	111	-80	17

‡: Worksop Town were deducted 3 points for fielding an ineligible player

o Opposition Own Goals for FC United:

James **Connelly**	21/09/2010	FC's 2nd v Burscough (NPLP)	A 2-0
Ashley **Lyth**	12/02/2011	FC's 4th v Whitby Town (NPLP)	H 4-0
James **Cotterill**	12/03/2011	FC's 2nd v Worksop Town (NPLP)	H 2-1
Sam **Denton**	15/03/2011	FC's 1st v North Ferriby United (NPLP)	A 1-1

NORTHERN PREMIER LEAGUE PREMIER DIVISION

Date	Opponents	Venue	Score	1	2	3	4	5	6	7	8	9	10	11
13.08	Stafford Rangers	A	2-0	Spencer J	Jacobs*	Neville L	Cottrell	Jones A	Stott 1	Roca*	Platt	Deegan	Wolfenden 1*	Battersby
17.08	North Ferriby United	H[1]	6-3 oo	Spencer J	Battersby	Neville L	Cottrell*	Jones A	Stott	Roca 1*	Platt	Deegan 1	Wolfenden 1*	Carr Mi
20.08	Chasetown	H	1-2	Spencer J	Battersby	Neville L	Cottrell	Chadwick	Stott	Roca*	Platt	Deegan*	Wolfenden 1	Carr Mi
24.08	Chester FC	A	1-2	Spencer J	Battersby	Neville L	Cottrell	Jones A	Stott	Deegan*	Platt*	Norton 1	Wolfenden	Carr Mi*
27.08	Buxton	A	4-0	Spencer J	Jacobs	Neville L	Cottrell*	Jones A 1	Stott	Roca	Platt	Norton 1	Wolfenden	Battersby*
29.08	Bradford Park Avenue	H[2]	5-2	Spencer J	Jacobs	Neville L 1	Grimshaw D*	Jones A 1	Stott	Roca*	Platt*	Norton	Wolfenden 1	Battersby
03.09	Rushall Olympic	H	0-0	Spencer J	Jacobs	Neville L	Cottrell	Jones A	Stott	Roca	Platt*	Norton	Wolfenden*	Battersby*
06.09	Kendal Town	A	1-3	Spencer J	Jacobs*	Neville L	Cottrell	Jones A	Stott	Roca*	Carr Mi	Norton	Wolfenden 1	Battersby*
09.09	Chorley	A	0-2	Spencer J	Jacobs*	Neville L	Cottrell	Jones A	Stott	Edwards A*	Carr Mi	Norton	Torpey*	Battersby*
14.09	Nantwich Town	H	1-3	Spencer J	Stott	Neville L	Platt	Jones A	Chadwick 1	Edwards A*	Carr Mi	Norton	Battersby	Grimshaw D
17.09	Woodley Sports (FAC:Q1)	H	1-1	Spencer J	Armstrong*	Neville L	Carr Mi	Jones A	Stott	Roca*	Platt 1	Norton	Deegan*	Grimshaw D
20.09	Woodley Sports (FAC:Q1R)	A	4-1	Spencer J	Battersby	Neville L	Carr Mi	Jones A 1	Stott	Roca 1	Platt	Norton 1*	Deegan 1*	Grimshaw D
24.09	Burscough	A	5-3	Spencer J	Battersby	Neville L	Carr Mi*	Jones A 1	Stott	Roca 2	Platt*	Norton 2	Torpey*	Grimshaw D
28.09	Whitby Town	H	3-0	Spencer J	Jacobs 1	Neville L	Cottrell	Jones A	Stott	Roca*	Battersby*	Norton	Deegan 2	Grimshaw D*
01.10	Lancaster City (FAC:Q2)	H	0-1	Spencer J	Jacobs	Neville L	Cottrell	Jones A	Stott	Roca	Battersby*	Norton	Deegan	Grimshaw D*
08.10	Marine	H[1]	1-1	Spencer J	Jacobs	Neville L	Cottrell	Jones A	Stott	Roca	Platt*	Deegan ■	Wolfenden 1*	Carr Mi*
11.10	Frickley Athletic	A	3-1 o	Spencer J	Jacobs*	Neville L	Cottrell	Jones A	Stott	Roca*	Carr Mi	Norton*	Wolfenden 1	Deegan 1
15.10	Chester FC	H	2-3	Spencer J	Jacobs	Neville L	Cottrell	Jones A ■	Stott	Roca 2*	Carr Mi	Norton	Wolfenden	Deegan*
18.10	Mossley (MPC:1)	A	1-2	Jones A	Battersby ■	Armstrong*	Platt	Chadwick	Brooks Ja	Edwards A*	Grimshaw D	Norton	Torpey 1	McGreevy*
22.10	Frickley Athletic (FAC:Q1)	A	4-0	Spencer J	Jacobs*	Neville L	Cottrell	Jones A 1*	Stott	Roca 1	Carr Mi 2	Norton	Wolfenden	Mulholland*
29.10	Stocksbridge Park Steels	A	2-2	Spencer J	Jacobs	Neville L	Cottrell	Stones	Stott	Roca	Carr Mi*	Norton 2	Wolfenden*	Mulholland*
05.11	Durham City (FAT:Q2)	A	1-1	Spencer J	Stott*	Jacobs	Cottrell	Jones A	Stones	Roca	Carr Mi*	Norton 1	Wolfenden*	Neville L
09.11	Durham City (FAT:Q2R)	H	3-1 e	Spencer J	Stott*	Jacobs	Cottrell	Jones A	Stones	Roca*	Platt	Norton 1	Deegan*	Neville L
12.11	Mickleover Sports	A	2-0	Spencer J	Jacobs	Neville L	Cottrell	Jones A	Stones	Roca*	Platt*	Norton	Stott	Mulholland
19.11	Worksop Town	A	3-2 o	Spencer J	Jacobs	Neville L 1	Cottrell	Jones A*	Stones	Roca	Platt 1*	Norton	Stott	Mulholland*
23.11	Kendal Town	H	1-0	Spencer J	Jacobs	Neville L	Cottrell	Stott	Stones	Roca*	Platt	Norton 1*	Holden ■	Mulholland*
27.11	Altrincham (FAT:Q3)	H	2-1	Spencer J	Jacobs	Neville L	Cottrell*	Jones A	Stones	Roca 1	Platt*	Norton 1	Stott	Mulholland*
29.11	Nantwich Town	A	1-1	Spencer J	Jacobs	Neville L	Carr Mi*	Jones A	Stones	Roca	Holden*	Deegan*	Stott	Johnson S
03.12	Chorley	H	0-0	Spencer J	Jacobs	Neville L	Cottrell*	Jones A	Stones	Roca*	Platt	Norton	Stott	Mulholland*
10.12	Guiseley (FAT:1)	A	0-2	Spencer J	Jacobs ■	Neville L	Platt*	Jones A	Stones	Roca*	Grimshaw D*	Norton	Stott	Mulholland
14.12	Burscough (LCC:3)	A	2-0	Spencer J	Jacobs	Neville L ■	Wolfenden*	Jones A	Stones	Roca*	Cottrell	Norton	Stott	Grimshaw D
17.12	Northwich Victoria	A	1-2	Spencer J	Jacobs	Neville L	Cottrell*	Jones A	Stott	Roca*	Cottrell	Norton 1	Grimshaw D*	Mulholland*
26.12	Ashton United	H	2-1	Spencer J	Armstrong*	Neville L 1	Stott	Jones A	Stones	Roca*	Platt	Norton 1	Wolfenden	Johnson S*
02.01	Bradford Park Avenue	A	5-2	Spencer J	Armstrong 1*	Grimshaw D*	Cottrell	Jones A 1	Stones	Wolfenden 1	Platt 1	Norton 1*	Stott	Johnson S
07.01	Stafford Rangers	H	1-2	Spencer J	Armstrong*	Jacobs	Platt	Jones A	Stones	Wolfenden*	Cottrell*	Norton 1	Stott	Johnson S
10.01	Chorley (LCC:4)	A	3-2 o	Spencer J	Jacobs	Cottrell	Tierney*	Jones A	Stones	Roca*	Wolfenden	Norton 1	Stott 1	Mulholland*
14.01	North Ferriby United	A	0-0	Spencer J	Jacobs	Cottrell	Tierney*	Jones A	Stones	Roca*	Wolfenden	Norton	Stott	Johnson S*
21.01	Chasetown	A	3-0	Spencer J	Jacobs*	Neville L	Cottrell	Jones A	Stones	Johnson S*	Wolfenden 1	Norton 1	Stott 1	Mulholland*
28.01	Hednesford Town	H	2-0	Spencer J	Jacobs	Battersby	Cottrell	Jones A	Stones	Roca*	Wolfenden 1*	Norton 1	Stott	Johnson S*
14.02	Frickley Athletic (LCC:QF)	A	1-3	Spencer J	Jacobs	Battersby*	Cottrell*	Jones A	Stones	Roca*	Wolfenden	Norton 1	Stott	Mulholland
18.02	Frickley Athletic	H	2-2	Spencer J	Jacobs*	Battersby*	Cottrell	Jones A	Stones	Roca 1	Wolfenden	Norton	Stott	Johnson S*
25.02	Marine	A	2-1	Spencer J	Jacobs	Battersby	Cottrell	Jones A 1	Stones	Roca*	Wolfenden 1*	Norton	Stott	Johnson S*
29.02	Matlock Town	H[1]	2-1 o	Spencer J	Jacobs*	Battersby	Cottrell	Jones A	Stones	Roca*	Wolfenden 1*	Norton	Stott	Johnson S*
03.03	Rushall Olympic	A	0-1	Spencer J	Jacobs*	Battersby*	Cottrell	Jones A	Stones	Neville L	Wolfenden	Norton	Stott	Johnson S
10.03	Stocksbridge Park Steels	H	3-0	Spencer J	Jacobs	Neville L	Cottrell*	Jones A	Stones	Roca*	Wolfenden 3*	Norton	Stott	Johnson S
17.03	Hednesford Town	A	2-1	Spencer J	Jacobs	Neville L 1	Cottrell	Jones A 1	Stones	Mulholland*	Wolfenden*	Norton	Stott	Johnson S
24.03	Worksop Town	H	3-1	Spencer J	Jacobs*	Neville L 1	Cottrell	Jones A	Stones	Roca*	Wolfenden 1 #	Norton 1 ■	Stott ■	Johnson S
31.03	Mickleover Sports	H[1]	4-0	Spencer J	Jacobs	Neville L	Cottrell	Jones A 1*	Stones*	Roca	Wolfenden 1	Norton 1*	Stott	Johnson S
07.04	Buxton	H	1-2	Spencer J	Jacobs	Neville L	Cottrell	Jones A	Stones	Roca*	Wolfenden	Battersby*	Platt*	Battersby
09.04	Ashton United	A	0-1	Spencer J	Jacobs	Neville L	Cottrell	Jones A	Stones	Roca	Wolfenden	Grimshaw D*	Platt	Johnson S*
14.04	Matlock Town	A	1-2 o	Spencer J	Jacobs	Neville L	Cottrell	Jones A	Stones	Roca*	Wolfenden	Grimshaw D*	Platt*	Mulholland
18.04	Burscough	H	1-1	Spencer J	Jacobs	Neville L	Cottrell	Jones A	Stones	Roca*	Wolfenden	Norton	Stott 1	Johnson S
21.04	Northwich Victoria	H	4-1	Spencer J	Jacobs	Neville L	Cottrell 1*	Stott	Stones	Roca	Wolfenden 2	Norton	Platt*	Johnson S 1
28.04	Chorley (PPO:SF)	A	1-0	Spencer J	Jacobs	Neville L	Cottrell	Jones A	Stones	Roca*	Wolfenden*	Norton 1	Stott	Johnson S*
06.05	Bradford Park Avenue (PPO:F)	A	0-1 e	Worsnop	Jacobs	Neville L	Cottrell	Jones A	Stones*	Roca*	Wolfenden	Norton	Stott	Johnson S*

#: Matthew Wolfenden was sent off in a case of mistaken identity against Worksop Town on 24/03/2012. The red card was later transferred to Dean Stott, who served the subsequent three-match suspension.

APPEARANCES & GOALS

Substitutes

Substitutes				Attendance
Chadwick	Grimshaw D	Carr Mi (2)	Torpey (7) Edwards A (10)	1,707
Chadwick	Grimshaw D (4)	Holden	**Torpey (10) 1** Edwards A (7)	1,532
Armstrong	Norton (9)	Holden	Torpey (7) Edwards A	2,049
Chadwick	Grimshaw D (8)	Metcalfe	Torpey (11) Roca (7)	3,219
Chadwick	**Grimshaw D (4) 1**	Carr Mi (11)	**Torpey (10) 1** Holden	904
Chadwick	Edwards A (7)	**Carr Mi (8) 1**	**Torpey (4) 1** Deegan	1,831
Chadwick	Grimshaw D	Carr Mi (11)	Torpey (8) Deegan (10)	2,445
Chadwick	Grimshaw D (2)	Platt	Torpey (11) Edwards A (7)	651
Chadwick	Grimshaw D (10)	Platt (2)	Armstrong Deegan (7) ■	1,074
Torpey	Wolfenden	Roca	Armstrong Deegan (7)	1,353
Chadwick	Battersby (2)	Edwards A	Howell (7) Kidd (10) Power J Brooks Ja	1,109
Chadwick	Torpey (10)	Edwards A	Howell Kidd (9) Armstrong Brooks Ja	328
Chadwick (8)	Jacobs (2)	Edwards A	Cottrell (4) McGreevy (7)	602
Chadwick	Armstrong	Carr Mi (11)	Platt (8) McGreevy (7)	1,408
Chadwick	Armstrong	Carr Mi (8)	Edwards A McGreevy Wolfenden (11) Platt	1,147
Chadwick	Battersby (11)	Grimshaw D (10)	Edwards A Kidd (8)	1,704
Chadwick	Battersby (2)	Grimshaw D (9)	Platt Mulholland (7)	497
Chadwick (7)	Battersby	Grimshaw D	Platt Mulholland (11)	3,142
Stott (11)	Neville L (3)	Wolfenden (7)	Howell Kidd	178
Chadwick (5)	Holden (11)	Grimshaw D	Platt Stones (2)	524
Battersby	Holden (10)	Grimshaw D (8)	Platt Walcott (11)	676
Deegan (2)	Holden	Grimshaw D	Platt (8) Mulholland (10)	533
Armstrong	**Holden (10) 1**	Grimshaw D (7)	Carr Mi **Mulholland (2) 1**	672
Armstrong	Holden (11)	Grimshaw D (8)	Walcott (7) Deegan	753
Armstrong	Holden (5)	Grimshaw D	Carr Mi (8) Deegan (11)	821
Armstrong	Walcott	Grimshaw D (11)	Carr Mi (7) Deegan (9)	1,517
Holden (4)	Wolfenden (11)	Grimshaw D	Carr Mi (8) Deegan	1,945
Armstrong	Wolfenden (8)	Grimshaw D (4)	Tierney **Norton (9) 1**	752
Johnson S (4)	Wolfenden (11)	Grimshaw D	Tierney (7) Deegan	2,075
Armstrong	Wolfenden (7)	Boland	Tierney (4) Deegan (8)	810
Armstrong	**Mulholland (4) 1**	Boland	Tierney Deegan (7)	147
Armstrong	Wolfenden (11)	Johnson S (10)	Farrimond Deegan (7)	1,114
Grimshaw D (11)	Tierney (2)	Boland	Mulholland (7) Deegan	1,926
Battersby (2)	Tierney (3)	Roca	Mulholland Deegan (9)	1,288
Grimshaw D	Tierney (8)	Roca (2)	Mulholland Deegan (7)	1,947
Grimshaw D (4)	Armstrong	Battersby (7)	Platt Deegan (11)	830
Grimshaw D (11)	Neville L (4) ■	Battersby	Platt Mulholland (7)	613
Grimshaw D	Tierney (7)	Battersby	Platt (2) Roca (11)	731
Grimshaw D	Tierney	Boland (11)	Platt (8) Mulholland (7)	1,816
Grimshaw D (7)	Warrender (3)	Boland	Platt (4) Howell	251
Grimshaw D	Warrender (2)	Cheetham	**Platt (3) 1** Mulholland (11)	1,791
Grimshaw D	Warrender	Cheetham	Platt (8) Mulholland (11)	1,111
Grimshaw D	Warrender	Neville L (11)	Platt (8) Mulholland (7)	1,458
Farrimond	Warrender (11)	Roca	Platt (2) Mulholland (3)	1,056
Grimshaw D (8)	Battersby	Cheetham	Platt (4) Mulholland (7)	1,999
Grimshaw D (11)	Battersby (8)	Cheetham	Platt (7) Armstrong	1,228
Grimshaw D	Battersby (2)	Cheetham	Platt (11) Mulholland (7)	2,873
Grimshaw D	Battersby	Cheetham	Platt (4) Mulholland (7)	614
Grimshaw D (5)	Battersby (6)	Cheetham	**Platt (9) 1** Mulholland	1,730
Grimshaw D (7)	Krou (10)	Cheetham	Kidd Mulholland (9)	2,279
Battersby	Krou	Cheetham	Kidd (11) Mulholland (9)	816
Battersby (9)	Krou (7)	Cheetham	Johnson S (10) Worsnop	1,319
Battersby	Grimshaw D	Cheetham	Platt Mulholland (7)	1,505
Battersby (10)	Grimshaw D (4)	Cheetham (11)	Worsnop Mulholland	2,542
Battersby (8)	Grimshaw D	Platt (11)	Worsnop **Mulholland (7) 1**	2,754
Battersby (8)	Grimshaw D (6)	Platt (7)	Cheetham Mulholland (11)	1,897

Player Appearances & Goals

Player	League		FAC & FAT		Other		Totals	
Paul **Armstrong**	3	1	1	0	1	0	5	1
Richard **Battersby**	18 (+8)	0	2 (+1)	0	2 (+2)	0	22 (+11)	0
Matthew **Boland**	0 (+1)	0	0	0	0	0	0 (+1)	0
James **Brooks**	0	0	0	0	1	0	1	0
Michael **Carr**	12 (+7)	1	4 (+2)	2	0	0	16 (+9)	3
David **Chadwick**	2 (+2)	1	0 (+1)	0	1	0	3 (+3)	1
Scott **Cheetham**	0 (+1)	0	0	0	0	0	0 (+1)	0
Jake **Cottrell**	37 (+1)	1	5	0	5	0	47 (+1)	1
Ben **Deegan**	9 (+8)	4	4 (+2)	1	0 (+2)	0	13 (+12)	5
Adam **Edwards**	2 (+4)	0	0	0	1	0	3 (+4)	0
Andrew **Farrimond**	0	0	0	0	0	0	0	0
Daniel **Grimshaw**	8 (+18)	1	4 (+1)	0	2 (+3)	1	14 (+22)	2
James **Holden**	2 (+3)	0	0 (+3)	1	0	0	2 (+6)	1
Sam **Howell**	0	0	0 (+1)	0	0	0	0 (+1)	0
Kyle **Jacobs**	35 (+1)	1	6	0	5	0	46 (+1)	1
Stephen **Johnson**	20 (+3)	1	0	0	2	0	22 (+3)	1
Adam **Jones**	38	7	8	2	6	0	52	9
Theo **Kidd**	0 (+2)	0	0 (+2)	0	0	0	0 (+4)	0
Cédric **Krou**	0 (+2)	0	0	0	0	0	0 (+2)	0
Ryan **McGreevy**	0 (+2)	0	0	0	1	0	1 (+2)	0
Scott **Metcalfe**	0	0	0	0	0	0	0	0
Astley **Mulholland**	9 (+15)	2	3 (+2)	1	2 (+3)	2	14 (+20)	5
Karl **Munroe**	0	0	0	0	0	0	0	0
Lee **Neville**	35 (+2)	5	8	0	3 (+1)	0	46 (+3)	5
Mike **Norton**	34 (+2)	16	8	4	6	3	48 (+2)	23
Nicky **Platt**	22 (+13)	4	5 (+1)	1	1 (+3)	0	28 (+17)	5
Joseph **Power**	0	0	0	0	0	0	0	0
Carlos **Roca**	34 (+3)	6	8	3	5	0	47 (+3)	9
James **Spencer**	42	0	8	0	4	0	54	0
Greg **Stones**	26	0	4 (+1)	0	5	0	35 (+1)	0
Dean **Stott**	39	3	8	0	5 (+1)	1	52 (+1)	4
Matthew **Tierney**	1 (+5)	0	0 (+1)	0	1	0	2 (+6)	0
Steve **Torpey**	2 (+8)	3	0 (+1)	0	1	1	3 (+9)	4
Jay **Walcott**	0 (+2)	0	0	0	0	0	0 (+2)	0
Danny **Warrender**	0 (+4)	0	0	0	0 (+1)	0	0 (+5)	0
Matthew **Wolfenden**	32 (+3)	20	2 (+3)	0	5 (+1)	0	39 (+7)	20
Jon **Worsnop**	0	0	0	0	1	0	1	0

FC United goals listed first. All games League unless stated otherwise:
FAC FA Cup **FAT** FA Trophy **MPC** Manchester FA Premier Cup
LCC Doodson Sport League Challenge Cup **PPO** Promotion Play-Offs
H Played at Gigg Lane (Bury FC) **H1** Played at Bower Fold (Stalybridge Celtic FC)
H2 Played at Tameside Stadium (Curzon Ashton FC) **e** After Extra Time
* Player Substituted **(2)** Substituted player's number Goalscorers in **bold**
■ Player Sent off **(+1)** Number of substitute appearances **#** Mistaken identity

	Team	Pld	W	D	L	F	A	GD	Pts
1	Chester FC ↑	42	31	7	4	102	29	+73	100
2	Northwich Victoria -3 points ↓	42	26	8	8	73	43	+30	‡83
3	Chorley	42	24	7	11	76	48	+28	79
4	Bradford Park Avenue ↑	42	24	6	12	77	49	+28	78
5	Hednesford Town	42	21	10	11	67	49	+18	73
6	FC UNITED OF MANCHESTER	42	21	9	12	83	51	+32	72
7	Marine	42	19	9	14	56	50	+6	66
8	Rushall Olympic	42	17	10	15	52	51	+1	61
9	North Ferriby United	42	16	10	16	56	70	−14	58
10	Nantwich Town -1 point	42	15	13	14	65	61	+4	‡57
11	Kendal Town	42	15	8	19	78	83	−5	53
12	Ashton United	42	15	8	19	61	67	−6	53
13	Buxton	42	15	8	19	64	77	−13	53
14	Matlock Town	42	12	14	16	52	54	−2	50
15	Worksop Town	42	13	10	19	56	76	−20	49
16	Stafford Rangers	42	12	12	18	60	65	−5	48
17	Whitby Town -1 point	42	12	11	19	57	80	−23	‡46
18	Stocksbridge Park Steels	42	10	12	20	57	75	−18	42
19	Frickley Athletic	42	10	12	20	48	69	−21	42
20	Chasetown ↓	42	10	11	21	50	75	−25	41
21	Mickleover Sports -3 points ↓	42	11	10	21	67	85	−18	‡40
22	Burscough ↓	42	5	11	26	54	104	−50	26

o Opposition Own Goals for FC United:

Nathan **Peat**	17/08/2011	FC's 2nd v North Ferriby United (NPLP)	H 6-3
Mark **Greaves**	17/08/2011	FC's 4th v North Ferriby United (NPLP)	H 6-3
Stuart **Ludlam**	11/10/2011	FC's 1st v Frickley Athletic (NPLP)	A 3-1
Luke **Shiels**	19/11/2011	FC's 3rd v Worksop Town (NPLP)	A 3-2
Wayne **Maden**	10/01/2012	FC's 2nd v Chorley (NPLCC:4)	A 3-2
Laurence **Gaughan**	29/02/2012	FC's 1st v Matlock Town (NPLP)	H 2-1
Adam **Yates**	14/04/2012	FC's 1st v Matlock Town (NPLP)	A 1-2

‡: All points deductions were due to clubs fielding ineligible players
Northwich Victoria were relegated to Division One South after being found guilty of failing to comply with League Rules relating to financial matters

NORTHERN PREMIER LEAGUE PREMIER DIVISION

Date	Opponents	Venue	Score	1	2	3	4	5	6	7	8	9	10	11
18.08	Grantham Town	A	4-2	Spencer J	Jacobs	Neville L	Birch*	Jones A 1	Stott	Roca 1*	Cottrell	Norton 1*	Wright 1	Wolfenden
21.08	Whitby Town	H	3-2	Spencer J	Jacobs	Neville L*	Birch	Jones A	Stott	Roca*	Cottrell 1	Norton 1	Wright	Wolfenden 1
25.08	Matlock Town	H	4-0	Spencer J	Jacobs 2	Neville L	Birch*	Jones A	Stott	Roca 1*	Cottrell	Norton 1	Wright	Wolfenden*
27.08	Witton Albion	A	1-1	Spencer J	Jacobs	Neville L	Birch	Jones A	Stott	Johnson S*	Cottrell	Norton	Wright*	Platt 1*
02.09	Hednesford Town	H¹	1-1	Spencer J	Jacobs	Cottrell	Birch	Jones A	Stott	Roca 1*	Platt*	Norton	Wright	Wolfenden*
05.09	Whitby Town	A	1-0	Spencer J	Jacobs	Cottrell*	Birch	Jones A	Stott	Roca*	Wolfenden 1	Norton	Wright	Johnson S*
09.09	Cammell Laird (FAC:Q1)	H	5-0 o	Worsnop	Jacobs*	Neville L 1	Birch	Jones A*	Stott	Johnson S	Platt	Norton 2	Wright 1*	Wolfenden
15.09	Nantwich Town	H	1-2	Spencer J	Jacobs	Neville L	Cheetham*	Jones A*	Stott	Roca	Cottrell	Norton	Wright	Wolfenden 1
18.09	Stafford Rangers	A	1-1	Spencer J	Jacobs	Neville L	Birch	Platt*	Stott	Roca*	Cottrell	Norton	Wright 1	Wolfenden
22.09	Salford City (FAC:Q2)	A	3-2	Spencer J ■	Jacobs	Platt 3*	Birch	Jones A*	Stott	Roca	Cottrell	Norton	Wright	Wolfenden*
29.09	Mossley (FAT:Q1)	H	3-3	Spencer J	Jacobs	Neville L*	Cheetham*	Jones A	Stott	Wolfenden*	Cottrell	Amadi 2	Wright 1	Platt
02.10	Mossley (FAT:Q1R)	A	3-1	Spencer J	Jacobs	Neville L	Birch 1	Jones A	Stott	Platt 1	Cottrell 1*	Norton*	Wright*	McGrath*
07.10	Kendal Town (FAC:Q3)	H	3-1	Worsnop	Jacobs	Neville L	Birch	Jones A 1	Stott 2	Platt	Cottrell*	Norton*	Wright	McGrath*
09.10	Mossley (MPC:1)	A	2-3	Worsnop	Armstrong	Neville L	Naughton	Munroe	Anderson*	Krou	Cheetham	Amadi 2	Daniels	Howell*
13.10	AFC Fylde	A	2-4	Spencer J	Jacobs*	Neville L	Birch	Jones A	Stott	McGrath	Cottrell*	Norton 1	Wright	Platt*
20.10	Hereford United (FAC:Q4)	H	0-2	Spencer J	Jacobs	Neville L	Birch*	Jones A	Stott	Wolfenden	Cottrell	Norton	Wright ■	Platt*
23.10	North Ferriby United	A	1-1	Spencer J	Jacobs	Neville L	Platt	Jones A	Stott	Wolfenden	Cottrell	Norton	Wright 1	Amadi*
27.10	Stamford (FAT:Q2)	A	1-2	Spencer J*	Jacobs	Neville L	Platt	Jones A	Stott	Wolfenden	Cottrell*	Norton 1	Wright	Amadi*
31.10	Ashton United	A	2-1	Worsnop	Jacobs	Neville L	Birch	Jones A	Stott	Wolfenden 2	Daniels*	Norton*	Wright	Platt*
04.11	Eastwood Town	H	4-1	Worsnop	Stott 1	Cottrell	Birch	Jones A 1*	Carr Ma	Wolfenden	Platt*	Norton 2*	Daniels	Neville L
10.11	Ilkeston	A	1-1	Spencer J	Stott	Cottrell	Birch*	Jones A	Carr Ma	Amadi*	Platt 1	Norton	Daniels	Neville L
17.11	Rushall Olympic	H	0-4	Spencer J	Stott	Cottrell	Birch	Jones A	Carr Ma*	Roca	Platt*	Norton	Daniels*	Neville L
20.11	Marine	H	0-1	Spencer J	Jacobs	Neville L*	Birch	Jones A	Stott	Wolfenden*	Tierney	Norton	Wright	Dawson*
24.11	Chorley	A	3-1	Spencer J	Jacobs	Neville L	Birch	Jones A	Stott	Wolfenden*	Tierney 1	Norton 1	Wright	Dawson*
01.12	Blyth Spartans	A	2-1	Spencer J	Jacobs	Neville L	Birch*	Jones A	Stott 1	Wolfenden	Tierney	Norton 1	Wright	Platt*
08.12	Hednesford Town	A	0-1	Spencer J	Jacobs*	Neville L	Chalmers*	Jones A	Stott	Wolfenden	Krou	Norton	Wright	Cottrell
15.12	Grantham Town	H	1-0	Spencer J	Jacobs	Neville L	Birch*	Jones A	Stott	Roca*	Cottrell	Norton	Wolfenden 1	Dawson*
26.12	*Witton Albion*	*H*	*0-1 a*	*Spencer J*	*Jacobs*	*Neville L*	*Birch*	*Jones A*	*Stott*	*Wolfenden*	*Tierney*	*Daniels*	*Wright*	*Krou*
05.01	Nantwich Town	A	3-2	Spencer J	Jacobs	Neville L	Birch	Jones A 1	Stott	Roca*	Chalmers*	Daniels 1	Wright	Wolfenden 1
12.01	Stafford Rangers	H	3-0	Spencer J	Jacobs	Neville L	Stott	Jones A	Horne*	Mulholland	Tierney*	Greaves 1	Wright 1	Wolfenden 1
30.01	Ashton United (LCC:3)	A	2-1	Worsnop	Jacobs	Cheetham	Cottrell	Jones A 1	Lacy	Mulholland	Krou*	Norton 1	Wright*	Fisher T*
02.02	Buxton	A	3-0	Spencer J	Jacobs	Neville L	Birch	Jones A	Stott	Wolfenden 1	Cottrell	Norton 2*	Wright*	Greaves*
09.02	AFC Fylde	H	2-1	Spencer J	Jacobs	Neville L	Tierney	Jones A	Stott	Wolfenden 2*	Cottrell	Norton*	Wright	Greaves*
12.02	Frickley Athletic	A	4-2	Spencer J	Jacobs	Neville L 1	Tierney ■	Jones A*	Stott	Wolfenden 1	Cottrell	Norton 1*	Wright	Greaves 1*
16.02	Marine	A	3-0	Spencer J	Jacobs	Cottrell	Birch	Neville L	Stott	Wolfenden	Tierney*	Norton*	Wright	Greaves 3*
19.02	Witton Albion (LCC:4)	A	3-4	Worsnop	Gray	Cheetham	Platt	Lacy	Stott 2	Mulholland	Krou*	Giggs 1*	Daniels	Walwyn*
23.02	Ilkeston	H	1-0	Spencer J	Jacobs	Neville L	Tierney*	Jones A 1	Stott	Wolfenden	Cottrell	Norton*	Wright*	Greaves
03.03	North Ferriby United	H¹	1-1	Spencer J	Jacobs	Neville L	Birch	Jones A	Stott	Wolfenden	Cottrell	Norton*	Wright*	Greaves 1
06.03	Matlock Town	A	2-2	Spencer J	Jacobs	Neville L*	Birch*	Jones A 2	Stott	Wolfenden	Cottrell	Norton*	Greaves	Mulholland
09.03	Chorley	H	1-3	Spencer J	Jacobs*	Neville L	Cottrell	Jones A	Stott	Mulholland	Daniels*	Greaves*	Wright	Wolfenden 1
16.03	Worksop Town	A	1-4	Spencer J	Jacobs	Neville L*	Birch	Jones A	Stott	Wolfenden 1	Cottrell	Norton	Daniels	Mulholland*
19.03	Buxton	H¹	1-2	Spencer J	Jacobs*	Cottrell	Stott	Jones A	Lacy	Wolfenden 1	Tierney	Norton*	Wright*	Greaves
23.03	Blyth Spartans	H	2-1	Spencer J	Stott	Neville L	Birch	Jones A	Gray*	Mulholland*	Fitzgerald*	Norton 1	Wright	Wolfenden
30.03	Kendal Town	A	5-1	Spencer J	Jacobs	Neville L	Birch*	Jones A	Stott 1	Wolfenden	Rodríguez*	Norton 1*	Wright 2	Greaves 1
01.04	Stocksbridge Park Steels	H	4-0	Worsnop	Jacobs	Cottrell	Birch 1*	Jones A	Neville L	Greaves	Rodríguez	Norton 1*	Wright*	Banks 1
06.04	Witton Albion	H	0-1	Worsnop	Jacobs	Neville L	Birch*	Jones A	Stott	Wolfenden	Cottrell*	Norton	Banks	Greaves*
09.04	Kendal Town	H	6-0	Worsnop	Stott	Daniels 3	Cottrell	Jones A*	Lacy	Roca*	Banks	Norton*	Wright	Wolfenden 1
13.04	Eastwood Town	A	2-2	Worsnop	Stott	Daniels	Cottrell	Jones A	Lacy	Wolfenden*	Banks 1	Giggs*	Wright	Walwyn*
16.04	Stocksbridge Park Steels	A	3-1	Worsnop	Jacobs	Neville L	Stott	Jones A 1	Lacy	Wolfenden*	Banks	Norton*	Wright 1	Daniels 1*
20.04	Worksop Town	H	1-0	Worsnop	Jacobs	Neville L	Stott	Jones A*	Lacy	Roca*	Banks*	Greaves	Wolfenden 1	Daniels
23.04	Ashton United	H	3-0	Worsnop	Jacobs	Neville L	Birch*	Stott 1	Lacy	Wolfenden 1*	Banks	Norton	Daniels 1	Mulholland*
27.04	Rushall Olympic	A	1-0	Worsnop	Jacobs	Cheetham*	Tierney	Stott 1	Masirika	Walwyn	Rodríguez	Norton*	Wright*	Giggs
04.05	Frickley Athletic	H	3-0	Worsnop	Birch	Daniels*	Rodríguez*	Lacy	Masirika	Mulholland	Tierney	Greaves 1*	Wright	Walwyn 1
07.05	Witton Albion (PPO:SF)	H	3-1	Worsnop	Jacobs	Neville L	Birch	Stott 1	Lacy*	Wolfenden 1*	Banks	Norton	Wright	Mulholland
11.05	Hednesford Town (PPO:F)	A	1-2	Worsnop	Jacobs	Neville L	Birch*	Stott	Masirika*	Wolfenden	Banks	Norton 1	Wright	Mulholland*

a: Match abandoned after 10 minutes due to a waterlogged pitch; appearances and goals are not counted in player totals.

APPEARANCES & GOALS

Player	League		FAC & FAT		Other		Totals	
Chris **Amadi**	2 (+6)	0	2 (+4)	2	1	2	5 (+10)	4
Charlie **Anderson**	0 (+1)	0	0 (+1)	0	1	0	1 (+2)	0
Paul **Armstrong**	0	0	0	0	1	0	1	0
Ollie **Banks**	7 (+2)	2	0	0	2	0	9 (+2)	2
Dave **Birch**	28 (+5)	1	5 (+1)	1	2	0	35 (+6)	2
Mathew **Carr**	3	0	0	0	0	0	3	0
Lewis **Chalmers**	2 (+1)	0	0	0	0	0	2 (+1)	0
Scott **Cheetham**	2 (+3)	0	1 (+2)	0	3	0	6 (+5)	0
Jake **Cottrell**	29 (+4)	1	6	1	1 (+3)	0	36 (+7)	2
Greg **Daniels**	13 (+14)	8	0 (+3)	0	2 (+1)	0	15 (+18)	8
Adam **Dawson**	3 (+1)	0	0	0	0	0	3 (+1)	0
Tom **Fisher**	0 (+5)	0	0	0	1	0	1 (+5)	0
Sam **Fitzgerald**	1	0	0	0	0	0	1	0
Rhodri **Giggs**	3 (+16)	1	0	0	1	1	4 (+16)	2
Travis **Gray**	1	0	0	0	1	0	2	0
Tom **Greaves**	15 (+7)	11	0	0	0 (+2)	0	15 (+9)	11
Daniel **Grimshaw**	0 (+3)	0	0	0	0	0	0 (+3)	0
Louis **Horne**	1	0	0	0	0	0	1	0
Sam **Howell**	0	0	0	0	1	0	1	0
Ryan **Howley**	0	0	0	0	0	0	0	0
Kyle **Jacobs**	35 (+2)	2	7	0	3	0	45 (+2)	2
Stephen **Johnson**	2 (+4)	0	1	0	0	0	3 (+4)	0
Adam **Jones**	37	7	7	1	1	1	45	9
Cédric **Krou**	1 (+9)	0	0 (+3)	0	3	0	4 (+12)	0
Lewis **Lacy**	7	0	0	0	3	0	10	0
Kevin **Masirika**	2	0	0	0	1	0	3	0
Phil **McGrath**	1	0	2 (+1)	0	0 (+1)	0	3 (+2)	0
Astley **Mulholland**	7 (+8)	0	0	0	4	1	11 (+8)	1
Karl **Munroe**	0	0	0	0	1	0	1	0
Connor **Naughton**	0	0	0	0	1	0	1	0
Lee **Neville**	35 (+3)	1	6 (+1)	1	3 (+1)	0	44 (+5)	2
Mike **Norton**	35 (+3)	15	6 (+1)	3	3 (+2)	2	44 (+6)	20
Nicky **Platt**	10 (+3)	2	7	4	1	0	18 (+3)	6
Carlos **Roca**	12 (+8)	3	1 (+3)	0	0	0	13 (+11)	3
Sergio **Rodríguez**	4	0	0	0	0	0	4	0
Ric **Smith**	0	0	0	0	0	0	0	0
James **Spencer**	31	0	5	0	0	0	36	0
Dean **Stott**	40	5	7	2	3	3	50	10
Mike **Taylor**	0	0	0	0	0	0	0	0
Matthew **Tierney**	11 (+4)	1	0	0	0 (+3)	0	11 (+7)	1
Matthew **Walwyn**	3 (+3)	1	0	0	1	0	4 (+3)	1
Matthew **Wolfenden**	35 (+2)	18	5	0	2	1	42 (+2)	19
Jon **Worsnop**	11	0	2	0	5	0	18	0
Jerome **Wright**	33 (+2)	7	7	2	3 (+1)	0	43 (+3)	9

Substitutes & Attendance

Substitutes							Attendance
Anderson	Cheetham (4)	Grimshaw D	Amadi (9)	Johnson S (7)			1,220
Anderson	Cheetham	Grimshaw D (3)	Krou	Johnson S (7)			1,562
Anderson	Cheetham	Grimshaw D	Platt (11)	Johnson S (7)			1,763
Anderson	Cheetham	Krou (7)	Wolfenden (11)	Roca (10)			1,352
Anderson	Cheetham	Grimshaw D (8)	Amadi (11)	Johnson S (7)			1,702
Anderson	Cheetham	Grimshaw D (3)	Amadi (11)	Platt (7)			482
Anderson (2)	Cheetham (5)	Grimshaw D	Amadi	Roca (10)	Cottrell	Spencer J	1,052
Anderson (5)	Platt (4)	Krou	Amadi (11)	Johnson S			1,969
Anderson	Cheetham	Krou (5)	Amadi (7)				814
Anderson	Cheetham	Krou (3)	Amadi (5)	Neville L (11)	Norton in goal from 90 mins		1,292
Birch	McGrath (3)	Krou	Norton (4)	Roca (7)			871
Daniels	Cheetham	Krou (8)	Amadi (10)	Roca (11)			405
Daniels (9)	Cheetham	Krou (11)	Amadi (8)	Anderson	Carr Ma	Howley	1,186
Norton (6)	McGrath (11)						258
Anderson	Cheetham	Krou (11)	Amadi (8)	Daniels (2) 1			1,418
Carr Ma	Cheetham	Krou	Amadi (11)	Daniels (4)	McGrath	Worsnop	2,212
Carr Ma	Cheetham	Krou	McGrath	Daniels (11)			538
Carr Ma	Cheetham (1)	Krou	Birch (8)	Daniels (11)	Birch in goal from 90 mins		749
Carr Ma	Tierney (11)	Krou (8)	Amadi	Fisher T (9)			503
Jacobs (5)	Roca (8)	Krou	Amadi	Fisher T (9)			1,692
Jacobs (7)	Horne	Krou (4)	Tierney	McGrath			1,015
Chalmers	Cheetham	Dawson (10)	Tierney (6)	Fisher T (8)			1,795
Chalmers	Horne	Roca (3)	Daniels (7)	Fisher T (11)			1,484
Chalmers	Platt	Krou (7)	Daniels (11)	Cottrell (4)			1,130
Chalmers (4)	Cheetham	Krou (11)*	Daniels	Cottrell (S)			617
Carr Ma	Cheetham	Fisher T (2)	Daniels (4)	Giggs			929
Chalmers	Krou	Tierney (4)	Daniels (11)	Giggs (7)			1,653
Chalmers	Cheetham	Lacy	Roca	Giggs			nk
Horne	Krou (11)	Greaves	Mulholland (7)	Giggs (8)			1,003
Birch (6)	Krou	Cottrell (8)	Roca	Giggs (7)			2,131
Neville L (10)	Smith R	Tierney (8)	Taylor Mi	Greaves (11)			229
Horne	Cheetham	Daniels (11)	Mulholland (9)	Giggs (9)			1,121
Horne	Cheetham	Daniels (11)	Mulholland (10)	Giggs (7)			2,042
Krou (11)	Cheetham	Daniels	Birch (5)	Giggs (9)			428
Lacy	Cheetham (8)	Daniels (11)	Mulholland	Giggs (9)			1,282
Birch	Neville L	Cottrell (8)	Wright (11)	Norton (9)			382
Birch (4)	Cheetham	Daniels (7)	Mulholland (10)	Giggs			1,929
Fitzgerald	Walwyn (10)	Daniels (9)	Mulholland	Giggs (7)			2,465
Fitzgerald	Walwyn	Daniels (9)	Wright (3)	Giggs (4)			613
Lacy	Walwyn (2)	Birch	Norton (8)	Giggs (9)			2,031
Fitzgerald	Walwyn (3)	Rodríguez	Wright	Greaves (11)			811
Fitzgerald	Neville L (2)	Birch	Mulholland (10)	Giggs (9)			1,501
Tierney	Rodríguez	Roca (6)	**Greaves (7) 1**	Giggs			1,730
Banks (4)	Cottrell	Roca (9)	Mulholland	Giggs (8)			710
Stott	**Daniels (9) 1**	Roca (10)	Wolfenden	Giggs (4)			1,659
Wright (4)	Daniels (11)	Roca (8)	Mulholland	Giggs			1,741
Neville L (5)	Birch	**Greaves (7) 1**	Mulholland (11)	Norton			1,517
Neville L	Birch (7)	**Greaves (11) 1**	Mulholland	Norton (9)			607
Rodríguez	Birch	Greaves (11)	Mulholland (7)	Giggs (9)			406
Cottrell (5)	Birch (7)	Norton	Mulholland	Giggs (8)			2,761
Cottrell	Tierney (4)	Greaves (11)	Roca (7)	Giggs			1,586
Neville L (3)	Birch	Greaves (9)	Mulholland (10)	Daniels			1,007
Neville L	Cottrell	**Norton (9) 1**	Wolfenden (3)	Banks (4)			2,124
Tierney (7)	Cottrell (11)	Greaves	Daniels (6)	Giggs			2,492
Tierney (4)	Cottrell (6)	Greaves (11)	Daniels	Giggs			4,412

Team		Pld	W	D	L	F	A	GD	Pts
1	North Ferriby United ↑	42	28	9	5	96	43	+53	93
2	Hednesford Town ↑	42	28	9	5	91	47	+44	93
3	FC UNITED OF MANCHESTER	42	25	8	9	86	48	+38	83
4	Witton Albion	42	24	8	10	85	57	+28	80
5	AFC Fylde	42	23	6	13	93	51	+42	75
6	Rushall Olympic	42	20	10	12	69	55	+14	70
7	Buxton	42	18	13	11	72	56	+16	67
8	Chorley	42	20	7	15	63	52	+11	67
9	Worksop Town	42	20	6	16	91	68	+23	66
10	Ashton United	42	15	14	13	71	66	+5	59
11	Marine	42	16	11	15	61	61	0	59
12	Ilkeston	42	15	13	14	67	55	+12	58
13	Whitby Town	42	16	9	17	68	72	−4	57
14	Nantwich Town	42	15	8	19	63	76	−13	53
15	Stafford Rangers	42	12	15	15	54	60	−6	51
16	Blyth Spartans	42	15	6	21	70	87	−17	51
17	Matlock Town	42	12	9	21	54	80	−26	45
18	Frickley Athletic	42	10	9	23	58	88	−30	39
19	Grantham Town	42	9	9	24	56	75	−19	36
20	Stocksbridge Park Steels	42	9	9	24	67	106	−39	36
21	Kendal Town ↓	42	9	6	27	65	112	−47	33
22	Eastwood Town ↓	42	3	6	33	36	121	−85	15

o Opposition Own Goal for FC United:
Mike **Grogan**   09/09/2012   FC's 4th v Cammell Laird (FAC:Q1)   H 5-0

FC United goals listed first.   All games League unless stated otherwise:
FAC FA Cup   **FAT** FA Trophy   **MPC** Manchester FA Premier Cup
LCC Doodson Sport League Challenge Cup   **PPO** Promotion Play-Offs
H Played at Gigg Lane (Bury FC)   **a** Match Abandoned
H[1] Played at Bower Fold (Stalybridge Celtic FC)
* Player Substituted   **(2)** Substituted player's number   Goalscorers in **bold**
■ Player Sent off   **(+1)** Number of substitute appearances

NORTHERN PREMIER LEAGUE PREMIER DIVISION

Date	Opponents	Venue	Score	1	2	3	4	5	6	7	8	9	10	11
17.08	Worksop Town	A	0-2	Worsnop	Brownhill	Neville L	Stott	Davies	Raglan	Wolfenden*	Banks	Daniels*	Wright*	Worsley
20.08	AFC Fylde	H	0-0	Spencer J	Brownhill*	Neville L	Stott	Davies	Raglan	Wolfenden	Banks	Norton*	Wright*	Worsley
24.08	Stamford	H	6-0	Spencer J	Brownhill	Neville L*	Stott	Davies	Raglan	Wolfenden 1*	Banks*	Greaves 3	Wright	Worsley
26.08	Trafford	A	3-2	Pearson	Brownhill	Birch	Davies*	Raglan	Wolfenden	Banks*	Norton	Mulholland 1*	Worsley
31.08	Grantham Town	A	5-1	Spencer J	Brownhill	Neville L 1	Stott	Pearson	Raglan	Wolfenden*	Banks*	Greaves 1*	Wright 1	Worsley
03.09	Witton Albion	H	3-1	Spencer J	Brownhill	Neville L	Stott 1	Pearson	Raglan	Wolfenden*	Banks 1*	Greaves 1*	Wright	Worsley ■
07.09	Rushall Olympic	H	0-2	Spencer J	Brownhill*	Neville L	Stott	Pearson	Raglan	Wolfenden	Mulholland*	Greaves*	Wright	Worsley
10.09	Frickley Athletic	A	2-1	Spencer J	Brownhill	Neville L	Stott	Pearson	Raglan*	Wolfenden	Banks	Greaves 2	Wright*	Worsley*
14.09	Chorley (FAC:Q1)	H	0-1	Spencer J	Brownhill	Neville L*	Stott	Pearson	Davies ■	Wolfenden	Daniels*	Greaves*	Wright	Worsley
21.09	Stafford Rangers	A	1-2	Spencer J	Brownhill	Birch*	Stott 1	Pearson	Davies	Wolfenden*	Byrne*	Greaves	Wright	Walwyn
24.09	New Mills (MPC:1)	A	3-3 p	Worsnop	Smith R	Neville L	Birch*	Dainty	Byrne	Mulholland 1	Van Gils 1	Daniels 1	Wright	Boland*
28.09	Whitby Town	H	1-3	Worsnop	Brownhill	Daniels	Birch	Pearson	Stott	Wolfenden*	Byrne*	Greaves	Wright 1	Mulholland
05.10	Marine	H[1]	1-0	Worsnop	Brownhill	Daniels 1	Birch	Pearson	Stott	Wolfenden	Worsley	Greaves*	Wright*	Mulholland
08.10	Nantwich Town	A	1-1	Worsnop	Brownhill	Daniels	Birch*	Pearson 1	Stott	Wolfenden	Worsley	Greaves*	Wright*	Mulholland
12.10	King's Lynn Town	A	0-0	Worsnop	Brownhill	Daniels*	Stott ■	Davies	Neville L	Wolfenden*	Worsley	Norton	Wright	Mulholland
15.10	Skelmersdale United	H	1-3	Worsnop	Brownhill	Daniels	Stott	Davies	Neville L	Wolfenden	Worsley*	Norton	Wright*	Mulholland
19.10	Witton Albion (FAT:Q1)	A	2-2	Worsnop	Brownhill	Neville L*	Rodríguez*	Pearson	Iqbal*	Wolfenden 1	Daniels	Norton	Greaves	Walwyn 1
26.10	Stocksbridge Park Steels	H	6-2	Worsnop	Brownhill	Neville L	Rodríguez	Davies	Iqbal	Wolfenden*	Daniels 2	Norton 2	Greaves*	Walwyn 1*
02.11	Witton Albion (FAT:Q1R)	H[2]	2-2 a	Worsnop	Brownhill	Neville L	Stott	Davies 1	Iqbal*	Wolfenden	Daniels	Norton 1	Byrne	Walwyn*
05.11	Witton Albion (FAT:Q1R)	H[3]	1-2	Worsnop	Brownhill*	Neville L ■	Stott*	Davies	Raglan	Wolfenden	Birch	Norton ■	Daniels*	Mulholland
09.11	Rushall Olympic	A	1-1	Worsnop	Brownhill	Neville L*	Stott	Davies	Raglan	Greaves	Birch	Norton 1*	Daniels*	Mulholland
12.11	Ramsbottom United (LCC:1)	A	2-1	Worsnop	Lacy	Brownhill	Stott*	Davies	Raglan	Greaves*	Birch	Norton 1	Daniels	Mulholland
16.11	Frickley Athletic	H	3-0 o	Worsnop	Brownhill	Neville L	Birch	Davies 1	Raglan	Giggs*	Daniels*	Greaves 1	Byrne	Mulholland
23.11	Matlock Town	A	1-1	Worsnop	Stott	Brownhill	Birch	Davies	Raglan	Giggs*	Wolfenden	Greaves 1	Byrne*	Mulholland
26.11	Droylsden	H	4-1	Worsnop	Stott 1	Brownhill	Birch*	Davies	Raglan	Wolfenden	Daniels*	Greaves 3*	Byrne	Mulholland
30.11	Blyth Spartans	H	3-0	Worsnop	Stott	Brownhill	Birch	Davies 1	Raglan	Wolfenden*	Daniels 1	Greaves 1*	Byrne	Mulholland
04.12	Ashton United (LCC:2)	H[1]	2-0	Spencer J	Pearson	Neville L	Stott*	Raglan	Lacy*	Giggs	Rodríguez*	Daniels 1	Byrne	Mulholland
07.12	Worksop Town	H	4-4	Worsnop	Brownhill	Neville L	Birch	Raglan	Lacy	Wolfenden 1	Daniels 1*	Greaves 2	Byrne	Mulholland
14.12	AFC Fylde	A	2-0	Spencer J*	Stott	Brownhill	Birch	Davies	Raglan	Wolfenden	Daniels 1	Greaves*	Byrne 1	Mulholland
21.12	Barwell	H	2-0	Wilczynski	Stott	Brownhill	Birch	Davies 1	Raglan	Wolfenden 1	Daniels*	Greaves*	Byrne	Mulholland
26.12	Ashton United	A	1-2	Wilczynski	Stott	Brownhill	Birch	Davies ■	Raglan	Wolfenden	Fox*	Norton 1*	Byrne	Greaves*
28.12	Buxton	A	2-0	Wilczynski	Stott	Brownhill	Birch	Davies	Raglan	Wolfenden 1*	Daniels*	Norton 1*	Byrne	Mulholland
04.01	Ilkeston	A	3-3	Carnell	Stott	Brownhill	Birch	Davies	Raglan	Wolfenden*	Daniels 1	Norton*	Byrne	Mulholland
14.01	Ossett Town (LCC:3)	A	2-1	Carnell	Birch	Brownhill	Rodríguez	Raglan*	Neville L	Giggs 1 ■	Worsley	Greaves	Daniels*	Walwyn*
18.01	Whitby Town	A	2-3	Carnell	Brownhill	Neville L	Birch*	Jones A 1	Stott	Mulholland	Daniels	Greaves 1	Byrne*	Mota*
21.01	Trafford	H	1-1	Carnell	Brownhill	Daniels*	Stott*	Raglan	Davies	Worsley	Byrne 1	Norton	Wright	Mota*
01.02	Marine	A	2-0	Carnell	Brownhill	Jones A	Birch*	Davies 1	Raglan	Daniels*	Byrne*	Norton	Wright 1	Greaves
18.02	Nantwich Town	H	2-1	Carnell	Brownhill	Jones A*	Stott	Davies	Raglan	Fox*	Byrne	Norton 1*	Wright	Greaves 1
22.02	Ilkeston	H	4-1	Carnell	Brownhill	Jones A	Stott	Davies	Raglan*	Wolfenden	Byrne	Norton*	Wright 2	Greaves 2
26.02	Carlton Town (LCC:QF)	A	1-2	Carnell	Brownhill	Neville L	Stott	Davies	Mulholland*	Wolfenden*	Byrne	Greaves 1	Wright	Giggs*
01.03	Droylsden	H	4-1	Carnell	Brownhill 1	Jones A 1*	Stott	Davies	Raglan	Wolfenden 1	Fox	Norton*	Wright 1	Greaves
04.03	Chorley	A	1-0	Carnell	Brownhill	Jones A*	Stott	Davies	Raglan	Wolfenden	Byrne	Norton	Wright	Greaves 1
08.03	Stocksbridge Park Steels	H	4-1	Carnell	Brownhill	Jones A*	Stott	Davies	Raglan 2	Wolfenden*	Byrne	Norton	Wright*	Greaves
15.03	King's Lynn Town	H	2-0	Carnell	Brownhill	Neville L	Stott	Davies	Raglan	Wolfenden	Byrne*	Norton 2	Wright	Greaves*
18.03	Stafford Rangers	H	4-0	Carnell	Brownhill	Neville L	Stott	Davies	Raglan 1	Wolfenden	Byrne*	Norton	Wright	Greaves 2*
22.03	Skelmersdale United	A	3-1	Carnell	Brownhill 1	Neville L	Stott	Davies	Raglan	Wolfenden*	Byrne*	Norton	Wright 1	Greaves 1*
25.03	Witton Albion	A	5-2	Carnell	Brownhill	Neville L	Stott	Davies	Raglan 1	Wolfenden 1*	Byrne*	Norton 1	Wright	Greaves 2*
29.03	Matlock Town	H	2-1	Carnell	Brownhill	Neville L	Stott	Davies	Raglan*	Wolfenden	Byrne*	Norton	Wright	Greaves 2*
05.04	Blyth Spartans	A	1-0	Carnell	Brownhill	Neville L	Stott	Davies	Jones A*	Wolfenden 1	Byrne	Norton*	Wright	Greaves
08.04	Chorley	H	2-2	Carnell	Brownhill	Neville L*	Stott	Davies	Raglan 1	Wolfenden	Byrne*	Norton*	Wright*	Greaves 1
12.04	Buxton	H	1-2	Carnell	Brownhill	Neville L*	Stott	Davies	Raglan	Wolfenden*	Byrne*	Norton*	Wright	Greaves 1
15.04	Grantham Town	H[1]	3-0	Carnell	Stott	Brownhill	Birch	Davies	Raglan	Wolfenden 2	Fox*	Daniels*	Mulholland*	Greaves 1
19.04	Stamford	A	3-2	Carnell	Brownhill	Neville L*	Stott*	Davies	Raglan	Wolfenden 1	Birch	Norton 2	Mulholland*	Greaves
21.04	Ashton United	H	3-2	Carnell	Brownhill	Jones A*	Stott	Davies	Raglan	Wolfenden	Byrne*	Norton 1*	Wright	Greaves
26.04	Barwell	A	3-0	Carnell	Brownhill	Lacy	Stott	Davies 1	Raglan	Wolfenden	Birch	Norton 1*	Wright	Greaves 1*
29.04	Ashton United (PPO:SF)	H	1-2 e	Carnell	Brownhill	Neville L	Stott	Davies	Raglan	Wolfenden	Birch	Norton*	Wright 1*	Greaves*

p: lost 4-5 on penalties (**scored:** Mulholland, Daniels, Neville L, Smith R **missed:** Poizer).   *a: Match abandoned after 75 minutes due to a waterlogged pitch; appearances and goals are not counted in player total*

APPEARANCES & GOALS

Substitutes					Attendance
ulholland	Birch	Walwyn (10)	Norton (9)	Greaves (7)	837
arson	Birch (2)	Walwyn (10)	Daniels	Greaves (9)	1,649
arson (3)	Birch	**Walwyn (8) 2**	Daniels	Mulholland (7)	1,629
o (5)	Giggs	**Walwyn (10) 1**	Daniels	**Greaves (8) 1**	1,374
o	Mulholland	**Walwyn (8) 2**	Daniels (7)	Norton (9)	739
o	Mulholland (7)	Giggs (9)	Daniels (8)	Norton	1,614
o	Davies (2)	Giggs (8)	Birch	Norton (9)	1,961
ulholland	Davies (6)	Giggs	Birch (11)	Norton (10) ■	420
o	Walwyn (3)	Giggs	Birch (8)	Norton (9) Byrne Worsnop	1,318
eville L	Daniels (8)	Giggs (7)	Mulholland	Norton (3)	1,052
oyle	Cooke D	Fowles	Taylor Mi (11)	Poizer (4)	275
mith R	Rodríguez	Giggs (7)	Van Gils	Walwyn (8)	1,524
nes A	Rodríguez (11)	Giggs	Byrne (9)	Walwyn (7)	1,528
eville L	Rodríguez	Norton (4)	Byrne (9)	Walwyn (11)	672
arson	Rodríguez (7)	Greaves	Byrne (3)	Walwyn (11)	1,440
arson	Rodríguez (10)	Greaves (11)	Byrne	**Walwyn (8) 1**	1,429
ott (3)	Davies (6)	Birch (4)	Byrne	Mulholland	693
arson	Van Gils	Giggs (7)	Byrne (10)	**Mulholland (11) 1**	1,542
arson	Rodríguez	Birch (6)	Greaves	Mulholland (11)	650
arson (2)	Rodríguez	**Greaves (4) 1**	Byrne	Walwyn (10)	369
earson	Rodríguez	Lacy (3)	Byrne (9)	Giggs (10)	539
earson	Rodríguez	Neville L	Byrne (4)	Giggs (7)	464
cy	Rodríguez	Wolfenden (7)	Norton (8)	Walwyn (11)	1,706
cy	Rodríguez (S)	Worsley (10)*	Daniels	Walwyn (7)	978
cy (9)	Rodríguez (4)	Fox (8)	Pearson	Giggs	754
cy	Rodríguez	Fox (7)	Mota (11)	Giggs (9)	1,690
rownhill (6) 1	Birch (4)	Worsley	Greaves (8)	Worsnop	282
earson	Rodríguez	Fox	Mota (11)	Norton (8)	1,600
eville L	Walwyn (11)	Fox (9)	Mota	Norton (1) Norton in goal from 45 mins	709
acy	Walwyn (9)	Fox	Mota (11)	Norton (8)	1,661
eville L (9)	Walwyn (11)	Daniels (8)	Rodríguez	Mulholland	1,008
eville L (7)	Walwyn (7)	Fox (8)	Rodríguez	Greaves (9)	1,112
eville L	Walwyn (11)	Fox	Mota (7)	**Greaves (9) 2**	974
right (5)	Byrne	Wolfenden (10)	Mulholland	**Norton (11) 1**	275
orsley (10)	Walwyn	Fox (11)	Giggs	Norton (4)	818
eville L (11)	Walwyn (3)	Fox	Jones A	Mulholland (7)	1,598
eville L	Stott (4)	Fox (8)	Worsley (7)	Mulholland	940
eville L (3)	Walwyn (9)	Wolfenden (7)	Mota	Mulholland	1,416
eville L (6)	Walwyn	Fox	Mota (7)	Mulholland (9)	1,863
aglan	Walwyn (11)	Fowles	Bower (7)	Norton (6)	336
eville L (3)	Walwyn (9)*	Mota	Bower	Mulholland (S)	1,974
eville L (3)	Fox	Mota	Bower	Mulholland	2,171
eville L (3) 1	Fox	Mota (7)	Bower	**Mulholland (10) 1**	891
nes A	Fox (8)	Mota	Walwyn	Mulholland (11)	2,083
nes A	Fox (8)	**Daniels (S) 1**	Walwyn (11)*	Mulholland	1,589
nes A	Fox (8)	Daniels (7)	Birch	Mulholland (11)	1,000
nes A	Fox	Daniels (11)	Birch (8)	Mulholland (7)	612
nes A (6)	Fox (8)	Daniels (11)	Hazel	Mulholland	2,044
acy (6)	Fox (8)	Daniels (9)	Hazel	Mulholland	932
ulkin	Fox (8)	Daniels (3) ■	Birch	Mulholland (10)	4,152
ones A	Fox (8)	Daniels (9)	Birch	Mulholland (7)	3,330
acy	Norton (9)	Hazel (10)	Byrne	Wright (8)	1,732
acy (3)	Fox	Daniels	Byrne (4)	Wright (10)	1,204
acy (8)	Fox	**Daniels (9) 1**	Hazel	Mulholland (3)	3,056
eville L	Fox	**Byrne (7) 1**	Hazel (11)	Mulholland (7)	1,709
iggs (9)	Fox	Byrne	Daniels (11)	Mulholland (10)	2,956

Player	League		FAC & FAT		Other		Totals	
Ollie Banks	7	1	0	0	0	0	7	1
Dave Birch	22 (+3)	0	1 (+2)	0	4 (+1)	0	27 (+6)	0
Matthew Boland	0	0	0	0	1	0	1	0
Connor Bower	0	0	0	0	0 (+1)	0	0 (+1)	0
Liam Brownhill	46	2	3	0	4 (+1)	1	53 (+1)	3
Callum Byrne	28 (+7)	3	0	0	3 (+1)	0	31 (+8)	3
Dave Carnell	21	0	0	0	3	0	24	0
Scott Cheetham	0	0	0	0	0	0	0	0
Cavell Coo	0 (+1)	0	0	0	0	0	0 (+1)	0
Daniel Cooke	0	0	0	0	0	0	0	0
Nick Culkin	0	0	0	0	0	0	0	0
Jordan Dainty	0	0	0	0	1	0	1	0
Greg Daniels	20 (+12)	9	3	0	4 (+1)	2	27 (+13)	11
Tom Davies	37 (+2)	5	2 (+1)	0	3	0	42 (+3)	5
Charlie Doyle	0	0	0	0	0	0	0	0
Jason Fowles	0	0	0	0	0	0	0	0
Joe Fox	4 (+13)	0	0	0	0	0	4 (+13)	0
Rhodri Giggs	2 (+7)	0	0	0	3 (+2)	1	5 (+9)	1
Tom Greaves	38 (+6)	34	2 (+1)	1	4 (+1)	1	44 (+8)	36
Jacob Hazel	0 (+2)	0	0	0	0	0	0 (+2)	0
Amjad Iqbal	1	0	1	0	0	0	2	0
Adam Jones	9 (+1)	2	0	0	0	0	9 (+1)	2
Lewis Lacy	2 (+5)	0	0	0	2	0	4 (+5)	0
Nelson Mota	2 (+6)	0	0	0	0	0	2 (+6)	0
Astley Mulholland	20 (+14)	3	1	0	4 (+1)	2	25 (+15)	5
Lee Neville	23 (+7)	2	3	0	5	0	31 (+7)	2
Mike Norton	27 (+12)	13	2 (+1)	0	2 (+2)	2	31 (+15)	15
Andy Pearson	9 (+1)	1	2 (+1)	0	1	0	12 (+2)	1
Jon Poizer	0	0	0	0	0 (+1)	0	0 (+1)	0
Charlie Raglan	37	5	1	0	4	0	42	5
Sergio Rodríguez	1 (+5)	0	0	0	2	0	4 (+5)	0
Ric Smith	0	0	0	0	1	0	1	0
James Spencer	9	0	1	0	1	0	11	0
Dean Stott	40 (+1)	3	2 (+1)	0	4	0	46 (+2)	3
Mike Taylor	0	0	0	0	0 (+1)	0	0 (+1)	0
Frank Van Gils	0	0	0	0	1	1	1	1
Matthew Walwyn	2 (+21)	7	1 (+2)	1	1 (+1)	0	4 (+24)	8
Ed Wilczynski	3	0	0	0	0	0	3	0
Matthew Wolfenden	40 (+2)	10	3	1	2 (+1)	0	45 (+3)	11
Chris Worsley	13 (+3)	0	1	0	1	0	15 (+3)	0
Jon Worsnop	13	0	2	0	2	0	17	0
Jerome Wright	30 (+2)	7	1	0	3 (+1)	1	34 (+3)	8

	Team	Pld	W	D	L	F	A	GD	Pts
1	Chorley ↑	46	29	10	7	107	39	+68	97
2	FC UNITED OF MANCHESTER	46	29	9	8	108	52	+56	96
3	AFC Fylde ↑	46	28	9	9	97	41	+56	93
4	Worksop Town	46	27	7	12	120	87	+33	88
5	Ashton United	46	24	8	14	92	62	+30	80
6	Skelmersdale United	46	24	5	17	92	79	+13	77
7	Rushall Olympic	46	21	12	13	79	65	+14	75
8	Blyth Spartans	46	20	12	14	79	78	+1	72
9	Whitby Town	46	18	16	12	82	64	+18	70
10	Trafford	46	20	8	18	77	73	+4	68
11	King's Lynn Town	46	20	8	18	76	77	−1	68
12	Matlock Town	46	18	13	15	61	53	+8	67
13	Buxton	46	16	14	16	63	60	+3	62
14	Barwell	46	17	11	18	62	67	−5	62
15	Grantham Town	46	17	10	19	77	78	−1	61
16	Witton Albion	46	17	9	20	77	80	−3	60
17	Ilkeston	46	17	8	21	81	77	+4	59
18	Stamford	46	17	7	22	75	85	−10	58
19	Nantwich Town	46	14	14	18	77	71	+6	56
20	Marine	46	13	14	19	78	76	−8	53
21	Frickley Athletic	46	12	13	21	62	80	−18	49
22	Stafford Rangers ↓	46	9	8	29	56	112	−56	35
23	Stocksbridge Park Steels ↓	46	5	8	33	60	130	−70	23
24	Droylsden ↓	46	2	3	41	40	182	−142	9

o Opposition Own Goal for FC United:
Steven **Gardner**   16/11/2013   FC's 1st v Frickley Athletic (NPLP)   H 3-0

FC United goals listed first.   All games League unless stated otherwise:
FAC FA Cup   **FAT** FA Trophy   **MPC** Manchester FA Premier Cup
LCC Doodson Sport League Challenge Cup   **PPO** Promotion Play-Offs
H Played at Gigg Lane (Bury FC)   **e** After Extra Time
H1 Played at Bower Fold (Stalybridge Celtic FC)   **p** Decided on penalties
H2 Played at Stainton Park (Radcliffe Borough FC)   **a** Match Abandoned
H3 Played at Wincham Park (Witton Albion FC)
* Player Substituted   **(2)** Substituted player's number   Goalscorers in **bold**
■ Player Sent off   **(+1)** Number of substitute appearances

NORTHERN PREMIER LEAGUE PREMIER DIVISION

Date	Opponents	Venue	Score	1	2	3	4	5	6	7	8	9	10	11
17.08	Barwell	A	0-0	Carnell	Stott	Daniels*	Birch	Pearson	Connor S*	Wolfenden	Byrne*	Greaves	Wright	Lindfield
19.08	Buxton	H¹	1-1	Carnell	Stott	Neville L*	Birch	Knowles	Pearson ■	**Wolfenden 1**	Byrne*	Daniels*	Wright	Lindfield
23.08	Belper Town	H¹	2-2	Carnell	Stott	Pearson*	Birch*	Lynch	Knowles	Wolfenden	Fox	**Norton 1**	Wright	Daniels*
25.08	Trafford	A	1-1	Carnell	Brownhill	Byrne	Stott	Lynch	**Knowles 1**	Mulholland*	Wolfenden	Norton*	Wright	Mota*
30.08	Ramsbottom	H¹	3-1	Carnell	Brownhill	Ashworth	Stott	Knowles	**Lynch 1**	Wolfenden	Byrne*	Bower*	Wright	**Greaves 2**
02.09	Blyth Spartans	A	1-0	Carnell	Brownhill	Ashworth	Stott	Knowles	Lynch	Wolfenden*	**Fox 1***	Norton*	Wright	Greaves
06.09	Marine	A	0-0	Carnell	Brownhill	Ashworth	Birch*	Stott	Lynch*	Wolfenden*	Byrne*	Norton	Wright	Greaves
09.09	Matlock Town	H¹	0-0	Carnell	Brownhill	Cheetham	Stott	Lynch	Ashworth	Wolfenden	Byrne	Norton*	Wright*	Greaves
14.09	Prescot Cables (FAC:Q1)	H¹	4-1	Carnell	Brownhill	Cheetham	Stott	**Lynch 1***	Ashworth	Wolfenden	Byrne	**Greaves 2***	Daniels	Welsh*
16.09	Frickley Athletic	A	1-4	Carnell	Brownhill	Cheetham	Stott	Lynch	Ashworth	Wolfenden	Byrne*	**Norton 1***	Daniels*	Welsh
20.09	Grantham Town	H¹	3-1	Carnell	Brownhill	Cheetham	Stott	Lynch	Ashworth	**Wolfenden 2**	**Byrne 1**	Greaves*	Daniels*	Welsh*
27.09	Lancaster City (FAC:Q2)	H¹	0-1	Carnell	Brownhill	Cheetham	Stott	Lynch	Ashworth	Wolfenden	Byrne	Greaves*	Daniels*	Welsh*
04.10	Whitby Town	H¹	2-0 o	Carnell	Brownhill	Lynch*	Stott	Knowles	Ashworth	Wolfenden	Fox*	Norton	Wright	**Welsh 1***
07.10	Radcliffe Borough (MPC:1)	A	1-1 p¹	Culkin	Pearson	Cheetham	Birch	Lynch*	Ashworth	Daniels	Byrne*	Greaves	**Brewster 1**	Walwyn*
11.10	Nantwich Town	A	2-1	Carnell	Brownhill	Lacy	Stott	Knowles	Ashworth	Wolfenden	Fox*	Norton*	Wright	Welsh*
14.10	Skelmersdale United	H¹	1-2	Carnell	Brownhill	Lacy	Stott	Knowles	Ashworth	Wolfenden*	Fox*	Norton	**Wright 1**	Welsh*
18.10	Ilkeston	A	1-3	Carnell	Brownhill	Lacy	Birch	Knowles*	Ashworth	Wolfenden	Fox*	Norton	**Wright 1**	Welsh*
21.10	Matlock Town	A	0-0	Carnell	Brownhill	Cheetham	Lynch	Knowles	Ashworth*	Wolfenden	Birch	Norton	Greaves*	Fox*
25.10	Rushall Olympic	H¹	0-0	Carnell	Brownhill	Cheetham ■	Lynch	Knowles*	Ashworth	Wolfenden	Birch	Norton*	Lindfield*	Fox*
28.10	Blyth Spartans	H¹	0-0	Carnell	Brownhill	Cheetham*	Lynch	Lacy	Ashworth	Wolfenden	Birch	Norton*	Lindfield	Fox*
02.11	Padiham (FAT:Q1)	H¹	2-0	Carnell	Brownhill	Lacy	Stott	Lynch*	Ashworth	Lindfield	Byrne	Greaves	**Wright 1***	Kay M*
04.11	Buxton	A	1-1	Carnell	**Stott 1**	Brownhill	Lacy	Knowles*	Ashworth	Wolfenden ■	Birch	Greaves*	Lindfield	Kay M*
08.11	Witton Albion	H¹	4-0	Carnell	Stott	Lacy*	Birch*	**Ashworth 1**	Byrne	**Wolfenden 2**	Daniels	Greaves	**Wright 1**	Lindfield*
10.11	Curzon Ashton (LCC:1)	A	0-0 p²	Carnell	Stott*	Cheetham	Lynch	Knowles	Ashworth	Brown T	Birch	Daniels	Kay M*	Walwyn*
15.11	Buxton (FAT:Q2)	H¹	2-0	Carnell	Stott	Lacy	Birch	Ashworth	Byrne*	**Wolfenden 2***	Daniels*	Greaves*	Wright	Lindfield
18.11	Frickley Athletic	H¹	3-2	Culkin	Stott	Lacy	Birch	Ashworth*	Byrne*	Van Gils*	Daniels	**Greaves 1**	Wright	**Lindfield**
22.11	Stourbridge	A	1-2	Carnell	Brownhill	Lacy	Stott	Knowles	Fox*	Van Gils	Daniels*	**Greaves 1**	Wright	Lindfield
29.11	Barwell (FAT:Q3)	A	1-1	Carnell	Brownhill	Lacy	Birch	Ashworth	**Byrne 1**	Van Gils*	Daniels	Greaves	Wright	Lindfield*
03.12	Barwell (FAT:Q3R)	H¹	3-2 o	Carnell	Brownhill	Lynch ■	Fox*	Knowles	Ashworth*	Wolfenden	**Byrne 1**	Greaves	Wright	Daniels
13.12	Harrogate Town (FAT:1)	H¹	4-0	Carnell	**Stott 2**	Cheetham	**Daniels 1***	Knowles	Ashworth	**Wolfenden 1**	Birch*	Greaves*	Byrne	Lindfield
26.12	Curzon Ashton	A	4-0	Carnell	Stott 1	Cheetham	Birch	Ashworth	Knowles*	**Wolfenden 1**	Byrne*	**Greaves 2**	Daniels	Lindfield*
28.12	King's Lynn Town	A	2-1	Carnell	Brownhill	Daniels*	Stott	**Lacy 1**	Ashworth	Wolfenden	Fox	**Greaves 1***	Wright	Lindfield*
01.01	Trafford	H²	3-0	Carnell	Brownhill	Daniels*	Byrne	Lacy	Ashworth	Wolfenden	Fox*	**Greaves 1**	Wright	**Lindfield 1**
03.01	Ashton United	A	2-0	Carnell	Brownhill	Lynch	Birch*	Brown T	Ashworth	**Wolfenden 1***	Kay M*	Greaves	Wright	**Lindfield 1**
10.01	Chorley (FAT:2)	A	3-3	Carnell	Brownhill	Lynch	Birch*	Brown T	Ashworth	**Wolfenden 1**	Byrne*	**Greaves 2**	Wright	Lindfield
13.01	Chorley (FAT:2R)	H²	1-0	Carnell	Brownhill	Lacy	Stott	Daniels*	Ashworth	Wolfenden*	Byrne*	**Greaves 1**	Wright	Lindfield
18.01	Nantwich Town	H¹	2-1	Carnell	Brownhill	Daniels*	Stott*	Lacy	Ashworth	Wolfenden	Byrne*	Payne	Wright	**Lindfield 1**
24.01	AFC Fylde (FAT:3)	H²	3-1	Carnell	Brownhill	Daniels*	Birch*	Lacy	Ashworth	Wolfenden	Brown T	Greaves*	**Wright 1**	**Lindfield 2**
07.02	Torquay United (FAT:QF)	A	0-1	Carnell	Brownhill	Daniels	Birch*	Lacy	Ashworth	Wolfenden*	Brown T*	Greaves	Wright	Lindfield
10.02	Barwell	H²	3-1	Carnell	Brownhill	Daniels*	Stott	Lacy	Ashworth	Wolfenden*	Byrne	Payne	Wright	**Lindfield 1**
14.02	Marine	H²	5-2	Carnell	Brownhill	Daniels*	**Birch 1***	Lacy	Ashworth*	**Wolfenden 1**	**Byrne 1**	**Payne 1**	Wright	**Lindfield 1**
17.02	Ashton United	H²	3-0	Carnell	**Brownhill 1**	Brown T*	Birch	Lacy	Ashworth	Wolfenden*	**Greaves 2**	Payne	Wright	Lindfield*
21.02	Belper Town	A	3-1	Carnell	Brownhill	Daniels	Stott*	Lacy	Ashworth	**Payne 1**	Byrne*	**Greaves 2**	Wright	Lindfield
24.02	Halesowen Town	H²	1-0	Carnell	Brownhill	**Daniels 1***	Stott	Lacy	Ashworth	Payne*	Byrne*	Greaves	Wright	Lindfield
28.02	Grantham Town	A	2-1	Carnell	Brownhill	**Daniels 1**	Stott	Lacy*	Ashworth	Wolfenden	Byrne*	Greaves	Wright	Payne*
03.03	Rushall Olympic	A	1-1	Carnell	Brownhill	Daniels*	Birch	Lacy	Ashworth	**Wolfenden 1***	Fallon	Greaves	Wright	Lindfield
07.03	King's Lynn Town	H²	3-1	Carnell	Stott	**Payne 1**	Birch	Lacy	Ashworth	Wolfenden*	Byrne*	Greaves*	Wright	**Lindfield 1**
10.03	Ilkeston	H²	2-2	Carnell	Brownhill	Payne*	Birch	Lacy	Ashworth*	Wolfenden*	Fallon	Daniels	**Wright 1**	Lindfield
14.03	Halesowen Town	A	1-0	Carnell	Brownhill	Daniels	Birch*	Lacy	Lynch	Wolfenden	Brown T	Greaves	Wright	**Lindfield 1**
17.03	Workington	H²	1-0	Carnell	Brownhill	Daniels	Fox*	**Lacy 1**	Lynch	Payne*	Byrne*	Greaves	Wright	Lindfield
21.03	Stamford	A	1-1	Carnell	Brownhill	Daniels	Stott	Lacy	Lynch	Wolfenden	Brown T*	**Payne 1**	Wright	Lindfield*
01.04	Whitby Town	A	4-0	Carnell	Brownhill	**Daniels 1**	Birch*	Lacy	Lynch	Wolfenden	Brown T*	**Greaves 1**	**Wright 1**	Lindfield
04.04	Ramsbottom	A	2-0	Carnell	**Stott 1**	Cheetham	Fox	Bayunu	Lynch*	Wolfenden	Byrne	Greaves*	**Fallon 1**	Payne
06.04	Curzon Ashton	H²	1-1	Carnell	Brownhill*	Daniels	Birch	Lacy	Ashworth	Fallon*	Byrne*	Greaves	Wright	**Lindfield 1**
11.04	Witton Albion	A	0-0	Carnell	Brownhill	Payne*	Birch*	Lacy	Ashworth	Wolfenden	Byrne	Greaves	Wright	Lindfield*
14.04	Skelmersdale United	A	0-1	Carnell	Brownhill	Daniels*	Stott	Lynch	Ashworth	Wolfenden*	Brown T	Fallon	Wright	Lindfield*
18.04	Stamford	H¹	3-1	Carnell	Brownhill	Daniels*	Stott	Lynch	Ashworth	Wolfenden*	Fallon	**Greaves 1***	Wright	**Lindfield 1**
21.04	Stourbridge	H²	1-0	Carnell	Brownhill	**Daniels 1***	Stott*	Lynch	Ashworth	Wolfenden*	Fallon	Greaves	Wright	Lindfield*
25.04	Workington	A	0-1	Carnell	Birch	Daniels	Cheetham	Fox	Bayunu	Walwyn	Brown T	Norton*	Byrne	Lindfield

p¹: lost 1-3 on penalties (**scored:** Lynch, **missed:** Daniels, Brewster, Greaves).   p²: lost 3-4 on penalties (**scored:** Lynch, Knowles, Wright **missed:** Daniels, Ashworth).

APPEARANCES & GOALS

...stitutes							Attendance
...etham	Knowles (6)	Fox (8)	Mulholland	Bower (3)			761
...etham	Greaves (9)	Fox (8)	Mulholland (3)	Bower			1,914
...rnhill (4)	Greaves (11) 1	Byrne	Pritchard (3)	Bower			1,849
...son	Greaves (11)	Fox (9)	Brown T	Daniels (7)			1,106
...etham	Neville L	Fox (8)	Norton (9)	Daniels (11)			1,917
...etham	Birch	Byrne (8)	Bower (9)	Daniels (7)			623
...etham	Brown T (6)	Walwyn	Bower (4)	Daniels (8)			1,142
...	Brown T	Walwyn (10)	Bower	Daniels (9)			1,844
...n (5)	Brown T	Walwyn (11) 1	Bower	Norton (9)	Wright	Culkin	1,001
...	Brown T	Walwyn (8)	Bower (10)	Greaves (9)			542
...son S (10)	Brown T	Walwyn	Bower (11)	Norton (9)			1,985
...son S	Brown T	Walwyn (9)	Bower	Norton (10)	Wright (11)	Culkin	1,033
...	Pearson (3)	Walwyn (11)	Byrne (8)	Daniels			1,971
...(4)	Brown T (8)	Hope	Bower (11)	Pritchard			325
...h	Brown T (8) 1	Walwyn	Brewster (9)	Greaves (11) 1			989
...h	Brown T (11)	Walwyn (8)	Brewster	Greaves (7)			1,843
...h	Brown T	Byrne (5)	Daniels (8)	Greaves (11)			775
...M (11)	Byrne	Daniels (6)	Welsh (10)				459
...M (5) 1	Wright (10)	Byrne	Daniels	Welsh (10)			1,928
...M (11)	Wright (3)	Byrne	Daniels (9)	Greaves			1,739
...enden (10)	Brown T	Fox	Daniels (5)	Walwyn (11) 1			624
...h	Byrne (9)	Fox (11)	Daniels (5)	Walwyn			810
...h (3)	Brown T (4)	Fox	Kay M	Walwyn (11)			1,988
...ht (2)	Byrne	Fox	Wolfenden (10)	Greaves (11)			415
...wles	Van Gils (8)	Fox (7)	Kay M (6)	Walwyn			1,002
...wles (5) 1	Brownhill	Fox (6)	Kay M (7)	Walwyn			1,634
...h	Ashworth	Birch	Kay M (6)	Walwyn (8)			1,444
...h	Brown T	Cheetham (7)	Stott	Walwyn (11)			420
...in	Brown T (4)	Cheetham	Van Gils	Walwyn (6) 1			503
...h	Brown T (4)	Fox (8)	Van Gils	Walwyn (9)			907
...(6)	Brown T (11)	Fox (8)	Van Gils	Walwyn			1,100
...h	Brown T (3)	Byrne	Van Gils (11)	Walwyn (9)			1,187
...h	Brown T (8)	Kay M (3)	Van Gils	Walwyn (11) 1			1,940
...in	Byrne (4)	Cheetham	Daniels (8)	Walwyn (7)			1,067
...	Stott (4)	Cheetham	Van Gils	Walwyn (8)			2,254
...h	Birch (5)	Cheetham	Brown T (8)	Walwyn			1,393
...h	Birch (4)	Greaves (3) 1	Brown T (8)	Walwyn			1,934
...h	Stott (4)	Norton (9)	Byrne	Walwyn (3)			1,732
...h	Stott (4)	Norton (8)	Byrne	Walwyn (7)			3,805
...h	Kay M	Fallon (11)	Greaves (3) 2	Walwyn (7)			1,810
...h (6)	Stott	Fallon (11)	Greaves (3)	Brown T			2,180
...h	Stott	Fallon (11)	Byrne (3)	Daniels (7)			2,273
...h	Fox (4)	Fallon (3)	Brown T (8)	Wolfenden			1,002
...h	Fox (3)	Fallon (8)	Brown T	Wolfenden (7)			2,007
...ch (5) 1	Fox	Fallon (8)	Brown T	Kay M (11)			844
...h	Fox (3)	Byrne	Payne (4)	Kay M (7)			555
...h	Fox	Byrne	Brown T (9)	Daniels (7) 1			2,458
...h (6)	Fox	Byrne	Brown T (7)	Greaves (3) 1			2,443
...anu (9)	Fox (4)	Byrne	Fallon (7)	Payne			1,478
...anu	Stott (4)	Brown T	Fallon (8)	Wolfenden (7)			2,349
...anu	Fox	Byrne (8)	Fallon (7)	Greaves (11)			974
...worth	Stott (4)	Byrne (8)	Fallon (7) 1	Payne			810
...worth (6)	Lindfield (9)	Brown T	Daniels	Walwyn (10)			2,079
...h	Stott (2)	Brown T (8)	Wolfenden (7)	Payne			3,071
...h	Stott	Brown T (4)	Fallon (3)	Daniels (11)			1,463
...ves (7)	Norton (3)	Byrne	Payne	Walwyn (11)			1,113
...	Norton (9)	Byrne (3)	Payne (7) 1	Birch			2,899
...	Norton	Byrne (3)	Payne (7)	Birch (4)			3,588
...t	Wright	Fallon (10)	Daniels (8)	Greaves (9)			2,603

Player	League		FAC & FAT		Other		Totals	
Luke Ashworth	35 (+1)	1	11	0	2	0	48 (+1)	1
Nia Bayunu	2 (+1)	0	0	0	0	0	2 (+1)	0
Dave Birch	23 (+2)	1	6 (+2)	0	2	0	31 (+4)	1
Connor Bower	1 (+5)	0	0	0	0 (+1)	0	1 (+6)	0
Michael Brewster	0 (+1)	0	0	0	1	1	1 (+1)	1
Tom Brown	7 (+13)	1	3 (+3)	0	1 (+1)	0	11 (+17)	1
Liam Brownhill	37 (+1)	1	9	0	0	0	46 (+1)	1
Callum Byrne	24 (+10)	2	9	2	1	0	34 (+10)	4
Dave Carnell	45	0	11	0	1	0	57	0
Scott Cheetham	9	0	3 (+2)	0	2	0	14 (+2)	0
Shaun Connor	1	0	0	0	0	0	1	0
Nick Culkin	1	0	0	0	0	0	2	0
Greg Daniels	27 (+14)	5	9 (+1)	1	2	0	38 (+15)	6
Rory Fallon	7 (+13)	2	0	0	0	0	7 (+13)	2
Joe Fox	15 (+11)	1	1 (+2)	0	0	0	16 (+13)	1
Tom Greaves	29 (+14)	20	11	5	1 (+1)	0	41 (+15)	25
Dean Hope	0	0	0	0	0	0	0	0
Stephen Johnson	0 (+1)	0	0	0	0	0	0 (+1)	0
Matty Kay	2 (+8)	1	1 (+1)	0	1	0	4 (+9)	1
James Knowles	14 (+2)	2	2	0	1	0	17 (+2)	2
Lewis Lacy	27 (+1)	2	6	0	0 (+1)	0	33 (+2)	2
Craig Lindfield	31 (+1)	10	8	2	0	0	39 (+1)	12
Chris Lynch (189)	21 (+4)	2	5	1	2	0	28 (+4)	3
Nelson Mota	1	0	0	0	0	0	1	0
Astley Mulholland	1 (+1)	0	0	0	0	0	1 (+1)	0
Lee Neville	1	0	0	0	0	0	1	0
Mike Norton	14 (+4)	2	0 (+4)	0	0	0	14 (+8)	2
Shelton Payne	13 (+3)	5	0	0	0	0	13 (+3)	5
Andy Pearson	3 (+1)	0	0	0	1	0	4 (+1)	0
John Pritchard	0 (+1)	0	0	0	0	0	0 (+1)	0
Dean Stott	30 (+3)	3	6 (+3)	2	1	0	37 (+6)	5
Frank Van Gils	2 (+1)	0	1 (+1)	0	0	0	3 (+2)	0
Matthew Walwyn	1 (+12)	1	0 (+9)	3	2	0	3 (+21)	4
Andy Welsh	6 (+2)	1	2	0	0	0	8 (+2)	1
Matthew Wolfenden	39 (+3)	9	9 (+1)	4	0 (+1)	0	48 (+5)	13
Jerome Wright	37 (+2)	5	8 (+1)	2	0 (+1)	0	45 (+4)	7

o Opposition Own Goals for FC United:

Richard Pell	04/10/2014	FC's 2nd v Whitby Town (NPLP)	H 2-0
Connor Gudger	03/12/2014	FC's 2nd v Barwell (FAT:Q3R)	H 3-2

#	Team	Pld	W	D	L	F	A	GD	Pts
1	FC UNITED OF MANCHESTER ↑	46	26	14	6	78	37	+41	92
2	Workington	46	27	9	10	63	39	+24	90
3	Ashton United	46	24	12	10	75	54	+21	84
4	Curzon Ashton ↑	46	23	14	9	79	46	+33	83
5	Ilkeston	46	22	15	9	79	56	+23	81
6	Blyth Spartans	46	21	16	9	84	54	+30	79
7	Skelmersdale United	46	21	10	15	58	48	+10	73
8	Barwell	46	21	10	15	69	63	+6	73
9	Rushall Olympic	46	21	9	16	76	64	+12	72
10	Buxton	46	18	17	11	70	57	+13	71
11	Halesowen Town	46	13	20	13	56	48	+8	59
12	Grantham Town	46	15	14	17	64	72	-8	59
13	Whitby Town	46	14	16	16	56	63	-7	58
14	Matlock Town	46	15	11	20	57	60	-3	56
15	Nantwich Town	46	16	7	23	61	76	-15	55
16	Stourbridge	46	14	11	21	59	72	-13	53
17	Ramsbottom United	46	15	8	23	66	80	-14	53
18	King's Lynn Town	46	14	10	22	60	81	-21	52
19	Frickley Athletic	46	14	12	20	60	73	-13	50
20	Stamford	46	13	11	22	56	75	-19	50
21	Marine	46	11	16	19	58	69	-11	49
22	Witton Albion ↓	46	14	7	25	58	86	-28	49
23	Trafford ↓	46	6	15	25	58	93	-35	33
24	Belper Town ↓	46	6	14	26	62	96	-34	32

FC United goals listed first. All games League unless stated otherwise:
FAC FA Cup   **FAT** FA Trophy   **MPC** Manchester FA Premier Cup
LCC Doodson Sport League Challenge Cup   **p** Decided on penalties
H¹ Played at Bower Fold (Stalybridge Celtic FC)
H² Played at Tameside Stadium (Curzon Ashton FC)
* Player Substituted   (2) Substituted player's number   Goalscorers in **bold**
■ Player Sent off   (+1) Number of substitute appearances

NATIONAL LEAGUE NORTH

Date	Opponents	Venue	Score	1	2	3	4	5	6	7	8	9	10	11
08.08	Gloucester City	A	0-1	Carnell	Brownhill	Daniels*	Birch*	Bayunu	Ashworth	Wolfenden*	Fallon	Greaves	Wright	Lindfield
11.08	Stockport County	H	1-2	Carnell	Brownhill	Brown T*	Stott	Bayunu	Ashworth	Wolfenden*	Fallon 1	Greaves	Wright	Lindfield
15.08	Tamworth	H	1-1	Carnell	Brownhill	Daniels*	Stott	Bayunu	Ashworth 1	Madeley*	Brown T*	Fallon	Wright ■	Lindfield
18.08	Chorley	A	0-3	Carnell	Brownhill	Stott	Birch*	Bayunu	Ashworth	Wolfenden*	Cooke S*	Greaves	Wright ■	Fallon
22.08	Brackley Town	H	3-2	Carnell	Brownhill	Stott	Cooke S*	Bayunu	Ashworth	Wolfenden 1	Madeley 1*	Greaves 1*	Wright	Lindfield
29.08	Hednesford Town	A	3-0	Carnell	Birch	Brownhill	Stott*	Bayunu 1	Ashworth	Wolfenden	Fallon	Greaves*	Cooke S 1	Lindfield
31.08	Curzon Ashton	H	3-3	Carnell	Birch	Brownhill	Thurston*	Bayunu	Ashworth 1	Wolfenden*	Fallon 1	Greaves	Cooke S	Lindfield
05.09	Lowestoft Town	A	4-1	Carnell	Brownhill	Daniels*	Stott	Bayunu	Ashworth	Madeley 2*	Fallon	Greaves 2	Cooke S*	Cheetham
12.09	Corby Town	H	1-0	Carnell	Brownhill	Daniels*	Stott	Bayunu	Ashworth	Madeley	Fallon	Greaves	Cooke S*	Cheetham
15.09	AFC Fylde	A	0-4	Carnell ■	Brownhill	Cheetham	Stott	Bayunu	Ashworth	Wolfenden*	Fallon	Greaves	Cooke S*	Madeley
19.09	Stalybridge Celtic	A	0-1	Carnell	Birch	Brown T*	Stott	Bayunu ■	Ashworth	Wolfenden*	Fallon	Greaves	Wright	Madeley
26.09	Witton Albion (FAC:Q2)	H	3-1	King L	Thurston	Fallon 1	Birch	Bayunu	Ashworth	Madeley 1*	Byrne*	Greaves	Wright	Lindfield
02.10	Worcester City	H	0-2	King L	Thurston	Fallon	Stott	Bayunu	Ashworth	Madeley	Cooke S*	Greaves	Wright	Lindfield
11.10	Buxton (FAC:Q3)	H	1-1	Carnell	Brownhill	Brown T*	Birch*	Lynch	Ashworth	Wolfenden	Fallon	Greaves 1	Wright	Lindfield
14.10	Buxton (FAC:Q3R)	A	2-0	Carnell	Brownhill	Daniels 1	Stott	Lynch*	Ashworth	Fallon*	Byrne	Greaves	Wright	Lindfield
17.10	North Ferriby United	A	0-1	Carnell	Brownhill	Daniels*	Sheridan	Lynch	Ashworth	Madeley*	Byrne*	Greaves	Wright	Fallon
24.10	Sporting Khalsa (FAC:Q4)	A	3-1	Carnell	Brownhill	Daniels 1*	Sheridan	Bayunu	Ashworth 1	Fallon	Byrne*	Greaves	Wright	Madeley
27.10	Glossop North End (MPC:1)	H	2-2 p	Culkin	Thurston	Cheetham	Birch*	Stott	Lynch	Lindfield 1*	Wolfenden*	Norton 1	Cooke S	Murray
31.10	Boston United	A	1-3	Carnell	Brownhill	Daniels*	Sheridan	Bayunu	Ashworth	Wolfenden 1	Byrne*	Greaves	Wright	Fallon*
03.11	AFC Telford United	H	1-3	Carnell	Brownhill	Daniels*	Stott	Bayunu	Ashworth	Wolfenden*	Sheridan	Greaves 1	Wright	Lindfield
09.11	Chesterfield (FAC:1)	H	1-4	Carnell	Brownhill	Thurston	Stott	Lynch	Ashworth 1	Fallon*	Sheridan*	Greaves	Wright	Lindfield
14.11	Gainsborough Trinity	H	1-2	Carnell	Thurston	Brownhill	Stott	Lynch	Ashworth	Fallon*	Sheridan	Greaves	Brown T*	Madeley
21.11	Nuneaton Town	A	2-2	Carnell	Thurston	Brownhill	Sheridan	Stott	Ashworth	Fallon*	Winter 1	Greaves 1*	Thomson G	Madeley
24.11	Stalybridge Celtic (MPC:QF)	H	3-4	Carnell	Thurston*	Daniels	Brown T*	Lynch	Stott	Wolfenden 1	Murray 1*	Lindfield 1	Cheetham	Patterson
27.11	AFC Telford United (FAT:Q3)	H	1-2	Carnell	Thurston	Brownhill*	Sheridan	Stott	Ashworth	Fallon	Winter	Greaves*	Thomson G 1	Madeley
05.12	Stockport County	A	2-1	Carnell	Stott	Thurston	Kay S	Smyth	Ashworth	Fallon 1	Winter	Greaves 1*	Thomson G*	Madeley
09.12	Nuneaton Town	H	3-2 o	Carnell	Stott	Thurston	Kay S	Smyth	Ashworth	Fallon	Winter	Greaves*	Thomson G 1*	Madeley
19.12	Gloucester City	H	1-2	Carnell	Stott	Thurston*	Kay S	Smyth	Ashworth	Fallon*	Winter	Greaves	Thomson G 1	Madeley
28.12	Hednesford Town	H	1-1	Carnell	Stott	Thurston	Kay S	Smyth	Ashworth	Wolfenden 1*	Sheridan*	Greaves	Thomson G	Winter
02.01	Bradford Park Avenue	H	2-1	Carnell	Stott	Brownhill	Kay S	Smyth	Ashworth	Wolfenden 1*	Sheridan*	Greaves*	Thomson G 1	Winter
09.01	Tamworth	A	1-1	Carnell	Stott	Brownhill	Kay S	Smyth ■	Ashworth	Wolfenden*	Sheridan	Greaves*	Thomson G 1*	Winter
16.01	Brackley Town	A	0-4	Carnell	Stott*	Brownhill	Kay S	Smyth	Ashworth	Lindfield	Sheridan	Greaves*	Thomson G	Winter
23.01	Lowestoft Town	H	6-1	Carnell	Brownhill	Chantler 1	Kay S	Lacy 1	Ashworth	Madeley 1*	Sheridan	Greaves 1*	Thomson G	Winter*
30.01	Harrogate Town	H	4-3	Carnell	Brownhill	Chantler	Kay S	Lacy	Ashworth	Madeley 1*	Sheridan 1*	Greaves 1*	Thomson G 1	Winter
09.02	AFC Telford United	A	1-5	Carnell*	Brownhill	Chantler	Kay S	Lacy	Ashworth	Madeley ■	Sheridan*	Greaves*	Thomson G 1	Winter
13.02	Alfreton Town	H	1-3	Forth	Brownhill*	Chantler	Kay S	Lacy*	Ashworth ■	Madeley 1	Brown T*	Daniels	Thomson G	Winter
17.02	Bradford Park Avenue	A	1-3	Forth	Thurston	Chantler	Eckersley*	Lacy	Ashworth	Kay S	Winter	Greaves*	Thomson G 1*	Daniels
20.02	Harrogate Town	A	0-5	Forth	Thurston*	Daniels	Winter	Smyth*	Eckersley	Kay S	Thomson G	Madeley	Wright*	Chantler
27.02	North Ferriby United	H	3-2	Carnell	Brownhill	Chantler	Kay S	Eckersley	Brown T	Wolfenden 2*	Winter	Greaves	Thomson G*	Daniels*
05.03	Worcester City	A	0-0	Carnell	Brownhill	Chantler	Kay S	Eckersley	Brown T	Wolfenden	Winter*	Greaves	Thomson G*	Daniels*
12.03	AFC Fylde	H	1-2	Carnell	Tonge	Chantler	Kay S	Eckersley	Brown T	Sheridan*	Winter 1	Greaves	Thomson G	Daniels
15.03	Solihull Moors	A	2-1	Carnell	Tonge	Chantler	Kay S	Eckersley	Ashworth	Sheridan	Winter	Johnson D*	Wright 1*	Thomson
19.03	Alfreton Town	A	1-0	Carnell	Tonge	Chantler	Kay S	Eckersley	Ashworth	Sheridan*	Winter	Johnson D*	Wright	Thomson
26.03	Chorley	H	2-0	Carnell	Tonge	Chantler	Kay S	Eckersley	Ashworth	Sheridan*	Winter	Johnson D 1*	Wright 1	Thomson
28.03	Curzon Ashton	A	0-0	Carnell	Tonge	Chantler	Kay S	Eckersley	Ashworth	Sheridan*	Winter	Johnson D	Wright	Thomson
02.04	Boston United	H	1-2	Carnell	Tonge	Chantler	Kay S	Eckersley	Ashworth	Sheridan 1	Winter*	Johnson D*	Wright	Thomson
09.04	Corby Town	A	3-2	Forth	Tonge	Chantler	Brown T	Kay S	Ashworth 1	Wolfenden*	Sheridan	Johnson D*	Wright*	Thomson
16.04	Stalybridge Celtic	H	0-1	Forth	Tonge	Chantler	Brown T*	Eckersley	Ashworth	Wolfenden*	Sheridan*	Johnson D	Wright 1	Thomson
23.04	Gainsborough Trinity	A	1-0	Forth	Tonge	Chantler	Brown T*	Eckersley	Ashworth	Wolfenden*	Sheridan	Johnson D*	Wright 1	Thomson
30.04	Solihull Moors	H	2-2	Carnell	Tonge	Chantler	Kay S	Eckersley	Ashworth	Brown T*	Sheridan	Greaves 2	Wright*	Thomson

p: won 6-5 on penalties (scored: Lynch, Thurston, Walwyn, Stott, Brownhill, Cheetham missed: Cooke S).

APPEARANCES & GOALS

Substitutes

					Attendance
ott	Byrne (4)	Brown T	Cooke S (3)	Murray (7)	1,451
ch	Daniels (7)	Madeley (11)	Cooke S	Murray (3)	3,199
ch	Greaves (8)	Wolfenden (5)	Cooke S (3)	Murray	3,580
ndfield	Byrne (4)	Daniels (8)	Madeley (7)	Murray	1,876
urston (4)	Birch	Daniels (9)	Byrne	Murray (8)	2,996
urston (4)	Norton	Daniels (9)	Madeley (11)	Murray	927
eetham (4)	Lynch	Daniels (11)	Madeley (7) 1	Murray	3,830
urston	Lindfield (7)	Birch	Wolfenden (3)	Murray (10)	1,154
urston (10)	Lynch	Birch	Wolfenden (3) 1	Murray	3,326
urston	Lynch (7)	Birch (11)	Daniels (10)	Murray	Lynch in goal from 55 mins	821
ndfield (7)	Lynch (3)	Byrne (11)	Daniels	Cooke S	1,775
own T(8)	Lynch	Wolfenden (7)	Daniels	Cooke S	Murray (11)	Cheetham	1,648
own T	Brownhill (2)	Wolfenden (11)	Daniels (8)	Birch	3,619
urston	Byrne (4)	Madeley (11)	Daniels	Cooke S (3)	Murray	King L	2,357
urston	Birch (5)	Madeley (11) 1	Walwyn	Cooke S (7)	Murray	King L	874
ott	Birch	Wolfenden (7)	Lindfield (3)	Cooke S (8)	951
ott (8)	Birch	Wolfenden (11)	Lindfield (3) 1	Cooke S	Thurston	Lynch	2,252
ownhill (4)	Bayunu	Brown T (8)	Greaves	Walwyn (7)	980
urston	Stott (8)	Lindfield	Madeley (3)	Patterson (11)	1,789
urston	Byrne	Fallon (11)	Madeley (3)	Patterson (7)	2,781
olfenden	Byrne (8)	Daniels (11)	Madeley	Patterson (7)	Brown T	Bayunu	2,916
olfenden (7)	Winter (10)	Daniels (11)	Lindfield	Patterson	3,301
olfenden	Brown T (7)	Daniels (11)	Lindfield	Patterson (9)	1,167
shworth	Brownhill (2)	Fallon (4)	Madeley (8)	Walwyn	695
olfenden	Brown T	Daniels (9)	Lindfield (3)	Patterson (11) ■	1,034
olfenden (10)	Brown T	Daniels (9)	Lindfield	Patterson (11)	4,797
olfenden (11)	Brown T	Daniels (10)	Lindfield	Patterson (9)	2,781
olfenden (3)	Brown T	Daniels (11)	Lindfield	Sheridan (7)	3,187
ownhill	Brown T	Daniels (7)	Lindfield (8)	Walwyn	3,421
urston	Brown T (8)	Daniels (7)	Lindfield (9)	Walwyn	3,379
urston (10)	Brown T	Daniels (7)	Lindfield (9)	Madeley	1,430
urston	Brown T	Daniels (9)	Walwyn	Madeley (2)	660
urston	Brown T (7)	Daniels (11) 1	Lindfield (9) 1	Stott	3,280
urston	Brown T (8)	Daniels (9)	Lindfield (7)	Stott	3,362
urston	Brown T	Daniels (9)	Lindfield (1)	Eckersley (8)	Madeley and Ashworth in goal	1,323
urston (8)	Wright (2)	Greaves	Wolfenden	Eckersley (5)	3,338
myth	Wright (4)	Brown T	Wolfenden (9)	Madeley (10)	619
ownhill	Lacy (5)	Brown T	Wolfenden (10)	Greaves (2)	1,357
urston (10)	Wright (7)	Walwyn	Lindfield (11) 1	Forth	3,419
urston (8)	Wright	Sheridan (11)	Madeley (10)	Forth	2,135
urston	Wright (7)	Brownhill	Walwyn	Forth	3,432
urston (11)	Brown T	Daniels (9)	Greaves	Wolfenden (10)	834
urston	Brown T (7)	Daniels	Greaves (9)	Wolfenden (11)	1,087
urston	Brown T (7)	Daniels	Greaves (9)	Wolfenden (11)	4,150
urston	Brown T	Daniels	Greaves (7)	Wolfenden (11)	1,692
urston	Brown T	Daniels (11)	Greaves (9)	Wolfenden (8)	3,544
ckersley	Walwyn (10)	Daniels (7)	Greaves (9)	Carnell named at no.1 but injured prior to kick-off	1,030
urston (4)	Winter (8)	Daniels	Greaves (7)	Carnell	3,451
alwyn	Winter (4)	Daniels (9)	Greaves (7)	Carnell	1,021
alwyn	Winter (7)	Daniels (11)	Madeley (10)	Forth	3,914

Appearances & Goals

Player	League		FAC & FAT		Other		Totals	
Luke Ashworth	38	3	6	2	0	0	44	5
Nia Bayunu	14	1	2	0	0	0	16	1
Dave Birch	5 (+1)	0	2 (+1)	0	1	0	8 (+2)	0
Tom Brown	12 (+6)	0	1 (+1)	0	1 (+1)	0	14 (+8)	0
Liam Brownhill	24 (+1)	0	5	0	0 (+2)	0	29 (+3)	0
Callum Byrne	2 (+3)	0	3 (+2)	0	0	0	5 (+5)	0
Dave Carnell	35	0	5	0	1	0	41	0
Chris Chantler	18	1	0	0	0	0	18	1
Scott Cheetham	3 (+1)	0	0	0	2	0	5 (+1)	0
Sean Cooke	8 (+3)	1	0 (+2)	0	1	0	9 (+5)	1
Nick Culkin	0	0	0	0	1	0	1	0
Greg Daniels	13 (+24)	1	2 (+2)	2	1	0	16 (+26)	3
Tom Eckersley	13 (+2)	0	0	0	0	0	13 (+2)	0
Rory Fallon	18 (+1)	3	6	1	0 (+1)	0	24 (+2)	4
Dylan Forth	6	0	0	0	0	0	6	0
Tom Greaves	31 (+9)	10	6	1	0	0	37 (+9)	11
Dale Johnson	8	1	0	0	0	0	8	1
Scott Kay	23	0	0	0	0	0	23	0
Lewis King	1	0	1	0	0	0	2	0
Lewis Lacy	5 (+1)	1	0	0	0	0	5 (+1)	1
Craig Lindfield	9 (+10)	3	4 (+2)	2	2	2	15 (+12)	7
Chris Lynch (189)	2 (+2)	0	3	0	0	0	7 (+2)	0
Sam Madeley	18 (+10)	9	3 (+2)	2	0 (+1)	0	21 (+13)	11
Cameron Murray	0 (+4)	0	0 (+1)	0	2	1	2 (+5)	1
Mike Norton	0	0	0	0	1	1	1	1
Rory Patterson	0 (+5)	0	0 (+2)	0	1	0	1 (+7)	0
Sam Sheridan	22 (+2)	2	3	0	0	0	25 (+2)	2
Tom Smyth	8	0	0	0	0	0	8	0
Dean Stott	20 (+1)	0	3 (+1)	0	2	0	25 (+2)	0
George Thomson	26	11	1	1	0	0	27	12
Adam Thurston	10 (+9)	0	3	0	2	0	15 (+9)	0
Dale Tonge	10	0	0	0	0	0	10	0
Matthew Walwyn	0 (+1)	0	0	0	0 (+1)	0	0 (+2)	0
Harry Winter	22 (+4)	2	1	0	0	0	23 (+4)	2
Matthew Wolfenden	18 (+16)	7	1 (+2)	0	2	1	21 (+18)	8
Jerome Wright	20 (+4)	3	5	0	0	0	25 (+4)	3

o Opposition Own Goal for FC United:
James Clifton 09/12/2015 FC's 3rd v Nuneaton Town (NLN) H 3-2

FC United goals listed first. All games League unless stated otherwise:
FAC FA Cup **FAT** FA Trophy **MPC** Manchester FA Premier Cup
H Played at Broadhurst Park (FC United Of Manchester)
* Player Substituted (2) Substituted player's number Scorers in **bold**
■ Player Sent off (+1) Number of substitute appearances

	Team	Pld	W	D	L	F	A	GD	Pts
1	Solihull Moors ↑	42	25	10	7	84	48	+36	85
2	North Ferriby United ↑	42	22	10	10	82	49	+33	76
3	AFC Fylde	42	22	9	11	76	53	+23	75
4	Harrogate Town	42	21	9	12	73	46	+27	72
5	Boston United	42	22	5	15	73	60	+13	71
6	Nuneaton Town -3 points	42	20	13	9	71	46	+25	‡70
7	Tamworth	42	16	15	11	55	45	+10	63
8	Chorley	42	18	9	15	64	55	+9	63
9	Stockport County	42	15	14	13	50	49	+1	59
10	Alfreton Town	42	15	13	14	58	54	+4	58
11	Curzon Ashton	42	14	15	13	55	52	+3	57
12	Stalybridge Celtic	42	14	11	17	62	75	−13	53
13	FC UNITED OF MANCHESTER	42	15	8	19	60	75	−15	53
14	Bradford Park Avenue	42	13	11	18	51	59	−8	50
15	Gloucester City	42	12	14	16	39	49	−10	50
16	Gainsborough Trinity	42	14	8	20	46	62	−16	50
17	Worcester City	42	12	12	18	55	61	−6	48
18	AFC Telford United	42	13	8	21	47	60	−13	47
19	Brackley Town	42	11	13	18	45	54	−9	46
20	Lowestoft Town ↓	42	12	10	20	48	69	−21	46
21	Hednesford Town ↓	42	8	14	20	50	77	−27	38
22	Corby Town ↓	42	7	11	24	47	93	−46	32

‡: Nuneaton Town were deducted 3 points for fielding an ineligible player

2016/17 RESULTS & LINE-UPS

NATIONAL LEAGUE NORTH

Date	Opponents	Venue	Score	1	2	3	4	5	6	7	8	9	10	11
06.08	Chorley	A	3-3	Carnell	Tonge	Chantler	Kay S	Eckersley	Ashworth	Sheridan*	Winter*	Greaves*	**Wright 1**	Thomson
09.08	AFC Telford United	H	0-0	Carnell	Tonge	Chantler	Kay S	Eckersley	Ashworth	Sheridan*	Winter*	Greaves*	Wright	Thomson G
12.08	Stockport County	H	2-0	Carnell	Tonge	Chantler	Kay S	Eckersley	Ashworth	**Wolfenden 1***	Sheridan*	Greaves*	Wright	Winter
16.08	Salford City	A	0-1	Carnell	Tonge	Chantler	Kay S	Eckersley	Ashworth	Wolfenden*	Sheridan*	Johnson D*	Gilchrist J	Winter
20.08	Worcester City	H	1-1	Carnell	Williams J*	Chantler	Kay S	Eckersley	Ashworth	Tonge	Sheridan*	**Johnson D 1**	Thomson G	Lowe*
27.08	Brackley Town	A	0-1	Carnell	Tonge	Chantler	Kay S	Eckersley	Ashworth	Wolfenden*	Sheridan*	Johnson D*	Thomson G	Lowe
29.08	Darlington 1883	H	2-3	Frith	Tonge	Chantler	Kay S	Eckersley	Ashworth	Glynn*	Lowe*	Greaves*	**Thomson G 1**	Gilchrist J
03.09	Boston United	A	3-2	Diba	Tonge	Chantler	Kay S	Eckersley	Ashworth	Wolfenden*	Sheridan*	**Greaves 2**	Thomson G*	Winter
06.09	Harrogate Town	A	1-3	Diba	Tonge	Chantler	Kay S	Eckersley	**Ashworth 1**	Wolfenden*	Lowe	Greaves*	Thomson G	Gilchrist J*
10.09	AFC Fylde	H	2-3	Diba	Tonge	Chantler	Kay S	Eckersley	Ashworth	Hooper*	Sheridan	Johnson D*	**Thomson G 1**	**Winter 1***
17.09	Ossett Town (FAC:Q2)	A	7-1	Carnell	Tonge	**Chantler 1**	Kay S	Eckersley	**Ashworth 3**	Wolfenden*	**Sheridan 1***	Greaves 1	**Thomson G 1***	Winter
24.09	Tamworth	A	1-1	Diba	Williams J	Chantler	Kay S	Eckersley	Ashworth	**Hooper 1**	Sheridan	Johnson D*	Thomson G	Winter*
27.09	Curzon Ashton	H	0-0	Diba	Williams J	Chantler	Kay S	Eckersley	Ashworth	Hooper*	Sheridan	Johnson D*	Thomson G	Winter
01.10	Harrogate Town (FAC:Q3)	H	3-3	Carnell	Tonge	Chantler	Kay S	Corbett	Ashworth	Williams J*	Sheridan	**Johnson D 1***	**Thomson G 1**	**Winter 1***
04.10	Harrogate Town (FAC:Q3R)	A	0-2	Carnell	Williams J	Tonge	Kay S	Eckersley	Ashworth	Gilchrist J*	Sheridan*	Johnson D*	Thomson G	Winter
08.10	Alfreton Town	H	4-3	Carnell	Williams J	Tonge*	Lowe	Eckersley*	**Ashworth 1**	**Wolfenden 1**	**Glynn 1**	Greaves*	**Thomson G 1**	Winter
15.10	AFC Telford United	A	0-1	Carnell	Williams J*	Chantler	Kay S	Corbett	Ashworth	Wolfenden*	Winter	Greaves*	Wright	Thomson G
18.10	Chadderton (MPC:1)	A	6-0	Carnell	Williams J	Chantler*	Kay S*	**Eckersley 1**	Ashworth	Wolfenden	Brown T*	**Greaves 2**	**Thomson G 3**	Gilchrist J
22.10	Kidderminster Harriers	A	2-0 o	Carnell	Tonge	Chantler	Kay S	Eckersley	**Ashworth 1**	Wolfenden*	Brown T*	Greaves*	Thomson G	Williams J
25.10	FC Halifax Town	A	1-3	Carnell	Tonge	Chantler	Kay S	Eckersley	Ashworth	Wolfenden*	Brown T*	Greaves	**Thomson G 1**	Williams J*
29.10	Gloucester City	H	2-4	Carnell	Tonge	Chantler	Kay S	Eckersley*	**Ashworth 1**	Wolfenden*	Winter	**Gilchrist J 1**	Wright	Thomson G
05.11	Bradford Park Avenue	H	2-3	Carnell	Tonge*	Chantler	Kay S	Eckersley*	Ashworth	Wolfenden*	Winter	**Gilchrist J 1**	Wright	**Thomson**
12.11	Stalybridge Celtic	A	4-2	Carnell	Tonge	Chantler	Brown T	Kay S	Baird	**Glynn 1***	Winter	**Gilchrist J 2***	**Wright 1**	Thomson G
16.11	Abbey Hey (MPC:QF)	A	3-1	Carnell	Williams J	Kisimba	Jones M	Baird	Ashworth	Wolfenden	Sheridan	**Greaves 3***	Arnison*	Winter*
19.11	Nuneaton Town	H	3-0	Carnell	Tonge	Chantler	Brown T*	Kay S	**Ashworth 1**	**Glynn 1***	Winter	Gilchrist J*	**Wright 1**	Thomson G
03.12	Gainsborough Trinity	A	2-1	Carnell	Tonge	Chantler	Brown T*	Kay S	Ashworth	Glynn*	**Winter 1**	Gilchrist J*	**Wright 1**	Thomson G
06.12	Nuneaton Town (FAT:Q3)	H	1-5	Carnell	Tonge	Chantler	Brown T*	Kay S	Ashworth	Glynn*	Winter*	**Gilchrist J 1**	Wright	Thomson G
17.12	Boston United	H	1-1	Carnell	Williams J	Brown T*	Winter	Kay S	Ashworth	Gilchrist J	Sheridan	Greaves*	Wright	**Thomson**
26.12	Altrincham	A	3-0	Basso	Tonge	Chantler	**Brown T 1**	Kay S	Ashworth	Sheridan*	Winter	**Gilchrist J 1***	Wright*	Thomson G
01.01	Altrincham	H	1-1	Basso	Tonge	Chantler	**Brown T 1**	Kay S	Ashworth ■	Glynn	Winter	**Gilchrist J 1***	Wright*	Thomson G
07.01	AFC Fylde	A	1-3	Basso	Tonge	Chantler	Brown T*	Kay S	Ashworth	Wolfenden*	**Winter 1**	Gilchrist J*	Wright	Thomson G
14.01	Worcester City	A	0-0	Basso	Tonge	Chantler	Brown T*	Kay S	Baird	Glynn*	Lowe	Gilchrist J*	Wright	Thomson G
21.01	Harrogate Town	H	2-2	Basso	Williams J	Chantler*	Brown T	Tonge	Baird	Wolfenden*	Sheridan*	**Gilchrist J 1**	Wright	Thomson G
28.01	Salford City	H	0-3	Basso	Tonge	Chantler*	Brown T*	Fagbola	Baird	Wolfenden*	Winter	Gilchrist J	Wright	Thomson G
07.02	West Didsbury & Chorlton (MPC:SF)	H	7-1	Basso	Tonge	Chantler	**Brown T 1**	Kay S	Ashworth	Glynn	Winter	**Gilchrist J 3***	Wright	Thomson G
11.02	Chorley	H	3-3	Basso ■	Tonge	Chantler*	Kay S	Ashworth	**Wolfenden 1***	Winter*	**Gilchrist J 1**	Wright	**Lowe 1***
18.02	Stockport County	A	1-2	Carnell	Williams J	Chantler ■	Brown T*	Kay S	Ashworth	Lowe	Winter	Gilchrist J	Arnison*	Glynn*
25.02	Gloucester City	A	3-2	Carnell	Williams J	Winter	Kay S	Corbett	Ashworth	Wolfenden*	**Lowe 2**	Gilchrist J*	Wright	Thomson G
04.03	Kidderminster Harriers	H	1-0	Carnell	Williams J	Winter	Kay S	Corbett	Ashworth	Wolfenden	Lowe*	Arnison*	Wright	Thomson G
11.03	Tamworth	H	1-0	Carnell	Williams J	Sheridan*	Kay S	Corbett	Ashworth	Wolfenden	**Lowe 1**	Arnison*	Wright	Thomson G
18.03	Alfreton Town	A	1-2	Carnell	Williams J	Sheridan*	Kay S	Corbett	Ashworth	Wolfenden*	Lowe	Arnison*	Wright	Thomson G
25.03	FC Halifax Town	H	0-3	Carnell	Williams J	Chantler	Kay S	Baird*	Ashworth	Glynn*	Lowe	Gilchrist J	Wright	Thomson G
27.03	Curzon Ashton	A	2-1	Basso	Tonge	Chantler	Kay S	Fagbola	Ashworth	**Wolfenden 1**	**Lowe 1***	Adeloye*	Wright	Wilkinson*
01.04	Stalybridge Celtic	H	2-2	Carnell	Tonge	Chantler*	Kay S	Fagbola	Ashworth	**Wolfenden 1**	Lowe	Adeloye*	Wright	Wilkinson*
08.04	Bradford Park Avenue	A	0-0	Schofield	Tonge	Chantler	Kay S	Fagbola	Ashworth	Wolfenden*	Lowe	Greaves	Wright*	Adeloye*
15.04	Brackley Town	H	1-2	Schofield	Tonge	Chantler*	Kay S	Fagbola	Ashworth	Thomson G*	**Lowe 1**	Gilchrist J*	Wright	Adeloye
17.04	Darlington 1883	A	2-4	Schofield	Williams J	Chantler	Kay S	Fagbola	Ashworth	Glynn*	Sheridan	Greaves*	**Brown T 1***	Wolfenden
22.04	Nuneaton Town	A	4-1	Schofield	Williams J	Chantler	Kay S	**Fagbola 1**	Ashworth*	**Wolfenden 1**	**Sheridan 1***	Adeloye*	Wright	Thomson G
29.04	Gainsborough Trinity	H	5-1	Schofield	Williams J	Chantler	Kay S*	Fagbola	Ashworth	**Wolfenden 2***	Sheridan*	Gilchrist J	**Wright 1**	Thomson G
04.05	Stalybridge Celtic (MPC:F)	N	1-0	Schofield	**Williams J 1**	Chantler	Kay S	Fagbola	Ashworth	Wolfenden*	Lowe	Adeloye*	Wright	Thomson G

APPEARANCES & GOALS

Substitutes						Attendance
liams J (8)	Lowe (7)	Glynn	Wolfenden	Gilchrist J (9)		1,947
liams J	Lowe	Glynn (7)	Wolfenden (8)	Gilchrist J (9)		2,124
liams J	Lowe (8)	Glynn	Johnson D (9) 1	Gilchrist J (7)		3,030
liams J	Lowe	Thomson G (8)	Madeley (7)	Greaves (9)		1,966
nter (2)	Glynn (8)	Wolfenden (11)	Gilchrist J	Greaves		2,328
liams J	Glynn (8)	Kisimba	Gilchrist J (7)	Greaves (9)		565
liams J	Winter (7)	Sheridan (8)	Wolfenden	Johnson D (9)		2,731
liams J	Lowe (8)	Glynn (10)	**Gilchrist J (7) 1**	Pratt		1,424
liams J	Kisimba	Glynn (7)	Johnson D (9)	Pratt (11)		1,094
liams J	Lowe (9)	Wolfenden	Gilchrist J (7)	Greaves (11)		2,284
liams J	Lowe (7)	Corbett	Gilchrist J (10)	Glynn (8)	Frith Pratt	694
wn T	Lowe (11)	Corbett	Gilchrist J (8)	Greaves (9)		1,105
ge	Lowe	Wolfenden (8)	Gilchrist J (9)	Greaves (7)		2,166
wn T (11)	Lowe (7)	Wolfenden	Gilchrist J	Greaves (9)	Frith Glynn	1,541
wn T	Lowe (8)	Wolfenden (7)	Glynn	Greaves (9)	Frith	881
wn T	Corbett (5)	Wright (3)	Gilchrist J	Johnson D (9)		2,528
wn T	Eckersley	Tonge (2)	Gilchrist J (7)	Johnson D (9)■		1,706
ght (3)	Corbett (4)	Tonge	Hill (8)	Johnson D		374
ght (7)	Corbett	Sheridan (8)	Hill	Gilchrist J (9)		2,177
ght (7)	Corbett	Sheridan (7)	Winter (11)	Gilchrist J		1,938
liams J	Corbett	Sheridan (7)	Brown T	Greaves (5)		2,499
liams J (2)	Corbett	Sheridan (5)	Brown T	Greaves (7)		2,397
liams J	Wolfenden (9)	Sheridan (7)	Arnison	Greaves (11)		1,466
r S	Wright	Hill (11)	Pratt (9)	Gilchrist J (10)		372
liams J	Sheridan (4)	Wolfenden (7)	Arnison	Greaves (9)		2,313
nge	Sheridan (4)	Wolfenden	Arnison (9)	Greaves (7)		762
liams J	Sheridan (4)	Wolfenden (7)	Arnison	Greaves (8)		736
rd	Glynn (3)	Jones M	Arnison (9)	Kisimba		2,393
liams J	Glynn (7)	Wolfenden (10)	Arnison	**Greaves (9) 1**		2,490
liams J	Baird	Wolfenden (9)	Lowe (11)	Greaves (10)		3,030
liams J	Glynn (7)	Jones M	Lowe (4)	Greaves (9)		2,821
liams J	Sheridan (4)	Arnison (9)	Wolfenden	Greaves (7)		803
dy	Lowe (8)	Arnison	Glynn (3)	Greaves (7)		2,367
liams J	Lowe	Sheridan (4)	Glynn (7)	Greaves (3)		4,158
liams J	Lowe (S)	Sheridan	**Wolfenden (11) 3**	Greaves (9)*		708
liams J	Wilkinson (4)	Sheridan (11)	Glynn (7)	Arnison	Sheridan in goal from 90 mins	2,403
nge	Wilkinson	Sheridan (4)	**Wright (11) 1**	Greaves (10)		5,630
wn T	Wilkinson (11)	Sheridan	Arnison (9)	**Greaves (7) 1**		795
wn T	Glynn	Sheridan (11)	Gilchrist J (8)	Greaves (9)		2,456
wn T	Glynn	Wilkinson (3)	Gilchrist J (9)	Greaves (11)		2,407
wn T	Chantler (7)	Wilkinson	Gilchrist J (3)	Greaves (9)		898
eloye (11)	Sheridan	Wilkinson (5)	Wolfenden (7)	Greaves		3,149
wn T	Sheridan (8)	Thomson G	Greaves (11)			829
wn T	Sheridan (11)	**Thomson G (3) 1**	Gilchrist J	Greaves (9)		2,375
wn T	Sheridan (10)	Thomson G (11)	Gilchrist J (7)	Glynn		566
wn T	Sheridan	Wolfenden (9)	Greaves (7)	Glynn (3)		2,823
nge	Wright	Lowe (10)	Thomson G (7)	**Adeloye (9) 1**		2,147
wn T	Jones M (8)	Lowe (9)	Greaves	Baird (6)		777
wn T	Jones M (4)	Lowe (8)	Greaves	Adeloye (7)		4,064
wn T	Jones M	Sheridan (7)	Greaves (9)	Gilchrist J (11)		1,592

Player	League		FAC & FAT		Other		Totals	
Tomi **Adeloye**	5 (+3)	1	0	0	1	0	6 (+3)	1
Gareth **Arnison**	4 (+4)	0	0	0	1	0	5 (+4)	0
Luke **Ashworth**	38	5	4	3	4	0	46	8
Sam **Baird**	5 (+1)	0	0	0	1	0	6 (+1)	0
Adriano **Basso**	8	0	0	0	1	0	9	0
Tom **Brown**	15	2	1 (+1)	0	2	1	18 (+1)	3
Dave **Carnell**	23	0	4	0	2	0	29	0
Chris **Chantler**	36 (+1)	0	3	1	3	0	42 (+1)	1
Zac **Corbett**	5 (+1)	0	1	0	0 (+1)	0	6 (+2)	0
Johny **Diba**	5	0	0	0	0	0	5	0
Tom **Eckersley**	17	0	0	0	1	1	20	1
Steeve **Eddy**	0	0	0	0	0	0	0	0
Jordan **Fagbola**	8	1	0	0	1	0	9	1
Ashley **Frith**	1	0	0	0	0	0	1	0
Jason **Gilchrist**	21 (+15)	10	2 (+1)	1	2 (+2)	3	25 (+18)	14
Kieran **Glynn**	10 (+12)	3	1 (+1)	0	1	0	12 (+13)	3
Tom **Greaves**	13 (+24)	4	1 (+3)	1	2 (+2)	5	16 (+29)	10
Chris **Hill**	0	0	0	0	0 (+2)	0	0 (+2)	0
James **Hooper**	3	1	0	0	0	0	3	1
Dale **Johnson**	6 (+5)	2	2	1	0	0	8 (+5)	3
Mike **Jones**	0 (+2)	0	0	0	1	0	1 (+2)	0
Scott **Kay**	39	0	4	0	3	0	46	0
Kisimba **Kisimba**	0	0	0	0	1	0	1	0
Nathan **Lowe**	17 (+11)	6	0 (+3)	0	1 (+1)	0	18 (+15)	6
Sam **Madeley**	0 (+1)	0	0	0	0	0	0 (+1)	0
Harry **Pratt**	0 (+1)	0	0	0	0 (+1)	0	0 (+2)	0
Ryan **Schofield**	5	0	0	0	1	0	6	0
Sam **Sheridan**	18 (+16)	1	3 (+1)	1	1 (+1)	0	22 (+18)	2
George **Thomson**	34 (+4)	15	4	2	3	3	41 (+4)	20
Dale **Tonge**	29 (+1)	0	4	0	1	0	34 (+1)	0
Greg **Wilkinson**	2 (+4)	0	0	0	0	0	2 (+4)	0
Jake **Williams**	18 (+2)	0	2	0	3	1	23 (+2)	1
Harry **Winter**	24 (+3)	3	4	1	2	0	30 (+3)	4
Matthew **Wolfenden**	25 (+9)	8	1 (+2)	0	3 (+1)	3	29 (+12)	11
Jerome **Wright**	28 (+4)	6	1	0	2 (+1)	0	31 (+5)	6

o Opposition Own Goal for FC United:
Keith **Lowe** 22/10/2016 FC's 1st v Kidderminster Harriers (NLN) A 2-0

FC United goals listed first. All games League unless stated otherwise:
FAC FA Cup **FAT** FA Trophy **MPC** Manchester FA Premier Cup
H Played at Broadhurst Park (FC United Of Manchester)
N Played at Boundary Park (Oldham Athletic FC)
* Player Substituted (2) Substituted player's number Goalscorers in **bold**
■ Player Sent off (+1) Number of substitute appearances

	Team	Pld	W	D	L	F	A	GD	Pts
1	AFC Fylde ↑	42	26	10	6	109	60	+49	88
2	Kidderminster Harriers	42	25	7	10	76	41	+35	82
3	FC Halifax Town ↑	42	24	8	10	81	43	+38	80
4	Salford City	42	22	11	9	79	44	+35	77
5	Darlington 1883 ‡	42	22	10	10	89	67	+22	76
6	Chorley	42	20	14	8	60	41	+19	74
7	Brackley Town	42	20	13	9	66	43	+23	73
8	Stockport County	42	19	16	7	59	41	+18	73
9	Tamworth	42	21	6	15	73	67	+6	69
10	Gloucester City	42	18	10	14	69	61	+8	64
11	Harrogate Town	42	16	11	15	71	63	+8	59
12	Nuneaton Town	42	14	13	15	69	71	-2	55
13	**FC UNITED OF MANCHESTER**	42	14	12	16	69	68	+1	54
14	Curzon Ashton	42	14	10	18	63	72	-9	52
15	Boston United	42	12	11	19	54	72	-18	47
16	Bradford Park Avenue	42	12	7	23	46	74	-28	43
17	AFC Telford United	42	10	12	20	38	57	-19	42
18	Alfreton Town	42	11	9	22	62	95	-33	42
19	Gainsborough Trinity	42	8	12	22	51	84	-33	36
20	Worcester City ↓	42	7	14	21	44	63	-19	35
21	Stalybridge Celtic ↓	42	8	5	29	40	89	-49	29
22	Altrincham ↓	42	4	9	29	39	91	-52	21

‡: Darlington 1883 were barred from entering the play-offs due to ground grading issues

NATIONAL LEAGUE NORTH

Date	Opponents	Venue	Score	1	2	3	4	5	6	7	8	9	10	11
05.08	Brackley Town	A	1-2	Allinson	Senior	Wisdom	Brown T*	Fagbola	Corbett	McCarthy	Lowe	Gilchrist J 1	Jones M*	St Juste*
08.08	Spennymoor Town	A	2-3	Allinson	Senior	Wisdom 1	Brown T	Fagbola	Corbett	McCarthy	Lowe	Gilchrist J 1*	Baker R*	Logan*
12.08	Kidderminster Harriers	H	1-2	Allinson	Senior	Wisdom 1	Brown T	Fagbola	Hughes	McCarthy	Lowe	Gilchrist J*	Baker R*	Logan*
15.08	Southport	A	3-3	Allinson	Senior	Wisdom	Kay S	Fagbola	Hughes	Hooper 1*	Lowe 1	Gilchrist J*	Connor M*	McCarthy
19.08	Bradford Park Avenue	A	0-3	Allinson	Senior	Wisdom	Kay S	Fagbola	Hughes	Hooper*	Lowe	Lacy	Brown T*	McCarthy
26.08	Boston United	H	2-1	Allinson	Brady*	Wisdom	Kay S	Fagbola	Hughes	Lindfield	Lowe 1	Gilchrist J*	Connor M*	McCarthy
28.08	York City	A	2-0	Allinson	Brady	Wisdom	Kay S	Fagbola	Hughes	Lindfield*	Lowe*	Gilchrist J 1	Connor M	McCarthy
02.09	Leamington	H	1-2	Allinson	Brady	Wisdom	Kay S 1	Fagbola	Hughes	Hooper*	Lowe	Gilchrist J*	Connor M*	McCarthy
05.09	Blyth Spartans	H	1-3	Allinson	Brady*	Wisdom	Kay S	Fagbola	Hughes	Logan	Connor M	Greaves	McCarthy*	Hooper*
09.09	Curzon Ashton	A	0-1	Allinson	Brady*	Wisdom	Kay S	Fagbola	Hughes	Connor M*	Irwin	Greaves*	McCarthy	Logan
13.09	Darlington	A	0-3	Allinson	Senior	Wisdom	Kay S	Fagbola	Hughes ■	Irwin*	Connor M ■	Greaves*	McCarthy	Logan*
16.09	Handsworth Parramore (FAC:Q2)	A	1-1	Allinson	Senior	Corbett	Kay S	Fagbola	Brady	Irwin 1	Connor M*	Gilchrist J	McCarthy*	Lindfield
19.09	Handsworth Parramore (FAC:Q2R)	H	6-2	Allinson	Senior	Corbett	Kay S*	Fagbola	Brady	Irwin	Connor M 1	Gilchrist J 1*	McCarthy 3	Lindfield*
24.09	Tamworth	H	3-1	Allinson	Brady	Wisdom	Kay S	Fagbola	Corbett	Senior	Irwin 1	Gilchrist J 2*	McCarthy*	Logan*
30.09	Stockport County (FAC:Q3)	A	3-3	Allinson	Brady	Wisdom	Kay S	Fagbola*	Corbett	Senior*	Connor M*	Gilchrist J 1	Irwin 1	Mantack
03.10	Stockport County (FAC:Q3R)	H	1-0	Allinson	Brady	Wisdom	Connor M ■	Corbett	Hughes ■	Mantack	Irwin	Greaves 1*	Gilchrist J*	Logan*
07.10	North Ferriby United	A	3-3	Allinson	Brady*	Wisdom	Kay S	Corbett	Hughes	Logan*	Irwin 1	Greaves 1	Gonzales	Walker T
14.10	AFC Telford United (FAC:Q4)	A	1-3	Allinson	Brady	Wisdom	Kay S	Fagbola	Corbett	Mantack*	Irwin	Greaves	McCarthy*	Walker T*
21.10	Chorley	A	0-1	Allinson	Mantack	Kay S	Brady	Corbett ■	Lindfield	Irwin*		Gonzales	Walker T	Kinsella*
28.10	Nuneaton Town	H	2-1	Allinson	Brady	Walker T	Kay S	Fagbola 1	Hughes	Logan	Glynn*	Greaves*	Gilchrist J 1	Lindfield*
04.11	Stockport County	A	1-4	Allinson	Brady*	Walker T	Kay S	Fagbola	Hughes	Logan	Connor M*	Greaves	Gilchrist J 1	Lindfield*
07.11	Salford City (MPC:QF)	A	3-0	Allinson	Senior*	Baird	Kay S	Brady	Hughes	Jones M	Glynn 1*	McCarthy	Gilchrist J 2*	Walker T
11.11	AFC Telford United	H	3-1	Allinson	Senior	Fagbola	Kay S	Hughes	Baird	Glynn*	Jones M*	Greaves 1	Gilchrist J 2*	Logan
14.11	Alfreton Town	H	3-2 o	Allinson	Senior	Fagbola*	Kay S	Baird	Hughes	Glynn 1	Irwin*	Greaves*	Gilchrist J 1	Logan
18.11	Gainsborough Trinity	A	0-1	Allinson	Senior	Corbett	Kay S	Hughes	Baird	Glynn*	Jones M	Greaves	McCarthy	Logan*
25.11	Marine (FAT:Q3)	A	0-1	Allinson	Senior	Corbett	Kay S	Baird	Hughes	Walker T	Jones M*	Greaves	McCarthy*	Lindfield
02.12	Harrogate Town	H	3-2	Allinson	Senior	Walker T*	Fagbola	Hughes	Corbett	Glynn	Kay S	Greaves 2	Irwin*	Lindfield
09.12	Brackley Town	H	1-1	Allinson	Senior	Walker T*	Fagbola	Hughes	Corbett	Glynn*	Kay S	Greaves	Irwin 1	Lindfield
23.12	Spennymoor Town	A	4-4	Allinson	Senior	Walker T*	Corbett	Fagbola 1	Hughes	Glynn*	Irwin	Greaves	McCarthy 2	Lindfield
26.12	Salford City	H	3-2	Allinson	Senior*	Walker T*	Fagbola	Hughes	Corbett 1	Glynn	Irwin	Greaves 1*	McCarthy 1	Lindfield
01.01	Salford City	A	2-2	Allinson	Senior	Walker T	Kay S	Fagbola	Corbett 1	Glynn*	Irwin	Greaves	McCarthy*	Lindfield*
07.01	Southport	H	1-0	Allinson	Senior	Corbett	Kay S	Baird	Fagbola	Glynn	Irwin	Greaves 1*	McCarthy*	Lindfield*
20.01	Blyth Spartans	A	1-1	Allinson	Senior	Wisdom*	Fagbola	Hughes	Corbett	Glynn*	Kay S	Greaves 1	Irwin	Lindfield
23.01	Kidderminster Harriers	A	0-4	Allinson	Senior	Wisdom	Fagbola	Hughes	Corbett ■	Jones M*	Kay S	Greaves*	Irwin*	McCarthy
27.01	Curzon Ashton	H	2-0	Allinson	Senior	Wisdom	Corbett*	Hughes	Baird	Glynn ■	Kay S	McCarthy 1	Irwin 1*	Lindfield*
03.02	Nuneaton Town	A	1-0	Allinson	Senior	Wisdom	Baird	Fagbola*	Hughes	Palmer*	Racchi	Greaves	McCarthy	Lindfield*
09.02	Chorley	H	0-0	Allinson	Senior	Wisdom*	Kay S	Baird	Hughes	Glynn	Racchi*	Greaves	McCarthy	Crawford*
13.02	Hyde United (MPC:SF)	A	1-0	Allinson	Tattum	Higham	Jones M	Fagbola	Baird*	Glynn*	Irwin*	Gilchrist A 1	Crawford	Lindfield
17.02	Stockport County	H	0-1	Allinson	Fagbola	Higham	Kay S	Hughes	Tattum	Glynn	Racchi	McCarthy*	Irwin	Lindfield*
24.02	AFC Telford United	A	0-1	Allinson	Senior	Higham	Kay S	Hughes	Baird	Glynn*	Racchi	Greaves*	Irwin*	King J
10.03	Harrogate Town	A	0-6	Allinson	Senior	Higham	Kay S	Hughes	Baird	Glynn*	Fagbola	Garner G*	King J	Irwin*
17.03	Boston United	A	4-4	Allinson	Senior	Higham	Kay S	Hughes	Baird*	McCarthy*	Racchi*	Greaves	Irwin	Lindfield
20.03	Gainsborough Trinity	H	1-0	Allinson	Senior	Higham	Kay S	Hughes	Fagbola	Crawford*	Irwin*	Greaves*	King J	Lindfield
24.03	Bradford Park Avenue	H	4-0	Allinson	Senior	Higham	Kay S	Hughes	Fagbola	Crawford*	Irwin	Greaves	King J 3*	Lindfield*
31.03	Leamington	A	0-1	Allinson	Senior	Higham	Kay S	Hughes	Fagbola	Glynn*	Racchi ■	Greaves	McCarthy	Garner G
07.04	Tamworth	A	2-0	Allinson	Senior	Higham	Kay S*	Hughes ■	Fagbola	Crawford*	Irwin	Greaves*	Garner G 1	Lindfield
14.04	Darlington	H	1-2	Allinson	Senior	Higham	Kay S 1	Fagbola	Baird	Glynn*	Irwin*	McCarthy	Tattum*	Lindfield
17.04	York City	H	1-0	Allinson	Senior	Higham	Kay S*	Baird	Fagbola	Glynn	Irwin*	McCarthy 1	Racchi*	Lindfield
21.04	Alfreton Town	A	0-1	Allinson	Senior*	Higham	Tattum	Fagbola	Baird	Glynn	Jones M*	Greaves*	Racchi	Gilchrist A
24.04	Trafford (MPC:F)	N	2-2 p	Allinson	Senior 1	Higham*	Kay S 1	Fagbola	Baird	Glynn	Racchi	Gilchrist A*	McCarthy*	Tattum
28.04	North Ferriby United	H	0-2	Allinson	Senior	Fagbola	Kay S*	Hughes	Baird	Simões*	Racchi*	Greaves	Palmer	Tattum

p: won 3-2 on penalties (scored: Greaves, Kay S, Glynn missed: Senior).

APPEARANCES & GOALS

Player	League		FAC & FAT		Other		Totals	
Steve **Affleck**	0 (+1)	0	0	0	0	0	0 (+1)	0
Lloyd **Allinson**	42	0	6	0	3	0	51	0
Sam **Baird**	14 (+1)	0	1	0	3	0	18 (+1)	0
Richie **Baker**	2 (+1)	0	0	0	0	0	2 (+1)	0
Adriano **Basso**	0	0	0	0	0	0	0	0
Danny **Brady**	10 (+2)	0	5	0	1	0	16 (+2)	0
Tom **Brown**	4 (+1)	0	0	0	0	0	4 (+1)	0
Michael **Connor**	8 (+2)	0	4	1	0	0	12 (+2)	1
Zac **Corbett**	15 (+1)	2	6	0	0	0	21 (+1)	2
Jamal **Crawford**	4 (+7)	0	0	0	1	0	5 (+7)	0
Jordan **Fagbola**	35 (+2)	2	4 (+1)	0	2	0	41 (+3)	2
Ashley **Frith**	0	0	0	0	0	0	0	0
Gerard **Garner**	3 (+3)	3	0	0	0	0	3 (+3)	3
Adam **Gilchrist**	1 (+3)	0	0	0	2	1	3 (+3)	1
Jason **Gilchrist**	12 (+1)	11	4 (+1)	2	1	2	17 (+2)	15
Kieran **Glynn**	20 (+6)	1	0 (+1)	0	3	1	23 (+7)	2
Sefton **Gonzales**	2	0	0	0	0	0	2	0
Tom **Greaves**	27 (+12)	8	3 (+3)	2	0 (+1)	0	30 (+16)	10
Luke **Higham**	11	0	0	0	2	0	13	0
James **Hooper**	4 (+5)	1	0 (+1)	0	0	0	4 (+6)	1
Matty **Hughes**	33	0	2 (+1)	0	1 (+1)	0	36 (+2)	0
Steve **Irwin**	24 (+4)	4	5	2	1	0	30 (+4)	6
Mike **Jones**	5 (+8)	0	1 (+1)	0	2	0	8 (+9)	0
Scott **Kay**	35	2	5	0	2	1	42	3
Jeff **King**	4 (+1)	4	0	0	0	0	4 (+1)	4
Tim **Kinsella**	1 (+4)	0	0	0	0	0	1 (+4)	0
Lewis **Lacy**	1	0	0	0	0	0	1	0
Craig **Lindfield**	21 (+9)	8	3 (+1)	1	1 (+1)	0	25 (+11)	9
Joel **Logan**	12 (+2)	0	1 (+3)	1	0 (+1)	0	13 (+6)	1
Nathan **Lowe**	8 (+1)	2	0	0	0	0	8 (+1)	2
Kallum **Mantack**	1	0	3	0	0	0	4	0
Connor **McCarthy**	26 (+9)	6	4 (+1)	3	2	0	32 (+10)	9
Callum **Nicholas**	0 (+1)	0	0 (+1)	0	0	0	0 (+2)	0
Sam **O'Donnell**	0	0	0	0	0	0	0	0
Tyrell **Palmer**	2 (+13)	0	0 (+1)	0	0 (+3)	0	2 (+17)	0
Danny **Racchi**	9 (+3)	0	0	0	1 (+1)	0	10 (+4)	0
Joel **Senior**	32 (+7)	0	4	0	2	1	38 (+7)	1
Elliot **Simões**	1 (+2)	0	0	0	0 (+1)	0	1 (+3)	0
Jason **St Juste**	1	0	0	0	0	0	1	0
Sam **Tattum**	4 (+7)	0	0	0	2	0	6 (+7)	0
Tom **Walker**	9 (+1)	1	2	0	1	0	12 (+1)	1
Danny **Wisdom**	19 (+1)	2	3	0	0	0	22 (+1)	2

Substitutes / Attendance

Substitutes				Attendance
Baker R (11)	Logan (10)	Glynn	Greaves (4)	654
St Juste	Lindfield (11)	Glynn (10)	Greaves (9)	1,602
St Juste	Lindfield (11)	Hooper (10)	Greaves (9)	1,946
Brown T (10)	**Lindfield (7) 1**	Logan	Greaves (9)	1,270
Brady (10)	Lindfield (11)	Logan	Greaves (11)	546
Irwin (10)	Hooper (9)	Logan	Greaves	1,688
Irwin (8)	Hooper (7)	Logan	**Greaves (11) 1**	3,411
Irwin (10)	Corbett	Logan	Greaves (9)	2,380
Irwin	Corbett	Lowe (11)	**Gilchrist J (10) 1**	1,491
Baird	Corbett	Hooper (7)	Kinsella (7)	723
Baird	Corbett	Hooper (9)	Kinsella (7)	1,178
Baird	Lacy	Hooper (10)	Greaves (8) — Jones M — Wisdom	434
Baird	Nicholas (4)	Hughes	Greaves (9) — Jones M — Wisdom	623
Baird	Nicholas (9)	Kinsella (10)	Greaves	1,770
Baird	Nicholas	McCarthy	**Greaves (8) 1** — Jones M — Hughes (5)	3,034
Baird	Nicholas	McCarthy	Fagbola (10) — Jones M (11) — Lindfield	1,688
Connor M (11)	Kinsella (7)	McCarthy	Fagbola	492
Baird	Logan (11)	Gilchrist J (10)	**Lindfield (7) 1** — Jones M — Nicholas	1,451
Fagbola (3)	McCarthy (8)	Gilchrist J	Greaves (11)	1,440
Jones M (9)	Connor M (8)	Kinsella	Frith	1,781
Jones M (8)	Glynn (11)	McCarthy	Frith	4,072
Logan (8)	Palmer (10)	Lindfield (2)	Greaves	714
Irwin (7)	Palmer (8)	Lindfield	McCarthy (10)	2,079
Walker T	Palmer (8)	Lindfield (9)	McCarthy	1,548
Walker T (9)	Palmer (7)	Lindfield (11)	Wisdom	782
Affleck	Palmer (8)	Glynn (10)	Wisdom	778
Jones M	Palmer (7)	McCarthy (11)	Wisdom (3)	2,394
Jones M	Palmer (7)	McCarthy (11)	Logan (3)	1,893
Jones M (3)	Palmer (11)	Tattum (7)	Affleck	795
Jones M (9)	Palmer	Tattum (2)	Affleck	3,041
Jones M	Palmer (7)	Tattum	Gilchrist A (10)	2,937
Jones M	Palmer (11)	Crawford (10)	Gilchrist A (9)	2,863
Jones M	Palmer (7)	Crawford (3)	McCarthy	985
Glynn (9)	Palmer (10)	Crawford (7)	Lindfield	1,375
Jones M (10)	Palmer (11)	Crawford (4)	Greaves	2,140
Jones M (7)	Gilchrist A	Crawford (11)	Basso	730
Jones M	Palmer (8)	Fagbola (3)	Lindfield	2,286
Hughes (6)	Palmer (7)	Racchi (8)	McCarthy	497
Jones M	Palmer	Gilchrist A (9)	Baird named at no.6 but injured prior to kick-off	3,084
Lindfield (7)	McCarthy (8)	Crawford (10)	Basso	1,186
Lindfield (11)	McCarthy	Crawford	Greaves (9)	1,547
Glynn	**Garner G (8) 1**	Crawford (6)	**King J (7) 1**	1,053
Glynn	Garner G (7)	McCarthy (9)	Basso	1,558
Glynn (11)	**Garner G (7) 1**	McCarthy (10)	Tattum	2,084
Simões	O'Donnell	Crawford	Tattum (7)	1,005
Simões	Glynn (7)	McCarthy (9)	Tattum (4)	962
Simões (8)	Racchi (7)	Gilchrist A	Greaves (10)	2,269
Simões	Tattum (4)	Jones M (8)	Greaves (10)	1,816
Simões (9)	Affleck (2)	Palmer (8)	O'Donnell	911
Simões (9)	Affleck	Palmer (3)	Greaves (10)	1,003
Higham	Affleck	Glynn (7)	McCarthy (8)	2,580

League Table

	Team	Pld	W	D	L	F	A	GD	Pts
1	Salford City ↑	42	28	7	7	80	45	+35	91
2	Harrogate Town ↑	42	26	7	9	100	49	+51	85
3	Brackley Town	42	23	11	8	72	37	+35	80
4	Kidderminster Harriers	42	20	12	10	76	50	+26	72
5	Stockport County	42	20	9	13	75	57	+18	69
6	Chorley	42	18	14	10	52	39	+13	68
7	Bradford Park Avenue	42	18	9	15	66	56	+10	63
8	Spennymoor Town	42	18	9	15	71	67	+4	63
9	Boston United	42	16	16	10	67	66	+1	60
10	Blyth Spartans	42	19	2	21	76	69	+7	59
11	York City	42	16	10	16	65	62	+3	58
12	Darlington	42	14	13	15	58	58	0	55
13	Nuneaton Town	42	14	13	15	50	57	-7	55
14	AFC Telford United	42	16	5	21	55	69	-14	53
15	Southport	42	14	8	20	60	72	-12	50
16	FC UNITED OF MANCHESTER	42	14	8	20	58	72	-14	50
17	Alfreton Town	42	14	7	21	67	71	-4	49
18	Curzon Ashton	42	12	13	17	52	66	-14	49
19	Leamington	42	13	10	19	51	65	-14	49
20	Gainsborough Trinity ↓	42	14	4	24	47	73	-26	46
21	Tamworth ↓	42	11	9	22	55	77	-22	42
22	North Ferriby United ↓	42	4	9	29	25	101	-76	21

53°31'00"N 02°10'49"W

o Opposition Own Goal for FC United:
Tom **Platt** | 14/11/2017 | FC's 3rd v Alfreton Town (NLN) | H 3-2

FC United goals listed first.　　All games League unless stated otherwise:
FAC FA Cup　　**FAT** FA Trophy　　**MPC** Manchester FA Premier Cup
H Played at Broadhurst Park (FC United Of Manchester)
N Played at Ewen Fields (Hyde United FC)　　p Decided on penalties
* Player Substituted　　(2) Substituted player's number　　Goalscorers in **bold**
■ Player Sent off　　(+1) Number of substitute appearances

NATIONAL LEAGUE NORTH

Date	Opponents	Venue	Score	1	2	3	4	5	6	7	8	9	10	11
04.08	Stockport County	A	1-5	Crellin	Senior*	O'Halloran	Barnes*	Baird	Lynch	Banister	Winter	Dickinson*	**Willoughby 1**	Logan
07.08	Ashton United	H	3-4	Crellin	Tattum	O'Halloran	Racchi	Ashworth	Lynch	Crawford*	**Winter 1**	Dickinson*	**Willoughby 1**	**Banister**
11.08	Boston United	H	0-3	Crellin	Senior	O'Halloran	Racchi	Ashworth	Lynch*	Crawford	Simões	Greaves	Willoughby	Tattum*
14.08	Altrincham	A	2-1	Crellin	Tattum	O'Halloran	Kay S	Baird	Lynch	Crawford	Racchi	**Dickinson 1**	**Willoughby 1**	Greaves*
25.08	Leamington	H	0-2	Crellin	Tattum	O'Halloran	Kay S	Lynch	Baird	Crawford*	Racchi*	Dickinson	Willoughby	Litchfield
27.08	Spennymoor Town	A	0-2	Crellin	Tattum	O'Halloran	Kay S	Lynch	Baird	Banister*	Winter*	Greaves	Willoughby	Logan*
02.09	Bradford Park Avenue	H	2-2	Crellin	Senior*	Logan*	O'Halloran	Ashworth	Lynch	Kay S	Baird*	**Willoughby 1**	**Litchfield 1**	Donohue
08.09	Southport	H	1-1	Carnell	Tattum	Thompson	Baird	Lynch*	O'Halloran	Jones M	Kay S	Mansell*	**Willoughby 1**	Donohue
11.09	Chester	A	0-0	Carnell	Tattum	Thompson	Baird	Priestley B	O'Halloran	Jones M	Kay S	Mansell*	Willoughby	Donohue
15.09	Guiseley	A	0-3	Carnell	Senior	Thompson*	Baird	Priestley B	O'Halloran	Jones M	Kay S	Winter*	Willoughby	Litchfield
22.09	Colne (FAC:Q2)	H	2-0	Carnell	Lynch	Thompson	Kay S	Priestley B	O'Halloran	Logan*	Winter	**Willoughby 1***	**Donohue 1**	Banister*
29.09	Nuneaton Borough	A	0-1	Carnell	Lynch*	Thompson	Jones M	Priestley B*	O'Halloran	Crawford	Winter	Willoughby	Donohue	Brierley*
06.10	Witton Albion (FAC:Q3)	H	1-2	Carnell*	Tattum	Thompson	Jones M	Lynch	O'Halloran	Crawford*	Winter ■	Willoughby ■	Donohue*	**Banister**
09.10	Glossop North End (MPC:1)	A	2-0	Perrin	Senior	Lonsdale	Jones M	Palinkas	O'Halloran	**Simões 2**	Brierley*	Mansell	Donohue	Banister*
13.10	Darlington	H	1-2	Perrin	Senior*	Thompson	Jones M*	Lynch	O'Halloran	Tattum ■	**Brierley 1***	Mansell ■	Donohue	Banister
20.10	Kidderminster Harriers	A	2-1	Allinson	Senior	Thompson	O'Halloran	Lynch	Lonsdale	Healey*	Brierley	Simões*	Donohue	**Banister**
27.10	Brackley Town	H	1-1	Allinson	Senior	Thompson	O'Halloran	Priestley B	**Potts 1**	Simões	Wallen	Mansell*	Donohue	Banister*
30.10	Alfreton Town	H	1-1	Allinson	Senior	Thompson	O'Halloran	Lynch	Potts	Simões*	**Wallen 1**	Mansell	Willoughby	Donohue*
03.11	Blyth Spartans	A	3-0	Allinson	Senior	Thompson	O'Halloran	Lynch	Potts	Simões*	Wallen	**Peers 1***	**Willoughby 1**	Donohue*
10.11	Hereford	A	3-1 o	Allinson	Senior	Thompson	O'Halloran	Lynch	Potts	Simões*	Wallen	**Peers 1***	**Willoughby 1**	Donohue*
13.11	Mossley (MPC:QF)	A	2-0 ‡	Allinson	Senior	Thompson	Palinkas	Lynch	Milligan*	Banister	Winter	Willoughby 1	Donohue*	**White R 1**
17.11	AFC Telford United	H	1-2	Allinson	Senior	Thompson	O'Halloran	Lynch	Potts	Simões	Wallen	**Peers 1**	Willoughby*	White R*
24.11	Hereford (FAT:Q3)	A	1-3	Allinson	Senior	White R	O'Halloran	Lynch	Potts*	Simoes	Wallen	Peers*	Willoughby	**Banister**
01.12	York City	A	0-2	Allinson	Senior	Richards	O'Halloran	Lynch	Potts	Simões	Wallen*	Peers*	Willoughby	Roache*
08.12	Curzon Ashton	H	2-0	Allinson	Senior	Richards	O'Halloran	Lynch	Potts	Simões*	**Wallen 1**	Peers	**Willoughby 1***	Donohue*
22.12	Leamington	A	2-2	Allinson	Senior	Richards	O'Halloran	Lynch	Potts	Peers*	**Wallen 1**	Sharp	**Willoughby 1**	Donohue*
26.12	Chorley	H	1-4	Allinson	Senior	Richards	O'Halloran	**Lynch 1**	Potts	Simões	Wallen	Sharp*	Willoughby	Donohue*
29.12	Spennymoor Town	H	1-3	Allinson	Senior	Richards	O'Halloran	Lynch*	**Potts 1**	Peers ■	Wallen*	Sharp	Winter	Donohue*
01.01	Chorley	A	0-4	Allinson	Palinkas*	Richards	O'Halloran	Lynch	Potts	Simões*	Winter	Peers	Willoughby	Donohue ■
05.01	Chester	H	0-2	Allinson	Morton	Richards*	O'Halloran	Lynch	Wallen*	Simões	Winter	Sharp	Willoughby	Banister
12.01	Bradford Park Avenue	A	3-2	Allinson	Morton	O'Halloran	Mohammed	Sass-Davies	Wallen	Simões*	Winter	**Willoughby 1**	**Sharp 1***	**Banister 1**
19.01	Ashton United	A	0-1	Allinson	Morton*	O'Halloran	Mohammed	Sass-Davies	Wallen*	Whitham*	Winter	Willoughby	Sharp	Banister
26.01	Stockport County	H	1-2	Allinson	Senior	O'Halloran*	Mohammed	Sass-Davies	Wallen*	Donohue*	Winter	**Willoughby 1**	Whitham	Banister
02.02	Boston United	A	1-2	Allinson	Morton	O'Halloran*	Mohammed	Sass-Davies	Wallen	Banister*	Whitham	Willoughby	**Sharp 1***	Donohue
09.02	Altrincham	H	1-2	Fisher A	Morton	Harris*	Mohammed	Sass-Davies	Winter*	Donohue	**Whitham 1**	Willoughby	Myers*	Peers
16.02	Guiseley	H	3-3	Fisher A	Morton	O'Halloran	Mohammed*	Sass-Davies	Lynch	Banister	Whitham	**Willoughby 2**	Sharp*	Winter*
23.02	Southport	A	0-0	Fisher A	Morton	O'Halloran	Harris	Sass-Davies	Lynch	Peers	Wallen	Willoughby	Whitham	Donohue*
02.03	Hereford	H	2-2	Fisher A	Morton	O'Halloran	Harris*	Sass-Davies	Lynch	Peers	Wallen	**Willoughby 1**	Whitham*	**Sharp 1***
09.03	AFC Telford United	A	3-1	Fisher A	Morton	O'Halloran	Mohammed	Lynch	Winter	Banister*	Wallen	**Willoughby 1***	Donohue*	McHale*
23.03	Curzon Ashton	A	1-3	Fisher A	Morton	O'Halloran	Mohammed	Lynch	Winter ■	Banister	Wallen	**Willoughby 1***	Donohue*	McHale*
26.03	York City	H	3-3	Fisher A	Morton	O'Halloran	Mohammed	Lynch	Winter	Banister	**Whitham 2***	**Willoughby 1**	Myers*	McHale*
30.03	Nuneaton Borough	H	0-4	Fisher A	Morton*	Harris	Mohammed	O'Halloran	Wallen*	Banister	Whitham	Willoughby	Myers	McHale*
06.04	Darlington	A	0-2	Fisher A	Lynch	O'Halloran	Mohammed	Palinkas	Potts*	Ozono*	Grimshaw J	Willoughby	West*	Peers
13.04	Kidderminster Harriers	H	0-1	Fisher A	Lynch	O'Halloran	Mohammed	Palinkas*	Potts*	Banister	Grimshaw J	Willoughby	Myers	West*
20.04	Alfreton Town	A	3-2	Fisher A	Peers	O'Halloran	Mohammed	**Baird 1**	Potts	Sharp*	Donohue*	**Willoughby 1**	**Myers 1***	Banister
22.04	Blyth Spartans	H	1-2	Fisher A	Peers*	O'Halloran	Mohammed	Baird	Potts	Sharp	Donohue*	Willoughby	Myers*	**Banister 1**
27.04	Brackley Town	A	0-1	Fisher A	Lynch	O'Halloran*	Mohammed	Baird	Potts	Sharp*	Winter	Willoughby	Myers	Jallow*

‡ FC United were removed from the Manchester FA Premier Cup after fielding a player without the requisite international clearance; Mossley were reinstated.

APPEARANCES & GOALS

Player	League		FAC & FAT		Other		Totals	
Steve **Affleck**	0	0	0	0	0	0	0	0
Lloyd **Allinson**	17	0	1	0	1	0	19	0
Luke **Ashworth**	3	0	0	0	0	0	3	0
Sam **Baird**	11 (+1)	1	0	0	0	0	11 (+1)	1
Jack **Banister**	19 (+14)	5	3	2	2	0	24 (+14)	7
Brad **Barnes**	1	0	0	0	0	0	1	0
Theo **Brierley**	3 (+3)	1	0	0	1	0	4 (+3)	1
Dave **Carnell**	4	0	2	0	0	0	6	0
David **Chadwick**	0	0	0	0	0 (+1)	0	0 (+1)	0
Jamal **Crawford**	5 (+11)	0	1 (+1)	0	0 (+2)	0	6 (+14)	0
Billy **Crellin**	7	0	0	0	0	0	7	0
Matt **Dempsey**	0 (+1)	0	0	0	0	0	0 (+1)	0
Liam **Dickinson**	4 (+3)	1	0	0	0	0	4 (+3)	1
Michael **Donohue**	24 (+9)	0	2	1	2	0	28 (+9)	1
Leighton **Egan**	0 (+2)	0	0	0	0 (+1)	0	0 (+3)	0
Andy **Fisher**	13	0	0	0	0	0	13	0
Tom **Greaves**	3 (+2)	0	0	0	0	0	3 (+2)	0
Jack **Grimshaw**	2 (+2)	0	0	0	0	0	2 (+2)	0
Bob **Harris**	4	0	0	0	0	0	4	0
Liam **Healey**	1	0	0	0	0	0	1	0
Josh **Hmami**	0 (+3)	0	0	0	0	0	0 (+3)	0
Salou **Jallow**	1 (+4)	0	0	0	0	0	1 (+4)	0
Mike **Jones**	5	0	1 (+1)	0	1	0	7 (+1)	0
Scott **Kay**	6	0	1	0	0	0	7	0
Henry **Limpitshi**	0 (+3)	0	0	0	0	0	0 (+3)	0
Brodie **Litchfield**	3 (+4)	1	0 (+1)	0	0	0	3 (+5)	1
Joel **Logan**	3 (+5)	0	1	0	0	0	4 (+5)	0
Cole **Lonsdale**	1	0	0	0	1	0	2	0
Chris **Lynch** (263)	31 (+1)	1	3	0	1	0	35 (+1)	1
Lewis **Mansell**	5 (+2)	1	0 (+1)	0	1	0	6 (+3)	1
Dominic **McGiveron**	0 (+3)	0	0	0	0	0	0 (+3)	0
Dominic **McHale**	4	0	1	0	0	0	4	1
Jamie **Milligan**	0 (+1)	0	0 (+1)	0	1	0	1 (+2)	0
Zehn **Mohammed**	15	0	0	0	0	0	15	0
Danny **Morton**	12	0	0	0	0	0	12	0
Louis **Myers**	7 (+3)	1	0	0	0	0	7 (+3)	1
Steve **O'Halloran**	41	0	3	0	1	0	45	0
Will **Ozono**	1 (+1)	0	0	0	0	0	1 (+1)	0
Jan **Palinkas**	3 (+2)	0	0	0	2	0	5 (+2)	0
Tom **Peers**	14 (+7)	5	1	0	0	0	15 (+7)	5
Jordan **Perrin**	1	0	0 (+1)	0	1	0	2 (+1)	0
Michael **Potts**	16 (+1)	2	1	0	0	0	17 (+1)	2
Billy **Priestley**	4	0	1	0	0	0	5	0
Danny **Racchi**	4	0	0	0	0	0	4	0
Caleb **Richards**	7	0	0	0	0	0	7	0
Rowan **Roache**	1	0	0 (+1)	0	0	0	1 (+1)	0
Sulaiman **Sajjad**	0	0	0	0	0	0	0	0
Billy **Sass-Davies**	8	0	0	0	0	0	8	0
Joel **Senior**	17 (+3)	0	1	0	2	0	20 (+3)	0
Chris **Sharp**	12 (+6)	3	0	0	0	0	12 (+6)	3
Elliot **Simões**	13 (+1)	0	1 (+2)	0	1 (+1)	2	15 (+4)	2
Sam **Tattum**	8 (+2)	0	1	0	0	0	9 (+2)	0
Lewis **Thompson**	11	0	2	0	1	0	14	0
Josh **Wallen**	20 (+4)	3	1	0	1	0	22 (+4)	3
Mark **West**	2	0	0	0	0	0	2	0
Ryan **White**	1 (+5)	0	1	0	1	1	3 (+5)	1
Dale **Whitham**	9 (+1)	3	0	0	0	0	9 (+1)	3
Kurt **Willoughby**	38 (+1)	18	3	1	1	1	42 (+1)	20
Harry **Winter**	17 (+3)	1	2	0	0	0	19 (+3)	1

Substitutes / Attendance

					Attendance
attum (2)	Dempsey (4)	Litchfield	Crawford (9)	Greaves	4,693
aird	Senior	Litchfield (11)	Logan (7)	Greaves (9)	1,526
aird (6)	Banister	Litchfield	Dickinson (11)	*Winter named at no.8 but injured prior to kick-off*	1,686
enior (11)	Banister	Litchfield	Ashworth	Palinkas	1,704
enior	Banister	Winter (8)	Logan (11)	Greaves (7)	1,727
fleck	Litchfield (7)	Crawford (8)	Simões (11)	Dickinson	863
fleck	Tattum (2)	Crawford (3)	Simões	Banister (8)	1,814
gan	Litchfield (9)	Crawford	Dickinson	Banister (5)	1,967
gan	Litchfield	Crawford (9)	Dickinson (9)	Banister	2,045
gan (3)	Tattum	Egan (8)	Dickinson (11)	Banister	907
anes M (7)	Tattum	Litchfield (9)	Dickinson	Simões (11) Baird Sajjad	1,130
enior (5)	Tattum	Litchfield (2)	Logan	Banister (11)	638
alinkas	Lonsdale	Simões (7)■	Logan	Mansell (10) Brierley Perrin (1)	1,234
fleck	Tattum	Thompson	Egan (8)	Crawford (11)	385
alinkas (4)	Lonsdale	Grimshaw J	Limpitshi (8)	Crawford (11)	1,978
fleck	Perrin	Egan (7)	Limpitshi (11)	Crawford (9)	1,860
alinkas	Perrin	Brierley	Limpitshi (9)	Crawford (11)	1,858
aird	Lonsdale	Brierley (11)	Banister	Crawford (7)	1,531
aird	Milligan	**Mansell (9) 1**	Banister (11)	Crawford (7)	832
aird	Milligan	Mansell (9)	Banister (7)	Crawford (11)	2,473
aird	Milligan	White R (11)	Brierley (8)	Banister (9)	2,583
alinkas	Sharp (7)	White R (11)	Brierley	Banister (10)	1,645
alinkas	Milligan	White R (11)	Brierley	Banister (7)	725
alinkas	Milligan	White R (7)	Peers (11)	Banister (9)	2,366
alinkas (5)	Milligan	White R (8)	Willoughby (11)	Banister	2,069
Wallen (2)	Milligan	White R	Sharp (7)	Banister	2,021
alinkas	Jallow (3)	Potts	Brierley	Donohue (6)	2,260
alinkas	Senior	Potts (7)	Brierley (11)	Crawford (9)	713
alinkas	Senior (2)	Hmami (6)	McGiveron (7)	Crawford	845
alinkas	Jallow	Hmami (7)	McGiveron (9)	Sharp (3)	2,987
alinkas	Peers (7)	Hmami (3)	McGiveron (10)	Crawford	1,071
ynch (3)	Allinson	Wallen (6)	McGiveron	Sharp (10)	2,215
enior	Allinson	Wallen (11)	Donohue (4)	**Peers (10) 1**	1,775
Mohammed	Allinson	Winter	Banister (11)	Sharp	1,665
Mohammed	Allinson	Winter (10)	Banister (4)	Donohue (11)	2,058
rimshaw J (7)	Allinson	Myers (9)	Sharp	**Peers (11) 1**	1,672
arris	Whitham (10)	Myers (9)	Sharp	Peers (11)	1,075
arris	Wallen (8)	Donohue (11)	Sharp (10)	Peers	1,670
ynch	Grimshaw J	Donohue (11)	Sharp (6)	Peers (2)	1,697
Wallen	Banister (7)	Donohue (10)	Sharp	Myers (6)	1,407
eers	Ozono (6)	Donohue (11)	Sharp	Jallow (5)	1,760
ogan (10)	Ozono	Grimshaw J (8)	Limpitshi	Jallow (7)	743
ogan (2)	Lynch	Grimshaw J	Winter (8)	Jallow (10)	1,971
ogan	Peers (3)	Grimshaw J	Banister (11)	Donohue (7)	945

League Table

	Team	Pld	W	D	L	F	A	GD	Pts
1	Stockport County ↑	42	24	10	8	77	36	+41	82
2	Chorley ↑	42	24	9	9	83	41	+42	81
3	Brackley Town	42	22	11	9	72	40	+32	77
4	Spennymoor Town	42	22	10	10	78	48	+30	76
5	Altrincham	42	20	11	11	85	56	+29	71
6	Blyth Spartans	42	20	9	13	74	62	+12	69
7	Bradford Park Avenue	42	18	11	13	71	61	+10	65
8	AFC Telford United	42	17	14	11	64	55	+9	65
9	Chester	42	17	11	14	60	62	−2	62
10	Kidderminster Harriers	42	17	9	16	68	62	+6	60
11	Boston United	42	17	7	18	62	60	+2	58
12	York City	42	16	10	16	58	63	−5	58
13	Leamington	42	13	15	14	57	60	−3	54
14	Southport	42	13	14	15	58	55	+3	53
15	Alfreton Town	42	13	12	17	53	67	−14	51
16	Darlington	42	12	14	16	56	62	−6	50
17	Hereford	42	11	16	15	47	58	−11	49
18	Curzon Ashton	42	13	10	19	44	71	−27	49
19	Guiseley	42	9	17	16	46	60	−14	44
20	Ashton United ↓	42	9	8	25	43	86	−43	35
21	**FC UNITED OF MANCHESTER** ↓	42	8	10	24	49	82	−33	34
22	Nuneaton Borough ↓	42	4	7	31	38	96	−58	19

○ Opposition Own Goal for FC United:

Harvey **Smith**	10/11/2018	FC's 2nd v Hereford (NLN)	A 3-1

FC United goals listed first.   All games League unless stated otherwise:

FAC FA Cup   **FAT** FA Trophy   **MPC** Manchester FA Premier Cup
H Played at Broadhurst Park (FC United Of Manchester)   ‡ Removed from cup
* Player Substituted   (2) Substituted player's number   Goalscorers in **bold**
■ Player Sent off   (+1) Number of substitute appearances

NORTHERN PREMIER LEAGUE PREMIER DIVISION 2019/20

Date	Opponents	Venue	Score	1	2	3	4	5	6	7	8	9	10	11
17.08	Grantham Town	A	2-3	Wharton	Morris A	Joyce*	Jones C	Doyle	Potts	Ennis*	Griffiths	**Rodney 1**	Carney*	**Linney 1**
20.08	Hyde United	H	1-2	Wharton	Carney	Joyce	Jones C	Dean T	Potts*	Ennis	Griffiths	Rodney	Lenehan*	**Linney 1**
24.08	Scarborough Athletic	H	0-1	Wharton	Jones C	Dodd	Doyle	Dean T*	Carney	Rodney*	Griffiths	Sharp	Ennis	Linney*
26.08	Radcliffe	A	1-1	Wharton	Jones C	Carney	Doyle	Dean T	Dodd	Lenehan*	Potts	**Linney 1***	Ennis*	Joyce
31.08	Morpeth Town	H	4-2	Wharton	Morris A	Dodd	Jones C	Dean T	Potts	Donohue*	Griffiths	**Owolabi 2***	**Ennis 2**	Linney*
03.09	Lancaster City	A	0-0	Wharton	Morris A	Dodd	Doyle	Dean T	Potts	Donohue	Griffiths ■	Owolabi*	Ennis*	Carney*
07.09	Atherton Collieries (FAC:Q1)	H	2-2	Wharton	Jones C	Dodd	Doyle	**Dean T 2**	Potts	Donohue*	Griffiths*	Owolabi	Ennis*	Linney
10.09	Atherton Collieries (FAC:Q1R)	A	1-0	Wharton	**Morris A 1**	Dodd	Jones C	Doyle	Potts	Donohue*	Lenehan	Owolabi	Linney*	Joyce
14.09	Stafford Rangers	A	0-0	Wharton	Morris A	Dodd	Jones C	Doyle	Potts	Donohue*	Lenehan*	Owolabi	Linney	Curran*
21.09	Warrington Town (FAC:Q2)	H	1-2	Wharton	Morris A	Dodd	Doyle	Dean T	Jones C	Rodney	Potts*	Owolabi	**Linney 1***	Carney*
24.09	Warrington Town	A	1-0	Wharton	Morris A	Dodd	Doyle	Dean T	Jones C	Babos*	Potts	Owolabi*	**Buckley 1**	Curran
28.09	Bamber Bridge	H	1-0	Wharton	Morris A	Dodd	Potts	Dean T*	Jones C	Babos	Curran	**Owolabi 1***	Buckley*	Linney
01.10	South Shields	H	0-2	Wharton	Morris A	Dodd	Doyle	Dean T*	Jones C	Babos*	Potts	Owolabi	Curran	Linney*
05.10	Stalybridge Celtic	A	3-2	Wharton	Morris A	Dodd	Griffiths	Doyle	Jones C	Babos*	Potts	**Owolabi 1**	Buckley*	Curran*
08.10	Radcliffe (MPC:1)	A	2-2 p¹	Belford	Barthram*	Joyce	Griffiths	Dean T	Jones C	**Rodney 1***	Lenehan	Buckley	**Donohue 1**	Ennis*
12.10	Buxton	H	7-0	Belford	Morris A	Dodd	Griffiths	Doyle	Jones C	Babos	Potts	**Owolabi 4***	**Buckley 1***	**Curran 1***
15.10	Basford United	H	1-3	Belford	Morris A	Dodd	Griffiths	Doyle	Jones C	Babos*	Potts	**Owolabi 1**	Buckley*	Ennis*
19.10	Atherton Collieries	A	3-2	Belford	Morris A	Dodd	Griffiths	Doyle	Jones C	Curran*	**Potts 1**	**Owolabi 1**	Buckley*	**Linney 1***
29.10	Radcliffe (FAT:Q1)	A	2-0	Belford	Morris A	Dodd	Griffiths	Doyle*	Jones C	Donohue	Potts*	**Owolabi 1**	Buckley*	**Linney 1**
02.11	Gainsborough Trinity	H	2-2	Belford	Morris A	Dodd	Lenehan*	Doyle	Jones C	Curran*	Potts	**Owolabi 1**	**Buckley 1***	Linney
09.11	Basford United (FAT:Q2)	H	3-1	Belford	Morris A	Dodd	Griffiths*	Doyle	Jones C	**Donohue 1***	Potts	Owolabi	**Ennis 1**	Linney*
12.11	Hyde United (MPC:QF)	A	3-0	Belford	Young	**Dodd 1**	Griffiths	Doyle	Jones C	Morris A	Lenehan	**Owolabi 1***	Curran*	Linney*
16.11	Witton Albion	A	3-3	Belford	Morris A	**Dodd 2**	Griffiths	Doyle	Jones C	Donohue*	**Potts 1**	Owolabi	Ennis*	Linney*
19.11	Glossop North End (LCC:1)	H	2-2 p²	Belford	Young*	**Dodd 1**	Griffiths	Doyle	Morris A	Curran	Lenehan	Buckley*	Ennis	**Linney 1**
23.11	Runcorn Linnets (FAT:Q3)	A	3-0	Belford	Morris A	**Dodd 1**	Griffiths	Doyle	Jones C	Donohue*	Potts	**Owolabi 2**	Curran*	Linney*
30.11	Lancaster City	H	3-2	Belford	Morris A	Dodd	Griffiths*	**Doyle 1**	Jones C	**Ennis 2***	Potts	Owolabi	Curran	Linney*
07.12	Matlock Town	H	5-2	Belford	Morris A	Dodd	Griffiths	**Doyle 1**	Jones C	Ennis*	Potts	**Owolabi 3***	Curran	**Linney 1***
14.12	Kettering Town (FAT:1)	H	2-1	Belford	Morris A	Dodd	Donohue*	Doyle	Jones C	Ennis*	Potts	**Owolabi 2**	Curran*	Linney
21.12	Grantham Town	H	4-0	Belford	**Morris A 1**	Dodd	Griffiths	Doyle	Jones C	Ennis*	**Potts 1***	**Owolabi 2**	Curran*	Linney
28.12	Ashton United	A	2-1	Belford	Morris A	Sikora	Griffiths	Doyle	Jones C	Ennis*	Potts*	Owolabi	Curran*	**Linney 1**
01.01	Radcliffe	H	3-2 o	Belford	Morris A	Dodd	Griffiths	Doyle	Jones C	S-Smith	**Potts 1**	**Owolabi 1***	Curran*	Linney*
04.01	Hyde United	A	5-1	Belford	Morris A	Dodd	Griffiths*	Doyle	**Jones C 1**	S-Smith*	Potts*	**Owolabi 2**	Curran	**Linney 2**
11.01	Barrow (FAT:2)	A	0-7	Belford	Morris A	Dodd	Griffiths	Doyle ■	Jones C	Ennis*	Potts*	Owolabi	Curran*	Linney
18.01	Whitby Town	A	2-1	Belford	Morris A	Dodd	Griffiths*	Lacy	Jones C	**Curran 1**	Potts	Owolabi	Lenehan*	Linney*
21.01	Sheffield (LCC:2)	H	1-2	Belford	Kerr	Dodd	Donohue*	Doyle	Lacy	S-Smith	Lenehan	Hawley*	Curran*	Ennis*
25.01	Buxton	A	2-2	Belford	Morris A	Dodd	Griffiths	Doyle	Jones C*	S-Smith*	Potts	Owolabi	Curran*	**Linney 1**
01.02	Mickleover Sports	H	3-3	Belford	Morris A	Dodd	Griffiths	Doyle	Elsdon	Ennis*	Potts	**Owolabi 1**	**H-Smith 1***	Linney*
04.02	Irlam (MPC:SF)	H	2-1	Belford	Donohue	Dodd	Griffiths	Morris A	Elsdon	**S-Smith 1**	Lenehan	Owolabi*	**Ennis 1***	H-Smith*
08.02	Basford United	A	1-1	Belford	Morris A	Dodd	Griffiths	Doyle	Elsdon	**Ennis 1***	Potts	Owolabi	Donohue*	Linney ■
18.02	Stafford Rangers	H	2-1	Belford	Morris A	Dodd	**Griffiths 1**	Doyle	Elsdon	Hawley*	Potts	Owolabi	Donohue*	S-Smith*
22.02	Bamber Bridge	A	0-3	Belford	Morris A	Dodd	Griffiths*	Elsdon	Jones C	Ennis*	Potts	Owolabi	T-Smith	Linney*
25.02	Nantwich Town	A	1-0	Belford	Kerr*	Dodd	**Morris A 1**	Doyle	Jones C	H-Smith*	Potts	Owolabi	Griffiths	Linney*
29.02	Warrington Town	H	4-4	Belford	Morris A	Dodd	Elsdon*	Doyle	**Jones C 1**	**H-Smith 1***	Potts	**Owolabi 1**	Griffiths	**Ennis 1***
07.03	Mickleover Sports	A	4-0	Belford	Morris A	**Dodd 1**	Griffiths	Doyle	Jones C	H-Smith*	Potts	**Owolabi 3***	T-Smith*	Ennis
14.03	South Shields	A	3-5	Belford	Morris A	Dodd	Griffiths	Doyle	Jones C	Ennis*	Potts	**Owolabi 3**	Donohue*	Linney*

p¹: won 4-2 on penalties (**scored**: Donohue, Griffiths, Curran, Lenehan, **missed**: none). p²: won 6-5 on penalties (**scored**: Ennis, Dodd, Linney, Morris A, Lenehan, Curran **missed**: Griffiths, Owolabi, Potts).

FC United goals listed first. | All games League unless stated otherwise:
FAC FA Cup | **FAT** FA Trophy | **MPC** Manchester FA Premier Cup
LCC Integro League Challenge Cup | **p** Decided on penalties
H Played at Broadhurst Park (FC United Of Manchester)
* Player Substituted | (2) Substituted player's number | Goalscorers in **bold**
■ Player Sent off | (+1) Number of substitute appearances

Due to the COVID-19 pandemic, the 2019/20 Northern Premier League competition was initially suspended on 16 March 2020 and formally abandoned on 26 March 2020, with all results from the season being officially expunged, and no promotion or relegation taking place to, from, or within the divisions. The 2020/21 Northern Premier League competition was suspended on 5 November 2020 and officially curtailed on 24 February 2021. On 13 October 2020, FC United were granted a walkover in the FA Cup third qualifying round after Alfreton Town were forced to withdraw from the fixture at Broadhurst Park due to a positive COVID-19 test within their squad.

NORTHERN PREMIER LEAGUE PREMIER DIVISION 2020/21

Date	Opponents	Venue	Score	1	2	3	4	5	6	7	8	9	10	11
19.09	Nantwich Town	H	1-1	Lavercombe	Lenehan	Dodd	Donohue	Doyle	Jones C	S-Smith*	Potts	Fowler	H-Smith*	Linney
22.09	Pontefract Collieries (FAC:Q1)	H	6-2	Lavercombe	**Morris A 1**	Dodd*	Griffiths	Doyle*	Stead	**Ennis 2**	Potts	**Cockerline 1***	**Donohue 1**	**Linney 1**
26.09	Scarborough Athletic	H	0-0	Lavercombe	Morris A	Dodd	Griffiths ■	Doyle	Jones C	Ennis*	Potts	Fowler*	Donohue	Linney*
29.09	Hyde United	H	2-2	Lavercombe	Morris A	Dodd	Griffiths	Doyle	Jones C	H-Smith*	Potts*	Cockerline	Donohue*	**Linney 1**
03.10	Curzon Ashton (FAC:Q2)	A	2-1	Lavercombe	Morris A	Dodd	Donohue	Doyle	Jones C	Penfold*	Potts	Fowler*	**Ennis 1**	**Linney 1***
17.10	Stafford Rangers	H	2-1	Lavercombe	Morris A	Dodd	Donohue	Doyle	Jones C	S-Smith*	Potts	**Cockerline 1**	Ennis*	Linney*
20.10	Lancaster City	H	1-1	Lavercombe	Morris A	Dodd	H-Smith*	Doyle	Jones C	S-Smith*	Potts	Fowler*	**Cockerline 1**	Linney
24.10	Guiseley (FAC:Q4)	H	2-1	Lavercombe	Morris A	Dodd	Griffiths	Doyle	Jones C	**Ennis 1***	Potts	Cockerline*	Simpson*	Linney
27.10	South Shields	A	0-1	Lavercombe	Morris A	Dodd	Griffiths*	Doyle	Jones C	Pemberton*	Potts	Fowler	Simpson*	S-Smith
31.10	Marske United (FAT:Q3)	H	2-3	Lavercombe	Morris A	Dodd	Griffiths	Woods	**Jones C 1**	Pemberton*	Donohue	**Fowler 1**	Ennis*	S-Smith
03.11	Warrington Town	H	3-1	Lavercombe	Donohue	Dodd	Griffiths ■	Morris A	**Jones C 1**	Pemberton*	Simpson	Fowler*	Ennis	**S-Smith 2***
07.11	Doncaster Rovers (FAC:1)	H	1-5	Lavercombe	Donohue	Dodd	Griffiths	Doyle	Jones C	Ennis*	Potts	**Linney 1**	Simpson*	S-Smith*

APPEARANCES & GOALS 2019/20

Player	League		FAC & FAT		Other		Totals	
Alex Babos	6	0	0	0	0	0	6	0
Jack Barthram	0	0	0	0	1	0	1	0
Cameron Belford	21	0	5	0	5	0	31	0
Jordan Buckley	7 (+5)	3	1 (+2)	0	2 (+1)	0	10 (+8)	3
Craig Carney	5 (+3)	0	1 (+2)	0	0	0	6 (+5)	0
Larnell Cole	0 (+1)	0	0	0	0	0	0 (+1)	0
Alex Curran	16 (+1)	2	3	0	3 (+1)	0	22 (+2)	2
Tom Dean	7	0	2	2	1	0	10	2
Adam Dodd	29	3	8	1	4	2	41	6
Michael Donohue	7 (+11)	1	6 (+2)	1	4	1	17 (+13)	3
Chris Doyle	28	2	8	0	3	0	39	2
Matty Elsdon	5 (+1)	0	0	0	1	0	6 (+1)	0
Paul Ennis	18 (+10)	10	4 (+3)	1	4 (+1)	2	26 (+14)	13
Luke Griffiths	26 (+4)	1	5	0	4 (+1)	0	35 (+5)	1
Rhain Hellawell	0 (+4)	0	0 (+1)	0	0	0	0 (+5)	0
Kyle Hawley	1 (+3)	0	1	0	1 (+1)	0	2 (+4)	1
Curtis Jones	28	2	8	0	2	0	38	2
James Joyce	3 (+2)	0	1	0	1	0	5 (+2)	0
Ben Kerr	1	0	0	0	1	0	2	0
Lewis Lacy	1	0	0	0	1	0	2	0
Jack Lenehan	5 (+17)	0	1 (+6)	0	5	0	11 (+23)	0
Regan Linney	24 (+5)	9	8	2	2 (+3)	1	34 (+8)	12
Aaron Morris	29	2	7	1	2	0	38	3
Louis Myers	0 (+2)	0	0 (+1)	0	0 (+1)	1	0 (+4)	1
Tunde Owolabi	28	27	8	6	2 (+3)	1	38 (+3)	34
Michael Potts	31 (+1)	4	8	0	0 (+2)	0	39 (+3)	4
Nialle Rodney	3 (+2)	1	1 (+1)	0	1	1	5 (+3)	2
Chris Sharp	1 (+5)	0	0 (+1)	0	0	0	1 (+6)	0
Jorge Sikora	1	0	0	0	0	0	1	0
Daniel T-Smith	2 (+3)	0	0	0	0	0	2 (+3)	0
Finlay S-Smith	4 (+8)	1	0 (+1)	0	2	1	6 (+9)	2
Morgan H-Smith	4 (+3)	3	0	0	1	0	5 (+3)	3
Paddy Wharton	11	0	3	0	0	0	14	0
Ashley Young	0 (+2)	0	0 (+3)	0	2	0	2 (+5)	0

o Opposition Own Goal for FC United:
Javid **Swaby-Neavin** 01/01/2020 FC's 2nd v Radcliffe (NPLP) H 3-2

Unused substitutes: Dylan **Blackledge** Josh **Brooks** Sandro **Da Costa**
Lenny **Fieldhouse** Mason **Walker** Keaton **Ward**

APPEARANCES & GOALS 2020/21

Player	League		FAC & FAT		Other		Totals	
David Chadwick	0 (+1)	0	0	0	0	0	0 (+1)	0
Dan Cockerline	3 (+3)	2	2 (+3)	1	0	0	5 (+6)	3
Kain Dean	0	0	0 (+1)	0	0	0	0 (+1)	0
Adam Dodd	7	0	5	0	0	0	12	0
Michael Donohue	5 (+1)	0	4	1	0	0	9 (+1)	1
Chris Doyle	6	0	4	0	0	0	10	0
Paul Ennis	3 (+3)	1	5	4	0	0	8 (+3)	5
Michael Fowler	5 (+2)	2	2 (+3)	1	0	0	7 (+5)	3
Luke Griffiths	4	0	4	0	0	0	8	0
Curtis Jones	7	1	4	1	0	0	11	2
Dan Lavercombe	7	0	5	0	0	0	12	0
Jack Lenehan	1 (+2)	0	0 (+1)	0	0	0	1 (+3)	0
Regan Linney	5	1	4	3	0	0	9	4
Aaron Morris	6	0	4 (+1)	0	0	0	10 (+1)	1
Tre Pemberton	2	0	1	0	0	0	3	0
Morgan Penfold	0 (+3)	0	1 (+1)	0	0	0	1 (+4)	0
Michael Potts	6	0	4	0	0	0	10	0
Jordan Simpson	2	0	2	0	0	0	4	0
Finlay S-Smith	5	2	2 (+2)	1	0	0	7 (+2)	3
Morgan H-Smith	3 (+3)	0	0 (+2)	0	0	0	3 (+5)	0
Tom Stead	0	0	1	0	0	0	1	0
Joe White	0 (+2)	0	0	0	0	0	0 (+2)	0
Calum Woods	0	0	1	0	0	0	1	0

Substitutes (2019/20)

						Attendance
...ehan (10)	Hellawell (3)	Myers (7)	Sharp	Walker M		810
...rris A	Hellawell (6)	Doyle	Sharp (10)	Walker M		1,811
...rris A	Hellawell (7)	Joyce (11)	Potts (5)	Lenehan	Donohue	1,532
...rris A	Hellawell	Griffiths (7)	Rodney (9)	Sharp (10)		1,228
...rce	Dean T	Lenehan (7)	Carney (11)	Sharp (9)		1,434
...rce	Jones C	Lenehan (11)	Linney (9)	Sharp (9)		522
...rce	Carney (10)	Lenehan	Hellawell (8)	Rodney (7)	Walker M Morris A	1,216
...an T	Carney (10)	Ennis (7)	Hellawell	Rodney	Walker M	947
...an T	Carney (8)	Blackledge	Hellawell (7)	Rodney (11)		936
...nohue (11)	Lenehan (8)	Blackledge	Hellawell	Belford	Sharp (10) Joyce	1,263
...nohue	Lenehan	Griffiths (7)	Linney (9)	Belford		702
...nohue (9)	Lenehan	Griffiths (10)	Carney (5)	Belford		1,543
...rce	Lenehan (11)	Griffiths (7)	Buckley (5)	Belford		1,349
...rce (11)	Lenehan (7)	**Ennis (10) 2**	Rodney	Belford		1,188
...dd	Doyle	Curran (2)	Owolabi (7)	Linney (11)		461
...nohue (9)	Lenehan	**Ennis (11) 1**	Rodney	Linney (10)		1,888
...nohue (10)	Lenehan (7)	Walker M	Rodney	Linney (9)	Curran injured in warm-up	1,402
...nohue	Lenehan (10)	Ennis (11)	Babos	Sharp (7)		1,019
...ung (8)	Lenehan (5)	Ennis (10)	Myers	Walker M		523
...ung	Donohue (4)	Ennis (10)	Myers (7)	Walker M		1,614
...ung (4)	Lenehan (11)	Buckley	Myers (7)	Walker M		907
...orris A	Potts	Buckley (7)	**Myers (11) 1**	Ennis (10)		277
...ung (11)	Lenehan	Buckley (7)	Curran (10)	Walker M		933
...nes C	Potts (2)	Owolabi (9)	Kerr	Walker M		372
...ung	Lenehan (7)	Buckley (11)	Kerr	Walker M	Ennis (10)	962
...ung (4)	Lenehan (11)	Donohue (7)	Kerr	Walker M		1,873
...ung	Lenehan (11)	Donohue (7)	Buckley (9)	Walker M		1,574
...ung (4)	Lenehan (10)	Kerr	Buckley (7)	Walker M		1,218
...kora	Lenehan	Donohue (8)	Buckley (7)	S-Smith (10)		1,701
...alker M	Lenehan (10)	**Donohue (8) 1**	Buckley	S-Smith (7)		1,502
...kora	Lenehan (10)	Donohue	Buckley (9)	Ennis (11)		2,124
...err	Lenehan (4)	Donohue (8)	Walker M	Ennis (7)		1,293
...err	Lenehan (8)	Donohue (7)	Hawley	**Hawley (4) 1**	S-Smith (10)	1,892
...err	Ennis (11)	Donohue	**Hawley (4) 1**	S-Smith (10)	Walker M Lacy	936
...orris A	Potts	Griffiths (4)	Owolabi (9)	Linney (10)		462
...err	Lenehan	Donohue (10)	Hawley (7)	**Ennis (6) 1**		1,206
...err	Lenehan (7)	Donohue	Hawley (11)	**S-Smith (10) 1**		1,747
...err	Potts (11)	Doyle	Hawley (9)	Linney (10)		484
...err	Lenehan (10)	H-Smith	Hawley	S-Smith (7)		901
...err	Lenehan (10)	**H-Smith (11) 1**	Ennis (7)	Walker M		1,336
...err	Lenehan (4)	H-Smith (7)	Cole (11)	Walker M		1,014
...sdon (2)	Lenehan	T-Smith (7)	Cole	Ennis (11)		580
...err	Lenehan (11)	T-Smith (4)	Linney	S-Smith (7)		2,088
...sdon	Lenehan	Donohue (10)	Linney (7)	S-Smith (9)		804
...sdon	Ward	T-Smith (10)	H-Smith	H-Smith (11)	S-Smith (7)	3,274

The top of the 2019/20 Premier Division table at the time of abandonment on 26 March:

	Team	Pld	W	D	L	F	A	GD	Pts
1	South Shields	33	21	6	6	64	34	+30	69
2	**FC UNITED OF MANCHESTER**	32	16	9	7	73	51	+22	57
3	Warrington Town	32	14	13	5	57	44	+13	55
4	Basford United	32	16	7	9	49	39	+10	55
5	Lancaster City	34	15	8	11	58	46	+12	53
6	Nantwich Town	31	15	7	9	55	39	+16	52

Unplayed 2019/20 fixtures:
...: Whitby Town, Stalybridge Celtic,
...antwich Town, Ashton United,
...therton Collieries, Witton Albion.
...: Scarborough Athletic,
...ainsborough Trinity, Matlock Town,
...orpeth Town. **N:** Trafford (MPC:F)

Substitutes (2020/21)

						Attendance
...ean K	Morris A	**Ennis (10) 1**	Brooks Jo	Cockerline (7)		547
...ean K (3)	S-Smith	Lenehan (5)	H-Smith	Fowler (9)	Fieldhouse	534
...ean K	Stead	Lenehan (11)	H-Smith (7)	Cockerline (9)		556
...nnis (10)	Stead	Lenehan (8)	S-Smith	**Fowler (7) 1**		600
...ean K	Stead	H-Smith (11)	S-Smith (7)	Cockerline (9)	Brooks Jo Da Costa	0
...ean K	White J	H-Smith (7)	Penfold (11)	**Fowler (10) 1**		600
...ean K (4)	White J	Brooks Jo	Penfold (7)	Ennis (9)		600
...-Smith (10)	White J	**S-Smith (7) 1**	Penfold	Fowler (9)	Brooks Jo Pemberton	600
...-Smith (10)	White J	Donohue (4)	Penfold (7)	Ennis		300
...-Smith	White J	Chadwick	Penfold (7)	Cockerline (10)	Brooks Jo Doyle injured in warm-up	600
...Woods	White J (7)	Chadwick (11)	Brooks Jo	Cockerline (9)		600
...Morris A (10)	White J	Stead	Fowler (11)	Cockerline (7)	Brooks Jo Pemberton	0

NORTHERN PREMIER LEAGUE PREMIER DIVISION

Date	Opponents	Venue	Score	1	2	3	4	5	6	7	8	9	10	11
14.08	Warrington Town	A	0-2	Lavercombe	Morris A	Dodd	Smith J*	Baker D	Jones C	Ennis*	Potts	Waddecar	Main	Linney*
17.08	Morpeth Town	H	3-0	Lavercombe	**Smith J 1**	Dodd	**Simpson 1***	Baker D	Morris A	**Ennis 1***	Potts	Waddecar*	Main	S-Smith
21.08	Buxton	H	1-1	Lavercombe	Smith J	Dodd	Simpson	Baker D	**Morris A 1**	Linney*	Potts	Cooke J*	Main*	S-Smith
24.08	South Shields	A	1-1	Lavercombe	Smith J	Dodd	Jones C*	Baker D	Morris A	Cooke J	Potts	Waddecar*	**Main 1**	S-Smith*
28.08	Hyde United	A	1-2	King L	Smith J	Dodd	Simpson*	Baker D	**Morris A 1**	Cooke J*	Potts	Ennis▪	Main	Linney*
30.08	Radcliffe	H	3-0	King L	Waddecar	**Dodd 1**	Ennis*	Baker D	Morris A	**Rain 1**	Potts	**Cooke J 1**	Main*	S-Smith*
04.09	Bootle (FAC:Q1)	A	2-2	Lavercombe	Rain	Dodd	Simpson*	Baker D	Morris A	S-Smith*	Potts	Waddecar	**Main 2**	Linney
07.09	Bootle (FAC:Q1R)	H	3-2	Lavercombe	Donohue	Dodd	**Rain 1**	Baker D	Morris A	**S-Smith 1**	Potts*	Waddecar*	Main	Pemberto
11.09	Stafford Rangers	H	1-3	Lavercombe	Morris A	Dodd	Donohue*	Baker D	Jones C	**S-Smith 1**	Potts	Cooke J*	Main	Linney
14.09	Bamber Bridge	H	1-0	Lavercombe	Donohue	Dodd	Jones C	Baker D	Morris A	Waddecar*	Potts	**Holmes 1***	Main	Ennis*
18.09	Blyth Spartans (FAC:Q2)	A	1-1	Lavercombe	Donohue*	Dodd	Jones C	Baker D	Morris A	S-Smith*	Potts	Holmes	**Main 1**	Linney*
21.09	Blyth Spartans (FAC:Q2R)	H	0-2	Lavercombe	Jones C*	Rain*	Dodd	Baker D	Morris A	Waddecar*	Potts	Holmes	Main	Ennis
25.09	Stalybridge Celtic	A	2-5	Lavercombe	Donohue	Dodd	Simpson*	Baker D	Morris A	Campbell*	Potts	**Holmes 2**	Main	Linney
28.09	Scarborough Athletic	H	6-0	Lavercombe	Waddecar	Dodd*	Donohue*	Baker D	Morris A	**Ennis 1**	Potts*	**Holmes 1**	**Main 2**	**Linney 1**
02.10	Matlock Town	A	0-1	Lavercombe	Waddecar*	Dodd	Donohue	Baker D	Morris A	Ennis*	Potts	Holmes	Main	Linney
05.10	Basford United	A	1-0	Lavercombe	Donohue	Dodd	Jones C	Baker D	Morris A	Ennis*	**Potts 1**	Holmes*	Main	Linney*
09.10	Nantwich Town	H	0-2	Lavercombe	Donohue*	Dodd	Jones C	Baker D	Morris A	Ennis*	Potts	Holmes*	Main	Linney
12.10	Lancaster City	A	0-1	Lavercombe	Smith J*	Dodd	Jones C	Baker D*	Morris A	Ennis	Potts*	Donohue	Main	Linney
16.10	Grantham Town	H	0-1	Lavercombe	Donohue	Dodd	White J*	Jones C	Morris A	Ennis*	Simpson	Campbell*	Main	Linney
23.10	Witton Albion	A	3-2 o	Lavercombe	Donohue	Dodd	Griffiths	**Baker D 1**	Jones C	Linney	Potts	Burns S*	Smith J*	**Hayes 1***
27.10	AKS Zly (EFT)	A	6-1	Lavercombe*	Donohue	**Dodd 1**	Baker D*	Morris A	Jones C	**Ennis 1***	Potts*	**Burns S 1**	**Holmes 3***	Bennett
30.10	Runcorn Linnets (FAT:Q3)	A	2-0	Lavercombe	Morris A	Dodd	Griffiths	Baker D	Jones C	Linney*	Potts	Waddecar*	**Burns S 1**	Major*
06.11	Gainsborough Trinity	H	3-2	Lavercombe	Morris A	**Dodd 1***	Griffiths	Baker D	Jones C	Hayes*	Potts	Holmes	**Burns S 1**	**Linney 1***
09.11	Whitby Town	A	0-1	Lavercombe	Morris A	Dodd*	Griffiths	Baker D	Jones C	Donohue*	Potts	Holmes*	Burns S	Linney
13.11	Marske United (FAT:1)	A	2-3	Lavercombe	Baker D	White J	Griffiths*	Morris A*	Jones C	Waddecar	Potts*	**Linney 1**	Holmes	**Ennis 1**
20.11	Atherton Collieries	A	1-2	Lavercombe	Donohue	White J*	Griffiths	Baker D	Morris A	Hayes	Smith J	**Holmes 1**	Ennis*	Linney*
27.11	Mickleover	H	2-0	Lavercombe	Donohue	White J*	Smith J	Baker D	**Morris A 1**	**Hayes 1**	Ennis	Waddecar	Holmes*	Linney*
11.12	Stafford Rangers	H		Lavercombe	White A	White J	Smith J	Morris A	Jones C	**Waddecar 2***	Griffiths	Holmes	Duckworth*	Ennis
18.12	Buxton	A	2-1	Lavercombe	Donohue	White A	Smith J	Morris A	**Jones C 1**	Waddecar	Griffiths	Linney	Wilson H*	Ennis
27.12	Ashton United	H	4-3	McMahon	**Donohue 1***	White A	Smith J	Morris A	Baker D	Waddecar	Griffiths	Linney	**Duckworth 2***	**Ennis 1***
01.01	Radcliffe	A	3-3	Lavercombe	Donohue	White A	Smith J	Morris A	Halls	Waddecar	Griffiths	**Linney 2**	Wilson H*	**Duckwort**
15.01	Bamber Bridge	A	0-0	Lavercombe	Halls	Dodd	Smith J	Morris A	Jones C	Waddecar	Griffiths*	Linney	Wilson H*	Donohue
22.01	Stalybridge Celtic	H	2-1	Lavercombe	Halls	Dodd	Smith J	Morris A	Jones C	Waddecar	Potts*	Linney	**Ennis 1***	**Bange 1***
25.01	Whitby Town	H	3-4 o	Lavercombe	Halls	Dodd	**Smith J 1**	**Morris A 1**	Jones C*	Donohue	Griffiths	Linney	Wilson H*	Duckworth
29.01	Grantham Town	A	2-1	Lavercombe	Halls	Dodd*	Smith J	Morris A	Jones C	Waddecar	Potts*	**Linney 1**	Griffiths*	Donohue
05.02	Witton Albion	H	2-0	Lavercombe	Halls	Dodd	Smith J	**Morris A 1**	Jones C	Donohue*	Potts	Linney	Ennis*	**Galloway**
08.02	Lancaster City	H	1-0	Lavercombe	Halls	Dodd	Smith J	Morris A	Jones C*	Waddecar	Griffiths	**Linney 1***	Ennis	Galloway
12.02	Gainsborough Trinity	A	2-3	Lavercombe	Waddecar	Dodd	Smith J	Morris A	Potts	Donohue*	Griffiths	**Linney 2**	Ennis*	Galloway
15.02	Warrington Town	H	0-1	Lavercombe	Donohue*	Dodd	Smith J	Morris A	Halls	Waddecar	Griffiths	Linney	Ennis*	Galloway
19.02	Scarborough Athletic	A	2-2	Lavercombe	Donohue	Dodd	**Griffiths 1**	Morris A	Halls	Galloway*	Potts	**Linney 1**	Ennis	Bange
26.02	Matlock Town	H	1-1	Lavercombe	Morris A	Dodd	Smith J	Halls	Sikora*	**Waddecar 1**	Griffiths	Linney	Ennis*	Bange
05.03	AKS Zly (EFT)	H	10-0	Lavercombe	Donohue	Dodd	Taylor C	Morris A*	Jones C*	**Galloway 1**	Potts	**Linney 3***	**Ennis 1***	**Duckworth**
12.03	Nantwich Town	A	0-2	Lavercombe	Smith J	Dodd	Griffiths*	Morris A	Sikora*	Waddecar*	Potts	Linney	Ennis	Bange
19.03	Basford United	H	3-2	Lavercombe	**Donohue 2**	Dodd	Smith J*	Morris A	Jones C	Galloway*	**Griffiths 1***	Linney	Ennis	Bange
26.03	Mickleover	A	3-3	Lavercombe	Donohue	Dodd	Griffiths*	Morris A	**Jones C 1**	Waddecar*	Potts	**Linney 1**	**Ennis 1**	Taylor C*
02.04	Atherton Collieries	H	2-0	Lavercombe	Morris A	Dodd	Smith J	Sikora	Jones C	Donohue	Potts	**Linney 1**	Ennis	**Askew 1***
06.04	Brera (EFT)	A	3-1	Hamer	**Waddecar 1***	Taylor C	Griffiths*	Morris A*	Sikora	Galloway*	McGee	Duckworth	**Ennis 1***	Bange*
09.04	Morpeth Town	A	0-1	Lavercombe	Donohue	Dodd	Smith J*	Morris A	Jones C	Waddecar*	Potts*	Linney	Ennis	Askew
16.04	South Shields	H	0-1	Lavercombe	Donohue	Dodd	Griffiths	Morris A	Jones C	Askew	Potts	Linney	Ennis*	McGee*
18.04	Ashton United	A	3-0	Lavercombe	Donohue	Dodd	Smith J*	Morris A	Jones C	Galloway	Potts	**Linney 3**	McGee*	Bange*
23.04	Hyde United	H	0-2	Lavercombe	Donohue	Dodd	Griffiths*	Morris A	Jones C	Waddecar*	Potts*	Linney	Ennis	Askew
04.05	Brera (EFT)	H	2-1	Lavercombe	Donohue*	Dodd*	Smith J	Morris A	Taylor C*	Waddecar	Potts*	**Galloway 1**	Ennis	**Askew 1**
11.06	Prague Raptors (EFT:F)	N	2-0	Lavercombe*	Donohue*	Askew	Smith J	McGee*	Jones C	**Waddecar 1***	Potts	Linney	Ennis	**Duckworth**

APPEARANCES & GOALS

Substitutes

substitutes					Attendance
Vhite J	Rain (4)	Simpson (7)	S-Smith (11)	Fieldhouse	1,105
White J (4)	Rain (9)	Jones C	Bennett (7)	Fieldhouse	1,522
anson (9)	Waddecar (10)	Ennis	Bennett (7)	Fieldhouse	1,797
ain	Simpson (4)	Ennis (11)	Linney (9)	Fieldhouse	2,362
ain (11)	Jones C	S-Smith (7)	Waddecar (4)	Fieldhouse	1,194
ennett	Simpson (4)■	H-Smith (10)	Linney (11)	Fieldhouse	1,803
ennett (4)	Smith J	H-Smith (7)	Donohue	Fieldhouse	1,381
ennett	Mulvey (8)	H-Smith (9)	**Linney (11) 1**	Fieldhouse	905
ain	Simpson (4)	H-Smith	Waddecar (9)	King L	1,696
ain	Cooke (9)	S-Smith (7)	Linney (11)	King L	1,525
ain (2)	Bennett	Ennis (7)	Waddecar (11)	Smith J	Chadwick	McDowell	1,169
onohue (2)	Bennett	S-Smith (3)	Linney (7)	Fieldhouse	Mulvey	947
ain	Jones C	Ennis (7)	Waddecar (4)	Mulvey	1,022
ain (3) 1	Simpson (4)	Campbell	Bennett (8)	Mulvey	1,457
ain (2)	Simpson	Campbell (7)	Bennett	Jones C	903
ain (11)	Simpson (9)	Campbell	Bennett	White J (7)	456
ain (7)	Simpson	Smith J (2)	Bennett	White J (9)	1,927
ain (2)	Simpson	Campbell	Mulvey (8)	White J (5)	582
ain	Sanyang (7)	Potts (4)	Baker D	Burns S (9)	1,744
White J (11)	Sanyang	Ennis (10)	Major	Holmes (9)	801
ain (4)	Waddecar (10)	Mulvey (8)	Deadman (7)	Brooks Jo (1)	n/k
ain	White J (7)	Bennett	Donohue (11)■	**Ennis (9) 1**	1,078
mith J (7)	White J (3)	Bennett	Waddecar	Ennis (11)	1,698
anyang	White J (3)	Bennett	Waddecar (9)	Ennis (7)	643
odd	Donohue (4)	Humphries (8)	Burns S (5)	Chadwick	1,006
anyang (3)	Waddecar (10)	Humphries	Da Silva (11)	Major	830
wen	Griffiths (3)	Duckworth (11)	Da Silva (10)	Major	1,564
aker D	Gooden	Humphries	Da Silva (10)	Major (7)	804
aker D	White J	Potts	**Duckworth (10) 1**	Major	1,309
ooden (2)	Brooks Jo	Jones C	Dodd (11)	Major (10)	2,279
ooden	White J	Potts (10)	Dodd	Major (11)	1,633
ooden	White J	Potts (8)	Duckworth (10)	Major	1,144
ooden	Donohue (11)	Griffiths	Duckworth (8)	Wilson H (10)	1,835
ooden	Ennis (6)	Potts	Waddecar (10)	Galloway (11)	1,573
ooden	Ennis (10)	Wilson H	Duckworth (3)	Galloway (8)	669
riffiths (10)	Humphries	Wilson H (11)	Duckworth	Waddecar (7)	1,867
Donohue	Humphries	Potts (6)	Duckworth (9)	Hamer	1,492
aylor C (7)	Humphries	Itota	Duckworth (10)	Owen	969
aylor C	Humphries	Potts (10)	Duckworth (2)	Unsworth	1,620
aylor C	Humphries	Smith J	Duckworth	Waddecar (7)	1,715
aylor C	Humphries	Potts (6)	Duckworth	Galloway (10)	1,873
mith J (6) 1	Humphries (5)	Griffiths (10)	Waddecar (11)	**Bange (9) 2**	Sikora	1,255
aylor C	Donohue (6)	Galloway (7)	Duckworth (4)	Hamer	1,005
aylor C	McGee (8)	Potts (8)	Waddecar (7)	Fieldhouse	2,068
sikora	McGee	Galloway (7)	Duckworth	Bange (4)	802
Griffiths	McGee	Galloway (11)	Waddecar (5)	Bange (10)	1,850
Dodd (5)	Jones C (10)	Potts (4)	Askew (2)	**Linney (11) 1**	Lavercombe	n/k
aylor C	Griffiths (4)	Galloway (8)	McGee	Bange (7)	734
sikora	Smith J	Galloway	Waddecar (11)	Bange (10)	2,198
sikora	Griffiths (4)	Ennis (10)	Waddecar	Askew (11)	901
smith J (8)	McGee	Galloway (7)	Bange (4)	Hamer	2,307
ones C (8)	McGee (3)	Griffiths (2)	Humphries (6)	Hamer (1)	870
aylor C (5)	Vincent (2)	Anderton (7)	Humphries (11)	Hamer (1)	n/k

Player Appearances & Goals

Player	League		FAC & FAT		Other		Totals	
Jack **Anderton**	0	0	0	0	0 (+1)	0	0 (+1)	0
Josh **Askew**	4 (+2)	1	0	0	1 (+1)	1	5 (+3)	2
Drew **Baker**	20	1	6	0	1	0	27	1
Ewan **Bange**	6 (+5)	1	0	0	1 (+1)	2	7 (+6)	3
Jack **Bennett**	0 (+3)	0	0 (+1)	0	1	0	1 (+4)	0
Josh **Brooks**	0	0	0	0	0 (+1)	0	0 (+1)	0
Sam **Burns**	3 (+1)	0	1 (+1)	1	1	1	5 (+2)	3
Hayden **Campbell**	2 (+1)	0	0	0	0	0	2 (+1)	0
Jamie **Cooke**	5 (+1)	1	0	0	0	0	5 (+1)	1
Vani **Da Silva**	0 (+3)	0	0	0	0	0	0 (+3)	0
Jimmy **Deadman**	0	0	0	0	0 (+1)	0	0 (+1)	0
Adam **Dodd**	36 (+1)	2	5	0	3 (+1)	1	44 (+2)	3
Michael **Donohue**	30 (+2)	4	2 (+3)	0	3	0	35 (+5)	4
Joe **Duckworth**	4 (+9)	4	0	0	2	2	6 (+9)	6
Paul **Ennis**	30 (+8)	5	2 (+2)	2	4	3	36 (+10)	10
Josh **Galloway**	7 (+8)	1	0	0	3	2	10 (+8)	3
Luke **Griffiths**	21 (+4)	2	2	0	1 (+2)	0	24 (+6)	2
Andy **Halls**	10	0	0	0	0	0	10	0
Ryan **Hamer**	0	0	0	0	1 (+1)	0	1 (+1)	0
Cian **Hayes**	4	2	0	0	0	0	4	2
Brad **Holmes**	11 (+1)	5	3	0	1	3	15 (+1)	8
Toby **Humphries**	0	0	0 (+1)	0	0 (+2)	0	0 (+3)	0
Curtis **Jones**	26	2	4	0	2 (+2)	0	32 (+2)	2
Lewis **King**	2	0	0	0	0	0	2	0
Dan **Lavercombe**	39	0	6	0	3	0	48	0
Regan **Linney**	37 (+3)	14	4 (+2)	2	1 (+1)	4	42 (+6)	20
Cedric **Main**	15	3	4	3	0	0	19	6
Jayden **Major**	0 (+3)	0	1	0	0	0	1 (+3)	0
Harry **McGee**	2 (+1)	0	0	0	1 (+1)	0	3 (+2)	0
George **McMahon**	1	0	0	0	0	0	1	0
Keaton **Mulvey**	0 (+1)	0	0 (+1)	0	0 (+1)	0	0 (+3)	0
Aaron **Morris**	41	5	6	0	4	0	51	5
Tre **Pemberton**	0	0	1	0	0	0	1	0
Michael **Potts**	29 (+7)	1	6	0	3 (+1)	0	38 (+8)	1
Matty **Rain**	1 (+8)	2	3 (+1)	1	0 (+1)	0	4 (+10)	3
Omar **Sanyang**	0 (+2)	0	0	0	0	0	0 (+2)	0
Jorge **Sikora**	3	0	0	0	1	0	4	0
Jordan **Simpson**	5 (+6)	1	1	0	0	0	6 (+6)	1
Finlay **S-Smith**	5 (+3)	1	3 (+1)	1	0	0	8 (+4)	2
Morgan **H-Smith**	0 (+1)	0	0 (+2)	0	0	0	0 (+3)	0
Jonathan **Smith**	27 (+3)	2	0	0	1 (+1)	1	28 (+4)	3
Chris **Taylor**	1 (+1)	0	0	0	3	0	4 (+1)	0
James **Vincent**	0	0	0	0	0 (+1)	0	0 (+1)	0
Alistair **Waddecar**	23 (+12)	3	5 (+1)	0	2 (+2)	1	30 (+15)	4
Andy **White**	4	0	0	0	0	0	4	0
Joe **White**	4 (+7)	0	1 (+1)	0	0	0	5 (+8)	0
Harry **Wilson**	4 (+2)	0	0	0	0	0	4 (+2)	0

League Table

	Team	Pld	W	D	L	F	A	GD	Pts
1	Buxton ↑	42	23	12	7	80	38	42	81
2	South Shields	42	23	9	10	71	40	31	78
3	Scarborough Athletic ↑	42	21	11	10	61	48	13	74
4	Matlock Town -1 point	42	21	10	11	59	36	23	72
5	Warrington Town	42	20	11	11	67	47	20	71
6	Bamber Bridge	42	21	6	15	67	59	8	69
7	Whitby Town	42	19	9	14	57	50	7	66
8	Stafford Rangers	42	15	16	11	55	39	16	61
9	FC UNITED OF MANCHESTER	42	18	7	17	66	57	9	61
10	Morpeth Town	42	17	10	15	67	59	8	61
11	Lancaster City	42	17	5	20	44	51	−7	56
12	Mickleover	42	15	10	17	54	65	−11	55
13	Nantwich Town	42	14	10	18	46	52	−6	52
14	Ashton United	42	13	12	17	50	59	−9	51
15	Radcliffe	42	15	6	21	56	73	−17	51
16	Gainsborough Trinity	42	12	14	16	40	52	−12	50
17	Hyde United	42	14	8	20	52	65	−13	50
18	Stalybridge Celtic -3 points	42	15	7	20	51	59	−8	49
19	Atherton Collieries	42	13	9	20	34	45	−11	48
20	Basford United	42	12	9	21	30	47	−17	45
21	Witton Albion ↓	42	12	7	23	48	78	−30	43
22	Grantham Town ↓	42	8	10	24	45	81	−36	34

Additional appearances: Jack **Gooden** Total 0 (+1) (in League), 0 goals
Jacob **Hanson** Total 0 (+1) (in League), 0 goals

Unused substitutes: David **Chadwick**   Lenny **Fieldhouse**   Silas **Itota**   Taylor **McDowell**   Tyler **Owen**   Will **Unsworth**

o Opposition Own Goals for FC United:
Greg **Hall**   23/10/2021   FC's 3rd v Witton Albion (NPLP)   A 3-2
Jake **Hackett**   25/01/2022   FC's 2nd v Whitby Town (NPLP)   H 3-4

FC United goals listed first.   All games League unless stated otherwise:
FAC FA Cup   **FAT** FA Trophy   **EFT** European FENIX Trophy
H Played at Broadhurst Park (FC United Of Manchester)
N Played at Stadio Romeo Neri, Rimini (Italy)
* Player Substituted   (2) Substituted player's number   Goalscorers in **bold**
■ Player Sent off   (+1) Number of substitute appearances

‡: Both points deductions were due to Matlock and Stalybridge fielding ineligible players

FC United Managers

Karl MARGINSON
22 June 2005 to 24 October 2017

(See player profile on p.136)

Tom GREAVES
24 October 2017 to 28 August 2018

(See player profile on p.175)

David CHADWICK
Caretaker, August to October 2018

(See player profile on p.123)

Roy SOULE   *Caretaker, August to September 2011*

Raised in Blackley, Roy was on schoolboy forms at Manchester United, where he was coached by Wilf McGuinness and John Aston Snr. and played in the Lancashire League. After a spell at Crewe Alexandra he played semi-professionally before beginning a long career in coaching. He managed non-league clubs Castleton Gabriels, Glossop North End, Caernarfon Town, Mossley and Droylsden and held coaching and scouting positions at Crewe, Rotherham United, Oldham Athletic and Grimsby Town. He spent several years in the USA as technical director of a club in Virginia, but would assist with FC United training sessions on his visits home. When he returned to Manchester in 2009, Roy was appointed as Karl Marginson's assistant, and stepped up to manage the team when Margy was struck by a kidney infection in August 2011. He left the club at the end of that term and later managed New Mills for three years, with his side knocking United out of the Manchester Premier Cup in 2013. Roy remained close to the Reds as a regular matchday expert summariser for FCUM Radio.

Neil REYNOLDS   Appointed 18 October 2018

Neil first played senior football for Darwen aged just 16, before spending a year as a professional at Plymouth Argyle. After returning to Darwen he went on to feature as an industrious midfielder for Bamber Bridge, Kendal Town, Rossendale United and Clitheroe, with whom he reached the FA Vase semi-final in 2001. After recovering from a serious knee injury, Reno scored a last-gasp winner in the final game of the season to clinch the North West Counties League title in 2004. At the age of 29 he was appointed as Clitheroe joint-manager in December 2006, and both played and managed against FC United the following term before reverting to playing in January 2009. Neil returned to Bamber Bridge later that year, and went on to join the coaching staff before becoming assistant to boss Neil Crowe in 2011. He was appointed manager in December 2016, and led his team to the Northern Premier League Challenge Cup at the end of that season, followed by promotion to the Premier Division a year later. Neil became FC boss in October 2018 with the side bottom of the table, but was unable to prevent relegation. He built a new-look attack-minded squad that launched an exciting promotion challenge in 2019/20, with the side top scorers and second in the league before the season was prematurely ended in March. The following term was also shortened in November 2020, but not before the Reds had reached the FA Cup 1st round for the third time in the club's history. At the end of his first full season Neil had led his team to their first silverware of his tenure by lifting the FENIX Trophy in Rimini in 2022.

373 players have represented FC United of Manchester in competitive first team matches

No.	Player	Seasons Played		LEAGUE Starts	(+Sub)	Goals	FA NATIONAL CUPS Starts	(+Sub)	Goals	OTHER CUPS / PLAY-OFFS Starts	(+Sub)	Goals	TOTALS Starts	(+Sub)	Goals
232	Tomi **Adeloye**	2016/17	(1)	5	(+3)	1	0	(+0)	0	1	(+0)	0	6	(+3)	1
259	Steve **Affleck**	2017/18	(1)	0	(+1)	0	0	(+0)	0	0	(+0)	0	0	(+1)	0
14	Will **Ahern**	2005/06 - 2006/07	(2)	25	(+10)	3	1	(+0)	0	1	(+0)	0	27	(+10)	3
46	Danny **Allen**	2006/07	(1)	3	(+2)	3	0	(+1)	0	0	(+1)	0	3	(+4)	3
234	Lloyd **Allinson**	2017/18 - 2018/19	(2)	59	(+0)	0	7	(+0)	0	4	(+0)	0	70	(+0)	0
150	Chris **Amadi**	2012/13	(1)	2	(+6)	0	2	(+4)	2	1	(+0)	2	5	(+10)	4
151	Charlie **Anderson**	2012/13	(1)	0	(+1)	0	0	(+1)	0	1	(+0)	0	1	(+2)	0
372	Jack **Anderton**	2021/22	(1)	0	(+0)	0	0	(+0)	0	0	(+1)	0	0	(+1)	0
139	Paul **Armstrong**	2011/12 - 2012/13	(2)	3	(+0)	1	1	(+0)	0	2	(+0)	0	6	(+0)	1
228	Gareth **Arnison**	2016/17	(1)	4	(+4)	0	0	(+0)	0	1	(+0)	0	5	(+4)	0
33	Sam **Ashton**	2006/07 - 2010/11	(5)	184	(+0)	1	30	(+0)	0	17	(+0)	0	231	(+0)	1
191	Luke **Ashworth**	2014/15 - 2018/19	(4)	114	(+1)	9	21	(+0)	5	6	(+0)	0	141	(+1)	14
370	Josh **Askew**	2021/22	(1)	4	(+2)	1	0	(+0)	0	1	(+1)	1	5	(+3)	2
108	Mark **Ayres**	2009/10 - 2010/11	(2)	5	(+5)	0	1	(+0)	0	1	(+0)	0	7	(+5)	0
318	Alex **Babos**	2019/20	(1)	6	(+0)	0	0	(+0)	0	0	(+0)	0	6	(+0)	0
55	Chris **Baguley**	2007/08 - 2008/09	(2)	43	(+12)	17	1	(+6)	0	8	(+3)	8	52	(+21)	25
62	Jamie **Baguley**	2007/08 - 2008/09	(2)	32	(+19)	5	1	(+0)	0	5	(+3)	0	38	(+22)	5
225	Sam **Baird**	2016/17 - 2018/19	(3)	30	(+3)	1	1	(+0)	0	4	(+0)	0	35	(+3)	1
342	Drew **Baker**	2021/22	(1)	20	(+0)	1	6	(+0)	0	1	(+0)	0	27	(+0)	1
239	Richie **Baker**	2017/18	(1)	2	(+1)	0	0	(+0)	0	0	(+0)	0	2	(+1)	0
28	Simon **Band**	2005/06	(1)	2	(+0)	0	0	(+0)	0	0	(+0)	0	2	(+0)	0
366	Ewan **Bange**	2021/22	(1)	6	(+5)	1	0	(+0)	0	1	(+1)	2	7	(+6)	3
264	Jack **Banister**	2018/19	(1)	19	(+14)	5	3	(+0)	2	2	(+0)	0	24	(+14)	7
166	Ollie **Banks**	2012/13 - 2013/14	(2)	24	(+2)	3	0	(+0)	0	2	(+0)	0	16	(+2)	3
262	Brad **Barnes**	2018/19	(1)	1	(+0)	0	0	(+0)	0	0	(+0)	0	1	(+0)	0
321	Jack **Barthram**	2019/20	(1)	0	(+0)	0	0	(+0)	0	1	(+0)	0	1	(+0)	0
229	Adriano **Basso**	2016/17	(1)	8	(+0)	0	0	(+0)	0	1	(+0)	0	9	(+0)	0
117	Richard **Battersby**	2010/11 - 2011/12	(2)	44	(+9)	0	6	(+2)	0	3	(+0)	0	53	(+13)	0
199	Nia **Bayunu**	2014/15 - 2015/16	(2)	16	(+1)	1	2	(+0)	0	0	(+0)	0	18	(+1)	1
320	Cameron **Belford**	2019/20	(1)	21	(+0)	0	5	(+0)	0	5	(+0)	0	31	(+0)	0
64	Colin **Bell**	2007/08	(1)	3	(+0)	0	0	(+0)	0	1	(+0)	0	4	(+0)	0
346	Jack **Bennett**	2021/22	(1)	0	(+3)	0	0	(+1)	0	1	(+0)	0	1	(+4)	0
149	Dave **Birch**	2012/13 - 2015/16	(4)	78	(+11)	2	14	(+6)	1	9	(+1)	0	101	(+18)	3
66	Micah **Bleau**	2007/08 - 2008/09	(2)	6	(+2)	0	0	(+0)	0	4	(+0)	0	10	(+2)	0
147	Matthew **Boland**	2011/12 - 2013/14	(2)	0	(+1)	0	0	(+0)	0	1	(+0)	0	1	(+1)	0
185	Connor **Bower**	2013/14 - 2014/15	(2)	1	(+5)	0	0	(+0)	0	0	(+2)	0	1	(+7)	0
243	Danny **Brady**	2017/18	(1)	10	(+2)	0	5	(+0)	0	1	(+0)	0	16	(+2)	0
195	Michael **Brewster**	2014/15	(1)	0	(+1)	0	0	(+0)	0	1	(+0)	1	1	(+1)	1
274	Theo **Brierley**	2018/19	(1)	3	(+3)	1	0	(+0)	0	1	(+0)	0	4	(+3)	1
144	James **Brooks**	2011/12	(1)	0	(+0)	0	0	(+0)	0	1	(+0)	0	1	(+0)	0
355	Josh **Brooks**	2021/22	(1)	0	(+0)	0	0	(+0)	0	0	(+1)	0	0	(+1)	0
24	Dave **Brown**	2005/06 - 2007/08	(3)	36	(+15)	4	0	(+1)	0	5	(+2)	1	41	(+18)	5
192	Tom **Brown**	2014/15 - 2017/18	(4)	38	(+20)	3	5	(+5)	0	4	(+2)	1	47	(+27)	4
168	Liam **Brownhill**	2013/14 - 2015/16	(3)	107	(+2)	3	17	(+0)	0	4	(+3)	1	128	(+5)	4
90	John **Buckley**	2008/09	(1)	0	(+0)	0	0	(+0)	0	0	(+1)	0	0	(+1)	0
319	Jordan **Buckley**	2019/20	(1)	7	(+5)	3	1	(+2)	0	2	(+1)	0	10	(+8)	3
130	Josh **Burke**	2010/11	(1)	0	(+0)	0	0	(+0)	0	0	(+1)	0	0	(+1)	0
60	Aaron **Burns**	2007/08	(1)	12	(+0)	6	0	(+0)	0	2	(+0)	2	14	(+0)	8
352	Sam **Burns**	2021/22	(1)	3	(+1)	1	1	(+1)	1	1	(+0)	1	5	(+2)	3
174	Callum **Byrne**	2013/14 - 2015/16	(3)	54	(+20)	5	12	(+2)	2	4	(+1)	0	70	(+23)	7
351	Hayden **Campbell**	2021/22	(1)	2	(+1)	0	0	(+0)	0	0	(+0)	0	2	(+1)	0
58	Adam **Carden**	2007/08 - 2009/10	(3)	54	(+17)	3	13	(+0)	0	6	(+1)	1	73	(+18)	4
18	Simon **Carden**	2005/06 - 2010/11	(6)	161	(+38)	57	16	(+8)	7	13	(+7)	3	190	(+53)	67
184	Dave **Carnell**	2013/14 - 2018/19	(5)	128	(+0)	0	22	(+0)	0	7	(+0)	0	157	(+0)	0
310	Craig **Carney**	2019/20	(1)	5	(+3)	0	1	(+2)	0	0	(+0)	0	6	(+5)	0
156	Mathew **Carr**	2012/13	(1)	3	(+0)	0	0	(+0)	0	0	(+0)	0	3	(+0)	0
136	Michael **Carr**	2011/12	(1)	12	(+7)	1	4	(+2)	2	0	(+0)	0	16	(+9)	3
15	David **Chadwick**	2005/06 - 2021/22	(10)	156	(+20)	19	16	(+2)	3	16	(+1)	2	188	(+23)	24
158	Lewis **Chalmers**	2012/13	(1)	2	(+1)	0	0	(+0)	0	0	(+0)	0	2	(+1)	0
210	Chris **Chantler**	2015/16 - 2016/17	(2)	54	(+1)	1	3	(+0)	1	3	(+0)	0	60	(+1)	2
93	Neil **Chappell**	2008/09	(1)	4	(+6)	1	0	(+0)	0	0	(+0)	0	4	(+6)	1
115	Scott **Cheetham**	2009/10 - 2015/16	(6)	14	(+6)	0	4	(+4)	0	8	(+0)	0	26	(+10)	0
333	Dan **Cockerline**	2020/21	(1)	3	(+3)	2	2	(+3)	1	0	(+0)	0	5	(+6)	3
330	Larnell **Cole**	2019/20	(1)	0	(+0)	0	0	(+0)	0	0	(+0)	0	0	(+0)	0
59	Theo **Coleman**	2007/08	(1)	0	(+0)	0	0	(+1)	0	0	(+0)	0	0	(+1)	0
31	Warren **Collier**	2005/06 - 2007/08	(2)	1	(+1)	0	0	(+0)	0	0	(+0)	0	1	(+1)	0
242	Michael **Connor**	2017/18	(1)	8	(+2)	0	4	(+0)	1	0	(+0)	0	12	(+2)	0
91	Shaun **Connor**	2008/09 - 2014/15	(2)	1	(+0)	0	0	(+0)	0	0	(+1)	0	1	(+1)	0
173	Cavell **Coo**	2013/14	(1)	0	(+1)	0	0	(+0)	0	0	(+0)	0	0	(+1)	0
347	Jamie **Cooke**	2021/22	(1)	5	(+1)	1	0	(+0)	0	0	(+0)	0	5	(+1)	1
200	Sean **Cooke**	2015/16	(1)	8	(+3)	1	0	(+2)	0	1	(+0)	0	9	(+5)	1
223	Zac **Corbett**	2016/17 - 2017/18	(2)	20	(+2)	2	7	(+0)	0	0	(+1)	0	27	(+3)	2
74	Martin **Cosgrave**	2007/08	(1)	0	(+0)	0	0	(+0)	0	0	(+2)	0	0	(+2)	0

No.	Player	Seasons Played		LEAGUE Starts	(+Sub)	Goals	FA NATIONAL CUPS Starts	(+Sub)	Goals	OTHER CUPS / PLAY-OFFS Starts	(+Sub)	Goals	TOTALS Starts	(+Sub)	Goals
101	Jake Cottrell	2009/10 - 2012/13	(4)	125	(+16)	7	26	(+3)	1	9	(+3)	0	160	(+22)	9
39	Liam Coyne	2006/07	(1)	5	(+3)	1	2	(+0)	0	0	(+0)	0	7	(+3)	1
8	Tony Coyne	2005/06	(1)	4	(+8)	0	0	(+0)	0	0	(+0)	0	4	(+8)	0
253	Jamal Crawford	2017/18 - 2018/19	(2)	9	(+18)	0	1	(+1)	0	1	(+2)	0	11	(+21)	0
260	Billy Crellin	2018/19	(1)	7	(+0)	0	0	(+0)	0	0	(+0)	0	7	(+0)	0
194	Nick Culkin	2014/15 - 2015/16	(2)	1	(+0)	0	0	(+0)	0	2	(+0)	0	3	(+0)	0
21	Tony Cullen	2005/06	(1)	14	(+9)	0	0	(+0)	0	2	(+1)	0	16	(+10)	0
317	Alex Curran	2019/20	(1)	16	(+1)	2	3	(+0)	0	3	(+1)	0	22	(+2)	2
176	Jordan Dainty	2013/14	(1)	0	(+0)	0	0	(+0)	0	1	(+0)	0	1	(+0)	0
153	Greg Daniels	2012/13 - 2015/16	(4)	73	(+64)	23	14	(+6)	3	9	(+2)	2	96	(+72)	28
359	Vani Da Silva	2021/22	(1)	0	(+3)	0	0	(+0)	0	0	(+0)	0	0	(+3)	0
169	Tom Davies	2013/14	(1)	37	(+2)	5	2	(+1)	0	3	(+0)	0	42	(+3)	5
157	Adam Dawson	2012/13	(1)	3	(+1)	0	0	(+0)	0	0	(+0)	0	3	(+1)	0
356	Jimmy Deadman	2021/22	(1)	0	(+0)	0	0	(+0)	0	0	(+1)	0	0	(+1)	0
335	Kain Dean	2020/21	(1)	0	(+0)	0	0	(+1)	0	0	(+0)	0	0	(+1)	0
314	Tom Dean	2019/20	(1)	7	(+0)	0	2	(+0)	2	1	(+0)	0	10	(+0)	2
100	Ben Deegan	2009/10 - 2011/12	(3)	40	(+34)	15	16	(+7)	8	3	(+2)	0	59	(+43)	23
267	Matt Dempsey	2018/19	(1)	0	(+1)	0	0	(+0)	0	0	(+0)	0	0	(+1)	0
131	Oliver Devenney	2010/11	(1)	0	(+6)	0	0	(+0)	0	0	(+0)	0	0	(+6)	0
265	Liam Dickinson	2018/19	(1)	4	(+3)	1	0	(+0)	0	0	(+0)	0	4	(+3)	1
220	Johny Diba	2016/17	(1)	5	(+0)	0	0	(+0)	0	0	(+0)	0	5	(+0)	0
85	Papis Dieyte	2008/09	(1)	3	(+6)	0	1	(+1)	1	1	(+0)	0	5	(+7)	1
315	Adam Dodd	2019/20 - 2021/22	(3)	72	(+1)	5	18	(+0)	1	7	(+1)	3	97	(+2)	9
269	Michael Donohue	2018/19 - 2021/22	(4)	66	(+23)	5	14	(+5)	3	9	(+0)	1	89	(+28)	9
306	Chris Doyle	2019/20 - 2020/21	(2)	34	(+0)	2	12	(+0)	0	3	(+0)	0	49	(+0)	2
360	Joe Duckworth	2021/22	(1)	4	(+9)	4	0	(+0)	0	2	(+0)	2	6	(+9)	6
211	Tom Eckersley	2015/16 - 2016/17	(2)	30	(+2)	0	2	(+0)	0	1	(+0)	1	33	(+2)	1
137	Adam Edwards	2011/12	(1)	2	(+4)	0	0	(+0)	0	1	(+0)	0	3	(+4)	0
273	Leighton Egan	2018/19	(1)	0	(+2)	0	0	(+0)	0	0	(+1)	0	0	(+3)	0
43	Lee Ellis	2006/07	(1)	0	(+1)	0	0	(+1)	0	0	(+0)	0	0	(+2)	0
327	Matty Elsdon	2019/20	(1)	5	(+1)	0	0	(+0)	0	1	(+0)	0	6	(+1)	0
6	Kevin Elvin	2005/06	(1)	18	(+1)	0	0	(+0)	0	4	(+0)	0	22	(+1)	0
114	Gage Eme	2009/10	(1)	0	(+4)	0	0	(+0)	0	0	(+0)	0	0	(+4)	0
307	Paul Ennis	2019/20 - 2021/22	(3)	51	(+21)	16	11	(+5)	7	8	(+1)	5	70	(+27)	28
230	Jordan Fagbola	2016/17 - 2017/18	(2)	43	(+2)	3	4	(+1)	0	3	(+0)	0	50	(+3)	3
198	Rory Fallon	2014/15 - 2015/16	(2)	25	(+14)	5	6	(+0)	1	0	(+1)	0	31	(+15)	6
155	Tom Fisher	2012/13	(1)	0	(+5)	0	0	(+0)	0	1	(+0)	0	1	(+5)	0
295	Andy Fisher	2018/19	(1)	13	(+0)	0	0	(+0)	0	0	(+0)	0	13	(+0)	0
127	Carl Fitton	2010/11	(1)	0	(+0)	0	0	(+0)	0	1	(+0)	0	1	(+0)	0
164	Sam Fitzgerald	2012/13	(1)	1	(+0)	0	0	(+0)	0	0	(+0)	0	1	(+0)	0
7	Craig Fleury	2005/06	(1)	1	(+0)	0	0	(+0)	0	0	(+0)	0	1	(+0)	0
212	Dylan Forth	2015/16	(1)	6	(+0)	0	0	(+0)	0	0	(+0)	0	6	(+0)	0
48	Liam Foster	2006/07 - 2008/09	(3)	42	(+4)	0	3	(+1)	0	12	(+0)	0	57	(+5)	0
332	Michael Fowler	2020/21	(1)	5	(+2)	2	2	(+3)	1	0	(+0)	0	7	(+5)	3
181	Joe Fox	2013/14 - 2014/15	(2)	19	(+24)	1	1	(+2)	0	0	(+0)	0	20	(+26)	1
89	Sam Freakes	2008/09	(1)	0	(+0)	0	0	(+0)	0	1	(+0)	0	1	(+0)	0
219	Ashley Frith	2016/17	(1)	1	(+0)	0	0	(+0)	0	0	(+0)	0	1	(+0)	0
367	Josh Galloway	2021/22	(1)	7	(+8)	1	0	(+0)	0	3	(+0)	2	10	(+8)	3
257	Gerard Garner	2017/18	(1)	3	(+3)	3	0	(+0)	0	0	(+0)	0	3	(+3)	3
83	Simon Garner	2008/09 - 2009/10	(2)	48	(+1)	2	12	(+0)	0	1	(+0)	0	61	(+1)	2
1	Barrie George	2005/06	(1)	28	(+0)	0	0	(+0)	0	4	(+0)	0	32	(+0)	0
56	Liam George	2007/08	(1)	1	(+3)	0	1	(+0)	0	1	(+0)	0	3	(+3)	0
36	Rhodri Giggs	2006/07 - 2013/14	(3)	32	(+33)	14	4	(+0)	0	9	(+3)	4	45	(+36)	18
252	Adam Gilchrist	2017/18	(1)	1	(+3)	0	0	(+0)	0	2	(+0)	1	3	(+3)	1
216	Jason Gilchrist	2016/17 - 2017/18	(2)	33	(+16)	21	6	(+2)	3	3	(+2)	5	42	(+20)	29
17	Ryan Gilligan	2005/06	(1)	3	(+4)	2	0	(+0)	0	1	(+0)	0	4	(+4)	2
218	Kieran Glynn	2016/17 - 2017/18	(2)	30	(+18)	4	1	(+2)	0	4	(+0)	1	35	(+20)	5
248	Sefton Gonzales	2017/18	(1)	2	(+0)	0	0	(+0)	0	0	(+0)	0	2	(+0)	0
364	Jack Gooden	2021/22	(1)	0	(+1)	0	0	(+0)	0	0	(+0)	0	0	(+1)	0
162	Travis Gray	2012/13	(1)	1	(+0)	0	0	(+0)	0	1	(+0)	0	2	(+0)	0
160	Tom Greaves	2012/13 - 2018/19	(7)	156	(+74)	87	23	(+7)	10	7	(+7)	6	186	(+88)	103
308	Luke Griffiths	2019/20 - 2021/22	(3)	51	(+8)	3	11	(+0)	0	5	(+3)	0	67	(+11)	3
138	Daniel Grimshaw	2011/12 - 2012/13	(2)	8	(+21)	1	4	(+1)	0	2	(+3)	1	14	(+25)	2
299	Jack Grimshaw	2018/19	(1)	2	(+2)	0	0	(+0)	0	0	(+0)	0	2	(+2)	0
71	Aaron Grundy	2007/08	(1)	6	(+0)	0	0	(+0)	0	2	(+0)	0	8	(+0)	0
365	Andy Halls	2021/22	(1)	10	(+0)	0	0	(+0)	0	0	(+0)	0	10	(+0)	0
371	Ryan Hamer	2021/22	(1)	0	(+0)	0	0	(+0)	0	1	(+1)	0	1	(+1)	0
72	Matt Hampson	2007/08	(1)	1	(+2)	0	0	(+0)	0	1	(+0)	0	2	(+2)	0
57	Cayne Hanley	2007/08	(1)	5	(+6)	0	1	(+2)	1	2	(+1)	1	8	(+9)	2
348	Jacob Hanson	2021/22	(1)	0	(+1)	0	0	(+0)	0	0	(+0)	0	0	(+1)	0
54	Anthony Hargreaves	2007/08	(1)	2	(+4)	1	0	(+2)	1	1	(+0)	0	3	(+6)	2
73	Kyle Harrop	2007/08	(1)	3	(+2)	0	0	(+0)	0	0	(+1)	0	3	(+3)	0
296	Bob Harris	2018/19	(1)	4	(+0)	0	0	(+0)	0	0	(+0)	0	4	(+0)	0
129	Jake Haslam	2010/11	(1)	0	(+1)	0	0	(+0)	0	0	(+1)	0	0	(+2)	0
186	Jacob Hazel	2013/14	(1)	0	(+2)	0	0	(+0)	0	0	(+0)	0	0	(+2)	0

No.	Player	Seasons Played		LEAGUE			FA NATIONAL CUPS			OTHER CUPS / PLAY-OFFS			TOTALS		
				Starts	(+Sub)	Goals	Starts	(+Sub)	Goals	Starts	(+Sub)	Goals	Starts	(+Sub)	Goals
325	Kyle **Hawley**	2019/20	(1)	1	(+3)	1	0	(+0)	0	1	(+1)	0	2	(+4)	1
354	Cian **Hayes**	2021/22	(1)	4	(+0)	2	0	(+0)	0	0	(+0)	0	4	(+0)	2
279	Liam **Healey**	2018/19	(1)	1	(+0)	0	0	(+0)	0	0	(+0)	0	1	(+0)	0
313	Rhain **Hellawell**	2019/20	(1)	0	(+4)	0	0	(+1)	0	0	(+0)	0	0	(+5)	0
122	Zach **Hibbert**	2010/11	(1)	6	(+0)	0	2	(+0)	0	0	(+0)	0	8	(+0)	0
255	Luke **Higham**	2017/18	(1)	11	(+0)	0	0	(+0)	0	2	(+0)	0	13	(+0)	0
224	Chris **Hill**	2016/17	(1)	0	(+0)	0	0	(+0)	0	0	(+2)	0	0	(+2)	0
293	Josh **Hmami**	2018/19	(1)	0	(+3)	0	0	(+0)	0	0	(+0)	0	0	(+3)	0
67	James **Holden**	2007/08 - 2011/12	(4)	30	(+23)	1	4	(+8)	2	2	(+0)	0	36	(+31)	3
349	Bradley **Holmes**	2021/22	(1)	11	(+1)	5	3	(+0)	0	1	(+0)	3	15	(+1)	8
16	Scott **Holt**	2005/06	(1)	1	(+3)	2	0	(+0)	0	0	(+0)	0	1	(+3)	2
222	James **Hooper**	2016/17 - 2017/18	(2)	7	(+5)	2	0	(+1)	0	0	(+0)	0	7	(+6)	2
159	Louis **Horne**	2012/13	(1)	1	(+0)	0	0	(+0)	0	0	(+0)	0	1	(+0)	0
68	Brad **Howard**	2007/08 - 2008/09	(2)	26	(+0)	0	0	(+0)	0	6	(+0)	1	32	(+0)	1
25	Josh **Howard**	2005/06 - 2007/08	(3)	44	(+13)	15	5	(+0)	2	10	(+4)	2	59	(+17)	19
75	Rob **Howarth**	2007/08 - 2008/09	(2)	1	(+3)	0	0	(+0)	0	0	(+0)	0	1	(+3)	0
141	Sam **Howell**	2011/12 - 2012/13	(2)	0	(+0)	0	0	(+1)	0	1	(+0)	0	1	(+1)	0
241	Matty **Hughes**	2017/18	(1)	33	(+0)	0	2	(+1)	0	1	(+1)	0	36	(+2)	0
358	Toby **Humphries**	2021/22	(1)	0	(+0)	0	0	(+1)	0	0	(+2)	0	0	(+3)	0
124	Glynn **Hurst**	2010/11	(1)	6	(+1)	2	3	(+1)	3	0	(+1)	0	9	(+2)	5
103	Abdirashid **Ibrahim**	2009/10	(1)	1	(+1)	0	0	(+1)	0	0	(+1)	0	1	(+3)	0
112	Stephanos **Ioannou**	2009/10	(1)	0	(+2)	0	0	(+0)	0	0	(+0)	0	0	(+2)	0
180	Amjad **Iqbal**	2013/14	(1)	1	(+0)	0	1	(+0)	0	0	(+0)	0	2	(+0)	0
244	Steve **Irwin**	2017/18	(1)	24	(+4)	4	5	(+0)	2	1	(+0)	0	30	(+4)	6
106	Kyle **Jacobs**	2009/10 - 2012/13	(4)	105	(+7)	3	22	(+0)	0	10	(+0)	0	137	(+7)	3
289	Salou **Jallow**	2018/19	(1)	1	(+4)	0	0	(+0)	0	0	(+0)	0	1	(+4)	0
65	Danny **Jarrett**	2007/08	(1)	2	(+1)	0	0	(+0)	0	0	(+0)	0	2	(+1)	0
214	Dale **Johnson**	2015/16 - 2016/17	(2)	14	(+5)	3	2	(+0)	1	0	(+0)	0	16	(+5)	4
146	Stephen **Johnson**	2011/12 - 2014/15	(3)	22	(+8)	1	1	(+0)	0	2	(+0)	0	25	(+8)	1
134	Adam **Jones**	2011/12 - 2013/14	(3)	84	(+1)	16	15	(+0)	3	7	(+0)	0	106	(+1)	20
305	Curtis **Jones**	2019/20 - 2021/22	(3)	61	(+0)	5	16	(+0)	1	4	(+2)	0	81	(+2)	6
227	Mike **Jones**	2016/17 - 2018/19	(3)	10	(+10)	0	2	(+2)	0	4	(+0)	0	16	(+12)	0
304	James **Joyce**	2019/20	(1)	3	(+2)	0	1	(+0)	0	1	(+0)	0	5	(+2)	0
110	Adam **Karim**	2009/10	(1)	0	(+1)	0	0	(+0)	0	0	(+0)	0	0	(+1)	0
196	Matty **Kay**	2014/15	(1)	2	(+8)	1	1	(+1)	0	1	(+0)	0	4	(+9)	1
208	Scott **Kay**	2015/16 - 2018/19	(4)	103	(+0)	2	10	(+0)	0	5	(+0)	1	118	(+0)	3
326	Ben **Kerr**	2019/20	(1)	1	(+0)	0	0	(+0)	0	1	(+0)	0	2	(+0)	0
140	Theo **Kidd**	2011/12	(1)	0	(+2)	0	0	(+2)	0	0	(+0)	0	0	(+4)	0
256	Jeff **King**	2017/18	(1)	4	(+1)	4	0	(+0)	0	0	(+0)	0	4	(+1)	4
204	Lewis **King**	2015/16 - 2021/22	(2)	3	(+0)	0	1	(+0)	0	0	(+0)	0	4	(+0)	0
245	Tim **Kinsella**	2017/18	(1)	1	(+4)	0	0	(+0)	0	0	(+0)	0	1	(+4)	0
226	Kisimba **Kisimba**	2016/17	(1)	0	(+0)	0	0	(+0)	0	1	(+0)	0	1	(+0)	0
188	James **Knowles**	2014/15	(1)	14	(+2)	2	2	(+0)	0	1	(+0)	0	17	(+2)	2
111	Cédric **Krou**	2009/10 - 2012/13	(3)	4	(+14)	0	0	(+3)	0	3	(+0)	0	7	(+17)	0
161	Lewis **Lacy**	2012/13 - 2019/20	(6)	43	(+7)	3	6	(+0)	0	6	(+1)	0	55	(+8)	3
331	Dan **Lavercombe**	2020/21 - 2021/22	(2)	46	(+0)	0	11	(+0)	0	3	(+0)	0	60	(+0)	0
312	Jack **Lenehan**	2019/20 - 2020/21	(2)	6	(+19)	0	1	(+7)	0	5	(+0)	0	12	(+26)	0
278	Henry **Limpitshi**	2018/19	(1)	0	(+3)	0	0	(+0)	0	0	(+0)	0	0	(+3)	0
187	Craig **Lindfield**	2014/15 - 2017/18	(3)	61	(+20)	21	15	(+3)	5	3	(+1)	2	79	(+24)	28
311	Regan **Linney**	2019/20 - 2021/22	(3)	66	(+8)	24	16	(+2)	7	3	(+4)	5	85	(+14)	36
268	Brodie **Litchfield**	2018/19	(1)	3	(+4)	1	0	(+1)	0	0	(+0)	0	3	(+5)	1
121	Colin **Little**	2010/11	(1)	1	(+2)	2	0	(+0)	0	0	(+0)	0	1	(+2)	2
97	Carl **Lomax**	2008/09 - 2009/10	(2)	10	(+3)	4	0	(+0)	0	0	(+0)	0	10	(+3)	4
40	Mike **Lomax**	2006/07	(1)	3	(+0)	0	0	(+1)	0	0	(+1)	0	3	(+2)	0
240	Joel **Logan**	2017/18 - 2018/19	(2)	15	(+7)	0	2	(+3)	1	0	(+1)	0	17	(+11)	1
276	Cole **Lonsdale**	2018/19	(1)	1	(+0)	0	0	(+0)	0	1	(+0)	0	2	(+0)	0
217	Nathan **Lowe**	2016/17 - 2017/18	(2)	25	(+12)	8	0	(+3)	0	1	(+1)	0	26	(+16)	8
189	Chris **Lynch**	2014/15 - 2015/16	(2)	23	(+6)	2	8	(+0)	1	4	(+0)	0	35	(+6)	3
263	Chris **Lynch**	2018/19	(1)	31	(+1)	1	3	(+0)	0	1	(+0)	0	35	(+1)	1
12	Darren **Lyons**	2005/06 - 2008/09	(3)	6	(+11)	3	0	(+1)	0	2	(+1)	0	8	(+13)	3
92	Jamie **Mack**	2008/09 - 2009/10	(2)	1	(+7)	3	0	(+3)	0	0	(+1)	0	1	(+11)	3
202	Sam **Madeley**	2015/16 - 2016/17	(2)	18	(+11)	9	3	(+2)	2	0	(+1)	0	21	(+14)	11
344	Cedric **Main**	2021/22	(1)	15	(+0)	3	4	(+0)	3	0	(+0)	0	19	(+0)	6
357	Jayden **Major**	2021/22	(1)	0	(+3)	0	1	(+0)	0	0	(+0)	0	1	(+3)	0
271	Lewis **Mansell**	2018/19	(1)	5	(+2)	1	0	(+1)	0	1	(+0)	0	6	(+3)	1
247	Kallum **Mantack**	2017/18	(1)	1	(+0)	0	3	(+0)	0	0	(+0)	0	4	(+0)	0
52	Karl **Marginson**	2006/07	(1)	0	(+1)	0	0	(+0)	0	0	(+0)	0	0	(+1)	0
99	Phil **Marsh**	2008/09 - 2009/10	(2)	37	(+6)	11	7	(+2)	2	1	(+0)	0	45	(+8)	13
167	Kevin **Masirika**	2012/13	(1)	2	(+0)	0	0	(+0)	0	1	(+0)	0	3	(+0)	0
237	Connor **McCarthy**	2017/18	(1)	26	(+9)	6	4	(+1)	3	2	(+0)	0	32	(+10)	9
22	Billy **McCartney**	2005/06	(1)	17	(+3)	0	0	(+0)	0	3	(+0)	0	20	(+3)	0
369	Harry **McGee**	2021/22	(1)	2	(+1)	0	0	(+0)	0	1	(+1)	0	3	(+2)	0
294	Dominic **McGiveron**	2018/19	(1)	0	(+3)	0	0	(+0)	0	0	(+0)	0	0	(+3)	0
152	Phil **McGrath**	2012/13	(1)	1	(+0)	0	2	(+1)	0	0	(+1)	0	3	(+2)	0
142	Ryan **McGreevy**	2011/12	(1)	0	(+2)	0	0	(+0)	0	1	(+0)	0	1	(+2)	0

No.	Player	Seasons Played		LEAGUE Starts	(+Sub)	Goals	FA NATIONAL CUPS Starts	(+Sub)	Goals	OTHER CUPS / PLAY-OFFS Starts	(+Sub)	Goals	TOTALS Starts	(+Sub)	Goals
298	Dominic McHale	2018/19	(1)	4	(+0)	1	0	(+0)	0	0	(+0)	0	4	(+0)	1
363	George McMahon	2021/22	(1)	1	(+0)	0	0	(+0)	0	0	(+0)	0	1	(+0)	0
119	Scott McManus	2010/11	(1)	36	(+0)	1	9	(+0)	0	2	(+0)	0	47	(+0)	1
30	Phil Melville	2005/06	(1)	7	(+0)	0	0	(+0)	0	0	(+0)	0	7	(+0)	0
27	Leon Mike	2005/06	(1)	3	(+2)	0	0	(+0)	0	1	(+0)	0	4	(+2)	0
283	Jamie Milligan	2018/19	(1)	0	(+1)	0	0	(+1)	0	1	(+0)	0	1	(+2)	0
9	Joz Mitten	2005/06	(1)	19	(+5)	7	0	(+0)	0	2	(+2)	0	21	(+7)	7
23	Paul Mitten	2005/06	(1)	1	(+2)	1	0	(+0)	0	0	(+2)	0	1	(+4)	1
290	Zehn Mohammed	2018/19	(1)	15	(+0)	0	0	(+0)	0	0	(+0)	0	15	(+0)	0
303	Aaron Morris	2019/20 - 2021/22	(3)	76	(+0)	7	17	(+1)	2	6	(+0)	0	99	(+1)	9
102	Ben Morris	2009/10	(1)	3	(+5)	0	0	(+0)	0	0	(+0)	0	3	(+5)	0
35	Alex Mortimer	2006/07 - 2007/08	(2)	36	(+0)	2	4	(+0)	0	4	(+0)	0	44	(+0)	2
288	Danny Morton	2018/19	(1)	12	(+0)	0	0	(+0)	0	0	(+0)	0	12	(+0)	0
95	Tunji Moses	2008/09 - 2009/10	(2)	22	(+5)	1	9	(+0)	0	0	(+0)	0	31	(+5)	1
182	Nelson Mota	2013/14 - 2014/15	(2)	3	(+6)	0	0	(+0)	0	0	(+0)	0	3	(+6)	0
143	Astley Mulholland	2011/12 - 2014/15	(4)	37	(+38)	5	4	(+2)	1	10	(+4)	5	51	(+44)	11
349	Keaton Mulvey	2021/22	(1)	0	(+1)	0	0	(+1)	0	0	(+1)	0	0	(+3)	0
123	Karl Munroe	2010/11 - 2012/13	(2)	15	(+2)	0	6	(+2)	0	1	(+0)	0	22	(+4)	0
201	Cameron Murray	2015/16	(1)	0	(+4)	0	0	(+1)	0	2	(+0)	1	2	(+5)	1
297	Louis Myers	2018/19 - 2019/20	(1)	7	(+5)	1	0	(+1)	0	0	(+1)	1	7	(+7)	2
154	Connor Naughton	2012/13	(1)	0	(+0)	0	0	(+0)	0	1	(+0)	0	1	(+0)	0
80	Dave Neville	2008/09 - 2009/10	(2)	11	(+10)	0	1	(+3)	0	1	(+0)	0	13	(+13)	0
116	Lee Neville	2010/11 - 2014/15	(5)	131	(+14)	8	23	(+1)	1	13	(+2)	0	167	(+17)	9
246	Callum Nicholas	2017/18	(1)	0	(+1)	0	0	(+1)	0	0	(+0)	0	0	(+2)	0
120	Mike Norton	2010/11 - 2015/16	(6)	151	(+21)	70	26	(+6)	15	13	(+4)	8	190	(+31)	93
5	Rob Nugent	2005/06 - 2009/10	(5)	136	(+7)	16	10	(+7)	1	13	(+3)	2	159	(+17)	19
51	John Ogden	2006/07	(1)	2	(+0)	0	0	(+0)	0	0	(+0)	0	2	(+0)	0
261	Steve O'Halloran	2018/19	(1)	41	(+0)	0	3	(+0)	0	1	(+0)	0	45	(+0)	0
32	Michael O'Neill	2005/06	(1)	1	(+0)	1	0	(+0)	0	0	(+0)	0	1	(+0)	1
3	Gareth Ormes	2005/06 - 2006/07	(2)	15	(+2)	0	0	(+0)	0	1	(+0)	0	16	(+2)	0
13	Adie Orr	2005/06 - 2006/07	(2)	24	(+15)	15	0	(+1)	0	4	(+0)	3	28	(+16)	18
113	Chris Ovington	2009/10 - 2010/11	(2)	10	(+9)	1	5	(+3)	1	1	(+0)	0	16	(+12)	2
316	Tunde Owolabi	2019/20	(1)	28	(+0)	27	8	(+0)	6	2	(+3)	1	38	(+3)	34
300	Will Ozono	2018/19	(1)	1	(+1)	0	0	(+0)	0	0	(+0)	0	1	(+1)	0
277	Jan Palinkas	2018/19	(1)	3	(+2)	0	0	(+0)	0	2	(+0)	0	5	(+2)	0
250	Tyrell Palmer	2017/18	(1)	2	(+13)	0	0	(+1)	0	0	(+3)	0	2	(+17)	0
118	Martin Parker	2010/11	(1)	17	(+0)	1	4	(+1)	0	0	(+1)	0	21	(+2)	1
11	Rory Patterson	2005/06 - 2015/16	(4)	97	(+14)	84	6	(+2)	4	17	(+1)	11	120	(+17)	99
197	Shelton Payne	2014/15	(1)	13	(+3)	5	0	(+0)	0	0	(+0)	0	13	(+3)	5
172	Andy Pearson	2013/14 - 2014/15	(2)	12	(+2)	1	2	(+1)	0	2	(+0)	0	16	(+3)	1
282	Tom Peers	2018/19	(1)	14	(+7)	5	1	(+0)	0	0	(+0)	0	15	(+7)	5
339	Tre Pemberton	2020/21 - 2021/22	(2)	2	(+0)	0	2	(+0)	0	0	(+0)	0	4	(+0)	0
336	Morgan Penfold	2020/21	(1)	0	(+3)	0	1	(+1)	0	0	(+0)	0	1	(+4)	0
275	Jordan Perrin	2018/19	(1)	1	(+0)	0	0	(+1)	0	1	(+0)	0	2	(+1)	0
41	Jamie Phoenix	2006/07	(1)	1	(+6)	2	0	(+1)	0	0	(+1)	0	1	(+8)	2
44	Nicky Platt	2006/07 - 2012/13	(6)	105	(+45)	15	22	(+5)	8	14	(+6)	3	141	(+56)	26
179	Jon Poizer	2013/14	(1)	0	(+0)	0	0	(+0)	0	0	(+1)	0	0	(+1)	0
280	Michael Potts	2018/19 - 2021/22	(4)	82	(+9)	7	19	(+0)	0	3	(+3)	0	104	(+12)	7
20	Phil Power	2005/06 - 2007/08	(3)	5	(+14)	4	0	(+1)	1	0	(+2)	1	5	(+17)	6
221	Harry Pratt	2016/17	(1)	0	(+1)	0	0	(+0)	0	0	(+1)	0	0	(+2)	0
272	Billy Priestley	2018/19	(1)	4	(+0)	0	1	(+0)	0	0	(+0)	0	5	(+0)	0
19	Phil Priestley	2005/06 - 2007/08	(2)	4	(+0)	0	0	(+0)	0	0	(+0)	0	4	(+0)	0
190	John Pritchard	2014/15	(1)	0	(+1)	0	0	(+0)	0	0	(+0)	0	0	(+1)	0
105	Ludovic Quistin	2009/10 - 2010/11	(2)	28	(+1)	0	4	(+0)	0	1	(+0)	0	33	(+1)	0
254	Danny Racchi	2017/18 - 2018/19	(2)	13	(+3)	0	0	(+0)	0	1	(+1)	0	14	(+4)	0
170	Charlie Raglan	2013/14	(1)	37	(+0)	5	1	(+0)	0	4	(+0)	0	42	(+0)	5
345	Matty Rain	2021/22	(1)	1	(+8)	2	3	(+1)	1	0	(+1)	0	4	(+10)	3
2	Mark Rawlinson	2005/06	(1)	10	(+4)	2	0	(+0)	0	0	(+1)	0	10	(+5)	2
128	Harrison Reeve	2010/11	(1)	0	(+0)	0	0	(+0)	0	0	(+1)	0	0	(+1)	0
286	Caleb Richards	2018/19	(1)	7	(+0)	0	0	(+0)	0	0	(+0)	0	7	(+0)	0
107	Adriano Rigoglioso	2009/10	(1)	3	(+3)	0	0	(+0)	0	0	(+0)	0	3	(+3)	0
285	Rowan Roache	2018/19	(1)	1	(+0)	0	0	(+1)	0	0	(+0)	0	1	(+1)	0
70	Nick Robinson	2007/08 - 2008/09	(2)	8	(+26)	5	0	(+2)	0	3	(+2)	0	11	(+30)	5
78	Carlos Roca	2008/09 - 2012/13	(5)	118	(+44)	33	29	(+6)	9	7	(+0)	0	154	(+50)	42
309	Nialle Rodney	2019/20	(1)	3	(+2)	1	1	(+1)	0	1	(+0)	1	5	(+3)	2
165	Sergio Rodriguez	2012/13 - 2013/14	(2)	5	(+5)	0	1	(+0)	0	2	(+0)	0	8	(+5)	0
49	Shaun Roscoe	2006/07 - 2007/08	(2)	30	(+2)	0	4	(+0)	0	7	(+0)	0	41	(+2)	0
76	Jamie Rother	2007/08	(1)	1	(+0)	0	0	(+0)	0	0	(+0)	0	1	(+0)	0
37	Stuart Rudd	2006/07 - 2007/08	(2)	61	(+4)	44	6	(+0)	3	9	(+3)	7	76	(+7)	54
47	Gary Sampson	2006/07	(1)	7	(+5)	2	0	(+1)	0	1	(+3)	0	8	(+9)	2
353	Omar Sanyang	2021/22	(1)	0	(+2)	0	0	(+0)	0	0	(+0)	0	0	(+2)	0
291	Billy Sass-Davies	2018/19	(1)	8	(+0)	0	0	(+0)	0	0	(+0)	0	8	(+0)	0
233	Ryan Schofield	2016/17	(1)	5	(+0)	0	0	(+0)	0	1	(+0)	0	6	(+0)	0
69	Danny Self	2007/08 - 2008/09	(2)	3	(+3)	0	0	(+1)	1	0	(+0)	0	3	(+4)	1
235	Joel Senior	2017/18 - 2018/19	(2)	49	(+10)	0	5	(+0)	0	4	(+0)	1	58	(+10)	1

No.	Player	Seasons Played		LEAGUE Starts	(+Sub)	Goals	FA NATIONAL CUPS Starts	(+Sub)	Goals	OTHER CUPS / PLAY-OFFS Starts	(+Sub)	Goals	TOTALS Starts	(+Sub)	Goals
45	Danny **Shannon**	2006/07	(1)	0	(+1)	1	0	(+0)	0	0	(+0)	0	0	(+1)	1
287	Chris **Sharp**	2018/19 - 2019/20	(2)	13	(+11)	3	0	(+1)	0	0	(+0)	0	13	(+12)	3
87	Grant **Shenton**	2008/09 - 2010/11	(3)	4	(+0)	0	0	(+0)	0	3	(+0)	0	7	(+0)	0
205	Sam **Sheridan**	2015/16 - 2016/17	(2)	40	(+18)	3	6	(+1)	1	1	(+1)	0	47	(+20)	4
324	Jorge **Sikora**	2019/20 - 2021/22	(2)	4	(+0)	0	0	(+0)	0	1	(+0)	0	5	(+0)	0
26	Chris **Simms**	2005/06	(1)	7	(+3)	3	0	(+0)	0	0	(+1)	0	7	(+8)	3
258	Elliot **Simões**	2017/18 - 2018/19	(2)	14	(+3)	0	1	(+2)	0	1	(+2)	2	16	(+7)	2
338	Jordan **Simpson**	2020/21 - 2021/22	(2)	7	(+6)	1	3	(+0)	0	0	(+0)	0	10	(+6)	1
84	Alex **Skidmore**	2008/09	(1)	3	(+4)	0	1	(+0)	0	1	(+0)	0	5	(+4)	0
341	Jonathan **Smith**	2021/22	(1)	27	(+3)	2	0	(+0)	0	1	(+1)	1	28	(+4)	3
175	Ric **Smith**	2013/14	(1)	0	(+0)	0	0	(+0)	0	1	(+0)	0	1	(+0)	0
38	Steve **Smith**	2006/07	(1)	2	(+12)	2	0	(+1)	0	0	(+0)	0	2	(+13)	2
328	Morgan **Homson-Smith**	2019/20 - 2021/22	(3)	7	(+7)	3	0	(+4)	0	1	(+0)	0	8	(+11)	3
323	Finlay **Sinclair-Smith**	2019/20 - 2021/22	(3)	14	(+11)	4	5	(+4)	2	2	(+0)	1	21	(+15)	7
329	Daniel **Trickett-Smith**	2019/20	(1)	2	(+3)	0	0	(+0)	0	0	(+0)	0	2	(+3)	0
209	Tom **Smyth**	2015/16	(1)	8	(+0)	0	0	(+0)	0	0	(+0)	0	8	(+0)	0
133	James **Spencer**	2011/12 - 2013/14	(3)	82	(+0)	0	14	(+0)	0	5	(+0)	0	101	(+0)	0
4	Steve **Spencer**	2005/06 - 2007/08	(3)	61	(+11)	5	8	(+0)	0	9	(+0)	0	78	(+11)	5
238	Jason **St Juste**	2017/18	(1)	1	(+0)	0	0	(+0)	0	0	(+0)	0	1	(+0)	0
334	Tom **Stead**	2020/21	(1)	0	(+0)	0	1	(+0)	0	0	(+0)	0	1	(+0)	0
145	Greg **Stones**	2011/12	(1)	26	(+0)	0	4	(+1)	0	5	(+0)	0	35	(+1)	0
98	Gary **Stopforth**	2008/09	(1)	0	(+2)	0	0	(+0)	0	0	(+0)	0	0	(+2)	0
135	Dean **Stott**	2011/12 - 2015/16	(5)	169	(+5)	14	26	(+5)	4	15	(+1)	4	210	(+11)	22
29	Dave **Swarbrick**	2005/06 - 2007/08	(3)	17	(+17)	3	1	(+0)	0	3	(+2)	0	21	(+19)	3
88	Nick **Swirad**	2008/09 - 2009/10	(2)	12	(+1)	0	2	(+0)	0	2	(+0)	0	16	(+1)	0
251	Sam **Tattum**	2017/18 - 2018/19	(2)	12	(+9)	0	1	(+0)	0	2	(+0)	0	15	(+9)	0
368	Chris **Taylor**	2021/22	(1)	1	(+1)	0	0	(+0)	0	3	(+0)	0	4	(+1)	0
34	Matty **Taylor**	2006/07 - 2007/08	(2)	45	(+0)	1	6	(+0)	0	4	(+1)	0	55	(+1)	1
178	Mike **Taylor**	2013/14	(1)	0	(+0)	0	0	(+0)	0	0	(+1)	0	0	(+1)	0
270	Lewis **Thompson**	2018/19	(1)	11	(+0)	0	2	(+0)	0	1	(+0)	0	14	(+0)	0
207	George **Thomson**	2015/16 - 2016/17	(2)	60	(+4)	26	5	(+0)	3	3	(+0)	3	68	(+4)	32
63	Peter **Thomson**	2007/08	(1)	0	(+5)	1	0	(+0)	0	1	(+0)	0	1	(+5)	1
203	Adam **Thurston**	2015/16	(1)	10	(+9)	0	3	(+0)	0	2	(+0)	0	15	(+9)	0
126	Matthew **Tierney**	2010/11 - 2012/13	(3)	19	(+10)	1	0	(+2)	0	4	(+3)	1	23	(+15)	2
96	Adam **Tong**	2008/09 - 2009/10	(2)	35	(+1)	6	9	(+0)	1	1	(+0)	1	45	(+1)	8
213	Dale **Tonge**	2015/16 - 2016/17	(2)	39	(+1)	0	4	(+0)	0	1	(+0)	0	44	(+1)	0
10	Steve **Torpey**	2005/06 - 2011/12	(3)	31	(+15)	16	0	(+1)	0	4	(+1)	5	35	(+17)	21
109	Angelos **Tsiaklis**	2009/10	(1)	4	(+4)	0	0	(+0)	0	0	(+0)	0	4	(+4)	0
61	Adam **Turner**	2007/08 - 2008/09	(2)	21	(+2)	1	5	(+0)	1	5	(+1)	0	31	(+3)	2
86	Tommy **Turner**	2008/09	(1)	9	(+2)	5	0	(+0)	0	1	(+0)	0	10	(+2)	5
177	Frank **Van Gils**	2013/14 - 2014/15	(2)	2	(+1)	0	1	(+1)	0	1	(+0)	1	4	(+2)	1
42	Fernando **Vaz Tê**	2006/07	(1)	0	(+1)	0	0	(+0)	0	0	(+0)	0	0	(+1)	0
373	James **Vincent**	2021/22	(1)	0	(+0)	0	0	(+0)	0	0	(+1)	0	0	(+1)	0
343	Alistair **Waddecar**	2021/22	(1)	23	(+12)	3	5	(+1)	0	2	(+2)	1	30	(+15)	4
132	Jay **Walcott**	2010/11 - 2011/12	(2)	0	(+2)	0	0	(+0)	0	0	(+1)	0	0	(+3)	0
249	Tom **Walker**	2017/18	(1)	9	(+1)	1	2	(+0)	0	1	(+0)	0	12	(+1)	1
281	Josh **Wallen**	2018/19	(1)	20	(+4)	3	1	(+0)	0	1	(+0)	0	22	(+4)	3
163	Matt **Walwyn**	2012/13 - 2015/16	(4)	6	(+37)	9	1	(+11)	4	4	(+2)	0	11	(+50)	13
82	Danny **Warrender**	2008/09 - 2011/12	(3)	38	(+2)	1	7	(+1)	0	1	(+1)	0	46	(+4)	1
193	Andy **Welsh**	2014/15	(1)	6	(+2)	1	2	(+0)	0	0	(+0)	0	8	(+2)	1
301	Mark **West**	2018/19	(1)	2	(+0)	0	0	(+0)	0	0	(+0)	0	2	(+0)	0
302	Paddy **Wharton**	2019/20	(1)	11	(+0)	0	3	(+0)	0	0	(+0)	0	14	(+0)	0
361	Andy **White**	2021/22	(1)	4	(+0)	0	0	(+0)	0	0	(+0)	0	4	(+0)	0
337	Joe **White**	2020/21 - 2021/22	(2)	4	(+9)	0	1	(+1)	0	0	(+0)	0	5	(+10)	0
284	Ryan **White**	2018/19	(1)	1	(+5)	0	1	(+0)	0	1	(+0)	1	3	(+5)	1
53	Dale **Whitehead**	2007/08 - 2008/09	(2)	8	(+1)	0	0	(+0)	0	1	(+0)	0	9	(+1)	0
292	Dale **Whitham**	2018/19	(1)	9	(+1)	3	0	(+0)	0	0	(+0)	0	9	(+1)	3
94	Tristram **Whitman**	2008/09	(1)	3	(+4)	1	0	(+0)	0	0	(+0)	0	3	(+4)	1
183	Ed **Wilczynski**	2013/14	(1)	3	(+0)	0	0	(+0)	0	0	(+0)	0	3	(+0)	0
232	Greg **Wilkinson**	2016/17	(1)	2	(+4)	0	0	(+0)	0	0	(+0)	0	2	(+4)	0
79	Danny **Williams**	2008/09 - 2009/10	(2)	9	(+21)	2	1	(+2)	0	0	(+0)	0	10	(+23)	2
215	Jake **Williams**	2016/17	(1)	18	(+2)	0	2	(+0)	0	3	(+0)	1	23	(+2)	1
266	Kurt **Willoughby**	2018/19	(1)	38	(+1)	18	3	(+0)	1	1	(+0)	1	42	(+1)	20
362	Harry **Wilson**	2021/22	(1)	4	(+2)	0	0	(+0)	0	0	(+0)	0	4	(+2)	0
77	Kyle **Wilson**	2008/09 - 2009/10	(2)	34	(+0)	25	5	(+0)	3	0	(+0)	0	39	(+0)	28
206	Harry **Winter**	2015/16 - 2018/19	(3)	63	(+10)	6	7	(+0)	1	2	(+0)	0	72	(+10)	7
236	Danny **Wisdom**	2017/18	(1)	19	(+1)	2	3	(+0)	0	0	(+0)	0	22	(+1)	2
125	Matthew **Wolfenden**	2010/11 - 2016/17	(7)	213	(+38)	83	22	(+11)	5	17	(+4)	6	252	(+53)	94
81	Jacob **Wood**	2008/09	(1)	2	(+0)	0	0	(+0)	0	0	(+0)	0	2	(+0)	0
340	Calum **Woods**	2020/21	(1)	0	(+0)	0	1	(+0)	0	0	(+0)	0	1	(+0)	0
171	Chris **Worsley**	2013/14	(1)	13	(+3)	0	1	(+0)	0	1	(+0)	0	15	(+3)	0
148	Jon **Worsnop**	2011/12 - 2013/14	(3)	24	(+0)	0	4	(+0)	0	8	(+0)	0	36	(+0)	0
50	Jerome **Wright**	2006/07 - 2016/17	(10)	310	(+18)	70	48	(+1)	7	18	(+5)	5	376	(+24)	82
322	Ashley **Young**	2019/20	(1)	0	(+2)	0	0	(+3)	0	2	(+0)	0	2	(+5)	0
104	Joe **Yoffe**	2009/10	(1)	7	(+13)	2	2	(+3)	2	1	(+0)	0	10	(+16)	4

373 players have represented FC United of Manchester in competitive first team matches

Their unique heritage number refers to the order in which they first appeared *(to find a player on an alphabetical list see pages 113-117)*

001 Barrie GEORGE

Born: 10/04/1986, Manchester
Debut: No.1 v Leek CSOB (A, NWCFL2), 13/08/2005

Goalkeeper

Season	LEAGUE			FA NATIONAL CUPS			OTHER CUPS / PLAY-OFFS			TOTALS		
	Starts	(+Sub)	Goals	Starts	(+Sub)	Goals	Starts	(+Sub)	Goals	Starts	(+Sub)	Goals
2005/06	28	(+0)	0				4	(+0)	0	32	(+0)	0
Totals	28	(+0)	0	0	(+0)	0	4	(+0)	0	32	(+0)	0

FC United's first ever goalkeeper, Wythenshawe-based Barrie began as a schoolboy at Manchester City and progressed via Altrincham's youth team to Radcliffe Borough. Hit the headlines in 2005 when he was chosen to play for England's partially-sighted team (rules allow a fully-sighted keeper), before joining up with FC United's first training sessions. With Phil Priestley attending a wedding, Barrie seized his big chance with a fantastic performance in the club's first friendly at Leigh, and further great displays in pre-season earned him the number one jersey when the league programme began at Leek. Quickly becoming a crowd favourite, his excellent form restricted Priestley to just one appearance with Barrie being the undisputed first choice netminder from September to March, with a run of six clean sheets in ten games being a personal highlight. Phil Melville then took over the gloves for much of the run-in, and the signing of Sam Ashton in July 2006 provided even stiffer competition. Beginning that season in the reserves, the consistency of Ashton meant Barrie was unable to regain his place in the side. In mid-September he was freed to join Salford City, for whom he lined up against FC in the FA Vase in November. He later had spells at Bacup Borough and New Mills before moving to live and work in China. He was back in Manchester to play for the FC United Old Boys in the club's 10th Anniversary celebration match against Leigh Genesis in July 2015, during which he brilliantly saved a penalty, and went on to play for Cheshire League side Linotype Cheadle Heath Nomads.

002 Mark RAWLINSON

Born: 09/06/1975, Bolton
Debut: No.2 v Leek CSOB (A, NWCFL2), 13/08/2005

Midfielder/Right-back

Season	LEAGUE			FA NATIONAL CUPS			OTHER CUPS / PLAY-OFFS			TOTALS		
	Starts	(+Sub)	Goals	Starts	(+Sub)	Goals	Starts	(+Sub)	Goals	Starts	(+Sub)	Goals
2005/06	10	(+4)	2				0	(+1)	0	10	(+5)	2
Totals	10	(+4)	2	0	(+0)	0	0	(+1)	0	10	(+5)	2

As well as having the honour of **captaining the team in FC United's first ever competitive match**, Mark was perhaps the best-known player in the initial squad. He started his career as a trainee at Manchester United in 1991, and helped the under-18s to the FA Youth Cup Final in 1993. Signing professional that summer, he spent two years in the reserves before joining Bournemouth in 1995. He made 90 senior appearances for the Dean Court outfit before switching to Exeter for the 2000/01 season, where he added a further 28 senior appearances. From there he dropped into non-league and saw service with Weymouth and Dorchester Town before heading back to the north-west. Capable of playing in a number of positions, he was expected to be a mainstay of the FC side and made a promising start to the season. He led the team out at Leek CSOB in August, and scored twice in the 7-1 victory over Eccleshall later that month. His time on the pitch was divided equally between right-back and midfield, but a series of niggling injuries from autumn onwards restricted his appearances and led to him hanging up his boots in the summer of 2006.

003 Gareth ORMES

Born: 03/02/1983, Pretoria (South Africa)
Debut: No.3 v Leek CSOB (A, NWCFL2), 13/08/2005

Full-back/Centre-back

Season	LEAGUE			FA NATIONAL CUPS			OTHER CUPS / PLAY-OFFS			TOTALS		
	Starts	(+Sub)	Goals	Starts	(+Sub)	Goals	Starts	(+Sub)	Goals	Starts	(+Sub)	Goals
2005/06	12	(+1)	0				1	(+0)	0	13	(+1)	0
2006/07	3	(+1)	0	0	(+0)	0	0	(+0)	0	3	(+1)	0
Totals	15	(+2)	0	0	(+0)	0	1	(+0)	0	16	(+2)	0

Despite being born and raised in South Africa, Gareth has his roots in the Manchester area as his parents are from Salford and Bolton. After representing Pretoria at schoolboy level and joining local team Rentmeester Rangers, he came over to England to play and ended up with Ramsbottom United. He had further spells with local teams Prestwich Heys, East Manchester and Salford City, where he was managed by Darren Lyons, who contacted him in June 2005 to join FC United's initial squad. He played at left-back in the first friendly at Leigh, and cemented his place as the team got the season off to a flyer. His attacking forays made him a crowd favourite until he was struck down by a double hernia in late October. He returned to the side in February before the injury struck again, and he was forced to rest on the sidelines as the team secured promotion and the championship. The form of new signing Alex Mortimer kept him out of the team in the early months of 2006/07 and he didn't return to the starting line-up until November, when he played three consecutive games at left-back, centre-back and right-back respectively. Soon after he signed again for Ramsbottom, for whom he faced FC when his former team-mates secured promotion in April 2007. He was back in an FC United shirt in July 2015 when he played for the Old Boys team in the club's 10th Anniversary celebration match against Leigh Genesis.

004 Steve SPENCER

Born: 06/10/1981, Manchester **Midfielder/Defender**
Debut: No.4 v Leek CSOB (A, NWCFL2), 13/08/2005 (scored 2)

Season	LEAGUE			FA NATIONAL CUPS			OTHER CUPS / PLAY-OFFS			TOTALS		
	Starts	(+Sub)	Goals	Starts	(+Sub)	Goals	Starts	(+Sub)	Goals	Starts	(+Sub)	Goals
2005/06	29	(+1)	4				3	(+0)	0	32	(+1)	4
2006/07	26	(+10)	1	4	(+0)	0	6	(+0)	0	36	(+10)	1
2007/08	6	(+0)	0	4	(+0)	0	0	(+0)	0	10	(+0)	0
Totals	**61**	**(+11)**	**5**	**8**	**(+0)**	**0**	**9**	**(+0)**	**0**	**78**	**(+11)**	**5**

In the 20th minute of FC United's first league game at Leek CSOB, Steve wrote himself into club folklore by **scoring the club's first competitive goal** with a long-range strike, and midway through the second half he scored again to put FC 3-2 ahead. A former schoolboy with Bolton Wanderers and young professional at Sheffield United, he drifted into non-league with first Leigh RMI, then Radcliffe Borough. Close friend Rob Nugent and former Radcliffe team-mate Karl Marginson persuaded him to join FC in July 2005, and he became an automatic choice in the centre of the park. Despite his initial goal threat, which also included another long-range stunner at home to Blackpool Mechanics, he concentrated more on the holding side of his game once Simon Carden had joined him in midfield. The Wythenshawe lad played that role to near-perfection on the march to promotion and the title, and such were his performances that he won the accolade of players' player of the season. His consistency continued in the second season when he was selected for all but one of the first 34 games, before a persistent hip problem mainly restricted him to appearances from the bench over the final two months. Despite some promising displays at the outset of 2007/08, Steve was unable to shake off his injury and reluctantly retired in October.

005 Robert NUGENT

Born: 27/12/1982, Bolton **Centre-back/Full-back**
Debut: No.5 v Leek CSOB (A, NWCFL2), 13/08/2005

Season	LEAGUE			FA NATIONAL CUPS			OTHER CUPS / PLAY-OFFS			TOTALS		
	Starts	(+Sub)	Goals	Starts	(+Sub)	Goals	Starts	(+Sub)	Goals	Starts	(+Sub)	Goals
2005/06	30	(+1)	4				1	(+1)	0	31	(+2)	4
2006/07	35	(+0)	8	4	(+0)	0	5	(+0)	2	44	(+0)	10
2007/08	34	(+0)	3	4	(+0)	1	7	(+1)	0	45	(+1)	4
2008/09	21	(+5)	0	0	(+2)	0	0	(+0)	0	21	(+7)	0
2009/10	16	(+1)	1	2	(+5)	0	0	(+1)	0	18	(+7)	1
Totals	**136**	**(+7)**	**16**	**10**	**(+7)**	**1**	**13**	**(+3)**	**2**	**159**	**(+17)**	**19**

Rob was a young professional at Sheffield United, before joining Northern Premier League side Ossett Town in 2003. A former season-ticket holder at Old Trafford and IMUSA member, he registered for FC United's initial trials in June 2005, but his previous football experience afforded him a place in the club's inaugural squad. He played in all of the first pre-season friendlies before starting the first eight league games at centre-back, during which he notched three goals. After spending October on the bench, he returned to the side at left-back, before switching to right-back where he became first choice until the end of the season. Despite this not being his preferred position, he still looked calm and assured while helping the team to win the title, scoring a further goal as promotion was secured at home to Chadderton. In the second season he was back at centre-back, becoming an automatic choice as his performances reached another level. He contributed an impressive haul of ten goals, which included a 35-yard screamer at home to Glossop North End and the winning goal in the Challenge Cup semi-final against Congleton Town. In one run in the spring he scored six goals in six games as the title was secured, and the team went on to win the double. He remained a model of consistency throughout 2007/08, despite having a number of different partners at the back during David Chadwick's absence. He scored the club's first ever goal in the FA Cup against Trafford, a crucial goal to seal the win at Curzon Ashton, and a brace at home to Lancaster City in the run-in to promotion. Injury problems at the start of 2008/09 kept him out until mid-September, but from the end of November he rarely missed a game, and the defence looked more secure with his presence. With Chadwick again suffering from injury, Rob captained the team for the last 11 games as they came within minutes of gaining a play-off place on the last day of the season. He also led the team in the first four matches of 2009/10, but this was to be his longest run in a frustrating injury-disrupted term. He played his 176th and final game at home to Matlock Town, when his perfectly weighted 40-yard pass was buried by Jerome Wright for the late winner. He later became a member of the FC United board.

006 Kevin ELVIN

Born: 22/05/1979, Coventry **Full-back/Centre-back**
Debut: No.6 v Leek CSOB (A, NWCFL2), 13/08/2005

Season	LEAGUE			FA NATIONAL CUPS			OTHER CUPS / PLAY-OFFS			TOTALS		
	Starts	(+Sub)	Goals	Starts	(+Sub)	Goals	Starts	(+Sub)	Goals	Starts	(+Sub)	Goals
2005/06	18	(+1)	0				4	(+0)	0	22	(+1)	0
Totals	**18**	**(+1)**	**0**	**0**	**(+0)**	**0**	**4**	**(+0)**	**0**	**22**	**(+1)**	**0**

A former Birmingham City schoolboy, Kevin had spells at Nuneaton Borough, Atherstone United, Sutton Coldfield Town, Stratford Town and Racing Club Warwick before playing in Australia with Sydney club AC United. After relocating to Manchester he joined FC United's initial training sessions in June 2005, and replaced injured skipper Billy McCartney in the first friendly at Leigh RMI. From then on he became an automatic choice, playing anywhere across the back four, until injury ended his season in February. Until then he boasted an impressive record of 18 wins, two draws and only two defeats from the games he started. Struggling to regain fitness as the 2006/07 season began, he played a handful of reserve games before departing for Trafford in February 2007.

007 Craig FLEURY

Born: 22/05/1976, Stockport
Debut: No.7 v Leek CSOB (A, NWCFL2), 13/08/2005

Right-winger

Season	LEAGUE Starts	(+Sub)	Goals	FA NATIONAL CUPS Starts	(+Sub)	Goals	OTHER CUPS / PLAY-OFFS Starts	(+Sub)	Goals	TOTALS Starts	(+Sub)	Goals
2005/06	1	(+0)	0				0	(+0)	0	1	(+0)	0
Totals	1	(+0)	0	0	(+0)	0	0	(+0)	0	1	(+0)	0

Part of FC United's inaugural squad, Craig's signing was something of a coup as he had played in the new Conference North for Ashton United during the previous season. A forward or winger who always scored his fair share of goals, he had also represented Cheadle Town, Warrington Town, Salford City, Woodley Sports, Curzon Ashton and Radcliffe Borough. At the first friendly at Leigh in July 2005 he impressed the watching Reds in the crowd with an exciting attacking display, setting up a number of chances with inviting crosses, and took this form into the final friendly at Flixton. It was therefore no surprise that he started the first league game at Leek CSOB, but unfortunately for Craig a first half injury led to him entering the record books as the club's first player to be substituted, and that was the last we saw of him in an FC United shirt. He later played for Witton Albion and in the Cheshire League with Middlewich Town before spells alongside his friend Joz Mitten at Prescot Cables, Rossendale United and Irlam.

008 Tony COYNE

Born: 12/03/1978, Manchester
Debut: No.8 v Leek CSOB (A, NWCFL2), 13/08/2005

Midfielder

Season	LEAGUE Starts	(+Sub)	Goals	FA NATIONAL CUPS Starts	(+Sub)	Goals	OTHER CUPS / PLAY-OFFS Starts	(+Sub)	Goals	TOTALS Starts	(+Sub)	Goals
2005/06	4	(+8)	0				0	(+0)	0	4	(+8)	0
Totals	4	(+8)	0	0	(+0)	0	0	(+0)	0	4	(+8)	0

Tony is the son of Peter Coyne, who played and scored for Manchester United's first team in 1976 just a couple of years after scoring for England Schoolboys at Wembley. He made his own way in semi-professional football as an industrious midfielder with Cheadle Town, Mossley, Flixton and Trafford before being part of FC United's first squad in July 2005. His performances in the friendlies earned him a starting berth for the first four league matches, but Simon Carden eventually took his place and his excellent form made it difficult for Tony to get back in. After several appearances from the bench he eventually moved back to Flixton in March 2006 in order to play regular football. He appeared against FC United the following season for Bacup Borough, before moving on to become assistant manager of Trafford when they won the North West Counties Football League title in 2007/08. His coaching career later took him to Manchester United, working with the schoolboys in the club's academy at Carrington.

010 Steve TORPEY

Born: 16/09/1981, Kirkby
Debut: No.10 v Leek CSOB (A, NWCFL2), 13/08/2005 (scored)

Left-winger

Season	LEAGUE Starts	(+Sub)	Goals	FA NATIONAL CUPS Starts	(+Sub)	Goals	OTHER CUPS / PLAY-OFFS Starts	(+Sub)	Goals	TOTALS Starts	(+Sub)	Goals
2005/06	29	(+0)	13				3	(+0)	4	32	(+0)	17
2010/11	0	(+7)	0	0	(+0)	0	0	(+1)	0	0	(+8)	0
2011/12	2	(+8)	3	0	(+1)	0	1	(+0)	1	3	(+9)	4
Totals	31	(+15)	16	0	(+1)	0	4	(+1)	5	35	(+17)	21

A versatile left-footed forward, Steve made FC United history by **scoring the club's first goal** with a fantastic strike in the friendly at Flixton in August 2005 He started his career as a young professional at Liverpool having represented England at schoolboy level (alongside Leon Mike), but his only taste of senior football was one game for Port Vale after moving there in 2001. The following year he joined the non-league circuit, spending most of the next three seasons with Prescot Cables and helping them to two promotions. After also spending some time with Altrincham in the new Conference North, he joined up with the FC United revolution as part of the club's first squad. His exciting play, mainly from the wing, endeared him to the crowd and he contributed 17 goals as the team stormed to the title. Among them was a hat-trick against New Mills in a cup-tie at Macclesfield, and some quite stunning efforts such as one against Nelson at Accrington. He continued these displays into the 2006 pre-season with an amazing goal in a friendly at Conference National side Halifax Town, who signed him three days later on a full-time contract. He spent two years at The Shay before moving into the Conference North with first Stalybridge Celtic, then AFC Telford United and Fleetwood Town. FC United were delighted to welcome Steve back to the club in the summer of 2010, but after just two brief appearances from the bench he suffered an early-season injury that ruled him out until March. He made a handful of further substitute appearances to help the team reach the play-off final, but he was unavailable for that match as the team suffered a narrow defeat. At the beginning of season 2011/12 it looked like he was getting back to his best with three goals in his first six matches, all from the bench, but his injury niggles still persisted and he was allowed to depart for Skelmersdale United in October 2011. As well as later becoming a respected coach with professional clubs, Steve has also represented England at Futsal. In July 2015 he played for the FC United Old Boys side in the club's 10th Anniversary celebration match against Leigh Genesis, where he was again amongst the goalscorers in the 3-3 draw.

009 Jonathan MITTEN

Born: 01/12/1976, Manchester
Debut: No.9 v Leek CSOB (A, NWCFL2), 13/08/2005 (scored)

Forward

Season	LEAGUE			FA NATIONAL CUPS			OTHER CUPS / PLAY-OFFS			TOTALS		
	Starts	(+Sub)	Goals	Starts	(+Sub)	Goals	Starts	(+Sub)	Goals	Starts	(+Sub)	Goals
2005/06	19	(+5)	7				2	(+2)	0	21	(+7)	7
Totals	**19**	**(+5)**	**7**	**0**	**(+0)**	**0**	**2**	**(+2)**	**0**	**21**	**(+7)**	**7**

Joz's place in FC United folklore was assured from the start, as it was he who recommended Karl Marginson as manager to the steering committee, and he subsequently became the first player to agree to be part of the squad. A cousin of team-mate Paul Mitten, Joz was a former season-ticket holder at Old Trafford who had played for local clubs Flixton, Trafford, Woodley Sports, Curzon Ashton and Radcliffe Borough, as well as spending a short spell in Australia with Manley Sea Warringah. He had spent the previous season in the new Conference North with Ashton United and Altrincham, helping the latter to promotion to the Conference National via the play-offs, but was happy to drop down five divisions such was his commitment to the FC United cause. An automatic choice to lead the line, beginning with the Leigh friendly in July 2005, Joz was overjoyed to score in the first league game at Leek CSOB and he became a firm crowd favourite. After Christmas, however, his appearances became intermittent with an increase in competition for places, but his contribution was always valuable when called upon in the run-in to the title, with a game-changing appearance from the bench away at Norton United being a particular highlight. Sadly his place could not be guaranteed for the second season and he moved back to Flixton in August 2006, and later saw service with Curzon Ashton, Trafford, Prescot Cables and Irlam, for whom he had a spell as manager. He played against FC on a handful of occasions and was always given a great reception by the fans, and in July 2015 he played in the club's 10th Anniversary celebration match against Leigh Genesis.

011 Rory PATTERSON

Born: 16/07/1984, Derry (Northern Ireland)
Debut: No.11 v Leek CSOB (A, NWCFL2), 13/08/2005

Forward

Season	LEAGUE			FA NATIONAL CUPS			OTHER CUPS / PLAY-OFFS			TOTALS		
	Starts	(+Sub)	Goals	Starts	(+Sub)	Goals	Starts	(+Sub)	Goals	Starts	(+Sub)	Goals
2005/06	25	(+5)	18				2	(+1)	1	27	(+6)	19
2006/07	37	(+1)	33	3	(+0)	2	5	(+0)	4	45	(+1)	39
2007/08	35	(+3)	33	3	(+0)	2	9	(+0)	6	47	(+3)	41
2015/16	0	(+5)	0	0	(+2)	0	1	(+0)	0	1	(+7)	0
Totals	**97**	**(+14)**	**84**	**6**	**(+2)**	**4**	**17**	**(+1)**	**11**	**120**	**(+17)**	**99**

An undisputed talent, during a rollercoaster career Rory played professional football in four countries and gained senior international caps. He started at Rochdale, making 18 appearances for them as a teenager before being released in 2004, despite being named the club's Young Player of the Year. He had spells the following season at Radcliffe Borough and Mossley and was considering his next move when former team-mate Karl Marginson invited him to join the FC United squad for the third friendly at Stalybridge. Taking to the field as a second-half substitute with an un-numbered shirt, he was immediately dubbed "Mr Mystery" and one of the club's first legends was born. He earned a starting berth for the first league game at Leek CSOB, and then scored the club's first home goal the following week against Padiham with a cheeky chipped penalty. This was a taste of things to come as Rory specialised in delighting the crowd with the spectacular, with controversy also sometimes in the mix. He received the club's first red card in the cup-tie at Colne, even though he had already been substituted, and picked up another later in the season. However the pure entertainment and goalscoring prowess that he contributed more than made up for his misdemeanours. He finished the first season as joint-top scorer with 18 goals, which included a memorable winner over challengers Winsford United and his first hat-trick against Leek, as the team won the league. His performances reached another level in the second season as he notched 39 goals on the way to winning the league and cup double. He continued to amaze, such as scoring from the kick-off immediately after Silsden had replied, and his tally included a four-goal haul past Glossop North End and hat-tricks in two successive games in April. His discipline greatly improved, which saw him rewarded with the captaincy when David Chadwick was absent, and he even took on the responsibility of keeping goal when Sam Ashton became injured at Newcastle Town. He surpassed this the next season by hitting 41 goals, including another four past Bridlington Town and a game-changing **club record seventh hat-trick** against Mossley on New Year's Day, a match he had started on the bench. He was captain for a long period due to Chadwick's injury, and finished the season by scoring in both play-off games as the team won a third successive promotion. In the summer of 2008 he signed for Bradford Park Avenue, then had a short spell with Droylsden before returning to his homeland to join Coleraine. Scoring another 41 goals earned him the title of Ulster Footballer of the Year, as well as his first full international cap for Northern Ireland and a transfer to Plymouth Argyle. Although he had been involved in the majority of matches, financial problems at the Devon club led to him joining Linfield, before signing for Derry City in January 2012. The highlight of his time at Brandywell was scoring twice to win the 2012 FAI Cup Final. His next move was to Cockburn City in Australia in February 2015, before he made a dramatic return to FC United in October. However, he was unfortunately unable to replicate the form of his first spell, and agonisingly remained stuck on 99 goals for the Reds, which remained the club record for a further two years. He returned to sign for Derry in December, where he was soon back amongst the goals when the Irish season began. He finished the 2016 campaign as the club's top scorer, but suffered a fractured ankle in the opening game of the following year, although he didn't realise that at the time and continued to train and play in the team for five weeks afterwards. In December 2017 he was appointed as Derry's first-team coach, a role he combined with playing duties, before moving to Northern Irish Premiership champions Crusaders in August 2018. After spells with intermediate level sides Ballymacash Rangers and Belfast Celtic, he returned to the top flight with Dungannon Swifts before being appointed player-manager of his local club Strabane Athletic in 2021.

012 Darren LYONS

Born: 09/11/1966, Manchester
Debut: Sub v Leek CSOB (A, NWCFL2), 13/08/2005

Right-winger/Forward

Season	LEAGUE			FA NATIONAL CUPS			OTHER CUPS / PLAY-OFFS			TOTALS		
	Starts	(+Sub)	Goals	Starts	(+Sub)	Goals	Starts	(+Sub)	Goals	Starts	(+Sub)	Goals
2005/06	5	(+8)	3				1	(+1)	0	6	(+9)	3
2006/07	1	(+3)	0	0	(+1)	0	0	(+0)	0	1	(+4)	0
2007/08	0	(+0)	0	0	(+0)	0	0	(+0)	0	0	(+0)	0
2008/09	0	(+0)	0	0	(+0)	0	1	(+0)	0	1	(+0)	0
Totals	6	(+11)	3	0	(+1)	0	2	(+1)	0	8	(+13)	3

Darren was appointed as Karl Marginson's first team coach just after FC United's formation in June 2005. The Middleton lad had started his career as a trainee at Oldham Athletic, but made his name as a flying non-league winger with Droylsden, Leek Town, Mossley, Accrington Stanley and Ashton United. His form attracted Bury, who signed him as a professional in 1992, and the following year he faced Manchester United in the FA Cup at Old Trafford. He moved to the Conference with Southport, before successful spells with Morecambe, Macclesfield Town (with whom he won the FA Trophy at Wembley in 1996) and Halifax Town, helping them to the Conference title in 1998. After representing Altrincham and Flixton, he moved into coaching as player-manager of East Manchester and Salford City before joining FC. He came off the bench in the first friendly at Leigh, and became **FC United's first substitute** in a competitive game when he came on at half-time at Leek CSOB. He brought his experience to the team with six starts and nine outings from the bench in the first season, also contributing three goals. A handful of games in 2006/07 followed as he focused on his coaching duties, but he played one last time in a cup-tie at Woodley Sports in December 2008, aged 42. He remained on the staff until leaving United along with Marginson in October 2017. He went on to coach at Wythenshawe Amateurs when they joined the North West Counties League in 2018, and later took temporary charge at Radcliffe under Marginson in 2020.

013 Adie ORR

Born: 22/02/1984, Manchester
Debut: Sub v Leek CSOB (A, NWCFL2), 13/08/2005 (scored)

Forward/Winger

Season	LEAGUE			FA NATIONAL CUPS			OTHER CUPS / PLAY-OFFS			TOTALS		
	Starts	(+Sub)	Goals	Starts	(+Sub)	Goals	Starts	(+Sub)	Goals	Starts	(+Sub)	Goals
2005/06	22	(+7)	15				4	(+0)	3	26	(+7)	18
2006/07	2	(+8)	0	0	(+1)	0	0	(+0)	0	2	(+9)	0
Totals	24	(+15)	15	0	(+1)	0	4	(+0)	3	28	(+16)	18

Adie was a young professional at Manchester City, despite growing up in Withington as a United fan, before his release in 2003. He had spells at Conference side Leigh RMI, and with the reserve teams of Altrincham and Witton Albion, but was without a club when he registered for FC United's initial player trials at Fallowfield in June 2005. Steve Eyre, his former coach at City, was there helping with the selection process, and recommended him to Karl Marginson straight away. Impressing in training, he was delighted to be selected to be part of the club's first squad, and was given his first taste of action as a substitute in the first friendly at his old club Leigh. He immediately endeared himself to the fans with his speed and movement, and earned a starting spot for the remaining friendlies, which he capped with a goal at Flixton. Although starting the league season on the bench, he came on to score at Leek, and ended August as the club's top scorer with five goals from four appearances. Rewarded with an extended run in the side from early October, he bagged **FC United's first ever hat-trick** in the cup-tie with Cheadle Town, which was sandwiched by braces against Daisy Hill and Nelson, and finished 2005 as joint top scorer with 16. After picking up a knock in mid-February he missed several games, but was fit for bench duties as promotion was secured. The explosive form of Stuart Rudd and Rory Patterson early in the second season restricted Adie to just two starts and nine substitute outings, and he moved on to Mossley in search of regular games in October. He later played for Chadderton and Runcorn Linnets.

014 William AHERN

Born: 04/02/1987, Islington
Debut: Sub v Leek CSOB (A, NWCFL2), 13/08/2005

Midfielder

Season	LEAGUE			FA NATIONAL CUPS			OTHER CUPS / PLAY-OFFS			TOTALS		
	Starts	(+Sub)	Goals	Starts	(+Sub)	Goals	Starts	(+Sub)	Goals	Starts	(+Sub)	Goals
2005/06	15	(+9)	3				1	(+0)	0	16	(+9)	3
2006/07	10	(+1)	0	1	(+0)	0	0	(+0)	0	11	(+1)	0
Totals	25	(+10)	3	1	(+0)	0	1	(+0)	0	27	(+10)	3

The youngest member of FC United's squad as the club began its inaugural season, Will had previously played as a schoolboy with Macclesfield Town and with his local club Urmston Town. He first appeared off the bench to wrap up the scoring in the final pre-season friendly at Flixton in August 2005, and also came on in the opening league game at Leek CSOB. After a spell out injured, his first start came at Darwen in November, and he kept his place for the next two games. Involved in every game from the start of the New Year, he scored his first goal in the memorable win at Blackpool Mechanics during a run of ten consecutive starts in the heart of midfield as the Reds romped to the title. So impressive were his displays that they earned him a trial with Grimsby Town in March 2006. Increased competition for places, coupled with a red card at Curzon Ashton, restricted his opportunities in the second season and he informed the club of his decision to leave in December 2006 in order to go travelling. He later had spells with Salford City, Irlam and Trafford, for whom he was shown a red card after being substituted in a bizarre incident when facing FC United on New Year's Day 2015. He went on to assist Wythenshawe Amateurs to gain promotion to the North West Counties League, and scoring the first goal under their new floodlights in 2018.

015 David CHADWICK

Born: 17/09/1977, Wigan
Debut: No.5 v Padiham (H, NWCFL2), 20/08/2005

Centre-back

Season	LEAGUE			FA NATIONAL CUPS			OTHER CUPS / PLAY-OFFS			TOTALS		
	Starts	(+Sub)	Goals	Starts	(+Sub)	Goals	Starts	(+Sub)	Goals	Starts	(+Sub)	Goals
2005/06	27	(+1)	6				3	(+0)	0	30	(+1)	6
2006/07	33	(+3)	4	2	(+0)	1	6	(+0)	1	41	(+3)	6
2007/08	27	(+0)	3	4	(+0)	0	3	(+0)	1	34	(+0)	4
2008/09	27	(+7)	0	5	(+0)	1	0	(+0)	0	32	(+7)	1
2009/10	23	(+3)	5	5	(+0)	1	0	(+0)	0	28	(+3)	6
2010/11	17	(+3)	0	0	(+1)	0	3	(+0)	0	20	(+4)	0
2011/12	2	(+2)	1	0	(+1)	0	1	(+0)	0	3	(+3)	1
2018/19	0	(+0)	0	0	(+0)	0	0	(+1)	0	0	(+1)	0
2020/21	0	(+1)	0	0	(+0)	0	0	(+0)	0	0	(+1)	0
2021/22	0	(+0)	0	0	(+0)	0	0	(+0)	0	0	(+0)	0
Totals	156	(+20)	19	16	(+2)	3	16	(+1)	2	188	(+23)	24

Having previously played alongside Karl Marginson at Salford City, the no-nonsense centre-back was earmarked by the manager to lead his new team from the beginning. However, David was already contracted to Prescot Cables, and it wasn't until after the first league game that they agreed to let their player of the year sign for FC United. The former Leigh RMI and Skelmersdale United man was installed as captain and led by example, consistently giving 100% effort to drive his team forward to the title. Not only was he solid in defence, he was a threat at the other end too, contributing vital goals such as a last-minute equaliser away to Cheadle Town and a winner away to Oldham Town. His form continued throughout 2006/07, with just 37 goals conceded in his 44 appearances as he led his charges to a league and cup double. In 2007/08 he was sidelined from October until the end of January, but returned to skipper the team through a congested fixture list to win the promotion play-off final, in which he powered home a header to put the Reds in front against Skelmersdale. In 2008/09 he missed just a handful of games until the end of February before injury struck again, but despite being less than 100% fit he was on the bench for most of the run-in as a place in the play-offs was narrowly missed. 2009/10 was a transitional season when a settled back four was rare, particularly when Chaddy had another three-month lay-off. Still struggling with niggles as 2010/11 began, he wasn't quite fit enough to progress beyond the bench as the manager built a new backline, and had a short loan at New Mills to build up his match fitness. He returned to make his first league start in January, and soon became a regular again as the team climbed the table to eventually reach the play-off final. With more competition for places, he was consigned mainly to the bench once again in 2011/12, and despite being in the squad for every game it was with some sadness that he was released at the end of October. He returned to Skelmersdale, before joining Stockport Sports and then having a spell as assistant manager to Phil Power at Salford. In the summer of 2016 he was appointed as manager of Chorley's newly-formed under-21 development squad, and led them to the Lancashire League West title in 2017. David made a welcome return to FC later that year, assuming responsibility for scouting and managing the club's nursery side Moston United in the Lancashire & Cheshire Amateur League. A change in structure saw him take charge of the club's new under-21 side in 2018, before he stepped up to first-team duties as caretaker manager after the resignation of Tom Greaves in August 2018. He steadied the ship somewhat with an unbeaten start, and was in charge for ten games until the appointment of Neil Reynolds in October. He remained part of the senior backroom staff, and remarkably returned to the field in an FC shirt once again, at the age of 41. Named as a substitute for the Manchester Premier Cup tie at Mossley in November, he replaced 38-year-old Jamie Milligan in the second half to make his first appearance for the club in seven years. When he came off the bench again in the last minute of the Broadhurst Park win over Warrington Town in November 2020 he became **FC United's oldest player at the age of 43**. He left his coaching role at the club in the summer of 2022.

016 Scott HOLT

Born: 22/03/1983, Manchester
Debut: Sub v Padiham (H, NWCFL2), 20/08/2005

Right-winger

Season	LEAGUE			FA NATIONAL CUPS			OTHER CUPS / PLAY-OFFS			TOTALS		
	Starts	(+Sub)	Goals	Starts	(+Sub)	Goals	Starts	(+Sub)	Goals	Starts	(+Sub)	Goals
2005/06	1	(+3)	2				0	(+0)	0	1	(+3)	2
Totals	1	(+3)	2	0	(+0)	0	0	(+0)	0	1	(+3)	2

Part of FC United's initial squad, and a keen supporter from the start, Scott was a forward or right winger from Droylsden who had caught the eye of coach Darren Lyons during spells with East Manchester and Chadderton. A substitute in the first friendly at Leigh in July 2005, a niggling thigh injury hampered his prospects for a starting berth, but he showed his potential with exciting appearances from the bench away to Winsford United and Ashton Town, when he scored twice. His persistence was rewarded with a start on the wing at home to Norton United, but this proved a bad day all round as the Reds slipped to their first defeat, and Scott was not involved after that. He spent time with Glossop North End later in the year while still training with FC United, but eventually left the club to join Trafford. He later played for Irlam, Mossley and AFC Emley.

017 Ryan GILLIGAN

Born: 26/09/1979, Manchester
Debut: Sub v Padiham (H, NWCFL2), 20/08/2005

Midfielder

Season	LEAGUE			FA NATIONAL CUPS			OTHER CUPS / PLAY-OFFS			TOTALS		
	Starts	(+Sub)	Goals	Starts	(+Sub)	Goals	Starts	(+Sub)	Goals	Starts	(+Sub)	Goals
2005/06	3	(+4)	2				1	(+0)	0	4	(+4)	2
Totals	3	(+4)	2	0	(+0)	0	1	(+0)	0	4	(+4)	2

A member of the club's initial squad, Ryan was a powerful midfielder previously with Altrincham and Flixton. He caught the eye of the crowd with an energetic display in the first friendly at Leigh in July 2005, and soon played his way into contention when the season began. A particularly memorable performance came from the bench away to Winsford United, and he also contributed two goals in his first six games. After a spell out with injury he found it difficult to break up the partnership of Steve Spencer and Simon Carden, and in December rejoined Flixton, for whom he played against FC United the following season. He later linked up with his friend Joz Mitten at Irlam, where he also had a spell as manager.

018 Simon CARDEN

Born: 26/10/1978, Manchester
Debut: Sub v Eccleshall (H, NWCFL2), 24/08/2005

Midfielder/Forward

Season	LEAGUE			FA NATIONAL CUPS			OTHER CUPS / PLAY-OFFS			TOTALS		
	Starts	(+Sub)	Goals	Starts	(+Sub)	Goals	Starts	(+Sub)	Goals	Starts	(+Sub)	Goals
2005/06	19	(+6)	17				3	(+0)	1	22	(+6)	19
2006/07	27	(+7)	12	3	(+0)	3	3	(+2)	1	33	(+9)	16
2007/08	20	(+13)	8	4	(+0)	1	6	(+2)	0	30	(+15)	9
2008/09	38	(+0)	11	5	(+0)	1	0	(+0)	0	43	(+0)	12
2009/10	32	(+2)	6	3	(+4)	2	0	(+1)	0	35	(+7)	8
2010/11	25	(+10)	3	1	(+4)	0	1	(+2)	0	27	(+16)	3
Totals	161	(+38)	57	16	(+8)	7	13	(+7)	3	190	(+53)	67

Simon spent time as a schoolboy with Manchester United, but started his career as a young professional at Stockport County. Able to play as an attacking midfielder or forward, he was a regular reserve on the fringes of the first team but was released in 1998. He made his way into non-league with Radcliffe Borough, where his performances attracted Accrington Stanley who signed him for a fee of £5,000. He enjoyed a successful time there, winning several trophies before a return to Radcliffe, who he also helped to a promotion. After a spell at Ashton United, Simon had a knee operation which kept him out of the game from early 2005, from which he was still recovering when former team-mate Karl Marginson and friend Joz Mitten persuaded him to join them at the start of the FC United adventure. After missing pre-season, he was gradually introduced to the team in the early league games, becoming a regular in midfield from late September. He proved his capabilities with a spectacular winner at home to Oldham Town, which set him on a tremendous run of 18 goals in 15 matches, including a hat-trick against New Mills and a **club record haul of five goals in a game** past Castleton Gabriels. A knee injury then kept him out for two months, but he returned to the squad for the run-in as promotion and the title were secured. A slight niggle kept him on the bench for the first game of 2006/07, but he emerged to score the club's first goal of that campaign, and his first of 13 in a 17 match run as he recaptured his form of the previous season to help the team to a league and cup double. More vital goals followed during 2007/08, when at times he was asked to play up front due to injuries as the team eventually earned promotion via the play-offs. Season 2008/09 saw Simon record his highest number of league appearances, missing just four games (none of which were won) as the team came within minutes of earning a place in the play-offs. His form in the second half of the season, when he averaged a goal every other game, was a major factor in the climb up the table. 2009/10 was a transitional season for the club, and a settled side proved difficult to field, but Simon remained one of the bedrocks of the team throughout the term, particularly over the winter when he was the most experienced player. As the team began to kick on again in 2010/11, he was consigned mainly to bench duties in the first half of the season, but he appeared in most games of the famous FA Cup run, including Rochdale and the Brighton replay. He earned a regular starting place again after the new year as the team began to steadily climb the table and ultimately reach the play-off final. However, after taking part in the 2011 pre-season, Simon decided to join his local club Trafford ahead of the new campaign, where he was once again amongst the goals. He ended his semi-professional career with a third spell at Radcliffe in 2014, but FC fans were delighted to see him play for the Old Boys XI in Broadhurst Park's opening game in May 2015.

019 Phil PRIESTLEY

Born: 30/03/1976, Wigan
Debut: No.1 v Winsford United (A, NWCFL2), 31/08/2005

Goalkeeper

Season	LEAGUE			FA NATIONAL CUPS			OTHER CUPS / PLAY-OFFS			TOTALS		
	Starts	(+Sub)	Goals	Starts	(+Sub)	Goals	Starts	(+Sub)	Goals	Starts	(+Sub)	Goals
2005/06	1	(+0)	0				0	(+0)	0	1	(+0)	0
2007/08	3	(+0)	0	0	(+0)	0	0	(+0)	0	3	(+0)	0
Totals	4	(+0)	0	0	(+0)	0	0	(+0)	0	4	(+0)	0

When FC United's first squad was announced in July 2005, Phil Priestley was one of two goalkeepers in the party. Being ten years older than Barrie George, it was expected that Phil would be the no.1. He came with experience of playing in the Football League for Rochdale and in the UEFA Cup for Bangor City, where he was named in the League Of Wales Team Of The Year in 2002. However, on the day of the club's first friendly at Leigh, Phil had to attend a wedding, allowing George to seize his chance with a great display. Restricted to just one league start during the first weeks of the season, Phil left the club amicably in September in order to play first team football and joined Radcliffe Borough. Later with Chorley, he returned to FC United as a coach and back-up for Sam Ashton in October 2007, and added a further three games to his tally before once again joining Radcliffe, for whom he played against FC United no fewer than four times in the space of a month later that term. During his career he was also on the books of Wigan Athletic, Atherton LR, Leyland Motors, Scarborough, Chester City, Prescot Cables, Stalybridge Celtic, Runcorn Linnets, Stockport Sports and AFC Blackpool. He remained active into his 40s as goalkeeping coach and cover at National League club Southport, as well as playing occasionally for Skelmersdale United.

020 Phil POWER

Born: 25/07/1966, Salford
Debut: Sub v Ashton Town (A, NWCFL2), 03/09/2005

Forward

Season	LEAGUE			FA NATIONAL CUPS			OTHER CUPS / PLAY-OFFS			TOTALS		
	Starts	(+Sub)	Goals	Starts	(+Sub)	Goals	Starts	(+Sub)	Goals	Starts	(+Sub)	Goals
2005/06	4	(+7)	2				0	(+1)	1	4	(+8)	3
2006/07	0	(+5)	2	0	(+1)	1	0	(+0)	0	0	(+6)	3
2007/08	1	(+2)	0	0	(+0)	0	0	(+1)	0	1	(+3)	0
Totals	5	(+14)	4	0	(+1)	1	0	(+2)	1	5	(+17)	6

A legend in north-west non-league football, Phil first made his name at Northwich Victoria, appearing for them at Wembley in the FA Trophy Final aged just 17. After a spell at neighbours Witton Albion, he became a professional at Crewe Alexandra in 1985, scoring twice on his debut against Burnley. He returned to non-league in 1987 with Horwich RMI, and then had an enjoyable spell in Malta with Sliema Wanderers. He came back to join Chorley, where he was in prolific form when suffering a badly broken leg that sidelined him for over a year. Once fit he played for Barrow and Stalybridge Celtic before signing for Macclesfield Town in 1993, where he had the best years of his career under Sammy McIlroy. They won the Conference twice in 1995 and 1997, and in between Phil also won his second FA Trophy by defeating former club Northwich at Wembley, and earned caps for the England C side. He was involved in the majority of games in the Silkmen's first season in the Football League, when they surprised many by winning promotion again in 1998. Only offered a short-term contract that summer, Phil left to join Altrincham and later had spells with Radcliffe Borough and Bacup Borough. In June 2005, his former Macclesfield colleague Karl Marginson appointed him as assistant manager upon FC United's formation. A colourful character who quickly became popular with the fans, he came off the bench during the first friendly at Leigh, and then made occasional appearances as substitute once the season began. He scored his first goal at his old ground Moss Rose in a cup-tie with New Mills in December, and was outstanding when appearing for the second half away to Blackpool Mechanics. This earned him a start in three of the next five games, in which he notched twice, and his experience was vital in helping the team to promotion. He made just six appearances from the bench in 2006/07, but still scored three goals, with the most memorable putting the nine men ahead against Quorn in the FA Vase. His powerful header in a win at Colne in April 2007 puts him in the record books as **FC United's oldest goalscorer** at the age of 40 years 263 days. He appeared four times in 2007/08 to help out in injury crises before concentrating on coaching. However, a cruciate injury limited his involvement and he left United in 2009, before managing Salford City.

021 Tony CULLEN

Born: 25/09/1973, Salford
Debut: Sub v Ashton Town (A, NWCFL2), 03/09/2005

Full-back

Season	LEAGUE			FA NATIONAL CUPS			OTHER CUPS / PLAY-OFFS			TOTALS		
	Starts	(+Sub)	Goals	Starts	(+Sub)	Goals	Starts	(+Sub)	Goals	Starts	(+Sub)	Goals
2005/06	14	(+9)	0				2	(+1)	0	16	(+10)	0
Totals	14	(+9)	0	0	(+0)	0	2	(+1)	0	16	(+10)	0

A hard tackling defensive player, Tony was a former young professional with Blackburn Rovers and Aston Villa before spells in non-league with Mossley, Altrincham and Salford City, where he played alongside several future FC United team-mates. His first appearance for the Reds was in the pre-season friendly at Flixton in August 2005, and he became a regular on the bench after the campaign began before gaining a run at right-back in November. His next sustained spell was at left-back for the title run-in, part of a defence that proved difficult to breach. At the end of the term he retired from playing duties in order to manage the club's newly-formed reserve team, and led them to the title in their first season. In October 2007 he stepped up to become first team coach, a role he held until December 2008 when he left the club to pursue business interests. Tony later became a successful tri-athlete and has participated in Ironman competitions around the world.

022 Billy McCARTNEY

Born: 16/04/1976, Manchester
Debut: Sub v Castleton Gabriels (A, NWCFL2), 17/09/2005

Centre-back

Season	LEAGUE			FA NATIONAL CUPS			OTHER CUPS / PLAY-OFFS			TOTALS		
	Starts	(+Sub)	Goals	Starts	(+Sub)	Goals	Starts	(+Sub)	Goals	Starts	(+Sub)	Goals
2005/06	17	(+3)	0				3	(+0)	0	20	(+3)	0
Totals	17	(+3)	0	0	(+0)	0	3	(+0)	0	20	(+3)	0

Billy went down in history as **FC United's first ever captain** when he led the team out in the friendly at Leigh in July 2005, but sadly for the North Manchester lad he had to leave the field early in proceedings due to a broken arm and dislocated shoulder. A former trainee with Rochdale, the solid centre-back had vast non-league experience from spells at Macclesfield Town, Oldham Town, Castleton Gabriels, Ramsbottom United, Trafford, Salford City, Chorley, Stalybridge Celtic, Mossley and Bacup Borough. Once he regained his fitness in September he enjoyed formidable partnerships with both David Chadwick and Dave Brown as the Reds extended their lead at the top of the table, with Billy boasting a record of just 18 goals conceded in his 23 appearances. Despite this he moved back to Trafford just before the 2006/07 season, and scored a late equaliser from the spot against United in the remarkable 4-4 draw in April. He later became player-coach at Salford City and then assistant manager at Ashton United. In July 2015 he captained the FC United Old Boys side in the club's 10th Anniversary celebration match against Leigh Genesis. Since retiring, Billy became an active member of local running club Salford Harriers, who used the Broadhurst Park ground as a base.

023 Paul MITTEN

Born: 22/12/1975, Stockport
Debut: Sub v Cheadle Town (A, NWCFLCC:1), 17/10/2005

Midfielder/Forward

Season	LEAGUE			FA NATIONAL CUPS			OTHER CUPS / PLAY-OFFS			TOTALS		
	Starts	(+Sub)	Goals	Starts	(+Sub)	Goals	Starts	(+Sub)	Goals	Starts	(+Sub)	Goals
2005/06	1	(+2)	1				0	(+2)	0	1	(+4)	1
Totals	1	(+2)	1	0	(+0)	0	0	(+2)	0	1	(+4)	1

Another inaugural squad member, Paul is the grandson of former Manchester United winger Charlie Mitten, who was part of the club's first great post-war side that lifted the FA Cup in 1948. His dad was also a reserve player at Old Trafford in the 1960s and Paul became the third generation to join United when he signed as a trainee in 1992. Sadly he suffered from injuries and was released in 1994, despite having a decent scoring record in the junior teams. He spent some time on professional forms with Coventry City but eventually found first team football in the non-league game with Stalybridge Celtic and Southport, for whom he was on the bench at Wembley for the 1998 FA Trophy Final. He moved on to Curzon Ashton, Mossley and Abbey Hey before joining FC United with his cousin Joz in July 2005. He started the first friendly at Leigh at right-back, but a combination of injuries kept him out of contention until October when he showed the fans what he could do with a lively display from the bench in the club's first cup-tie. This earned him a start when he replaced Joz up front for the home game with Nelson, and he didn't disappoint by opening the scoring with a tremendous curling shot from outside the area. Unfortunately his injury hoodoo struck again and he was forced to leave the action just after half-time. He returned in November to make three further substitute appearances, the final one being in the 10-2 over Castleton Gabriels, before deciding to leave FC due to increasing work and family commitments just before his 30th birthday in December 2005.

024 David BROWN

Born: 15/09/1972, Heywood
Debut: Sub v Nelson (H, NWCFL2), 22/10/2005

Centre-back

Season	LEAGUE			FA NATIONAL CUPS			OTHER CUPS / PLAY-OFFS			TOTALS		
	Starts	(+Sub)	Goals	Starts	(+Sub)	Goals	Starts	(+Sub)	Goals	Starts	(+Sub)	Goals
2005/06	18	(+5)	1				2	(+0)	0	20	(+5)	1
2006/07	13	(+8)	3	0	(+0)	0	1	(+2)	1	14	(+10)	4
2007/08	5	(+2)	0	0	(+1)	0	2	(+0)	0	7	(+3)	0
Totals	36	(+15)	4	0	(+1)	0	5	(+2)	1	41	(+18)	5

After being on schoolboy forms at Manchester United, Dave turned down an apprenticeship at Rochdale in order to concentrate on his studies. After graduating from university he entered the non-league circuit, playing for various local clubs such as Leigh RMI, Accrington Stanley, Trafford, Mossley, Castleton Gabriels, Radcliffe Borough and Salford City, where he played with several future FC United team-mates including Karl Marginson. Capable of playing in midfield or the centre of defence, he also spent an enjoyable summer in Canada with Lethbridge Bulldogs. As the 2005/06 season began, Dave thought his playing days were over, but he was invited to train with FC in September, and signed for the club soon after. Making his first appearance from the bench, his first start came at Darwen and he marked the occasion by opening the scoring. Thereafter he featured in virtually every game as the team romped to the title. After playing in the 2006 pre-season, he spent a brief spell back at Salford but returned to the Reds in October to be a valuable member of the squad as they won the league and cup double. He particularly enjoyed his goals at Colne in the cup and at home to Maine Road. He became player-coach in the summer of 2007, helping the team in a further ten matches before hanging up his boots. After a stint managing Rochdale Town, he returned to FC's coaching staff to work at various times with the youths, reserves and particularly the first team. He left the club in November 2016 in order to take a break from football for family reasons. In September 2017 he gathered together most of the inaugural season's squad to take part in a charity match at Broadhurst Park to help raise money for treatment for his partner Natalie.

025 Joshua HOWARD

Born: 15/11/1980, Ashton-under-Lyne   Winger
Debut: No.7 v Colne (A, NWCFLCC:2), 13/11/2005

Season	LEAGUE			FA NATIONAL CUPS			OTHER CUPS / PLAY-OFFS			TOTALS		
	Starts	(+Sub)	Goals	Starts	(+Sub)	Goals	Starts	(+Sub)	Goals	Starts	(+Sub)	Goals
2005/06	16	(+2)	5				3	(+0)	0	19	(+2)	5
2006/07	24	(+8)	9	4	(+0)	1	4	(+2)	2	32	(+10)	12
2007/08	4	(+3)	1	1	(+0)	1	3	(+2)	0	8	(+5)	2
Totals	44	(+13)	15	5	(+0)	2	10	(+4)	2	59	(+17)	19

A tremendously gifted attacking midfield player, Josh started his career as a young professional at Manchester United, where he graduated to the reserve team before his release in the summer of 2000. He began playing non-league football with local clubs Stalybridge Celtic and Hyde United before settling at Mossley, whom he helped to promotion to the Northern Premier League in 2004. He joined FC United in November 2005, and quickly became an automatic choice on the right side of midfield, playing a key role as the team went on to lift the title. His attacking play excited the crowd as he set up numerous goals and scored five himself, including the goal of the season with a 40-yard strike from the touchline at home to Darwen. He showed his versatility in the second season by switching between right and left wings, and also appearing as an attacking central midfielder. He contributed twelve goals to help the team to the double, saving the best for last with a tremendous run and finish for the winner in the cup final against Curzon Ashton. Injuries unfortunately hindered Josh during 2007/08, putting him out of contention from September until January, and then from the end of March onwards, but he still scored memorable goals in the club's first FA Cup tie against Trafford and his last home appearance against Radcliffe Borough. He left the club in the summer of 2008 to sign for New Mills, and later played for Runcorn Linnets.

026 Chris SIMMS

Born: 10/10/1966, Salford   Midfielder
Debut: Sub v Flixton (A, NWCFL2), 26/12/2005

Season	LEAGUE			FA NATIONAL CUPS			OTHER CUPS / PLAY-OFFS			TOTALS		
	Starts	(+Sub)	Goals	Starts	(+Sub)	Goals	Starts	(+Sub)	Goals	Starts	(+Sub)	Goals
2005/06	7	(+7)	3				0	(+1)	0	7	(+8)	3
Totals	7	(+7)	3	0	(+0)	0	0	(+1)	0	7	(+8)	3

After initially guesting for FC United in the pre-season friendly at Flixton in August 2005, Chris eventually joined the club in December after quitting as player-manager of Maine Road. Despite being a massive Red, he had made over 500 appearances for the Chorlton club over 22 years, interrupted by spells in the Northern Premier League with Hyde United and Trafford, as well as a short time with Lower Hutt City in New Zealand. He became the club's oldest debutant at 39 years and 77 days, a record that stood for exactly 11 years until it was beaten by Adriano Basso. His vast non-league experience brought a calm assurance to midfield, and he contributed vital goals to help secure promotion. At the end of the term Chris became manager of the club's newly-formed youth team, a post he held until 2008, and proudly saw a number of his charges go on to represent the first team. He continued to play occasional games for Maine Road well into his 40s, before becoming a schoolboy academy coach at Manchester United.

027 Leon Depasois-MIKE

Born: 04/09/1981, Manchester   Forward
Debut: No.9 v Winsford United (H, NWCFL2), 02/01/2006

Season	LEAGUE			FA NATIONAL CUPS			OTHER CUPS / PLAY-OFFS			TOTALS		
	Starts	(+Sub)	Goals	Starts	(+Sub)	Goals	Starts	(+Sub)	Goals	Starts	(+Sub)	Goals
2005/06	3	(+2)	0				1	(+0)	0	4	(+2)	0
2006/07	0	(+0)	0	0	(+0)	0	0	(+0)	0	0	(+0)	0
Totals	3	(+2)	0	0	(+0)	0	1	(+0)	0	4	(+2)	0

Leon was a powerfully built but very skilful centre forward who had represented England at schoolboy and youth level and had attended the FA National School at Lilleshall. He was a big United fan, but started his career at Manchester City, where he made two Football League appearances. He spent loan spells at Oxford United and Halifax Town before joining Aberdeen in February 2002 for a fee of £50,000. He made an instant impact with the Dons faithful by scoring on his debut against Dundee United at Pittodrie in a live TV game. Further highlights of his stay in Scotland included a winning goal on his first start against Dunfermline, facing Hertha Berlin in the UEFA Cup and netting a goal against Rangers. Upon his release in 2003 he headed back to Manchester and surprisingly chose to play non-league football with Mossley, where he scored 37 goals in his two seasons there. Having not appeared during 2005/06 he signed for FC United in December and made his debut in the memorable home win over Winsford United in the first game of 2006. His appearances were sporadic as he searched for match fitness, but his effort and technique could not be faulted when he was on the pitch in a red shirt. He started the second season with a few reserve matches and was called up to the bench for the club's first match in the FA Vase, but the partnership of Rory Patterson and Stuart Rudd was hard to break up and Leon eventually left to join Flixton in January 2007. Later that year he retired from playing to study for a law degree at university, before returning to the game as a regional manager at the Quinton Fortune Academy and as a youth coach at Oldham Athletic. In May 2022 he became manager at North West Counties League side Burscough.

028 Simon BAND

Born: 01/01/1977, Macclesfield
Debut: No.9 v Daisy Hill (A, NWCFL2), 11/02/2006

Forward

Season	LEAGUE			FA NATIONAL CUPS			OTHER CUPS / PLAY-OFFS			TOTALS		
	Starts	(+Sub)	Goals	Starts	(+Sub)	Goals	Starts	(+Sub)	Goals	Starts	(+Sub)	Goals
2005/06	2	(+0)	0				0	(+0)	0	2	(+0)	0
Totals	2	(+0)	0	0	(+0)	0	0	(+0)	0	2	(+0)	0

Simon is a former Congleton Town, Buxton, Atherton LR and Trafford centre-forward who signed for FC United in February 2006 after a notable display in a friendly at Glossop North End. He made an impressive debut leading the line in the away victory against Daisy Hill the following weekend, and kept the number nine shirt for the memorable trip to Bloomfield Road to face Blackpool Mechanics. Unfortunately he picked up an injury during the first half and had to be withdrawn at the interval, and this proved to be his last appearance in a competitive match for the Reds. After featuring in several friendly matches before the end of the campaign, he left the club in the summer and reverted to playing local amateur football.

029 David SWARBRICK

Born: 14/04/1984, Barrow-in-Furness
Debut: Sub v Flixton (H, NWCFL2), 15/03/2006

Winger/Forward

Season	LEAGUE			FA NATIONAL CUPS			OTHER CUPS / PLAY-OFFS			TOTALS		
	Starts	(+Sub)	Goals	Starts	(+Sub)	Goals	Starts	(+Sub)	Goals	Starts	(+Sub)	Goals
2005/06	7	(+2)	1				0	(+0)	0	7	(+2)	1
2006/07	6	(+7)	2	0	(+0)	0	2	(+0)	0	8	(+7)	2
2007/08	4	(+8)	0	1	(+0)	0	1	(+2)	0	6	(+10)	0
Totals	17	(+17)	3	1	(+0)	0	3	(+2)	0	21	(+19)	3

A pacy winger with a tremendous work rate, Dave signed in March 2006 after impressing and scoring against FC United when we hosted his team Holker Old Boys at Altrincham in February. His energetic attacking play brought a different dimension to the team for the run-in to the title, and this kept him in the team for the beginning of the second season. Unfortunately injuries ruled him out of contention for two long spells, but he still made a valuable contribution to a second successive championship, such as with his two goals in six minutes away to Atherton Collieries. Season 2007/08 frustratingly followed a similar pattern and Dave left the club in November to play for first Barrow and then Lancaster City in order to improve his fitness. He returned ahead of the transfer deadline in March 2008, when the team still had 12 games to play in less than a month, and helped achieve a second place finish and eventual promotion via the play-offs. He returned to Lancaster in the summer of 2008 and also later played for New Mills, AFC Fylde and Kendal Town. He was still hitting the net back at Holker Old Boys in 2016/17, when he finished as the team's top scorer. Dave was a popular player with FC United fans, and even more so with the management team who couldn't help but praise his dedication in travelling down from Barrow for every training session. He was deservedly invited to play for the Old Boys XI in the opening game at Broadhurst Park in May 2015.

031 Warren COLLIER

Born: 13/06/1986, Manchester
Debut: No.2 v Chadderton (A, NWCFL2), 19/04/2006

Right-back/Right-winger

Season	LEAGUE			FA NATIONAL CUPS			OTHER CUPS / PLAY-OFFS			TOTALS		
	Starts	(+Sub)	Goals	Starts	(+Sub)	Goals	Starts	(+Sub)	Goals	Starts	(+Sub)	Goals
2005/06	1	(+0)	0				0	(+0)	0	1	(+0)	0
2007/08	0	(+1)	0	0	(+0)	0	0	(+0)	0	0	(+1)	0
Totals	1	(+1)	0	0	(+0)	0	0	(+0)	0	1	(+1)	0

Warren had been playing in the Manchester League for Monton Amateurs when he first appeared for FC United in a friendly at Glossop North End in February 2006, in which he scored the side's opening goal. Comfortable on the right side of defence or attack, he made his debut at right-back at Boundary Park against Chadderton in April, soon after the league title had been secured. For the second season he was a mainstay of the newly-formed reserve team where he headed both the appearance and goalscoring charts as the team recorded a league and cup double. He reprised that role in 2007/08, helping the reserves secure a second successive title, and was rewarded with a first team call up at Radcliffe Borough in April, almost two years to the day since his previous appearance. When the reserve side was disbanded in the summer of 2008, the club arranged for Warren and several of his team-mates to sign for Bacup Borough in order to gain further experience of first team football in the North West Counties League. He deservedly won the Supporters Player Of The Year in his first season, before joining his local club Trafford in 2010, where he played for four seasons.

030 Phil MELVILLE

Born: 10/01/1973, Manchester
Debut: No.1 v Leek CSOB (H, NWCFL2), 18/03/2006

Goalkeeper

Season	LEAGUE			FA NATIONAL CUPS			OTHER CUPS / PLAY-OFFS			TOTALS		
	Starts	(+Sub)	Goals	Starts	(+Sub)	Goals	Starts	(+Sub)	Goals	Starts	(+Sub)	Goals
2005/06	7	(+0)	0				0	(+0)	0	7	(+0)	0
Totals	7	(+0)	0	0	(+0)	0	0	(+0)	0	7	(+0)	0

Phil had been a junior with Sheffield United and Rotherham United before entering non-league with spells at Radcliffe Borough, Mossley and Salford City, where he was in a successful team with several future FC United colleagues. He joined the Reds in October 2005, and waited patiently as cover for Barrie George until he was drafted into the team for the run-in to the first campaign. He helped to bring a reassuring presence to the defence, which conceded just four goals in his seven games as first promotion, and then the championship, were secured. He was part of the squad at the start of 2006/07, but the form of new signing Sam Ashton meant that opportunities were limited, and so Phil left to join Oldham Town. He later moved to Bacup Borough, where he also had a coaching role, before becoming assistant manager to Rhodri Giggs at Salford City in 2010.

032 Michael O'NEILL

Born: 22/08/1987, Manchester
Debut: No.8 v Chadderton (A, NWCFL2), 19/04/2006 (scored)

Midfielder

Season	LEAGUE			FA NATIONAL CUPS			OTHER CUPS / PLAY-OFFS			TOTALS		
	Starts	(+Sub)	Goals	Starts	(+Sub)	Goals	Starts	(+Sub)	Goals	Starts	(+Sub)	Goals
2005/06	1	(+0)	1				0	(+0)	0	1	(+0)	1
Totals	1	(+0)	1	0	(+0)	0	0	(+0)	0	1	(+0)	1

Michael was already a member and active fan from FC United's formation when he signed for the club in February 2006. Aged just 18, he had been playing in the Manchester League for Gregorians when he first appeared for FC United in a friendly at Glossop North End. An impressive display that night, as well as in further friendlies at Woodley Sports and Congleton Town, marked him out as one for the future. He made his senior debut in midfield at Boundary Park against Chadderton in April, and marked the occasion by scoring the team's first goal in a 3-2 win. He began the second season as part of the newly-formed reserve team, but moved on to join Maine Road in search of a higher standard of football. He later returned to Gregorians, before spending several years in the USA where he coached and played part-time. When back home Michael could sometimes be seen at FC United matches selling the influential fanzine *Red Issue*. After returning to England he became a youth coach at Oldham Athletic.

033 Sam ASHTON

Born: 09/10/1986, Bolton
Debut: No.1 v St Helens Town (A, NWCFL1), 12/08/2006

Goalkeeper

Season	LEAGUE			FA NATIONAL CUPS			OTHER CUPS / PLAY-OFFS			TOTALS		
	Starts	(+Sub)	Goals	Starts	(+Sub)	Goals	Starts	(+Sub)	Goals	Starts	(+Sub)	Goals
2006/07	40	(+0)	0	4	(+0)	0	6	(+0)	0	50	(+0)	0
2007/08	33	(+0)	0	4	(+0)	0	9	(+0)	0	46	(+0)	0
2008/09	42	(+0)	0	5	(+0)	0	0	(+0)	0	47	(+0)	0
2009/10	35	(+0)	0	9	(+0)	0	1	(+0)	0	45	(+0)	0
2010/11	34	(+0)	1	8	(+0)	0	1	(+0)	0	43	(+0)	1
Totals	184	(+0)	1	30	(+0)	0	17	(+0)	0	231	(+0)	1

Sam began his career as a young professional with boyhood heroes Bolton Wanderers, and had even played for their reserve team before leaving school. He made his first-team debut in an FA Cup tie at Watford in January 2006, when he was brought on as a late substitute to play not in goal, but up front. That summer he was released by the Trotters and made his way to FC United, where some impressive pre-season displays made him the undisputed number one. He and his defence made an excellent start to the league campaign by conceding just one goal, a penalty, in the first eight matches. He missed just two games in the entire season, as he helped the team to the league and cup double. He had two separate month-long spells out with injury in 2007/08, but was fit for the extraordinary run of fixtures late in the season that saw the President's Cup win and promotion earned via the play-offs. He missed just one game the following season, a Challenge Cup tie, as the team came within minutes of reaching the play-offs, with his late-season form being a major factor in the climb up the table. In the transitional season of 2009/10, he was ever-present until being given a rest in April, with a standout performance coming in the FA Cup replay win at Stalybridge. The following season was extremely eventful for the club, and Sam was involved in many of the major headlines. He helped the team to reach the FA Cup first round, and was outstanding in the unforgettable win over Rochdale, but he then went one better in the next round by saving a late penalty at Brighton to earn a replay. In January he even managed to get on the scoresheet with a long kick from his own area at Retford United. He also experienced the lows with a red card at home to Northwich Victoria in April, which brought a three-match suspension, his return being the play-off final that ended in a narrow defeat at Colwyn Bay. After featuring in the early pre-season games in 2011, he moved on to Skelmersdale United and helped them to promotion in 2013 before joining Chorley, and faced FC in some epic battles over the next four seasons. A cruciate knee injury in October 2016 ruled him out for the rest of the season, and he spent time on loan at Kendal Town and Ramsbottom United during his rehabilitation in 2017/18. He left Chorley at the end of that campaign to sign a permanent deal with Ramsbottom, whom he helped to the West Division play-offs. He moved on to Lancaster City in the summer of 2019, and twice kept goal against FC United in the Northern Premier League in 2019/20. After a short spell with Radcliffe, he moved on to help Macclesfield to the North West Counties League title at the end of their first season in 2021/22.

034 Matthew TAYLOR

Born: 05/12/1980, Manchester
Debut: No.2 v St Helens Town (A, NWCFL1), 12/08/2006

Right-back

Season	LEAGUE			FA NATIONAL CUPS			OTHER CUPS / PLAY-OFFS			TOTALS		
	Starts	(+Sub)	Goals	Starts	(+Sub)	Goals	Starts	(+Sub)	Goals	Starts	(+Sub)	Goals
2006/07	32	(+0)	0	4	(+0)	0	4	(+0)	0	40	(+0)	0
2007/08	13	(+0)	1	2	(+0)	0	0	(+1)	0	15	(+1)	1
Totals	45	(+0)	1	6	(+0)	0	4	(+1)	0	55	(+1)	1

A speedy right-back from Moss Side, Matty had represented Manchester Boys before making his name on the local non-league circuit during long spells with Hyde United, Trafford and Mossley. He played for Woodley Sports in a friendly against FC United in March 2006 and moved to the Reds that summer. His displays in both defence and going forward quickly won over the fans, particularly a heroic performance in the FA Vase against Quorn when he soldiered on despite being clearly injured as the nine men in red were cruelly denied in the last minute of extra-time. When fit he was an automatic choice in the number two shirt as the team stormed to the league and cup double. Unfortunately, injury issues during 2007/08 restricted him to just 16 appearances and he had to take a break from the game. A short spell at New Mills followed in order for him to regain some match fitness before he returned to training with FC United, but he failed to return to the line-up and joined the Millers permanently in 2008. He later had a spell with Salford City.

035 Alex MORTIMER

Born: 28/11/1982, Manchester
Debut: No.3 v St Helens Town (A, NWCFL1), 12/08/2006

Left-back/Midfielder

Season	LEAGUE			FA NATIONAL CUPS			OTHER CUPS / PLAY-OFFS			TOTALS		
	Starts	(+Sub)	Goals	Starts	(+Sub)	Goals	Starts	(+Sub)	Goals	Starts	(+Sub)	Goals
2006/07	34	(+0)	2	4	(+0)	0	4	(+0)	0	42	(+0)	2
2007/08	2	(+0)	0	0	(+0)	0	0	(+0)	0	2	(+0)	0
Totals	36	(+0)	2	4	(+0)	0	4	(+0)	0	44	(+0)	2

A former schoolboy at Manchester United, Alex signed professional for Leicester City and became a regular in the reserves. He joined Shrewsbury Town in 2002 and played in Division Three, before a spell in Ireland at St Patrick's Athletic. He returned to the north-west and joined the non-league circuit with Southport, before helping Hyde United to promotion in 2005. After recovering from injury he linked up with his local team Flixton, where he first came to the attention of FC United fans during our tussles in the first season. He joined the Reds in the summer of 2006 and was immediately installed at left-back and began to make a vital contribution at both ends of the pitch. His corner taking was of the highest quality, leading to a good number of goals, and he hit the back of the net himself with a free-kick away to Atherton LR and an unstoppable penalty to equalise at home to Ramsbottom United on Boxing Day. He had missed just one game by the turn of the year before a couple of spells out with injury and suspension, but he was in the team for the crucial promotion, title and cup-winning matches. He began 2007/08 in the side, but in September moved on to Curzon Ashton, for whom he was on the losing side twice against FC United. After a long spell at Salford City and stints at Radcliffe Borough and Mossley, he again faced FC with Droylsden and later became player-coach at AFC Darwen.

037 Stuart RUDD

Born: 10/10/1976, Wigan
Debut: No.9 v St Helens Town (A, NWCFL1), 12/08/2006 (scored)

Forward

Season	LEAGUE			FA NATIONAL CUPS			OTHER CUPS / PLAY-OFFS			TOTALS		
	Starts	(+Sub)	Goals	Starts	(+Sub)	Goals	Starts	(+Sub)	Goals	Starts	(+Sub)	Goals
2006/07	39	(+1)	37	4	(+0)	3	5	(+0)	4	48	(+1)	44
2007/08	22	(+3)	7	2	(+0)	0	4	(+3)	3	28	(+6)	10
Totals	61	(+4)	44	6	(+0)	3	9	(+3)	7	76	(+7)	54

A goal machine who began his career in the youth team at Wigan Athletic, Stuart settled into the non-league game with Westhoughton Town before beginning a long association with Skelmersdale United. His impressive stats took him into the Northern Premier League with Burscough for a record fee of £2,500, but despite a promising start he failed to settle and returned to Skelmersdale. Once back his goalscoring exploits were soon breaking records and by 2006 he had bagged 230 in 315 games for the club. That summer he joined FC United, and made a great start with a goal on his debut at St Helens Town. He carried on scoring throughout the season as the team won the double, although he was suspended for the Challenge Cup Final. Altogether he struck 44 times, a haul that included four hat-tricks and the club's first goal in the FA Vase at Brodsworth. Amongst his most crucial were goals in both league matches against closest challengers Curzon Ashton, a double to beat Maine Road in the first 'mini-derby', and another brace past Congleton Town in the Challenge Cup Semi-Final. After a slow start to 2007/08 that was disrupted by suspension, he was just getting into his stride when he was sidelined for over three months with an injury picked up in the FA Trophy at Bradford Park Avenue. He returned in late January to net from the bench in two successive cup-ties, but it wasn't until late March that the goals began to flow again, starting with a dramatic last-minute winner with an overhead kick at Woodley Sports. In April his late strike sealed the President's Cup win, and he ended the season helping the Reds to beat former club Skelmersdale in the play-off final. That summer he moved on to Bradford PA, for whom he played against FC, before spells with Witton Albion, Salford City, Guiseley, Rhyl, Leigh Genesis, Woodley Sports and Winsford United. He later became a coach at Salford.

036 Rhodri GIGGS

Born: 02/04/1977, Cardiff
Debut: No.7 v St Helens Town (A, NWCFL1), 12/08/2006

Winger/Forward

Season	LEAGUE			FA NATIONAL CUPS			OTHER CUPS / PLAY-OFFS			TOTALS		
	Starts	(+Sub)	Goals	Starts	(+Sub)	Goals	Starts	(+Sub)	Goals	Starts	(+Sub)	Goals
2006/07	27	(+10)	13	4	(+0)	0	5	(+1)	2	36	(+11)	15
2012/13	3	(+16)	1	0	(+0)	0	1	(+0)	1	4	(+16)	2
2013/14	2	(+7)	0	0	(+0)	0	3	(+2)	1	5	(+9)	1
Totals	32	(+33)	14	4	(+0)	0	9	(+3)	4	45	(+36)	18

An exciting Welsh-born attacker, Rhodri had been raised in Swinton after his father signed to play for the town's professional Rugby League club. He began his career on a YTS scheme with Torquay United, where he played for the first team in friendly matches, before spending a short time at Livingston. He eventually made his name in the non-league game after returning to the north-west with an enjoyable spell at Salford City alongside several future FC United players, including Karl Marginson. He spent time in the League Of Wales with Bangor City and Aberystwyth Town, before returning to England with Kidsgrove Athletic and Bacup Borough. He next settled at Mossley, whom he helped to two promotions and picked up their Player of the Year award before joining FC United in the summer of 2006. Stationed mainly on the right wing, he also led the line effectively, combining pace, trickery and an impressive aerial ability. His outstanding form continued in a red shirt as he scored 15 goals to help the team to the league and cup double, with a personal highlight being a hat-trick at home to former club Salford. After playing much of the 2007 pre-season, he decided to move to Curzon Ashton in August, and scored against the Reds at Gigg Lane the following March. He later played for New Mills and Bacup again before returning to Salford, where he eventually became player-manager in October 2010. He resigned in April 2012, and then joined up again with FC United in a player-coach capacity that summer. Now in the twilight of his playing career, he made the most of his appearances from the bench over the next two terms, helping the team to reach the play-offs each time. Rhodri hung up his boots in the summer of 2014 and became the manager the club's reserve team, a post he held until 2017.

038 Steve SMITH

Born: 09/06/1984, Salford
Debut: Sub v St Helens Town (A, NWCFL1), 12/08/2006

Midfielder

Season	LEAGUE			FA NATIONAL CUPS			OTHER CUPS / PLAY-OFFS			TOTALS		
	Starts	(+Sub)	Goals	Starts	(+Sub)	Goals	Starts	(+Sub)	Goals	Starts	(+Sub)	Goals
2006/07	2	(+12)	2	0	(+1)	0	0	(+0)	0	2	(+13)	2
Totals	2	(+12)	2	0	(+1)	0	0	(+0)	0	2	(+13)	2

An energetic central midfielder from Walkden, Steve began his career on a scholarship at Rochdale, alongside Rory Patterson. He was released in 2003 and made his way into the Conference with Leigh RMI, for whom he faced FC United in the club's first ever game in July 2005. His tigerish performance made an impression with the fans and management alike, and he signed for the Reds a year later after a spell with Lancaster City. The quality available to compete for midfield places restricted him to mainly substitute appearances, but he contributed a goal on his home debut against Nelson, and also netted from 30 yards on his first start away to Trafford at Altrincham. The arrival of Nicky Platt increased competition for his position and he moved on to Leek Town later in the autumn in search of regular football. He later faced FC United in the colours of Witton Albion and Flixton, and also had spells at Warrington Town, Newcastle Town, Winsford United, Bacup Borough, Leigh Genesis and Salford City.

039 Liam COYNE

Born: 08/05/1987, Manchester
Debut: Sub v St Helens Town (A, NWCFL1), 12/08/2006

Centre-back

Season	LEAGUE			FA NATIONAL CUPS			OTHER CUPS / PLAY-OFFS			TOTALS		
	Starts	(+Sub)	Goals	Starts	(+Sub)	Goals	Starts	(+Sub)	Goals	Starts	(+Sub)	Goals
2006/07	5	(+3)	1	2	(+0)	0	0	(+0)	0	7	(+3)	1
Totals	5	(+3)	1	2	(+0)	0	0	(+0)	0	7	(+3)	1

Standing at 6'6", towering centre-back Liam was on schoolboy forms with Rochdale, but was playing open-age first-team football with local club Trafford at the age of 16. Showing maturity beyond his years, he was signed by Conference side Leigh RMI, and impressed for them against FC United in the historic first friendly in July 2005. When his contract expired the following summer, the Reds snapped him up and he was a regular squad member at the beginning of 2006/07. Despite fierce competition for a place, he started the club's first FA Vase match in September, and his first goal sealed the win over Bacup Borough a week later. After a further handful of appearances he started the FA Vase game against Quorn, but was controversially sent off just after half-time, with the Reds later reduced to nine men and cruelly beaten in the last minute of extra-time. This was his last action for the club as he was unable to regain his place after suspension and he rejoined Leigh, initially on loan to regain match fitness. He later served Winsford United, Warrington Town, Chorley, Witton Albion, Mossley, New Mills and Salford City. He then became the first player to play for both FC United and AFC Liverpool, captaining them to two North West Counties Trophy wins, before switching his attention to Gaelic Football.

040 Mike LOMAX

Born: 06/12/1979, Manchester
Debut: No.2 v Flixton (H, NWCFL1), 30/08/2006

Right-back

Season	LEAGUE			FA NATIONAL CUPS			OTHER CUPS / PLAY-OFFS			TOTALS		
	Starts	(+Sub)	Goals	Starts	(+Sub)	Goals	Starts	(+Sub)	Goals	Starts	(+Sub)	Goals
2006/07	3	(+0)	0	0	(+1)	0	0	(+1)	0	3	(+2)	0
2007/08	0	(+0)	0	0	(+0)	0	0	(+0)	0	0	(+0)	0
Totals	3	(+0)	0	0	(+1)	0	0	(+1)	0	3	(+2)	0

Mike started his career as a trainee at Premiership club Blackburn Rovers, before becoming a professional with Macclesfield Town in 1998. The Withington lad was a key defender for the reserves and was awarded his senior debut as an early substitute in the last Division Two game of 1998/99. He was released later that year and began his non-league odyssey with Winsford United, before a spell playing in Singapore. Upon his return to Manchester he joined Hyde United in 2002, which was followed by stints with Trafford, Salford City and Woodley Sports before he arrived at FC United in July 2006. An excellent tackler with a good turn of pace, he made five appearances but was unable to gain a regular place in an excellent defence and moved back to Winsford in February 2007. After a brief return to the Reds early in 2007/08, he left again in October, going on to play for New Mills and Glossop North End.

041 Jamie PHOENIX

Born: 15/01/1984, Manchester
Debut: Sub v Flixton (H, NWCFL1), 30/08/2006

Left-winger

Season	LEAGUE			FA NATIONAL CUPS			OTHER CUPS / PLAY-OFFS			TOTALS		
	Starts	(+Sub)	Goals	Starts	(+Sub)	Goals	Starts	(+Sub)	Goals	Starts	(+Sub)	Goals
2006/07	1	(+6)	2	0	(+1)	0	0	(+1)	0	1	(+8)	2
Totals	1	(+6)	2	0	(+1)	0	0	(+1)	0	1	(+8)	2

A tricky and pacy winger from Wythenshawe, Jamie was a schoolboy at Manchester City and Bolton Wanderers before beginning his non-league adventure with Altrincham. Spells with Nantwich Town and Stafford Rangers followed, before he registered for FC United's initial player trials in June 2005. However, he chose to stay at Stafford for another year, finally joining the Reds in August 2006. He made a fast impact with a goal in his second game against Congleton Town, and another on his first start against Glossop North End. Although seen as a flamboyant player, he also contributed to hard-fought wins away at Newcastle Town and Maine Road, before disappearing from contention in the new year. He then had a nomadic career that included playing in Vietnam, Oman, Malaysia, Bulgaria, Portugal and Thailand before spells with Northwich Victoria and Alsager Town.

042 Fernando VAZ TÊ

Born: 08/07/1985, Bissau (Guinea-Bissau)
Debut: Sub v Abbey Hey (H, NWCFL1), 13/09/2006

Midfielder

Season	LEAGUE			FA NATIONAL CUPS			OTHER CUPS / PLAY-OFFS			TOTALS		
	Starts	(+Sub)	Goals	Starts	(+Sub)	Goals	Starts	(+Sub)	Goals	Starts	(+Sub)	Goals
2006/07	0	(+1)	0	0	(+0)	0	0	(+0)	0	0	(+1)	0
Totals	0	(+1)	0	0	(+0)	0	0	(+0)	0	0	(+1)	0

The brother of Portugal under-21 striker Ricardo Vaz Tê, who at the time was playing for Bolton Wanderers, Fernando was raised in Lisbon and had played in the Portuguese lower leagues before heading to Manchester in 2006. He joined up with FC United that summer, and soon impressed with his powerful performances in central midfield for the new reserve team, where he missed only a handful of games as a league and cup double was won. He earned a call-up to the first team, where he made his debut from the bench in September, but this was his only appearance at that level. He went back to Portugal to play for Rio Maior in 2007, before venturing to the Cypriot Second Division with Chalkanoras Idaliou the following summer. He later had stints with Portuguese clubs Mirandela, Monsanto, Alcanenense and Vilaverdense.

045 Danny SHANNON

Born: 26/08/1987, Manchester
Debut: Sub v Squires Gate (H, NWCFL1), 14/10/2006 (scored)

Forward

Season	LEAGUE			FA NATIONAL CUPS			OTHER CUPS / PLAY-OFFS			TOTALS		
	Starts	(+Sub)	Goals	Starts	(+Sub)	Goals	Starts	(+Sub)	Goals	Starts	(+Sub)	Goals
2006/07	0	(+1)	1	0	(+0)	0	0	(+0)	0	0	(+1)	1
Totals	0	(+1)	1	0	(+0)	0	0	(+0)	0	0	(+1)	1

Danny joined FC United as a left-winger in the summer of 2006 after spells at Woodley Sports and Accrington Stanley, but was converted into a central striker during his early weeks in the club's new reserve team. The switch paid off as he was quickly amongst the goals, and his form earned a first-team call-up against Squires Gate in October. He came on as a substitute after an hour, and marked the occasion by scoring with a thumping diving header in the last minute. The rest of the term was spent helping to win a league and cup double with the reserves, for whom he also played in 2007/08 before going to play at a higher level for Atherton Collieries. He later appeared in Conference North for Workington, returned to face FC United with Woodley Sports, and also played at Rossendale United, Curzon Ashton, Trafford, Winsford United, Radcliffe Borough and 1874 Northwich.

043 Lee ELLIS

Born: 29/03/1989, Manchester
Debut: Sub v Abbey Hey (H, NWCFL1), 13/09/2006

Forward

Season	LEAGUE			FA NATIONAL CUPS			OTHER CUPS / PLAY-OFFS			TOTALS		
	Starts	(+Sub)	Goals	Starts	(+Sub)	Goals	Starts	(+Sub)	Goals	Starts	(+Sub)	Goals
2006/07	0	(+1)	0	0	(+1)	0	0	(+0)	0	0	(+2)	0
Totals	**0**	**(+1)**	**0**	**0**	**(+1)**	**0**	**0**	**(+0)**	**0**	**0**	**(+2)**	**0**

A bustling forward with good control and a powerful shot, Lee became the first FC United player to appear for each of the senior, reserve and youth teams. The Gorton lad was with Oldham Athletic and Manchester City as a schoolboy before a spell at Curzon Ashton. He joined the Reds in 2006 when the development teams were set up, and had a rapid progression through the ranks with a first-team debut early in the season. Aged just 17, he was the youngest player to appear in the senior team at the time, which remained a record for over two years. For most of the term he led the line for the under-18s, before top-scoring for the second string in 2007/08. He then moved to Bacup Borough along with a number of his young colleagues for more senior experience.

044 Nicky PLATT

Born: 05/12/1987, Ashton-under-Lyne
Debut: Sub v St Helens Town (H, NWCFL1), 11/10/2006

Midfielder

Season	LEAGUE			FA NATIONAL CUPS			OTHER CUPS / PLAY-OFFS			TOTALS		
	Starts	(+Sub)	Goals	Starts	(+Sub)	Goals	Starts	(+Sub)	Goals	Starts	(+Sub)	Goals
2006/07	19	(+7)	6	1	(+1)	0	4	(+1)	1	24	(+9)	7
2007/08	26	(+4)	3	2	(+2)	1	7	(+1)	2	35	(+7)	6
2008/09	3	(+4)	0	0	(+0)	0	0	(+0)	0	3	(+4)	0
2010/11	25	(+14)	0	7	(+1)	2	1	(+1)	0	33	(+16)	2
2011/12	22	(+13)	4	5	(+1)	1	1	(+3)	0	28	(+17)	5
2012/13	10	(+3)	2	7	(+0)	4	1	(+0)	0	18	(+3)	6
Totals	**105**	**(+45)**	**15**	**22**	**(+5)**	**8**	**14**	**(+6)**	**3**	**141**	**(+56)**	**26**

A midfielder from Dukinfield, Nicky had been at Liverpool's schoolboy academy before taking a scholarship at Burnley. Released in 2006, he spent a short time with Stalybridge Celtic before joining FC United in October. He quickly settled in and was involved in virtually every game until the end of the season as the team won the league and cup double. He contributed some vital goals, not least crucial penalties in the promotion-winning game at Ramsbottom United and in the Challenge Cup Final against Curzon Ashton. His cool head came to the rescue once more a year later when he equalised from the spot in the play-off final against Skelmersdale United to send the club on the way to promotion. In July 2008 he was tempted back to Stalybridge to play in the Conference North, but he returned to FC United the following March and played in the run-in as the team narrowly missed qualifying for the play-offs. In the summer of 2009 he headed to Australia to join Mandurah City, but a year later he was back for a third spell with the Reds. He soon became a regular back in midfield, and hit the national headlines with the opening goal in the unforgettable FA Cup first round win at Rochdale, a trick he then went on to repeat in the next round at Brighton. These were in fact his only goals of the season as he took on more of a holding role in midfield as FC reached the play-off final. He helped the team to the same stage in each of the next two terms, and got back amongst the goals when playing as an attacking midfielder, notably with a hat-trick in the FA Cup at Salford City. Unfortunately he suffered a bad facial injury in a win at Blyth Spartans in December 2012 and was unable to regain his place in the side when fit. He moved on to Nantwich Town in search of regular football, and later also played for New Mills, Witton Albion, Stockport County and Salford. In the summer of 2013 Nicky was in the Great Britain men's football team that earned silver medals at the World University Games in Russia. After scoring for the Old Boys XI in the Broadhurst Park opener in May 2015, Nicky trained with FC before signing for Bamber Bridge in November. He returned to Nantwich in March 2016, then joined Trafford in July before moving to Glossop North End in November. He joined a large contingent of ex-Reds at Ashton United in 2017, where he was part of the team that won promotion to the National League North by winning the Northern Premier League Play-Offs in 2018. He later played for Hyde United and Mossley, and also featured in the North West Counties for West Didsbury & Chorlton and New Mills.

046 Danny ALLEN

Born: 18/01/1988, Stockport
Debut: Sub v Glossop North End (H, NWCFL1), 28/10/2006

Forward

Season	LEAGUE			FA NATIONAL CUPS			OTHER CUPS / PLAY-OFFS			TOTALS		
	Starts	(+Sub)	Goals	Starts	(+Sub)	Goals	Starts	(+Sub)	Goals	Starts	(+Sub)	Goals
2006/07	3	(+2)	3	0	(+1)	0	0	(+1)	0	3	(+4)	3
2007/08	0	(+0)	0	0	(+0)	0	0	(+0)	0	0	(+0)	0
Totals	**3**	**(+2)**	**3**	**0**	**(+1)**	**0**	**0**	**(+1)**	**0**	**3**	**(+4)**	**3**

A nippy striker with an impressive strike rate, Danny was in the Oldham Athletic and Manchester City academies, but a knee injury sadly ruined his chance of a professional career. Once recovered, he had a spell at his local club Chadderton, before joining FC United in the summer of 2006. Initially playing in the new reserve team, his form earned a senior call-up in the autumn. He marked his first start by hitting a hat-trick at home to Stone Dominoes in November, and also got the final touch to the last goal but it was credited to Rory Patterson. He appeared in a few more games in December before returning to help the reserves to a league and cup double. In 2007/08, injury restricted him to a solitary call-up to the senior bench for the FA Trophy replay, but he won a second successive reserves title. After being involved with the first team's 2008 pre-season, he moved on to New Mills in September, and later played for Glossop North End and Woodley Sports before another knee injury halted his football activities altogether. He then worked as a fitness trainer.

047 Gary SAMPSON

Born: 13/09/1982, Manchester
Debut: Sub v Nantwich Town (A, NWCFLCC:2), 11/11/2006

Midfielder

Season	LEAGUE			FA NATIONAL CUPS			OTHER CUPS / PLAY-OFFS			TOTALS		
	Starts	(+Sub)	Goals	Starts	(+Sub)	Goals	Starts	(+Sub)	Goals	Starts	(+Sub)	Goals
2006/07	7	(+5)	2	0	(+1)	0	1	(+3)	0	8	(+9)	2
Totals	7	(+5)	2	0	(+1)	0	1	(+3)	0	8	(+9)	2

Raised in Hulme and Stretford, Gary realised his boyhood ambition by signing as a young professional with Manchester United. A regular in the youth teams, he graduated to the reserves before being released in 2002. After trials with Bury and Macclesfield Town, he entered non-league with Accrington Stanley and scored on his debut, but was unable to earn a regular place in a settled side. He went on to join Radcliffe Borough in 2003, where he had an enjoyable time in a team that contained Karl Marginson, Dave Brown, Simon Carden, Steve Spencer, Rory Patterson and Richard Battersby. In 2005 he was considering his career options outside football, and went on to join the Royal Marines. However, after his training period he decided not to sign up permanently and returned to Manchester in October 2006, whereupon he joined FC United. He showed his tigerish but skilful qualities when selected in midfield, with his most memorable display being when he emerged from the bench to score twice against Curzon Ashton in a vital top-of-the-table clash in February. He ended the season with league and cup winner's medals, but surprisingly returned to Radcliffe in the summer where he became a regular in a wing-back role. He faced FC United no fewer than five times the following season, and again for Radcliffe in 2010 after a short spell with Salford City. Gary has since become a respected Academy Coach back at Manchester United.

048 Liam FOSTER

Born: 04/09/1987, Salford
Debut: No.2 v Ramsbottom United (H, NWCFL1), 26/12/2006

Right-back

Season	LEAGUE			FA NATIONAL CUPS			OTHER CUPS / PLAY-OFFS			TOTALS		
	Starts	(+Sub)	Goals	Starts	(+Sub)	Goals	Starts	(+Sub)	Goals	Starts	(+Sub)	Goals
2006/07	6	(+2)	0	0	(+0)	0	2	(+0)	0	8	(+2)	0
2007/08	26	(+2)	0	2	(+0)	0	10	(+0)	0	38	(+2)	0
2008/09	10	(+0)	0	1	(+1)	0	0	(+0)	0	11	(+1)	0
Totals	42	(+4)	0	3	(+1)	0	12	(+0)	0	57	(+5)	0

Liam began his career on a YTS at Stockport County, progressing to make his senior debut as a substitute in League Two against Lincoln City in February 2006. Unfortunately the Eccles lad was released that summer, and he linked up with FC United, initially as part of the club's new reserve side. He proved an able deputy for Matty Taylor when called up to the first team, and went on to appear in ten games, all of which were won, as the team won the league and cup double. With Taylor's injury problems in 2007/08, Liam made the right-back spot his own and was an instrumental figure as promotion was earned via the play-offs. Showing excellent defensive awareness, his speciality was the goal-line clearance, and he saved at least a dozen certain goals from being conceded. He began 2008/09 as first choice in the number two shirt until sidelined by injury, and by the time he was fit he faced competition for his place from Danny Warrender. He still managed another run of games in the autumn before injury struck again and once fit he was unable to break back into a settled defence. He moved on to Salford City in January 2009, initially to gain match fitness with the intention of returning to FC, but he stayed with his local club for two seasons. He later joined Prestwich Heys, where he became part of the team that gained promotion to the North West Counties League by winning the Manchester League in 2015/16.

049 Shaun ROSCOE

Born: 15/08/1986, Manchester
Debut: No.3 v Newcastle Town (H, NWCFL1), 30/12/2006

Left-back

Season	LEAGUE			FA NATIONAL CUPS			OTHER CUPS / PLAY-OFFS			TOTALS		
	Starts	(+Sub)	Goals	Starts	(+Sub)	Goals	Starts	(+Sub)	Goals	Starts	(+Sub)	Goals
2006/07	7	(+2)	0	0	(+0)	0	3	(+0)	0	10	(+2)	0
2007/08	23	(+0)	0	4	(+0)	0	4	(+0)	0	31	(+0)	0
Totals	30	(+2)	0	4	(+0)	0	7	(+0)	0	41	(+2)	0

A former schoolboy with Rochdale, Shaun became a young professional at Bury, where he became a regular member of their reserves until injury halted his progress. The Middleton lad then had a short spell with Accrington Stanley before joining up with FC United in the summer of 2006. Initially a member of the club's new reserve team, he became involved with the senior squad before Christmas and made 12 appearances as the team won the league and cup double. Affectionately dubbed "The Sheriff" by a section of fans, he became first choice at left-back early in the following season, emerging as a stand-out performer in an increasingly unsettled back line. Assured on the ball, he also provided an outlet going forward, as his storming run and cross to set up the opener in the memorable Manchester Premier Cup win at Droylsden will testify. After an injury at Christmas, he struggled to regain a regular place in the side until the run-in, when he helped the team reach the play-offs, but another injury near the end of the semi-final ruled him out of the final. After featuring in the 2008 pre-season, he was not selected for first team duties when the campaign began, and moved on to New Mills in September. He later had stints at Bacup Borough, Rossendale United, Oldham Town, Trafford, Salford City, Connah's Quay Nomads and Ashton United.

050 Jerome WRIGHT

Born: 29/10/1985, Manchester
Debut: No.10 v Atherton Collieries (A, NWCFL1), 06/01/2007

Left-winger/Left-back

Season	LEAGUE Starts	(+Sub)	Goals	FA NATIONAL CUPS Starts	(+Sub)	Goals	OTHER CUPS / PLAY-OFFS Starts	(+Sub)	Goals	TOTALS Starts	(+Sub)	Goals
2006/07	18	(+0)	8	0	(+0)	0	0	(+0)	0	18	(+0)	8
2007/08	39	(+0)	6	4	(+0)	0	9	(+1)	3	52	(+1)	9
2008/09	36	(+1)	6	5	(+0)	0	0	(+0)	0	41	(+1)	9
2009/10	33	(+1)	9	9	(+0)	1	0	(+0)	0	42	(+1)	10
2010/11	36	(+2)	13	8	(+0)	2	1	(+0)	1	45	(+2)	16
2012/13	33	(+2)	7	7	(+0)	2	3	(+1)	0	43	(+3)	9
2013/14	30	(+2)	7	1	(+0)	0	3	(+1)	1	34	(+3)	8
2014/15	37	(+2)	5	8	(+1)	2	0	(+1)	0	45	(+4)	7
2015/16	20	(+4)	3	5	(+0)	0	0	(+0)	0	25	(+5)	3
2016/17	28	(+4)	6	1	(+0)	0	2	(+1)	0	31	(+5)	6
Totals	**310**	**(+18)**	**70**	**48**	**(+1)**	**7**	**18**	**(+5)**	**5**	**376**	**(+24)**	**82**

Jerome was a schoolboy at Oldham Athletic, but joined Maine Road upon leaving school. He went straight into the first team, and was the club's player of the season in his first term. After a long lay-off with a serious knee injury, he regained his place and impressed the FC United management in the first 'mini-derby' played at Stalybridge in November 2006. He became United's own when he joined the Reds a month later, and soon settled in to the side by creating and scoring several goals, his most important being in the promotion-clinching game at Ramsbottom. Over the next four years he rarely missed a game, helping the team to a further promotion and another cup win in 2008, reaching the play-off final in 2011, as well as memorable FA Cup runs. He also contributed his fair share of goals, such as his spectacular winner in the FA Cup replay at Stalybridge in 2009, and strikes in two play-off semi-finals. He had a particularly impressive term in 2010/11, with 16 goals and many more assists, which attracted the interest of Chester, who signed him that summer. He came back to FC a year later and was once again an integral player as the team reached the FA Cup 4th Qualifying Round and a third successive play-off final. His importance to the side grew in 2013/14, despite a long lay-off due to a broken arm between October and January. His adaptability saw him play as an orthodox winger, left-back and wing-back as the team stormed up the table before just missing out on the title and automatic promotion by a single point. In the early months of 2014/15 he again alternated between positions, before settling at left-back when the manager stuck with a flat back-four. His displays earned him the Manager's Player of the Season award as the team finally won promotion and the Northern Premier League title. Jerome was named as FC's captain in the summer of 2015, and proudly led the team out to commence their first season at Broadhurst Park in the National League North. His own campaign had a mixed start as he was sent off in successive games to earn a five-match suspension. Jerome put in a captain's performance in the FA Cup first round tie with Chesterfield, but another broken arm near the end of the match sidelined him for three months. He was mainly eased back

from the bench, before returning to the wing in spectacular fashion when scoring in the first minute of the superb win at champions-elect Solihull Moors. The club's highest appearance maker went on to hit further priceless goals in wins over Chorley and Gainsborough Trinity and ended the season well as the team achieved a mid-table finish. He again captained the side in 2016/17, but after beginning the term with a goal on the opening day at Chorley he then missed two months through injury. He was soon back amongst the goals, notching in three consecutive league wins. Thereafter he was absent from the starting line-up on just two occasions, and on one of those he came on to score a penalty at Stockport County. He also scored in the last league game of the season at home to Gainsborough, before celebrating his **club record 400th appearance for FC United** by lifting the Manchester Premier Cup in May. Later that month he signed a contract to play for Altrincham in 2017/18, but moved on to join Ramsbottom United before the season had commenced. In 2018 he moved to Hyde United, before returning to the North West Counties League with his local side Wythenshawe Town in January 2019.

051 John OGDEN

Born: 17/10/1978, Bury
Debut: No.1 v Stone Dominoes (A, NWCFL1), 24/03/2007

Goalkeeper

Season	LEAGUE Starts	(+Sub)	Goals	FA NATIONAL CUPS Starts	(+Sub)	Goals	OTHER CUPS / PLAY-OFFS Starts	(+Sub)	Goals	TOTALS Starts	(+Sub)	Goals
2006/07	2	(+0)	0	0	(+0)	0	0	(+0)	0	2	(+0)	0
Totals	**2**	**(+0)**	**0**	**0**	**(+0)**	**0**	**0**	**(+0)**	**0**	**2**	**(+0)**	**0**

A goalkeeper with a good reputation in north-west non-league circles after stints at Clitheroe and Salford City, John linked up with FC United in October 2006 to provide cover between the sticks after the squad lost both Barrie George and Phil Melville. However, Sam Ashton was proving to be a colossus in the green jersey, meaning John had to wait patiently for his chance. He was given an opportunity in late March, and was delighted to keep a clean sheet on his debut, with his next game being at home against Trafford, which ended in an extraordinary 4-4 draw. He featured for the Reds in the 2007 pre-season, but was looking to play regularly so joined Ramsbottom United for the new campaign. He later lined up for Rossendale United and Bacup Borough.

052 Karl MARGINSON

Born: 11/11/1970, Manchester
Debut: Sub v Formby (H, NWCFL1), 28/04/2007

Forward

Season	LEAGUE Starts	(+Sub)	Goals	FA NATIONAL CUPS Starts	(+Sub)	Goals	OTHER CUPS / PLAY-OFFS Starts	(+Sub)	Goals	TOTALS Starts	(+Sub)	Goals
2005/06	0	(+0)	0				0	(+0)	0	0	(+0)	0
2006/07	0	(+1)	0	0	(+0)	0	0	(+0)	0	0	(+1)	0
Totals	0	(+1)	0	0	(+0)	0	0	(+0)	0	0	(+1)	0

Hailing from Miles Platting, Karl had spells as a junior at Stockport County, Tranmere Rovers and Blackpool, where he played in the FA Youth Cup, before making his name in non-league as a left-sided attacker with Droylsden, Curzon Ashton and Ashton United. His performances soon attracted the professional clubs and he signed for Rotherham United in March 1993, making his debut in Division Two just a few weeks later at Swansea City. He earned a regular place early in 1993/94 and scored his first goal at Doncaster Rovers before dropping out through injury. Once recovered, it was not until a change of manager the following season that he got back in, but after succumbing to another injury he was released in the summer of 1995. He joined Conference champions Macclesfield Town, who had been denied promotion to the Football League due to ground issues, and along with Darren Lyons and Phil Power he was part of the squad that won the 1996 FA Trophy. He moved on to Chorley and then helped Barrow to promotion to the Conference before joining Stalybridge Celtic, but after a promising start he suffered a cruciate injury. He fought back to fitness and joined Hyde United, then spent an enjoyable time at Salford City, where he played alongside several of his future FC United charges. Spells at Radcliffe Borough, Bacup Borough and Flixton followed as Karl was looking to get into the coaching side of the game, and another unfortunate cruciate injury accelerated his progress. In the summer of 2005, when the steering committee of FC United were forming the club, they approached Joz Mitten for advice on choosing a manager, and he had no hesitation in recommending Margy, who was appointed on 22nd June. He proved to be the perfect man for the job, building a team from scratch and leading them to promotion and the North West Counties League Division Two title in the first season. His team went one better the next year by winning the double of the North West Counties Division One title and the League Challenge Cup with victory over Curzon Ashton. In the last league game of that campaign at home to Formby, he named himself as a substitute, and finally to rapturous applause took to the field in a red shirt when he replaced Simon Carden for the last 20 minutes. He had more than earned it, and almost crowned the occasion with a goal or two. Thereafter he concentrated on managing, and led his team through another successful season in 2007/08 when they won yet another promotion, this time from the Northern Premier League Division One North via a play-off final victory over Skelmersdale United. They also won another final by overcoming Radcliffe Borough in the League President's Cup. The Northern Premier League Premier Division was the next level up, but it proved to be a tough nut to crack for Margy's men. They came agonisingly close to reaching the promotion play-offs at the first attempt, but they were denied by late goals on the season's last day. The next season was notable for a run to the 4th qualifying round of the FA Cup, but any hopes of challenging for promotion were realistically over before spring began. A handful of quality additions gave a squad that provided a memorable campaign in 2010/11. The team became famous nationally for the dramatic win at Rochdale in the FA Cup 1st round, then drawing at League One leaders Brighton & Hove Albion in the 2nd round before going out in the replay. Back on league duty, the Reds stormed up the table to finish 4th and reach the play-off final, where they were narrowly beaten by a late goal at Colwyn Bay. There followed similar final defeats in both 2012 and 2013, before another tremendous run of results took FC to the brink of the title in 2014, only for them to be pipped by a point at the end and then lose out on the play-offs again. The Reds finally won promotion from the Northern Premier League in 2015 when another tremendous sequence of results led to them winning the title on a memorable evening at the Tameside Stadium in April. Earlier in the season Marginson had also led his men to the FA Trophy quarter-final, where they were unlucky to bow out at Torquay United. Soon after the club's move to Broadhurst Park the team reached the FA Cup 1st round again, and Karl led them to two 13th place finishes in the National League North, as well as winning the Manchester Premier Cup in 2017. He drastically overhauled the squad that summer, but the changes failed to have the desired effect and the team made the worst start to a campaign of his tenure. After collecting just 11 points from the first 14 games, Karl and FC United parted company by mutual consent on 24th October 2017. He returned to the game in November 2018 for a spell as Head Of Football Operations at Radcliffe.

054 Anthony HARGREAVES

Born: 07/12/1979, Ashton-under-Lyne
Debut: No.9 v Lancaster City (A, NPL1N), 18/08/2007

Forward

Season	LEAGUE Starts	(+Sub)	Goals	FA NATIONAL CUPS Starts	(+Sub)	Goals	OTHER CUPS / PLAY-OFFS Starts	(+Sub)	Goals	TOTALS Starts	(+Sub)	Goals
2007/08	2	(+4)	1	0	(+2)	1	1	(+0)	0	3	(+6)	2
Totals	2	(+4)	1	0	(+2)	1	1	(+0)	0	3	(+6)	2

A creative attacker previously with Altrincham, Hyde United, Trafford and Cammell Laird, Anthony joined FC United in July 2007 after a successful season with Flixton, for whom he had scored against the Reds in December 2006. With Stuart Rudd suspended, he started the first game of the season and impressed with his intelligent movement, but despite netting twice in nine appearances he was unable to dislodge the established partnership of Rudd and Rory Patterson. Consequently, he left the club in September 2007 in order to secure regular first-team football and headed back to Flixton, followed by spells at Runcorn Linnets, Irlam and Maine Road. He later became an academy coach at Manchester City and Macclesfield Town, before venturing to the USA to coach at FC Long Island.

053 Dale WHITEHEAD

Born: 10/10/1986, Salford
Debut: No.4 v Lancaster City (A, NPL1N), 18/08/2007

Midfielder

Season	LEAGUE			FA NATIONAL CUPS			OTHER CUPS / PLAY-OFFS			TOTALS		
	Starts	(+Sub)	Goals	Starts	(+Sub)	Goals	Starts	(+Sub)	Goals	Starts	(+Sub)	Goals
2007/08	2	(+1)	0	0	(+0)	0	1	(+0)	0	3	(+1)	0
2008/09	6	(+0)	0	0	(+0)	0	0	(+0)	0	6	(+0)	0
Totals	8	(+1)	0	0	(+0)	0	1	(+0)	0	9	(+1)	0

A tough-tackling midfielder also capable of filling in at the back, Dale began his career in the youth team at Bolton Wanderers, where he came through the ranks alongside Sam Ashton. Upon his release he joined up with his local club Salford City, for whom he impressed when inflicting FC United's first defeat of the 2006/07 season. His battling qualities were evident from the start, but he also showed there was more to his game when his rasping 30-yard shot struck the bar with Ashton beaten. He signed for the Reds in July 2007, and started the first two games of the season before being sidelined with a dislocated shoulder. The injury took longer than expected to heal, and he missed the rest of the campaign, but returned fully fit in the summer of 2008 ready to start again. He was rewarded with a starting berth in six of the first seven games of 2008/09 before his injury curse struck again, and for the second year running he suffered a premature end to his campaign.

055 Chris BAGULEY

Born: 01/09/1987, Salford
Debut: Sub v Lancaster City (A, NPL1N), 18/08/2007

Midfielder

Season	LEAGUE			FA NATIONAL CUPS			OTHER CUPS / PLAY-OFFS			TOTALS		
	Starts	(+Sub)	Goals	Starts	(+Sub)	Goals	Starts	(+Sub)	Goals	Starts	(+Sub)	Goals
2007/08	30	(+7)	9	0	(+3)	0	7	(+3)	8	37	(+13)	17
2008/09	13	(+5)	8	1	(+3)	0	1	(+0)	0	15	(+8)	8
Totals	43	(+12)	17	1	(+6)	0	8	(+3)	8	52	(+21)	25

An intelligent attacking playmaker, Chris spent several years in the Manchester United Academy, earning England under-16 caps before joining Oldham Athletic, where his progress was soon rewarded with a professional contract. After his release he joined FC United in July 2007, where he was gradually introduced to the team from the bench in the opening stages of the season. His breakthrough match was when he converted two near-identical free-kicks to clinch a 2-1 win over Wakefield, and from then on he was usually the creative hub of the team. His goal haul included further crucial strikes at Radcliffe Borough (twice), and an amazing injury-time equaliser against promotion rivals Bamber Bridge. He also emerged from the bench to open the scoring late on in the President's Cup Final, and finished the season by sealing victory over Skelmersdale United in the promotion play-off final. He began 2008/09 in similar fashion, with a late equaliser from the bench in the opening game, and had played his way back into the team when he picked up a needless red card at Bradford Park Avenue. Upon returning from suspension, he scored an impressive number of goals, memorably playing his part in the incredible comeback to draw 5-5 with Cammell Laird and the dramatic win over Marine. However, he was unable to gain a further sustained run in the side, and left the club in January 2009 to play in Cyprus, and then with Mandurah City in Australia. He later played for Leigh Genesis, Trafford, Salford City, Rossendale United, New Mills and Ramsbottom United, before facing FC several times in the colours of Ashton United. He went on to feature for Stalybridge Celtic, Glossop North End, Buxton and Wythenshawe Town, but mainly played alongside brothers Mark and Jamie at Prestwich Heys, where he also became part of the backroom staff as a UEFA licensed coach.

056 Liam GEORGE

Born: 02/02/1979, Luton
Debut: No.7 v Alsager Town (H, NPLCC:1), 05/09/2007

Right-winger

Season	LEAGUE			FA NATIONAL CUPS			OTHER CUPS / PLAY-OFFS			TOTALS		
	Starts	(+Sub)	Goals	Starts	(+Sub)	Goals	Starts	(+Sub)	Goals	Starts	(+Sub)	Goals
2007/08	1	(+3)	0	1	(+0)	0	1	(+0)	0	3	(+3)	0
Totals	1	(+3)	0	1	(+0)	0	1	(+0)	0	3	(+3)	0

A talented attacker with a wealth of professional experience, Liam began his career at his local club Luton Town, and made his Football League debut at the age of 18. He qualified to represent the Republic of Ireland, and in 1998 he scored the winning penalty to defeat Germany in the European Youth Championship, but a broken leg stalled his progress soon after. He bounced back to earn a regular place in 1999/2000, when he was top scorer at Kenilworth Road, and he maintained his position the following term until injury struck again. Thereafter he became a journeyman with short periods at Clydebank, Bury, Boston United, St Patrick's Athletic and York City, followed by a season in the US and spells at a host of non-league clubs in the south. He ventured north in 2006 when he enrolled at the University of Salford to study for a Physiotherapy degree, and after a short time at Hyde United he joined FC in September 2007. Despite a lively start, he moved on in October, signing for Barton Rovers close to his Bedfordshire home.

057 Cayne HANLEY

Born: 10/05/1988, Manchester
Debut: No.9 v Alsager Town (H, NPLCC: 1), 05/09/2007
Forward/Right-winger

Season	LEAGUE			FA NATIONAL CUPS			OTHER CUPS / PLAY-OFFS			TOTALS		
	Starts	(+Sub)	Goals	Starts	(+Sub)	Goals	Starts	(+Sub)	Goals	Starts	(+Sub)	Goals
2007/08	5	(+6)	0	1	(+2)	1	2	(+1)	1	8	(+9)	2
Totals	5	(+6)	0	1	(+2)	1	2	(+1)	1	8	(+9)	2

A powerful forward from Fallowfield, Cayne was a prolific scorer in the youth team at Burnley, but his progress was halted by a back injury and he was released in 2006. After short spells with Kidderminster Harriers, Hyde United and Stalybridge Celtic, he linked up with FC United in September 2007, and earned a regular place the following month. Replacing the injured Stuart Rudd early on at Bradford, he put in a man of the match performance before finding a niche on the right wing, most memorably when heading the Reds in front in the fantastic win at Droylsden. His exciting potential caught the eye of Conference outfit Northwich Victoria, and he went to try his luck at the higher level in January 2008 along with team-mate Aaron Burns. He was later on the books at Leigh Genesis, Woodley Sports, Padiham, Salford City and Droylsden, and he faced FC whilst at Buxton.

058 Adam CARDEN

Born: 24/07/1985, Liverpool
Debut: No.7 v Woodley Sports (H, NPL1N), 22/09/2007
Right-winger/Right-back

Season	LEAGUE			FA NATIONAL CUPS			OTHER CUPS / PLAY-OFFS			TOTALS		
	Starts	(+Sub)	Goals	Starts	(+Sub)	Goals	Starts	(+Sub)	Goals	Starts	(+Sub)	Goals
2007/08	11	(+12)	2	1	(+0)	0	6	(+1)	1	18	(+13)	3
2008/09	30	(+4)	1	5	(+0)	0	0	(+0)	0	35	(+4)	1
2009/10	13	(+1)	0	7	(+0)	0	0	(+0)	0	20	(+1)	0
Totals	54	(+17)	3	13	(+0)	0	6	(+1)	1	73	(+18)	4

Adam first experienced senior football as a 17-year-old for Southport in the Conference, and soon after he had a trial at Manchester City. He moved on to Runcorn, then Accrington Stanley, where a torn cartilage sidelined him for eight months. Once recovered, he switched to Burscough, whom he helped to the Northern Premier League title in 2007, before joining FC United that September. A promising start was derailed through injury, and most of his appearances were from the bench until the season's closing stages. The moment that proved he was back to his best was when he struck a dramatic last-minute winner with his first touch at home to Newcastle Blue Star, and he also contributed further important strikes against Lancaster City and in the play-off semi-final against Bamber Bridge. Another injury delayed his start to 2008/09, but he soon established himself as first-choice right-winger, with his displays earning a trial with AFC Bournemouth. He ended the season at right-back, and filled both roles in the early part of 2009/10 when he was ever-present until late October. He then surprisingly left the club in November, signing for Altrincham soon after, and subsequently played for Northwich Victoria, Kendal Town, AFC Fylde, Nantwich Town, Skelmersdale United, Stalybridge Celtic and Witton Albion. In 2015 he was part of the Old Boys team that played in FC United's 10th Anniversary game against Leigh Genesis in Atherton. The following year linked up with Warrington Town, who were managed by his brother Paul, and was in their team that was defeated in the Northern Premier League Premier Division Promotion Play-Off Final in 2018.

060 Aaron BURNS

Born: 08/11/1987, Manchester
Debut: No.9 v Clitheroe (A, NPL1N), 16/10/2007 (scored 2)
Forward

Season	LEAGUE			FA NATIONAL CUPS			OTHER CUPS / PLAY-OFFS			TOTALS		
	Starts	(+Sub)	Goals	Starts	(+Sub)	Goals	Starts	(+Sub)	Goals	Starts	(+Sub)	Goals
2007/08	12	(+0)	6	0	(+0)	0	2	(+0)	2	14	(+0)	8
Totals	12	(+0)	6	0	(+0)	0	2	(+0)	2	14	(+0)	8

FC United's capture of Aaron in October 2007 was something of a coup, as he had finished the previous season as top-scorer for Manchester United's reserves. Released in the summer after three years as a full-timer at Old Trafford, he spent part of the summer playing for Afturelding in Iceland before linking up with Cardiff City, but the Welsh club were unable to offer a contract. His pedigree meant he was in demand, but a complicated situation due to having been registered in two different countries meant that until January 2008 he could only sign for clubs at Northern Premier League level or below. He duly joined FC on a short-term arrangement, and although his debut was delayed by a week whilst awaiting international clearance, it was worth waiting for as he struck within six minutes and later added another in a great win at Clitheroe. A week later he hit a screamer in the memorable win at Droylsden, and when he completed a 12-minute hat-trick against Rossendale United in mid-November he had bagged eight times in his first seven games. They turned out to be his last goals as he failed to register in the next seven, and when January came he moved into the Conference with Northwich Victoria. He later had short spells with Altrincham, Droylsden, Connah's Quay and Marine, before becoming established at Ashton United and Nantwich Town, scoring several times for both clubs against FC. In 2015 he joined Conference North side Chorley, and later that year linked up with Trafford. In 2016/17 he was named in the Northern Premier League First Division North 'Team of the Season', before moving back up a level with Stalybridge Celtic. However after just seven games he rejoined Trafford, where he was again top scorer as they reached the promotion play-offs. He was an unused substitute as his team lost on penalties to FC United in the 2018 Manchester Premier Cup Final. He moved to Radcliffe in February 2019, and was in the squad that won the Northern Premier League Division One West play-off final before further returns to Droylsden, Northwich Victoria and Nantwich preceded spells at Ramsbottom United and 1874 Northwich.

059 Theo COLEMAN

Born: 05/05/1989, Manchester
Debut: Sub v Bradford Park Avenue (H, FAT:PR), 10/10/2007

Left-winger

Season	LEAGUE			FA NATIONAL CUPS			OTHER CUPS / PLAY-OFFS			TOTALS		
	Starts	(+Sub)	Goals	Starts	(+Sub)	Goals	Starts	(+Sub)	Goals	Starts	(+Sub)	Goals
2007/08	0	(+0)	0	0	(+1)	0	0	(+0)	0	0	(+1)	0
Totals	0	(+0)	0	0	(+1)	0	0	(+0)	0	0	(+1)	0

A pacy and tricky winger from Fallowfield, Theo spent several years in the Manchester United academy, and was in the Greater Manchester team that shared the English Schools FA Inter-County Trophy in 2005. He became a trainee at Rochdale, and impressed enough to make a Football League debut at the age of just 16. Despite his early promise, he was released in 2007, and after a trial at Bury he linked up with his cousin, Cayne Hanley, at FC United. He was drafted into the squad for the FA Trophy match at Bradford Park Avenue, where he was an unused substitute, but was thrown into the fray in the replay as the Reds sought to get back into the game. This proved to be his only appearance for the club, and he signed for Salford City in January 2008. The following season he made a brief return to Rochdale, where he featured in the reserves, before later having a spell at Mossley.

061 Adam TURNER

Born: 31/12/1986, Manchester
Debut: Sub v Clitheroe (A, NPL1N), 16/10/2007

Centre-back

Season	LEAGUE			FA NATIONAL CUPS			OTHER CUPS / PLAY-OFFS			TOTALS		
	Starts	(+Sub)	Goals	Starts	(+Sub)	Goals	Starts	(+Sub)	Goals	Starts	(+Sub)	Goals
2006/07	0	(+0)	0	0	(+0)	0	0	(+0)	0	0	(+0)	0
2007/08	3	(+1)	1	0	(+0)	0	4	(+1)	0	7	(+2)	1
2008/09	18	(+1)	0	5	(+0)	1	1	(+0)	0	24	(+1)	1
Totals	21	(+2)	1	5	(+0)	1	5	(+1)	1	31	(+3)	2

A commanding centre-back from Stretford, Adam joined FC United's reserve squad in the summer of 2006 and only missed a handful of games as the team romped to a league and cup double. His displays caught the eye of Karl Marginson, who called him up to the first-team bench in April 2007 for the promotion-clinching match at Ramsbottom United. He made his senior debut six months later, and earned his first start in November against Bradford Park Avenue. His entrance to the team was dramatic, as he gave away a penalty but soon scored the equaliser, before harshly receiving a red card in his second start at Mossley. After serving his suspension his involvement was solely in cup-ties, until his call-up to deputise for skipper David Chadwick in the promotion play-off semi-final against Bamber Bridge. He put in a fantastic performance, and although Chadwick was back for the final, Adam was rewarded with an appearance from the bench to see the Reds home. He established himself in 2008/09, missing just three of the first 23 games through injury and suspension, with his highlight being despatching the injury-time winner against Radcliffe Borough in the FA Trophy. When Rob Nugent returned from a long lay-off, Adam was rested for a few games in January, but surprisingly chose to move on to Bacup Borough in order to keep playing regularly. He later turned out for Trafford and Salford City.

062 Jamie BAGULEY

Born: 12/12/1984, Salford
Debut: Sub v Ossett Albion (H, NPL1N), 27/10/2007

Midfielder/Winger/Forward

Season	LEAGUE			FA NATIONAL CUPS			OTHER CUPS / PLAY-OFFS			TOTALS		
	Starts	(+Sub)	Goals	Starts	(+Sub)	Goals	Starts	(+Sub)	Goals	Starts	(+Sub)	Goals
2007/08	24	(+6)	3	0	(+0)	0	5	(+3)	0	29	(+9)	3
2008/09	8	(+13)	2	1	(+0)	0	0	(+0)	0	9	(+13)	2
Totals	32	(+19)	5	1	(+0)	0	5	(+3)	0	38	(+22)	5

Jamie followed his younger brother Chris to FC United in October 2007, but his name was already familiar to the club's fans as he had hit Salford City's last-minute equaliser at The Willows a year earlier. He too had earlier spent several years on the books at Manchester United, before being released at 16 and signing a YTS at Stockport County, which progressed to a professional deal. Despite becoming a member of the senior squad, he was released in 2004 and joined the non-league ranks, initially with Altrincham, before settling at Radcliffe Borough where he became a team-mate of Karl Marginson. After a spell with Woodley Sports he joined Salford, before moving to FC, where he became a reliable performer capable of bringing his quality to a number of positions. Initially used out wide, he also played up front and dropped into central midfield, from where he struck his first goal for the club – a crucial equaliser at Woodley. For the play-offs he also filled in at left-back, and did a sterling job as promotion was clinched. He began 2008/09 with some good performances, the highlight being his winner at Buxton, before picking up a cartilage injury in September that ruled him out for four months. He announced his return by sealing the win at Leigh Genesis, but his action thereafter was usually from the bench. He moved on to Leigh that summer, and also had spells at Trafford, Salford and Radcliffe before facing FC whilst playing for New Mills. In July 2015 he played for FC United Old Boys in the club's 10th Anniversary celebration match against Leigh. He went on to carve a niche at Prestwich Heys, becoming a vital component of the team that gained promotion to the North West Counties League by winning the Manchester League in 2015/16. He was part of the team that won the First Division Trophy in 2018, but missed their defeat in the Promotion Play-Off Semi-Final a few days later. He moved on to Wythenshawe Town in March 2019.

063 Peter THOMSON

Born: 30/06/1977, Manchester
Debut: Sub v Ossett Albion (H, NPL1N), 27/10/2007 (scored)

Forward

	LEAGUE			FA NATIONAL CUPS			OTHER CUPS / PLAY-OFFS			TOTALS		
Season	Starts	(+Sub)	Goals	Starts	(+Sub)	Goals	Starts	(+Sub)	Goals	Starts	(+Sub)	Goals
2007/08	0	(+5)	1	0	(+0)	0	1	(+0)	0	1	(+5)	1
Totals	0	(+5)	1	0	(+0)	0	1	(+0)	0	1	(+5)	1

A powerful centre-forward from Whitefield, Peter began his career as a professional at Bury before making his name in non-league during a prolific spell at Lancaster City. His impressive scoring form earned a move to Dutch side NAC Breda for a fee of £25,000, but a broken leg curtailed his progress. Luton Town brought him back in 2000 for £100,000, and he made his Football League debut for the Bedfordshire club. After a loan period at Rushden & Diamonds, he returned to non-league with Morecambe before having further successful spells at Southport, Lancaster and Stafford Rangers. After brief stops at Barrow and Altrincham, the massive Red joined FC United in October 2007 and immediately felt at home, which was evident when he scored on his debut against Ossett Albion. Due to the form of the other strikers he was mainly used from the bench, but unluckily when the opportunity arose a recurring calf problem kept him sidelined and ultimately led to his premature retirement from football in 2008.

064 Colin BELL

Born: 29/01/1983, Rochdale
Debut: No.5 v Bamber Bridge (H, NPLPC:2), 31/10/2007

Centre-back

	LEAGUE			FA NATIONAL CUPS			OTHER CUPS / PLAY-OFFS			TOTALS		
Season	Starts	(+Sub)	Goals	Starts	(+Sub)	Goals	Starts	(+Sub)	Goals	Starts	(+Sub)	Goals
2007/08	3	(+0)	0	0	(+0)	0	1	(+0)	0	4	(+0)	0
Totals	3	(+0)	0	0	(+0)	0	1	(+0)	0	4	(+0)	0

A versatile defensive player from Heywood, Colin began his career as a trainee at Rochdale. After being released he spent time with Bury before joining the non-league game with first Chester City, followed by a spell at Radcliffe Borough. He then took his talents into the League Of Wales with TNS, and had been playing for Carmarthen Town when he signed up for FC United in October 2007. With David Chadwick injured, Colin initially built up a good partnership with Rob Nugent as the defence conceded just one goal in his first three games. However, an injury sustained in his fourth outing put him on the sidelines and he decided to take some time out of football later that season in order to recover.

065 Danny JARRETT

Born: 16/05/1981, Bury
Debut: No.6 v Bradford Park Avenue (H, NPL1N), 24/11/2007

Centre-back

	LEAGUE			FA NATIONAL CUPS			OTHER CUPS / PLAY-OFFS			TOTALS		
Season	Starts	(+Sub)	Goals	Starts	(+Sub)	Goals	Starts	(+Sub)	Goals	Starts	(+Sub)	Goals
2007/08	2	(+1)	0	0	(+0)	0	0	(+0)	0	2	(+1)	0
Totals	2	(+1)	0	0	(+0)	0	0	(+0)	0	2	(+1)	0

A tall centre-back also able to play in midfield, Danny began his non-league career at Altrincham before joining Northwich Victoria. He then moved to Southport, where a broken leg in his very first game left him sidelined for over two years. After a spell with Witton Albion, he switched to Winsford United and helped them to win the North West Counties Division Two in 2006/07. He signed for FC United during an injury crisis in November 2007, but despite his valiant efforts the inexperienced backline continued to leak goals and he lost his place to the returning Rob Nugent. He moved on to Woodley Sports early in 2008, and faced FC twice before the end of the season. He later turned out for Colwyn Bay, Llandudno and Prescot Cables before a long spell with Rhyl. In July 2016 he joined Runcorn Town, and helped them to challenge for the North West Counties League title in each of the following two seasons. After a short spell at Barnton he was appointed as player/assistant-manager back at Runcorn Town in 2019.

066 Micah BLEAU

Born: 09/11/1987, Bradford
Debut: No.5 v Radcliffe Borough (A, NPL1N), 26/12/2007

Centre-back

	LEAGUE			FA NATIONAL CUPS			OTHER CUPS / PLAY-OFFS			TOTALS		
Season	Starts	(+Sub)	Goals	Starts	(+Sub)	Goals	Starts	(+Sub)	Goals	Starts	(+Sub)	Goals
2007/08	5	(+2)	0	0	(+0)	0	4	(+0)	0	9	(+2)	0
2008/09	1	(+0)	0	0	(+0)	0	0	(+0)	0	1	(+0)	0
Totals	6	(+2)	0	0	(+0)	0	4	(+0)	0	10	(+2)	0

A former Halifax Town defender, Micah signed for FC United during a defensive injury crisis in December 2007. He initially helped to steady the ship in tandem with Rob Nugent, and the team drew one and won four of his first five games. Once skipper David Chadwick returned, his chances were fewer but he still contributed to the second-place finish that led to promotion via the play-offs. He played in the first game of 2008/09, before moving back over the Pennines to AFC Emley in September. He later played for Sheffield FC, Hemsworth MW, Goole, Wakefield, Farsley, Worksop Town, Winterton Rangers, Thackley, Albion Sports and Frickley Athletic, for whom he played against FC in 2013. Micah has also emulated Steve Torpey in representing England at Futsal.

067 James HOLDEN

Born: 16/10/1986, Manchester **Midfielder/Right-back**
Debut: Sub v Radcliffe Borough (A, NPL1N), 26/12/2007

Season	LEAGUE			FA NATIONAL CUPS			OTHER CUPS / PLAY-OFFS			TOTALS		
	Starts	(+Sub)	Goals	Starts	(+Sub)	Goals	Starts	(+Sub)	Goals	Starts	(+Sub)	Goals
2007/08	1	(+5)	0	0	(+0)	0	1	(+0)	0	2	(+5)	0
2009/10	10	(+4)	0	0	(+0)	0	0	(+0)	0	10	(+4)	0
2010/11	17	(+11)	1	4	(+5)	1	1	(+0)	0	22	(+16)	2
2011/12	2	(+3)	0	0	(+3)	1	0	(+0)	0	2	(+6)	1
Totals	30	(+23)	1	4	(+8)	2	2	(+0)	0	36	(+31)	3

Jimmy spent his schoolboy years on the books of Manchester United, then Bury, but injury dashed his hopes of a professional contract and so he joined the youth team at Altrincham. His first taste of first-team football came with Ashton United, where he established himself as a tough-tackling but creative midfielder that could also operate at full-back. He began 2007/08 with Chorley, facing FC United in September, before making a switch to the Reds in December. He had what would have been a last-minute winner disallowed on his debut, but a niggling injury prevented him from establishing himself in the team that won promotion. He moved on to Conference North outfit Vauxhall Motors in the summer, and became a key figure in their engine room before having a brief spell the following season at Welsh club Bala Town. He returned to FC in January 2010, and earned a spot at right-back as the season drew to a close. With a good pre-season behind him, he became a key member of the squad in 2010/11, and it was his first goal for the club against Radcliffe Borough that began the famous FA Cup run. In fact he became something of a lucky charm as the team lost just three of the matches that he started on the way to reaching the promotion play-off final, with a personal highlight being the spectacular volley that opened the scoring against Whitby Town. He found opportunities limited at the start of 2011/12 and signed for Curzon Ashton, but made another return to the Reds in October. He played his part in a good unbeaten run, which included netting past Durham City in the FA Trophy, but picked up a needless red card against Kendal Town. He was unable to re-establish himself after his suspension, and moved to Altrincham in January. He later played for Salford City, whom he captained against FC in 2012, as well as Stockport Sports and Droylsden, and after a break from the game returned to play at amateur level.

068 Bradley HOWARD

Born: 16/11/1986, Salford **Left-back/Centre-back**
Debut: No.3 v Curzon Ashton (A, NPL1N), 29/12/2007

Season	LEAGUE			FA NATIONAL CUPS			OTHER CUPS / PLAY-OFFS			TOTALS		
	Starts	(+Sub)	Goals	Starts	(+Sub)	Goals	Starts	(+Sub)	Goals	Starts	(+Sub)	Goals
2007/08	19	(+0)	0	0	(+0)	0	6	(+0)	1	25	(+0)	1
2008/09	7	(+0)	0	0	(+0)	0	0	(+0)	0	7	(+0)	0
Totals	26	(+0)	0	0	(+0)	0	6	(+0)	1	32	(+0)	1

A former schoolboy with Bolton Wanderers, Bradley first played in non-league at Trafford, but was unattached when he attended training at FC United with long-term friends Chris and Jamie Baguley. Karl Marginson liked what he saw from the calm and classy performer, and once he had regained his fitness he was rewarded with a debut at table-topping Curzon Ashton in December 2007. He helped the team to a terrific win, although the boycott meant there were few fans there to witness it. Thereafter he missed just a handful of games, mainly at left-back but also as cover at centre-back, as the team secured the runners-up spot. He was excellent as the Reds lifted the President's Cup, although he missed both promotion play-off matches with a suspension picked up playing Sunday football. He played the first seven games of 2008/09 before a niggling injury prompted the manager to sign Simon Garner, and Bradley left the club soon after to concentrate on his career as a model, actor and singer. He was back on the semi-professional circuit in 2016/17 playing alongside several of his former FC team-mates for Prestwich Heys in their first season back in the North West Counties League.

069 Danny SELF

Born: 22/10/1981, Manchester **Right-back/Midfielder**
Debut: Sub v Curzon Ashton (A, NPL1N), 29/12/2007

Season	LEAGUE			FA NATIONAL CUPS			OTHER CUPS / PLAY-OFFS			TOTALS		
	Starts	(+Sub)	Goals	Starts	(+Sub)	Goals	Starts	(+Sub)	Goals	Starts	(+Sub)	Goals
2007/08	0	(+1)	0	0	(+0)	0	0	(+0)	0	0	(+1)	0
2008/09	3	(+2)	0	0	(+1)	1	0	(+0)	0	3	(+3)	1
Totals	3	(+3)	0	0	(+1)	1	0	(+0)	0	3	(+4)	1

Once a Manchester City and Oldham Athletic schoolboy, Danny played for Manchester League sides Springhead and East Manchester, where he was managed by Darren Lyons. The Droylsden lad moved up to the North West Counties League with Maine Road, establishing himself as an energetic midfielder with a keen eye for goal. He signed for FC United in December 2007, and made his debut as a late substitute in the superb win at Curzon Ashton, although very few Reds were there to see it due to the agreed boycott. He played for Maine Road for the rest of the season, before linking up again with FC in the summer of 2008. He began the term as a regular on the bench, before being pressed into action as a makeshift right-back. Reverting to midfield, he scored in the FA Cup defeat by Nantwich Town, but further opportunities were limited and he moved on to Mossley in October, later returning to Maine Road.

070 Nick ROBINSON

Born: 15/11/1982, London
Debut: Sub v Mossley (H, NPL1N), 01/01/2008

Forward/Midfielder

Season	LEAGUE			FA NATIONAL CUPS			OTHER CUPS / PLAY-OFFS			TOTALS		
	Starts	(+Sub)	Goals	Starts	(+Sub)	Goals	Starts	(+Sub)	Goals	Starts	(+Sub)	Goals
2007/08	7	(+15)	3	0	(+0)	0	2	(+2)	0	9	(+17)	3
2008/09	1	(+11)	2	0	(+2)	0	1	(+0)	0	2	(+13)	2
Totals	8	(+26)	5	0	(+2)	0	3	(+2)	0	11	(+30)	5

After being on schoolboy forms at Bolton Wanderers, Nick made his way onto the non-league circuit with Irlam, before joining his local side Salford City. He caught the attention of FC United by bagging the injury-time winner at The Willows in October 2006, and he also opened the scoring in the return match at Gigg Lane later that season. He scored past the Reds again for Woodley Sports in September 2007, so Karl Marginson moved to snap him up on New Year's Eve when squad reinforcements were needed. Thereafter he featured in every match, bar President's Cup ties for which he was ineligible, as he helped the team achieve promotion via the play-offs. He showed his great versatility by filling several positions, usually up front, but also in midfield, out wide, and occasionally he came off the bench to play at the back. He was unable to break into the starting line-up on a regular basis in 2008/09, and actually left United in September for a very brief sojourn with Conference North side Vauxhall Motors. He returned in early October, before producing his two most memorable moments in a red shirt. With the team 2-5 down at home to Cammell Laird in November, he was thrown on with 20 minutes remaining, and crossed for Chris Baguley to make it 4-5, then in the last minute he stretched out a leg to poke home a dramatic equaliser. A month later he slammed home a last-minute winner against Marine, but then left the club to play in Australia in January 2009.

071 Aaron GRUNDY

Born: 21/01/1988, Bolton
Debut: No.1 v Skelmersdale United (H, NPL1N), 16/02/2008

Goalkeeper

Season	LEAGUE			FA NATIONAL CUPS			OTHER CUPS / PLAY-OFFS			TOTALS		
	Starts	(+Sub)	Goals	Starts	(+Sub)	Goals	Starts	(+Sub)	Goals	Starts	(+Sub)	Goals
2007/08	6	(+0)	0	0	(+0)	0	2	(+0)	0	8	(+0)	0
Totals	6	(+0)	0	0	(+0)	0	2	(+0)	0	8	(+0)	0

Aaron joined FC United from landlords Bury on a short-term loan in February 2008 after Sam Ashton suffered a nasty hand injury. He had been at Gigg Lane since leaving school, and had made his senior debut aged just 17 in October 2005. He had made a total of six first-team appearances by the summer of 2007, when he picked up an ankle injury as he was challenging for the no.1 spot. The move to FC suited both club and player as he needed regular competitive action, and he made a fantastic start by keeping three consecutive clean sheets and being named as the league's Goalkeeper of the Month. His performances were pivotal in the team picking up crucial points against promotion rivals Skelmersdale United, Bamber Bridge and Curzon Ashton on their way to winning the play-offs. He returned to Bury in March when Ashton recovered, before being released in the summer and signing for Conference North side Burscough. After further spells with Warrington Town, Cambridge United, Fleetwood Town and Witton Albion he linked up with Chorley, where ironically he would share netminding duties with Sam Ashton.

073 Kyle HARROP

Born: 22/04/1987, Oldham
Debut: Sub v Goole (A, NPLPC:SF), 08/03/2008

Right-back/Midfielder

Season	LEAGUE			FA NATIONAL CUPS			OTHER CUPS / PLAY-OFFS			TOTALS		
	Starts	(+Sub)	Goals	Starts	(+Sub)	Goals	Starts	(+Sub)	Goals	Starts	(+Sub)	Goals
2006/07	0	(+0)	0	0	(+0)	0	0	(+0)	0	0	(+0)	0
2007/08	3	(+2)	0	0	(+0)	0	0	(+1)	0	3	(+3)	0
2008/09	0	(+0)	0	0	(+0)	0	0	(+0)	0	0	(+0)	0
Totals	3	(+2)	0	0	(+0)	0	0	(+1)	0	3	(+3)	0

Hailing from Chadderton, Kyle had previously been a member of the youth team at Curzon Ashton when he joined FC United's fledgling reserve squad in the summer of 2006. As a combative midfielder he was a standout performer as the team stormed to the title, and earned a call-up to the first-team bench for the league game at Nantwich Town in February 2007. When he finally made his full debut over a year later, he was selected to play at right-back, and it was in this position that he added to his appearances in the hectic run-in to 2007/08. He began the following season named on the bench, but in September 2008 he joined several of his former second-string colleagues at Bacup Borough to earn more first-team experience. He later had spells at Rossendale United, Trafford, Nantwich Town and Australian clubs Sorrento and Mandurah, before facing FC with Ashton United and Ramsbottom United. He was later on the books at Manchester League side Royton Town and North West Counties League outfits Chadderton and Avro.

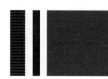

072 Matthew HAMPSON

Born: 21/10/1986, Oldham
Debut: No.4 v Goole (A, NPLPC:SF), 08/03/2008

Midfielder

Season	LEAGUE			FA NATIONAL CUPS			OTHER CUPS / PLAY-OFFS			TOTALS		
	Starts	(+Sub)	Goals	Starts	(+Sub)	Goals	Starts	(+Sub)	Goals	Starts	(+Sub)	Goals
2007/08	1	(+2)	0	0	(+0)	0	1	(+0)	0	2	(+2)	0
Totals	1	(+2)	0	0	(+0)	0	1	(+0)	0	2	(+2)	0

Matt had played for local club Oldham Athletic and FC United's landlords Bury at youth and reserve level before he linked up with the Reds in 2007. The Royton lad became a fixture in the centre of midfield for the reserves, where his tidy and intelligent passing helped the team to a second successive championship. He earned a senior call-up in March, and was something of a lucky charm as the team won three and drew one of his four games on the way to earning promotion and lifting the President's Cup. Along with a number of second-string colleagues, he moved on to Bacup Borough in the summer of 2008 for regular football. He had two spells there across five seasons, interrupted by stints at Oldham Boro, Ashton Athletic and Runcorn Linnets. In 2013 he joined New Mills, and faced FC United in a Manchester Premier Cup tie in September.

074 Martin COSGRAVE

Born: 16/04/1988, Manchester
Debut: Sub v Goole (A, NPLPC:SF), 08/03/2008

Forward

Season	LEAGUE			FA NATIONAL CUPS			OTHER CUPS / PLAY-OFFS			TOTALS		
	Starts	(+Sub)	Goals	Starts	(+Sub)	Goals	Starts	(+Sub)	Goals	Starts	(+Sub)	Goals
2007/08	0	(+0)	0	0	(+0)	0	0	(+2)	0	0	(+2)	0
Totals	0	(+0)	0	0	(+0)	0	0	(+2)	0	0	(+2)	0

A pacy striker from Middleton, Martin had played in the junior teams at Bury before joining FC United in the summer of 2006. He began with the new reserve team, where he gained a regular place in the second half of the season and earned winner's medals in both league and cup. The goals continued to flow at that level in 2007/08 as a second successive title was won, and he was rewarded with a senior call-up in March. He twice came on as a substitute in semi-finals, in the League President's Cup at Goole and the Manchester Premier Cup at Radcliffe Borough. In the summer he joined Bacup Borough, along with a number of his reserve team colleagues, in order to play first-team football in the North West Counties League. He remained there for several seasons and later had spells with Ramsbottom United and Mossley.

075 Rob HOWARTH

Born: 07/08/1979, Bolton
Debut: No.4 v Radcliffe Borough (A, NPL1N), 15/04/2008

Midfielder

Season	LEAGUE			FA NATIONAL CUPS			OTHER CUPS / PLAY-OFFS			TOTALS		
	Starts	(+Sub)	Goals	Starts	(+Sub)	Goals	Starts	(+Sub)	Goals	Starts	(+Sub)	Goals
2007/08	1	(+0)	0	0	(+0)	0	0	(+0)	0	1	(+0)	0
2008/09	0	(+3)	0	0	(+0)	0	0	(+0)	0	0	(+3)	0
Totals	1	(+3)	0	0	(+0)	0	0	(+0)	0	1	(+3)	0

A tenacious defensive midfielder who had spent time on schoolboy forms with Bolton Wanderers, Rob had played the majority of his football in the West Lancashire League before a spell with Darwen. He came along to train with FC United with his friend Sam Ashton, and impressed sufficiently to be signed on in March 2008. He made his debut in a win at Radcliffe Borough during the busy conclusion to the season, and was a regular on the bench in the opening months of the following campaign. With increasing competition for places, he dropped out of contention and moved on to join Atherton Laburnum Rovers in January 2009.

076 Jamie ROTHER

Born: 08/03/1989, Manchester
Debut: No.8 v Radcliffe Borough (A, NPL1N), 15/04/2008

Midfielder

Season	LEAGUE			FA NATIONAL CUPS			OTHER CUPS / PLAY-OFFS			TOTALS		
	Starts	(+Sub)	Goals	Starts	(+Sub)	Goals	Starts	(+Sub)	Goals	Starts	(+Sub)	Goals
2007/08	1	(+0)	0	0	(+0)	0	0	(+0)	0	1	(+0)	0
Totals	1	(+0)	0	0	(+0)	0	0	(+0)	0	1	(+0)	0

A dynamic midfielder from Middleton, Jamie joined FC United in the summer of 2006 as part of the club's first youth team squad. His performances earned a call-up to the reserves midway through the season, and he became a regular member of the second string throughout 2007/08. He was rewarded with a first-team debut during the hectic run-in to the season, and he didn't disappoint when assisting a crucial victory at Radcliffe Borough. In August 2008 he joined Bacup Borough, along with several other reserve team colleagues, in order to experience more competitive football, and his all-action style and long-range goals became a feature in the North West Counties League. He later faced FC during a long spell at Salford City, and also for New Mills and Ramsbottom United, whom he helped to the Northern Premier League West Division play-offs in 2019.

077 Kyle WILSON

Born: 14/11/1985, Birkenhead | Forward
Debut: No.9 v Matlock Town (H, NPLP), 16/08/2008 (scored 2)

Season	LEAGUE Starts	(+Sub)	Goals	FA NATIONAL CUPS Starts	(+Sub)	Goals	OTHER CUPS / PLAY-OFFS Starts	(+Sub)	Goals	TOTALS Starts	(+Sub)	Goals
2008/09	27	(+0)	21	5	(+0)	3	0	(+0)	0	32	(+0)	24
2009/10	7	(+0)	4	0	(+0)	0	0	(+0)	0	7	(+0)	4
Totals	34	(+0)	25	5	(+0)	3	0	(+0)	0	39	(+0)	28

A prolific goalscorer, Kyle began his career as a young professional at Crewe Alexandra, where he earned caps for the England under-19 side and spent a loan period at Altrincham. He was released in 2006 and joined Barrow, where his father Phil was manager, but after a promising start he suffered a cruciate injury that sidelined him for almost a year. After short spells with Witton Albion, Fleetwood Town and Droylsden, he joined Skelmersdale United, and played against FC United in the 2008 promotion play-off final. His next appearance was for the Reds, whom he joined that July, and he made a great start with two goals within the first 20 minutes of his debut. His excellent form maintained almost a goal-a-game record throughout the autumn, and by December he was the leading scorer in all professional and semi-pro leagues in England. Particular highlights included a hat-trick against Whitby Town, two in a great 3-0 win over table-topping Hednesford Town, and a superb late winner at Boston United. There was also a memorable double within four minutes against Witton Albion that included **FC United's fastest ever goal** after just **14 seconds**. A bad knee injury in January 2009 ended his season, but his exploits earned a move to Macclesfield Town in May. He made his long-awaited Football League debut in August, but was unable to break into the starting line-up and came back on loan to FC in January 2010. A hat-trick at Nantwich Town brought back memories of the previous season and he returned to Macclesfield refreshed, but was released in the summer and returned to the non-league circuit with Hyde. He later faced FC whilst playing for Nantwich and Witton, and also featured for Chester, Bangor City and Conwy Borough.

078 Carlos ROCA

Born: 04/09/1984, Manchester | Winger/Forward
Debut: No.10 v Matlock Town (H, NPLP), 16/08/2008

Season	LEAGUE Starts	(+Sub)	Goals	FA NATIONAL CUPS Starts	(+Sub)	Goals	OTHER CUPS / PLAY-OFFS Starts	(+Sub)	Goals	TOTALS Starts	(+Sub)	Goals
2008/09	26	(+11)	10	4	(+1)	0	1	(+0)	0	31	(+12)	10
2009/10	28	(+7)	8	9	(+0)	5	0	(+0)	0	37	(+7)	13
2010/11	18	(+15)	6	7	(+2)	1	1	(+0)	0	26	(+17)	7
2011/12	34	(+3)	6	8	(+0)	3	5	(+0)	0	47	(+3)	9
2012/13	12	(+8)	3	1	(+3)	0	0	(+0)	0	13	(+11)	3
Totals	118	(+44)	33	29	(+6)	9	7	(+0)	0	154	(+50)	42

Arguably the most skilful player to have pulled on the red shirt, Carlos was a tricky attacker from Withington who spent time in the academies of Manchester City and Bolton Wanderers before becoming a young professional with Oldham Athletic. After making seven appearances in the Football League, he was released and joined Conference side Carlisle United, before further spells at Northwich Victoria, Stalybridge Celtic and Altrincham. He signed for FC United in July 2008, and was soon delighting the fans and getting amongst the goals, particularly his double strikes at Ossett Town and against high-flying Ilkeston Town, and his memorable hat-trick against Ashton United. He was an integral member of the team that narrowly missed out on a play-off spot in 2009, and carried this form into the next campaign with notable strikes in the FA Cup and FA Trophy runs and a dramatic last-gasp winner against Stocksbridge Park Steels. In 2010/11 his most productive spell coincided with the incredible FA Cup run, in which he scored the winner against Barrow to set up the unforgettable first-round trip to Rochdale. A niggling injury restricted his outings after Christmas, and he was mainly used as an impact substitute, most effectively when enabling the club's first-ever win over Bradford Park Avenue and burying a lovely curler past Burscough. 2011/12 was perhaps his most consistent campaign, as he missed just a handful of matches on the way to a second successive play-off final heartbreak. He assumed the mantle of the team's main penalty-taker, but strikes like his screamer against Altrincham in the FA Trophy still showcased his eye for the spectacular. A promising start to 2012/13, when he struck three goals in his first four starts, was affected by injury, which was then exacerbated by a broken foot in January which ruled him out for almost three months. When he returned, the team were fighting to maintain their play-off position, affording fewer opportunities to regain peak fitness during the run-in. Upon the conclusion of the season, he decided on a change of scenery and made a switch to Chorley, before moving into the Welsh Premier League with Rhyl. He left the semi-professional game in 2014 to concentrate on his coaching career, but FC fans were delighted to see him play for the Old Boys XI in the first game at Broadhurst Park in May 2015. Carlos was part of a consortium that purchased Stockport Town in 2019, before he became Director of Football at newly-formed Macclesfield FC in October 2020.

079 Danny WILLIAMS

Born: 15/01/1988, Wigan
Debut: No.11 v Matlock Town (H, NPLP), 16/08/2008

Left-winger

Season	LEAGUE Starts	(+Sub)	Goals	FA NATIONAL CUPS Starts	(+Sub)	Goals	OTHER CUPS / PLAY-OFFS Starts	(+Sub)	Goals	TOTALS Starts	(+Sub)	Goals
2008/09	7	(+15)	2	1	(+2)	0	0	(+0)	0	8	(+17)	2
2009/10	2	(+6)	0	0	(+0)	0	0	(+0)	0	2	(+6)	0
Totals	9	(+21)	2	1	(+2)	0	0	(+0)	0	10	(+23)	2

Danny first became acquainted with FC United when he was introduced as a substitute for Daisy Hill in one of our earliest home games in October 2005. The lad from Leigh had spent four years on schoolboy forms at Wigan Athletic before joining the non-league ranks, and was named North West Counties Player of the Season before joining the Reds in July 2008. With Jerome Wright injured, he began the season in the starting line-up on the left wing, before mainly being used from the bench. He was recalled to the team in October and marked the occasion with a goal at Frickley Athletic before suffering a broken leg three days later at Whitby Town. After a period of rehabilitation, he returned to the squad to help the ultimately unsuccessful push for a play-off place, but he did his bit by firing a last-gasp winner in the penultimate game at title-chasing Ilkeston Town to set up the final day showdown. He began 2009/10 as a regular in the squad, but the consistency of Wright limited his opportunities and he made the switch to Clitheroe in October. He later moved to Kendal Town, for whom he scored a last-minute winner against FC in April 2012, before a spell in the Conference North with Chester. His progress was noted by Scottish Premiership outfit Inverness Caledonian Thistle, who signed him to a contract in August 2013, and he scored his first professional goal in January 2014 with the winner against Aberdeen. In a successful three-season spell he was part of the team that won the Scottish Cup at Hampden Park in 2015. In March 2016 he signed a pre-contract agreement to play the following season for Dundee, and he helped them to retain their place in the Premiership. He had a frustrating start to 2017/18, with just three substitute appearances to his name before leaving the club in November. He returned to England to link up with Accrington Stanley in January, but despite struggling to break into a settled side that were crowned League Two champions he was offered a contract for 2018/19. After a three-month loan spell at AFC Fylde he made just one more substitute appearance for Accrington before returning to the National League with FC Halifax Town on a free transfer in 2019. He remained for two years before emigrating in 2021 to coach at Dubai City.

080 David NEVILLE

Born: 18/07/1986, Manchester
Debut: Sub v Matlock Town (H, NPLP), 16/08/2008

Midfielder

Season	LEAGUE Starts	(+Sub)	Goals	FA NATIONAL CUPS Starts	(+Sub)	Goals	OTHER CUPS / PLAY-OFFS Starts	(+Sub)	Goals	TOTALS Starts	(+Sub)	Goals
2008/09	9	(+8)	0	1	(+1)	0	0	(+0)	0	10	(+9)	0
2009/10	2	(+2)	0	0	(+2)	0	1	(+0)	0	3	(+4)	0
Totals	11	(+10)	0	1	(+3)	0	1	(+0)	0	13	(+13)	0

A feisty playmaker from Middleton, Dave had been on schoolboy forms at Oldham Athletic, but he made his way in non-league during spells at Oldham Town and Bangor City. He linked up with FC United in July 2008, and helped to create the late equaliser on his debut within a minute of entering the fray. Used mainly from the bench in the first half of the campaign, he earned a regular place in January, and the team won six of his seven starts before a fractured leg kept him out of the line-up. He joined Witton Albion in July 2009, where he played alongside younger brother Lee, before making a return to FC in October. Unfortunately he was unable to regain a regular spot in the side, and moved on to Salford City in December.

081 Jacob WOOD

Born: 13/12/1989, Salford
Debut: No.6 v Bradford Park Avenue (A, NPLP), 01/09/2008

Centre-back

Season	LEAGUE Starts	(+Sub)	Goals	FA NATIONAL CUPS Starts	(+Sub)	Goals	OTHER CUPS / PLAY-OFFS Starts	(+Sub)	Goals	TOTALS Starts	(+Sub)	Goals
2008/09	2	(+0)	0	0	(+0)	0	0	(+0)	0	2	(+0)	0
Totals	2	(+0)	0	0	(+0)	0	0	(+0)	0	2	(+0)	0

A former Stockport County trainee, Jacob joined FC United early in 2008/09 after a short spell at Stalybridge Celtic. The versatile defender from Walkden impressed in training and came into contention due to injuries and suspension. He was given a baptism of fire as recently departed hero Rory Patterson put the Reds to the sword to win the points for Bradford Park Avenue, but emerged from the game with a lot of credit from the manager. His second match also ended in defeat, after which he did not emerge from the bench as defensive reinforcements were brought in. He went on to play for Runcorn Linnets, Ashton Athletic, Radcliffe Borough and Droylsden, and faced FC for Salford City and New Mills, where he was named Players' Player of the Season. He later joined Prestwich Heys, where he became part of the team that gained promotion to the North West Counties League by winning the Manchester League in 2015/16, and he was almost an ever-present in their first three seasons at the higher level. He captained Heys to victory in the NWCFL First Division Trophy in 2018, and opened the scoring against Cammell Laird in the final, before suffering defeat by the same opponents in the Promotion Play-Off Semi-Final a few days later. He was appointed as player/assistant-manager by Prestwich in 2019, but a change in leadership at the club saw him depart for Avro towards the end of the year. He went on to join Cheadle Town in 2022.

082 Danny WARRENDER

Born: 28/04/1986, Manchester   **Right-back/Centre-back/Midfielder**
Debut: No.2 v Nantwich Town (A, FAC:Q1), 13/09/2008

Season	LEAGUE			FA NATIONAL CUPS			OTHER CUPS / PLAY-OFFS			TOTALS		
	Starts	(+Sub)	Goals	Starts	(+Sub)	Goals	Starts	(+Sub)	Goals	Starts	(+Sub)	Goals
2008/09	26	(+0)	1	5	(+0)	0	0	(+0)	0	31	(+0)	1
2009/10	12	(+0)	0	2	(+1)	0	1	(+0)	0	15	(+1)	0
2011/12	0	(+2)	0	0	(+0)	0	0	(+1)	0	0	(+3)	0
Totals	38	(+2)	1	7	(+1)	0	1	(+1)	0	46	(+4)	1

Danny began his career as a young professional at Manchester City, where he made great strides through the youth teams to become a regular in the reserves. The Blackley lad made his Football League debut in a loan period at Blackpool, a move that was later made permanent, but he was surprisingly released in 2006. After spells with Rossendale United, for whom he faced FC United in 2007, and in the USA with San Francisco Seals, he joined the Reds in September 2008. Usually deployed at right-back, he also had a couple of runs in midfield, and his ability and experience was a massive factor in the team very nearly gaining a play-off spot. He was an automatic choice in the early months of 2009/10, when the team boasted an impressive defensive record, until being sidelined with a hip injury. Soon after he returned, the injury flared again and he decided to take a break from football in December, before making a comeback with Ramsbottom United in 2010. He rejoined FC in February 2012, but only appeared from the bench before returning to Ramsbottom, with whom he won promotion to the Northern Premier League Premier Division and again lined up against his former FCUM team-mates.

083 Simon GARNER

Born: 15/08/1982, Blackburn   **Left-back**
Debut: No.3 v Nantwich Town (A, FAC:Q1), 13/09/2008

Season	LEAGUE			FA NATIONAL CUPS			OTHER CUPS / PLAY-OFFS			TOTALS		
	Starts	(+Sub)	Goals	Starts	(+Sub)	Goals	Starts	(+Sub)	Goals	Starts	(+Sub)	Goals
2008/09	32	(+0)	2	4	(+0)	0	0	(+0)	0	36	(+0)	2
2009/10	16	(+1)	0	8	(+0)	0	1	(+0)	0	25	(+1)	0
Totals	48	(+1)	2	12	(+0)	0	1	(+0)	0	61	(+1)	2

The nephew of former Manchester United and England star Mike Duxbury, Simon spent several years on schoolboy forms at Blackburn Rovers, but was not offered a YTS contract upon leaving school. He joined the youth team at hometown club Accrington Stanley, before moving on to Great Harwood Town, Clitheroe, Kendal Town and Prescot Cables. Making his name as a left-back who was also comfortable in midfield, he progressed into the Conference North with Hyde United, Stalybridge Celtic and Fleetwood Town before joining FC United in September 2008. He missed only a handful of games, through suspension and injury, and helped to settle the side as they very nearly secured a play-off spot. He scored his first goal for the club at Frickley Atheltic with a sublime, curling 30-yard free-kick, and repeated the trick to earn a last-gasp point at high-flying Hednesford Town. He missed just one game before Christmas in 2009/10, contributing to the FA Cup and FA Trophy runs, before surprisingly choosing to leave the club in January for a fresh challenge. He linked up with FC Halifax Town, and bagged the winner against the Reds the following December. He later played for Chorley and Northwich Victoria before returning to Clitheroe in 2013 and spending almost three seasons as player-manager. In the summer of 2016 he joined Altrincham as player-coach, but left along with the manager at the end of August and signed for Trafford, where along with several other former FC players he and his new team narrowly missed out on a Northern Premier League Division One North play-off spot.

084 Alex SKIDMORE

Born: 03/10/1989, Bolton   **Left-back**
Debut: Sub v Worksop Town (H, NPLP), 20/09/2008

Season	LEAGUE			FA NATIONAL CUPS			OTHER CUPS / PLAY-OFFS			TOTALS		
	Starts	(+Sub)	Goals	Starts	(+Sub)	Goals	Starts	(+Sub)	Goals	Starts	(+Sub)	Goals
2008/09	3	(+4)	0	1	(+0)	0	1	(+0)	0	5	(+4)	0
Totals	3	(+4)	0	1	(+0)	0	1	(+0)	0	5	(+4)	0

After spending time as a schoolboy in the academies of both Manchester United and Bolton Wanderers, Alex joined Blackburn Rovers as a youth trainee at the age of 16. As competition for places in his favoured midfield role intensified, he spent a loan period with Rochdale, but a cartilage injury curtailed his progress and he was released by Blackburn in the summer of 2008. He joined FC United in September and became a regular member of the matchday squad, providing cover for the left side. He was elevated to the starting line-up due to Simon Garner's suspension and brief injury, and he performed admirably, particularly in the win over high-flying Ilkeston Town. However, the form of Garner and Jerome Wright limited his opportunities and he moved on to Salford City in the New Year in search of regular football.

085 Papis DIEYTE

Born: 28/08/1988, Malicounda Bambara (Senegal)   Midfielder
Debut: Sub v Ilkeston Town (H, NPLP), 29/10/2008

Season	LEAGUE			FA NATIONAL CUPS			OTHER CUPS / PLAY-OFFS			TOTALS		
	Starts	(+Sub)	Goals	Starts	(+Sub)	Goals	Starts	(+Sub)	Goals	Starts	(+Sub)	Goals
2008/09	3	(+6)	0	1	(+1)	1	1	(+0)	0	5	(+7)	1
Totals	**3**	**(+6)**	**0**	**1**	**(+1)**	**1**	**1**	**(+0)**	**0**	**5**	**(+7)**	**1**

A powerful midfielder from Senegal, Papis moved to Worsley with his English wife and initially earned a trial with Bolton Wanderers. That was unsuccessful, but his brother-in-law was an FC United fan and recommended him to the club in September 2008. He impressed the management team enough to sign him, although his registration was delayed by several weeks until he obtained a work permit. He was gradually introduced from the bench as he became acclimatised to the weather and pace of the game, but his all-action style and willingness to shoot from distance quickly endeared him to the crowd. He earned a run of starts from mid-November, but they coincided with a downturn in results, although he did manage to score in the FA Trophy defeat to Boston United. The return to contention of Dave Neville and Tunji Moses limited his opportunities and he was only used sparingly from the bench in the New Year, before moving on to Rossendale United in the summer. He later played for Trafford, Droylsden and Corby Town.

086 Tommy TURNER

Born: 06/10/1983, Salford   Forward
Debut: No.11 v Hednesford Town (H, NPLP), 29/11/2008

Season	LEAGUE			FA NATIONAL CUPS			OTHER CUPS / PLAY-OFFS			TOTALS		
	Starts	(+Sub)	Goals	Starts	(+Sub)	Goals	Starts	(+Sub)	Goals	Starts	(+Sub)	Goals
2008/09	9	(+2)	5	0	(+0)	0	1	(+0)	0	10	(+2)	5
Totals	**9**	**(+2)**	**5**	**0**	**(+0)**	**0**	**1**	**(+0)**	**0**	**10**	**(+2)**	**5**

A former midfielder in Accrington Stanley's youth team, Tommy developed into a proven goalscorer in the area's non-league circles. He first came to FC United's attention when he opened the scoring for Salford City in the FA Vase game in 2006, and followed that up with a further strike at Gigg Lane later that season. He signed for the Reds in November 2008 after a great start to the season at Bacup Borough, and went straight into the side for the superb win over table-toppers Hednesford Town. He was soon amongst the goals, registering in the eventful win over Marine, bagging a double to claim the points at Worksop Town, and heading the dramatic last-minute winner against Guiseley. However, despite his impressive statistics, he surprisingly chose to return to Bacup in February 2009. He later had spells at New Mills, Trafford, Runcorn Linnets and Atherton Collieries.

087 Grant SHENTON

Born: 28/01/1991, Manchester   Goalkeeper
Debut: No.1 v Woodley Sports (A, NPLCC:3), 02/12/2008

Season	LEAGUE			FA NATIONAL CUPS			OTHER CUPS / PLAY-OFFS			TOTALS		
	Starts	(+Sub)	Goals	Starts	(+Sub)	Goals	Starts	(+Sub)	Goals	Starts	(+Sub)	Goals
2008/09	0	(+0)	0	0	(+0)	0	1	(+0)	0	1	(+0)	0
2009/10	3	(+0)	0	0	(+0)	0	0	(+0)	0	3	(+0)	0
2010/11	1	(+0)	0	0	(+0)	0	2	(+0)	0	3	(+0)	0
Totals	**4**	**(+0)**	**0**	**0**	**(+0)**	**0**	**3**	**(+0)**	**0**	**7**	**(+0)**	**0**

Grant is a Newton Heath lad who joined FC United's youth team in 2008 from Maine Road. He was the last line of defence as the under-18s won a tremendous hat-trick of trophies, by which time he had already made his senior debut as a 17-year-old in a League Cup tie at Woodley Sports in December. He made a further three appearances as the 2009/10 season drew to a close, and was then pressed into action a year later due to Sam Ashton's suspension. He would have played at Matlock Town, if it weren't for his brother's wedding, but he lined up against Kendal Town and saved a last-minute penalty, although the rebound was subsequently converted. The biggest match of his career came three days later when he lined up at Bradford Park Avenue in the play-off semi-final, and kept a clean sheet as the Reds recorded a tremendous victory. After featuring during the 2011 pre-season, the signing of James Spencer meant that he would still be second choice, and so he accepted the offer of a two-year contract with Ramsbottom United, where he knew he would gain valuable experience. He helped his new club to the North West Counties League title in 2012, and also to promotion to the Northern Premier League Premier Division in 2014, which allowed him to face his former FC colleagues in two league games in 2014/15. He spent a total of five seasons with Ramsbottom, during which he became the club's record appearance maker and was captain of the side in his final term. He switched to Ashton United in the summer of 2016, but a broken arm kept him on the sidelines and he moved on to Stalybridge Celtic in October. He played against FC United in the two National League North encounters but his new side unfortunately finished the campaign in the relegation places. He joined up with Trafford in the summer of 2017, and was instrumental in them reaching the promotion play-offs in 2017/18. He had a terrific game against FC United in the 2018 Manchester Premier Cup Final, but although he saved Joel Senior's penalty in the shoot-out he was unable to prevent the trophy returning to Moston. He returned to National League North when signing a contract for Chester in the summer of 2018, and kept two clean sheets against FC during a solid campaign. However, back in the Northern Premier League with Buxton in 2019/20, Grant was the unlucky stopper on the wrong end of United's 7-0 victory at Broadhurst Park in October. He rejoined Stalybridge in November 2020, initially on loan before a permanent switch, but his return there was blighted by injury and he moved to North West Counties League outfit Avro in 2022.

088 Nick SWIRAD

Born: 28/05/1991, Oldham
Debut: No.6 v Woodley Sports (A, NPLCC:3), 02/12/2008

Centre-back

Season	LEAGUE Starts	(+Sub)	Goals	FA NATIONAL CUPS Starts	(+Sub)	Goals	OTHER CUPS / PLAY-OFFS Starts	(+Sub)	Goals	TOTALS Starts	(+Sub)	Goals
2008/09	0	(+0)	0	0	(+0)	0	1	(+0)	0	1	(+0)	0
2009/10	12	(+1)	0	2	(+0)	0	1	(+0)	0	15	(+1)	0
Totals	12	(+1)	0	2	(+0)	0	2	(+0)	0	16	(+1)	0

Already a keen FC United supporter, Nick joined the club's youth team in the summer of 2007 and established himself in the centre of defence. He was a key component as the under-18s won a hat-trick of trophies in 2008/09, by which time he had already made his first-team debut in a League Cup tie at Woodley Sports and also been named on the bench in a couple of league matches. His big breakthrough came in November 2009 when he was drafted in for the FA Trophy replay at home to Lancaster City, and gave a terrific performance in the 1-0 victory. He kept his place for the next six games, until the return of David Chadwick prompted a short loan switch to Rossendale United. Returning to the line-up in March, he played the majority of matches until the season's end, but after featuring in pre-season friendlies in 2010 he moved on to New Mills for more experience. In an excellent 2010/11 campaign, he helped his new club win the North West Counties League title, whilst picking up both Manager's and Players' Player of the Season. He went on to represent Mossley and Ashton United, before facing FC three times for Stocksbridge Park Steels. He then became a footballing globetrotter, playing and coaching in New York and Tasmania before settling in Malaysia. There he has played for Johor Darul Ta'zim, Melaka United, PKNS, Selangor and Sri Pahang, plus Nongbua Pitchaya in Thailand. In 2019 he earned his first call-up to the Malaysian national squad.

089 Sam FREAKES

Born: 21/08/1991, Manchester
Debut: No.11 v Woodley Sports (A, NPLCC:3), 02/12/2008

Left-winger

Season	LEAGUE Starts	(+Sub)	Goals	FA NATIONAL CUPS Starts	(+Sub)	Goals	OTHER CUPS / PLAY-OFFS Starts	(+Sub)	Goals	TOTALS Starts	(+Sub)	Goals
2008/09	0	(+0)	0	0	(+0)	0	1	(+0)	0	1	(+0)	0
Totals	0	(+0)	0	0	(+0)	0	1	(+0)	0	1	(+0)	0

Sam joined FC United when his father, Peter, was appointed as youth team manager in July 2008, and the Moston lad settled into the left-wing spot for the under-18s. He provided his fair share of goals in an attacking team, and was rewarded with a starting berth for the senior side's League Cup tie at Woodley Sports in December, which made him the **youngest player to start a game for the club**. His progress was halted by a broken leg in March 2009, but he recovered sufficiently to emerge from the bench in the youth team's last game of the season, the Manchester Youth Cup Final, which they won to complete a fantastic hat-trick of trophies. He moved on to continue his recovery at Trafford, and later also played for Salford City, Oldham Boro, Radcliffe Borough, Ashton United, Glossop North End, Ramsbottom United and Bamber Bridge. He twiced lined up against FC in the colours of Droylsden in 2013/14, and later featured for 1874 Northwich, Congleton Town and Padiham.

090 John BUCKLEY

Born: 24/07/1991, Manchester
Debut: Sub v Woodley Sports (A, NPLCC:3), 02/12/2008

Midfielder

Season	LEAGUE Starts	(+Sub)	Goals	FA NATIONAL CUPS Starts	(+Sub)	Goals	OTHER CUPS / PLAY-OFFS Starts	(+Sub)	Goals	TOTALS Starts	(+Sub)	Goals
2008/09	0	(+0)	0	0	(+0)	0	0	(+1)	0	0	(+1)	0
Totals	0	(+0)	0	0	(+0)	0	0	(+1)	0	0	(+1)	0

John joined up with FC United's under-18s in 2008, and the Ancoats lad soon caught the eye as a midfielder with an eye for goal. His progress was rewarded with a place on the bench for the first team's League Cup tie at Woodley Sports in December, when he replaced fellow youth teamer Sam Freakes at half-time. This was his only senior outing for the club, but he played a significant part as the youths won an incredible hat-trick of trophies in 2008/09, lifting the North West Youth Alliance league title and Open Cup, as well as the Manchester FA Youth Cup. After featuring in several pre-season games in 2009 and 2010, he moved on to continue his football development with Daisy Hill, Trafford, Mossley, Oldham Borough and Cheadle Town.

091 Shaun CONNOR

Born: 28/05/1991, Stockport
Debut: Sub v Woodley Sports (A, NPLCC:3), 02/12/2008

Centre-back

Season	LEAGUE			FA NATIONAL CUPS			OTHER CUPS / PLAY-OFFS			TOTALS		
	Starts	(+Sub)	Goals	Starts	(+Sub)	Goals	Starts	(+Sub)	Goals	Starts	(+Sub)	Goals
2008/09	0	(+0)	0	0	(+0)	0	0	(+1)	0	0	(+1)	0
2014/15	1	(+0)	0	0	(+0)	0	0	(+0)	0	1	(+0)	0
Totals	1	(+0)	0	0	(+0)	0	0	(+1)	0	1	(+1)	0

Shaun is part of a footballing family that has produced three generations to have represented Stockport County. He joined FC United in 2008, and was part of the exciting youth team that clinched a trophy treble in 2008/09. By then, he had already made his first-team debut as a substitute in the League Cup tie at Woodley Sports, along with several of his junior colleagues. To gain further experience he joined Atherton Collieries, before switching to Radcliffe Borough, where he established himself at centre-back in a long spell. He often featured in the line-up with his twin brother, Mark, at the club where their father Joe had earned league success in 1997. After enrolling at Sheffield University, he spent time at Ossett Town, for whom he faced FC in January 2014. His performances hadn't gone unnoticed by Karl Marginson, who brought him back to the club in July 2014, and his pre-season displays earned a starting berth for the season opener at Barwell. Unfortunately he suffered a knee injury after just 11 minutes which subsequently ruled him out for the rest of the term, although he was seen at the majority of home matches cheering his team-mates on to the Northern Premier League title.

092 Jamie MACK

Born: 07/03/1991, Manchester
Debut: Sub v Woodley Sports (A, NPLCC:3), 02/12/2008

Forward

Season	LEAGUE			FA NATIONAL CUPS			OTHER CUPS / PLAY-OFFS			TOTALS		
	Starts	(+Sub)	Goals	Starts	(+Sub)	Goals	Starts	(+Sub)	Goals	Starts	(+Sub)	Goals
2008/09	0	(+0)	0	0	(+0)	0	0	(+1)	0	0	(+1)	0
2009/10	1	(+7)	3	0	(+3)	0	0	(+0)	0	1	(+10)	3
Totals	1	(+7)	3	0	(+3)	0	0	(+1)	0	1	(+11)	3

A former Oldham Athletic schoolboy, Jamie joined FC United in the summer of 2008 as part of the youth team squad, and as captain he led the side to a fantastic treble in 2008/09. A prolific marksman, the Blackley lad also finished the season as the North West Youth Alliance league's top goalscorer, by which time he had already made his first-team debut as a substitute in a League Cup tie at Woodley Sports. He became a regular member of the senior squad the following season, and whilst he only started one game, he was named on the bench for over half of the fixtures, and netted three times in the process. His first goal for the Reds, in a home win over Marine in August 2009, made him FC United's youngest goalscorer at the time. He spent a spell on loan the following season at Rochdale Town, before later turning out for Ramsbottom United and Oldham Town.

093 Neil CHAPPELL

Born: 18/11/1985, Manchester
Debut: Sub v Ashton United (A, NPLP), 26/12/2008

Midfielder

Season	LEAGUE			FA NATIONAL CUPS			OTHER CUPS / PLAY-OFFS			TOTALS		
	Starts	(+Sub)	Goals	Starts	(+Sub)	Goals	Starts	(+Sub)	Goals	Starts	(+Sub)	Goals
2008/09	4	(+6)	1	0	(+0)	0	0	(+0)	0	4	(+6)	1
Totals	4	(+6)	1	0	(+0)	0	0	(+0)	0	4	(+6)	1

Neil was a player well known to FC United, having captained Maine Road in both 'mini-derby' matches in 2006/07, and also lining up for Radcliffe Borough in five of the six encounters between December 2007 and October 2008. In between, he spent a short spell at Ashton United, who became the team he faced on his debut soon after following close friend Jerome Wright in signing for the Reds in December 2008. The Wythenshawe lad could boast an impressive scoring record from midfield, which he proved by netting on his first start for the club against Leigh Genesis. With competition for places intensifying, he moved back to Maine Road, where he eventually broke their goalscoring record in April 2014. He also had stints with Salford City, Glossop North End and 1874 Northwich, where he helped the fan-owned club to their first trophy in April 2016. He switched to Atherton Collieries midway through the following campaign, and helped them to the 2017 North West Counties Premier Division title before signing for Congleton Town. He made another return to Maine Road in March 2018, but was unable to help prevent their relegation from the North West Counties League top flight. He later linked up with rivals West Didsbury & Chorlton, Cheadle Town and Wythenshawe Amateurs.

094 Tristram WHITMAN

Born: 09/06/1980, Nottingham
Debut: Sub v Boston United (A, NPLP), 10/01/2009

Forward

Season	LEAGUE Starts	(+Sub)	Goals	FA NATIONAL CUPS Starts	(+Sub)	Goals	OTHER CUPS / PLAY-OFFS Starts	(+Sub)	Goals	TOTALS Starts	(+Sub)	Goals
2008/09	3	(+4)	1	0	(+0)	0	0	(+0)	0	3	(+4)	1
Totals	3	(+4)	1	0	(+0)	0	0	(+0)	0	3	(+4)	1

A well travelled non-league striker who gained caps for the England 'C' semi-professional team, Tristram first emerged at Arnold Town, before a £10,000 transfer to Doncaster Rovers, whom he helped to promotion back into the Football League in 2003. He then moved to Scarborough, followed by a productive period at Tamworth, before spells with Crawley Town, Hinckley United, Alfreton Town, Farsley Celtic and Bradford Park Avenue. He was at Eastwood Town when he joined FC United on a loan basis in January 2009, and helped the Reds to two wins when appearing from the bench. His first start yielded a goal in an unfortunate defeat at Witton Albion, but after attacking reinforcements were introduced he returned to his parent club in March. He subsequently saw service with Carlton Town, Hucknall Town, Grantham Town, Bedworth United and Rainworth Miners Welfare.

095 Tunji MOSES

Born: 12/09/1983, Manchester
Debut: Sub v Prescot Cables (H, NPLP), 17/01/2009

Midfielder

Season	LEAGUE Starts	(+Sub)	Goals	FA NATIONAL CUPS Starts	(+Sub)	Goals	OTHER CUPS / PLAY-OFFS Starts	(+Sub)	Goals	TOTALS Starts	(+Sub)	Goals
2008/09	14	(+3)	1	0	(+0)	0	0	(+0)	0	14	(+3)	1
2009/10	8	(+2)	0	9	(+0)	0	0	(+0)	0	17	(+2)	0
Totals	22	(+5)	1	9	(+0)	0	0	(+0)	0	31	(+5)	1

Tunji is the son of former Manchester United star Remi Moses, but he had already made his own impression on FC United fans with his battling performances for Salford City in the clashes of 2006/07. In his youth he had been an exceptional ice hockey player, representing Great Britain, and played non-league football for Oldham Town, Flixton and Rossendale United where he established himself as a hard tackling central midfielder. He signed for the Reds in July 2008, but his debut was delayed until the following January by a suspension and a training ground injury. Once he regained his fitness he earned a regular place, and was instrumental in a long unbeaten run that very nearly earned a play-off spot. His own highlight was scoring his first goal for the club with a thumping header in the victory over North Ferriby United. He began 2009/10 in the starting line-up before missing a handful of games through injury, but yet again his return coincided with an upturn in results as he helped the team reach the final qualifying rounds of both the FA Cup and FA Trophy. Unfortunately he decided to take a break from football in December 2009, and although he did return to the club to play some part in the 2010 pre-season, he didn't stay once the competitive action got underway. He later resurfaced at Curzon Ashton before switching to Hyde, whom he helped to the Conference North title in 2012 and to retain their Conference status the year after. He then joined Stockport County, and FC fans next saw him when he played in the opening game at Broadhurst Park, in which he scored the first goal for the Old Boys XI. Later that summer he returned to Salford, and helped them to promotion to the National League North, before moving on to Ashton United in 2016. The following year he signed for North West Counties League new boys Prestwich Heys, featuring alongside several other former FC United players.

096 Adam TONG

Born: 21/04/1982, Manchester
Debut: No.6 v Guiseley (H, NPLP), 31/01/2009

Centre-back

Season	LEAGUE Starts	(+Sub)	Goals	FA NATIONAL CUPS Starts	(+Sub)	Goals	OTHER CUPS / PLAY-OFFS Starts	(+Sub)	Goals	TOTALS Starts	(+Sub)	Goals
2008/09	16	(+0)	3	0	(+0)	0	0	(+0)	0	16	(+0)	3
2009/10	19	(+1)	3	9	(+0)	1	1	(+0)	1	29	(+1)	5
Totals	35	(+1)	6	9	(+0)	1	1	(+0)	1	45	(+1)	8

A towering defender from Urmston, Adam attracted FC United's attention with his commanding displays for Bamber Bridge in four crucial encounters in the 2007/08 promotion fight. He had made his way in non-league with West Lancashire League side Charnock Richard, before joining the ambitious Fleetwood Town, where he won the North West Counties League. Moving on to Burscough, he scored in a win over Gillingham in the FA Cup in November 2005, but unfortunately suffered a broken leg in the next round at Burton Albion. He signed for the Reds in January 2009, and played every game until the end of the season as the team narrowly missed out on a play-off spot. A big influence in the improved defensive record, he was also a threat at the other end of the pitch, not just with his aerial ability but also with his huge long throws. His most memorable strike, though, was not a header, but a 35-yard screamer at Ashton United in the FA Trophy. After playing a part in all but three matches in 13 months, he left FC in February 2010 in order to pursue a career in Western Australia. He had a long spell with Perth club Balcatta, before spells with local rivals Bayswater City, Inglewood United and ECU Joondalup.

097 Carl LOMAX

Born: 19/01/1981, Bury **Forward**
Debut: No.9 v Leigh Genesis (H, NPLP), 14/02/2009 (scored)

Season	LEAGUE			FA NATIONAL CUPS			OTHER CUPS / PLAY-OFFS			TOTALS		
	Starts	(+Sub)	Goals	Starts	(+Sub)	Goals	Starts	(+Sub)	Goals	Starts	(+Sub)	Goals
2008/09	9	(+2)	4	0	(+0)	0	0	(+0)	0	9	(+2)	4
2009/10	1	(+1)	0	0	(+0)	0	0	(+0)	0	1	(+1)	0
Totals	10	(+3)	4	0	(+0)	0	0	(+0)	0	10	(+3)	4

A strong and mobile striker previously with Radcliffe Borough, Bacup Borough and Colne, Carl had faced FC United with his local club Ramsbottom United and Clitheroe. After a spell at Hyde United he signed for the Reds in January 2009, and made an immediate impact with a goal on his debut against Leigh Genesis. Despite a couple of injuries he contributed a reasonable return of four goals in an unbeaten run that almost earned the team a play-off spot. After looking sharp in the 2009 pre-season, he started the first league game against Boston United, and came off the bench at Bradford Park Avenue two days later before suffering a nasty bout of flu. Upon his recovery he picked up a series of niggling injuries, and so rejoined Ramsbottom to regain match fitness. He later played for Bamber Bridge and Rossendale United before returning again to Ramsbottom and also later featuring for Barnoldswick Town.

098 Gary STOPFORTH

Born: 08/09/1986, Burnley **Midfielder**
Debut: Sub v Frickley Athletic (H, NPLP), 14/03/2009

Season	LEAGUE			FA NATIONAL CUPS			OTHER CUPS / PLAY-OFFS			TOTALS		
	Starts	(+Sub)	Goals	Starts	(+Sub)	Goals	Starts	(+Sub)	Goals	Starts	(+Sub)	Goals
2008/09	0	(+2)	0	0	(+0)	0	0	(+0)	0	0	(+2)	0
Totals	0	(+2)	0	0	(+0)	0	0	(+0)	0	0	(+2)	0

Gary began his career at Blackburn Rovers, progressing to the reserves before being released in 2007 and entering non-league with Clitheroe. His battling midfield displays earned his Manager's Player of the Year award, and he also impressed against FC United, prompting the Reds to sign him in March 2009. However, he only appeared twice from the bench before moving to the USA for a summer with New Orleans Jesters. He spent the following term with Kendal Town, and after another American summer with Baton Rouge Capitals, he returned to join AFC Fylde. There followed a productive spell at Ramsbottom United, as well as another summer with New Orleans before he moved to Salford City in 2015. He helped them to two successive promotions before joining Stockport County in 2016, for whom he faced FC at Broadhurst Park in August. In 2017 he moved to Australia to play for Mitchelton in the Brisbane Premier League, before a return to Stockport. He faced FC again in the four encounters in both league and FA Cup in 2017/18, before work commitments saw him join his local club Colne. He returned to National League North with Chester in 2018, and despite a knee injury in December ending his campaign he was given a deal for the following season. He later rejoined Clitheroe, where he had a spell as joint player-manager alongside another former FC player, Billy Priestley.

099 Phil MARSH

Born: 15/11/1986, Whiston **Forward/Midfielder/Right-back**
Debut: No.9 v Hednesford Town (A, NPLP), 21/03/2009

Season	LEAGUE			FA NATIONAL CUPS			OTHER CUPS / PLAY-OFFS			TOTALS		
	Starts	(+Sub)	Goals	Starts	(+Sub)	Goals	Starts	(+Sub)	Goals	Starts	(+Sub)	Goals
2008/09	8	(+0)	1	0	(+0)	0	0	(+0)	0	8	(+0)	1
2009/10	29	(+6)	10	7	(+2)	2	1	(+0)	0	37	(+8)	12
Totals	37	(+6)	11	7	(+2)	2	1	(+0)	0	45	(+8)	13

Phil made history on 21st March 2009 when he became the **first player to appear in the first-team for both Manchester United and FC United of Manchester**. The St. Helens lad had come through the ranks at Old Trafford, but his progress was halted by a serious injury sustained in a road accident when he was just 17. His long road to recovery was rewarded with a senior bow in a League Cup tie at Crewe Alexandra in October 2006, but he was released at the end of that season and signed for Blackpool. His injury curse struck again as a broken metatarsal prevented him from reaching the first team, and he moved into the non-league circuit in 2008 with Northwich Victoria, then Hyde United. He was with Leigh Genesis when Karl Marginson first attempted to sign him in February 2009, but he stayed put and scored a hat-trick against the Reds later that week in a surprise win for his team. This only strengthened the manager's resolve, and he finally got his man the following month. His class shone through immediately as he helped the team to an unbeaten run that almost earned a play-off spot. Injury delayed his start to 2009/10, but his season came to life with a tremendous hat-trick against Nantwich Town, followed by a cool finish in the exciting FA Cup draw with Stalybridge Celtic. This campaign was one of transition, and on occasion Phil was asked to bring his creativity into midfield, and even filled in at right-back. He was unable to find his scoring touch on a regular basis, however, and chose to move on in the summer. He regained his form at Stalybridge, before moving into the Conference with Forest Green Rovers, then Hereford United, for whom he faced FC in the FA Cup in 2012. He later played for Guiseley, Barrow, Salford City and Ashton United before moving into the Welsh Premier League with Cefn Druids and then Bala Town. He came back across the border in October 2016 to join Altrincham, before linking up with North West Counties League pacesetters Runcorn Town. He returned to Wales in October 2017 to join Rhyl before signing for Droylsden in July 2018, but was sidelined due to a prolonged international clearance delay. He moved to Clitheroe in March 2019 and later became player-coach at his local side Pilkington after they joined the North West Counties League.

100 Ben DEEGAN

Born: 13/07/1988, Manchester
Debut: Sub v Boston United (H, NPLP), 15/08/2009

Forward

Season	LEAGUE			FA NATIONAL CUPS			OTHER CUPS / PLAY-OFFS			TOTALS		
	Starts	(+Sub)	Goals	Starts	(+Sub)	Goals	Starts	(+Sub)	Goals	Starts	(+Sub)	Goals
2009/10	26	(+6)	9	7	(+2)	3	1	(+0)	0	34	(+8)	12
2010/11	5	(+20)	2	5	(+3)	4	2	(+0)	0	12	(+23)	6
2011/12	9	(+8)	4	4	(+2)	1	0	(+2)	0	13	(+12)	5
Totals	40	(+34)	15	16	(+7)	8	3	(+2)	0	59	(+43)	23

A big centre-forward from Wythenshawe, Ben started on the non-league circuit at Altrincham, before establishing himself at Flixton. He was no stranger to FC United after opening the scoring for Ashton United in December 2008, and took little persuasion to link up with the Reds in July 2009. His wholehearted commitment quickly made him a huge fan favourite, and he played a crucial role in the team reaching the final qualifying rounds of both national competitions in his first season. He got the FA Cup run going with the opening goal at Sheffield, before bagging the winner at North Ferriby United in the next round, while his extra-time winner over Lancaster City ensured progress in the FA Trophy. His most prolific spell began in February, when ironically he partnered the man he was brought in to replace, Kyle Wilson, who had returned for a loan spell. Ben's five goals in five games were a major reason why the club decided not to extend Wilson's stay. He began 2010/11 alongside new signing Michael Norton, but after an injury remained on the bench for a few games. He returned to the line-up in spectacular fashion with a hat-trick in the FA Trophy win over Newcastle Town, which ensured he kept his place for the FA Cup tie with Barrow. He then had the game of his life in the famous win over Rochdale, where his neat turn on the left helped to set up Jake Cottrell's screamer. After starring in both games with Brighton & Hove Albion, he lost his place through suspension, and a change of team shape in the New Year meant he became a permanent substitute as the Reds chased promotion. In April 2011 his legendary status soared even higher when he emerged from the bench to take over in goal when Sam Ashton was dismissed in a crucial encounter with Northwich Victoria. His first task was to face a penalty, which he amazingly saved, and not only did he go on to pull off further stops, it was also his long kick that was seized upon by Norton to fire the winning goal. He then scored twice in the next three matches to seal wins over Frickley Athletic and

Marine, before playing the entire game in goal at Matlock Town and helping the team to a vital 2-1 win. His luck ran out in the unsuccessful play-off final at Colwyn Bay, but he began 2011/12 in the team before a niggling injury restricted his game time. When back to fitness he hit a purple patch with four goals in five starts before serving a suspension, after which his opportunities were limited, and he joined New Mills in January 2012. He later had two further spells with Ashton United, plus stints at Nantwich Town, Droylsden, Trafford and Warrington Town, where he won the Northern Premier League Division One North in 2015/16. He joined Glossop North End in July 2017, and was their top goalscorer before moving to Hyde United in March 2018 and helping them to promotion from the Northern Premier League Division One North. He later had a short spell at Ramsbottom United.

104 Joe YOFFE

Born: 26/05/1987, Manchester
Debut: Sub v Ashton United (A, FAT:Q1), 17/10/2009

Forward

Season	LEAGUE			FA NATIONAL CUPS			OTHER CUPS / PLAY-OFFS			TOTALS		
	Starts	(+Sub)	Goals	Starts	(+Sub)	Goals	Starts	(+Sub)	Goals	Starts	(+Sub)	Goals
2009/10	7	(+13)	2	2	(+3)	2	1	(+0)	0	10	(+16)	4
Totals	7	(+13)	2	2	(+3)	2	1	(+0)	0	10	(+16)	4

Joe was was a prolific striker in the Stockport County academy, before venturing to the USA to embark on a scholarship at Embry-Riddle University in Florida. He further honed his instincts on the college circuit, before returning home upon graduating and having trials at several professional clubs. Frustrated by delays resulting from international clearance and registration deadlines, he signed for Cheadle Town, but soon needed a sterner challenge and so linked up with close friend Carlos Roca at FC United in October 2009. He was introduced gradually as a substitute, before making his mark with a double strike inside 20 minutes of his first start in the FA Trophy tie at Lancaster City. Further goals contributed to a point at Whitby Town and a win at Durham City, but he was unable to earn a regular place and moved on in the summer of 2010. He later had spells in Canada with Ottawa Fury, Crevillente Deportivo in Spain, Galway United in Ireland, Bayswater City in Australia, Dutch side RKSV Halsteren, Icelandic clubs Selfoss and Grindavík, and back home with AFC Telford United and Droylsden.

101 Jake COTTRELL

Born: 02/05/1988, Manchester
Debut: Sub v Boston United (H, NPLP), 15/08/2009

Midfielder/Left-back

Season	LEAGUE Starts	(+Sub)	Goals	FA NATIONAL CUPS Starts	(+Sub)	Goals	OTHER CUPS / PLAY-OFFS Starts	(+Sub)	Goals	TOTALS Starts	(+Sub)	Goals
2009/10	23	(+8)	1	6	(+2)	0	1	(+0)	0	30	(+10)	1
2010/11	36	(+3)	4	9	(+1)	1	2	(+0)	0	47	(+4)	5
2011/12	37	(+3)	1	5	(+0)	0	5	(+0)	0	47	(+1)	1
2012/13	29	(+4)	1	6	(+0)	1	1	(+3)	0	36	(+7)	2
Totals	125	(+16)	7	26	(+3)	2	9	(+3)	0	160	(+22)	9

After being on the books of Rochdale as a schoolboy, Jake began playing non-league football with Oldham Town, and the Middleton lad's performances were enough to attract FC United, who signed him in July 2009. He spent the majority of the first two months of the campaign as a substitute as he acclimatised to the higher level, but then became a virtual ever-present until the end of the season. His remarkable displays led to the club awarding him a contract, and he went on to make a deserved clean sweep of the Player of the Season awards.

He carried this form into 2010/11, and began to get amongst the goals too, beginning with a long-range chip against Retford United and the unforgettable FA Cup screamer at Rochdale that saw him voted as Player of the Round. He claimed an automatic spot as the team's creative force as they marched through to the ultimately unsuccessful play-off final at Colwyn Bay. The following season followed a similar route for the energetic midfielder, with a last-gasp play-off final defeat at Bradford Park Avenue, but he had hardly missed a game and was one of the standout performers yet again. He was still the midfield kingpin as 2012/13 began, but also showed his versatility with a number of games at left-back. This possibly affected his momentum, as for the final two months of the season he was unable to string together a run of games in midfield and found himself on the bench as the team lost a third successive play-off final at Hednesford Town in May. The next month he decided on a switch to Chorley, and became a mainstay in the side that pipped United to the Northern Premier League title in 2014 and continued to challenge for further promotions. He went on to face the Reds in some classic encounters in the FA Cup, the FA Trophy, Northern Premier League and National League North, and also lined up for the Old Boys XI in the opening game at Broadhurst Park in May 2015. He earned a further promotion in 2019 in the Chorley side that won the play-offs to reach the National League. He had played over 300 times for the club before moving to Ashton United in 2020, and later played for Avro and Workington.

102 Ben MORRIS

Born: 02/10/1989, Oldham
Debut: Sub v Retford United (A, NPLP), 22/08/2009

Left-back/Midfielder

Season	LEAGUE Starts	(+Sub)	Goals	FA NATIONAL CUPS Starts	(+Sub)	Goals	OTHER CUPS / PLAY-OFFS Starts	(+Sub)	Goals	TOTALS Starts	(+Sub)	Goals
2009/10	3	(+5)	0	0	(+0)	0	0	(+0)	0	3	(+5)	0
Totals	3	(+5)	0	0	(+0)	0	0	(+0)	0	3	(+5)	0

Ben began his career as a young professional at Manchester City, where he progressed to the reserves prior to being released in 2009. Comfortable playing at left-back or in midfield, the Middleton lad linked up with FC United that summer, and was a constant member of the squad during the first two months of the season. With fierce competition for places, he disappeared from contention, before returning to the fold later in the campaign and adding to his appearances. He left the club in 2010, and later played for Trafford while embarking on a career as a fitness trainer.

103 Abdirashid IBRAHIM

Born: 05/04/1987, Mogadishu (Somalia)
Debut: Sub v Nantwich Town (H, NPLP), 07/10/2009

Winger/Forward

Season	LEAGUE Starts	(+Sub)	Goals	FA NATIONAL CUPS Starts	(+Sub)	Goals	OTHER CUPS / PLAY-OFFS Starts	(+Sub)	Goals	TOTALS Starts	(+Sub)	Goals
2009/10	1	(+1)	0	0	(+1)	0	0	(+1)	0	1	(+3)	0
Totals	1	(+1)	0	0	(+1)	0	0	(+1)	0	1	(+3)	0

The son of a FIFA referee who moved his family from Somalia to Norway, Abdi came to Manchester soon after his younger brother, Abdisalam, joined the youth team at Manchester City. A talented player in his own right, he was an exciting and speedy attacker capable of playing through the middle or out wide. After impressing for FC United in the 2009 pre-season, his competitive debut was delayed whilst awaiting international clearance, but he became a regular in the squad during the autumn. However, he was unable to establish himself and left the club in January 2010, later linking up with Rossendale United.

105 Ludovic QUISTIN

Born: 24/05/1984, Les Abymes (Guadeloupe)   **Full-back**
Debut: No.2 v North Ferriby United (A, NPLP), 27/10/2009

Season	LEAGUE			FA NATIONAL CUPS			OTHER CUPS / PLAY-OFFS			TOTALS		
	Starts	(+Sub)	Goals	Starts	(+Sub)	Goals	Starts	(+Sub)	Goals	Starts	(+Sub)	Goals
2009/10	24	(+0)	0	3	(+0)	0	1	(+0)	0	28	(+0)	0
2010/11	4	(+1)	0	1	(+0)	0	0	(+0)	0	5	(+1)	0
Totals	28	(+1)	0	4	(+0)	0	1	(+0)	0	33	(+1)	0

Ludo was a versatile player with a mountain of experience with numerous clubs, as well as international caps for his native Guadeloupe. Comfortable playing in a number of positions, he was best as a marauding full-back, and moved to England in his late teens, attending trials at several professional clubs. He played for various non-league outfits around the south and midlands, before relocating to the north-west and signing for FC United in October 2009. His first few games were at right-back, before he became first choice on his favoured left in the New Year. This coincided with an impressive eight-match unbeaten run, before the season ultimately ended in disappointment. He missed the first few months of 2010/11 after injuring his knee in a friendly at Cliftonville, and was pitched back into action for the FA Cup 2nd round replay with Brighton & Hove Albion. He was unable to claim a regular place after Lee Neville's return to the team, and linked up with Conference outfit Forest Green Rovers in February 2011.

In May 2012, the club was devastated to hear that Ludo had lost his life in a motorbike accident back home in Guadeloupe. Football had lost an enthusiastic and popular player who will be remembered by all those who had the pleasure to play alongside him.

106 Kyle JACOBS

Born: 18/10/1986, Manchester   **Full-back/Centre-back**
Debut: No.2 v Stocksbridge Park Steels (A, NPLP), 23/01/2010

Season	LEAGUE			FA NATIONAL CUPS			OTHER CUPS / PLAY-OFFS			TOTALS		
	Starts	(+Sub)	Goals	Starts	(+Sub)	Goals	Starts	(+Sub)	Goals	Starts	(+Sub)	Goals
2009/10	12	(+2)	0	0	(+0)	0	0	(+0)	0	12	(+2)	0
2010/11	23	(+2)	0	9	(+0)	0	2	(+0)	0	34	(+2)	0
2011/12	35	(+1)	1	6	(+0)	0	5	(+0)	0	46	(+1)	1
2012/13	35	(+2)	2	7	(+0)	0	5	(+0)	0	45	(+2)	2
Totals	105	(+7)	3	22	(+0)	0	10	(+0)	0	137	(+7)	3

Kyle began his football education in the colours of local club Moston Juniors, before he spent several years in the academy of Oldham Athletic, where he was rewarded with a YTS contract after leaving school. Despite progressing to the fringes of the first team, he was released in May 2005 and signed for Mansfield Town, for whom he made five appearances in the Football League. In August 2006 he moved to Macclesfield Town, but despite making the bench was not called into action and shortly afterwards joined Welsh side Bangor City. He went on to play for Porthmadog and Welshpool Town before a bad ankle injury sidelined him for almost a year. After a brief stint at Kendal Town, he joined FC United in January 2010, when his arrival coincided with a great run of five wins and three draws. After a spell out with injury, he resumed his right-back role as the season drew to a disappointing close. He began 2010/11 in great form, starting each of the first 20 games, and assuming the team captaincy, a role that he proudly held for the momentous FA Cup victory at Rochdale and both games in the following round against Brighton & Hove Albion. After sustaining an injury on New Year's Day he was sidelined for two months, but returned for the tremendous run-in that took the team to the promotion play-off final. His injury jinx struck again after just 13 minutes of the 2011/12 season, and again a month later, but he returned to the line-up in spectacular fashion by notching his first goal for the club with a cracker from long-range against Whitby Town. Thereafter he was rarely missing as he led his team once again to the play-off final, which ended in heartache in the last minute of extra-time at Bradford Park Avenue. He was again a model of consistency in 2012/13, which he began by leading the team to three straight victories, during which he scored twice against Matlock Town on his 100th appearance for the Reds. United also reached the final qualifying round of the FA Cup, but despite impressive form in the league they lost a third successive play-off final, this time at Hednesford Town. This was Kyle's last game for the club, as he accepted a contract offer from Stockport County in June 2013. He later played for Chorley, Ashton United, Trafford, Glossop North End and Colwyn Bay. After a brief return to Ashton United, he moved to Ramsbottom United in September 2018 and helped his team to reach the Northern Premier League Division One West play-offs before joining North West Counties side Avro in 2019.

107 Adriano RIGOGLIOSO

Born: 28/05/1979, Liverpool
Debut: Sub v Stocksbridge Park Steels (A, NPLP), 23/01/2010

Forward/Midfielder

Season	LEAGUE Starts	(+Sub)	Goals	FA NATIONAL CUPS Starts	(+Sub)	Goals	OTHER CUPS / PLAY-OFFS Starts	(+Sub)	Goals	TOTALS Starts	(+Sub)	Goals
2009/10	3	(+3)	0	0	(+0)	0	0	(+0)	0	3	(+3)	0
Totals	3	(+3)	0	0	(+0)	0	0	(+0)	0	3	(+3)	0

Although known as a cultured attacking player, Adriano actually began his career with Liverpool as a trainee goalkeeper. After being released he began his non-league journey playing outfield with Marine, before moving into the Conference for a long spell with Morecambe. His performances attracted the attention of professional clubs, and in November 2003 he signed for Doncaster Rovers, making his Football League debut the following month and being a regular member of their squad that gained promotion to the third tier. Thereafter his appearances were mainly from the bench, and he returned to Morecambe in 2006, via a short loan stint with Southport. He then had a successful spell at Forest Green Rovers before short stays at Grays Athletic and Colwyn Bay. He joined FC United in December 2009, and although his quality was evident he picked up a straight red card within 20 minutes of his first start. After returning from suspension he was unable to claim a regular spot, making just one further start, and rejoined Colwyn Bay in March. He later faced FC for Ashton United and Marine, before playing for Rhyl, Conwy Borough and Northwich Victoria.

108 Mark AYRES

Born: 17/05/1985, Salford
Debut: Sub v Frickley Athletic (A, NPLP), 20/02/2010

Centre-back

Season	LEAGUE Starts	(+Sub)	Goals	FA NATIONAL CUPS Starts	(+Sub)	Goals	OTHER CUPS / PLAY-OFFS Starts	(+Sub)	Goals	TOTALS Starts	(+Sub)	Goals
2009/10	4	(+3)	0	0	(+0)	0	0	(+0)	0	4	(+3)	0
2010/11	1	(+2)	0	1	(+0)	0	1	(+0)	0	3	(+2)	0
Totals	5	(+5)	0	1	(+0)	0	1	(+0)	0	7	(+5)	0

As a teenager Mark was on the books at Blackpool, and the Walkden lad was also part of the Salford Boys team that beat Cardiff at Old Trafford to win the National Schools Cup. He began in non-league with Flixton, where he faced FC United four times in the club's first three seasons, before moving to Salford City. He joined the Reds in February 2010, and was set for a regular spot in central defence when he had to have a wisdom tooth operation. He returned before the end of the term, and was fit to start 2010/11, but extra competition for places limited his outings. He started in the league win at Ossett Town and the FA Trophy victory over Colwyn Bay, and was a valued member of the squad for the historic FA Cup matches with Rochdale and Brighton & Hove Albion. However, he moved on in January 2011 in search of regular football, linking up with Irlam, before a further stint at Salford. He faced FC again for Droylsden and Ramsbottom United, and also played for Radcliffe Borough, Atherton Collieries, Colne, Prestwich Heys, Padiham and Northwich Victoria.

109 Angelos TSIAKLIS

Born: 02/10/1989, Nicosia (Cyprus)
Debut: Sub v Ossett Town (H, NPLP), 03/03/2010

Midfielder

Season	LEAGUE Starts	(+Sub)	Goals	FA NATIONAL CUPS Starts	(+Sub)	Goals	OTHER CUPS / PLAY-OFFS Starts	(+Sub)	Goals	TOTALS Starts	(+Sub)	Goals
2009/10	4	(+4)	0	0	(+0)	0	0	(+0)	0	4	(+4)	0
Totals	4	(+4)	0	0	(+0)	0	0	(+0)	0	4	(+4)	0

A Cypriot midfielder, Angelos began his career as a young professional at Manchester City, where he was a member of the side that won the FA Youth Cup in 2008, along with another future FC United player Scott Kay. After winning under-21 caps for his country, he made his senior club debut during a loan spell with Conference side Wrexham the following season. He later moved to the Welsh club on a permanent basis, but he became a free agent late in 2009. Karl Marginson was alerted to his availability by youth team player and family friend Stephanos Ioannou, and he signed for FC in February 2010. He became a regular member of the squad during the closing stages of the season, and earned a starting berth for four consecutive matches in April where he showed some class with his neat passing ability. He returned to Cyprus in the summer to sign a contract with Anorthosis Famagusta, and later helped Enosis Neon Paralimni to promotion to the top flight in 2015. The following year he moved back to his home city to play for Olympiakos Nicosia, where he won another promotion.

110 Adam Docker-KARIM

Born: 17/11/1985, Rochdale
Debut: Sub v Buxton (A, NPLP), 06/03/2010

Centre-back

Season	LEAGUE			FA NATIONAL CUPS			OTHER CUPS / PLAY-OFFS			TOTALS		
	Starts	(+Sub)	Goals	Starts	(+Sub)	Goals	Starts	(+Sub)	Goals	Starts	(+Sub)	Goals
2009/10	0	(+1)	0	0	(+0)	0	0	(+0)	0	0	(+1)	0
Totals	0	(+1)	0	0	(+0)	0	0	(+0)	0	0	(+1)	0

A giant central defender or striker, Adam was on the books at Bury as a teenager before progressing through the youth and reserve teams at Altrincham. He made his way into the Welsh Premier League with Bangor City, before a switch to Porthmadog, where he gained international recognition with a call-up to play for Pakistan in the World Cup qualifiers. After short spells with Chorley and Salford City, he joined FC United in February 2010, but only appeared once on the pitch, as a half-time substitute in the defeat at Buxton. The following season saw him turn out for Chadderton and Ashton United, and in 2013 he played for Droylsden in the Conference North.

111 Cédric KROU

Born: 25/07/1991, Paris (France)
Debut: Sub v Matlock Town (A, NPLP), 16/03/2010

Midfielder

Season	LEAGUE			FA NATIONAL CUPS			OTHER CUPS / PLAY-OFFS			TOTALS		
	Starts	(+Sub)	Goals	Starts	(+Sub)	Goals	Starts	(+Sub)	Goals	Starts	(+Sub)	Goals
2009/10	3	(+3)	0	0	(+0)	0	0	(+0)	0	3	(+3)	0
2011/12	0	(+2)	0	0	(+0)	0	0	(+0)	0	0	(+2)	0
2012/13	1	(+9)	0	0	(+3)	0	3	(+0)	0	4	(+12)	0
Totals	4	(+14)	0	0	(+3)	0	3	(+0)	0	7	(+17)	0

After spending time in the Paris Saint-Germain youth academy, Cédric came to Manchester to study English, and was spotted by Karl Marginson while coaching at Manchester College. A strapping centre-back or defensive midfielder with a good turn of pace, he was introduced to the FC United team in the latter stages of the 2009/10 season whilst still aged just 18. After a spell at Trafford, he returned to the Reds in March 2012, making a couple of appearances from the bench in the run-in, before becoming a regular squad member in 2012/13. With his starts mainly restricted to cup games, he signed for Conference North side Droylsden in February 2013. He later faced FC with Trafford and Ramsbottom United, where he won promotion to the Northern Premier League Premier Division in 2014. He joined Northwich Victoria a year later, before venturing to Latvia to play for Higher League club BFC Daugavpils in 2016. He then made another return to FC United in March 2017, but did not feature in the squad before the season ended. He later had short spells at Mossley, Abbey Hey and Avro.

112 Stephanos IOANNOU

Born: 04/06/1992, Limassol (Cyprus)
Debut: Sub v Matlock Town (A, NPLP), 16/03/2010

Forward/Midfielder

Season	LEAGUE			FA NATIONAL CUPS			OTHER CUPS / PLAY-OFFS			TOTALS		
	Starts	(+Sub)	Goals	Starts	(+Sub)	Goals	Starts	(+Sub)	Goals	Starts	(+Sub)	Goals
2009/10	0	(+2)	0	0	(+0)	0	0	(+0)	0	0	(+2)	0
Totals	0	(+2)	0	0	(+0)	0	0	(+0)	0	0	(+2)	0

An attacker or midfielder from Cyprus, Stephanos joined up with FC United's youth team in the autumn of 2009, after being discovered by Karl Marginson when the manager was coaching at Manchester College. He made sufficient progress to be rewarded with a senior bow in March 2010, whilst still aged just 17. His debut came away at Matlock Town, where family friend Angelos Tsiaklis plus fellow student Cédric Krou both sat alongside him on the bench. His second appearance was in the last game of the season at home to the same opponents. He finished the campaign by netting the winning goal in the Manchester FA Youth Cup Final, before moving on in the summer.

113 Chris OVINGTON

Born: 10/08/1990, Leeds
Debut: Sub v Hucknall Town (H, NPLP), 20/03/2010

Winger

Season	LEAGUE Starts	(+Sub)	Goals	FA NATIONAL CUPS Starts	(+Sub)	Goals	OTHER CUPS / PLAY-OFFS Starts	(+Sub)	Goals	TOTALS Starts	(+Sub)	Goals
2009/10	6	(+3)	0	0	(+0)	0	0	(+0)	0	6	(+3)	0
2010/11	4	(+6)	1	5	(+3)	1	1	(+0)	0	10	(+9)	2
Totals	10	(+9)	1	5	(+3)	1	1	(+0)	0	16	(+12)	2

A pacy winger, Chris was in the Manchester United academy before becoming a professional at Leeds United, where he played regularly in the reserves. After loans at local non-league clubs Farsley Celtic and Guiseley, he was released and signed part-time with Garforth Town. He created several goals for main striker Tom Greaves, before moving up a level with Bradford Park Avenue. He signed for FC United in March 2010 and began most of the remaining games on the right wing as the season fizzled out. He played his part in the team winning the first three games of 2010/11 and then scored his first goal for FC at former side Bradford PA. With Carlos Roca in superb form, his chances were limited, but he was a regular name on the bench as United made excellent progress in both FA competitions. His volley opened the scoring in the FA Trophy win over Colwyn Bay, whilst in the FA Cup he emerged from the bench on the historic night at Rochdale and then started both games with Brighton & Hove Albion. The arrival of Matthew Wolfenden increased the competition for places, so Chris moved to Buxton in February 2011, and faced against his former team-mates a month later. He later played for Ossett Town, Stocksbridge Park Steels, Goole, Harrogate Railway Athletic, Hemsworth Miners Welfare, Campion and Nostell Miners Welfare.

114 Gage EME

Born: 28/04/1992, Manchester
Debut: Sub v Hucknall Town (H, NPLP), 20/03/2010

Forward

Season	LEAGUE Starts	(+Sub)	Goals	FA NATIONAL CUPS Starts	(+Sub)	Goals	OTHER CUPS / PLAY-OFFS Starts	(+Sub)	Goals	TOTALS Starts	(+Sub)	Goals
2009/10	0	(+4)	0	0	(+0)	0	0	(+0)	0	0	(+4)	0
Totals	0	(+4)	0	0	(+0)	0	0	(+0)	0	0	(+4)	0

A pacy striker from Moss Side, Gage was formerly in the schoolboy academy at Crewe Alexandra before linking up with Abbey Hey. He caught the eye with his goalscoring exploits for FC United's youth team during the 2009/10 season, and was rewarded with a promotion to the senior ranks in March. He emerged from the bench in four matches in the run-in, and then finished the campaign by helping the under-18s to retain the Manchester FA Youth Cup. He featured again for the first team during the pre-season build-up in the summer of 2010, before going on to experience further senior football in spells at North West Counties League sides Congleton Town and Cheadle Town.

115 Scott CHEETHAM

Born: 30/12/1992, Manchester
Debut: Sub v Burscough (A, NPLP), 10/04/2010

Left-back/Midfielder

Season	LEAGUE Starts	(+Sub)	Goals	FA NATIONAL CUPS Starts	(+Sub)	Goals	OTHER CUPS / PLAY-OFFS Starts	(+Sub)	Goals	TOTALS Starts	(+Sub)	Goals
2009/10	0	(+1)	0	0	(+0)	0	0	(+0)	0	0	(+1)	0
2010/11	0	(+0)	0	0	(+0)	0	1	(+0)	0	1	(+0)	0
2011/12	0	(+1)	0	0	(+0)	0	0	(+0)	0	0	(+1)	0
2012/13	2	(+3)	0	1	(+2)	0	3	(+0)	0	6	(+5)	0
2013/14	0	(+0)	0	0	(+0)	0	0	(+0)	0	0	(+0)	0
2014/15	9	(+0)	0	3	(+2)	0	2	(+0)	0	14	(+2)	0
2015/16	3	(+1)	0	0	(+0)	0	2	(+0)	0	5	(+1)	0
Totals	14	(+6)	0	4	(+4)	0	8	(+0)	0	26	(+10)	0

When Scott came on to make his senior debut for FC United at Burscough in April 2010, he became the youngest player to represent the first team at the time. Able to play at left-back or in midfield, the Openshaw lad joined the club in 2009 via the link-up with the Manchester College. During a successful twelve month spell he helped the youth team to win the Manchester FA Youth Cup in 2010, the North West Youth Alliance title in 2011, and also earned caps for England Schools under-18s. He remained a regular senior squad member apart from a spell on loan at Trafford in 2011/12, and a season helping the new reserve team to the Lancashire League title in 2013/14. His patience was rewarded with an extended run in the side at left-back in 2014/15, as he helped the Reds to finally win promotion from the Northern Premier League. He ended the term with a championship medal, and played in the historic opening matches at Broadhurst Park. His start to 2015/16 was delayed by illness, which sidelined him when he would have deputised for the suspended Jerome Wright. He came back from the bench against Curzon Ashton when the Reds struck two late goals to earn an unlikely point, and then helped the team shoot up the table with six points in the next two outings. He dropped out of contention when Wright returned, and thereafter featured only in the Manchester Premier Cup, in which he scored United's final penalty in the shoot-out win over Glossop North End. He moved on to Mossley in December in search of first-team football.

116 Lee NEVILLE

Born: 06/04/1988, Manchester   Left-back/Centre-back/Midfielder
Debut: No.3 v Marine (A, NPLP), 22/08/2010

Season	LEAGUE			FA NATIONAL CUPS			OTHER CUPS / PLAY-OFFS			TOTALS		
	Starts	(+Sub)	Goals	Starts	(+Sub)	Goals	Starts	(+Sub)	Goals	Starts	(+Sub)	Goals
2008/09	0	(+0)	0	0	(+0)	0	0	(+0)	0	0	(+0)	0
2010/11	37	(+2)	0	6	(+0)	0	2	(+0)	0	45	(+2)	0
2011/12	35	(+2)	5	8	(+0)	0	3	(+1)	0	46	(+3)	5
2012/13	35	(+3)	1	6	(+1)	1	3	(+1)	0	44	(+5)	2
2013/14	23	(+7)	2	3	(+0)	0	5	(+0)	0	31	(+7)	2
2014/15	1	(+0)	0	0	(+0)	0	0	(+0)	0	1	(+0)	0
Totals	**131**	**(+14)**	**8**	**23**	**(+1)**	**1**	**13**	**(+2)**	**0**	**167**	**(+17)**	**9**

After spending time in the academies of Oldham Athletic and Rochdale, Lee joined Bury on a YTS contract, but left the club at the age of 17. A few months later he was back at Gigg Lane, lining up for Oldham Town against FC United in the club's first season, where he gave an impressive attacking display from the left wing. After playing sporadically over the next couple of seasons, he gained a regular place in 2008/09, and in March of that season he joined older brother Dave at FC to provide cover if required. Both brothers began the following season with Witton Albion and were reunited later at Salford City, before Lee made a return to the Reds in July 2010. Despite preferring a midfield role, he began the season at left-back in a new-look defence, and took to his new position superbly. He started every game until suffering a broken foot at the end of October, which unfortunately caused him to miss the unforgettable FA Cup games with Rochdale and Brighton & Hove Albion. He returned to the team in January, not missing another match until the end of the campaign, helping the Reds to storm up the table and reach the promotion play-off final. He carried this consistency into 2011/12, again missing only a handful of games, mainly due to suspension from two red cards. He also added goals to his game, with his aerial ability a particular threat at set-pieces, and the team won all of the games in which he scored on the way to a second play-off heartbreak. He continued to be first-choice left-back in 2012/13, when he showed his versatility by also lining up on the left of midfield and in the centre of defence. A third successive play-off final defeat ensued, and in 2013/14 a niggling injury and a change in formation saw him spend more time on the bench. However, he did eventually prove to be the ideal choice as the left of the new back-three, and helped the team to win 12 consecutive matches to storm to the top of the table. Unfortunately, they eventually lost the title by a point and were then unsuccessful in the play-offs once more. After playing just once in the opening games of 2014/15, Lee moved on to Salford in August in search of regular football, before switching to Ramsbottom United, where he faced his former FC team-mates in April. The following month he played in the first game at Broadhurst Park as part of the Old Boys XI. He joined Hyde in the summer of 2015, before linking up with Trafford the following January. In June 2017 he signed for Stalybridge Celtic, but returned to Trafford in January 2018 and helped them to reach the Northern Premier Division One North promotion play-offs. In 2019, after a brief spell at Avro, he finally tasted play-off success with Radcliffe before a spell at Droylsden the following term.

117 Richard BATTERSBY

Born: 12/09/1979, Bolton   Full-back/Midfielder
Debut: No.4 v Marine (A, NPLP), 22/08/2010

Season	LEAGUE			FA NATIONAL CUPS			OTHER CUPS / PLAY-OFFS			TOTALS		
	Starts	(+Sub)	Goals	Starts	(+Sub)	Goals	Starts	(+Sub)	Goals	Starts	(+Sub)	Goals
2010/11	26	(+1)	0	4	(+1)	0	1	(+0)	0	31	(+2)	0
2011/12	18	(+8)	0	2	(+1)	0	2	(+0)	0	22	(+11)	0
Totals	**44**	**(+9)**	**0**	**6**	**(+2)**	**0**	**3**	**(+0)**	**0**	**53**	**(+13)**	**0**

Richard was a young professional at Oldham Athletic, where he played regularly in the reserves before dropping into the Northern Premier League with Radcliffe Borough. In a productive five-year spell he played alongside Karl Marginson, and became a hero by despatching the winning penalty in a promotion play-off final shootout. His displays as a right wing-back earned a move to Northwich Victoria in 2005, where he won the Conference North title in his first season. After a spell with Altrincham he returned to Radcliffe, and faced FC United at Gigg Lane in October 2008. He repeated this experience a year later with Stalybridge Celtic, before linking up with the Reds in July 2010. He missed just three of the first 13 games, playing either in central midfield or on the right, but took a break in October due to family issues. He made an unexpected return for the famous FA Cup win at Rochdale, playing out of position at left-back. Despite being short of match fitness, he gave a colossal performance against the odds, which included a crucial second half goal-line clearance. After the tragic loss of fiancée Jenna in January 2011, Richard's return the following month coincided with five straight victories as the team stormed up the table. He put in another assured performance to help the team to a fantastic victory in the play-off semi-final at Bradford Park Avenue, but remained on the bench for the final. He was on the team sheet, usually from the start, for the first 19 matches of 2011/12, before losing his place due to a suspension. After a short loan at Trafford, he returned in the New Year and helped the team to another play-off final. He moved back to Radcliffe in the summer before hanging up his boots in 2013. However, United fans were pleased to see him play for the Old Boys XI in the first game at Broadhurst Park in May 2015.

118 Martin PARKER

Born: 29/09/1984, Ashton-under-Lyne
Debut: No.5 v Marine (A, NPLP), 22/08/2010

Centre-back

	LEAGUE			FA NATIONAL CUPS			OTHER CUPS / PLAY-OFFS			TOTALS		
Season	Starts	(+Sub)	Goals	Starts	(+Sub)	Goals	Starts	(+Sub)	Goals	Starts	(+Sub)	Goals
2010/11	17	(+0)	1	4	(+1)	0	0	(+1)	0	21	(+2)	1
Totals	17	(+0)	1	4	(+1)	0	0	(+1)	0	21	(+2)	1

After a spell in the Manchester City academy in his early teens, Martin emerged in non-league with Curzon Ashton, where he broke into the first team at the age of 17. The Denton lad was progressing well until he was sidelined for three years due to tendonitis, before he resumed playing at Glossop North End. Normally a classy centre-back, he was also often played up front, and was amongst the goals as he helped his side reach the FA Vase Final at Wembley in 2009. Unfortunately, he remained an unused substitute on the day as his team-mates lost to Whitley Bay. He put that disappointment behind him the following term with a terrific campaign in which he reverted to defence and caught the eye of FC United. He joined the Reds in July 2010, and went straight into the line-up as the team made a great start to the new season. He opened the scoring with an early header to set up the third successive win against Retford United, and kept his place until an unfortunate run of defeats in September. He spent most of the famous FA Cup run on the bench, but returned to the side for the replay with Brighton & Hove Albion in December. He largely remained there until breaking a foot in February, only returning for the promotion play-off final defeat at Colwyn Bay. After featuring in pre-season friendlies in 2011, he moved on to Clitheroe in August, before lining up for Salford City and Radcliffe Borough the following term. He later returned to Glossop, helping them to win the North West Counties League and finally playing at Wembley as they again reached the FA Vase Final in 2015. The same month he played for the Old Boys XI in the opening game at Broadhurst Park, and faced FC later in the year in the Manchester Premier Cup, but was unfortunate to miss the deciding penalty in the shoot-out. He later featured for Abbey Hey and Ramsbottom United.

119 Scott McMANUS

Born: 28/05/1989, Bury
Debut: No.6 v Marine (A, NPLP), 22/08/2010

Centre-back

	LEAGUE			FA NATIONAL CUPS			OTHER CUPS / PLAY-OFFS			TOTALS		
Season	Starts	(+Sub)	Goals	Starts	(+Sub)	Goals	Starts	(+Sub)	Goals	Starts	(+Sub)	Goals
2010/11	36	(+0)	1	9	(+0)	0	2	(+0)	0	47	(+0)	1
Totals	36	(+0)	1	9	(+0)	0	2	(+0)	0	47	(+0)	1

After spending part of his teenage years in the Manchester United academy, Scott drifted into non-league and was with Curzon Ashton when he was offered a route back into the full-time game with Crewe Alexandra in 2008. He became a regular member of their reserve team at left-back, before being called up to make his Football League debut in April 2009 in an unfamiliar midfield role. He made a total of six senior appearances for the Cheshire club, in which he scored with an unstoppable long-range drive at Stockport County, before being released. He linked up with his local team, Prestwich Heys of the Manchester League, in order to maintain his fitness, before joining FC United in the summer of 2010. He quickly established himself as a centre-back in the new-look defence, and had a tremendous season in which he missed very few games. He was ever-present until November, playing a crucial role as the team progressed in both FA competitions. He was part of the team that beat Rochdale in the unforgettable FA Cup first round tie, but he received a red card with FC leading at Brighton & Hove Albion in the next round. On his return from suspension the team began a charge up the league, and he scored with a bullet header against Frickley Athletic in the dramatic run-in. The promotion bid ultimately ended in play-off final defeat, after which he left the club to join Conference North new boys FC Halifax Town. He became a vital member of their team, helping them to promotion in 2013 and cementing his place in the history books when netting a spectacular strike to win the FA Trophy Final at Wembley in May 2016. He was sidelined for most of the next campaign after suffering a cruciate injury, but returned towards the end of the season to make his 250th appearance for the Yorkshire club. In May 2018 he moved on to Coalville Town, close to his new home in Leicestershire, and spent two years with the Southern League Central side before retiring from football in the summer of 2020.

121 Colin LITTLE

Born: 04/11/1972, Manchester
Debut: Sub v Retford United (H, NPLP), 28/08/2010 (scored 2)

Forward

	LEAGUE			FA NATIONAL CUPS			OTHER CUPS / PLAY-OFFS			TOTALS		
Season	Starts	(+Sub)	Goals	Starts	(+Sub)	Goals	Starts	(+Sub)	Goals	Starts	(+Sub)	Goals
2010/11	1	(+2)	2	0	(+0)	0	0	(+0)	0	1	(+2)	2
Totals	1	(+2)	2	0	(+0)	0	0	(+0)	0	1	(+2)	2

Colin is a Wythenshawe lad who first made his name in non-league circles with Rossendale United and Hyde United, before joining the professional ranks with Crewe Alexandra in 1996. He made over 200 appearances for the Cheshire club, the majority of which were in the second tier after he helped them to promotion in 1997. A quick and lively attacker, he was capable of playing on the wing or in a central striking position, and contributed a decent return of goals. After a brief loan spell at Mansfield Town he joined Macclesfield Town in 2003, staying for a year before returning to non-league with Halifax Town. Shortly after he began a long and successful association with Altrincham, for whom he scored over a century of goals, before leaving in 2010 to devote more time to his coaching role at Manchester United's academy. He linked up with FC United that summer, and scored a stunning brace when making his debut as a substitute against Retford United. However, after two further appearances he left due to the pressures of his role at Carrington, and re-signed for Altrincham, before short stints with New Mills and Witton Albion.

120 Michael NORTON

Born: 20/01/1981, Ashton-under-Lyne
Debut: No.9 v Marine (A, NPLP), 22/08/2010 (scored 2)

Forward

Season	LEAGUE			FA NATIONAL CUPS			OTHER CUPS / PLAY-OFFS			TOTALS		
	Starts	(+Sub)	Goals	Starts	(+Sub)	Goals	Starts	(+Sub)	Goals	Starts	(+Sub)	Goals
2010/11	41	(+0)	24	10	(+0)	8	1	(+0)	0	52	(+0)	32
2011/12	34	(+2)	16	8	(+0)	4	6	(+0)	3	48	(+2)	23
2012/13	35	(+3)	15	6	(+1)	3	3	(+2)	2	44	(+6)	20
2013/14	27	(+12)	13	2	(+1)	0	2	(+2)	2	31	(+15)	15
2014/15	14	(+4)	2	0	(+4)	0	0	(+0)	0	14	(+8)	2
2015/16	0	(+0)	0	0	(+0)	0	1	(+0)	1	1	(+0)	1
Totals	151	(+21)	70	26	(+6)	15	13	(+4)	8	190	(+31)	93

After being on schoolboy forms with Bury, Michael began playing non-league football in the Manchester League for East Manchester, before spending a short spell at Droylsden. The lad from Stalybridge established himself as prolific goalscorer with Woodley Sports, where his exploits earned him a trial at Nottingham Forest, but after a minor injury they failed to offer him a contract. In 2005 he joined Curzon Ashton, where he notched over 200 goals in a terrific five-year spell. His strikes helped the club to reach the FA Vase semi-final and win promotion from the North West Counties League in 2007, and also to reach the promotion play-offs in the Northern Premier League's Division One North in each of the following three seasons. He had been a thorn in the side of FC United on several occasions, and after a couple of approaches it was with relief that he finally joined the Reds in June 2010. He scored twice on his debut at Marine, the first of 32 goals in an unforgettable season for both club and player. He made the national headlines when he stroked home the injury-time winner at Rochdale in the FA Cup, before embarking on a terrific spree in the New Year that shot United into the play-offs. His goals won points in numerous matches, but a harsh dismissal at Chasetown in April led to his suspension for the play-off final, where he was sorely missed. The ban delayed his start to 2011/12, but he was soon amongst the goals as the Reds once again challenged for promotion. His highlights would be the FA Trophy winner against Altrincham and the terrific solo goal at Chorley that helped FC into the play-off final. He began 2012/13 on fire, but ultimately suffered play-off agony again when his goal at Hednesford Town in the play-off final was not enough to save the Reds from defeat. The arrival of Tom Greaves brought competition for his place, and he had to wait until October to register his first goal of 2013/14. His momentum was then delayed by suspension, and the form of Greaves restricted him to the bench. He did however become a hero for a different reason in December 2013 when he played the entire second half in goal at AFC Fylde, keeping a clean sheet in the fantastic win. He regained his place at Christmas, and soon after the manager altered the team's formation, which accommodated both of his deadly strikers. This was the catalyst for the Reds to go on a tremendous 12-match winning streak that took them to the top of the table, but ultimately they lost out in the play-offs again, with both Norton and Greaves limping out of the semi-final. Worse was to come on the injury front for Mike the following season when he suffered a serious knee ligament injury in a clash against Blyth Spartans in October that effectively ended his season. He briefly returned to feature as a late substitute in the FA Trophy ties with Fylde and Torquay United before undergoing further rehabilitation, eventually getting back onto the teamsheet for the final four games as FC finally clinched promotion by winning the Northern Premier League title. After a short loan spell at Trafford in September 2015, Mike returned to score his first goal at Broadhurst Park in the Manchester Premier Cup against Glossop North End, before leaving to rejoin former club Curzon in November. His final tally of 93 goals puts him fourth in the club's all-time scorers' list, and he also had another strike wiped from his record when the FA Trophy replay with Witton Albion was abandoned in November 2013. He switched to Glossop in the summer of 2016, where he appeared alongside several other former Reds, and also went on to play a single game for Ashton United in December 2017. He joined North West Counties League newcomers Avro the following term and helped them to the final of the First Division Cup, before being appointed joint manager of New Mills alongside close friend and former team-mate Dave Birch in September 2019.

122 Zach HIBBERT

Born: 28/06/1988, Whangarei (New Zealand)
Debut: No.1 v Ashton United (A, NPLP), 30/08/2010

Goalkeeper

Season	LEAGUE			FA NATIONAL CUPS			OTHER CUPS / PLAY-OFFS			TOTALS		
	Starts	(+Sub)	Goals	Starts	(+Sub)	Goals	Starts	(+Sub)	Goals	Starts	(+Sub)	Goals
2010/11	6	(+0)	0	2	(+0)	0	0	(+0)	0	8	(+0)	0
Totals	6	(+0)	0	2	(+0)	0	0	(+0)	0	8	(+0)	0

Born in the southern hemisphere but raised in Wigan, Zach was a schoolboy at Wigan Athletic before joining Burscough, where he made the first team aged just 17. After loan spells with Fleetwood Town, Ashton United, Colwyn Bay and Lancaster City, he faced FC United with Prescot Cables in 2008 before signing a short-term contract for Football League side Accrington Stanley in January 2009. He provided cover on the bench until the end of the term before returning to non-league with Chorley, being named their Player of the Season. He joined the Reds in July 2010 as competition for Sam Ashton, and was given an early opportunity with eight games from late August to early October. Two of those were at the start of the famous run to the FA Cup second round, with Zach being on the bench for the others after Ashton regained his place. Needing regular football, he moved on to Clitheroe in January 2011, before joining Southport and playing for them in the Conference. He later lined up against FC for Skelmersdale United, and had further spells at Salford City, Stalybridge Celtic, back at Clitheroe and Prescot, as well as at Ashton Town. In July 2015 he played for the FC United Old Boys team in the club's 10th Anniversary game against Leigh Genesis, and spent part of the match playing in the back four.

125 Matthew WOLFENDEN

Born: 23/07/1987, Oldham
Debut: No.11 v Colwyn Bay (H, FAT:Q2), 30/10/2010

Midfielder/Forward

Season	LEAGUE			FA NATIONAL CUPS			OTHER CUPS / PLAY-OFFS			TOTALS		
	Starts	(+Sub)	Goals	Starts	(+Sub)	Goals	Starts	(+Sub)	Goals	Starts	(+Sub)	Goals
2010/11	24	(+3)	11	1	(+3)	0	3	(+0)	1	28	(+6)	12
2011/12	32	(+3)	20	2	(+3)	0	5	(+1)	0	39	(+7)	20
2012/13	35	(+2)	18	5	(+0)	0	2	(+0)	1	42	(+2)	19
2013/14	40	(+2)	10	3	(+0)	1	2	(+1)	0	45	(+3)	11
2014/15	39	(+3)	9	9	(+1)	4	0	(+1)	0	48	(+5)	13
2015/16	18	(+16)	7	1	(+2)	0	2	(+0)	1	21	(+18)	8
2016/17	25	(+9)	8	1	(+2)	0	3	(+1)	3	29	(+12)	11
Totals	213	(+38)	83	22	(+11)	5	17	(+4)	6	252	(+53)	94

Matthew began his career with local club Oldham Athletic, and became their youngest ever senior player in November 2003 aged just 16. He continued in the youth and reserve teams over the next two seasons, with occasional first-team substitute appearances. He became a regular squad member in 2006/07, and scored his first goal in the promotion play-off semi-final, although the team were ultimately defeated. His appearances were more frequent the following term as the Latics just missed out on a play-off spot, but a couple of injuries wrecked his 2008/09 campaign and he was released to join Conference side Wrexham. His sole season there was also disrupted by injury, and he was a free agent when he signed for FC United in October 2010. He was gradually introduced to the team during the autumn as he regained his match fitness, before really establishing himself in the New Year. His first goal for the club was the winner against Ashton United that kick-started the team's march to the play-off places, and the Reds won every game in which he scored. He began a great purple patch in February that produced seven goals in five games, including a hat-trick at Nantwich Town, but his most important strike was giving United an early lead in the promotion play-off semi-final at Bradford Park Avenue. He began 2011/12 in terrific form by scoring in each of the first three games, including the first goal scored in the entire league in the first minute of the opening day, and then after a couple of autumn injury lay-offs he once again became the team's talisman after Christmas. He played in every game, either up front, out wide or in central midfield, and notched 13 goals in 19 matches to finish as the team's top league scorer, although they lost out in the play-offs again. The next campaign followed a similar pattern, as he maintained a great goalscoring record but suffered play-off final agony for the third consecutive year. He was the matchwinner against Whitby Town, Ashton United, Grantham Town, AFC Fylde and Worksop Town, but he saved his best goal for last with the outrageous 40-yard screamer against Witton Albion in the play-off semi-final. A more withdrawn position saw his scoring figures drop in the opening months of 2013/14, before the team's new formation put him as the link between midfield and the front two as they went on a 12-match winning run, although promotion remained elusive. Wolfy scored FC's first goal of the 2014/15 season, a momentous campaign in which he was the team's top scorer in the fantastic run to the FA Trophy quarter-final. In the league his strikes set the Reds up for crucial victories over Grantham Town, Witton and Ashton United as they finally earned promotion to the Conference North by winning the Northern Premier League title. In 2015/16 his appearances were split between the starting line-up and substitutes' bench, but he still boasted a decent scoring rate with some important strikes. His first goal of the season against Brackley Town set the Reds up for their first ever win at Broadhurst Park, and his late winner against Corby Town also clinched the second. He twice opened the scoring over the festive period against Hednesford Town and Bradford PA to help earn vital points, and then returned from injury to hit a double in the dramatic win over North Ferriby United in February. He began 2016/17 on the bench, but marked his first start by opening the scoring with a smart volley in the terrific win over Stockport County. After netting against Alfreton Town in October he had his longest run of starts, but then was mainly on the bench until the New Year. He then hit a good run of form, beginning by hitting the club's fastest hat-trick in the space of just seven minutes against West Didsbury & Chorlton in the Manchester Premier Cup. Five goals in the final month of the season included a late winner at Curzon Ashton and a double against Gainsborough Trinity that at the time took Matthew into second place in the list of the club's all-time highest goalscorers. He ended the campaign with a winner's medal in the Manchester Premier Cup Final, played on his old home ground at Boundary Park, before leaving United to join Stalybridge Celtic in July 2017. He moved to Radcliffe in the summer of 2019, and opened the scoring against FC in the first of three games he played against the Reds during the 2019/20 season. He later linked up with several former FC colleagues at North West Counties League side Avro.

PLAYER PROFILES

123 Karl MUNROE

Born: 23/09/1979, Manchester
Debut: Sub v Radcliffe Borough (H, FAC:Q1), 11/09/2010

Centre-back

Season	LEAGUE Starts	(+Sub)	Goals	FA NATIONAL CUPS Starts	(+Sub)	Goals	OTHER CUPS / PLAY-OFFS Starts	(+Sub)	Goals	TOTALS Starts	(+Sub)	Goals
2010/11	15	(+2)	0	6	(+2)	0	0	(+0)	0	21	(+4)	0
2012/13	0	(+0)	0	0	(+0)	0	1	(+0)	0	1	(+0)	0
Totals	15	(+2)	0	6	(+2)	0	1	(+0)	0	22	(+4)	0

After impressing for Manchester Boys, Karl signed on YTS forms at Swansea City, and made his Football League debut in 1998. The Cheetham Hill lad returned north a year later to join Macclesfield Town, where he played 136 senior games, mostly in midfield before moving back into defence, until his release in 2004. After suffering a broken leg at Conference side Halifax Town, he regained fitness in a short stint at Northwich Victoria before playing almost a century of games for Altrincham. After spells at Droylsden, Hyde United and Leigh Genesis, Karl signed for FC United in August 2010, gaining a regular spot the following month. He played a crucial role in the famous FA Cup run, with terrific displays in the wins over Barrow and Rochdale. His most memorable match was arguably in the second round at Brighton & Hove Albion, where in a colossal display he repelled the hosts time and again with towering headers, brave tackles and goal-line clearances. Injuries restricted his outings in the New Year, but he still played his part in some important wins as the Reds chased promotion. His last major contribution to the season was in a superb defensive display to protect emergency goalkeeper Ben Deegan at Matlock Town in a win that sealed FC's play-off spot. He stayed on the books for the next two seasons, but with a flourishing business and coaching career he featured just once more, in a Manchester Premier Cup tie at Mossley in October 2012. In 2017 Karl played for the Manchester United Legends team, alongside childhood friend Wes Brown in a testimonial for former United and Swansea defender Alan Tate.

124 Glynn HURST

Born: 17/01/1976, Barnsley
Debut: Sub v Stocksbridge Park Steels (H, NPLP), 18/09/2010 (scored)

Forward

Season	LEAGUE Starts	(+Sub)	Goals	FA NATIONAL CUPS Starts	(+Sub)	Goals	OTHER CUPS / PLAY-OFFS Starts	(+Sub)	Goals	TOTALS Starts	(+Sub)	Goals
2010/11	6	(+1)	2	3	(+1)	3	0	(+1)	0	9	(+2)	5
Totals	6	(+1)	2	3	(+1)	3	0	(+1)	0	9	(+2)	5

Born in Yorkshire, Glynn spent most of his childhood in South Africa, and won under-23 caps for his adopted country. He came back to England to sign as a trainee for Tottenham Hotspur, before a professional breakthrough at hometown club Barnsley. Initially a defender, he became a battling but clever forward, but struggled to make a mark in the Football League. He regained his confidence at non-league Emley before a prolific spell in Scotland at Ayr United. He returned south with Stockport County in 2001 before successful stints with Chesterfield, Notts County, Shrewsbury Town and Bury. He returned to non-league in 2009 with Gainsborough Trinity, then switched to Hyde United before joining FC United in September 2010. He scored within two minutes of coming on for his debut against Stocksbridge Park Steels, and then notched both goals against Gainsborough in the FA Cup. He scored again in the next round, but a knock in the win over Barrow kept him on the bench for the famous win at Rochdale. After three further outings the injury resurfaced, and in January 2011 he retired from football to train as a teacher. He returned to the game in 2019 as coach of Marine's reserves and had a spell as manager of North West Counties League club Ashton Town in 2020.

126 Matthew TIERNEY

Born: 11/10/1992, Manchester
Debut: Sub v Hinckley United (H, FAT:Q3), 20/11/2010

Midfielder

Season	LEAGUE Starts	(+Sub)	Goals	FA NATIONAL CUPS Starts	(+Sub)	Goals	OTHER CUPS / PLAY-OFFS Starts	(+Sub)	Goals	TOTALS Starts	(+Sub)	Goals
2010/11	7	(+1)	0	0	(+1)	0	3	(+0)	1	10	(+2)	1
2011/12	1	(+5)	0	0	(+1)	0	1	(+0)	0	2	(+6)	0
2012/13	11	(+4)	1	0	(+0)	0	0	(+3)	0	11	(+7)	1
Totals	19	(+10)	1	0	(+2)	0	4	(+3)	1	23	(+15)	2

A powerful midfielder also able to operate in the centre of defence, Matty signed a professional contract with Manchester City aged 17, but a disagreement saw him leave the club shortly afterwards. In May 2010 he played against FC United in the Manchester Youth Cup Final for his local club Wythenshawe Juniors, and was invited to join the Reds for the following term. He helped the under-18s to the North West Youth Alliance title, but his major achievement was becoming an established member of the senior squad after making his debut in November. He became **FC United's youngest goalscorer** when he netted on his first start in the League Cup at Ashton United, but received a red card on his second start at Hucknall Town. Thereafter he played his part in some crucial victories as FC chased promotion, and was deservedly named in the line-up for both play-off matches. A youth team sending-off saw him suspended for the opening months of 2011/12, which limited his appearances as he tried to regain match fitness. He found game time with Salford City for the remainder of the campaign, before beginning 2012/13 at Radcliffe Borough. He returned to United in October 2012, and within a month had scored a storming long-range free-kick to gain a late win at Chorley. He was once again an important member of the squad that narrowly missed out on promotion, and featured in both play-off encounters. The following campaign he returned to Salford, and also turned out for Stockport Sports, Mossley and Winsford United. FC fans were delighted to see him play for the Old Boys XI in Broadhurst Park's opening match, and even more so when he featured in the 2015 pre-season preparations, although injury unfortunately kept him sidelined for the entire 2015/16 campaign.

127 Carl FITTON

Born: 16/09/1992, Oldham
Debut: No.3 v Ashton United (A, NPLCC:3), 22/11/2010

Left-back

Season	LEAGUE			FA NATIONAL CUPS			OTHER CUPS / PLAY-OFFS			TOTALS		
	Starts	(+Sub)	Goals	Starts	(+Sub)	Goals	Starts	(+Sub)	Goals	Starts	(+Sub)	Goals
2010/11	0	(+0)	0	0	(+0)	0	1	(+0)	0	1	(+0)	0
Totals	0	(+0)	0	0	(+0)	0	1	(+0)	0	1	(+0)	0

Carl joined FC United's youth team in 2009 after previously being on schoolboy forms at Manchester City and Leeds United. The Middleton lad became the team's regular left-back as they retained the Manchester FA Youth Cup in 2010, and picked up more silverware the following season by winning the North West Youth Alliance title. His cultured displays were rewarded with a first-team debut in November 2010 in a League Cup tie at Ashton United. He went on to join Salford City in July 2011, where he played for two seasons before representing Rochdale Town, New Mills and Radcliffe Borough. He then became a regular for Prestwich Heys after the club returned to the North West Counties League in 2016. He picked up a winner's medal in the NWCFL First Division Trophy in 2018, before suffering defeat in the Promotion Play-Off Semi-Final a few days later.

128 Harrison REEVE

Born: 21/09/1992, Bury
Debut: Sub v Ashton United (A, NPLCC:3), 22/11/2010

Midfielder

Season	LEAGUE			FA NATIONAL CUPS			OTHER CUPS / PLAY-OFFS			TOTALS		
	Starts	(+Sub)	Goals	Starts	(+Sub)	Goals	Starts	(+Sub)	Goals	Starts	(+Sub)	Goals
2010/11	0	(+0)	0	0	(+0)	0	0	(+1)	0	0	(+1)	0
Totals	0	(+0)	0	0	(+0)	0	0	(+1)	0	0	(+1)	0

Before Harrison joined FC United's youth team in 2010, he had already made a name for himself by taking part in the TV show "Wayne Rooney's Street Striker". The Heywood lad then impressed for the under-18s as they won the North West Youth Alliance title in the 2010/11 campaign. By then he had already made his senior debut as a half-time substitute for Ben Deegan in the League Cup tie at Ashton United in November, and three days later he scored in a fund-raising friendly at Irlam. He was also named on the bench for the League match with Mickleover Sports in March, but remained an unused substitute. He moved on to further his development with Rochdale Town, before becoming a Physical Training Instructor in the RAF.

129 Jake HASLAM

Born: 21/07/1993, Salford
Debut: Sub v Ashton United (A, NPLCC:3), 22/11/2010

Left-back/Midfielder

Season	LEAGUE			FA NATIONAL CUPS			OTHER CUPS / PLAY-OFFS			TOTALS		
	Starts	(+Sub)	Goals	Starts	(+Sub)	Goals	Starts	(+Sub)	Goals	Starts	(+Sub)	Goals
2010/11	0	(+1)	0	0	(+0)	0	0	(+1)	0	0	(+2)	0
Totals	0	(+1)	0	0	(+0)	0	0	(+1)	0	0	(+2)	0

Jake joined FC United's youth team in 2009, whilst still at school, and helped the under-18s twice win the North West Youth Alliance and Manchester FA Youth Cup during his time with the squad. A left-sided player who operated at full-back or further up the pitch, he used the ball well and his progress was rewarded with a senior debut as a substitute in the League Cup tie at Ashton United in November 2010. He returned to the bench at Stocksbridge Park Steels in February 2011, and then replaced hat-trick hero Matthew Wolfenden for the latter stages of the win at Nantwich Town a few days later. He went on to play in the Cheshire League for Billinge and with Manchester League side Hindsford.

130 Joshua BURKE

Born: 04/02/1993, Bury
Debut: Sub v Ashton United (A, NPLCC:3), 22/11/2010

Midfielder

Season	LEAGUE			FA NATIONAL CUPS			OTHER CUPS / PLAY-OFFS			TOTALS		
	Starts	(+Sub)	Goals	Starts	(+Sub)	Goals	Starts	(+Sub)	Goals	Starts	(+Sub)	Goals
2010/11	0	(+0)	0	0	(+0)	0	0	(+1)	0	0	(+1)	0
Totals	0	(+0)	0	0	(+0)	0	0	(+1)	0	0	(+1)	0

Josh joined up with FC United's youth team in 2009 after spending time in the academy at his local club Bury. He soon established himself as an energetic box-to-box midfielder, and helped the under-18s to win the Manchester FA Youth Cup and North West Youth Alliance title in his time with the squad. His performances earned a senior call-up to the first team in November 2010, and he came off the bench to make his debut in the League Cup tie at Ashton United. He furthered his development with loan spells at Irlam and Radcliffe Borough later that season, before having spells the following campaign at Ramsbottom United and Mossley. He returned to FC to play for the re-introduced reserve team in 2013/14, before later settling at Bacup Borough.

131 Oliver DEVENNEY

Born: 22/12/1991, Blackburn
Debut: Sub v Whitby Town (H, NPLP), 12/02/2011

Midfielder

Season	LEAGUE			FA NATIONAL CUPS			OTHER CUPS / PLAY-OFFS			TOTALS		
	Starts	(+Sub)	Goals	Starts	(+Sub)	Goals	Starts	(+Sub)	Goals	Starts	(+Sub)	Goals
2010/11	0	(+6)	0	0	(+0)	0	0	(+0)	0	0	(+6)	0
Totals	0	(+6)	0	0	(+0)	0	0	(+0)	0	0	(+6)	0

Oliver began his football career as a trainee at Burnley, before being released at the age of 18 and joining the non-league ranks with Clitheroe. A classy, ball-playing midfielder, he joined FC United in February 2011, and made six appearances from the bench as the Reds pushed for promotion. He participated in the pre-season programme ahead of 2011/12, but rejoined Clitheroe where he was able to stake a claim for a regular place. He later faced FC in the colours of Nantwich Town, before once again linking up briefly with the Reds in the 2014 pre-season. He went on to play for Mossley, before signing for Nelson after recovering from an ankle injury.

132 Jay WALCOTT

Born: 05/01/1993, Manchester
Debut: Sub v Colwyn Bay (A, NPLPPO:F), 02/05/2011

Right-winger

Season	LEAGUE			FA NATIONAL CUPS			OTHER CUPS / PLAY-OFFS			TOTALS		
	Starts	(+Sub)	Goals	Starts	(+Sub)	Goals	Starts	(+Sub)	Goals	Starts	(+Sub)	Goals
2010/11	0	(+0)	0	0	(+0)	0	0	(+1)	0	0	(+1)	0
2011/12	0	(+2)	0	0	(+0)	0	0	(+0)	0	0	(+2)	0
Totals	0	(+2)	0	0	(+0)	0	0	(+1)	0	0	(+3)	0

A rapid attacker from Longsight, Jay had spent time in the Manchester United academy and at Woodley Sports. He first joined FC United in 2009 whilst attending the Manchester College, where he was called up to the British Colleges National Squad, and was a regular in the under-18 team in 2010/11 that won the North West Youth Alliance title. He was still an unknown quantity when he was introduced as a late substitute in the promotion play-off final at Colwyn Bay in May 2011, but still had time to impress with a couple of surging runs. He joined Mossley in the summer to gain more senior experience, and did well enough there to be signed back on again with the Reds in October. He made two further substitute appearances before continuing his education at Salford City, but he was briefly back at FC playing for the reformed reserve team in 2013/14. He later linked up with Northwich Flixton Villa.

133 James SPENCER

Born: 11/04/1985, Manchester
Debut: No.1 v Stafford Rangers (A, NPLP), 13/08/2011

Goalkeeper

Season	LEAGUE			FA NATIONAL CUPS			OTHER CUPS / PLAY-OFFS			TOTALS		
	Starts	(+Sub)	Goals	Starts	(+Sub)	Goals	Starts	(+Sub)	Goals	Starts	(+Sub)	Goals
2011/12	42	(+0)	0	8	(+0)	0	4	(+0)	0	54	(+0)	0
2012/13	31	(+0)	0	5	(+0)	0	0	(+0)	0	36	(+0)	0
2013/14	9	(+0)	0	1	(+0)	0	1	(+0)	0	11	(+0)	0
Totals	82	(+0)	0	14	(+0)	0	5	(+0)	0	101	(+0)	0

A tall goalkeeper with an imposing presence, James was still a trainee at his local club Stockport County when he was pitched into the first team against Watford in English football's second tier at the age of just 16 in April 2002, and didn't look out of place in a 2-1 win. He earned a professional contract ten days later on his 17th birthday and eventually became first choice by the age of 19. However, a change of manager saw his appearances dwindle and he moved to Rochdale in 2007. He began the season with a good run in the line-up, but was sidelined with a stress fracture of the hip and was unable to reclaim his place. He regained his fitness during a short loan at Chester City, before moving into non-league with Northwich Victoria in 2009, with whom he faced FC United twice in 2010/11. He made the switch to the Reds in July 2011, and was ever-present as the team reached the promotion play-off final. However he was ruled out by a domestic accident on the eve of the game, where FC were beaten in the last-minute of extra-time. He was fit to take his place for the start of 2012/13, and only missed a handful of games, due to suspension after a dismissal at Salford City and an injury sustained at Stamford, until the run-in of the latest promotion bid. During the first half of 2013/14 he shared duties with Jon Worsnop, but disaster struck on his return at AFC Fylde in December when a bad knee injury ended his campaign, and this proved to be his last senior match.

134 Adam JONES

Born: 03/02/1986, Manchester
Debut: No.5 v Stafford Rangers (A, NPLP), 13/08/2011

Centre-back

Season	LEAGUE			FA NATIONAL CUPS			OTHER CUPS / PLAY-OFFS			TOTALS		
	Starts	(+Sub)	Goals	Starts	(+Sub)	Goals	Starts	(+Sub)	Goals	Starts	(+Sub)	Goals
2011/12	38	(+0)	7	8	(+0)	2	6	(+0)	0	52	(+0)	9
2012/13	37	(+0)	7	7	(+0)	1	1	(+0)	1	45	(+0)	9
2013/14	9	(+1)	2	0	(+0)	0	0	(+0)	0	9	(+1)	2
Totals	**84**	**(+1)**	**16**	**15**	**(+0)**	**3**	**7**	**(+0)**	**1**	**106**	**(+1)**	**20**

Adam had spent time as a teenager in Bristol City's academy while living in the south-west. After moving back north he played for the youth team at Mossley, before joining Stalybridge Celtic, where he progressed to the first team. In 2005 he joined Curzon Ashton, and was part of the team that won promotion from the North West Counties League in 2007, reached the semi-final of the FA Vase, and beat Football League side Exeter City in the FA Cup first round in 2008. After playing against FC United in some classic encounters, he joined the Reds in July 2011 and became the rock on which the defence was built, missing just four games all season as the team reached the promotion play-off final. His contribution wasn't confined to the back, as he hit nine goals, including a dramatic last-minute winner at Marine and a crucial header in the win at rivals Hednesford Town. He even played in goal at Mossley in the Manchester Premier Cup tie! He carried his form into 2012/13, when he scored the team's first goal of the season at Grantham Town, and helped to keep the Reds in the promotion hunt with a late winner against Ilkeston and a brace at Matlock Town. An bad Achilles injury kept him out for the run-in, and in his absence FC lost another play-off final. He returned to contention in October 2013, but made a temporary switch to Nantwich Town to build up his match fitness. He was recalled in January 2014 and marked his return with a goal at Whitby Town. The manager accommodated Adam, Tom Davies and Charlie Raglan in a 3-5-2 formation which triggered the start of a 12-match winning run that fired the Reds to the top of the table. However, Adam lost his place to Lee Neville and after the promotion hopes were ultimately dashed once more, he chose to move on in the summer. He made a return to Nantwich, where he faced FC again, before a mid-season switch to Trafford. He was on the move again in 2015/16, starting the term with Hyde United before signing for Shaw Lane Aquaforce in October. By February he was back at Hyde, and in January 2017 moved to Glossop North End. He returned to Stalybridge in the summer but by September was back at Glossop, before joining Mossley in June 2018. After a short spell playing under old colleagues Mike Norton and Dave Birch for New Mills, he hung up his boots to take over as manager at North West Counties League side Stockport Town in November 2019.

135 Dean STOTT

Born: 05/10/1989, Burnley
Debut: No.6 v Stafford Rangers (A, NPLP), 13/08/2011 (scored)

Right-back/Centre-back/Midfielder

Season	LEAGUE			FA NATIONAL CUPS			OTHER CUPS / PLAY-OFFS			TOTALS		
	Starts	(+Sub)	Goals	Starts	(+Sub)	Goals	Starts	(+Sub)	Goals	Starts	(+Sub)	Goals
2011/12	39	(+0)	3	8	(+0)	0	5	(+1)	1	52	(+1)	4
2012/13	40	(+0)	5	7	(+0)	2	3	(+0)	3	50	(+0)	10
2013/14	40	(+1)	3	2	(+1)	0	4	(+0)	0	46	(+2)	3
2014/15	30	(+3)	3	6	(+3)	2	1	(+0)	0	37	(+6)	5
2015/16	20	(+1)	0	3	(+1)	0	2	(+0)	0	25	(+2)	0
Totals	**169**	**(+5)**	**14**	**26**	**(+5)**	**4**	**15**	**(+1)**	**4**	**210**	**(+11)**	**22**

A product of the Burnley academy, Dean joined his hometown club on a scholarship after leaving school, and established himself at right-back in the youth team. He was released in 2008, but was picked up by Preston North End, where he signed as a professional and spent a season playing for their reserve team. He joined the non-league ranks with Hyde United in 2009, where he spent two years in the Conference North before signing for FC United in July 2011. Despite Dean having played the vast majority of his football at right-back, the manager felt that his speed and excellent reading of the game would make him an ideal partner for Adam Jones, and so it was at centre-back that he made his debut in red, and marked the occasion with a goal. Those same qualities prompted a further positional switch in November when he was deployed as a holding midfielder, a role he kept for the majority of the remaining matches. He also added another string to his bow by becoming the team's penalty-taker. He reverted to central defence for the majority of 2012/13, and led the team's appearance chart as they chased promotion. His coolly-converted penalty against Witton Albion saw the Reds home in the play-off semi-final, but they suffered final heartbreak for the third year running. The departure of Kyle Jacobs and injury to Jones led to Dean being deservedly appointed as team captain in 2013/14, and he once again mainly played in midfield as he skippered FC to another unlucky play-off defeat. He continued to lead by example in the memorable 2014/15 campaign, taking the team to the FA Trophy quarter-final and along the way scoring from the halfway line in the thrashing of Harrogate Town. His proudest moments were undoubtedly finally clinching promotion and lifting the Northern Premier League title in April, before leading the team out against Benfica in Broadhurst Park's official opening game the following month. Dean remained largely as first choice in midfield in the opening months of 2015/16, before reinforcements in that area coupled with a defensive crisis saw him revert firstly to centre-back before a run at right-back. This coincided with a good run of results, but increased competition for places plus extra working commitments saw him drop out of the team, and he signed for Colne in March 2016. He helped his new team to win the North West Counties League the following month, before switching to Ramsbottom United, where he was made captain ahead of the 2017/18 term.

136 Michael CARR

Born: 06/02/1983, Crewe
Debut: Sub v Stafford Rangers (A, NPLP), 13/08/2011

Midfielder

Season	LEAGUE			FA NATIONAL CUPS			OTHER CUPS / PLAY-OFFS			TOTALS		
	Starts	(+Sub)	Goals	Starts	(+Sub)	Goals	Starts	(+Sub)	Goals	Starts	(+Sub)	Goals
2011/12	12	(+7)	1	4	(+2)	2	0	(+0)	0	16	(+9)	3
Totals	12	(+7)	1	4	(+2)	2	0	(+0)	0	16	(+9)	3

An energetic midfielder, Michael made his Football League debut for Macclesfield Town in 2002, and was a squad regular for a couple of seasons. He entered non-league in 2005 with Northwich Victoria, gaining several caps for the England C team and earning a professional return with Morecambe in 2008. After a promising start he lost his place through injury and dropped back to the Conference with Kidderminster Harriers. He faced FC United with both Stalybridge Celtic and his local club Nantwich Town, before joining the Reds in July 2011. He appeared as an early substitute on the opening day before earning a starting spot, and showed his scoring prowess with a long-range screamer against Bradford Park Avenue and a double at Frickley Athletic. Despite playing a part in all but four matches, he was unable to gain a prolonged run in the side and moved to Stafford Rangers in December. He captained his new team against FC the following month, before later playing for Kidsgrove Athletic and Alsager Town.

137 Adam EDWARDS

Born: 27/09/1989, Salford
Debut: Sub v Stafford Rangers (A, NPLP), 13/08/2011

Right-winger

Season	LEAGUE			FA NATIONAL CUPS			OTHER CUPS / PLAY-OFFS			TOTALS		
	Starts	(+Sub)	Goals	Starts	(+Sub)	Goals	Starts	(+Sub)	Goals	Starts	(+Sub)	Goals
2011/12	2	(+4)	0	0	(+0)	0	1	(+0)	0	3	(+4)	0
Totals	2	(+4)	0	0	(+0)	0	1	(+0)	0	3	(+4)	0

Adam was a right-winger with blistering pace, whose brother Gary was part of FC United's first reserve team in 2006. A former Oldham Athletic junior, he starred for his local team Prestwich Heys in the Manchester League, before earning rave reviews for Chadderton in the North West Counties League. He was snapped up by the Reds in July 2011, and after some exciting pre-season displays he was a regular substitute early in the season. His highlight was coming on to set up a goal for Matthew Wolfenden in the thrashing of rivals Bradford Park Avenue, before he was handed the no.7 shirt for two consecutive games. Unfortunately both ended in defeat as the team was missing some key players, and he returned to the bench. He was afforded just one more opportunity, in the Manchester Premier Cup tie at Mossley, before making a return to Chadderton in order to play regular football. He later had spells at Clitheroe and Trafford.

138 Daniel GRIMSHAW

Born: 18/03/1986, Manchester
Debut: Sub v North Ferriby United (H, NPLP), 17/08/2011

Midfielder/Left-back

Season	LEAGUE			FA NATIONAL CUPS			OTHER CUPS / PLAY-OFFS			TOTALS		
	Starts	(+Sub)	Goals	Starts	(+Sub)	Goals	Starts	(+Sub)	Goals	Starts	(+Sub)	Goals
2011/12	8	(+18)	1	4	(+1)	0	2	(+3)	1	14	(+22)	2
2012/13	0	(+3)	0	0	(+0)	0	0	(+0)	0	0	(+3)	0
Totals	8	(+21)	1	4	(+1)	0	2	(+3)	1	14	(+25)	2

Daniel is a Blackley lad who was on the books at Rochdale as a schoolboy before joining Altrincham's youth team. After being on the periphery of the senior squad he moved to Rossendale United, before settling with Manchester League side Avro. He signed for FC United in July 2011, where his versatility was expected to provide cover in midfield and at left-back, but after scoring at Buxton in only his third outing as a substitute, he was rewarded with a run in the starting line-up. He contributed well to good wins over Bradford Park Avenue, Woodley Sports, Burscough and Whitby Town before going back to the bench, then returned to the team in various roles over the festive period. The rest of the term was spent with him largely as a substitute as the team reached the play-off final, but he would have been proud that his name was missing from the teamsheet on just two occasions throughout the entire campaign. He remained as a regular on the bench at the start of 2012/13, before he was lured to New Mills in September where he was able to establish himself. A year later he scored in a penalty shoot-out for his new club against the Reds in the Manchester Premier Cup, before moving on to play for Mossley, Droylsden, Glossop North End, Abbey Hey and Brighouse Town. In July 2018 he made a return to Avro ahead of their first ever season in the North West Counties League, and helped them to the First Division Cup Final.

139 Paul ARMSTRONG

Born: 30/04/1986, Manchester
Debut: No.2 v Woodley Sports (H, FAC:Q1), 17/09/2011

Full-back

Season	LEAGUE			FA NATIONAL CUPS			OTHER CUPS / PLAY-OFFS			TOTALS		
	Starts	(+Sub)	Goals	Starts	(+Sub)	Goals	Starts	(+Sub)	Goals	Starts	(+Sub)	Goals
2011/12	3	(+0)	1	1	(+0)	0	1	(+0)	0	5	(+0)	1
2012/13	0	(+0)	0	0	(+0)	0	1	(+0)	0	1	(+0)	0
Totals	3	(+0)	1	1	(+0)	0	2	(+0)	0	6	(+0)	1

Paul was a young professional at Oldham Athletic, but a badly broken jaw ultimately led to his release. After loan spells at Barrow and Mossley, the Moston lad dropped into non-league football permanently with Hyde United, establishing himself as a tough and versatile defender. He went on to feature for Ashton United, Flixton, and Welsh club Connah's Quay, but work commitments restricted his outings and he settled at Manchester League side Avro. He signed for FC United in July 2011, and mainly provided defensive cover on the bench until a run of three consecutive starts over the festive period. He helped the Reds to crucial wins over Ashton and Bradford Park Avenue, in which he scored with an outrageous chip, but thereafter was mainly sidelined through injury for the rest of the term. After playing in the Manchester Premier Cup defeat at Mossley the following season, he linked up with former FC coach Roy Soule at New Mills. A badly broken leg ended his playing days in December 2013, after which he became Soule's assistant. He returned to Ashton United as coach in 2015, before moving to Manchester League side Avro in a similar capacity and helping to guide them to the Manchester League title in 2018. This earned promotion to the North West Counties League, and in their first season they were runners-up in the First Division Cup.

140 Theo KIDD

Born: 15/09/1993, Salford
Debut: Sub v Woodley Sports (H, FAC:Q1), 17/09/2011

Forward

Season	LEAGUE			FA NATIONAL CUPS			OTHER CUPS / PLAY-OFFS			TOTALS		
	Starts	(+Sub)	Goals	Starts	(+Sub)	Goals	Starts	(+Sub)	Goals	Starts	(+Sub)	Goals
2011/12	0	(+2)	0	0	(+2)	0	0	(+0)	0	0	(+4)	0
Totals	0	(+2)	0	0	(+2)	0	0	(+0)	0	0	(+4)	0

Theo joined FC United's youth team in the summer of 2011, after scoring against them the previous season for Altrincham, where he had made the bench for the first team. His exciting displays soon caught the eye of Karl Marginson, and the skilful pacy striker was called up for senior duty just after his 18th birthday in September. He emerged from the bench during the FA Cup draw with Woodley Sports and also in the replay three days later. His league bow soon followed during the draw with Marine, and he added to his first-team appearances when he was brought on at Ashton United in the run-in. He ended his days in the under-18s by helping the team to win a hat-trick of trophies: the North West Youth Alliance league title and Open Cup, and the Manchester FA Youth Cup in May 2012. Later that year he moved to Salford City to gain further senior experience, but he was back at FC playing for the re-introduced reserve team in August 2013. Theo then embarked on a course at Leeds University, where he played the majority of his competitive football until the completion of his degree. After a short spell on the books at Witton Albion, he was back amongst the goals in the North West Counties League with Atherton Laburnum Rovers in 2017, and later with Prestwich Heys and West Didsbury & Chorlton.

141 Sam HOWELL

Born: 11/08/1994, Bolton
Debut: Sub v Woodley Sports (H, FAC:Q1), 17/09/2011

Midfielder

Season	LEAGUE			FA NATIONAL CUPS			OTHER CUPS / PLAY-OFFS			TOTALS		
	Starts	(+Sub)	Goals	Starts	(+Sub)	Goals	Starts	(+Sub)	Goals	Starts	(+Sub)	Goals
2011/12	0	(+0)	0	0	(+1)	0	0	(+0)	0	0	(+1)	0
2012/13	0	(+0)	0	0	(+0)	0	1	(+0)	0	1	(+0)	0
Totals	0	(+0)	0	0	(+1)	0	1	(+0)	0	1	(+1)	0

An energetic midfielder usually found on the right, Sam joined FC United from Daisy Hill in the spring of 2011, and went on to play in the youth team's run-in to clinch the North West Youth Alliance championship. When he made his senior debut as a last-minute substitute in the FA Cup tie against Woodley Sports in September 2011, he was just 17 years and 37 days old. This made him the club's youngest ever player, a record he held for almost ten years until it was broken by Jack Bennett in 2021. In 2011/12 he helped the under-18s to regain their title, whilst also adding the Open Cup and Manchester FA Youth Cup to their trophy haul. He was named on the bench for three further cup games that season, whilst also experiencing North West Counties League football in a loan spell back at Daisy Hill. He made his first start in the Manchester Premier Cup tie at Mossley in October 2012, before furthering his education with spells at Ramsbottom United, Barnoldswick Town, Nelson and Winsford United. He faced FC for Radcliffe Borough in October 2014, before becoming a regular at Mossley and later playing for Burscough, Colne, Glossop North End, Padiham and Atherton Laburnum Rovers. He also forged a career in football as a qualified coach, which included working for Burnley FC.

142 Ryan McGREEVY

Born: 05/09/1991, Salford
Debut: Sub v Burscough (A, NPLP), 24/09/2011

Forward

Season	LEAGUE			FA NATIONAL CUPS			OTHER CUPS / PLAY-OFFS			TOTALS		
	Starts	(+Sub)	Goals	Starts	(+Sub)	Goals	Starts	(+Sub)	Goals	Starts	(+Sub)	Goals
2011/12	0	(+2)	0	0	(+0)	0	1	(+0)	0	1	(+2)	0
Totals	**0**	**(+2)**	**0**	**0**	**(+0)**	**0**	**1**	**(+0)**	**0**	**1**	**(+2)**	**0**

A nippy and clever striker, Ryan spent time in the academies of Stockport County and Manchester City before becoming a trainee at Preston North End. The Eccles lad then ventured to the USA on a scholarship at Notre Dame College in Ohio, before returning to the UK for a short spell at Rhyl. He joined FC United in September 2011, and looked to be a promising addition in his three appearances as he created chances and was unlucky not to score himself. However he picked up an injury in October and moved to Clitheroe the following month in search of regular football. He later had a productive spell with Irlam in the North West Counties League before joining Manchester League side Prestwich Heys.

143 Astley MULHOLLAND

Born: 19/01/1988, Manchester
Debut: Sub v Frickley Athletic (A, NPLP), 11/10/2011

Winger

Season	LEAGUE			FA NATIONAL CUPS			OTHER CUPS / PLAY-OFFS			TOTALS		
	Starts	(+Sub)	Goals	Starts	(+Sub)	Goals	Starts	(+Sub)	Goals	Starts	(+Sub)	Goals
2011/12	9	(+15)	2	3	(+2)	1	2	(+3)	2	14	(+20)	5
2012/13	7	(+8)	0	0	(+0)	0	4	(+0)	1	11	(+8)	1
2013/14	20	(+14)	3	1	(+0)	0	4	(+1)	2	25	(+15)	5
2014/15	1	(+1)	0	0	(+0)	0	0	(+0)	0	1	(+1)	0
Totals	**37**	**(+38)**	**5**	**4**	**(+2)**	**1**	**10**	**(+4)**	**5**	**51**	**(+44)**	**11**

As a teenager Astley was in the academy at Leeds United before the Wythenshawe lad joined the Altrincham youth team. He first made his name in non-league during a productive spell with Abbey Hey before Ashton United took him into the Northern Premier League in 2009. He was unable to establish himself and left the following summer, when he first lined up for FC United in pre-season games. After a brief stop at Salford City, he enjoyed a great campaign at Flixton where he scored 42 goals and was deservedly named as the North West Counties League Player of the Season. He then moved back to Altrincham in the Conference North, but just after scoring his first goal for the club he finally signed for FC in October 2011. The pacy attacker, capable of playing on either wing or centrally, immediately caught the eye with some exciting displays. He was soon amongst the goals, sealing the FA Trophy win over Durham City and then bagging a quick-fire brace at Mickleover Sports, and also created numerous chances, most memorably the cross that was headed home by Michael Norton to knock Altrincham out of the Trophy. Although he was named on the teamsheet for every game in the New Year, he was mainly confined to substitute duties. Even so, within minutes of emerging from the bench in the closing stages of the promotion play-off semi-final at Chorley he scored a wonderful solo goal to confirm United's passage to the final. Unsure of a regular spot, he moved back to Ashton United in the summer of 2012, and faced FC during the autumn, before returning to the Reds in January 2013. He was again mainly on the bench, but he forced his way into the side near the end of the season. He justified his place by scoring in the play-off semi-final for the second year running, again with a solo effort against Witton Albion, before the team lost a third successive final. He began 2013/14 as a bench regular again, before celebrating his first start with a goal at Trafford. He then earned a run of 19 starts in 22 games, helping the Reds to some crucial wins as they kept in touch with the leaders. However in the New Year he was the main victim of the 3-5-2 formation as FC hit the top of the table with 12 consecutive wins. They ultimately lost out in the play-offs again, and after a slow start to 2014/15 the manager decided to freshen up the squad and allowed Astley to leave. He returned to the Conference North with Chorley, before ending the season scoring goals again for Trafford. He spent 2015/16 with Glossop North End, and reminded FC fans of his ability in the Manchester Premier Cup at Broadhurst. After a brief spell at Hyde United the following season, he returned to Glossop before joining Colwyn Bay in March 2017. He was their

top scorer in 2017/18, which earned him a contract with full-time National League North side Barrow for the next campaign. However, he was unable to gain a regular place and after a loan spell at Hyde United he returned to Colwyn Bay, before linking up with Mossley in June 2019. Unfortunately he suffered a broken leg during pre-season, and once recovered featured for North West Counties League sides Cheadle Town and Stockport Town as he recovered his fitness. He later had a short spell with Radcliffe before making returns to Mossley and then Trafford in 2020.

Astley's elder brother Kyle tragically lost his life at the age of 19 in 2005 after suffering a cardiac arrest whilst playing football. In 2016 Astley launched a petition urging the Football Association to make it mandatory for easily accessible defibrillators to be installed at all non-league grounds, as well as parks with football pitches, and to ensure that fully-trained personnel are always on hand. His #defibrillators4grassroots campaign returned to the public eye in 2021 when Denmark's Christian Eriksen collapsed during a game at the European Championships.

144 James BROOKS

Born: 11/11/1993, Bolton
Debut: No.6 v Mossley (A, MPC:1), 18/10/2011

Centre-back

Season	LEAGUE Starts	(+Sub)	Goals	FA NATIONAL CUPS Starts	(+Sub)	Goals	OTHER CUPS / PLAY-OFFS Starts	(+Sub)	Goals	TOTALS Starts	(+Sub)	Goals
2011/12	0	(+0)	0	0	(+0)	0	1	(+0)	0	1	(+0)	0
Totals	0	(+0)	0	0	(+0)	0	1	(+0)	0	1	(+0)	0

James was captain of FC United's youth team when he first appeared on a senior team sheet as substitute for both FA Cup ties with Woodley Sports in September 2011. The following month he made his senior debut in central defence in a Manchester Cup tie at Mossley, three weeks before his 18th birthday. Later that term, he led the under-18s to a hat-trick of trophies as they won the North West Youth Alliance league title and Open Cup, plus the Manchester FA Youth Cup. He was named as coach Dave Brown's youth team player of the year, and was also called up by the England Colleges national football squad. He continued his football education with Daisy Hill in 2012/13, before joining Atherton Laburnum Rovers, one of his local clubs. He moved across town to Atherton Collieries in 2014, and helped them to the North West Counties Premier Division title in 2017. He later played for Prestwich Heys before making a return to Atherton LR.

145 Greg STONES

Born: 04/05/1982, Birkenhead
Debut: Sub v Frickley Athletic (A, FAT:Q1), 22/10/2011

Centre-back

Season	LEAGUE Starts	(+Sub)	Goals	FA NATIONAL CUPS Starts	(+Sub)	Goals	OTHER CUPS / PLAY-OFFS Starts	(+Sub)	Goals	TOTALS Starts	(+Sub)	Goals
2011/12	26	(+0)	0	4	(+1)	0	5	(+0)	0	35	(+1)	0
Totals	26	(+0)	0	4	(+1)	0	5	(+0)	0	35	(+1)	0

Previously on schoolboy forms at Tranmere Rovers, Greg began playing senior football for another local side, Poulton Victoria, in the West Cheshire League, where he made his name as a tall and powerful central midfielder who could also play at the back. He moved to the Welsh Premier League with Rhyl in 2004, and played in the UEFA Champions League qualifiers for them and his next club, TNS. He later moved into the Northern Premier League with spells at Stafford Rangers, Cammell Laird, Colwyn Bay and Chester, before he signed for FC United in October 2011. He made his debut as a substitute at Frickley Athletic, and took the place of the suspended Adam Jones a week later. He then forged a great partnership with Jones in all but three games for the remainder of the campaign as they helped the Reds to reach the promotion play-off final. His commanding presence in defence helped build the foundations to claim many crucial points, and his terrific long throw also created numerous chances at the other end. He left the club at the end of the season, returning to Wales to play for Prestatyn Town in July 2012, before heading back to Rhyl. He announced his retirement in April 2016.

146 Stephen JOHNSON

Born: 03/09/1987, Liverpool
Debut: No.11 v Nantwich Town (A, NPLP), 29/11/2011

Winger

Season	LEAGUE Starts	(+Sub)	Goals	FA NATIONAL CUPS Starts	(+Sub)	Goals	OTHER CUPS / PLAY-OFFS Starts	(+Sub)	Goals	TOTALS Starts	(+Sub)	Goals
2011/12	20	(+3)	1	0	(+0)	0	2	(+0)	0	22	(+3)	1
2012/13	2	(+4)	0	1	(+0)	0	0	(+0)	0	3	(+4)	0
2014/15	0	(+1)	0	0	(+0)	0	0	(+0)	0	0	(+1)	0
Totals	22	(+8)	1	1	(+0)	0	2	(+0)	0	25	(+8)	1

A former schoolboy with Tranmere Rovers, Stephen became a trainee at Stoke City, but family commitments dictated a move back to Liverpool and so he joined the non-league scene with Burscough. After a spell at Vauxhall Motors he established himself at his local club Prescot Cables, before a move to Welsh Premier League club Caernarfon Town. He gained FC United's attention when he opened the scoring for Marine in the clash at Bower Fold in October 2011. Less than two months later he joined the Reds, and quickly became an automatic choice. A fast and tricky winger with an extremely accurately cross from either foot, he created numerous chances for his fellow forwards as the team reached the promotion play-off final, where they were beaten by a last-minute goal in extra-time. He began 2012/13 on the bench, but had started three of the first eight games when he left the club in September in search of regular football. He linked up with Ashton United, and faced FC twice later in the term, before returning to the Reds during pre-season in 2013. However, before he played a competitive game he moved again, this time to Nantwich Town. He began a third spell with the club in September 2014, but only featured once from the bench before disappearing from contention.

147 Matthew BOLAND

Born: 01/09/1993, Salford
Debut: Sub v Hednesford Town (H, NPLP), 28/01/2012

Forward

Season	LEAGUE Starts	(+Sub)	Goals	FA NATIONAL CUPS Starts	(+Sub)	Goals	OTHER CUPS / PLAY-OFFS Starts	(+Sub)	Goals	TOTALS Starts	(+Sub)	Goals
2011/12	0	(+1)	0	0	(+0)	0	0	(+0)	0	0	(+1)	0
2013/14	0	(+0)	0	0	(+0)	0	1	(+0)	0	1	(+0)	0
Totals	0	(+1)	0	0	(+0)	0	1	(+0)	0	1	(+1)	0

Matty gained a football education over several years in the Manchester United academy. After a spell with Oldham Athletic, the lively forward linked up with FC United's youth team and impressed sufficiently to earn a call-up to the senior squad for the FA Trophy game at Guiseley in December 2011. He made his debut from the bench the following month in the win over high-flying Hednesford Town, before returning to the under-18s and helping them to win a hat-trick of trophies: the North West Youth Alliance league title and Open Cup, and the Manchester FA Youth Cup. He spent the following term gaining experience at Daisy Hill, but was back with the Reds in July 2013 as part of the re-introduced reserve team. An incredible 12 goals in just seven games earned him a first start for the first team in the Manchester Premier Cup at New Mills, before linking up with Atherton Laburnum Rovers. He finished the 2013/14 season at Salford City before moving on to Atherton Collieries. In July 2015 he played in FC United's 10th Anniversary celebration match against Leigh Genesis, where he opened the scoring. He later became a prolific goalscorer in the North West Counties League over several seasons with Irlam, before later featuring for West Didsbury & Chorlton, Avro, Winsford United and Padiham.

148 Jon WORSNOP

Born: 13/01/1983, Bradford
Debut: No.1 v Bradford Park Avenue (A, NPLPPO:F), 06/05/2012

Goalkeeper

Season	LEAGUE Starts	(+Sub)	Goals	FA NATIONAL CUPS Starts	(+Sub)	Goals	OTHER CUPS / PLAY-OFFS Starts	(+Sub)	Goals	TOTALS Starts	(+Sub)	Goals
2011/12	0	(+0)	0	0	(+0)	0	1	(+0)	0	1	(+0)	0
2012/13	11	(+0)	0	2	(+0)	0	5	(+0)	0	18	(+0)	0
2013/14	13	(+0)	0	2	(+0)	0	2	(+0)	0	17	(+0)	0
Totals	24	(+0)	0	4	(+0)	0	8	(+0)	0	36	(+0)	0

Jon began his career with local club Bradford City, where he was awarded a professional contract and progressed to the first-team bench. He was released in 2002 and began his non-league odyssey in the Conference with Chester City, before switching to League of Wales side Aberystwyth Town. After spells at Droylsden, Leigh RMI, Witton Albion and Ossett Town he returned to his home city with ambitious Bradford Park Avenue, for whom he faced FC United in six titanic battles between 2007 and 2009. He also kept goal against FC for Guiseley and Worksop Town, before joining the Reds himself in March 2012 to provide cover in case of injury to James Spencer. Unfortunately for the previously ever-present Spencer, that injury did arise in a domestic accident on the eve of the promotion play-off final in May, and so Jon was pitched in to make his debut against his old club, Bradford PA. He performed very well, and had kept a clean sheet for 119 minutes when his friend Tom Greaves slid home the last-minute winner to condemn United to a second successive play-off final defeat. He mainly played second fiddle again in 2012/13, until an injury to Spencer in March ruled him out of the run-in, and Jon grabbed his chance to concede just four goals in the last nine league games as the team reached the play-offs again. He started 2013/14 as no.1, but two errors at Worksop gifted his old club the points and Spencer took over. He regained the shirt in late September and kept his place until December when Spencer was recalled, and so Jon answered a late call from Conference side Alfreton Town to play for them on an emergency loan. So impressive was his performance that they immediately offered him a contract to remain, and so his stay at FC United came to an end. He made a return to Chester the following summer, where he was first choice for two seasons before linking up with Warrington Town in October 2016. However, he was soon on the move once more when he returned to Bradford Park Avenue, and yet again lined up twice against FC in National League North encounters. He left BPA again in June 2017 to sign for York City, and faced FC when the Reds won their first away game of the season. He was appointed to the coaching staff at York in October, but left the club the following month to join Southport, for whom he was once again beaten by old mate Greaves in FC's 1-0 win at Broadhurst Park in January 2018. He spent the next campaign back at Guiseley before later signing for Ashton United, Grantham Town and Clitheroe. He returned to Chester as player-coach in the summer of 2020, before retiring in 2022.

151 Charlie ANDERSON

Born: 24/06/1991, Manchester
Debut: Sub v Cammell Laird (H, FAC:Q1), 09/09/2012

Centre-back

Season	LEAGUE Starts	(+Sub)	Goals	FA NATIONAL CUPS Starts	(+Sub)	Goals	OTHER CUPS / PLAY-OFFS Starts	(+Sub)	Goals	TOTALS Starts	(+Sub)	Goals
2012/13	0	(+1)	0	0	(+1)	0	1	(+0)	0	1	(+2)	0
Totals	0	(+1)	0	0	(+1)	0	1	(+0)	0	1	(+2)	0

The son of former Manchester United and England legend Viv Anderson, Charlie was a striker on schoolboy forms at Macclesfield Town before becoming a semi-professional defender with Abbey Hey, Ashton United and Flixton. He linked up with FC United in July 2012, and provided defensive cover on the bench for the majority of matches during the first two months of the season. He was a popular member of the squad, but the settled back four restricted him to just three appearances before he moved on to join Winsford United in order to play regularly. His impressive performances for the Cheshire club saw him follow their manager to Mossley in 2013, where he became a lynchpin of the side in defence or midfield over the following two years.

149 David BIRCH

Born: 14/01/1981, Ashton-under-Lyne   **Midfielder/Right-back**
Debut: No.4 v Grantham Town (A, NPLP), 18/08/2012

Season	LEAGUE			FA NATIONAL CUPS			OTHER CUPS / PLAY-OFFS			TOTALS		
	Starts	(+Sub)	Goals	Starts	(+Sub)	Goals	Starts	(+Sub)	Goals	Starts	(+Sub)	Goals
2012/13	28	(+5)	1	5	(+1)	1	2	(+0)	0	35	(+6)	2
2013/14	22	(+3)	0	1	(+2)	0	4	(+1)	0	27	(+6)	0
2014/15	23	(+2)	1	6	(+2)	0	2	(+0)	0	31	(+4)	1
2015/16	5	(+1)	0	2	(+1)	0	1	(+0)	0	8	(+2)	0
Totals	78	(+11)	2	14	(+6)	1	9	(+1)	0	101	(+18)	3

After spending several years as a schoolboy in the Manchester United academy, Dave had a brief spell at Stockport County before he began playing non-league football with Glossop North End. It was during a long and successful period with Curzon Ashton that he really established himself, captaining the team to promotion from the North West Counties League in 2007, and also reaching the FA Vase semi-final and the 2nd round of the FA Cup. The Denton lad faced FC United on five occasions during his time in blue, lining up either at right-back or in his preferred holding midfield position, and even took over in goal for the second half in 2008 when custodian Dave Carnell was injured. He switched to Hyde in 2011, where despite being relegation favourites he skippered his new club to the 2012 Conference North title, before signing for FC that summer. He made a great start with the Reds, not tasting defeat until his 12th game and rarely missing a match in the first half of the season. As the promotion push continued, his appearances tended to coincide with three points, but the luck ran out when the team narrowly lost another promotion play-off final. Much of the opening stages of 2013/14 were spent as the senior presence on the bench, before his experience was called upon mid-season to keep the promotion challenge burning. Sidelined through injury just after the team began the momentous 12-match winning run, he returned to the squad as the season reached the climax, but his presence was not enough to prevent a fourth consecutive play-off heartbreak. Season 2014/15 saw Dave effectively in a job-share with Dean Stott, as for much of the season the midfield berth and captaincy were alternated between the pair. Whilst Stott lifted the trophy when the Northern Premier League title was finally won, Birch skippered the side in the FA Trophy quarter-final at Torquay United, in the first game as champions at Workington, and also had the honour of leading the team out for the first game at Broadhurst Park in May against the Old Boys XI. He began 2015/16 in the line-up as the team embarked upon their first season in the National League North, but was only used sporadically and spent most of his time on the bench. Shortly after captaining the side against his former club Glossop in the Manchester Premier Cup, Dave signed for another of his old clubs, Hyde United, on a dual-registration basis, before announcing his retirement from football in December 2015. He returned to the game in September 2019 when he was appointed as joint manager of North West Counties club New Mills alongside close friend and former team-mate Mike Norton.

Dave Birch is the only player to feature both for and against FC as an outfield player and an emergency replacement goalkeeper. As Curzon Ashton captain, he replaced future Reds colleague Dave Carnell at half-time at Gigg Lane on 05/03/2008 (left). For United, he took over in goal from the injured James Spencer in the 64th minute of the FA Trophy tie at Stamford on 27/10/2012 (right).

150 Chris AMADI

Born: 13/11/1983, Oldham   **Forward**
Debut: Sub v Grantham Town (A, NPLP), 18/08/2012

Season	LEAGUE			FA NATIONAL CUPS			OTHER CUPS / PLAY-OFFS			TOTALS		
	Starts	(+Sub)	Goals	Starts	(+Sub)	Goals	Starts	(+Sub)	Goals	Starts	(+Sub)	Goals
2012/13	2	(+6)	0	2	(+4)	2	1	(+0)	2	5	(+10)	4
Totals	2	(+6)	0	2	(+4)	2	1	(+0)	2	5	(+10)	4

Although born in Oldham, Chris was raised in Nigeria from the age of six after his parents returned to their homeland. He began playing football in Port Harcourt with Dolphins FC, where he signed professional terms and helped them to win the Nigerian Premier League and Cup double in 2004. His form earned him call-ups for his country's under-18 and under-23 squads before he returned to north-west England upon completion of his university degree. Short spells at Conference North side Burscough, Leigh Genesis and Warrington Town in 2008/09 were followed by an enjoyable season with Chorley. His next move was to Ashton United, where he came to the attention of FC United when he scored a great solo goal against the Reds in December 2011. He signed for FC in July 2012, and was gradually introduced from the bench in the early stages of the campaign. He marked each of his first two starts with braces, and interestingly both were against Mossley, one in the FA Trophy and the other in the Manchester Premier Cup. However, increased competition for places limited his opportunities and he returned to Ashton United in November. He later turned out for Nantwich Town and Droylsden, before linking up with Hyde United in the summer of 2016.

152 Phil McGRATH

Born: 07/04/1992, Banbridge (N. Ireland)
Debut: Sub v Mossley (H, FAT:Q1), 29/09/2012

Winger

	LEAGUE			FA NATIONAL CUPS			OTHER CUPS / PLAY-OFFS			TOTALS		
Season	Starts	(+Sub)	Goals	Starts	(+Sub)	Goals	Starts	(+Sub)	Goals	Starts	(+Sub)	Goals
2012/13	1	(+0)	0	2	(+1)	0	0	(+1)	0	3	(+2)	0
Totals	1	(+0)	0	2	(+1)	0	0	(+1)	0	3	(+2)	0

A Northern Ireland youth international, Phil began his career as a young professional with Oldham Athletic, but his progress was hampered by a series of long-term injuries. His patient determination was rewarded with a Football League debut in April 2011, but a second cruciate ligament injury ruined the following term and he was released in 2012. He joined FC United in September that year, and was introduced as a 71st minute substitute with the Reds trailing 0-3 at home to Mossley in the FA Trophy. He played his part in a remarkable comeback, and earned a starting place for the replay, which he kept for the FA Cup tie with Kendal Town. Still a little short of match fitness, he moved on to Salford City in December, but sadly his injury jinx struck again and he was forced to give up playing. He qualified as a coach and returned to Oldham to work in the club's Academy, before making a playing comeback with North West Counties League side Chadderton in 2020.

153 Greg DANIELS

Born: 21/01/1993, Salford
Debut: Sub v Kendal Town (H, FAC:Q3), 07/10/2012

Forward/Midfielder

	LEAGUE			FA NATIONAL CUPS			OTHER CUPS / PLAY-OFFS			TOTALS		
Season	Starts	(+Sub)	Goals	Starts	(+Sub)	Goals	Starts	(+Sub)	Goals	Starts	(+Sub)	Goals
2012/13	13	(+14)	8	0	(+3)	0	2	(+1)	0	15	(+18)	8
2013/14	20	(+12)	9	3	(+0)	0	4	(+1)	2	27	(+13)	11
2014/15	27	(+14)	5	9	(+1)	1	2	(+0)	0	38	(+15)	6
2015/16	13	(+24)	1	2	(+2)	2	1	(+0)	0	16	(+26)	3
Totals	73	(+64)	23	14	(+6)	3	9	(+2)	2	96	(+72)	28

A former player in the Manchester City academy, Greg went on to join Macclesfield Town, where his prolific scoring form in the youth and reserve teams earned a professional contract and a call-up to the first-team bench. After a loan spell with non-league Newcastle Town, his progress was hampered by a knee injury, and he was one of a large number of players released when the Cheshire club lost their Football League status in 2012. The Crumpsall-raised lad linked up with FC United in September that year, and made an excellent impression in his early appearances, which were mostly as a substitute. Able to play up front or as an attacking midfielder, he demonstrated his prowess in both positions with numerous assists and some important goals as the Reds chased promotion. He notched a crucial late winner at Nantwich Town, and bagged five goals in five games in the run-in that included a hat-trick against Kendal Town. Impressive pre-season performances in 2013 saw him chosen to lead the line for the first game of the season, but a long autumn run in midfield produced his best displays. Amongst his goals were vital strikes against Marine and Fylde, before he missed over a month through injury just as the team began the amazing 12-match winning run. He marked his comeback with a superb strike as a substitute against Stafford Rangers, and his dramatic injury-time header against Ashton United took the title race to the final day. Although he had to wait until December to register his first goal of 2014/15, he proved he still had the knack for important strikes. He settled a tight encounter with Halesowen Town that took the Reds to the top of the table for the first time, before scoring one of the most famous and important goals in the club's history by heading the winner against Stourbridge that clinched the Northern Premier League title. In May 2015 he went on to score twice in the opening game at Broadhurst Park against the Old Boys XI. After beginning 2015/16 in the starting line-up, he mainly featured from the bench in the opening weeks of the campaign, but still made important contributions as the team began to climb the table. He got back amongst the goals in October with FA Cup strikes at Buxton and Sporting Khalsa that helped the Reds to reach the first round proper. His only goal in the league was a great individual effort in the biggest win of the season against Lowestoft Town in January, and the following month his patience was rewarded with his longest run of six consecutive starts. Thereafter his contributions were exclusively from the bench as the team preserved their status in the National League North. Greg announced that he was leaving FC in June 2016, with the intention of going travelling, and after his return early the following year had spells at Trafford and Ramsbottom United. In 2020 he signed for North West Counties League side Cheadle Town, managed by former FC colleague Liam Brownhill. Later that year he scored the first competitive goal for newly-formed fan-owned club Bury AFC, before moving to Prestwich Heys in October 2021.

'154 Connor NAUGHTON

Born: 03/10/1993, Manchester
Debut: No.4 v Mossley (A, MPC:1), 09/10/2012

Midfielder

Season	LEAGUE			FA NATIONAL CUPS			OTHER CUPS / PLAY-OFFS			TOTALS		
	Starts	(+Sub)	Goals	Starts	(+Sub)	Goals	Starts	(+Sub)	Goals	Starts	(+Sub)	Goals
2012/13	0	(+0)	0	0	(+0)	0	1	(+0)	0	1	(+0)	0
Totals	0	(+0)	0	0	(+0)	0	1	(+0)	0	1	(+0)	0

A midfielder from Urmston who was a junior member of FC United, Connor became a driving force of the youth team's highly successful 2011/12 campaign when they won a hat-trick of trophies: the North West Youth Alliance league title and Open Cup, and the Manchester FA Youth Cup. His performances were rewarded by being signed on first-team forms in March that season, before making his senior debut in the Manchester Premier Cup tie at Mossley in October 2012. His impressive display kept him on the fringes of the squad, before he was sent to gain more competitive experience in the North West Counties League with Rochdale Town. He went on to represent Stockport Sports, Salford City, St Helens Town, Irlam, Cheadle Town, Chadderton and Barnton, and also often featured in a defensive capacity.

'155 Tom FISHER

Born: 28/06/1992, Manchester
Debut: Sub v Ashton United (A, NPLP), 31/10/2012

Forward

Season	LEAGUE			FA NATIONAL CUPS			OTHER CUPS / PLAY-OFFS			TOTALS		
	Starts	(+Sub)	Goals	Starts	(+Sub)	Goals	Starts	(+Sub)	Goals	Starts	(+Sub)	Goals
2012/13	0	(+5)	0	0	(+0)	0	1	(+0)	0	1	(+5)	0
Totals	0	(+5)	0	0	(+0)	0	1	(+0)	0	1	(+5)	0

A striker from Wythenshawe, Tom was a young professional with Stockport County, where he made his Football League debut at the age of 16. He became a regular squad member two seasons later, when he scored his first senior goal, but was released when County were relegated to the Conference in 2011. He moved to Macclesfield Town, where he appeared only once as they also lost their League status in 2012, before joining the non-league ranks himself with spells at Hyde and Droylsden. He joined FC United in October 2012, and went straight into the squad for the trip to Ashton United. He looked confident on the ball when called upon, but was unable to establish himself in the line-up and dropped from contention after his only start in a Manchester Premier Cup tie, again at Ashton. He resurfaced on the semi-professional circuit with Nantwich Town in the summer of 2015, and later featured for Mossley, Winsford United and local North West Counties League side Wythenshawe Amateurs.

'156 Mathew CARR

Born: 23/12/1992, Bury
Debut: No.6 v Eastwood Town (H, NPLP), 04/11/2012

Centre-back

Season	LEAGUE			FA NATIONAL CUPS			OTHER CUPS / PLAY-OFFS			TOTALS		
	Starts	(+Sub)	Goals	Starts	(+Sub)	Goals	Starts	(+Sub)	Goals	Starts	(+Sub)	Goals
2012/13	3	(+0)	0	0	(+0)	0	0	(+0)	0	3	(+0)	0
Totals	3	(+0)	0	0	(+0)	0	0	(+0)	0	3	(+0)	0

A tall central defender from Radcliffe, Mathew was on schoolboy forms with Manchester City, before becoming a young professional at Oldham Athletic. Upon his release he joined the non-league ranks with Clitheroe, before a spell at Stocksbridge Park Steels. He joined FC United in October 2012, and was given an opportunity in three consecutive games the following month. He defended well, and provided a goal threat at the other end, but was withdrawn at the break with the team needing to get back into the game against Rushall Olympic. He dropped out of contention thereafter, and following a return to Clitheroe he went on to feature for Droylsden, Mossley, Radcliffe Borough and Prestwich Heys. He rejoined Radcliffe in the summer of 2018 and was in the squad that won the Northern Premier League Division One West play-offs the following year, before returning to Prestwich.

OUR FLAG STAYS RED

COURSE YOU CAN MALCOLM

157 Adam DAWSON

Born: 05/10/1992, Oldham
Debut: Sub v Rushall Olympic (H, NPLP), 17/11/2012

Winger

Season	LEAGUE			FA NATIONAL CUPS			OTHER CUPS / PLAY-OFFS			TOTALS		
	Starts	(+Sub)	Goals	Starts	(+Sub)	Goals	Starts	(+Sub)	Goals	Starts	(+Sub)	Goals
2012/13	3	(+1)	0	0	(+0)	0	0	(+0)	0	3	(+1)	0
Totals	3	(+1)	0	0	(+0)	0	0	(+0)	0	3	(+1)	0

A fast and skilful winger, Adam was on the books at Liverpool as a schoolboy, before completing a scholarship at hometown club Bury. In June 2011 he signed his first professional contract with Wigan Athletic, but was released after making his senior debut the following year on loan at Accrington Stanley. After playing a game for Bacup Borough he joined FC United in November 2012, and his debut display as a half-time substitute was the highlight of a disappointing encounter. This earned him a starting place for three of the next five matches, but injury niggles saw him withdrawn on each occasion and he did not feature after Christmas. He moved to Conference side Barrow in March 2013, and then after a short stint with Nelson was snapped up by Leicester City, where he featured regularly in their reserve team. After loan spells at Notts County, Nuneaton Town and Bristol Rovers in 2014/15, he signed for Kidderminster Harriers in the summer. Another loan period followed, this time at Tranmere Rovers, before a permanent return to Nuneaton in March 2016. However he did not make an appearance there and moved on to Eastleigh in June, and then back to Tranmere in November. After a loan spell at Darlington in 2017 he moved to Southport, and came on as a substitute against FC in January 2018. During the following season he spent time at AFC Telford United, Chester and Macclesfield Town, before again entering the fray at Broadhurst Park whilst on loan at Radcliffe in January 2020. Later in the year he moved to Cyprus to play for Achyronas Liopetriou, before returning to the Northern Premier League for spells at Radcliffe and Bamber Bridge in 2021/22.

158 Lewis CHALMERS

Born: 04/02/1986, Manchester
Debut: Sub v Blyth Spartans (A, NPLP), 01/12/2012

Midfielder

Season	LEAGUE			FA NATIONAL CUPS			OTHER CUPS / PLAY-OFFS			TOTALS		
	Starts	(+Sub)	Goals	Starts	(+Sub)	Goals	Starts	(+Sub)	Goals	Starts	(+Sub)	Goals
2012/13	2	(+1)	0	0	(+0)	0	0	(+0)	0	2	(+1)	0
Totals	2	(+1)	0	0	(+0)	0	0	(+0)	0	2	(+1)	0

A former schoolboy at Manchester City and Accrington Stanley, Lewis rose through the ranks in senior football at Altrincham. The energetic midfielder's displays earned him caps for the England C semi-professional team, before he was snapped up by Aldershot Town in June 2007. In his first season there he played an important role as the team won the Conference title, and he was a regular for large parts of their first two seasons in the Football League. After loan spells with Crawley Town and Oxford United, he returned north to sign for Macclesfield Town in June 2010, where despite a promising first season he had an injury-hit 2011/12 campaign which coincided with the club's relegation back into non-league. After a stint at Radcliffe Borough, he joined FC United in November 2012, but was unable to establish himself with the Reds. He made just two starts amidst fierce competition for places, and moved on to Droylsden in January 2013. After a brief return to Macclesfield he later featured for Stamford, Nantwich Town, New Mills, Stafford Rangers, Trafford and Northwich Villa.

159 Louis HORNE

Born: 28/05/1991, Bradford
Debut: No.6 v Stafford Rangers (H, NPLP), 12/01/2013

Centre-back

Season	LEAGUE			FA NATIONAL CUPS			OTHER CUPS / PLAY-OFFS			TOTALS		
	Starts	(+Sub)	Goals	Starts	(+Sub)	Goals	Starts	(+Sub)	Goals	Starts	(+Sub)	Goals
2012/13	1	(+0)	0	0	(+0)	0	0	(+0)	0	1	(+0)	0
Totals	1	(+0)	0	0	(+0)	0	0	(+0)	0	1	(+0)	0

A versatile left-sided defender, Louis was a young professional at Bradford City, for whom he made one Football League appearance. After loan spells with Barrow and Fleetwood Town, he switched permanently to non-league with FC Halifax Town, and went on to feature for Hinckley United, Buxton, Vauxhall Motors and Northwich Victoria, for whom his only appearance was as a late substitute against FC United in December 2011. He signed for the Reds from Goole in November 2012, initially providing cover on the bench before making his debut in January 2013. Unfortunately he picked up an injury that forced his half-time withdrawal, and that proved to be his only outing before moving to Scarborough Athletic in February. He later went on to line up for Mossley, Goole again, Ossett Town, Harrogate Railway Athletic, Frickley Athletic, Ossett Albion and Liversedge.

160 Tom GREAVES

Born: 23/04/1985, Bradford
Debut: No.9 v Stafford Rangers (H, NPLP), 12/01/2013 (scored)

Forward

Season	LEAGUE			FA NATIONAL CUPS			OTHER CUPS / PLAY-OFFS			TOTALS		
	Starts	(+Sub)	Goals	Starts	(+Sub)	Goals	Starts	(+Sub)	Goals	Starts	(+Sub)	Goals
2012/13	15	(+7)	11	0	(+0)	0	0	(+2)	0	15	(+9)	11
2013/14	38	(+6)	34	2	(+1)	1	4	(+1)	1	44	(+8)	36
2014/15	29	(+14)	20	11	(+0)	5	1	(+1)	0	41	(+15)	25
2015/16	31	(+9)	10	6	(+0)	1	0	(+0)	0	37	(+9)	11
2016/17	13	(+24)	4	1	(+3)	1	2	(+2)	5	16	(+29)	10
2017/18	27	(+12)	8	3	(+3)	2	0	(+1)	0	30	(+16)	10
2018/19	3	(+2)	0	0	(+0)	0	0	(+0)	0	3	(+2)	0
Totals	156	(+74)	87	23	(+7)	10	7	(+7)	6	186	(+88)	103

Formerly with Bridlington Town, Guiseley, Woodley Sports, Ossett Town and Garforth Town, Tom became a thorn in FC United's side when playing for Bradford Park Avenue. He bagged a late hat-trick to sink the Reds in September 2010, before bundling home the dramatic last-minute winner in the promotion play-off final in May 2012. When news of his availability reached Karl Marginson, it was with some relief that he crossed the Pennines to join FC in January 2013. He capped his debut by scoring with an astonishing volley against Stafford Rangers, and hit a further 10 strikes as the team reached another play-off final. His goals were responsible for crucial points earned against Marine, North Ferriby United, Blyth Spartans and Eastwood Town, but he was unable to repeat his promotion-clinching exploits of the previous year. He got off the mark for 2013/14 with a hat-trick against Stamford, and then hit a purple patch in November with eight goals in five games. He was virtually unstoppable in the New Year, when a change in the team's formation allowed him to partner Michael Norton and contributed to a remarkable 12-match winning run. His dramatic injury-time winner at Chorley in March kept the title hopes alive, as did his late equaliser against the same opponents a month later. That was one of 11 goals in 10 games in the run-in, but ultimately the Reds lost out in the play-offs again after Tom limped out of the semi-final against Ashton United. He suffered a slower start to 2014/15, with late equalisers against Belper Town and Nantwich Town, and a brace against Ramsbottom United being highlights of the early months. He burst into life on Boxing Day with a double at Curzon Ashton, beginning a run of 14 goals in 13 games that included two at Chorley in the FA Trophy, and the winner in the subsequent replay. In the league he hit another vital late equaliser against Nantwich and further braces against Barwell, Ashton and Belper to put the Reds within reach of top spot. A late equaliser against Ilkeston consolidated the lead, before Tom settled the nerves against Stamford, setting the team up to clinch the title in the next game with Stourbridge. In May he was named Northern Premier League Player of the Season by the Non-League Paper, before making history by **scoring the first goal at Broadhurst Park** against the Old Boys XI. His scoring rate fell in the National League North in 2015/16, but he still netted at important times, such as the first winning goal in Moston against Brackley Town, the opener at Nuneaton Town, the winner at Stockport County and the dramatic equaliser against Harrogate Town. He was also appointed as vice-captain, and led the team out on many occasions. Despite featuring on the teamsheet for all but one fixture in 2016/17, the majority of his appearances were as a substitute. He shared the no.9 shirt with Dale Johnson until October, when Jason Gilchrist claimed the place, and he made just four starts during the rest of the season. Even so, he hit a hat-trick to defeat Abbey Hey in the Manchester Premier Cup, and equalised at Gloucester City in February. Tom was again on the bench for the first eight matches of 2017/18, although in one of them he came on to open the scoring in the terrific win at York City. He was given three starts in September, but the team was in poor form and he was allowed to join Ramsbottom United on a dual registration. After just one game, he was back on the FC bench and came on to score during the dramatic FA Cup comeback at Stockport County. In the midweek replay he struck the winner as the nine men amazingly progressed at the start of a historic month for both him and the club. When Marginson left on 24th October, Tom became caretaker-manager, with the role made permanent after he won four of his first five games. A terrific run followed around Christmas, as the Reds picked up points against the top teams and with Tom equalling and then breaking Rory Patterson's long-standing **club goalscoring record** with his 99th and 100th goals in the closing stages of the 3-2 win over Harrogate Town. He also struck the winners over Salford City and Southport, before guiding the team to safety and retaining the Manchester Premier Cup with a penalty shoot-out victory over Trafford in April. He was rewarded with an extension to his contract to manage the team in the 2018/19 campaign, and rebuilt the squad over the summer. He started three of the first six games, but his side lost five of those and so Tom resigned as manager in late August. He joined Hyde United later in the week, before moving in November to newly-formed Ossett United, where he also had a spell as joint caretaker-manager. In 2020 he switched to another new club, Bury AFC, for whom he scored at Broadhurst Park in a friendly in July 2021. He rediscovered his touch as a prolific striker at Ossett and Bury, where his achievements mean that Tom holds the distinction of being the record goalscorer for three separate fan-owned clubs. He moved on to local side Thackley in 2022.

162 Travis GRAY

Born: 30/11/1993, Manchester
Debut: No.2 v Witton Albion (A, NPLCC:4), 19/02/2013

Right-back

Season	LEAGUE			FA NATIONAL CUPS			OTHER CUPS / PLAY-OFFS			TOTALS		
	Starts	(+Sub)	Goals	Starts	(+Sub)	Goals	Starts	(+Sub)	Goals	Starts	(+Sub)	Goals
2012/13	1	(+0)	0	0	(+0)	0	1	(+0)	0	2	(+0)	0
Totals	1	(+0)	0	0	(+0)	0	1	(+0)	0	2	(+0)	0

A right-sided defender from Middleton, Travis was in the Greater Manchester team that won the National Under-16s Cup in 2010. He joined Stoke City on a scholarship that summer, and became a regular in their youth team. He was released in 2012, and spent part of the pre-season with FC United before joining Northwich Victoria. He finally signed for the Reds in February 2013, and put in an encouraging display on his debut in a League Cup tie at Witton Albion. The following month he was drafted in at the last minute to make his league bow against Blyth Spartans, but despite again performing well he was unluckily sacrificed as FC chased an equaliser. That proved to be his final action in a United shirt, as he moved on to feature for Northwich Flixton Villa and Stockport Sports.

161 Lewis LACY

Born: 22/10/1994, Manchester
Debut: No.6 v Ashton United (A, NPLCC:3), 30/01/2013

Centre-back/Forward

Season	LEAGUE Starts	(+Sub)	Goals	FA NATIONAL CUPS Starts	(+Sub)	Goals	OTHER CUPS / PLAY-OFFS Starts	(+Sub)	Goals	TOTALS Starts	(+Sub)	Goals
2012/13	7	(+0)	0	0	(+0)	0	3	(+0)	0	10	(+0)	0
2013/14	2	(+5)	0	0	(+0)	0	2	(+0)	0	4	(+5)	0
2014/15	27	(+1)	2	6	(+0)	0	0	(+1)	0	33	(+2)	2
2015/16	5	(+1)	1	0	(+0)	0	0	(+0)	0	5	(+1)	1
2017/18	1	(+0)	0	0	(+0)	0	0	(+0)	0	1	(+0)	0
2019/20	1	(+0)	0	0	(+0)	0	1	(+0)	0	2	(+0)	0
Totals	43	(+7)	3	6	(+0)	0	6	(+1)	0	55	(+8)	3

A product of Moston Juniors, FC United's partner club at Broadhurst Park, Lewis also played in the academies of Manchester City and Rochdale as a schoolboy. In September 2011, at the age of just 16, he played once for Ashton United in the Northern Premier League, but came to FC's attention when facing the club's youth team for Moston in the Manchester FA Youth Cup Final in 2012. He switched sides that summer, and initially played up front before establishing himself as a commanding central defender. His progress was rewarded with a first-team call-up when he was named as a substitute against Witton Albion match on Boxing Day 2012, although his hopes of a debut were dashed when the game was forced into an early abandonment. He made his senior bow the following month in a League Cup tie at Ashton United, and then came to the fore in April when starting six of the final seven league games, which included four clean sheets, as the Reds cemented a play-off spot. Facing Witton in the semi-final, he suffered a leg injury in a bad challenge during the first half that sadly ruled him out of the final, where his presence was sorely missed. He regained his sharpness with loan spells at Trafford, Ramsbottom United and Curzon Ashton during 2013/14, before returning to help United to a fourth successive play-off place. A niggling injury delayed his start to 2014/15, but after returning in October he was missing from the teamsheet on just four occasions for the remainder of the fantastic campaign, in which he developed a great partnership with Luke Ashworth. He was particularly impressive in the narrow defeat at Torquay United in the FA Trophy, and in ensuring clean sheets in the run-in at Whitby Town and Witton Albion. At the other end, his first goal for the club proved to be the winner at King's Lynn Town, and he also bagged the only goal of the crucial encounter with Workington that arguably settled the destination of the title. He played most of the pre-season games in 2015, before taking up a scholarship at Syracuse University in upstate New York. However, he was back at FC in January 2016, and marked his return by scoring against Lowestoft Town. He also performed well in the dramatic comeback win over Harrogate Town, but the next four games were all lost amidst a defensive injury crisis, and Lewis did not feature again that season. He linked up with local side Chadderton in July 2016, and was a regular in both defence and attack in their North West Counties League campaign. He returned once again to United for pre-season in 2017, when he mainly featured up front in the friendlies. He performed well enough to join the squad and was selected in the no.9 shirt for the defeat at Bradford Park Avenue in August, but this was his only outing before joining Glossop North End the following month. He signed for Radcliffe in June 2018, and crowned a successful season with a man of the match display as his team won the Northern Premier League Division One West play-off final. After a spell at NWCFL side Avro, he began a fourth stint at FC in January 2020. He earned praise from Neil Reynolds for his display when stepping in to the centre of defence for the hard-fought win at Whitby Town, and he kept his position for the League Challenge Cup loss to Sheffield a few days later. However, he did not feature in the squad after that and later returned to play for Avro.

163 Matthew WALWYN

Born: 23/06/1990, Blackpool
Debut: No.11 v Witton Albion (A, NPLCC:4), 19/02/2013

Winger/Forward

Season	LEAGUE Starts	(+Sub)	Goals	FA NATIONAL CUPS Starts	(+Sub)	Goals	OTHER CUPS / PLAY-OFFS Starts	(+Sub)	Goals	TOTALS Starts	(+Sub)	Goals
2012/13	3	(+3)	1	0	(+0)	0	1	(+0)	0	4	(+3)	1
2013/14	2	(+21)	7	1	(+2)	1	1	(+1)	0	4	(+24)	8
2014/15	1	(+12)	1	0	(+9)	3	2	(+0)	0	3	(+21)	4
2015/16	0	(+1)	0	0	(+0)	0	0	(+1)	0	0	(+2)	0
Totals	6	(+37)	9	1	(+11)	4	4	(+2)	0	11	(+50)	13

The son of former York City, Blackpool and Carlisle United striker Keith Walwyn, Matt was on schoolboy forms at Blackburn Rovers before joining his local non-league club Kirkham & Wesham. The tall and pacy attacker assisted three promotions, from the West Lancashire League, through the North West Counties and into the Northern Premier League, by which time they were known as AFC Fylde. Whilst still aged 17, he emerged from the bench in the 2008 FA Vase Final at Wembley with his side trailing, and hit two late goals to win the trophy. He left to join Skelmersdale United in 2011, but soon moved to Chorley, where he first encountered FC United as both sides chased promotion. In the early months of 2012/13 he played for Northwich Victoria and Conference North side Droylsden, but was hampered by a hernia injury. A free agent when he signed for FC in February 2013, although still not fully fit he managed four starts and opened his scoring account with a spectacular strike in the last league game of the season against Frickley Athletic. He did well in the 2013 pre-season, before coming off the bench to hit five goals in three appearances (totalling just 75 minutes) before the end of August. He remained a regular impact substitute as care was taken with his fitness, and when his patience was rewarded with two consecutive starts in October he scored in both. However, his injury jinx continued and he twice pulled a hamstring within minutes of coming off the bench, with the second ruling him out for the rest of the term. Matt suffered another injury-hit campaign in 2014/15, when his only league start came in the last game of the season. He maintained his reputation as FC's "supersub" though, by notching four goals, most memorably the dramatic injury-time winner in the FA Trophy replay against Barwell. He made just two substitute outings in 2015/16, but was called up to play for Saint Kitts and Nevis in the World Cup qualifiers, and won his first cap in their historic win over Andorra in November. He took part in the 2016 pre-season, but did not feature once the campaign was underway.

164 Sam FITZGERALD

Born: 28/10/1993, Manchester
Debut: No.8 v Blyth Spartans (H, NPLP), 23/03/2013

Midfielder

	LEAGUE			FA NATIONAL CUPS			OTHER CUPS / PLAY-OFFS			TOTALS		
Season	Starts	(+Sub)	Goals	Starts	(+Sub)	Goals	Starts	(+Sub)	Goals	Starts	(+Sub)	Goals
2012/13	1	(+0)	0	0	(+0)	0	0	(+0)	0	1	(+0)	0
Totals	1	(+0)	0	0	(+0)	0	0	(+0)	0	1	(+0)	0

A dynamic midfielder from Middleton, Sam was part of the Greater Manchester team that won the National under-16s Cup in 2010 before launching his career on a scholarship at Oldham Athletic. After captaining the youth team and becoming a regular in the reserves, he was released in 2012, and linked up with FC United in February 2013. After warming the bench for several matches, he was drafted into the starting line-up against Blyth Spartans, and impressed with his link-up play. A slight injury kept him out for the remainder of the campaign, but he was back for the 2013/14 pre-season before featuring in a number of reserve team games. He moved on to Droylsden in October for further first-team experience, before also featuring for Salford City, Ashton United, Abbey Hey, New Mills, Stockport Sports and Radcliffe Borough. He also spent a summer in the USA with Springfield Demize, and in early 2016 moved to Australia to play for Brisbane Premier League side Mitchelton, before switching to rivals Western Pride. After returning home he signed for Chadderton in February 2018, before joining Wythenshawe Town in the summer ahead of their inaugural campaign in the North West Counties League. He also later featured for Avro and New Mills.

165 Sergio RODRIGUEZ Suárez

Born: 16/02/1991, Gijón (Spain)
Debut: No.8 v Kendal Town (A, NPLP), 30/03/2013

Midfielder

	LEAGUE			FA NATIONAL CUPS			OTHER CUPS / PLAY-OFFS			TOTALS		
Season	Starts	(+Sub)	Goals	Starts	(+Sub)	Goals	Starts	(+Sub)	Goals	Starts	(+Sub)	Goals
2012/13	4	(+0)	0	0	(+0)	0	0	(+0)	0	4	(+0)	0
2013/14	1	(+5)	0	1	(+0)	0	2	(+0)	0	4	(+5)	0
Totals	5	(+5)	0	1	(+0)	0	2	(+0)	0	8	(+5)	0

An inventive Spanish midfielder, Sergio progressed through the ranks in his homeland with Real Avilés to play in Segunda División B. Keen to try his luck in England, he drove all the way to Manchester to trial with FC United, impressing enough to sign for the club in March 2013. He started four games, which produced maximum points, in the run-in as the team reached a third successive play-off final. Injury delayed his start to 2013/14, but he again proved a lucky charm as the Reds lost just one match in which he was involved. However, he was unable to gain a regular berth and moved on in January 2014 to Welsh Premier side Rhyl, linking up with his friend Carlos Roca. He later came back to the Northern Premier League with New Mills, before returning to Spain to play for Tercera División clubs CD Praviano and CD Colunga.

166 Oliver BANKS

Born: 21/09/1992, Rotherham
Debut: Sub v Kendal Town (A, NPLP), 30/03/2013

Midfielder

	LEAGUE			FA NATIONAL CUPS			OTHER CUPS / PLAY-OFFS			TOTALS		
Season	Starts	(+Sub)	Goals	Starts	(+Sub)	Goals	Starts	(+Sub)	Goals	Starts	(+Sub)	Goals
2012/13	7	(+2)	2	0	(+0)	0	2	(+0)	0	9	(+2)	2
2013/14	7	(+0)	1	0	(+0)	0	0	(+0)	0	7	(+0)	1
Totals	14	(+2)	3	0	(+0)	0	2	(+0)	0	16	(+2)	3

Ollie began his professional career at Rotherham United, the club where his father Ian had played alongside Karl Marginson. The cultured midfield player scored within minutes of coming on as a substitute on his Football League debut in May 2011, before loan spells at non-league clubs Sheffield, Buxton and Stalybridge Celtic. He joined the semi-professional ranks permanently in 2012 with Gainsborough Trinity, but left after a frustrating spell to play for Scarborough Athletic. His performances earned a further switch to North Ferriby United in January 2013, and he appeared as a late substitute for them against FC United in March. Knowing that he was too good to sit on the bench regularly, Marginson made an approach, and Ollie signed for the Reds later that month. He made a quick impact with a goal on his first start, and became the team's stylish playmaker as they reached the promotion play-off final. He carried his impressive form into 2013/14, and it was no surprise that he was attracted the attention of Chesterfield, who took him back into the professional game in September. Within six months he was appearing at Wembley in the Football League Trophy Final, and although an injury during the game finished his season, he earned a League Two championship medal as his team won promotion to the third tier. After a short loan spell at Northampton Town, he returned to help Chesterfield reach the 2015 League One play-offs. In November 2015 he emerged from the bench against FC in the FA Cup first round tie at Broadhurst Park, and scored his side's fourth goal. He moved back over the Pennines to sign for Oldham Athletic in July 2016 and featured in the majority of matches during his first season. He lost his place early in 2017/18, and embarked on a two-month loan spell with National League side Tranmere Rovers in November 2017. He moved up a level to League Two with another loan stint at Swindon Town from January 2018 until the end of the season. He was released by Oldham in May 2018 and signed permanently for Tranmere, who had since won the National League play-offs and been promoted back to League Two. A year later he appeared at Wembley again as Tranmere were promoted via the play-offs for the second year running. He moved on to Barrow in January 2021 during their first term back in the Football League, but cancelled his contract in June 2022 and rejoined Chesterfield, now in the National League.

167 Kevin MASIRIKA

Born: 07/05/1995, Köln (Germany)
Debut: No.6 v Rushall Olympic (A, NPLP), 27/04/2013

Centre-back

Season	LEAGUE			FA NATIONAL CUPS			OTHER CUPS / PLAY-OFFS			TOTALS		
	Starts	(+Sub)	Goals	Starts	(+Sub)	Goals	Starts	(+Sub)	Goals	Starts	(+Sub)	Goals
2012/13	2	(+0)	0	0	(+0)	0	1	(+0)	0	3	(+0)	0
Totals	2	(+0)	0	0	(+0)	0	1	(+0)	0	3	(+0)	0

A tall central defender who was in the schoolboy ranks at FC Köln, Kevin moved with his family to Little Hulton, and was signed on a scholarship contract by Rochdale. In March 2013, towards the end of his second term, he joined FC United on a work experience loan to provide cover in case of injuries during the run-in. When Adam Jones was ruled out of the closing stages, Kevin was given an opportunity at Rushall Olympic, where he looked confident and assured against his physical opponents. Another clean sheet followed against Frickley Athletic, and when Lewis Lacy was stretchered off in the play-off semi-final win over Witton Albion, Kevin was drafted in for the final at Hednesford Town. Sadly, the Reds made a bad start and he was sacrificed before half-time as the team looked to recover a two-goal deficit. He was released by Rochdale a few weeks later, and spent part of the 2013 pre-season with FC, before linking up with Droylsden. He later featured for Irlam, Stockport Sports, New Mills and Bacup Borough.

168 Liam BROWNHILL

Born: 28/11/1986, Manchester
Debut: No.2 v Worksop Town (A, NPLP), 17/08/2013

Full-back

Season	LEAGUE			FA NATIONAL CUPS			OTHER CUPS / PLAY-OFFS			TOTALS		
	Starts	(+Sub)	Goals	Starts	(+Sub)	Goals	Starts	(+Sub)	Goals	Starts	(+Sub)	Goals
2013/14	46	(+0)	2	3	(+0)	0	4	(+1)	1	53	(+1)	3
2014/15	37	(+1)	1	9	(+0)	0	0	(+0)	0	46	(+1)	1
2015/16	24	(+1)	0	5	(+0)	0	0	(+2)	0	29	(+3)	0
Totals	107	(+2)	3	17	(+0)	0	4	(+3)	1	128	(+5)	4

Liam began his football education with Stockport County, where he served a YTS scholarship before being released at the age of 18. He then began his semi-professional career in the Welsh Premier League with Bangor City, before switching to Connah's Quay. He moved closer to his Altrincham home to sign for Witton Albion, where in a successful spell he was rewarded with caps for the England C team. In 2008 he joined Droylsden, where he played in the Conference North for three seasons and was part of the team that reached the 2nd round of the FA Cup. He joined Chester in 2011, and helped them to two wins over FC United on the way to winning the 2012 Northern Premier League title, before returning to Bangor and sampling ties in the Europa League. He joined FC in July 2013, and proved to be an inspired signing who was ever-present during the league campaign as the Reds narrowly missed out on promotion. He established himself at right-back, although as a genuinely two-footed player he was equally at home on the left, and for the second half of the season his attacking qualities were used effectively in a wing-back role. He set up numerous chances, either from set-pieces or crossing in open play, and also got amongst the goals, particularly when sealing the excellent win at Skelmersdale United. A niggling injury delayed his start to 2014/15, but he again became a model of consistency which saw him rewarded with the captaincy on several occasions. Part of the defence with the best record in the league, he still ventured forward, most notably with a fantastic goal in the crunch clash with Ashton United, and his tremendous crossfield ball against Stourbridge that enabled Craig Lindfield to centre for Greg Daniels to head the title-winning goal. At the beginning of 2015/16, Liam was appointed as the team's vice-captain, and went on to wear the armband on many occasions due to Jerome Wright's suspension and injury. Despite often featuring when less than fully fit, he started the majority of games at the higher level where his quality and experience proved invaluable. However, new additions in both full-back positions saw him drop to the bench, and he spent the final weeks of the season back in the Northern Premier League on loan at Ashton United. He helped them to the promotion play-offs once more before making a permanent summer switch. However, he was soon on the move again when he joined Trafford early in the new season, linking up with several other former Reds and narrowly missing out on a play-off place. He later featured for Glossop North End, Abbey Hey, Ramsbottom United and Wythenshawe Town before being appointed as joint manager of North West Counties League club Cheadle Town in September 2019.

169 Tom DAVIES

Born: 18/04/1992, Warrington
Debut: No.5 v Worksop Town (A, NPLP), 17/08/2013

Centre-back

Season	LEAGUE			FA NATIONAL CUPS			OTHER CUPS / PLAY-OFFS			TOTALS		
	Starts	(+Sub)	Goals	Starts	(+Sub)	Goals	Starts	(+Sub)	Goals	Starts	(+Sub)	Goals
2013/14	37	(+2)	5	2	(+1)	0	3	(+0)	0	42	(+3)	5
Totals	37	(+2)	5	2	(+1)	0	3	(+0)	0	42	(+3)	5

After training at the Manchester United and Blackburn Rovers academies, Tom entered non-league football aged 16 with his local Cheshire League club, Grappenhall Sports. Whilst studying for his A-levels he also played for Runcorn Town and Warrington Town, before embarking on a degree course at Northumbria University, and representing Team Northumbria in the Northern League. Despite lining up in defence, he had an outstanding goalscoring record, including bagging a brace in a cup final at Newcastle United's St James's Park. After graduating, he returned to the north-west and linked up with FC United in the summer of 2013, where his impressive pre-season displays earned a starting place when the league campaign commenced. After missing several games through injury and suspension, he was rarely sidelined from October onwards, and developed a great relationship with Charlie Raglan as the team stormed towards the top of the table. He scored five crucial goals, all of which contributed to victories, and it came as little surprise when he was offered a contract by Football League side Fleetwood Town in March 2014. He remained with the Reds until the end of the season, when they again lost out in the play-offs, before beginning his professional career. With a very large squad, he encountered fierce competition for places at his new club, and spent time on loan at Alfreton Town, Lincoln City and Southport. He moved on to Accrington Stanley in May 2015, and established himself in the side that unluckily lost out in the League Two promotion play-offs a year later. He joined Portsmouth in July 2016, and went one better by being part of the squad that lifted the League Two title in 2017. He switched to Coventry City in August 2017, and had another successful season. He was in the team that beat Premier League side Stoke City in the FA Cup, but was suspended as his team-mates won the League Two Play-Off Final at Wembley in May 2018. Despite being a regular squad member during the League One campaign in 2018/19, he was released by Coventry in the summer and joined Bristol Rovers. In January 2021 he signed on loan for Barrow, on the same day as former FC team-mate Ollie Banks, before moving on to fellow League Two side Tranmere Rovers in the summer.

170 Charlie RAGLAN

Born: 28/04/1993, Manchester
Debut: No.6 v Worksop Town (A, NPLP), 17/08/2013

Centre-back

Season	LEAGUE			FA NATIONAL CUPS			OTHER CUPS / PLAY-OFFS			TOTALS		
	Starts	(+Sub)	Goals	Starts	(+Sub)	Goals	Starts	(+Sub)	Goals	Starts	(+Sub)	Goals
2013/14	37	(+0)	5	1	(+0)	0	4	(+0)	0	42	(+0)	5
Totals	37	(+0)	5	1	(+0)	0	4	(+0)	0	42	(+0)	5

After spending his early years in Poynton, Charlie spent most of his childhood living in Tenerife, where his father ran a furniture business. After leaving school on the island, he returned to England to begin a YTS scholarship at Port Vale, where he earned a professional contract and progressed to the first-team bench. He had a loan spell at Conference North side Hinckley United, which was made permanent in the summer of 2012, before switching to Nantwich Town. He linked up with FC United on the post-season trip to Babelsberg in May 2013, and signed on for the club for the following season. He began the campaign as an automatic choice in the centre of defence, before being sidelined for two months with a fractured ankle. He returned in November, and hardly missed another game as he developed a great relationship with Tom Davies, which was a vital component in the team's surge up the table. He also added goals to his game in the run-in, the most memorable of which was his thundering volley that began the comeback in the top of the table clash with Chorley. His displays attracted the attention of Football League clubs, and in April 2014 it was announced that he was to join former team-mate Ollie Banks at Chesterfield. He made his debut against old club Port Vale in August, and scored his first goal against the same opponents in January 2015, before helping his new club to reach the League One promotion play-offs. The following season he entered the fray as a substitute at Broadhurst Park when Chesterfield faced FC in the FA Cup first round. He spent the majority of 2016/17 on loan to League One rivals Oxford United, who came close a play-off spot whilst his parent club finished bottom of the table. He joined Oxford on a permanent deal in the summer, however he ruptured ligaments on the eve of the season and played just two further games for them. After loan spells in League Two at his first club Port Vale and then Cheltenham Town, he signed for the latter on a free transfer in May 2019. He helped them to reach the League Two play-offs a year later, before they went one better with promotion as champions in 2021.

171 Chris WORSLEY

Born: 23/09/1987, Oldham
Debut: No.11 v Worksop Town (A, NPLP), 17/08/2013

Midfielder

Season	LEAGUE			FA NATIONAL CUPS			OTHER CUPS / PLAY-OFFS			TOTALS		
	Starts	(+Sub)	Goals	Starts	(+Sub)	Goals	Starts	(+Sub)	Goals	Starts	(+Sub)	Goals
2013/14	13	(+3)	0	1	(+0)	0	1	(+0)	0	15	(+3)	0
Totals	13	(+3)	0	1	(+0)	0	1	(+0)	0	15	(+3)	0

Chris became known as an energetic box-to-box midfielder with an eye for goal during a long spell with Curzon Ashton, where his versatility also saw him operate in defence. Whilst at the Tameside Stadium he played against FC United several times, and helped his team to win promotion to the Northern Premier League and reach the FA Vase semi-final in 2007. In 2008 he opened the scoring as Curzon defeated Football League outfit Exeter City in the first round of the FA Cup, before they bowed out in the next round against Kidderminster Harriers. In 2011 he switched to neighbours Hyde, and was an integral part of the team that lifted the Conference North title the following year. He then moved to FC Halifax Town, where he won a second successive promotion to the Conference, this time via the play-offs. However, he moved on again before playing at that level, when he signed for FC United in July 2013. He began the season well, being an automatic choice for the first nine games and only being forced to sit out due to a harsh red card in the win over Witton Albion. But after being carried off against Skelmersdale United in October, he was only able to make sporadic appearances as he attempted to recover, before being ruled out for the remainder of the season with a knee ligament injury.

172 Andy PEARSON

Born: 21/12/1989, Manchester
Debut: Sub v Stamford (H, NPLP), 24/08/2013

Centre-back/Full-back

Season	LEAGUE			FA NATIONAL CUPS			OTHER CUPS / PLAY-OFFS			TOTALS		
	Starts	(+Sub)	Goals	Starts	(+Sub)	Goals	Starts	(+Sub)	Goals	Starts	(+Sub)	Goals
2013/14	9	(+1)	1	2	(+1)	0	1	(+0)	0	12	(+2)	1
2014/15	3	(+1)	0	0	(+0)	0	1	(+0)	0	4	(+1)	0
Totals	12	(+2)	1	2	(+1)	0	2	(+0)	0	16	(+3)	1

Andy spent time on schoolboy forms with Bolton Wanderers before joining Wigan Athletic on a YTS scholarship. The Urmston lad progressed to the reserve team, but was released in 2009 and began his non-league journey with Altrincham. He earned a regular place when he moved into the Welsh Premier League with Rhyl, before joining Hyde and helping them to the Conference North title in 2012. After a loan spell at Guiseley, he linked up with FC United in August 2013, and initially provided defensive cover on the bench. He took his opportunity when it came in a sustained run during the early autumn, which he capped by opening the scoring at Nantwich Town in October. Two months later he joined Nantwich in search of a regular spot, and faced the Reds in February 2014. In July he made a return to FC, and was named in the starting line-up for the first three games of the 2014/15 campaign. The Reds remained unbeaten, but a red card against Buxton meant a suspension for Andy, and he was unable to regain his place thereafter. He once again switched to Nantwich in October, before returning to Hyde in February 2015, where he unfortunately suffered two successive relegations. He moved on to sign for his local side Trafford in November 2016.

173 Cavell COO-Richards

Born: 07/08/1987, Manchester
Debut: Sub v Trafford (A, NPLP), 26/08/2013

Full-back

Season	LEAGUE			FA NATIONAL CUPS			OTHER CUPS / PLAY-OFFS			TOTALS		
	Starts	(+Sub)	Goals	Starts	(+Sub)	Goals	Starts	(+Sub)	Goals	Starts	(+Sub)	Goals
2013/14	0	(+1)	0	0	(+0)	0	0	(+0)	0	0	(+1)	0
Totals	0	(+1)	0	0	(+0)	0	0	(+0)	0	0	(+1)	0

A speedy and skilful defender, Cavell began his career as a trainee with Crewe Alexandra and was part of the side that reached the FA Youth Cup semi-final in 2004. After his release the Didsbury lad joined the non-league game with Altrincham, and had stints at Witton Albion, Droylsden, Halifax Town and Curzon Ashton before a successful spell with Mossley. He joined FC United in July 2013, and earned plaudits for his impressive pre-season displays. However, he was unlucky to make just one appearance, as a substitute during the win at Trafford, before moving on in September for regular football with Ashton United. He faced the Reds four times later that season, performing extremely well on each occasion, in particular when his new club defeated FC with a last-gasp extra-time winner in the promotion play-off semi-final. In October 2014 he joined Salford City, where he won promotion to the Northern Premier League's top tier and was included in the First Division North's 'Team of the Season'. He returned to Ashton United in the summer of 2015, and helped them to reach the promotion play-offs once again in 2016. After a spell sidelined through injury he later featured for West Didsbury & Chorlton, Glossop North End and Cheadle Town whilst also pursuing a career as a rap music artist.

174 Callum BYRNE

Born: 05/02/1992, Liverpool
Debut: No.8 v Stafford Rangers (A, NPLP), 21/09/2013

Midfielder

Season	LEAGUE			FA NATIONAL CUPS			OTHER CUPS / PLAY-OFFS			TOTALS		
	Starts	(+Sub)	Goals	Starts	(+Sub)	Goals	Starts	(+Sub)	Goals	Starts	(+Sub)	Goals
2013/14	28	(+7)	3	0	(+0)	0	3	(+1)	0	31	(+8)	3
2014/15	24	(+10)	2	9	(+0)	2	1	(+0)	0	34	(+10)	4
2015/16	2	(+3)	0	3	(+2)	0	0	(+0)	0	5	(+5)	0
Totals	54	(+20)	5	12	(+2)	2	4	(+1)	0	70	(+23)	7

Callum was a young professional at Rochdale, where the cultured playmaker advanced to the first-team substitutes' bench before loan spells at Trafford and Mossley. He entered non-league permanently with Hyde in 2011, forming a midfield trio with Dave Birch and Chris Worsley as they won the 2012 Conference North title. After a loan stint at Colwyn Bay, Callum joined FC United in September 2013, but most of his early months were spent being introduced from the bench as he regained his match sharpness. He began a sustained run in midfield in November which coincided with an upturn in results. The following month he hit his first goal for the club to seal the terrific win at Fylde, and in the New Year was an integral part of the team that very nearly won promotion. He was the main man pulling the strings in midfield in the first half of 2014/15, particularly when scoring against Barwell in both FA Trophy games when it seemed the Reds were about to be eliminated on each occasion. Thereafter he started most of the games as the team stormed to the top of the table with a remarkable winning run, but also played his part from the bench when needed. He was introduced for the final few minutes against Stourbridge and did an excellent job of maintaining possession as the team won the game and the Northern Premier League title. After finding games hard to come by in 2015/16, Callum left the club in November, shortly after appearing as a substitute in the FA Cup 1st Round tie with Chesterfield.

175 Richard SMITH

Born: 18/02/1994, Bury
Debut: No.2 v New Mills (A, MPC:1), 24/09/2013

Right-back

Season	LEAGUE			FA NATIONAL CUPS			OTHER CUPS / PLAY-OFFS			TOTALS		
	Starts	(+Sub)	Goals	Starts	(+Sub)	Goals	Starts	(+Sub)	Goals	Starts	(+Sub)	Goals
2012/13	0	(+0)	0	0	(+0)	0	0	(+0)	0	0	(+0)	0
2013/14	0	(+0)	0	0	(+0)	0	1	(+0)	0	1	(+0)	0
Totals	0	(+0)	0	0	(+0)	0	1	(+0)	0	1	(+0)	0

An adaptable defender or midfielder originally on the books of Bury, Ric joined FC United's youth team in 2011 and was an integral part of their highly successful 2011/12 campaign when they won a hat-trick of trophies. He was rewarded by signing first-team forms in March 2012, before he was first named on the senior bench in January 2013. After a stint gaining experience at Daisy Hill, he returned to make his debut the following season in the Manchester Premier Cup tie at New Mills, where he showed maturity beyond his years by coolly scoring a penalty in the shoot-out. After spells at Stockport Sports and Salford City, he established himself at Radcliffe Borough, where he was appointed captain in 2015. He moved up a division in 2016 to join Ashton United, where he further demonstrated his versatility with stints up front and even took over in goal on one occasion. After a spell out injured in 2017/18 he spent a month on loan at Atherton Collieries before returning to the Ashton team. However he lost his place and returned to Radcliffe in March 2018, and was part of the squad that won promotion to the Northern Premier League's top division in 2019. He faced FC in three competitions in 2019/20, and his late headed equaliser in the Manchester Premier Cup in October took the tie to penalties. He rejoined Atherton Collieries in the summer of 2020, but with the league season curtailed due to the COVID-19 pandemic he was recruited by Warrington Rylands when their FA Vase campaign resumed in April 2021. He helped them to the Wembley final, and was in the team that lifted the trophy with a 3-2 win over Binfield. He stayed with them for 2021/22, when they continued their progression by winning the Northern Premier League Division One West.

Richard's dad, Robin, was a former professional goalkeeper who coached the young FC United custodians for over three years. Robin sadly passed away in August 2014, and the club observed a minute's silence at the next home game in honour of a much loved member of the backroom staff.

176 Jordan DAINTY

Born: 05/02/1993, Wigan
Debut: No.5 v New Mills (A, MPC:1), 24/09/2013

Centre-back

Season	LEAGUE			FA NATIONAL CUPS			OTHER CUPS / PLAY-OFFS			TOTALS		
	Starts	(+Sub)	Goals	Starts	(+Sub)	Goals	Starts	(+Sub)	Goals	Starts	(+Sub)	Goals
2010/11	0	(+0)	0	0	(+0)	0	0	(+0)	0	0	(+0)	0
2013/14	0	(+0)	0	0	(+0)	0	1	(+0)	0	1	(+0)	0
Totals	0	(+0)	0	0	(+0)	0	1	(+0)	0	1	(+0)	0

Jordan joined FC United's youth team in 2009, and enjoyed a successful time with the under-18s by helping them to win the Manchester FA Youth Cup in 2010 and the North West Youth Alliance League in 2011. His progress was rewarded with a call-up to the first-team bench for the trip to Nantwich Town in March 2011, but he had to wait for another 2½ years to make his senior debut in the Manchester Premier Cup at New Mills. In the meantime the Pemberton lad had furthered his development with spells in the North West Counties League at Rochdale Town and Oldham Boro, and he then went on to establish himself at his local club Wigan Robin Park.

177 Frank VAN GILS

Born: 21/01/1995, Den Haag (Netherlands)
Debut: No.8 v New Mills (A, MPC:1), 24/09/2013 (scored)

Midfielder

Season	LEAGUE			FA NATIONAL CUPS			OTHER CUPS / PLAY-OFFS			TOTALS		
	Starts	(+Sub)	Goals	Starts	(+Sub)	Goals	Starts	(+Sub)	Goals	Starts	(+Sub)	Goals
2013/14	0	(+0)	0	0	(+0)	0	1	(+0)	1	1	(+0)	1
2014/15	2	(+1)	0	1	(+1)	0	0	(+0)	0	3	(+2)	0
Totals	2	(+1)	0	1	(+1)	0	1	(+0)	1	4	(+2)	1

Frank began his football education in his homeland with Feyenoord's academy, before coming to England and joining the system at Manchester City. A small, fast and skilful player able to fulfil various attacking roles, he linked up with FC United through the club's partnership with the Manchester College. The Ardwick resident was an integral part of the team that reached the British Colleges National Final in 2012, and later that year was selected for the England Colleges national football squad. His progress was rewarded with a senior FC call-up for the Manchester Premier Cup tie at New Mills in September 2013, and he marked the occasion by getting on the scoresheet. He was an unused substitute for two further matches before returning to the reserve team, and helping them to win the Lancashire League and Cup double. He came back into senior contention in November 2014, and impressed onlookers with his lively and creative displays, which included a standout performance and an assist at Stourbridge. He gained further experience on loan at Radcliffe Borough later in the season, but was back with the Reds to join the title-winning celebrations and play in the historic opening games at Broadhurst Park. He remained in FC's reserves during 2015/16, save for a brief loan spell back in the Northern Premier League with Hyde United in February. He rejoined Radcliffe on a permanent basis in August 2016, before returning to the Netherlands with amateur clubs SV Oosterheem and FC Boshuizen.

178 Michael TAYLOR

Born: 29/12/1994, Manchester
Debut: Sub v New Mills (A, MPC:1), 24/09/2013

Midfielder

Season	LEAGUE			FA NATIONAL CUPS			OTHER CUPS / PLAY-OFFS			TOTALS		
	Starts	(+Sub)	Goals	Starts	(+Sub)	Goals	Starts	(+Sub)	Goals	Starts	(+Sub)	Goals
2012/13	0	(+0)	0	0	(+0)	0	0	(+0)	0	0	(+0)	0
2013/14	0	(+0)	0	0	(+0)	0	0	(+1)	0	0	(+1)	0
Totals	0	(+0)	0	0	(+0)	0	0	(+1)	0	0	(+1)	0

A versatile player from Chorlton-cum-Hardy, Mike joined FC United's youth team in 2012 as part of the club's link with the Manchester College. In a successful 2012/13 campaign he helped the under-18s to runners-up spot in the North West Youth Alliance, captained Manchester FA to the FA County Youth Cup Final, and was selected for the England Colleges national football squad. His progress was noted by Karl Marginson, who named him as a substitute for the first team's League Cup trip to Ashton United in January, although he remained on the bench. In September the following season he was once again called up for senior duty for the Manchester Premier Cup tie at New Mills, where he played the last half-hour and almost snatched a dramatic late winner, before the Reds eventually lost on penalties. He played the remainder of the season in the reformed reserve team, where he showed his versatility by turning out in defence, midfield and attack, and won the Lancashire League and Cup double. He went on to play in the North West Counties League with his local club West Didsbury & Chorlton, and later linked up with Wythenshawe Town.

179 Jonathan POIZER

Born: 25/10/1994, Manchester
Debut: Sub v New Mills (A, MPC:1), 24/09/2013

Left-winger/Forward

Season	LEAGUE			FA NATIONAL CUPS			OTHER CUPS / PLAY-OFFS			TOTALS		
	Starts	(+Sub)	Goals	Starts	(+Sub)	Goals	Starts	(+Sub)	Goals	Starts	(+Sub)	Goals
2013/14	0	(+0)	0	0	(+0)	0	0	(+1)	0	0	(+1)	0
Totals	0	(+0)	0	0	(+0)	0	0	(+1)	0	0	(+1)	0

A left-sided attacking player from Chorlton-cum-Hardy, Jon joined FC United's youth team in 2011, and played a prominent role as they won the North West Youth Alliance title and Open Cup, and the Manchester FA Youth Cup in May 2012. The following season the Manchester College student helped the under-18s to runners-up spot in the league, played for Manchester in the FA County Youth Cup Final, and was selected to play for Greater Manchester Colleges. In September 2013 he was called up for senior duty for the Manchester Premier Cup match at New Mills, where he entered the fray as a last-minute substitute as the tie descended towards a penalty shoot-out. He bravely stepped up to take one of FC's spot-kicks, but unfortunately his effort went over the bar and the Reds were eliminated shortly afterwards. He played the remainder of the term in the reserve team, showing his versatility by lining up at left-back, left-wing and up front, and hit 19 goals as the youngsters won the Lancashire League and Cup double. He then continued his football education in the North West Counties League with Northwich Flixton Villa and his local side West Didsbury & Chorlton, for whom he played against FC in the Manchester Premier Cup semi-final at Broadhurst Park in February 2017. He switched to Wythenshawe Town the following year when they joined the North West Counties League.

180 Amjad IQBAL

Born: 22/06/1982, Bradford
Debut: No.6 v Witton Albion (A, FAT:Q1), 19/10/2013

Centre-back

	LEAGUE			FA NATIONAL CUPS			OTHER CUPS / PLAY-OFFS			TOTALS		
Season	Starts	(+Sub)	Goals	Starts	(+Sub)	Goals	Starts	(+Sub)	Goals	Starts	(+Sub)	Goals
2013/14	1	(+0)	0	1	(+0)	0	0	(+0)	0	2	(+0)	0
Totals	1	(+0)	0	1	(+0)	0	0	(+0)	0	2	(+0)	0

A former Bradford City academy player, Amjad made his name in non-league with Thackley, before captaining Farsley Celtic to four promotions in five seasons to reach the Conference. In this successful phase of his career he also earned international caps for Pakistan, representing the homeland of his parents in World Cup qualifiers. In March 2009 he joined Bradford Park Avenue, and lined up against FC United in both defence and midfield in Northern Premier League matches. The following year he switched to the newly-reformed Farsley AFC, before returning to Bradford PA, but a dislocated shoulder and two leg breaks sidelined him for long periods. He signed for FC in October 2013 and made his debut in the FA Trophy draw at Witton Albion. His league bow followed a week later, and he also played in the abandoned replay against Witton before dropping out of contention with first a groin injury, then a chest infection. After leaving semi-professional football he concentrated on his career as a chemistry lecturer.

181 Joe FOX

Born: 03/12/1991, York
Debut: Sub v Droylsden (A, NPLP), 26/11/2013

Midfielder

	LEAGUE			FA NATIONAL CUPS			OTHER CUPS / PLAY-OFFS			TOTALS		
Season	Starts	(+Sub)	Goals	Starts	(+Sub)	Goals	Starts	(+Sub)	Goals	Starts	(+Sub)	Goals
2013/14	4	(+13)	0	0	(+0)	0	0	(+0)	0	4	(+13)	0
2014/15	15	(+11)	1	1	(+2)	0	0	(+0)	0	16	(+13)	1
Totals	19	(+24)	1	1	(+2)	0	0	(+0)	0	20	(+26)	1

As a schoolboy Joe was on the books of hometown club York City, as well as Leeds United, before becoming a young professional with Hull City. He was part of their youth team that won the North East Youth Alliance title in 2010, before his progress was halted by a long-term injury which led to his release. He joined the non-league ranks with Hyde, before spells at Worksop Town and Ossett Albion, where he established himself as a midfielder capable of fulfilling various roles. He faced FC United twice in the colours of Frickley Athletic in the autumn of 2013, and impressed sufficiently in the second encounter that the Reds signed him a few days later. He mainly featured as a substitute as the team chased promotion in 2013/14, but he was given a run in the side during the first half of 2014/15. He scored his first goal to clinch three vital points at Blyth Spartans, and his long throw also provided the team with another attacking weapon. Increased competition for places restricted his appearances in the New Year, but he still provided outstanding performances when called upon, such as in the crucial narrow wins over Halesowen Town and Workington in March. He ended the season with a deserved Northern Premier League winner's medal, and played in the showcase opening games at Broadhurst Park, before moving on to Scarborough Athletic in the summer. In 2016 he moved to Australia to play in the New South Wales Premier League for Manly United, where he also became head coach of their schools academy.

182 Nelson MOTA

Born: 16/09/1989, Bondy (France)
Debut: Sub v Blyth Spartans (H, NPLP), 30/11/2013

Winger

	LEAGUE			FA NATIONAL CUPS			OTHER CUPS / PLAY-OFFS			TOTALS		
Season	Starts	(+Sub)	Goals	Starts	(+Sub)	Goals	Starts	(+Sub)	Goals	Starts	(+Sub)	Goals
2013/14	2	(+6)	0	0	(+0)	0	0	(+0)	0	2	(+6)	0
2014/15	1	(+0)	0	0	(+0)	0	0	(+0)	0	1	(+0)	0
Totals	3	(+6)	0	0	(+0)	0	0	(+0)	0	3	(+6)	0

A tricky and pacy French winger, Nelson began his football career in his native country with Niort, before featuring for Lilas, Saint-Maur and Paris FC. He moved to Spain, where he played for CD Rota, Atlético Sanluqueño and Conil CF, before his travels brought him to Manchester in the summer of 2013. After trials with several clubs, he joined Salford City early in the 2013/14 season, where he quickly impressed with some exciting performances. He caught the eye of the FC United scouts, who moved to persuade him to sign for the Reds in November. Introduced as a late substitute against Blyth Spartans, he won a penalty within minutes, and went on to provide another dimension to the team's play with further cameo appearances. He was rewarded with starts in January against Whitby Town and Trafford, but despite performing well he became a victim of the change in formation, and was confined to the bench for the remainder of the campaign. After starting the draw at Trafford in August 2014, he was released by the club and moved on to Ramsbottom United, before switching to Darlington 1883 and helping them to promotion from the Northern Premier League Division One North.

183 Ed WILCZYNSKI

Born: 13/09/1994, Huddersfield
Debut: No.1 v Barwell (H, NPLP), 21/12/2013

Goalkeeper

Season	LEAGUE			FA NATIONAL CUPS			OTHER CUPS / PLAY-OFFS			TOTALS		
	Starts	(+Sub)	Goals	Starts	(+Sub)	Goals	Starts	(+Sub)	Goals	Starts	(+Sub)	Goals
2013/14	3	(+0)	0	0	(+0)	0	0	(+0)	0	3	(+0)	0
Totals	3	(+0)	0	0	(+0)	0	0	(+0)	0	3	(+0)	0

FC United were faced with a goalkeeping crisis in December 2013 with James Spencer's injury, and Jon Worsnop's departure. The club swooped to sign Ed on a month's loan from Huddersfield Town, where he was in his first year as a professional. He performed admirably during his short stay, keeping two clean sheets in three matches which earned six vital points. After the signing of Dave Carnell, Ed returned to his parent club to continue his development, which included further loan spells with Trafford, Hyde, Sheffield and Bishop Auckland. After his release by Huddersfield he joined AFC Fylde in August 2016, before swiftly returning to Bishop Auckland. He joined Darlington 1883 in January 2017, and was on the bench for FC's league visit in April. He later kept goal for Shaw Lane AFC, Trafford, Clitheroe, Ossett United, Liversedge, Yorkshire Amateur and Eccleshill United, and also for the newly-formed North West Counties League side Bury AFC in their first competitive match in September 2020.

184 David CARNELL

Born: 18/04/1985, Münster (Germany)
Debut: No.1 v Ilkeston (A, NPLP), 04/01/2014

Goalkeeper

Season	LEAGUE			FA NATIONAL CUPS			OTHER CUPS / PLAY-OFFS			TOTALS		
	Starts	(+Sub)	Goals	Starts	(+Sub)	Goals	Starts	(+Sub)	Goals	Starts	(+Sub)	Goals
2013/14	21	(+0)	0	0	(+0)	0	3	(+0)	0	24	(+0)	0
2014/15	45	(+0)	0	11	(+0)	0	1	(+0)	0	57	(+0)	0
2015/16	35	(+0)	0	5	(+0)	0	1	(+0)	0	41	(+0)	0
2016/17	23	(+0)	0	4	(+0)	0	2	(+0)	0	29	(+0)	0
2018/19	4	(+0)	0	2	(+0)	0	0	(+0)	0	6	(+0)	0
Totals	128	(+0)	0	22	(+0)	0	7	(+0)	0	157	(+0)	0

Dave is a former Manchester United academy goalkeeper who began in non-league with Oldham Town, and faced FC United twice in our inaugural 2005/06 season. He moved on to Hyde United, and had a short spell with Stalybridge Celtic, before a successful period at Curzon Ashton. With the Tameside outfit he reached the FA Vase semi-final and won promotion from the North West Counties League in 2007. He again lined up against the Reds in the Northern Premier League Division One North, when his first-half injury in March 2008 arguably tipped the match in FC's favour. The following season he kept goal in Curzon's run to the 2nd round of the FA Cup, defeating Football League club Exeter City along the way, but his dismissal proved crucial in their eventual elimination at Kidderminster Harriers. Along with several team-mates, he switched to Hyde in 2011, and won the 2012 Conference North title. Carnell's heroics were a major factor in Hyde's retention of Conference status for 2013/14, before he was sidelined by a hamstring injury in October. A replacement was signed in his absence, and so when FC needed a keeper due to the loss of both Jon Worsnop and James Spencer in December, Dave jumped at the chance to join the club. Despite his presence, the team dropped points in his first three league games, before clicking into gear with a 12-match winning run that saw them hit the top of the table. Just eight goals were conceded in this period, and although the promotion challenge was ultimately unsuccessful, most observers were delighted with the calming presence and abilities of the new custodian. He carried this consistency into the 2014/15 campaign, when he missed just two games and was vital to the team finally winning the Northern Premier League title. They boasted the best defensive record in the division, and Dave kept a remarkable 20 clean sheets as he was named in the league's team of the season. He was again a standout performer in 2015/16, and had quite an eventful campaign. On the opening day he saved a penalty at Gloucester City, but just as the team seemed to have adjusted to the higher league he was unfortunately sent off at AFC Fylde. In February his first-half injury at Telford led to another heavy defeat, but once back he kept four clean sheets in six games as the team's best run of the season eased the relegation fears. He had a frustrating 2016/17 with three spells on the sidelines. He began the season in similar fashion to the previous one by saving a penalty on the opening day at Chorley, but he suffered

his first injury at the end of August. After his return in October he produced one of the best displays of his career in the tremendous 2-0 win at Kidderminster Harriers. Another issue at Christmas led to FC signing Adriano Basso, who kept goal until receiving a red card at home to Chorley in February. Dave returned with a man-of-the-match performance at Stockport County, and remained in terrific form until his injury jinx struck again in April and he sat out the rest of the campaign. He was initially part of FC's squad for 2017/18, but left in July and joined Ashton United, where he once again won promotion to the National League North via the play-offs. He returned to FC United as short-term cover in September 2018, and performed well in adding a further six appearances to his record before signing for Trafford on a dual-registration basis in November. He rejoined Ashton United in August 2019, before later signing for former colleagues Mike Norton and Dave Birch at New Mills. In May 2021 it was announced that Dave was making a further return to FC United to combine a coaching role with cover for the established custodian Dan Lavercombe. However, despite featuring in three pre-season friendlies, he picked up an injury during the summer that prevented any further involvement with the Reds. His only senior outing during the season was alongside several other former United players for Avro in the North West Counties League.

185 Connor BOWER

Born: 17/03/1995, Bradford
Debut: Sub v Carlton Town (A, NPLCC:QF), 26/02/2014

Forward

Season	LEAGUE			FA NATIONAL CUPS			OTHER CUPS / PLAY-OFFS			TOTALS		
	Starts	(+Sub)	Goals	Starts	(+Sub)	Goals	Starts	(+Sub)	Goals	Starts	(+Sub)	Goals
2013/14	0	(+0)	0	0	(+0)	0	0	(+1)	0	0	(+1)	0
2014/15	1	(+5)	0	0	(+0)	0	0	(+1)	0	1	(+6)	0
Totals	1	(+5)	0	0	(+0)	0	0	(+2)	0	1	(+7)	0

Pacy forward Connor joined Bradford City as a scholar, but despite boasting an decent scoring record in the youth team, he was released in 2013 and joined the non-league circuit with Garforth Town. He joined FC United in February 2014, and made his debut as a late substitute in the League Cup tie at Carlton Town. He remained on the bench for the next three games before heading to Sweden, where he spent three months playing for BK Sport. He returned to the Reds in July, and his impressive pre-season displays earned him a regular squad place at the outset of 2014/15. However, he was unable to gain a prolonged run in the side and moved to Ossett Town in October 2014. The following month he switched to neighbours Ossett Albion, where his exploits earned a move to National League North side Harrogate Town. He later played for Frickley Athletic, Mossley and Worsbrough Bridge Athletic.

186 Jacob HAZEL

Born: 15/04/1994, Bradford
Debut: Sub v Grantham Town (H, NPLP), 15/04/2014

Forward

Season	LEAGUE			FA NATIONAL CUPS			OTHER CUPS / PLAY-OFFS			TOTALS		
	Starts	(+Sub)	Goals	Starts	(+Sub)	Goals	Starts	(+Sub)	Goals	Starts	(+Sub)	Goals
2013/14	0	(+2)	0	0	(+0)	0	0	(+0)	0	0	(+2)	0
Totals	0	(+2)	0	0	(+0)	0	0	(+0)	0	0	(+2)	0

The son of Karl Marginson's former Rotherham United team-mate Des Hazel, Jacob was in the schoolboy academies at Bradford City and Halifax Town before becoming a professional with Chesterfield. He made his senior debut as a substitute against Oldham Athletic in September 2012, before being rewarded with a first start a few days later at York City. Later in that campaign he spent time on loan at non-league sides Matlock Town and Workington, before spending a productive summer scoring goals in Norway for SK Sprint-Jeløy. After further loan spells with Buxton and Bradford Park Avenue, he linked up with FC United on a similar arrangement in March 2014, in order to provide fresh legs in reserve for the promotion run-in. He was called from the bench twice and impressed with his touch and movement, prompting the Reds to invite him to sign permanently when Chesterfield released him in June. He featured in several pre-season games for FC that summer, but chose to link up instead with Salford City, before later playing for Ashton United, Mickleover Sports and Frickley Athletic. He signed for Gainsborough Trinity in the summer of 2016, but in the early stages of the season he joined Farsley Celtic on a loan deal. In December he switched to Scarborough Athletic, and helped them to the Northern Premier League First Division North promotion play-offs. He also emulated his father by making his international debut for Saint Kitts and Nevis in a friendly match with Estonia in November 2016. He returned to Frickley in June 2017, and scored 46 goals to help his team reach the Northern Premier League First Division South promotion play-offs the next year. He moved up a level in 2020 with Whitby Town, for whom he bagged the winner in his side's dramatic 4-3 win at Broadhurst Park in January 2022. He ended 2021/22 as the division's top scorer before being snapped up by National League North side Darlington in the summer.

188 James KNOWLES

Born: 21/05/1983, Dewsbury
Debut: Sub v Barwell (A, NPLP), 17/08/2014

Centre-back

Season	LEAGUE			FA NATIONAL CUPS			OTHER CUPS / PLAY-OFFS			TOTALS		
	Starts	(+Sub)	Goals	Starts	(+Sub)	Goals	Starts	(+Sub)	Goals	Starts	(+Sub)	Goals
2014/15	14	(+2)	2	2	(+0)	0	1	(+0)	0	17	(+2)	2
Totals	14	(+2)	2	2	(+0)	0	1	(+0)	0	17	(+2)	2

Able to play in midfield or central defence, James was in the Blackburn Rovers academy before going into non-league with Garforth Town. After coaching and playing in the USA, he returned to play for the successful Farsley Celtic team that reached the Conference. His next stop was Bradford Park Avenue, where he first faced FC United in some epic battles. He scored against the Reds in August 2009 and captained his team to a last-gasp play-off final victory in May 2012. He joined Halifax Town that summer, and won another promotion to the Conference in his one season there before returning to Park Avenue. He joined FC in July 2014, but despite him scoring his first goal at Trafford his early months were disrupted by a groin injury. After burying a superb diving header past Frickley Athletic in November, he looked set for a long run until suffering a horrific leg break at Curzon Ashton on Boxing Day. He trained with the squad in 2015/16, but was released in November in order to find game time and eventually returned to Farsley. He began a third spell at Bradford in October 2016, and faced FC again in league matches. He joined Scarborough Athletic in November 2017 before ending the season with Ossett Albion. He spent the following campaign helping the newly-formed Ossett United to reach the Northern Premier League Division One East promotion play-offs, and for a spell was the team's joint caretaker-manager along with Tom Greaves when Andy Welsh resigned in November 2019. He moved to Northern Counties East League side Emley in 2020.

187 Craig LINDFIELD

Born: 07/09/1988, Birkenhead
Debut: No.11 v Barwell (A, NPLP), 17/08/2014

Winger/Forward

Season	LEAGUE			FA NATIONAL CUPS			OTHER CUPS / PLAY-OFFS			TOTALS		
	Starts	(+Sub)	Goals	Starts	(+Sub)	Goals	Starts	(+Sub)	Goals	Starts	(+Sub)	Goals
2014/15	31	(+1)	10	8	(+0)	2	0	(+0)	0	39	(+1)	12
2015/16	9	(+10)	3	4	(+2)	2	2	(+0)	2	15	(+12)	7
2017/18	21	(+9)	8	3	(+1)	1	1	(+1)	0	25	(+11)	9
Totals	**61**	**(+20)**	**21**	**15**	**(+3)**	**5**	**3**	**(+1)**	**2**	**79**	**(+24)**	**28**

As a young professional at Liverpool, Craig won the FA Youth Cup in 2006 and again in 2007, when he scored the opening goal against Manchester United. The England under-19 cap had loan spells in League Two at Notts County, Chester City, Bournemouth and Accrington Stanley, before signing for Macclesfield Town in December 2009. He returned to Accrington in July 2010, but a knee injury meant he was mainly a substitute in his first season, with a short loan at Kidderminster Harriers to regain match fitness. He established himself in 2011/12, playing the majority of matches, and remained a regular until an injury midway through the following term. When his contract ended in June 2013, he returned to Chester and played in the Conference, before joining FC United in June 2014. A bad knee injury in just his second game sidelined him for two months, but his return inspired the team's upturn in form. He scored his first goal for the club against Frickley Athletic in November, but a late red card in the same game earned a one-match suspension. Thereafter he missed just one more game, and was integral in the run to the FA Trophy quarter-final and the charge to the top of the table. His two early goals against Fylde set up the trip to Torquay United, whilst in the league he hit double figures, often cutting in from the wing and curling the ball into the far corner. He scored late winners against Nantwich Town and Halesowen Town, and also struck at vital times against Ashton United, Barwell, Marine, King's Lynn Town, Curzon Ashton and Stamford. He also created many goals, most notably the inch-perfect cross nodded home by Greg Daniels against Stourbridge that won the Northern Premier League title. Niggling injuries restricted his efforts in 2015/16, but he still hit vital goals, such as the

dramatic injury-time winner against North Ferriby United in February, just minutes after he came on as a substitute. A few days later he went to Ashton United on loan, before joining Marine in June. In February 2017 he switched to Trafford, but returned to join the Reds during the summer. He scored his first goal back in the draw at Southport in August, but minor knocks prevented a sustained run until Tom Greaves took over in October. He scored against Harrogate Town, Spennymoor Town and Salford City in the terrific sequence of results around Christmas, and hit form again in spring. His goals against Boston United, Gainsborough Trinity and Tamworth were crucial in easing the relegation fears, before he once again departed the club at the end of the season. During the next term he lined up for Nantwich, Curzon Ashton, Runcorn Town and Radcliffe, where he was in the team that won the Northern Premier League Division One West play-offs. He returned to Marine in 2019 before later spells at Runcorn Linnets and Cymru North side Colwyn Bay.

189 Chris LYNCH

Born: 31/01/1991, Blackburn
Debut: No.5 v Belper Town (H, NPLP), 23/08/2014

Centre-back

Season	LEAGUE			FA NATIONAL CUPS			OTHER CUPS / PLAY-OFFS			TOTALS		
	Starts	(+Sub)	Goals	Starts	(+Sub)	Goals	Starts	(+Sub)	Goals	Starts	(+Sub)	Goals
2014/15	21	(+4)	2	5	(+0)	1	2	(+0)	0	28	(+4)	3
2015/16	2	(+2)	0	3	(+0)	0	2	(+0)	0	7	(+2)	0
Totals	**23**	**(+6)**	**2**	**8**	**(+0)**	**1**	**4**	**(+0)**	**0**	**35**	**(+6)**	**3**

Chris developed in the youth system at Burnley, where the central defender from Darwen earned a professional contract and became a mainstay in the reserve team. At the age of 18 he had a loan spell with Conference club Chester City, but his progress stalled when he ruptured his anterior cruciate ligament. He was released by Burnley in 2011, and signed for Conference North outfit Stalybridge Celtic, where his impressive displays led to a move to Southport in the summer of 2012. He gained a regular place in the Conference side before damaging a cartilage, and then suffering another cruciate injury in the July 2013. After missing a whole year of football, he joined FC United in August 2014 on an initial one-month loan deal that became a permanent move the following month. After helping the team to two draws in his first two matches, he scored his first goal for the club in his third against Ramsbottom United to seal the first win of what would be a terrific season. Many of his early games were spent as one of three centre-backs, but after serving a suspension due to a red card against Barwell in the FA Trophy he became the unlucky player to lose out when the manager reverted to a back four. He reminded everyone of his presence when coming off the bench to score the deciding goal at Grantham Town, before regaining his place for the vital last push as the Northern Premier League title was won. He ended the campaign by playing in the opening matches at Broadhurst Park in May. Beginning 2015/16 with an injury, his first appearance of the term was in unusual circumstances as a substitute goalkeeper at AFC Fylde. After a handful of starts, increased competition for defensive spots led to him moving on to Clitheroe in December. He linked up with Colne in July 2016 and hardly missed a game over the next two seasons. He appeared as a half-time substitute against FC in the FA Cup at Broadhurst in September 2018, before later moving into the North West Counties League with Padiham and AFC Darwen.

190 John PRITCHARD

Born: 29/09/1995, Manchester
Debut: Sub v Belper Town (H, NPLP), 23/08/2014

Midfielder

Season	LEAGUE			FA NATIONAL CUPS			OTHER CUPS / PLAY-OFFS			TOTALS		
	Starts	(+Sub)	Goals	Starts	(+Sub)	Goals	Starts	(+Sub)	Goals	Starts	(+Sub)	Goals
2014/15	0	(+1)	0	0	(+0)	0	0	(+0)	0	0	(+1)	0
Totals	0	(+1)	0	0	(+0)	0	0	(+0)	0	0	(+1)	0

A versatile left-sider from Levenshulme, John was in Manchester United's academy before turning professional at Oldham Athletic. He was denied a goal by the crossbar on his Football League debut as a substitute against Colchester United in December 2013, prior to his release the next summer. He joined FC United in July 2014, and came on to help the Reds to win a late point on his debut the following month against Belper Town. Despite impressing in the reserve team this was his only senior involvement, and for more experience he joined Trafford in January 2015. He went on to play at New Mills, Ramsbottom United, Northwich Victoria, Stockport Town and West Didsbury & Chorlton, showing adaptaly by featuring at left-back as well as in midfield. He returned to the Northern Premier League's top level in 2017 with Ashton United, where he was a mainstay of the side that won promotion to the National League North in 2018. He moved to Chester in the summer and made a promising start before joining Buxton on loan until the end of the term, helping them to the Northern Premier League play-off semi-final. In May 2019 he returned to Ashton United, where he was in the side that lost to FC in December. He went on to link up with Matlock Town, Radcliffe, Cheadle Heath Nomads and Wythenshawe Town.

192 Tom BROWN

Born: 01/10/1994, Bolton
Debut: Sub v Marine (A, NPLP), 06/09/2014

Midfielder

Season	LEAGUE			FA NATIONAL CUPS			OTHER CUPS / PLAY-OFFS			TOTALS		
	Starts	(+Sub)	Goals	Starts	(+Sub)	Goals	Starts	(+Sub)	Goals	Starts	(+Sub)	Goals
2014/15	7	(+13)	1	3	(+3)	0	1	(+1)	0	11	(+17)	1
2015/16	12	(+6)	0	1	(+1)	0	1	(+1)	0	14	(+8)	0
2016/17	15	(+0)	2	1	(+1)	0	2	(+0)	1	18	(+1)	3
2017/18	4	(+1)	0	0	(+0)	0	0	(+0)	0	4	(+1)	0
Totals	38	(+20)	3	5	(+5)	0	4	(+2)	1	47	(+27)	4

Tom captained the Blackburn Rovers under-18 side, winning their Young Player of the Year award and stepping up to the under-21s, but two bad knee injuries precipitated his release in 2014. He joined FC United in August, and was still relatively unknown when he came on to hit a vital late winner at Nantwich Town in October. He was heavily involved in Matt Walwyn's dramatic last-minute clincher against Barwell in the FA Trophy, and after impressive cameos in December was given several starts in the New Year. His display in the Trophy win over AFC Fylde ensured he kept his place for the trip to Torquay United, where he produced another excellent performance. He spent the rest of the term sharing duties with Callum Byrne, but played his part in the team's fantastic run to the top of the table and the eventual lifting of the Northern Premier League title. Apart from two spells out injured in the autumn, he remained a regular squad member in 2015/16, but increased competition in midfield kept him mainly on the bench until the closing months of the campaign. He began 2016/17 late due to injury, with his first appearance not arriving until October. His first start was later that month at Chadderton, and he then started 17 of the next 20 games which constituted his best run for the club. He notched his first goal for over two years with a stunning volley at Altrincham on Boxing Day, and also scored at home for the first time against West Didsbury & Chorlton. Tactical changes saw him drop to the bench in February, and he featured just once before the term ended, although he marked that with a goal at Darlington 1883 in April. He began 2017/18 leading the side at Brackley Town, but had moved to Stalybridge Celtic before the end of August. He joined Radcliffe in February 2019, and was in the squad that won the Northern Premier League Division One West play-offs. He was on the losing side when FC won in the FA Trophy in October 2019, before later playing for Colne and in the North West Counties League for Daisy Hill, and New Mills under fellow former Reds Mike Norton and Dave Birch.

193 Andy WELSH

Born: 24/01/1983, Manchester
Debut: No.11 v Prescot Cables (H, FAC:Q1), 14/09/2014

Midfielder/Left-winger

Season	LEAGUE			FA NATIONAL CUPS			OTHER CUPS / PLAY-OFFS			TOTALS		
	Starts	(+Sub)	Goals	Starts	(+Sub)	Goals	Starts	(+Sub)	Goals	Starts	(+Sub)	Goals
2014/15	6	(+2)	1	2	(+0)	0	0	(+0)	0	8	(+2)	1
Totals	6	(+2)	1	2	(+0)	0	0	(+0)	0	8	(+2)	1

Raised in Dukinfield, Andy made his Football League debut for Stockport County in October 2001, and later that season was in the team that famously beat Manchester City. After a loan spell at Macclesfield Town, he claimed the left-wing spot two seasons later, and attracted the attention of Sunderland, signing for them in November 2004. He scored on his full debut, and helped the team to promotion to the Premier League at the end of the term. He recorded 14 top-flight appearances the following season, including a start against boyhood heroes Manchester United. After two loan periods at Leicester City, he moved to Canada to play for MLS side Toronto FC in March 2007. He returned to England with Blackpool, before three happy seasons with Yeovil Town. After injury-hit stints at Carlisle United and Scunthorpe United, Andy signed for the Reds in September 2014. Despite initially being short of full match fitness, his ability was obvious, and after he scored against Whitby Town it seemed he would be key to FC's attack for some time. However, tactical changes saw him drop to the bench and he moved to Farsley in November. He joined Ossett Albion as player-coach in 2017, and later became the first-ever manager of newly-formed Ossett United in 2018, and of Bury AFC upon their formation in 2020.

191 Luke ASHWORTH

Born: 04/12/1989, Bolton
Debut: No.3 v Ramsbottom United (H, NPLP), 30/08/2014

Centre-back

Season	LEAGUE Starts	(+Sub)	Goals	FA NATIONAL CUPS Starts	(+Sub)	Goals	OTHER CUPS / PLAY-OFFS Starts	(+Sub)	Goals	TOTALS Starts	(+Sub)	Goals
2014/15	35	(+1)	1	11	(+0)	0	2	(+0)	0	48	(+1)	1
2015/16	38	(+0)	3	6	(+0)	2	0	(+0)	0	44	(+0)	5
2016/17	38	(+0)	5	4	(+0)	3	4	(+0)	0	46	(+0)	8
2018/19	3	(+0)	0	0	(+0)	0	0	(+0)	0	3	(+0)	0
Totals	114	(+1)	9	21	(+0)	5	6	(+0)	0	141	(+1)	14

A tall central defender from Little Lever, Luke was a schoolboy at Oldham Athletic before leading Wigan Athletic's youth team. He made his League One debut on loan to Leyton Orient in August 2008, before making the move permanent in January 2009. He switched to League Two side Rotherham United in July 2010, but was released a year later to join Conference North side Harrogate Town. After a spell at FC Halifax Town, he joined Hyde for their first season in the Conference, and missed just one game as they avoided relegation. They did go down in 2013/14, but Luke was loaned to Chester for the season's closing stages. He joined FC United in August 2014, and helped the Reds to their first win of the season on his debut. From that point he was virtually ever-present until the spring, missing just once when he dropped to the bench with a slight injury. His return was the start of a long successful run that saw the team reach the FA Trophy quarter-final and the top of the table. He suffered a foot injury against Ilkeston in March, but was back for the run-in as the Northern Premier League title was secured. He carried his form into 2015/16 as he missed just four games through suspension. He also provided a threat at the other end of the pitch, contributing five goals which included earning the first point of the season at home to Tamworth, and the late consolation in the FA Cup against Chesterfield. He missed only four matches again in 2016/17 and scored eight goals, including an FA Cup hat-trick at Ossett Town and vital winners against Alfreton Town and Kidderminster Harriers. He ended the term with a Manchester Premier Cup winner's medal, before signing for Stalybridge Celtic in the summer. He returned to the Reds a year later, but left again after just three further outings to join Ashton United in September. He was on the winning side against FC in January 2019, although both clubs were relegated at the end of the season, after which he switched to Radcliffe.

194 Nick CULKIN

Born: 06/07/1978, York
Debut: No.1 v Radcliffe Borough (A, MPC:1), 17/10/2014

Goalkeeper

Season	LEAGUE Starts	(+Sub)	Goals	FA NATIONAL CUPS Starts	(+Sub)	Goals	OTHER CUPS / PLAY-OFFS Starts	(+Sub)	Goals	TOTALS Starts	(+Sub)	Goals
2013/14	0	(+0)	0	0	(+0)	0	0	(+0)	0	0	(+0)	0
2014/15	1	(+0)	0	0	(+0)	0	1	(+0)	0	2	(+0)	0
2015/16	0	(+0)	0	0	(+0)	0	1	(+0)	0	1	(+0)	0
Totals	1	(+0)	0	0	(+0)	0	2	(+0)	0	3	(+0)	0

Nick was a YTS trainee at hometown club York City when he was signed by Manchester United for £100,000 in September 1995. He progressed through the youth and reserve teams and was first named as a substitute for the first team in December 1997. He sat on the bench in a total of 18 senior games, which included European Cup ties with Valencia and Real Madrid, the 1999 European Super Cup, and two Charity Shields, but was only called into action on one occasion. He made it onto the pitch in the last minute of a victory at Arsenal in August 1999 as a replacement for the injured Raimond van der Gouw, and only had time to take the resulting free-kick before the full-time whistle went. In all likelihood he holds the record for the shortest United senior career, of which he is extremely proud! He went on to have loan spells at Hull City, Bristol Rovers and Livingston before leaving Old Trafford to join Queens Park Rangers in July 2002. He began the season in the team, but a couple of freak training ground injuries left him sidelined. He recovered to regain the shirt for a three-month run before suffering major cartilage damage to his knee, which after several comeback attempts eventually led to his retirement from professional football in 2005. He began playing at non-league level in 2010 when he joined Radcliffe Borough, and in an enjoyable spell there he was named in the Northern Premier League Division One North Team of the Year and also faced FC United in an FA Cup tie. After a stint with Prescot Cables he linked up with the Reds in March 2014 to provide cover for the final push towards promotion, and was named on the bench for the crunch clash with Chorley in April. In October of the following season he made his debut for the club in a cup-tie at former side Radcliffe, and in doing so emulated Phil Marsh to be only **the second player to have represented both Uniteds in a competitive fixture**. An immensely popular character with team-mates, staff and fans, Nick continued to provide back-up to Dave Carnell whilst also helping Paul Chapman in coaching the club's goalkeepers. He ended the season by playing in Broadhurst Park's opening matches, keeping goal for the Old Boys XI and then entering the fray in the closing stages against Benfica. He featured just once in 2015/16, against Glossop North End in the Manchester Premier Cup, when his penalty save helped the Reds to win a shoot-out decider for the first time in the club's history. Thereafter reverting to just coaching, Nick left the club when Karl Marginson's reign in charge ended in October 2017, and he later returned to coach at Radcliffe.

195 Michael BREWSTER

Born: 17/01/1996, Manchester **Midfielder**
Debut: No.10 v Radcliffe Borough (A, MPC:1), 17/10/2014 (scored)

Season	LEAGUE Starts	(+Sub)	Goals	FA NATIONAL CUPS Starts	(+Sub)	Goals	OTHER CUPS / PLAY-OFFS Starts	(+Sub)	Goals	TOTALS Starts	(+Sub)	Goals
2014/15	0	(+1)	0	0	(+0)	0	1	(+0)	1	1	(+1)	1
Totals	0	(+1)	0	0	(+0)	0	1	(+0)	1	1	(+1)	1

Michael spent time as a schoolboy in the academies at both Manchester City and Manchester United, before joining Oldham Athletic on a YTS scholarship. The Blackley lad became a mainstay in the youth team before fracturing a fibula in November 2013, and he was released at the end of that term. Along with team-mate John Pritchard, he joined FC United in July 2014, and his impressive displays in the reserve team earned him a senior call-up for the Manchester Premier Cup tie at Radcliffe Borough in October. He marked the occasion by opening the scoring in the first half, but later in the evening he hit the bar in the penalty shoot-out as the Reds were eliminated. A few days later he emerged from the bench to help United claim a late win over Nantwich Town, and was an unused substitute for the next game against Skelmersdale United. His progress was noted by Scottish Premier League side St Mirren, who signed him on a professional contract to play for their Development League side in January 2015. After gaining valuable experience in Scotland, he returned south in the summer to join Conference club Southport, and later spent time on loan at Colwyn Bay, Witton Albion and Skelmersdale. In the summer of 2016 he linked up with Pritchard again when they both signed for Northwich Victoria, although by the end of the year he had switched to ambitious Barnsley outfit Shaw Lane AFC. He moved on again in February 2017 to join Marine, and was in their team that knocked FC United out of the FA Trophy in November 2017. He joined Droylsden the following summer, where he was appointed as captain, before facing FC with both Atherton Collieries and Ashton United. He helped the latter club to lift their 16th Manchester Premier Cup at Broadhurst Park in 2022. A qualified coach, Michael's career took him to work at the Manchester United Foundation.

196 Matthew KAY

Born: 02/11/1987, Manchester **Midfielder**
Debut: Sub v Matlock Town (A, NPLP), 21/10/2014

Season	LEAGUE Starts	(+Sub)	Goals	FA NATIONAL CUPS Starts	(+Sub)	Goals	OTHER CUPS / PLAY-OFFS Starts	(+Sub)	Goals	TOTALS Starts	(+Sub)	Goals
2014/15	2	(+8)	1	1	(+1)	0	1	(+0)	0	4	(+9)	1
Totals	2	(+8)	1	1	(+1)	0	1	(+0)	0	4	(+9)	1

An attacking midfielder with an exceptional goalscoring record, Matty was a YTS trainee with Rochdale before beginning his non-league journey with Ashton United. The Oldham resident then had spells with Woodley Sports, Ramsbottom United and Salford City before a productive two years at Mossley, where he won Supporters' Player of the Year and twice finished top scorer. He moved on to Curzon Ashton in 2011, where he maintained a decent scoring return despite some injury lay-offs. A loan stint at West Didsbury & Chorlton helped his return to fitness, before he made a switch to FC United in October 2014. He made his bow as a late substitute at Matlock Town, before entering the fray during the first half for his home debut against Rushall Olympic, when he was credited with the winning goal in a tight encounter. Despite Matty impressing with his movement and late runs into the box, niggling injuries and fierce competition for places meant he was unable to force his way into the starting line-up. He linked up with Cheadle Town on a loan arrangement in March 2015, before signing for Trafford in the summer. Later in the year he returned to West Didsbury & Chorlton, where he became a permanent fixture in the side. He reminded FC of his ability when he hit a long-range equaliser in the Manchester Premier Cup Semi-Final at Broadhurst Park in February 2017. His performances earned a move back to Mossley in the summer of 2018, but he returned to 'West' and became assistant manager and briefly interim manager before the end of the year.

197 Shelton PAYNE

Born: 04/02/1989, Cardiff **Winger/Forward**
Debut: No.9 v Nantwich Town (H, NPLP), 18/01/2015

Season	LEAGUE Starts	(+Sub)	Goals	FA NATIONAL CUPS Starts	(+Sub)	Goals	OTHER CUPS / PLAY-OFFS Starts	(+Sub)	Goals	TOTALS Starts	(+Sub)	Goals
2014/15	13	(+3)	5	0	(+0)	0	0	(+0)	0	13	(+3)	5
Totals	13	(+3)	5	0	(+0)	0	0	(+0)	0	13	(+3)	5

A very fast and skilful attacker, Shelton trialled with Cardiff City and Crystal Palace before embarking on a nomadic non-league adventure in his native Wales with Dinas Powys and Port Talbot Town. He ventured north for spells with Colwyn Bay, Chorley, Hyde and Barrow, but undoubtedly his happiest and most productive period was with Trafford, where he led the scoring charts and picked up numerous awards. His highlight there was scoring five times against Droylsden in the FA Cup, and he also scored twice in four matches against FC United. Despite Trafford struggling during 2014/15, he was still amongst the league's top scorers, and when manager Garry Vaughan resigned in January 2015 Shelton followed him to sign for FC. He made his debut against Nantwich Town, when he created the last-minute winner, and his style brought an added dimension to the team's attacking options. He scored five goals as the Reds stormed up the table to clinch the Northern Premier League title, and finished the season by playing in the opening matches at Broadhurst Park. However, he decided to move on again during the summer, and later had short spells with Salford City, Ramsbottom United, Curzon Ashton, Hednesford Town, Chorley, 1874 Northwich, Ashton United, Radcliffe, Prestwich Heys and New Mills. He also had stints back in Wales with Connah's Quay Nomads and Rhyl.

198 Rory FALLON

Born: 03/10/1989, Stockport
Debut: Sub v Barwell (H, NPLP), 10/02/2015

Midfielder

Season	LEAGUE			FA NATIONAL CUPS			OTHER CUPS / PLAY-OFFS			TOTALS		
	Starts	(+Sub)	Goals	Starts	(+Sub)	Goals	Starts	(+Sub)	Goals	Starts	(+Sub)	Goals
2014/15	7	(+13)	2	0	(+0)	0	0	(+0)	0	7	(+13)	2
2015/16	18	(+1)	3	6	(+0)	1	0	(+1)	0	24	(+2)	4
Totals	25	(+14)	5	6	(+0)	1	0	(+1)	0	31	(+15)	6

Rory comes from a family with a strong footballing pedigree, as he is the son of former Droylsden player-manager Mark Fallon, and nephew of Martin O'Neill, who won the European Cup with Nottingham Forest, played in the World Cup with Northern Ireland, and managed several teams including Leicester City, Celtic, Aston Villa and Republic of Ireland. Rory began in non-league football with Loughborough University in the Midland Alliance whilst studying for a degree, which was coupled with a short spell at Hyde. He first played for FC United in a pre-season friendly at Chadderton in July 2012, before signing for Witton Albion and facing the Reds soon after. He moved to Trafford in March 2013, and helped them to promotion from the Northern Premier League Division One North at the end of that season. He again impressed when facing FC in the higher division, and when manager Garry Vaughan resigned in January 2015, Rory followed him and team-mate Shelton Payne to sign for United. He featured in every remaining match, initially from the bench before his exciting attacking midfield displays earned him a starting berth for some of the important encounters in the run-in. After claiming his first goal for the club at Whitby Town, he was particularly impressive when scoring again at Ramsbottom United and in the vital games at home to Stamford and Stourbridge that sealed the Northern Premier League title. He began 2015/16 as he finished the previous term, and was arguably the team's standout performer in the first half of the season. He **scored the first competitive goal at Broadhurst Park** against Stockport County, and further haunted his hometown club at Edgeley Park in December when opening the scoring and providing the cross for Tom Greaves to head the winner. In between he also stroked home the dramatic late equaliser at home to Curzon Ashton, and hit one of the goals of the season to wrap up the FA Cup win over Witton Albion. Unfortunately he picked up a knee injury just before Christmas that required surgery and brought a premature end to his season. After sustaining another injury in training, he announced he was leaving the club in October 2016 ahead of a cruciate reconstruction operation. He returned to the game in July 2017 with Curzon Ashton, but regained his fitness in autumn spells at Runcorn Linnets and Mossley. He moved to North West Counties side 1874 Northwich in January 2018, and helped them to reach the FA Vase semi-final. He joined Wythenshawe Amateurs the following term, then signed for former FC colleague Liam Brownhill at Cheadle Town in January 2020. He returned to the Northern Premier League Division One with Glossop North End in 2021.

Rory Fallon's shot hits the back of the Stockport County as he scores the first competitive goal at Broadhurst Park

199 Nia BAYUNU

Born: 22/02/1990, London
Debut: Sub v Halesowen Town (A, NPLP), 15/03/2015

Centre-back

Season	LEAGUE			FA NATIONAL CUPS			OTHER CUPS / PLAY-OFFS			TOTALS		
	Starts	(+Sub)	Goals	Starts	(+Sub)	Goals	Starts	(+Sub)	Goals	Starts	(+Sub)	Goals
2014/15	2	(+1)	0	0	(+0)	0	0	(+0)	0	2	(+1)	0
2015/16	14	(+0)	1	2	(+0)	0	0	(+0)	0	16	(+0)	1
Totals	16	(+1)	1	2	(+0)	0	0	(+0)	0	18	(+1)	1

Nia first linked up with FC United in 2007/08 when he played for the club's youth team and was coached by Karl Marginson at the Manchester College. The Moss Side lad went on to play first-team football the following season for Woodley Sports and Leigh Genesis, for whom he appeared against the Reds as a substitute in January 2009. Later that year he began a long association with Trafford, establishing himself as a commanding central defender and going on to become the third-highest appearance maker in the club's history. He was pivotal in their promotion from the Northern Premier League Division One North in 2013, when he was voted Supporters Player of the Year. He was also handed the captaincy, and went on to impress in a further four encounters with FC before making a return to the Reds in February 2015. He made his long-awaited debut for the club as a substitute in the vital win at Halesowen Town in March, but his role in the squad was mainly as defensive cover as the team clinched the Northern Premier League title. He ended the campaign by featuring against Benfica in Broadhurst Park's official opening match in May, before starting the first 13 matches in the back line the following term. After some strong performances, he was unable to reclaim a regular place after a suspension, and once again left the club in November 2015 to sign for Ramsbottom United. He moved to North West Counties side West Didsbury & Chorlton in 2016, and was selected to face FC in the Manchester Premier Cup semi-final in February 2017. Unfortunately he was forced to sit out the game after succumbing to an injury during the warm-up. He later featured for Wythenshawe Town.

200 Sean COOKE

Born: 03/09/1992, Crewe
Debut: Sub v Gloucester City (A, NLN), 08/08/2015

Midfielder

Season	LEAGUE			FA NATIONAL CUPS			OTHER CUPS / PLAY-OFFS			TOTALS		
	Starts	(+Sub)	Goals	Starts	(+Sub)	Goals	Starts	(+Sub)	Goals	Starts	(+Sub)	Goals
2015/16	8	(+3)	1	0	(+2)	0	1	(+0)	0	9	(+5)	1
Totals	8	(+3)	1	0	(+2)	0	1	(+0)	0	9	(+5)	1

Sean began his career on a youth scholarship with Crewe Alexandra, but was released at the age of 18 and linked up with local side Nantwich Town, where his father Dave had been a long-serving player and manager. The creative attacking midfielder soon became a thorn in the side of FC United, scoring three times in four meetings, and his displays earned a place in the NPL Premier Division Team of the Year and a move to ambitious AFC Fylde. He moved up to the Conference North to join Telford United in May 2013, but spent loan spells back at former clubs Fylde and Nantwich during his time there. He linked up with the Reds in July 2015, and began the club's first Conference North season on the bench before earning a starting spot that coincided with the team climbing the table. He played his part in a run of 13 points gained from five matches, his highlight being the impudent chip that sealed the 3-0 win at Hednesford Town. However, he lost his place as the team lost form, and his missed penalty in the Manchester Premier Cup shoot-out win over Glossop North End was his last kick in a red shirt. He returned to Nantwich in November to aid their promotion push, and played a crucial role as they reached the FA Trophy semi-final in 2016. He remained a consistent goal provider as his team continued to challenge for promotion from the Northern Premier League, and went on to score against FC at Broadhurst Park in September 2020.

201 Cameron MURRAY

Born: 21/03/1995, Halifax
Debut: Sub v Gloucester City (A, NLN), 08/08/2015

Winger

Season	LEAGUE			FA NATIONAL CUPS			OTHER CUPS / PLAY-OFFS			TOTALS		
	Starts	(+Sub)	Goals	Starts	(+Sub)	Goals	Starts	(+Sub)	Goals	Starts	(+Sub)	Goals
2015/16	0	(+4)	0	0	(+1)	0	2	(+0)	1	2	(+5)	1
Totals	0	(+4)	0	0	(+1)	0	2	(+0)	1	2	(+5)	1

Cameron was a schoolboy at Leeds United and Bradford City before moving to Spain on a football scholarship in 2011. An injury ended his time there, and after playing for FC United during pre-season in 2012, he signed as a young professional at York City. The small and tricky wideman made his senior debut as a substitute against Rotherham United in the Football League Trophy in October 2013. After a loan spell at Frickley Athletic, he joined non-league permanently with Scarborough Athletic in February 2015. He linked up again with FC that summer, and was a regular on the bench in the opening two months of the season. He was introduced as a substitute four times in the first eight games, but thereafter his appearances were limited to cup ties. He was unlucky not to score in the FA Cup against Witton Albion when his effort ricocheted off the upright, before he started both Manchester Premier Cup ties. He scored a wonderful goal to equalise in the defeat to Stalybridge Celtic, but that was his last involvement in a red shirt as he dropped out of contention. His performance had impressed the opponents, however, and he signed for Stalybridge in January 2016. In the early weeks of the following season he joined Brighouse Town, before returning to Scarborough and helping them to the Northern Premier League Division One North play-offs. After spells at Tadcaster Albion and Farsley Celtic, he moved south to join Dorchester Town in 2018. He switched to Weymouth in January 2019, and helped them to two promotions from the Southern League through to the National League in 2020.

203 Adam THURSTON

Born: 13/10/1994, Manchester
Debut: Sub v Brackley Town (H, NLN), 22/08/2015

Full-back/Midfielder

Season	LEAGUE			FA NATIONAL CUPS			OTHER CUPS / PLAY-OFFS			TOTALS		
	Starts	(+Sub)	Goals	Starts	(+Sub)	Goals	Starts	(+Sub)	Goals	Starts	(+Sub)	Goals
2015/16	10	(+9)	0	3	(+0)	0	2	(+0)	0	15	(+9)	0
Totals	10	(+9)	0	3	(+0)	0	2	(+0)	0	15	(+9)	0

After being a schoolboy in the Manchester United academy, Adam joined Preston North End on a scholarship. The Heaton Mersey lad was released in 2013, and first played for FC United in pre-season friendly matches that summer. He eventually signed for Conference club Hyde, where he impressed despite suffering successive relegations. He finally joined the Reds in July 2015, and helped the team to their first win at Broadhurst Park on his debut against Brackley Town in August. He became a regular on the bench during the opening months of the season, with occasional starts mainly at right-back, including an impressive performance in the Manchester Premier Cup tie with Glossop North End. He was rewarded with a surprise call-up to play in midfield in the FA Cup first round against Chesterfield, which was his first of nine consecutive starts. The next four were at right-back, before he switched to the left in an emergency, during which he contributed to an improved sequence of results that earned four points from table-toppers Nuneaton Town and a great win at Stockport County. Increased competition for places saw Adam mainly on the bench in the New Year, with his most memorable contribution being a crunching tackle and precise through ball to set up Craig Linfield's dramatic injury-time winner over North Ferriby United. He spent the summer of 2016 in the USA with USL Premier Development League club Alberquerque Sol, before returning to Hyde in September. He moved abroad again in January 2017 to play for South Adelaide Panthers, and helped them to win promotion to the South Australia State League. He went on to play in New Zealand with Hawke's Bay United, Canterbury United and Eastern Suburbs, with a brief return to South Adelaide and a stint with FC's Northern Premier League rivals South Shields in between.

202 Sam MADELEY

Born: 04/06/1990, Manchester
Debut: Sub v Stockport County (H, NLN), 11/08/2015

Winger/Forward

	LEAGUE			FA NATIONAL CUPS			OTHER CUPS / PLAY-OFFS			TOTALS		
Season	Starts	(+Sub)	Goals	Starts	(+Sub)	Goals	Starts	(+Sub)	Goals	Starts	(+Sub)	Goals
2015/16	18	(+10)	9	3	(+2)	2	0	(+1)	0	21	(+13)	11
2016/17	0	(+1)	0	0	(+0)	0	0	(+0)	0	0	(+1)	0
Totals	18	(+11)	9	3	(+2)	2	0	(+1)	0	21	(+14)	1

A tremendously skilful forward or winger, Sam scored prolifically in the youth team at local club Altrincham before venturing to the USA on a scholarship at Trevecca Nazarene University in Nashville, Tennessee. He returned to England and brought his talents to the non-league circuit with Woodley Sports, Nantwich Town, Hyde and Ashton United, where his knack for spectacular strikes soon made him a terrace favourite. He moved to Mossley in 2012, where he was leading scorer with 20 goals, followed by a short spell at Glossop North End. He next linked up with Droylsden, for whom he scored against FC United in March 2014, before spending the following season helping ambitious Salford City to the Northern Premier League Division One North title.

Sam joined the Reds in August 2015, and made his debut in Broadhurst Park's first competitive match against Stockport County. He was soon amongst the goals, with his first in the team's first National League North win against Brackley Town. The following week he struck the goal of the season with an astonishing volley against Curzon Ashton, and two minutes later his amazing piece of skill and cross picked out Rory Fallon to bury the dramatic equaliser. A double strike in the next game at Lowestoft Town included a tremendous overhead kick, and later that month he scored FC's first FA Cup goal in Moston against Witton Albion. Another screamer sealed the replay win at Buxton in the same competition, which was a welcome relief during a run of league defeats. A well taken equaliser against Gainsborough Trinity in November was ultimately in vain, but an upturn in results included a great win over league leaders Nuneaton Town in which Sam opened the scoring. He spent a short spell on the sidelines with injury over the festive period, but scored again on his return to the starting line-up against Lowestoft Town as the team recorded their biggest win of the season. The following week he bagged the winner in the dramatic comeback win over Harrogate Town as the Reds came from three goals down to claim the points. His next game was even more eventful as he took over in goal at AFC Telford United when Dave Carnell was injured. After making a couple of good saves he was then controversially sent off, with the referee inflicting the double punishment of also awarding a penalty. After serving the inevitable suspension, he was unfortunately sidelined with injury during March and April, only making a return to action in the last game of the season against Solihull Moors. He made just one appearance the following term before moving up a division with Macclesfield Town, who sent him on subsequent loan spells to Stalybridge Celtic, Nantwich and Warrington Town. He played against FC for Curzon Ashton in 2017/18, before later featuring for Ramsbottom United, Droylsden, Glossop and Winsford United.

204 Lewis KING

Born: 08/05/1993, Derby
Debut: No.1 v Witton Albion (H, FAC:Q2), 26/09/2015

Goalkeeper

	LEAGUE			FA NATIONAL CUPS			OTHER CUPS / PLAY-OFFS			TOTALS		
Season	Starts	(+Sub)	Goals	Starts	(+Sub)	Goals	Starts	(+Sub)	Goals	Starts	(+Sub)	Goals
2015/16	1	(+0)	0	1	(+0)	0	0	(+0)	0	2	(+0)	0
2021/22	2	(+0)	0	0	(+0)	0	0	(+0)	0	2	(+0)	0
Totals	3	(+0)	0	1	(+0)	0	0	(+0)	0	4	(+0)	0

Lewis began his career as a scholar at hometown club Derby County before turning professional at Sunderland. He first played non-league football on loan at Conference club Stockport County, which was made permanent in the summer of 2012. The following year he had a spell with Eastwood Town before joining Boston United, and then spent 2014/15 at Stalybridge Celtic. He initially featured for FC United in two pre-season friendly matches in July 2015, before linking up with Matlock Town. He returned to the Reds in September to cover for Dave Carnell's injury and suspension, and played in the FA Cup victory over Witton Albion and the league defeat to Worcester City. In November he joined Glossop North End, and he later played for Northwich Victoria before moving to Mickleover Sports in the summer of 2016. He returned to Stalybridge a year later but after just three games he went back to Mickleover in September 2017. He signed for Stafford Rangers in May 2019, and faced FC three times in the Northern Premier League, keeping a clean sheet in one game and saving a Paul Ennis penalty in another. He moved to Hanley Town in 2021, but rejoined United in August that year as an emergency signing to provide cover when Dan Lavercombe was taken ill. He doubled his Reds tally with another two outings before taking a break from the game in October in order to focus on his business. Lewis became a local hero in Derby in May 2018 when he helped to rescue a neighbour from a house fire.

205 Sam SHERIDAN

Born: 30/11/1989, Manchester
Debut: No.4 v North Ferriby United (A, NLN), 17/10/2015

Midfielder

Season	LEAGUE			FA NATIONAL CUPS			OTHER CUPS / PLAY-OFFS			TOTALS		
	Starts	(+Sub)	Goals	Starts	(+Sub)	Goals	Starts	(+Sub)	Goals	Starts	(+Sub)	Goals
2015/16	22	(+2)	2	3	(+0)	0	0	(+0)	0	25	(+2)	2
2016/17	18	(+16)	1	3	(+1)	1	1	(+1)	0	22	(+18)	2
Totals	40	(+18)	3	6	(+1)	1	1	(+1)	0	47	(+20)	4

Sam excelled as a cultured midfielder in a similar mould to his uncles: Darren, who played in the Premier League for Barnsley, and John, who played in the World Cup for Ireland. Sam himself earned caps for the Ireland under-19 team whilst he was a young professional in the reserves at Bolton Wanderers. After a loan period at his local club Altrincham, he returned to the Conference with Stockport County in 2011, which was also interrupted with a short temporary spell at Southport. In 2013 he joined Barrow, helping them to the Conference North title in 2015 before linking up with Chorley that summer. However, he was unable to gain a regular spot and moved to FC United in October. He settled into the side straight away, and apart from a couple of spells out with illness and injury, was a regular in the starting line-up. His vision and passing brought an added dimension to the team's options, and he was one of the standout performers for the remainder of the term. He was particularly dominant in tight encounters against Alfreton Town, Chorley, Curzon Ashton and Gainsborough Trinity as the Reds picked up hard-earned points. He bagged two memorable goals, the first in the dramatic comeback win over Harrogate Town, and also hit a spectacular volley against Boston United. He made a good start to 2016/17, starting 13 of the first 15 matches and scoring a great goal at Ossett Town in the FA Cup. After a short spell out injured, he spent much of the remainder of the campaign as a substitute, and on one of those occasions he finished the match in goal against Chorley when Adriano Basso was sent off. He started the final three league games, and opened the scoring in the win at Nuneaton Town, before coming off the bench in the Manchester Premier Cup Final. In May 2017 he returned to Altrincham, but after a brief loan at Stalybridge Celtic he went on to help Ashton United to reach the National League North via the play-offs. He starred as Ashton won in Moston in August 2018, and also performed superbly in defensive roles when the clubs met again after their relegations back to the Northern Premier League. He was part of the Ashton team that won the Manchester Premier Cup at Broadhurst Park in April 2022.

206 Harry WINTER

Born: 10/06/1989, Manchester
Debut: Sub v Gainsborough Trinity (H, NLN), 14/11/2015

Midfielder

Season	LEAGUE			FA NATIONAL CUPS			OTHER CUPS / PLAY-OFFS			TOTALS		
	Starts	(+Sub)	Goals	Starts	(+Sub)	Goals	Starts	(+Sub)	Goals	Starts	(+Sub)	Goals
2015/16	22	(+4)	2	1	(+0)	0	0	(+0)	0	23	(+4)	2
2016/17	24	(+3)	3	4	(+0)	0	2	(+0)	0	30	(+3)	4
2018/19	17	(+3)	1	2	(+0)	0	0	(+0)	0	19	(+3)	1
Totals	63	(+10)	6	7	(+0)	1	2	(+0)	0	72	(+10)	7

A tall, energetic central midfielder from Stretford, Harry first played senior non-league football for his local club Trafford, where he captained the side at the age of just 19. His impressive displays earned a move up the divisions to Conference North club Northwich Victoria in August 2009, before a switch to ambitious FC Halifax Town the following spring. His time there was disrupted by a serious knee injury that sidelined him for almost a year, and upon his recovery he had brief stints at Hyde and Matlock Town before joining AFC Fylde in February 2012. He helped the Lancashire club to two promotions, from the Northern Premier League Division One North through to the Conference North, and faced FC United in four classic encounters, before switching to rivals Chorley in the summer of 2014. He again lined up against the Reds in the FA Trophy games in January 2015, and narrowly missed out on another promotion with his new club at the end of that season. After a short loan at Ashton United in the autumn of 2015, he made the move to Broadhurst Park in November when the Reds were searching for midfield reinforcements. His back post header put United two goals ahead in his first start at league leaders Nuneaton Town, before he helped the team to victory over the same opponents as well as Stockport County in December. Along with fellow new boys Sam Sheridan and Scott Kay, he added a solidity to the midfield as the team gradually gelled to provide the platform for some good runs of results that eventually secured their National League North status for another season. Harry continued to be a towering presence in the engine room in 2016/17, particularly in the autumn and winter months. His unstoppable injury-time strike won the points in a dramatic finish at Gainsborough Trinity, and he added further goals against Fylde (twice) and Harrogate Town in the FA Cup. He also demonstrated his adaptability by playing the second half at home to Altrincham as an emergency centre-back. He would have been amongst the front-runners for the player of the season award, but he left to join Stockport in March, just two weeks after captaining the Reds against them at Edgeley Park. He faced FC twice in the FA Cup in 2017/18 before being released in May 2018 and returning to Broadhurst Park. He was appointed as United's skipper as the campaign began, and scored on his first home appearance to put the Reds in front against Ashton United. However he was restricted by injury during the opening month, and then received a red card in the FA Cup tie with Witton Albion in October. The following month he returned to Trafford on loan in order to regain match fitness, before returning to FC over the festive period. He played the majority of fixtures until a second dismissal of the season at Curzon Ashton brought a four-match ban, and only returned for the final two games as the team's relegation from the National League North was confirmed. He moved on to Radcliffe in the summer of 2019, and captained them three times against FC during the following season.

207 George THOMSON

Born: 19/05/1992, Sheffield   Midfielder/Forward
Debut: No.10 v Nuneaton Town (A, NLN), 21/11/2015

Season	LEAGUE			FA NATIONAL CUPS			OTHER CUPS / PLAY-OFFS			TOTALS		
	Starts	(+Sub)	Goals	Starts	(+Sub)	Goals	Starts	(+Sub)	Goals	Starts	(+Sub)	Goals
2015/16	26	(+0)	11	1	(+0)	1	0	(+0)	0	27	(+0)	12
2016/17	34	(+4)	15	4	(+0)	2	3	(+0)	3	41	(+4)	20
Totals	60	(+4)	26	5	(+0)	3	3	(+0)	3	68	(+4)	32

George is an attacking midfielder who started his career on a scholarship with Nottingham Forest. After being released he joined the Glenn Hoddle Academy in Spain, where as part of his development he gained senior league experience with Jerez Industrial. He moved back to England in 2011, beginning his non-league journey with spells at Hinckley United and Histon while studying at Loughborough University. His displays during a successful spell with King's Lynn Town, where he faced FC United three times and was leading scorer, earned a contract with Conference club Chester in January 2015. Despite many lively displays, he was on the fringes in 2015/16 as the struggling team became more defensive, and he jumped at the chance to join FC on loan in November. Offering an added dimension to the attack, his arrival was the catalyst for an improved sequence of results. He hit the bar on his debut at league leaders Nuneaton Town, but he was soon amongst the goals, with his strikes contributing to great wins over Nuneaton and Bradford Park Avenue, and earning a valuable point at Tamworth. He signed permanently in January, and later that month he began the amazing comeback against Harrogate Town as the Reds recovered from three goals down to win 4-3. He scored the decider at champions-elect Solihull Moors in March and followed that up by hitting the winner at Alfreton Town as the team began a great run to ease the relegation fears. His double strike at Corby Town in April effectively sealed FC's status in the National League North for another term, and he ended his first campaign in red as the club's top scorer and Player of the Season. He continued to be United's star man in 2016/17, when with 20 goals he was top scorer for the second year running. He held that position from the first day of the season when his double at Chorley included the team's first goal of the campaign. Most of his strikes were long-range efforts from outside the box, where he was able to take advantage of his explosive shooting power, and several of them earned points late on in games. He hit spectacular late equalisers at home to Boston United, Harrogate Town and Stalybridge Celtic, and bagged the only goal of the game against promotion chasers Kidderminster Harriers. He got the Manchester Premier Cup run started with a hat-trick at Chadderton, and finished the season with a winners medal in the competition before signing for Harrogate in May. He went on to face FC twice, finishing on the losing side at Broadhurst Park but gaining revenge with a hat-trick in United's heavy defeat in March 2018. He ended the term in the Harrogate side that won the National League North promotion play-offs, and was virtually ever-present as they reached the National League play-offs in 2019. Despite the curtailment of the 2019/20 season, the National League play-offs were contested in the summer. In the Wembley final, an early goal from George put Harrogate ahead as they beat Notts County to reach the Football League for the first time.

208 Scott KAY

Born: 18/09/1989, Ashton-under-Lyne   Midfielder/Centre-back
Debut: No.4 v Stockport County (A, NLN), 05/12/2015

Season	LEAGUE			FA NATIONAL CUPS			OTHER CUPS / PLAY-OFFS			TOTALS		
	Starts	(+Sub)	Goals	Starts	(+Sub)	Goals	Starts	(+Sub)	Goals	Starts	(+Sub)	Goals
2015/16	23	(+0)	0	0	(+0)	0	0	(+0)	0	23	(+0)	0
2016/17	39	(+0)	0	4	(+0)	0	3	(+0)	0	46	(+0)	0
2017/18	35	(+0)	2	5	(+0)	0	2	(+0)	1	42	(+0)	3
2018/19	6	(+0)	0	1	(+0)	0	0	(+0)	0	7	(+0)	0
Totals	97	(+0)	2	10	(+0)	0	5	(+0)	1	118	(+0)	3

Scott is a product of the academy at Manchester City, where he signed his first professional contract and was part of the team that won the FA Youth Cup in 2008. Able to play in midfield or defence, the Denton lad became a mainstay of the reserve side, but was released in 2011 and joined Macclesfield Town. In a season with the Cheshire club he made several appearances in the Football League, before spending the following term on the books of Huddersfield Town. He dropped into the non-league game with a loan spell at Southport in 2013, before returning to Macclesfield, who by that time were also in the Conference, for the 2013/14 season. He then spent the following term back at Southport, before linking up with Mossley in September 2015. His quality and experience stood out in the Northern Premier League Division One, and he soon moved back up the leagues when he joined FC United in December. He made his debut in the terrific win at Stockport County, and brought a calm assurance to the defensive midfield role. From thereon in Scott missed just two games, and was particularly instrumental during the upturn of results in early spring that helped secure the team's National League North status. He also demonstrated his versatility by performing extremely well at centre-back on four occasions. As he was still dual-registered, he ended the season by playing one more game for Mossley, helping them to win the Manchester Premier Cup in April. He continued to be a model of consistency again in 2016/17, being absent for just four matches and spending more time on the pitch in league games than any other player. He was his usual industrious self in the holding midfield role, before being pressed into service as a central defender between November and February. He ended the season by winning the Manchester Premier Cup again, and was appointed captain by Karl Marginson for 2017/18. He was again an automatic pick when available, and also scored his first goals for the club. The first two were both in home defeats, but the most important was a bullet header in the Manchester Premier Cup Final. He later also converted in the penalty shoot-out to ensure he lifted the trophy for the third year running. He wasn't initially part of the squad for the 2018/19 season, but made a surprise reappearance to help FC to their first win of the campaign at Altrincham in August. He left the club the following month to take a break from the game, but resurfaced at Ashton United a few weeks later. He was on the winning side against FC in January 2019, although both clubs were ultimately relegated at the end of the term, and also went on to skipper Glossop North End against the Reds in the Northern Premier League Challenge Cup at Broadhurst Park in November 2019.

209 Tom SMYTH

Born: 18/03/1991, Southport
Debut: No.5 v Stockport County (A, NLN), 05/12/2015

Centre-back

Season	LEAGUE			FA NATIONAL CUPS			OTHER CUPS / PLAY-OFFS			TOTALS		
	Starts	(+Sub)	Goals	Starts	(+Sub)	Goals	Starts	(+Sub)	Goals	Starts	(+Sub)	Goals
2015/16	8	(+0)	0	0	(+0)	0	0	(+0)	0	8	(+0)	0
Totals	8	(+0)	0	0	(+0)	0	0	(+0)	0	8	(+0)	0

A former forward, Tom was converted to centre-back as a young professional at Preston North End. He moved to Accrington Stanley for 2010/11, and played in the Football League before entering non-league with Workington, Northwich Victoria and Colwyn Bay, where he was a mainstay in the Welsh club's Conference North defence for two years. He moved to Chorley in 2014, helping them to the Conference North play-off final and facing FC United twice in the FA Trophy before injury struck. He returned to fitness with loans at Ashton United and Trafford in the early stages of 2015/16, before joining FC in December. He made his debut in the tremendous win at Stockport County, and built a great understanding with Luke Ashworth that brought much needed stability to the backline. This was interrupted by a suspension for a red card at Tamworth, and his bad luck resurfaced when he suffered a cruciate injury minutes into his return at Harrogate Town that prematurely ended his campaign. His rehabilitation continued for the whole of 2016/17, before he featured in several pre-season games for FC in 2017. Another injury scuppered his chance of a permanent return to the squad and he instead dropped into the Northern Premier League Division One North when he signed for Clitheroe in September.

210 Chris CHANTLER

Born: 16/12/1990, Stockport
Debut: No.3 v Lowestoft Town (H, NLN), 23/01/2016 (scored)

Left-back

Season	LEAGUE			FA NATIONAL CUPS			OTHER CUPS / PLAY-OFFS			TOTALS		
	Starts	(+Sub)	Goals	Starts	(+Sub)	Goals	Starts	(+Sub)	Goals	Starts	(+Sub)	Goals
2015/16	18	(+0)	1	0	(+0)	0	0	(+0)	0	18	(+0)	1
2016/17	36	(+1)	0	3	(+0)	1	3	(+0)	0	42	(+1)	1
Totals	54	(+1)	1	3	(+0)	1	3	(+0)	0	60	(+1)	2

When Chris made his debut for Manchester City on his 20th birthday as a late substitute away at Juventus in the Europa League, he became the first player to progress all the way from the club's under-8 academy team to the senior side. The Cheadle Hulme lad switched to Carlisle United in 2011, featuring regularly in the League One side, either at left-back or in midfield, before spells on the sidelines with a series of injuries. He moved further north in 2014 to join Scottish Premiership side Kilmarnock, where he established himself in the team with 29 appearances before suffering a knee injury in March 2015. He was surprisingly released at the end of the term, and after a short spell at Macclesfield Town Chris signed for FC United in January 2016. He opened the scoring on his debut against Lowestoft Town, and was named man-of-the-match as the team racked up their biggest win of the term. Thereafter he was ever-present until the end of the season, helping to steady the defence and supporting the attack down the left, most notably when setting up George Thomson's winner in the crunch clash at Alfreton Town. He was amongst the highest appearance makers in 2016/17, with his main absence being due to a red card in the last minute of the defeat at his local club Stockport County. He continued to offer a threat going forward, with memorable crosses converted by Matthew Wolfenden at home to Stockport and Tom Greaves at Boston United. He also notched his second goal for the club with a well-taken finish at Ossett Town in the FA Cup. He was in the team that won the Manchester Premier Cup in May, before moving to newly-promoted National League North rivals Spennymoor Town. He faced FC in both league meetings in 2017/18 as his new team agonisingly missed out on a promotion play-off place by virtue of goal difference, before later spells at Ossett United and Colne.

211 Tom ECKERSLEY

Born: 06/12/1991, Altrincham
Debut: Sub v AFC Telford United (A, NLN), 09/02/2016

Centre-back

Season	LEAGUE			FA NATIONAL CUPS			OTHER CUPS / PLAY-OFFS			TOTALS		
	Starts	(+Sub)	Goals	Starts	(+Sub)	Goals	Starts	(+Sub)	Goals	Starts	(+Sub)	Goals
2015/16	13	(+2)	0	0	(+0)	0	0	(+0)	0	13	(+2)	0
2016/17	17	(+0)	0	2	(+0)	0	1	(+0)	1	20	(+0)	1
Totals	30	(+2)	0	2	(+0)	0	1	(+0)	1	33	(+2)	1

Tom progressed through the academy at Bolton Wanderers, where he signed his first professional contract in 2010 and became a reserve team regular. In 2012 he moved to Accrington Stanley, playing senior games in the Football League, League Cup and League Trophy, before loan spells at Conference clubs Stockport County and Barrow. He switched permanently to non-league with Tamworth in 2013, and went on to face FC United in the colours of Rushall Olympic, AFC Fylde and Curzon Ashton. He also spent time with Witton Albion and Glossop North End, either side of a spell on the sidelines with a broken leg. He linked up with FC in January 2016, and made his debut as a half-time substitute in difficult circumstances at AFC Telford United when the Reds went through three goalkeepers. His next few outings also ended in disappointing defeats amidst a defensive injury crisis, but results improved from late February as Tom built up partnerships with Scott Kay and Luke Ashworth. The new-found solidity at the back saw the team climb the table and ease the relegation fears, and was crowned with three successive clean sheets in late-March. Tom's height was also an asset at the other end of the pitch, and he scored his first goal for the club in the Manchester Premier Cup tie at Chadderton in October 2016. However, after partnering Ashworth in all but two of the opening 22 games of 2016/17, he surprisingly took a break from football in November to spend more time with his family. He returned to the game in the summer of 2017 with Ashton United, and later lined up for Radcliffe Borough and Ramsbottom United.

212 Dylan FORTH

Born: 14/11/1996, Ashton-under-Lyne
Debut: No.1 v Alfreton Town (H, NLN), 13/02/2016

Goalkeeper

Season	LEAGUE			FA NATIONAL CUPS			OTHER CUPS / PLAY-OFFS			TOTALS		
	Starts	(+Sub)	Goals	Starts	(+Sub)	Goals	Starts	(+Sub)	Goals	Starts	(+Sub)	Goals
2015/16	6	(+0)	0	0	(+0)	0	0	(+0)	0	6	(+0)	0
Totals	**6**	**(+0)**	**0**	**0**	**(+0)**	**0**	**0**	**(+0)**	**0**	**6**	**(+0)**	**0**

A goalkeeper from Hattersley, Dylan was a schoolboy with Blackburn Rovers before two years as a scholar at Aston Villa. Released in 2015, he joined National League side Chester, before signing for FC United in January 2016. He was immediately loaned to Northern Premier League First Division outfit Witton Albion for more senior experience, before a recall in February to cover for Dave Carnell. In a period of defensive uncertainty, his first three matches ended in defeat, and although he had performed well, he dropped out once Carnell was fit. He was afforded another chance in April at Corby Town when Carnell pulled up in the warm-up, and later that month kept his first clean sheet for United in the win at Gainsborough Trinity. After featuring in FC's pre-season programme, he joined Hyde United in August 2016, before spells at Northwich Victoria, Stockport Town and Glossop North End. He kept goal for Runcorn Linnets as they won the North West Counties League and promotion to the Northern Premier League Division One West in 2018, before moving to Mossley the following year and later signing for New Mills.

213 Dale TONGE

Born: 07/05/1985, Doncaster
Debut: No.2 v AFC Fylde (H, NLN), 12/03/2016

Right-back

Season	LEAGUE			FA NATIONAL CUPS			OTHER CUPS / PLAY-OFFS			TOTALS		
	Starts	(+Sub)	Goals	Starts	(+Sub)	Goals	Starts	(+Sub)	Goals	Starts	(+Sub)	Goals
2015/16	10	(+0)	0	0	(+0)	0	0	(+0)	0	10	(+0)	0
2016/17	29	(+1)	0	4	(+0)	0	1	(+0)	0	34	(+1)	0
Totals	**39**	**(+1)**	**0**	**4**	**(+0)**	**0**	**1**	**(+0)**	**0**	**44**	**(+1)**	**0**

Adept at playing in several positions, Dale came through the ranks at Barnsley to make his Football League debut in April 2004. His initial starts came the following season in midfield, but he established himself with long runs at right-back before suffering a knee injury in 2006. Thereafter he was unable to regain a regular spot, and after a short loan spell at Gillingham he switched to Rotherham United in May 2007. He was an automatic choice for the next two terms, before a broken foot again left him sidelined for almost a year. Once fully-fit again, he was back to help the side with their bids to advance from League Two, but was on the fringes when they won promotion in 2013 and joined Torquay United on a free transfer that summer. His first year in Devon saw the Gulls drop into the National League, and he remained at that level when joining Chester in 2015. Later that year he had a short spell at Stockport County before signing for FC United in March 2016. He was ever-present for the final ten games, with his experience proving crucial as the Reds maintained their status in the National League North. A terrific victory at runaway league leaders Solihull Moors came in his second game, before wins over Alfreton Town and Chorley and a draw at Curzon Ashton saw the team record three successive clean sheets for the first time in 2015/16. He was rarely missing for much of 2016/17 either, usually at right-back although he was also used at left-back, centre-back and in midfield. He captained the side several times during the autumn, but lost his place to Jake Williams in February and started just four more games before leaving FC in May. He went on to hold senior coaching positions at Barnsley, Heart Of Midlothian, Scunthorpe United and Peterborough United.

214 Dale JOHNSON

Born: 03/05/1985, Ashton-under-Lyne
Debut: No.9 v Solihull Moors (A, NLN), 15/03/2016

Forward

Season	LEAGUE			FA NATIONAL CUPS			OTHER CUPS / PLAY-OFFS			TOTALS		
	Starts	(+Sub)	Goals	Starts	(+Sub)	Goals	Starts	(+Sub)	Goals	Starts	(+Sub)	Goals
2015/16	8	(+0)	1	0	(+0)	0	0	(+0)	0	8	(+0)	1
2016/17	6	(+5)	2	2	(+0)	1	0	(+0)	0	8	(+5)	3
Totals	**14**	**(+5)**	**3**	**2**	**(+0)**	**1**	**0**	**(+0)**	**0**	**16**	**(+5)**	**4**

A tall and mobile centre-forward, Dale began at Woodley Sports before joining Hyde United in 2004, making over 200 appearances. His prolific form earned a loan to Conference side Droylsden in 2008, and he stayed at that level with a switch to Altrincham that summer. He soon became a regular starter until a ruptured cruciate ligament in September 2009 sidelined him for the remainder of the season. He rejoined Hyde in 2010 and was back amongst the goals before further returns to both Altrincham and Droylsden. He aided Halifax Town's promotion to the Conference in 2013, and after a loan at Barrow moved to Ashton United in November 2013. He hit a late winner against FC a few weeks later, and also broke Reds hearts with a dramatic injury-time equaliser in the promotion play-off semi-final in April. He began 2014/15 at Salford City, but returned to Ashton in November, and helped them to the play-offs again. He endured an injury-hit 2015/16, and was still not 100% fit when he signed for FC United in March. His debut was the terrific win at champions-elect Solihull Moors, and he added an extra dimension to the team's attack as they began a great run of results. His personal highlight was a classy finish for his first goal that sealed the fantastic win over Chorley. He marked his first appearance of 2016/17 by deflecting Nathan Lowe's volley home to seal the superb win over Stockport County, and opened the scoring in the next home game against Worcester City. He struck in the FA Cup against Harrogate Town soon after a man-of-the-match performance against Curzon Ashton, but was sent off in injury time at AFC Telford United in October. This was his last action for United as work commitments restricted his availability once his suspension was served. He joined Glossop North End in February, and was soon back amongst the goals in a team containing several other former FC stars.

215 Jake WILLIAMS

Born: 03/10/1994, Leicester
Debut: Sub v Chorley (A, NLN), 06/08/2016

Right-back

Season	LEAGUE Starts	(+Sub)	Goals	FA NATIONAL CUPS Starts	(+Sub)	Goals	OTHER CUPS / PLAY-OFFS Starts	(+Sub)	Goals	TOTALS Starts	(+Sub)	Goals
2016/17	18	(+2)	0	2	(+0)	0	3	(+0)	1	23	(+2)	1
Totals	18	(+2)	0	2	(+0)	0	3	(+0)	1	23	(+2)	1

The son of former Stockport County, Coventry City and Plymouth Argyle defender Paul Williams, pacy right-back Jake was also adept at providing an attacking threat further forward. His first taste of senior football was in the North West Counties League as a teenager at Glossop North End, before dropping into the Cheshire League with Wythenshawe Town. He scored in their Manchester FA Amateur Cup triumph at Boundary Park in 2015, at the end of a campaign in which the club won all of their 39 matches. He had a trial that summer with League One club Fleetwood Town, before joining Ashton United. During the next few months he also linked up with Buxton, Mossley and Boston United, before settling at New Mills. He joined FC United in July 2016, and was a regular in the matchday squad when the season began. His initial patience was rewarded with a run of nine consecutive starts from the end of September, before he spent most of the winter back on the bench. He reclaimed the no.2 shirt in February, and his form earned a call-up to a National League North representative side to play the British Army in March. Unfortunately he had to drop out with an injury that also kept him out of FC's next four games – the only matches in the entire campaign that his name was missing from the teamsheet. He recovered for the run-in, and ended the season in spectacular fashion with his first goal for the club. Although it was probably a mis-hit cross that deceived the goalkeeper, it pleased all at FC as it was the only goal of the game to win the Manchester Premier Cup. After featuring in most of the pre-season outings in 2017, he signed for Buxton in August on a dual-registration basis before switching to Radcliffe Borough.

216 Jason GILCHRIST

Born: 17/12/1994, St. Helens
Debut: Sub v Chorley (A, NLN), 06/08/2016

Forward

Season	LEAGUE Starts	(+Sub)	Goals	FA NATIONAL CUPS Starts	(+Sub)	Goals	OTHER CUPS / PLAY-OFFS Starts	(+Sub)	Goals	TOTALS Starts	(+Sub)	Goals
2016/17	21	(+15)	10	2	(+1)	1	2	(+2)	3	25	(+18)	14
2017/18	12	(+1)	11	4	(+1)	2	1	(+0)	2	17	(+2)	15
Totals	33	(+16)	21	6	(+2)	3	3	(+2)	5	42	(+20)	29

Jason spent ten years as a schoolboy in the Manchester City academy, before joining Burnley on a scholarship upon leaving school in 2011. He was top scorer in the under-18 team for the next two seasons, the highlight of which was his sensational hat-trick at Old Trafford that knocked his favourite club Manchester United out of the FA Youth Cup in December 2012. His first senior experience was on loan with Conference North side Droylsden in March 2013, after which he signed his first professional contract at Turf Moor. He continued to score regularly in the Development Squad, and was rewarded with a three-month loan spell at Accrington Stanley in February 2015, during which he made his Football League debut. He had a further loan stint at National League outfit Chester in January 2016, before being released by Burnley that summer. He linked up with FC United in July, and announced his arrival with a hat-trick in a friendly at Mossley, which earned him a place on the bench when the season began. He marked only his second start with his first goal for the club, an opportunistic inch-perfect chip from over 30 yards out at home to Darlington 1883, and then bagged the winner the week after at Boston United. After a patient wait for a regular place, he took his chance when it arrived in October and hit 12 goals in a run of 17 starts. They included the club's fastest hat-trick within 23 minutes of the kick-off against West Didsbury & Chorlton in the Manchester Premier Cup in February, and he ended the term with a winners medal in that competition. He was amongst the goals from the start of 2017/18, scoring in each of the first two games, and bagged another spectacular strike from near the right touchline against Tamworth in September. He wasn't always picked to start under Karl Marginson, but hit form with seven goals in Tom Greaves' first five games in charge. They included the first goal under the new manager and a terrific brace against AFC Telford United, the second being an outrageous 40-yard screamer. A week later he was transferred to Southport for a club record fee, and scored a hat-trick on his debut for them. He ended the season as top scorer for both clubs, as well as the whole National League North, and also played for the England C team against Wales. Goals were harder to come by in 2018/19, with a missed penalty at Broadhurst Park in September being typical of his luck. He was transfer-listed and loaned to Stockport County, but made just one substitute appearance as they went on to clinch the National League North title. He signed a contract with South Shields in the summer of 2019, and scored in both fixtures against FC United as his team stormed twelve points clear at the top of the Northern Premier League table in March 2020 before the season was abandoned shortly afterwards. With his employers again inactive, he was loaned to National League North side York City in January 2021, and made that move permanent in June. However, in December he moved on to Buxton, for whom he made his first start in their home loss to FC. Despite that setback, he helped his new side to win the 2021/22 Northern Premier League title.

217 Nathan LOWE

Born: 24/03/1996, Wigan
Debut: Sub v Chorley (A, NLN), 06/08/2016

Midfielder

Season	LEAGUE			FA NATIONAL CUPS			OTHER CUPS / PLAY-OFFS			TOTALS		
	Starts	(+Sub)	Goals	Starts	(+Sub)	Goals	Starts	(+Sub)	Goals	Starts	(+Sub)	Goals
2016/17	17	(+11)	6	0	(+3)	0	1	(+1)	0	18	(+15)	6
2017/18	8	(+1)	2	0	(+0)	0	0	(+0)	0	8	(+1)	2
Totals	25	(+12)	8	0	(+3)	0	1	(+1)	0	26	(+16)	8

Nathan emerged through the academy at Burnley, and was in their youth team that defeated Manchester United at Old Trafford in the FA Youth Cup in 2012, courtesy of a hat-trick from future FC team-mate Jason Gilchrist. At the end of his scholarship he signed a professional contract, and spent two seasons in the development squad whilst also training and travelling with the first team. After a long injury lay-off, his contract was cancelled in March 2016, and he linked up with the Reds that summer. He began the season on the bench, and made an impression seconds after coming on against Stockport County when his long-range shot was deflected in by Dale Johnson to seal the three points. By mid-October he had made a handful of starts, until a cartilage injury kept him out until New Year's Day. January was mainly spent on the bench before his season began in earnest in February when he hit his first credited goal for the club with a spectacular strike against Chorley. He managed to top that a fortnight later at Gloucester City when a sublime chip reduced the arrears, before he lobbed the goalkeeper from inside his own half to win the game with three minutes to go. He was at it again at home to Tamworth when he hit the winner with a 30-yard rocket with virtually the last kick of the game to celebrate signing a contract with the club earlier in the day. Another long-range strike turned the game at Curzon Ashton, and he ended the season with a winners medal in the Manchester Premier Cup. He opened his account for 2017/18 with a cool 20-yard finish in the August draw at Southport, which inspired the opponents to sign him for an undisclosed fee in September. He played against FC in the return fixture at Broadhurst in January 2018, but soon after he linked up with Spennymoor Town on a loan arrangement until the end of the season. He began 2018/19 in the Southport team, but his contract was cancelled in October. He joined ambitious big spenders South Shields and helped them to the Northern Premier League play-off final in 2019. He took delight in beating FC twice the next term as his team looked certain to claim the title before the season was halted. When the following campaign at our level suffered a similiar fate, he returned to the National League North in January 2021 on loan to Darlington. He repeated that move in March 2022 before joining their divisional rivals Kidderminster Harriers upon his release by South Shields in May.

218 Kieran GLYNN

Born: 14/11/1997, Oldham
Debut: Sub v AFC Telford United (H, NLN), 09/08/2016

Midfielder

Season	LEAGUE			FA NATIONAL CUPS			OTHER CUPS / PLAY-OFFS			TOTALS		
	Starts	(+Sub)	Goals	Starts	(+Sub)	Goals	Starts	(+Sub)	Goals	Starts	(+Sub)	Goals
2016/17	10	(+12)	3	1	(+1)	0	1	(+0)	0	12	(+13)	3
2017/18	20	(+6)	1	0	(+1)	0	3	(+0)	1	23	(+7)	2
Totals	30	(+18)	4	1	(+2)	0	4	(+0)	1	35	(+20)	5

Kieran came to FC United's attention through the club's link with Hopwood Hall College in Rochdale, where he was vice-captain of the Football Academy team that won all of their fixtures in 2015/16. When it became evident that he wasn't attached to another senior club, the Reds offered him a contract to be part of the squad for the 2016/17 campaign. His displays in pre-season impressed onlookers who agreed that the club had unearthed a raw diamond with the way he effortlessly glided past opponents. The youngster from Shaw was introduced mainly as a substitute in the first two months of the term, but was still voted as FC's star performer on a couple of occasions. He marked only his second start with a goal inside three minutes against Alfreton Town in October, but then was frustratingly sidelined as he waited to speak to a surgeon about a suspected ACL injury sustained two years previously. He returned at Stalybridge Celtic in November to score again in another majestic performance, and repeated the trick a week later when his smart turn and shot gave United the lead in the win over Nuneaton Town. With three goals in three games, the club moved quickly in December to extend his contract until the end of 2017/18. He gave further virtuoso displays, particularly when pulling the strings at Altrincham and in the Manchester Premier Cup win over West Didsbury & Chorlton, but injury disrupted the rest of his campaign. He missed most of the pre-season programme in 2017 and was given just 16 minutes as a substitute under Karl Marginson before being sent on loan to North West Counties side Padiham. When Tom Greaves took over as manager he put Kieran straight back in the team, and he rewarded that faith with two goals in his first four starts - the second of which was a wonderful overhead kick on his 20th birthday to begin the superb comeback win over Alfreton Town. In December he scored during a trial game for Crewe Alexandra's under-23 side, and eventually became a full-time player when FC accepted an offer from National League new boys Salford City for his transfer in May 2018. He started just three games in his first season, all in the FA Trophy, and had time on loan at Chorley and in National League South with Woking. He spent the whole of the 2019/20 term out on loan again, with spells at Southport and Northern Premier League side Scarborough Athletic. He returned permanently to the latter in May after his release by Salford, and was in their line-up when they visited Broadhurst Park in September 2020, for FC's 6-0 win a year later, and also the 2-2 draw in Yorkshire in February 2022. He ended that season successfully as part of the team that won the play-offs to earn promotion to the National League North.

219 Ashley FRITH

Born: 02/06/1994, Stockport
Debut: No.1 v Darlington 1883 (H, NLN), 29/08/2016

Goalkeeper

Season	LEAGUE			FA NATIONAL CUPS			OTHER CUPS / PLAY-OFFS			TOTALS		
	Starts	(+Sub)	Goals	Starts	(+Sub)	Goals	Starts	(+Sub)	Goals	Starts	(+Sub)	Goals
2016/17	1	(+0)	0	0	(+0)	0	0	(+0)	0	1	(+0)	0
2017/18	0	(+0)	0	0	(+0)	0	0	(+0)	0	0	(+0)	0
Totals	1	(+0)	0	0	(+0)	0	0	(+0)	0	1	(+0)	0

A tall and agile goalkeeper from Marple, Ashley was in the schoolboy academies at Blackburn Rovers and Manchester City. His first senior football was as a 16-year-old for Glossop North End, where he became a regular the following season. He joined Hyde in January 2012, making his bow as a late replacement for Dave Carnell in front of over 2,200 fans in a narrow loss at Mansfield Town. He started five Conference matches in total for Hyde, either side of loans at Northern Premier League clubs AFC Fylde and Ashton United in 2013. He played for Mossley in 2014/15, before linking up with FC United the following spring, when he registered for the reserves. After a short loan spell at Radcliffe Borough, he covered for Carnell again at home to Darlington 1883 in August 2016. He overcame early nerves as the team recovered a two-goal deficit, but had no chance with an unfortunate late deflected winner. Thereafter he was on the bench for FA Cup matches, and was also back-up in 2017/18 without adding to his solitary appearance.

220 Johny DIBA Musangu

Born: 12/10/1997, Mbuji-Mayi (DR Congo)
Debut: No.1 v Boston United (A, NLN), 03/09/2016

Goalkeeper

Season	LEAGUE			FA NATIONAL CUPS			OTHER CUPS / PLAY-OFFS			TOTALS		
	Starts	(+Sub)	Goals	Starts	(+Sub)	Goals	Starts	(+Sub)	Goals	Starts	(+Sub)	Goals
2016/17	5	(+0)	0	0	(+0)	0	0	(+0)	0	5	(+0)	0
Totals	5	(+0)	0	0	(+0)	0	0	(+0)	0	5	(+0)	0

Johny is a Congolese-born goalkeeper who was raised in Rochdale, and attracted the attention of his hometown club when he played in the final of the English National Schools Cup. Whilst still at school he attended England training camps at the National Football Centre, and also won the English Schools FA Inter-County Trophy with Greater Manchester. He joined Rochdale on a scholarship, and was dramatically pitched into action as a substitute during the League One match at Chesterfield in August 2014, still aged just 16. His progress was further rewarded with his first professional contract in November. He joined FC United on a one-month loan deal in September 2016, impressing on his debut in the fine away win at Boston United and playing five National League North matches for the club in total. In March 2017 he began another loan at Glossop North End, playing in the remainder of their Northern Premier League Division One North fixtures. He was released by Rochdale in the summer, and played in some of FC's pre-season friendly games before going on to feature for Ashton United and Mossley.

222 James HOOPER

Born: 10/02/1997, Manchester
Debut: No.7 v AFC Fylde (H, NLN), 10/09/2016

Winger/Forward

Season	LEAGUE			FA NATIONAL CUPS			OTHER CUPS / PLAY-OFFS			TOTALS		
	Starts	(+Sub)	Goals	Starts	(+Sub)	Goals	Starts	(+Sub)	Goals	Starts	(+Sub)	Goals
2016/17	3	(+0)	1	0	(+0)	0	0	(+0)	0	3	(+0)	1
2017/18	4	(+5)	1	0	(+1)	0	0	(+0)	0	4	(+6)	1
Totals	7	(+5)	2	0	(+1)	0	0	(+0)	0	7	(+6)	2

James began his career at Rochdale, where he was named youth team Player of the Season and signed a professional contract shortly after his first call-up to the senior squad in April 2015. The lad from Altrincham made his Football League debut in November the following season as a substitute at Gillingham, and his performance was rewarded with starts in the next two matches. Thereafter he was unable to progress beyond the bench, and so came to FC United on loan in September 2016, just a week after club-mate Johny Diba made the same move. The Wythenshawe-born attacker immediately impressed with his pacy and direct play from wide positions, although his debut was unfortunately curtailed by injury just after the interval. He returned for the next league fixture at Tamworth, when he earned the Reds a point with a tremendous late equaliser, but after one further outing he was recalled to Spotland. He linked up with Stockport County on a further loan in October, before being released by his parent club in January. After a short trial spell, he signed for Carlisle United in March 2017 until the end of the season, and was a member of their squad that reached the League Two promotion play-offs. He became a free agent in the summer, and played against FC in a friendly for Salford City in July, before signing for the Reds again, this time on a permanent basis, the following month. His long-range strike opened the scoring when FC earned their first points of the campaign at Southport on his first start, and he came close to adding to his tally in the following games, particularly when hitting the bar in the win over Boston United. He was one of FC's most exciting attacking threats, but was surprisingly allowed to leave in late September to join Radcliffe Borough in the Northern Premier League Division One North. He finally joined Salford on a one-year deal in July 2018, but started just two Manchester Premier Cup ties at left-back, before moving to Chorley in November, where he was on the bench as they won promotion to the National League via the play-offs. In 2019/20 he faced FC twice with Radcliffe, and during a busy campaign he also linked up with Ashton United, West Didsbury & Chorlton, Altrincham and Witton Albion before later featuring for Atherton Collieries.

221 Harry PRATT

Born: 24/09/1997, Rochdale
Debut: Sub v Harrogate Town (A, NLN), 06/09/2016

Forward

Season	LEAGUE			FA NATIONAL CUPS			OTHER CUPS / PLAY-OFFS			TOTALS		
	Starts	(+Sub)	Goals	Starts	(+Sub)	Goals	Starts	(+Sub)	Goals	Starts	(+Sub)	Goals
2016/17	0	(+1)	0	0	(+0)	0	0	(+1)	0	0	(+2)	0
Totals	0	(+1)	0	0	(+0)	0	0	(+1)	0	0	(+2)	0

A tall and mobile forward, Harry came through the ranks to join hometown club Rochdale on a scholarship deal. They initially released him in 2016, but he was invited back to train with the first team that summer. However, his trial was unsuccessful and so he linked up with FC United instead, first appearing and scoring in a friendly at Nelson in July. His competitive debut came from the bench at Harrogate Town in September, but with the team usually fielding just one recognised striker Harry found it difficult to establish himself. Despite a decent scoring record for the reserves, he only got one other senior appearance, from the bench in the Manchester Premier Cup tie at Abbey Hey in November. In between those two outings, he had played on loan at Northern Premier League side Clitheroe, along with team-mate Kisimba Kisimba. He joined Chorley in January 2017, playing for their under-21 side under David Chadwick, before going on to feature for 1874 Northwich, Colne, Chadderton, Droylsden and Padiham. After a fruitful spell at Mossley, he moved up a level to join Hyde United in 2022, and started their win over FC at Broadhurst at the end of the season.

223 Zac CORBETT

Born: 14/05/1996, Crewe
Debut: No.5 v Harrogate Town (H, FAC:Q3), 01/10/2016

Centre-back/Left-back

Season	LEAGUE			FA NATIONAL CUPS			OTHER CUPS / PLAY-OFFS			TOTALS		
	Starts	(+Sub)	Goals	Starts	(+Sub)	Goals	Starts	(+Sub)	Goals	Starts	(+Sub)	Goals
2016/17	5	(+1)	0	1	(+0)	0	0	(+1)	0	6	(+2)	0
2017/18	15	(+1)	2	6	(+0)	0	0	(+0)	0	21	(+1)	2
Totals	20	(+2)	2	7	(+0)	0	0	(+1)	0	27	(+3)	2

Zac is a former Stoke City and Crewe Alexandra schoolboy who also featured in the youth team at Nantwich Town. The versatile left-sided player moved to Northern Premier League rivals Witton Albion in 2014, and faced FC twice playing at left-back and in midfield. He switched to Colwyn Bay the following year, before moving to Welsh Premier League side Rhyl in January 2016. He joined the Reds that summer, and made his first appearance in a friendly at his former club, although his competitive debut was delayed by international clearance and injury. He made his bow in the FA Cup against Harrogate Town, and was unlucky to have a header cleared off the line. After a stint mainly warming the bench he spent another spell on the sidelines when he required knee surgery due to a cist in November. He returned to the team in February with four consecutive starts, the first three of which were all won, but the injury jinx struck again and he sat out the remainder of the season. He started the first two games of 2017/18 and performed well, but then remained on the bench until a recall in mid-September. That coincided with the team remaining unbeaten in six games, but he blotted his copybook with a needless sending-off in the defeat at Chorley, which signalled an end to Karl Marginson's time as manager. After serving his suspension he was recalled by Tom Greaves, and really came into his own as one of three centre-backs during the terrific run in December and January. After a few near misses he scored his first goal for the club in spectacular style with a long-range rocket to equalise in the Boxing Day win over league leaders Salford City, and he levelled again in the 2-2 draw against the same opponents on New Year's Day. He was unfortunate to pick up a second red card in the defeat at Kidderminster Harriers, but worse was to follow when he was then ruled out for the rest of the season through injury. In May 2018 he became the third FC player in just eight months to sign for Southport on a full-time deal, but after being named just once on the bench his contract was cancelled in October 2018. The following season he linked up with both Warrington Town and Buxton.

224 Chris HILL

Born: 06/10/1997, Bolton
Debut: Sub v Chadderton (A, MPC:1), 18/10/2016

Midfielder

Season	LEAGUE			FA NATIONAL CUPS			OTHER CUPS / PLAY-OFFS			TOTALS		
	Starts	(+Sub)	Goals	Starts	(+Sub)	Goals	Starts	(+Sub)	Goals	Starts	(+Sub)	Goals
2016/17	0	(+0)	0	0	(+0)	0	0	(+2)	0	0	(+2)	0
Totals	0	(+0)	0	0	(+0)	0	0	(+2)	0	0	(+2)	0

Chris joined FC United's reserve team soon after leaving school in the summer of 2014, and soon earned a regular place as an attacking midfielder. His progress was rewarded with a couple of outings in the first team's pre-season friendlies in 2015, before he captained the Reds in the 6-2 win over Southport in the first FA Youth Cup tie to be held at Broadhurst Park. He remained a regular starter for the reserves over the next two seasons, and was called up to make his senior debut as a substitute in the Manchester Premier Cup tie at Chadderton in October 2016. He also came on in the next round at Abbey Hey, and in between was on the bench for the league game at Kidderminster Harriers. In January 2017 he joined Northern Premier League Division One North side Radcliffe Borough on loan, and remained at that level in 2017/18 when he featured for Skelmersdale United. He went on to command a regular place for Ashton Town in the North West Counties League, and also had a spell with Irlam.

225 Sam BAIRD

Born: 20/04/1999, Bolton
Debut: No.6 v Stalybridge Celtic (A, NLN), 12/11/2016

Centre-back

Season	LEAGUE			FA NATIONAL CUPS			OTHER CUPS / PLAY-OFFS			TOTALS		
	Starts	(+Sub)	Goals	Starts	(+Sub)	Goals	Starts	(+Sub)	Goals	Starts	(+Sub)	Goals
2016/17	5	(+1)	0	0	(+0)	0	1	(+0)	0	6	(+1)	0
2017/18	14	(+1)	0	1	(+0)	0	3	(+0)	0	18	(+1)	0
2018/19	11	(+1)	1	0	(+0)	0	0	(+0)	0	11	(+1)	1
Totals	**30**	**(+3)**	**1**	**1**	**(+0)**	**0**	**4**	**(+0)**	**0**	**35**	**(+3)**	**1**

Sam joined FC United's Academy after leaving school in 2015, and was in the team at right-back for Broadhurst Park's first FA Youth Cup tie against Southport that September. He was moved over to centre-back as the season progressed, and also went on to appear in the reserve team several times. He played in every match, and was also named as captain, as the under-18s reached the FA Youth Cup 1st round for the first time in the club's history in 2016/17. Along with team-mate Kamahl Fuller, he was selected for trials for the England Colleges team, before being called up to the first team in the midst of a defensive crisis in November. He went straight into the centre of defence for the trip to Stalybridge Celtic, where he was voted FC's star man in the 4-2 victory, and kept his place for the Manchester Premier Cup win at Abbey Hey. He returned to the team for three consecutive games in January, and was once again man of the match in the 0-0 draw at Worcester City. His displays caught the eye of Premier League club Burnley, who invited him for a trial, but unfortunately he suffered a groin injury there that sidelined him for a month, although he recovered to make a further two senior appearances before the season ended. Sam was often an unused substitute in the early months of 2017/18 before new boss Tom Greaves brought him back into the side in November, and his performances were rewarded with an extension to his contract until May 2019. Thereafter he was absent from the matchday squad just four times, due to an injury in March, before finishing the season strongly. He picked up his first senior winners medal as part of the team that retained the Manchester Premier Cup in April 2018 by defeating Trafford on penalties after a 2-2 draw. He started eight of the first ten games of 2018/19 before surprisingly being allowed to join Droylsden on loan in September. He was recalled by new boss Neil Reynolds in October, but remained an unused substitute before rejoining Droylsden in December on a deal that was extended until the end of the season. He performed well in a settled side before another dramatic recall to FC in April 2019 for the trip to Alfreton Town, where he headed his first goal for the club to claim a late win. He also started the final two games of the term before joining good friend Michael Jones at Trafford in May. Sam helped his new team to the Manchester Premier Cup Final, where they were due to face FC United before the 2019/20 season was abandoned. He moved up to the Northern Premier League's top division with Ashton United in August 2020, and was in the side that lost to FC in April 2022. He experienced a happier return to Broadhurst Park when helping his club to claim their 16th Manchester Premier Cup triumph that month.

227 Michael JONES

Born: 19/11/1998, Manchester
Debut: No.4 v Abbey Hey (A, MPC:QF), 16/11/2016

Midfielder

Season	LEAGUE			FA NATIONAL CUPS			OTHER CUPS / PLAY-OFFS			TOTALS		
	Starts	(+Sub)	Goals	Starts	(+Sub)	Goals	Starts	(+Sub)	Goals	Starts	(+Sub)	Goals
2016/17	0	(+2)	0	0	(+0)	0	1	(+0)	0	1	(+2)	0
2017/18	5	(+8)	0	1	(+1)	0	2	(+0)	0	8	(+9)	0
2018/19	5	(+0)	0	1	(+1)	0	1	(+0)	0	7	(+1)	0
Totals	**10**	**(+10)**	**0**	**2**	**(+2)**	**0**	**4**	**(+0)**	**0**	**16**	**(+12)**	**0**

Mike is a tall and powerful midfielder who can also play at centre-back. He joined FC United's Academy after leaving school in 2015, and featured in the two FA Youth Cup ties held at Broadhurst Park that September. He missed just one game in the youth team, and was also ever-present in the reserves from October onwards. He played in every match as the under-18s reached the FA Youth Cup 1st round for the first time in the club's history in 2016/17, and also represented Manchester FA in the FA County Youth Cup. He was called up to the senior squad in November, and made his debut in central midfield in the Manchester Premier Cup win at Abbey Hey. In December he signed a contract to remain with the club until the summer of 2018. He appeared from the bench in the final two league games of the season before picking up a winner's medal as an unused substitute in the Manchester Premier Cup Final in May. Mike began the 2017/18 campaign in the starting line-up at Brackley Town, but his only other appearance under Karl Marginson was as a half-time substitute in the FA Cup replay at home to Stockport County in October. That night he belied his tender age with a dominant display to repel the visitors as the nine men of FC held on for a memorable 1-0 victory. He became heavily involved once Tom Greaves took over as manager, missing just one of his first seven games in charge with an injury. He was particularly impressive in the Manchester Premier Cup win at Salford City and the league win over AFC Telford United, when his clever flick sent Jason Gilchrist clear to score his first of the afternoon. He was an ever-present in the matchday squad until February 2018, and soon after was sent to Northern Premier League side Mossley on loan in order to gain more experience. However, he was disappointed to be given just ten minutes as a substitute during his month there and returned to United in April. He came off the bench to help protect the 1-0 lead over York City that ensured the team's place in National League North for another season, before collecting his second successive Manchester Premier Cup winner's medal, although he was once again an unused substitute against Trafford. After completing pre-season with the Reds, he began 2018/19 on loan at North West Counties League side Padiham, before being recalled to Broadhurst Park by caretaker-manager David Chadwick in September. He was the team's star performer on his return at home to Southport, and featured in eight consecutive games before suffering a first half injury against Darlington. He was named on the bench twice by new boss Neil Reynolds, before joining Stalybridge Celtic on a month's loan in December. Opportunities were limited back at FC in the New Year as the struggling team looked for experience, and so Mike returned to the Northern Premier League with Trafford in February 2019. He was on course for another Manchester Premier Cup Final with his local club, where ironically they would face FC United, only for the 2019/20 season to be abandoned in March.

PLAYER PROFILES

226 Kisimba KISIMBA

Born: 23/10/1997, DR Congo
Debut: No.3 v Abbey Hey (A, MPC:QF), 16/11/2016

Full-back

Season	LEAGUE			FA NATIONAL CUPS			OTHER CUPS / PLAY-OFFS			TOTALS		
	Starts	(+Sub)	Goals	Starts	(+Sub)	Goals	Starts	(+Sub)	Goals	Starts	(+Sub)	Goals
2016/17	0	(+0)	0	0	(+0)	0	1	(+0)	0	1	(+0)	0
Totals	0	(+0)	0	0	(+0)	0	1	(+0)	0	1	(+0)	0

Kisimba came through the ranks at his local club Rochdale, where he signed as a scholar after twice experiencing success in national school competitions. With St Cuthberts RC High he reached the final of the English National Schools Cup, and went on to win the English Schools FA Inter-County Trophy with Greater Manchester at Coventry's Ricoh Arena in 2014. He was still just 16 years of age when he was called up to the first-team bench for a Football League Trophy tie against Walsall in October 2014, but this was his only involvement at senior level. The diminutive dynamo remained a regular in the reserve and youth teams, alongside future FC United team-mates Harry Pratt, Johny Diba and James Hooper, until his release in 2016. He joined the Reds during pre-season, and showed his versatility in friendly and reserve team matches by playing in both defensive and attacking midfield roles. He was named on the first-team bench in a couple of early-season fixtures, before joining Northern Premier League First Division North club Clitheroe on dual registration terms in October. He returned to make his FC debut as a left-back in the Manchester Premier Cup win at Abbey Hey in November, but this was his only appearance in the senior side. He signed for Northern Premier League outfit Marine in February 2017, featuring mainly in either full-back position. He also later linked up with Glossop North End, Mossley, Chadderton and Padiham.

228 Gareth ARNISON

Born: 18/09/1986, Whitehaven
Debut: No.10 v Abbey Hey (A, MPC:QF), 16/11/2016

Forward

Season	LEAGUE			FA NATIONAL CUPS			OTHER CUPS / PLAY-OFFS			TOTALS		
	Starts	(+Sub)	Goals	Starts	(+Sub)	Goals	Starts	(+Sub)	Goals	Starts	(+Sub)	Goals
2016/17	4	(+4)	0	0	(+0)	0	1	(+0)	0	5	(+4)	0
Totals	4	(+4)	0	0	(+0)	0	1	(+0)	0	5	(+4)	0

A tall centre-forward, Gareth boasted an excellent goalscoring record for non-league clubs in his native Cumbria. He played most of his football in the Conference North, particularly with Workington, where he struck 127 times in three separate spells spanning eleven seasons. He switched to Northern Premier League side Kendal Town in 2007, before returning a year later and remaining until moving to Barrow in 2013. A debilitating illness sidelined him the following summer, so he returned to Workington in October 2014 and twice faced FC as his team finished runners-up to United in the Northern Premier League that term. He helped them to reach the play-offs again the season after, before his illness caused him to miss most of the pre-season programme and led to his eventual release in August. As he lived in Manchester, he began training with FC and signed formally in October 2016. He was a regular member of the matchday squad until March, mainly featuring from the bench, and after contributing to a great comeback win at Gloucester City in February he was rewarded by starting the next three matches. Unfortunately, he was unable to open his scoring account for the club and remained on the sidelines thereafter before being released in the summer. After another spell out of the game he returned to Kendal in February 2018, and was soon back scoring goals again before a brief stint at Witton Albion.

229 Adriano BASSO

Born: 18/04/1975, Jundiaí (Brazil)
Debut: No.1 v Altrincham (A, NLN), 26/12/2016

Goalkeeper

Season	LEAGUE			FA NATIONAL CUPS			OTHER CUPS / PLAY-OFFS			TOTALS		
	Starts	(+Sub)	Goals	Starts	(+Sub)	Goals	Starts	(+Sub)	Goals	Starts	(+Sub)	Goals
2016/17	8	(+0)	0	0	(+0)	0	1	(+0)	0	9	(+0)	0
2017/18	0	(+0)	0	0	(+0)	0	0	(+0)	0	0	(+0)	0
Totals	8	(+0)	0	0	(+0)	0	1	(+0)	0	9	(+0)	0

FC United's first South American player, Adriano began his career with Ponte Preta and Atlético Paranaense in his native Brazil, before venturing to England where his wife was studying. After a trial with Arsenal, he joined Isthmian League side St Albans City in 2004, but soon moved to Conference club Woking. His displays earned a switch to Bristol City in October 2005, where he was voted BBC West's Footballer of the Year as they won promotion to the Championship the following term. In 2008 he kept goal in the Championship Play-Off Final at Wembley as the Robins lost to Hull City. He remained first choice during the next season, but he left Ashton Gate in 2010 after 182 appearances. In January 2011 he joined Wolverhampton Wanderers on a short-term deal, but did not make the Premier League side. He returned to the Championship with Hull, before moving to California in 2012 to play for NPSL club SC Corinthians USA. He initially lined up for FC in two pre-season friendlies in July 2016, but instead signed a contract with National League South side Truro City. He returned north in December, and became the **oldest player to make his Reds debut**, aged 41 years 252 days. His experience was often vital behind a young and makeshift defence, with his highlight being a late penalty save to earn a draw at Worcester City. However, his copybook was blotted with an injury-time red card against Chorley that led to the visitors earning a point. That looked to be his last action for FC as Dave Carnell excelled during his suspension, and Adriano joined League Two side Hartlepool United as a goalkeeping coach in March. However, an injury to Carnell led to an unexpected call-up for the trip to Curzon Ashton, where he helped United to a memorable away win. He linked up with the club again for pre-season in 2017, and was an unused substitute in eight matches during the season. He also provided cover for both Radcliffe Borough and Ashton United before furthering his coaching career at Nuneaton Borough, Grantham Town and Sheffield Wednesday.

230 Jordan FAGBOLA

Born: 01/12/1993, Manchester
Debut: No.5 v Salford City (H, NLN), 28/01/2017

Centre-back

Season	LEAGUE Starts	(+Sub)	Goals	FA NATIONAL CUPS Starts	(+Sub)	Goals	OTHER CUPS / PLAY-OFFS Starts	(+Sub)	Goals	TOTALS Starts	(+Sub)	Goals
2016/17	8	(+0)	1	0	(+0)	0	1	(+0)	0	9	(+0)	1
2017/18	35	(+2)	2	4	(+1)	0	2	(+0)	0	41	(+3)	2
Totals	43	(+2)	3	4	(+1)	0	3	(+0)	0	50	(+3)	3

After being part of the Greater Manchester team that won the National under-16s Cup in 2010, Jordan began his career as a scholar with Rochdale, where he was given a first-team squad number in his second year. He was released in 2012, and linked up with Stockport County, where he was one of the star performers in his first season as they suffered relegation from the Conference. After three years he moved to Colwyn Bay, where he spent a year in the Northern Premier League before moving back into the National League with newly promoted Solihull Moors in August 2016. He played 26 games for the Midlands outfit, including a run to the FA Cup 2nd round, before returning north to sign for FC United in January 2017. He performed well on his debut against Salford City, despite the team's defeat, but was unfortunate to be ruled out by injury for the next two months. After returning in March, he settled well in the centre of defence, and also hit his first goal for the club in the win at Nuneaton Town. He ended the campaign with a Manchester Premier Cup winner's medal against Stalybridge Celtic in May. Jordan was missing from the teamsheet for just one match during the 2017/18 campaign, starting all but ten games and also captaining the side on three occasions. He was usually part of a back four, but also looked comfortable when asked to bring the ball out of defence when Tom Greaves selected three centre-backs. He claimed the goal that effectively sealed the first win under Greaves against Nuneaton in October, and he also scored with a header from distance to begin the comeback in the extraordinary 4-4 draw at Spennymoor Town in December. He picked up a Manchester Premier Cup winner's medal for the second consecutive year as part of the team that defeated Trafford after a penalty shoot-out decider in April 2018, but left the club in the summer to join Hyde United. He faced FC three times with his new club during 2019/20, but later suffered a ruptured achilles that ruled him out of the following campaign. He recovered to reclaim a regular place, and twice emerged victorious against FC United during the 2021/22 season.

231 Greg WILKINSON

Born: 03/10/1989, Manchester
Debut: Sub v Chorley (H, NLN), 11/02/2017

Midfielder

Season	LEAGUE Starts	(+Sub)	Goals	FA NATIONAL CUPS Starts	(+Sub)	Goals	OTHER CUPS / PLAY-OFFS Starts	(+Sub)	Goals	TOTALS Starts	(+Sub)	Goals
2016/17	2	(+4)	0	0	(+0)	0	0	(+0)	0	2	(+4)	0
Totals	2	(+4)	0	0	(+0)	0	0	(+0)	0	2	(+4)	0

Greg was in the Manchester United academy for several years before joining Curzon Ashton's youth team and playing in the Manchester League for East Manchester. He was signed by Stalybridge Celtic in 2007, where he became the club's youngest ever captain and made 165 appearances either side of a short loan spell at Chorley. In 2013 he moved to Altrincham, where he contributed several important goals, most memorably the winner against Guiseley in the 2014 Conference North promotion play-off final, just 22 seconds after coming off the bench. He featured mainly as a substitute in the Conference, and dropped back down a level to join Stockport County on loan in January 2015. He initially linked up with FC United that summer when he played in several pre-season friendlies, but instead signed a contract for AFC Telford United. He had an injury-disrupted season there and was released the following summer, before rejoining Altrincham. Soon after facing FC twice over the festive period, the intelligent midfielder with an eye for a forward pass finally signed for the Reds in January 2017. He helped the team to three wins and two draws in six outings, but his injury jinx struck against former team Stalybridge in April. This sidelined him for the rest of the campaign and he was released in May, before returning to Bower Fold the following month. He later played for Wythenshawe Town in the North West Counties League.

232 Tomi ADELOYE

Born: 17/02/1996, Sidcup
Debut: Sub v FC Halifax Town (H, NLN), 25/03/2017

Forward

Season	LEAGUE Starts	(+Sub)	Goals	FA NATIONAL CUPS Starts	(+Sub)	Goals	OTHER CUPS / PLAY-OFFS Starts	(+Sub)	Goals	TOTALS Starts	(+Sub)	Goals
2016/17	5	(+3)	1	0	(+0)	0	1	(+0)	0	6	(+3)	1
Totals	5	(+3)	1	0	(+0)	0	1	(+0)	0	6	(+3)	1

A tall, fast and mobile forward, Tomi began his career at Charlton Athletic, but switched to Millwall in December 2013. The following summer he joined Stoke City, where he played in their under-21 team either side of a loan spell at Macclesfield Town. He was released in June 2015 and moved into non-league with stints at Chelmsford City, Dover, Leatherhead and Welling United. He returned north to join Altrincham in January 2017, playing four times before linking up with FC United the following month. After scoring twice in a reserve match, he featured in each of the last nine games of the season, bringing pace and strength to the attack. He scored his only senior goal for the club at Darlington 1883 and helped the team to win the Manchester Premier Cup Final against Stalybridge Celtic in May. He left FC in the summer, and continued his nomadic football journey. He went on to play in the National League with Hartlepool United, Dagenham & Redbridge, Ebbsfleet United and Barnet, in the National League South for St. Albans City and Whitehawk, and in Scotland for Lowland League club East Kilbride and Championship side Ayr United.

233 Ryan SCHOFIELD

Born: 11/12/1999, Huddersfield

Debut: No.1 v Bradford Park Avenue (A, NLN), 08/04/2017

Goalkeeper

Season	LEAGUE			FA NATIONAL CUPS			OTHER CUPS / PLAY-OFFS			TOTALS		
	Starts	(+Sub)	Goals	Starts	(+Sub)	Goals	Starts	(+Sub)	Goals	Starts	(+Sub)	Goals
2016/17	5	(+0)	0	0	(+0)	0	1	(+0)	0	6	(+0)	0
Totals	5	(+0)	0	0	(+0)	0	1	(+0)	0	6	(+0)	0

Ryan joined the schoolboy academy of local club Huddersfield Town at under-9 level and progressed to sign a scholarship deal in 2016. Just before leaving school he played in the under-21 Professional Development League 2 play-off final, where he made some impressive saves as the Terriers beat Sheffield United to win the national title. After attending an England training camp for promising young goalkeepers earlier in the year, he was called up to his country's under-18 squad in November, before earning his first cap and keeping a clean sheet in a win over Qatar in March 2017. He was a virtual ever-present in the Town youth team in 2016/17, as well as stepping up to the under-23s, and was rewarded with his first professional contract soon after his 17th birthday in December. He joined FC United on an initial emergency seven-day loan deal in April after an injury to Dave Carnell, and became the club's **youngest ever first team goalkeeper**, as well as the **youngest player to start a league game,** when he lined up for his debut at Bradford Park Avenue. After keeping a clean sheet, the loan was extended and he played in each of the season's remaining fixtures. That included being given the nod for the Manchester Premier Cup final against Stalybridge Celtic, where his goal remained intact again as he picked up another winner's medal. In the summer he played for England under-20s as they won the prestigious Toulon Tournament, where he saved a penalty in the final's shoot-out. Back at Huddersfield, he was elevated to work with the senior squad after they were promoted to the Premier League for the 2017/18 season, before embarking on a month's loan at FC's National League North rivals AFC Telford United in January 2018. A year later he began another temporary spell, with Notts County in League Two, but was unable to prevent the world's oldest professional club from losing their Football League status after 131 years. He made his Huddersfield debut in the League Cup against Lincoln City in August 2019, and kept a clean sheet on his Championship bow for the club at home to Middlesbrough in October. A later loan at Scottish Premiership side Livingston was cut short after he picked up an injury on his debut in January 2020. He returned to make 30 Championship appearances for Huddersfield's in the 2020/21 season, and also began the following term as first choice before losing his place.

234 Lloyd ALLINSON

Born: 07/09/1993, Rothwell

Debut: No.1 v Brackley Town (A, NLN), 05/08/2017

Goalkeeper

Season	LEAGUE			FA NATIONAL CUPS			OTHER CUPS / PLAY-OFFS			TOTALS		
	Starts	(+Sub)	Goals	Starts	(+Sub)	Goals	Starts	(+Sub)	Goals	Starts	(+Sub)	Goals
2017/18	42	(+0)	0	6	(+0)	0	3	(+0)	0	51	(+0)	0
2018/19	17	(+0)	0	1	(+0)	0	1	(+0)	0	19	(+0)	0
Totals	59	(+0)	0	7	(+0)	0	4	(+0)	0	70	(+0)	0

Lloyd progressed through the youth system to become a young professional at Huddersfield Town. He was first named as substitute goalkeeper for a senior match in October 2010 against Peterborough United in the Football League Trophy, just months after he had left school. He got his first taste of first-team football in a loan spell at Northern Premier League side Ilkeston the following campaign, and returned there for a similar stint in 2013/14. He was regularly named on the bench for Huddersfield in the Football League Championship over the next two seasons, and finally made his debut as a first-half substitute on the final day of the 2015/16 season. He was released shortly after, and signed an initial six-month contract with Chesterfield in August 2016. He made his debut against Wolverhampton Wanderers in the EFL Trophy, where he played alongside former FC defender Charlie Raglan, and started all five of the club's games in that competition during the campaign. He also started five matches in League One, but was released at the end of the season following Chesterfield's relegation. He signed for FC United in June 2017, and was installed as first choice ahead of the new campaign. Despite the team suffering the worst start in the club's history at that point, the form of the new custodian was one of the few plus points as he often kept the score respectable even in defeat. Clean sheets were few and far between, but when they did arrive he more than earned them, particularly in the terrific wins at York City and in the FA Cup at home to Stockport County. His contract was extended in November to commit him to the club until May 2019, and his form continued into 2018. Terrific displays against Southport, Curzon Ashton, Chorley, Gainsborough Trinity and York in particular earned vital points in the fight to avoid relegation, and a superb save in the Manchester Premier Cup Final penalty shoot-out against Trafford helped bring the trophy back to Moston. He ended the term having played every minute of every single game, and deservedly picked up some of the club's Player Of The Season awards. He was performing well in the 2018 pre-season friendlies until a self-inflicted hand injury on the eve of the campaign rendered him unavailable for the first 15 games. He returned for the superb win at Kidderminster Harriers in October, and looked to be back to his best with great displays the following month against Blyth Spartans, AFC Telford United, Hereford and Mossley (where he saved a penalty). However a series of errors around the festive period led to a loss of confidence and he dropped to the bench in favour of loanee Andy Fisher in February 2019. In March he joined Nantwich Town on loan to aid their Northern Premier League promotion push, but conceded an unfortunate own-goal in their unsuccessful play-off semi-final. He moved to Guiseley in the summer, before spells with Northern Premier League sides Matlock Town, Ashton United, Hyde United and Gainsborough Trinity, for whom he lined up at Broadhurst in November 2019. He later featured for Scarborough Athletic, Ramsbottom United, Nostell Miners Welfare and Pontefract Collieries.

235 Joel SENIOR

Born: 24/06/1999, Stockport
Debut: No.2 v Brackley Town (A, NLN), 05/08/2017

Right-back

Season	LEAGUE			FA NATIONAL CUPS			OTHER CUPS / PLAY-OFFS			TOTALS		
	Starts	(+Sub)	Goals	Starts	(+Sub)	Goals	Starts	(+Sub)	Goals	Starts	(+Sub)	Goals
2017/18	32	(+7)	0	4	(+0)	0	2	(+0)	1	38	(+7)	1
2018/19	17	(+3)	0	1	(+0)	0	2	(+0)	0	20	(+3)	0
Totals	49	(+10)	0	5	(+0)	0	4	(+0)	1	58	(+10)	1

A former schoolboy with Oldham Athletic, Joel got his first taste of senior football when making his debut in the North West Counties League for Maine Road in September 2015, just months after leaving school. He made such great strides that he earned a regular place that season, and in 2016/17 he was voted as the division's best right-back at the annual awards. His performances alerted FC United boss Karl Marginson, and he was invited to participate in the 2017 pre-season programme, with his tenacity and energy rewarded with the no.2 shirt for the season's opener. He started the first five games, but the new-look team made a terrible start and he dropped to the bench for the next five. During his next run he was also tried further forward, where he demonstrated

his attacking threat when his cross was headed home by Jason Gilchrist to open the scoring against Tamworth. He was on the bench during October, but was brought back in by new boss Tom Greaves for the Manchester Premier Cup tie at Salford City and thereafter was an automatic choice. Greaves favoured a 3-5-2 formation at this point, and Joel suited the right-wing-back role perfectly. He got forward at every opportunity and went close to opening his goalscoring account particularly in the great run over the festive period. He also cleared a number of goalbound shots off the line as his defensive awareness matured, and he was one of the standout performers in the run-in as the team's place in the National League North was secured for another season. He picked a great time to score his first goal for the club when he hammered home the second equaliser against Trafford in the Manchester Premier Cup Final, and although his penalty was later saved in the shoot-out he capped a great campaign by picking up a winner's medal. He was also awarded a couple of the club's Player Of The Season awards, and was attracting the attention of professional clubs. He made a slow start to 2018/19 due to injury and inconsistent form, with a calamitous own goal at home to Bradford Park Avenue symptomatic of his luck. He fought back to reclaim a regular place in October, and hit top form again in the team's good run of results over the following weeks. His pinpoint crosses created goals at Kidderminster Harriers and Hereford,

and he also showed his ability from free-kicks with a couple of efforts going very close. However, uncertainty over his week-to-week contract saw new boss Neil Reynolds bring in Danny Morton in January, and Joel started just one further game before moving to Curzon Ashton the following month. After a trial at Burnley, he spent 2019/20 on a full-time contract with the Premier League club's under-23 side, but his time there was disrupted by injury. He signed for National League side Altrincham in September 2020, where his impressive displays earned a player of the season award and a return to the professional ranks. He was signed by League Two club Carlisle United in January 2022. He made his Football League debut against Hartlepool United, but in just his fourth game suffered a knee injury that ruled him out for the rest of the season.

237 Connor McCARTHY

Born: 06/04/1995, Liverpool
Debut: No.7 v Brackley Town (A, NLN), 05/08/2017

Forward

Season	LEAGUE			FA NATIONAL CUPS			OTHER CUPS / PLAY-OFFS			TOTALS		
	Starts	(+Sub)	Goals	Starts	(+Sub)	Goals	Starts	(+Sub)	Goals	Starts	(+Sub)	Goals
2017/18	26	(+9)	6	4	(+1)	3	2	(+0)	0	32	(+10)	9
Totals	26	(+9)	6	4	(+1)	3	2	(+0)	0	32	(+10)	9

Connor began in non-league with Northern Premier League Division One North side Prescot Cables, who saw him playing Sunday football in 2013. After a productive season he moved up a level to Skelmersdale United, for whom he was on the winning side against FC United in October 2014. After a spell on dual registration terms with North West Counties side Widnes, he moved into the National League with Southport in February 2015, and also earned a call-up to an England C training camp. The following season he had two separate loan spells with AFC Telford United, and faced FC again twice in the National League North. He made the switch permanent in September 2016, and struck the winner against the Reds the following month. Whilst not a prolific goalscorer, his work rate made him a fan favourite but he was unable to maintain a regular place and

moved on loan to Warrington Town in February 2017. He was released by Telford at the end of the season and was signed by Karl Marginson on a contract with FC United for the 2017/18 campaign. His effort ensured he started the first 14 games, and whilst his own scoring touch took a while to arrive, he was often involved in the build-up to goals. He laid on the team's first two strikes of the season for Jason Gilchrist, and James Hooper's shot took a touch off him to open the scoring at his former club Southport. Later in that game his cross was swept home by Craig Lindfield as the Reds earned their first point of the season. The following week he got his first credited goal with a cool finish as FC won for the first time against Boston United. He had a goal disallowed in the FA Cup at Handsworth Parramore, but got his revenge with a hat-trick in the replay. He spent a few weeks mainly warming the bench, but came on to great effect in the final minute against Harrogate Town, just in time to cross for Tom Greaves to hit his 100th goal for the club and seal the terrific win. He was at his best over Christmas, bagging a double in the great comeback to draw 4-4 at Spennymoor Town, and heading United's first equaliser in another superb 3-2 win over league leaders Salford City. He sealed the win over Curzon Ashton in January, but was then unable to sustain a run in the side. He got one more goal, which was the crucial winner over York City that maintained FC United's place in the division, and he also picked up a winner's medal in the Manchester Premier Cup Final. He joined Runcorn Linnets in September 2018, before returning to help Warrington to the Northern Premier League play-offs. He rejoined Linnets in August 2019, and came off the bench against FC in the FA Trophy in November. He moved on to City Of Liverpool FC in December 2020.

236 Danny WISDOM

Born: 11/04/1989, Blackpool
Debut: No.3 v Brackley Town (A, NLN), 05/08/2017

Left-back

Season	LEAGUE Starts	(+Sub)	Goals	FA NATIONAL CUPS Starts	(+Sub)	Goals	OTHER CUPS / PLAY-OFFS Starts	(+Sub)	Goals	TOTALS Starts	(+Sub)	Goals
2017/18	19	(+1)	2	3	(+0)	0	0	(+0)	0	22	(+1)	2
Totals	19	(+1)	2	3	(+0)	0	0	(+0)	0	22	(+1)	2

After playing in the Blackpool schoolboy teams, Danny became a professional for two seasons at Morecambe. He dropped into non-league with Kendal Town in 2008, initially at left-back before cementing a place on the left side of midfield. He faced FC United several times in the Northern Premier League in a Kendal side that the Reds often found difficult to beat. He moved on to Northwich Victoria in 2012, before a brief return to Kendal in 2014. He soon moved on to Skelmersdale United, where he was part of the only team to inflict a league double in FC's 2014/15 title-winning season. At the end of that term he moved on to Stalybridge Celtic, and again became a thorn in FC's side when he bagged the winner at Broadhurst Park in April 2016. After Celtic's relegation from National League North in 2017 he signed a contract with FC United for the 2017/18 season. Despite the team's poor start, Danny began well and scored in each of the first two home games of the season. A well-placed, right-footed curler equalised against Spennymoor Town, before he opened the scoring with a header against Kidderminster Harriers. He was an automatic choice at left-back before picking up an injury at Chorley in Karl Marginson's last game in charge, and he didn't start a game for Tom Greaves until January. He was playing himself back into form, with his display in the home win over Curzon Ashton a particular highlight, before disaster struck. Chasing a through ball against Chorley in February, his leg buckled and he was stretchered off with a snapped achilles that ended to his campaign. After 12 months on the sidelines, he returned to the game with Bamber Bridge in February 2019 and played twice against FC the following season.

238 Jason ST JUSTE

Born: 21/09/1985, Leeds
Debut: No.11 v Brackley Town (A, NLN), 05/08/2017

Left-winger

Season	LEAGUE Starts	(+Sub)	Goals	FA NATIONAL CUPS Starts	(+Sub)	Goals	OTHER CUPS / PLAY-OFFS Starts	(+Sub)	Goals	TOTALS Starts	(+Sub)	Goals
2017/18	1	(+0)	0	0	(+0)	0	0	(+0)	0	1	(+0)	0
Totals	1	(+0)	0	0	(+0)	0	0	(+0)	0	1	(+0)	0

An experienced left-winger, Jason began in non-league with Garforth Town in 2003. In November 2004 he was signed by Darlington, featuring 15 times in League Two and scoring two brilliant goals, including the winner at Grimsby Town. In 2005 he joined Southampton, but he failed to appear in their senior side and returned to Garforth in 2006. He first faced FC United in August 2007, when he hit the only goal in our first home game in the Northern Premier League. He moved to Norway for a spell with Sandnes Ulf in 2009, before a short stay at Chester. He joined FC Halifax Town in 2011, where he showed versatility by often lining up at left-back during a two-year stay. After spells at Bradford Park Avenue, Whitehawk and Farsley, he joined North Ferriby United in 2014. He was named as Man-Of-The-Match in the FA Trophy Final as his side defeated Wrexham on penalties at Wembley, and also gained his first international caps for Saint Kitts and Nevis in a memorable season. After a short spell at AFC Fylde he rejoined Bradford PA in September 2015 and faced the Reds again in the National League North, which he also did the following term for Boston United. He signed for FC in July 2017, and started the season opener at Brackley Town. However, he was withdrawn after 63 minutes and spent the next two games on the bench. He joined Northern Premier League Division One North side Trafford on dual registration in September, and went back over the Pennines in December to join Ossett Town. He later played for Northern Counties East League sides Yorkshire Amateur and Emley.

239 Richie BAKER

Born: 29/12/1987, Burnley
Debut: Sub v Brackley Town (A, NLN), 05/08/2017

Midfielder

Season	LEAGUE Starts	(+Sub)	Goals	FA NATIONAL CUPS Starts	(+Sub)	Goals	OTHER CUPS / PLAY-OFFS Starts	(+Sub)	Goals	TOTALS Starts	(+Sub)	Goals
2017/18	2	(+1)	0	0	(+0)	0	0	(+0)	0	2	(+1)	0
Totals	2	(+1)	0	0	(+0)	0	0	(+0)	0	2	(+1)	0

Richie had several schoolboy years playing in the Manchester United academy as a right-back, before moving into midfield when he signed on a scholarship with Preston North End. He was released in 2006 and joined Bury, where he became an established League Two player making over 100 appearances in four seasons at Gigg Lane. He moved to Oxford United in July 2010, but started just one senior match before dropping into the Conference with Barrow in February 2011. He was a regular for over two years until their relegation in 2013, when he switched to Tamworth, where he suffered a second successive demotion the next term. He began 2014/15 in the Conference North with Stockport County, before switching to AFC Fylde in March 2015. He faced FC United four times in their colours over the next two campaigns, which included scoring a free-kick past substitute goalkeeper Chris Lynch in September 2015. He was released after Fylde's promotion in 2017, and signed a contract with the Reds that summer. His debut came from the bench in the opening day defeat at Brackley Town, before he started the next two games. He was withdrawn through injury just after the break in the third straight loss against Kidderminster Harriers, and feeling that he was unable to do himself justice in a red shirt he graciously cancelled his contract in early September. Later that month he joined rivals Curzon Ashton, where he settled better and soon contributed a couple of goals. He was still unable to regain peak fitness, however, and was released in May 2018. After assisting Lancaster City, he helped Colne to the Northern Premier League West Division play-offs, before later spells at Padiham, Ramsbottom United and Clitheroe.

240 Joel LOGAN

Born: 25/01/1995, Manchester
Debut: Sub v Brackley Town (A, NLN), 05/08/2017

Winger/Full-back

Season	LEAGUE Starts	(+Sub)	Goals	FA NATIONAL CUPS Starts	(+Sub)	Goals	OTHER CUPS / PLAY-OFFS Starts	(+Sub)	Goals	TOTALS Starts	(+Sub)	Goals
2017/18	12	(+2)	0	1	(+3)	1	0	(+1)	0	13	(+6)	1
2018/19	3	(+5)	0	1	(+0)	0	0	(+0)	0	4	(+5)	0
Totals	15	(+7)	0	2	(+3)	1	0	(+1)	0	17	(+11)	1

Joel was on academy forms at Bolton Wanderers, who spotted the Ardwick lad playing for renowned local club Fletcher Moss Rangers, before joining Rochdale as a scholar upon leaving school. He progressed to make his senior debut at the age of 17 as a substitute in a League Two encounter at Plymouth Argyle in October 2012, and remained on the fringes of the first team that season. He joined Conference side Southport on loan in November 2013, and then began a similar spell with Stalybridge Celtic in Conference North in March 2014. He was back in the Rochdale squad the following season, and made his first start in the famous FA Cup 3rd round win over Nottingham Forest in January 2015. He was sent on another loan spell in August 2015, this time to National League side Wrexham, for whom he first appeared in a friendly against FC United at Broadhurst Park. He was unable to regain a senior spot on his return to Rochdale and was released in June 2016, before linking up with Northern Premier League side Hednesford Town in August. He was back in the National League with Guiseley in November, but only featured as a substitute before joining FC Halifax Town on loan in March 2017. His sole outing was against FC in Moston before he joined the Reds in July. His debut came from the bench on the season's opening day, before he started the first two home games during which he was involved in much of the team's attacking threats. He then spent the next five matches as an unused substitute before becoming more involved in September. He emerged from the bench in the first half of the FA Cup replay with Handsworth Parramore, and within four minutes had smashed home his first goal for the club. He was one of the stars of the first few games under Tom Greaves, shining initially on the right wing before being asked to fill in at left wing-back. During this run he was instrumental in the dramatic comeback victory over Alfreton Town when his last-minute cross was deflected home for the winning goal. In December he signed a contract with the club until May 2019, but a recurrence of an injury before Christmas kept him on the sidelines for the rest of the season. He began 2018/19 in the starting line-up, but was unable to recapture either his form or full match fitness before another injury ruled him out in October. He joined Northern Premier League side Hednesford Town on a month's loan in December, and didn't return to the FC United squad until the trip to Alfreton Town in April, when he emerged from the bench to help the team gain a terrific win. He moved on to Hyde United in June 2019, and played in their win at Broadhurst Park in August before his season was ended by a knee injury in October.

241 Matty HUGHES

Born: 01/04/1992, Salford
Debut: No.6 v Kidderminster Harriers (H, NLN), 12/08/2017

Centre-back

Season	LEAGUE Starts	(+Sub)	Goals	FA NATIONAL CUPS Starts	(+Sub)	Goals	OTHER CUPS / PLAY-OFFS Starts	(+Sub)	Goals	TOTALS Starts	(+Sub)	Goals
2017/18	33	(+0)	0	2	(+1)	0	1	(+1)	0	36	(+2)	0
Totals	33	(+0)	0	2	(+1)	0	1	(+1)	0	36	(+2)	0

As a highly rated young central defender, Matty became a regular in the reserves at Rochdale whilst still at school. He attracted the attention of Scottish giants Celtic, who paid a significant fee to take him on a scholarship in 2008. After early injury setbacks he returned to captain a successful under-19 side, before being released and joining Conference side Fleetwood Town in 2011. However, he was unable to gain a place as the club won the title and he spent much of the 2011/12 season on loan at Conference North club Colwyn Bay. He dropped into the Northern Premier League with AFC Fylde in the summer of 2012, and faced FC United three times in his two years there. After helping them to promotion to the Conference North, he switched to Stalybridge Celtic in June 2014, where he became captain in a three-year stay. He led his team against FC five times, and twice scored at Broadhurst Park in Manchester Premier Cup and National League North encounters. Karl Marginson had been interested in Matty for a while and he finally got his man in May 2017. Personal commitments delayed his debut, but he seemed to have reached top form by the end of August, particularly during the excellent 2-0 win at York City. However, a poor run in early September saw four straight defeats, during which he picked up a number of yellow cards. Two in one game at Darlington led to an early bath, and he was also dismissed early on in his next start against Stockport County in the FA Cup replay. By the time his suspension was over, Tom Greaves had taken over as manager and Matty grew in stature as the team worked hard to recover from the poor start. He was installed as vice-captain and started every league game for which he was available. An accumulation of bookings led to a further ban in January, and he was gutted to miss most of April after unluckily receiving his third red card late on at Tamworth, after an immense performance. He moved on to Hyde United in June 2018, and later had a short loan spell at Trafford before facing FC three times in three different competitions for Radcliffe in 2019/20.

242 Michael CONNOR

Born: 10/09/1989, Manchester
Debut: No.10 v Southport (A, NLN), 15/08/2017

Midfielder

Season	LEAGUE Starts	(+Sub)	Goals	FA NATIONAL CUPS Starts	(+Sub)	Goals	OTHER CUPS / PLAY-OFFS Starts	(+Sub)	Goals	TOTALS Starts	(+Sub)	Goals
2017/18	8	(+2)	0	4	(+0)	1	0	(+0)	0	12	(+2)	1
Totals	8	(+2)	0	4	(+0)	1	0	(+0)	0	12	(+2)	1

Previously on Manchester City's books, Michael was playing Sunday football when Mossley took him for a short stint in the Northern Premier League Division One North in September 2008. After winning the Cheshire League with Woodley, the powerful midfielder from Openshaw joined Conference North side Northwich Victoria in 2009. He faced FC United in the FA Cup 4th qualifying round that October, with his team eventually reaching the 2nd round. After failing to recapture his form the next term, he ripped up his contract to join his local club Droylsden in December 2010, before a brief return to Northwich in September 2012. He linked up with Ashton United in February 2013, but off-field issues a few months later necessitated a long spell out of the game. Karl Marginson had long been an admirer, and when he heard that Michael was playing again at amateur level he moved to finally get him to FC in August 2017. He was terrific as the Reds stormed into a 3-1 lead on his debut at Southport, but had been substituted before the hosts grabbed their two late goals. United then won their next two games with Mike in the side, against Boston United and at York City, before again losing a potential point against Leamington after he had gone off. This was the first of four straight defeats the effects of his long lay-off perhaps started to show as he picked up several bookings for mistimed tackles, culminating in a dismissal at Darlington that reduced FC to nine men. He seemed to have recovered well when he scored his first goal for the club against Handsworth Parramore in the FA Cup a week later, but was sent off again before half-time in the next round against Stockport County, once more leaving United with nine men. He featured in the first two games after Tom Greaves replaced Marginson in October, but feeling like he hadn't done himself justice at FC he went to Glossop North End on a dual registration basis to recover his sharpness. However, he was shown another red card just 12 minutes into his debut, and didn't play again at semi-professional level until he joined New Mills in 2020. He also later featured for Cheadle Town.

243 Danny BRADY

Born: 20/05/1988, Blackburn
Debut: Sub v Bradford Park Avenue (A, NLN), 19/08/2017

Right-back/Centre-back

Season	LEAGUE Starts	(+Sub)	Goals	FA NATIONAL CUPS Starts	(+Sub)	Goals	OTHER CUPS / PLAY-OFFS Starts	(+Sub)	Goals	TOTALS Starts	(+Sub)	Goals
2017/18	10	(+2)	0	5	(+0)	0	1	(+0)	0	16	(+2)	0
Totals	10	(+2)	0	5	(+0)	0	1	(+0)	0	16	(+2)	0

Danny was a late arrival to the semi-professional game, having mainly played local amateur football until gaining a place at Northern Premier League Division One North side Clitheroe in 2014. Under the leadership of former FC United defender Simon Garner, he soon became a terrace favourite with his wholehearted approach, whether deployed in the centre of defence, at full-back or in a defensive midfield role. He was appointed the team's captain for the 2016/17 season, and had another colossal campaign that prompted Karl Marginson to sign him for FC in June 2017. He made a great start by heading the winning goal on his first appearance in a red shirt in the pre-season friendly against Bohemians in Dublin. Personal commitments ruled him out of contention in early August until he made his debut as a substitute at Bradford Park Avenue. He then started 16 of the next 17 matches, with 12 of those coming at right-back where his older head was preferred over the youthful Joel Senior. In that position he played his part in some terrific displays, most notably the second half in the FA Cup at Stockport County as FC came back from three down, and the subsequent replay when the nine Reds won through against the odds. He did look more assured in central defence, and in that role was United's best player in Marginson's last game in charge, at Chorley in October, when he was denied a goal by the crossbar. He started the first three games under Tom Greaves, but rejoined Clitheroe in November where he knew he would be guaranteed games in his favoured centre-back position. He moved to Stalybridge Celtic in June 2018 and was appointed as club captain, but left in January 2019 and retired from football.

246 Callum NICHOLAS

Born: 15/09/1997, Manchester
Debut: Sub v Handsworth Parramore (H, FAC:Q2R), 19/09/2017

Midfielder

Season	LEAGUE Starts	(+Sub)	Goals	FA NATIONAL CUPS Starts	(+Sub)	Goals	OTHER CUPS / PLAY-OFFS Starts	(+Sub)	Goals	TOTALS Starts	(+Sub)	Goals
2017/18	0	(+1)	0	0	(+1)	0	0	(+0)	0	0	(+2)	0
Totals	0	(+1)	0	0	(+1)	0	0	(+0)	0	0	(+2)	0

An attacking midfielder from Urmston, Callum played at Manchester United's academy for several years, but wasn't offered a scholarship and instead switched to rivals Liverpool in 2014. He became a regular member of their under-18 side, but unfortunately he suffered with injuries in his second season and was released in 2016. The following summer he linked up with FC United, where his combination of flair and high work-rate impressed in the pre-season friendlies. He was signed as part of the squad ahead of the 2017/18 season, but briefly left the club in order to undergo a trial at Cardiff City. He was back in September and finally appeared in the first team with substitute appearances in the wins over Handsworth Parramore and Tamworth. However he moved on in November, having been unable to establish a place in the squad, and eventually joined Radcliffe Borough in the New Year. After a short spell with Mossley he joined North West Counties side Irlam in 2019, and performed well for them in their narrow defeat to FC in the Manchester Premier Cup at Broadhurst Park in February 2020. He later linked up with 1874 Northwich and Avro.

244 Steve IRWIN

Born: 29/09/1990, Liverpool   Midfielder
Debut: Sub v Boston United (H, NLN), 26/08/2017

Season	LEAGUE Starts	(+Sub)	Goals	FA NATIONAL CUPS Starts	(+Sub)	Goals	OTHER CUPS / PLAY-OFFS Starts	(+Sub)	Goals	TOTALS Starts	(+Sub)	Goals
2017/18	24	(+4)	4	5	(+0)	2	1	(+0)	0	30	(+4)	6
Totals	24	(+4)	4	5	(+0)	2	1	(+0)	0	30	(+4)	6

Steve came through the ranks to earn a professional contract at Liverpool, where he had been a substitute in the side that won the FA Youth Cup against Manchester United in 2007. He progressed to captain the reserves, before being released in the summer of 2011. Deciding to try his luck overseas, he signed for Dutch Eerste Divisie club Telstar, but left the club due to homesickness just weeks after making his senior debut. He moved back abroad in September 2012 for a three-month stint with Finnish Premier League club FF Jaro, and had a trial with AaB Aalborg in Denmark in August 2014, before a long spell without a senior club whilst he developed his coaching career. He next surfaced in a playing capacity at Northern Premier League side Skelmersdale United in February 2017 to help in their ultimately unsuccessful fight against relegation, before joining FC United in August, where he linked up with former colleague Craig Lindfield. He was gradually introduced from the bench as he built up his match fitness, but was already a terrace favourite when he established himself in the starting line-up. His workrate and inventiveness impressed onlookers, as did his calmness under pressure when expertly despatching penalties. Five of his goals were from the spot, which included earning a vital point against Brackley Town, as well as the late equaliser to seal the terrific FA Cup comeback at Stockport County. His other goal was an absolute peach, a 25-yard screamer into the top corner at North Ferriby United. He had a couple of short spells out whilst crocked, but when fit he was an automatic choice in the line-up until the team's place in the National League North was secured in April. He signed for Stalybridge Celtic in September 2018, but soon moved to Marine, where he experienced the club's first ever relegation. He later played for Warrington Rylands.

245 Tim KINSELLA

Born: 29/07/1994, Manchester   Forward
Debut: Sub v Curzon Ashton (A, NLN), 09/09/2017

Season	LEAGUE Starts	(+Sub)	Goals	FA NATIONAL CUPS Starts	(+Sub)	Goals	OTHER CUPS / PLAY-OFFS Starts	(+Sub)	Goals	TOTALS Starts	(+Sub)	Goals
2017/18	1	(+4)	0	0	(+0)	0	0	(+0)	0	1	(+4)	0
Totals	1	(+4)	0	0	(+0)	0	0	(+0)	0	1	(+4)	0

Tim became a prolific scorer over several terms for Whalley Range in the Lancashire & Cheshire Amateur League. He was brought into the North West Counties League by Irlam in 2017, and hit the ground running with three goals in his first six matches in semi-professional football. His progress alerted Karl Marginson, who signed him for FC United in September. He was introduced from the bench at Curzon Ashton, and almost made it a dream debut when he rounded the goalkeeper, but could only hit the side netting from a tight angle. With the team playing five games in the FA Cup over the next month, he was unable to establish a run in the squad having already played in the competition in August. His patience was rewarded with a start at Chorley, but it was a miserable day as the Reds fell to a defeat that ended Marginson's reign. Although Tim was named on the bench for the first match under Tom Greaves, he remained unused and left the club in November. After just a week on the books of Winsford United, he returned to Irlam and developed a front-line partnership with former FC striker Matty Boland, with both bagging hat-tricks before the end of the season. He went on to have a productive spell with Wythenshawe Amateurs in 2018/19, before reverting to amateur level back at Whalley Range.

247 Kallum MANTACK

Born: 01/05/1998, Wolverhampton   Full-back/Winger
Debut: No.11 v Stockport County (A, FAC:Q3), 30/09/2017

Season	LEAGUE Starts	(+Sub)	Goals	FA NATIONAL CUPS Starts	(+Sub)	Goals	OTHER CUPS / PLAY-OFFS Starts	(+Sub)	Goals	TOTALS Starts	(+Sub)	Goals
2017/18	1	(+0)	0	3	(+0)	0	0	(+0)	0	4	(+0)	0
Totals	1	(+0)	0	3	(+0)	0	0	(+0)	0	4	(+0)	0

Kallum is a product of the youth system at Oldham Athletic, where he progressed to sign his first professional contract in April 2016. A full-back or midfielder from Wythenshawe, he was awarded a senior debut on the right wing against Wigan Athletic in the Football League Cup in August 2016, before beginning a loan spell with Alfreton Town the following month. He played against FC United in a National League North fixture at Broadhurst Park shortly afterwards, and his loan was extended until January 2017. He played twice for Oldham, in League One and the EFL Trophy, in August 2017 before joining FC on loan in September. His debut was delayed by illness and came in the FA Cup at Stockport County when the Reds came from three down at the break to draw 3-3. He kept his place for the replay when United memorably won 1-0 with nine men, and his next game was also in the FA Cup at AFC Telford United where he almost scored with a long-range shot. After featuring in the defeat at Chorley, he returned to his parent club at the end of his loan, but almost immediately joined Stockport on a similar arrangement. Coincidentally, his debut for them was against FC as an early substitute, and he scored his new side's third goal before the break. Just minutes after hitting County's winner against Alfreton on Boxing Day he suffered a broken fibula and dislocated ankle that brought an end to his season. He was released by Oldham in May 2018 and returned to Stockport, where he scored against FC again on the season's opening day. After a trial at Blackburn Rovers, he had spells at Altrincham, Ashton United and Curzon Ashton before facing FC again in the colours of Stalybridge Celtic in October 2019.

248 Sefton GONZALES

Born: 21/12/1991, Chorley
Debut: No.10 v North Ferriby United (A, NLN), 07/10/2017

Forward

Season	LEAGUE			FA NATIONAL CUPS			OTHER CUPS / PLAY-OFFS			TOTALS		
	Starts	(+Sub)	Goals	Starts	(+Sub)	Goals	Starts	(+Sub)	Goals	Starts	(+Sub)	Goals
2017/18	2	(+0)	0	0	(+0)	0	0	(+0)	0	2	(+0)	0
Totals	2	(+0)	0	0	(+0)	0	0	(+0)	0	2	(+0)	0

A big, strong centre-forward, Sefton initially made his name with Kendal Town before linking up with Droylsden, but he got his first sustained run at Clitheroe under former FC defender Simon Garner. His form earned a move into National League North with Stockport County in 2015, when he faced United in the first competitive game at Broadhurst Park. After a month's loan to Salford City, he returned to Clitheroe before joining his hometown club Chorley in the summer of 2016. He made his debut in the first game of the season against FC, and opened the scoring after just ten minutes. Later that season he spent a month each with Colne and Stalybridge Celtic before rejoining Stockport in February 2017. At the end of the term he signed for Altrincham, but returned to Clitheroe due to work commitments before kicking a ball. He joined FC United in September 2017, but featured just twice before moving on to Droylsden in November. In 2018/19 he was the Northern Premier League West Division's 2nd highest scorer with 22 goals, before rejoining Colne for the following season. However he left after being the victim of an unsavoury comment by a club official and signed for South Shields in December 2019. He later linked up with Matlock Town and Ramsbottom United before returning to Clitheroe.

249 Tom WALKER

Born: 12/12/1995, Salford
Debut: No.10 v North Ferriby United (A, NLN), 07/10/2017 (scored)

Left-back/Left-winger

Season	LEAGUE			FA NATIONAL CUPS			OTHER CUPS / PLAY-OFFS			TOTALS		
	Starts	(+Sub)	Goals	Starts	(+Sub)	Goals	Starts	(+Sub)	Goals	Starts	(+Sub)	Goals
2017/18	9	(+1)	1	2	(+0)	0	1	(+0)	0	12	(+1)	1
Totals	9	(+1)	1	2	(+0)	0	1	(+0)	0	12	(+1)	1

Tom progressed through the Bolton Wanderers youth system to make his Football League Championship debut against Leeds United in January 2015. Two months later he claimed his first goal against Wigan Athletic on just his third start, and played in every game from then until the end of the season. He featured a further eight times in 2015/16, but started just once as the struggling side were relegated to League One. He joined rivals Bury on loan in August 2016, playing 15 times for the Gigg Lane club before his release by Bolton in May 2017. He linked up with Stockport County, who signed him on a short-term deal in August, but let him go the following month after just five substitute appearances. He joined FC United in October, and made a great start by opening the scoring with a lovely finish on his debut at North Ferriby United. He started the last three games of Karl Marginson's reign on the left wing, but was asked to fill in at left-back when Tom Greaves made his first selection against Nuneaton Town. This developed into a left wing-back role for the Manchester Premier Cup win at Salford City, and after a couple of games out through illness he was back in that position for the great sequence of results over the festive period, when he was arguably the team's best player. His corners provided the first two goals in the memorable win over high-flying Harrogate Town, the second of which was headed home by Greaves for his 99th goal for the club. He was man-of-the-match against second placed Brackley Town, before two outstanding performances against Salford that would change the course of his career. His crosses led to the equaliser and the winner from Greaves in the 3-2 home win on Boxing Day, before another solid display in the 2-2 draw on New Year's Day prompted Salford to offer him a full-time contract days later. He missed just one game for his hometown club and scored six goals as they claimed the National League North title, and was named in the division's Team Of The Year along with former FC team-mate Jason Gilchrist. Tom capped a wonderful season by scoring a stunning goal on his debut for the England C team against Ireland in Dublin in May. He earned further caps the following year, and was part of the Salford squad that reached the Football League by winning the 2019 National League play-off final at Wembley. He had four outings in League Two, and seven in that division in 2020/21 for Harrogate Town, but subsequently played mainly back in the National League in spells at Stockport, AFC Fylde, Notts County and Altrincham.

250 Tyrell PALMER

Born: 05/10/1997, Manchester
Debut: Sub v Salford City (A, MPC:QF), 07/11/2017

Midfielder

	LEAGUE			FA NATIONAL CUPS			OTHER CUPS / PLAY-OFFS			TOTALS		
Season	Starts	(+Sub)	Goals	Starts	(+Sub)	Goals	Starts	(+Sub)	Goals	Starts	(+Sub)	Goals
2017/18	2	(+13)	0	0	(+1)	0	0	(+3)	0	2	(+17)	0
Totals	2	(+13)	0	0	(+1)	0	0	(+3)	0	2	(+17)	0

Tyrell joined Bolton Wanderers on a scholarship after leaving school in 2014, and was a regular in the under-18 side before being released in 2016. The following year he joined FC United's reserve side, and his impressive displays in the Lancashire & Cheshire Amateur League for junior partner club Moston United earned a deal with the senior team in November 2017. He made his debut from the bench in the Manchester Premier Cup win at Salford City, and became a constant in the matchday squad for the next four months. His pace, energy and drive from midfield caught the eye, particularly a right wing run and cross for Connor McCarthy to seal the home win over Curzon Ashton in January. Along with team-mate Michael Jones, he joined Mossley on loan in March 2018, and played six times in the Northern Premier League Division One North. He returned to United in April and featured in the last three games of the season, which included a substitute appearance in the Manchester Premier Cup Final against Trafford which the Reds won on penalties. However, despite featuring in pre-season, he sustained a broken ankle that halted his semi-professional career.

251 Sam TATTUM

Born: 03/09/1996, Salford
Debut: Sub v Spennymoor Town (A, NLN), 23/12/2017

Full-back/Midfielder

	LEAGUE			FA NATIONAL CUPS			OTHER CUPS / PLAY-OFFS			TOTALS		
Season	Starts	(+Sub)	Goals	Starts	(+Sub)	Goals	Starts	(+Sub)	Goals	Starts	(+Sub)	Goals
2017/18	4	(+7)	0	0	(+0)	0	2	(+0)	0	6	(+7)	0
2018/19	8	(+2)	0	1	(+0)	0	0	(+0)	0	9	(+2)	0
Totals	12	(+9)	0	1	(+0)	0	2	(+0)	0	15	(+9)	0

Sam came through the ranks to join Manchester City on a scholarship in 2013. The Worsley lad also won caps for Wales at under-17 level, but suffered an injury-hit first year in full-time football. He recovered to be almost ever-present in 2014/15 and was awarded a professional contract at the end of the term. After several outings in the reserves, he was released in 2016 and after trials at Blackburn Rovers, AFC Fylde and Sheffield Wednesday he joined National League North side Stalybridge Celtic in September. Unfortunately, on his very first start against Droylsden a terrible tackle broke his leg and ankle and sidelined him for over a year. He returned to the game when he signed for FC United in December 2017, and in his first two outings the team won points from losing positions after he emerged as a substitute. He came on for his debut with 21 minutes to go at Spennymoor Town with FC trailing 2-4, and within seven minutes the scores were level at 4-4. The Reds also hit two late goals soon after he was introduced to beat league leaders Salford City 3-2 on Boxing Day. In January he joined Padiham on a dual registration basis, and played seven games in the North West Counties League to improve his fitness when not on United duty. His first start for FC was in the Manchester Premier Cup semi-final win at Hyde United, and he was a regular squad member during the season's run-in. He played an important part in each of the last seven fixtures, and was one of three players who played without payment in the last three games after FC's relegation fears were allayed. He was a member of the team that brought the Manchester Premier Cup back to Broadhurst Park with a penalty shoot-out win over Trafford in the final in April. His cross was converted by Kurt Willoughby for FC's first goal of 2018/19, just three minutes after he came off the bench on the season's opening day. He played in each of the first nine games and was a regular in the squad until a harsh red card against Darlington in October. Two weeks later he signed on a dual registration basis for Northern Premier League side Marine, before spells abroad in Sweden with Syrianska and in Norway with Brattvåg.

252 Adam GILCHRIST

Born: 18/05/1989, St. Helens
Debut: Sub v Salford City (A, NLN), 01/01/2018

Forward/Winger

	LEAGUE			FA NATIONAL CUPS			OTHER CUPS / PLAY-OFFS			TOTALS		
Season	Starts	(+Sub)	Goals	Starts	(+Sub)	Goals	Starts	(+Sub)	Goals	Starts	(+Sub)	Goals
2017/18	1	(+3)	0	0	(+1)	0	2	(+0)	1	3	(+3)	1
Totals	1	(+3)	0	0	(+1)	0	2	(+0)	1	3	(+3)	1

Adam signed for FC United in December 2017, soon after his younger brother Jason had left to join Southport. Able to play up front or wide on either side, Adam came to the Reds with over 10 years experience at North West Counties League and Northern Premier League levels. His first senior outings were with Radcliffe Borough, before spells at his local club St. Helens Town, Marine, Ashton Athletic and Burscough. He made his United debut as a late substitute in the 2-2 draw at league leaders Salford City on New Year's Day 2018, before making club history the following weekend against Southport when he and Jason became the first set of brothers to face each other in an FC fixture. He marked his first start with the only goal at Hyde United in the Manchester Premier Cup semi-final in February, before joining Hyde on a dual registration basis in March. He struck the winner for them at Tadcaster Albion later that month, before returning to FC in April when he was one of the players who lined up for free in order to help to alleviate the club's financial position. He was rewarded by starting the Manchester Premier Cup Final against Trafford, and deservedly earned his winners medal. He joined Runcorn Linnets in August 2018, but returned to Ashton Athletic in November and was a standout performer in the North West Counties League over the next two seasons before a switch to rivals Pilkington in 2020. Adam is also a UEFA B qualified football coach.

253 Jamal CRAWFORD

Born: 26/11/1997, Manchester
Debut: Sub v Southport (H, NLN), 07/01/2018

Winger/Forward

Season	LEAGUE			FA NATIONAL CUPS			OTHER CUPS / PLAY-OFFS			TOTALS		
	Starts	(+Sub)	Goals	Starts	(+Sub)	Goals	Starts	(+Sub)	Goals	Starts	(+Sub)	Goals
2017/18	4	(+7)	0	0	(+0)	0	1	(+0)	0	5	(+7)	0
2018/19	5	(+11)	0	1	(+1)	0	0	(+2)	0	6	(+14)	0
Totals	9	(+18)	0	1	(+1)	0	1	(+2)	0	11	(+21)	0

As a schoolboy Jamal was an extremely talented athlete, who finished 2nd in the UK for his age group in the long jump in 2012. At the same time he was also making his way in football as part of the academy at Burnley, where he signed as a scholar upon leaving school in 2014. Pacy and skilful, he was a potent attacking threat in the under-18 team, but was released in the summer of 2016 before joining Welsh Premier League side Llandudno later that year. He returned to Manchester at the end of the season and linked up with FC United's junior partner club Moston United. His performances in the Lancashire & Cheshire Amateur League saw him quickly elevated to join the senior squad in November 2017, although his first-team bow was delayed as the club awaited international clearance. He came off the bench for his debut in the win over Southport in January 2018, and almost made a dream start with his first touch, but his superb header was kept out by former FC goalkeeper Jon Worsnop. He continued to excite as a substitute, and was given his first start on the wing in February against Chorley. He kept his place for the Manchester Premier Cup semi-final win at Hyde United, and played his part in the build-up to Adam Gilchrist's winning goal. After a spell on the sidelines, he was introduced as a half-time replacement with the Reds three goals down at Boston United, and was instrumental in the comeback for an amazing 4-4 draw. His reward was starting the vital home games with Gainsborough Trinity and Bradford Park Avenue, and he was involved in breaking the deadlock in both as United collected six crucial points. An injury at Tamworth in April unfortunately ended his season, but he had done enough to be given a new contract in May for the 2018/19 campaign. He started four of the first five games in 2018/19, and was particularly impressive as the Reds picked up their first points of the season at Altrincham. However, during the autumn he more often appeared off the bench. He almost opened his goalscoring account in the superb win at Kidderminster Harriers, only for his shot to strike the bar. After month-long loan spells at Northern Premier League sides Stalybridge Celtic and Widnes, Jamal cancelled his FC United contract at the end of March 2019 and spent the last month of the season with Chester, featuring three times in National League North. He moved on to Hyde United, and came off the bench twice against FC in 2019/20 before later spells with Curzon Ashton, Atherton Collieries, Bamber Bridge, Glossop North End, Trafford and Widnes.

254 Danny RACCHI

Born: 22/11/1987, Halifax
Debut: No.8 v Nuneaton Town (A, NLN), 03/02/2018

Midfielder

Season	LEAGUE			FA NATIONAL CUPS			OTHER CUPS / PLAY-OFFS			TOTALS		
	Starts	(+Sub)	Goals	Starts	(+Sub)	Goals	Starts	(+Sub)	Goals	Starts	(+Sub)	Goals
2017/18	9	(+3)	0	0	(+0)	0	1	(+1)	0	10	(+4)	0
2018/19	4	(+0)	0	0	(+0)	0	0	(+0)	0	4	(+0)	0
Totals	13	(+3)	0	0	(+0)	0	1	(+1)	0	14	(+4)	0

Danny progressed through the Huddersfield Town youth ranks to sign a professional contract in 2006, and made his senior debut as a substitute in a League One draw with Port Vale in March 2007. After five further appearances from the bench, he joined Bury on a free transfer in July 2008 and played in a number of defensive and midfield roles in two years at Gigg Lane. After a short spell at Wrexham he signed for Conference rivals York City in September 2010, where he made a promising start but left the club in April 2011 after losing his regular place. In July 2011 he signed for Scottish Premier League club Kilmarnock, where he became a valued member of the squad. He bagged his first goal away at Celtic in December before scoring a late winner against St. Mirren the following week. He had earned a regular spot early in 2012/13, but was sidelined by a knee injury in October. He regained fitness, only to be floored by a rare virus later in the year, and thereafter he was unable to force his way back into the side. He was released amidst a contractual dispute in April 2013, and moved to Iceland to play for Valur that summer. He returned to England for a short spell with Conference North side Hyde in January 2015, before starting the following season with hometown club FC Halifax Town. He switched to Tamworth in October 2015 before moving to Torquay United in January 2016. He was a popular figure in Devon, but was released in the summer and then had a long spell out of the game after suffering injuries to both knees. He began training with FC United in December 2017, and was registered to play when the team were short of midfield options. He proved a useful addition to the squad, although he understandably tired towards the end of games after his long lay-off. Despite that, he was involved in all but two matches, one of which when he was suspended after an unfortunate red card at Leamington. He further endeared himself to the Reds faithful as one of the players who played the last three games of the season for no wages, and he deservedly picked up a Manchester Premier Cup winner's medal. His gesture and efforts were rewarded with a place in the squad for 2018/19, although he was somewhat controversially omitted from the teamsheet on the season's opening day. He was back in the starting line-up for the next four matches, which included the first win of the season at Altrincham, but left FC at the end of August. He linked up with Curzon Ashton in January 2019, before later moving into the Northern Premier League with Hednesford Town. He captained Grantham Town to a win against FC United on the opening day of the 2019/20 season and later had spells with Ilkeston Town and Brighouse Town.

255 Luke HIGHAM

Born: 21/10/1996, Blackpool
Debut: No.3 v Hyde United (A, MPC:SF), 13/02/2018

Left-back

Season	LEAGUE			FA NATIONAL CUPS			OTHER CUPS / PLAY-OFFS			TOTALS		
	Starts	(+Sub)	Goals	Starts	(+Sub)	Goals	Starts	(+Sub)	Goals	Starts	(+Sub)	Goals
2017/18	11	(+0)	0	0	(+0)	0	2	(+0)	0	13	(+0)	0
Totals	11	(+0)	0	0	(+0)	0	2	(+0)	0	13	(+0)	0

Luke progressed through the ranks at his local club Blackpool, where he was a season-ticket holder, to sign as a professional in May 2015. The tall left-back made his senior debut against Port Vale in the Football League Trophy in October 2015, and later in the campaign he started the final 11 League One fixtures, although the side were unable to avoid relegation. His only senior appearances the following season were in the EFL Trophy, but he did have two loan spells in National League North with Nuneaton Town and then AFC Telford United. He joined Fleetwood Town on a free transfer in July 2017, but again played just one EFL Trophy game before joining FC United on loan in February 2018 after Danny Wisdom's injury. He made his debut for the Reds in the Manchester Premier Cup semi-final win at Hyde United, and kept the no.3 shirt until picking up a winner's medal in the final against Trafford in April. He began the next season with Colne before moving to Australia to play for Moreland City. After returning to England in 2020 he had spells on the books at Lancaster City, Marine and Bamber Bridge, for whom he twice faced FC in 2021/22.

256 Jeff KING

Born: 19/12/1995, Liverpool
Debut: No.11 v AFC Telford United (A, NLN), 24/02/2018

Midfielder/Forward

Season	LEAGUE			FA NATIONAL CUPS			OTHER CUPS / PLAY-OFFS			TOTALS		
	Starts	(+Sub)	Goals	Starts	(+Sub)	Goals	Starts	(+Sub)	Goals	Starts	(+Sub)	Goals
2017/18	4	(+1)	4	0	(+0)	0	0	(+0)	0	4	(+1)	4
Totals	4	(+1)	4	0	(+0)	0	0	(+0)	0	4	(+1)	4

As an attacking midfielder who could also lead the line, Jeff came through the youth teams at Altrincham, where his uncle John is a legendary former captain and manager. After a spell on loan at Prescot Cables in March 2014, he played for Nantwich Town, Kendal Town and Trafford in 2014/15, then Ashton United and Witton Albion the following season. He joined Droylsden in August 2016, where he came to the attention of Bolton Wanderers, who signed him for their under-23 side in November. He was given a full professional contract in July 2017 and made his debut in September in the League Cup against West Ham United. He was given two further senior outings before joining FC United on a month's loan in February 2018. The team failed to score during his first two games, and were behind again when he scored within four minutes of coming on at Boston United to contribute to an amazing comeback. The final game of his loan came against Bradford Park Avenue a week later, and he signed off in style by scoring a hat-trick of set-pieces. His first was a wonderful free-kick, whereas his second took a wicked deflection off the defensive wall. He completed his treble by audaciously chipping a penalty over the goalkeeper to complete the 4-0 victory. He signed for Scottish Premiership club St Mirren in June 2018, but left by mutual consent in January 2019 and joined National League side FC Halifax Town for the 2019/20 season. He was converted into an attacking right-back before switching to Chesterfield in 2021, and helping them to the National League play-offs in 2022.

257 Gerard GARNER

Born: 02/11/1998, Liverpool
Debut: No.9 v Harrogate Town (A, NLN), 10/03/2018

Forward

Season	LEAGUE			FA NATIONAL CUPS			OTHER CUPS / PLAY-OFFS			TOTALS		
	Starts	(+Sub)	Goals	Starts	(+Sub)	Goals	Starts	(+Sub)	Goals	Starts	(+Sub)	Goals
2017/18	3	(+3)	3	0	(+0)	0	0	(+0)	0	3	(+3)	3
Totals	3	(+3)	3	0	(+0)	0	0	(+0)	0	3	(+3)	3

Gerard is a former Liverpool academy striker, who came to the club's attention after scoring 73 times in a season for the city's schoolboys' team to break a record held by Wayne Rooney. After leaving school he became a scholar at Fleetwood Town, and progressed to sign professional terms in March 2017. He began 2017/18 on loan at Southport, but was an unused substitute in four National League North matches, one of which was against FC United. He had a further loan spell at Northern Premier League Division One North side Bamber Bridge in November 2017, before embarking on his third temporary stint when he linked up with FC on March 2018. He had a debut to forget as the team slumped to the club's record defeat, but he went on to score on each of the next three Saturdays. He came off the bench to reduce the deficit as the Reds came back to draw 4-4 at Boston United, before bagging the third at home to Bradford Park Avenue. In the dying seconds at Tamworth he coolly stroked the ball home to seal an unexpected victory, but that was his last act in an FC shirt. A few days later he scored for Fleetwood against Bury in the Lancashire Cup Final but suffered a broken jaw just minutes later that prematurely ended his campaign. He continued to progress at Fleetwood over the next two terms, during which he made his Football League debut and scored his first senior goal, and he was rewarded with a new contract in March 2019. After another loan spell in the National League North with Gateshead in October 2020, he returned to be a regular member of the Fleetwood squad.

258 Elliot SIMÕES Inácio

Born: 20/12/1999, Amadora (Portugal)
Debut: Sub v Darlington (H, NLN), 14/04/2018

Winger/Forward

Season	LEAGUE			FA NATIONAL CUPS			OTHER CUPS / PLAY-OFFS			TOTALS		
	Starts	(+Sub)	Goals	Starts	(+Sub)	Goals	Starts	(+Sub)	Goals	Starts	(+Sub)	Goals
2017/18	1	(+2)	0	0	(+0)	0	0	(+1)	0	1	(+3)	0
2018/19	13	(+1)	0	1	(+2)	0	1	(+1)	2	15	(+4)	2
Totals	14	(+3)	0	1	(+2)	0	1	(+2)	2	16	(+7)	2

Previously in the academies of both Benfica and Sporting Lisbon in his homeland, Elliot joined the FC United academy in 2016 and developed into a regular goalscorer during his two years in the youth and college teams. He was selected to represent Manchester County FA in February 2018, and the following month he was one of four youth graduates to sign registration forms for the senior side. He was named on the bench for the visit to Leamington, and featured in every subsequent matchday squad until the end of the season. He made his bow in the closing stages against Darlington, before producing exciting attacking displays at Alfreton Town and against Trafford when the Reds won the Manchester Premier Cup Final. He was rewarded with a starting spot in the final National League North fixture of the season against North Ferriby United. After starting against Boston United as a late replacement for the injured Harry Winter, he was eased in from the bench in the early stages of 2018/19. Inexperience was probably a factor in an injury-time dismissal in the FA Cup tie against Witton Albion, but he made up for it three days later by grabbing both goals in the Manchester Premier Cup win at Glossop North End. Having played, and scored, in a full game for the under-21 side the night before, he returned to the senior side to lead the line in the tremendous win at Kidderminster Harriers in October. Thereafter he became an automatic choice on the wing for new boss Neil Reynolds, particularly with thrilling performances against Alfreton, Blyth Spartans and Hereford. He signed a contract for the club in December, but by then was already attracting the attention of Football League clubs. It wasn't long before one pounced, as Elliot signed for Barnsley for an undisclosed fee in January 2019. He was handed a Championship debut as a substitute against Swansea City in October, and scored his first goal in just his third outing when he equalised in a televised game at Derby County in January 2020. He remained in the senior squad for the rest of the term, and also for the early months of 2020/21, during which he made a senior international debut for Angola against Mozambique. He joined League One side Doncaster Rovers on loan in January 2021, before moving to French Ligue 2 side AS Nancy Lorraine in August.

259 Steve AFFLECK

Born: 27/11/1999, Manchester
Debut: Sub v Alfreton Town (A, NLN), 21/04/2018

Right-back

Season	LEAGUE			FA NATIONAL CUPS			OTHER CUPS / PLAY-OFFS			TOTALS		
	Starts	(+Sub)	Goals	Starts	(+Sub)	Goals	Starts	(+Sub)	Goals	Starts	(+Sub)	Goals
2017/18	0	(+1)	0	0	(+0)	0	0	(+0)	0	0	(+1)	0
2018/19	0	(+0)	0	0	(+0)	0	0	(+0)	0	0	(+0)	0
Totals	0	(+1)	0	0	(+0)	0	0	(+0)	0	0	(+1)	0

A right-back from Middleton, Steve joined FC United's academy in the summer of 2016, and was integral to the under-18s reaching the FA Youth Cup 1st round in his first season. He also broke into the reserve team, before making further strides in 2017/18. His stunning 35-yard strike was the highlight of the FA Youth Cup win at Burscough, and he was soon promoted to the senior squad. He was named on the bench for the FA Trophy trip to Marine in November, and just after his 18th birthday he signed a contract with the club until May 2019. Along with youth team colleague Sam O'Donnell, he went on loan to North West Counties League side West Didsbury & Chorlton in January 2018, drawing great praise from their management and fans in a dozen outings. He came back to the Reds in April to make his debut as a substitute at Alfreton Town, and was also on the bench for the Manchester Premier Cup Final win over Trafford and the last National League North fixture of the season. He was an unused substitute in four further games the following term, before cancelling his contract in November. He initially rejoined West Didsbury & Chorlton, but switched to Chadderton in January 2019.

260 Billy CRELLIN

Born: 30/01/2000, Blackpool
Debut: No.1 v Stockport County (A, NLN), 04/08/2018

Goalkeeper

Season	LEAGUE			FA NATIONAL CUPS			OTHER CUPS / PLAY-OFFS			TOTALS		
	Starts	(+Sub)	Goals	Starts	(+Sub)	Goals	Starts	(+Sub)	Goals	Starts	(+Sub)	Goals
2018/19	7	(+0)	0	0	(+0)	0	0	(+0)	0	7	(+0)	0
Totals	7	(+0)	0	0	(+0)	0	0	(+0)	0	7	(+0)	0

Billy became the first player from the youth academy at his local club Fleetwood Town to sign a professional contract, and was also the club's first player to represent England at youth level. He was in his country's squad when they won the under-17 World Cup in India in October 2017, and also travelled to the under-19 European Championship in 2018. He joined FC United on an emergency youth loan in July 2018 as cover for the injured Lloyd Allinson, and started the first seven games of the campaign. Despite the team picking up just four points, the teenage keeper grew in confidence with a series of fine saves, particularly at Spennymoor Town, the win at Altrincham and the home draw with Bradford Park Avenue. He was recalled by his parent club in September and went straight onto the bench for the subsequent League One fixtures before making his senior debut against Rochdale in the Football League Trophy the following month. He began 2019/20 on loan in the National League at Chorley, and earned an England under-20 cap in October. The following month he began a run of eight games in the Fleetwood first team, which included a victory on his Football League bow against Tranmere Rovers. He spent 2020/21 on loan in League Two with Bolton Wanderers, before moving into the Premier League in January 2022 when he signed for Everton, to initially feature for their under-23 side.

261 Stephen O'HALLORAN

Born: 29/11/1987, Cork (Ireland)   Left-back/Centre-back
Debut: No.3 v Stockport County (A, NLN), 04/08/2018

Season	LEAGUE			FA NATIONAL CUPS			OTHER CUPS / PLAY-OFFS			TOTALS		
	Starts	(+Sub)	Goals	Starts	(+Sub)	Goals	Starts	(+Sub)	Goals	Starts	(+Sub)	Goals
2018/19	41	(+0)	0	3	(+0)	0	1	(+0)	0	45	(+0)	0
Totals	41	(+0)	0	3	(+0)	0	1	(+0)	0	45	(+0)	0

After leaving school in Ireland, Steve came over to England to join Premiership giants Aston Villa as a scholar, and was promoted to the first team squad after signing a professional contract in 2006. He made his senior debut on loan for League Two side Wycombe Wanderers that November, and played for them against Chelsea in the 2007 League Cup semi-final. That summer he gained two full international caps against Ecuador and Bolivia on Ireland's tour of the USA, and was named as his country's under-21 player of the season a year later. After a month's loan at Championship club Southampton, he joined Leeds United in League One on a smiliar arrangement in February 2008. Unfortunately, he sustained a serious ACL injury whilst warming up for what would have been his debut at Swindon Town, and was sidelined for several months. Once recovered he returned to the Championship with Swansea City on another loan in November 2008, but he suffered another ACL injury the following month. He eventually worked his way back to fitness in Villa's reserves, before a free transfer to Coventry City in June 2010. However, he struggled to establish himself and moved to Carlisle United a year later, but had another injury-disrupted season. He dropped into the Conference with Nuneaton Town in 2012, then joined Stockport County after their demotion to the Conference North in 2013. He extended his contract the following year, before moving to Northern Premier League club Salford City in 2015. He equalised with a rare goal against Hartlepool United in the FA Cup 2nd round, and struck again later in the term when his team secured promotion to National League North. He faced FC United in 2016/17, and again in 2017/18 after rejoining Stockport. He joined the Reds on a contract in June 2018 and scored in a friendly against Airbus UK at Broadhurst. After his official debut at former club Stockport he missed just one league game, and two in total, during the entire campaign. Appointed as vice-captain, he spent the first month of the season at left-back before moving across to the centre in September, mainly partnering Chris Lynch. The two experienced campaigners combined well, particularly during the good run of results in the autumn, and at the other end it was from O'Halloran's cross that Lynch equalised against Chorley. Steve reverted to left-back for the superb win at Bradford Park Avenue in January 2019, and pretty much held that position until the end of the season. He moved on to Stalybridge Celtic in June, and became player-assistant manager before retiring in May 2022. Steve is also a qualified physiotherapist, having graduated from the University of Salford in 2016.

265 Liam DICKINSON

Born: 04/10/1985, Salford   Forward
Debut: No.9 v Stockport County (A, NLN), 04/08/2018

Season	LEAGUE			FA NATIONAL CUPS			OTHER CUPS / PLAY-OFFS			TOTALS		
	Starts	(+Sub)	Goals	Starts	(+Sub)	Goals	Starts	(+Sub)	Goals	Starts	(+Sub)	Goals
2018/19	4	(+3)	1	0	(+0)	0	0	(+0)	0	4	(+3)	1
Totals	4	(+3)	1	0	(+0)	0	0	(+0)	0	4	(+3)	1

As a schoolboy Liam played in the academies at Blackpool, Bolton Wanderers and Blackburn Rovers, but he did not immediately progress into full-time football after leaving school. He joined the amateur circuit with Irlam in the Manchester League, before becoming semi-professional in the North West Counties League with Trafford, and later at Woodley Sports. After a successful trial, he signed for Stockport County in November 2005, and made his League Two debut in January 2006, when he took just five minutes to score against Cheltenham Town after coming off the bench. He began to establish himself as a powerful centre-forward, before enjoying the most prolific campaign of his career in 2007/08. He hit 21 goals and was County's player of the season, and scored the winning goals in the promotion play-off semi-final against Wycombe Wanderers and the final against Rochdale at Wembley. His performances prompted Championship side Derby County to pay £750,000 for his services in July 2008, but he never played a senior game for them and instead served consecutive loan spells with Huddersfield Town, Blackpool and Leeds United. He was transferred to Brighton & Hove Albion in July 2009, and was a regular in the Seagulls' squad until joining Peterborough United on loan in February 2010. He moved on a permanent deal to Barnsley in June 2010, but after just four appearances embarked on further loan spells with Walsall and Rochdale. He initially agreed a contract with Plymouth Argyle in July 2011, but instead signed for Southend United, where he finally got a long run in a settled side that missed automatic promotion from League Two by just one point. Unfortunately, his season had been ended by a broken ankle in March 2012, and he was released that summer. The ankle took time to properly heal, and after two unsuccessful trials at Port Vale he eventually returned to the non-league game with a return to Stockport in 2013. He later featured for Guiseley and Bradford Park Avenue between three spells with Stalybridge Celtic, for whom he played against FC United in November 2016. He was delighted to link up with FC in July 2018 as the Reds were looking for a physical presence up front, and showed that he was more than just a target man when he netted with a sumptuous 30-yard chip in the home friendly with Rochdale. He equalised with a towering header at Altrincham, and was named man of the match as the team earned their first points of the season. He also came close with an overhead kick in the draw at Chester. However, he was released by caretaker boss David Chadwick in September, before signing for Northern Premier League side Droylsden the following month.

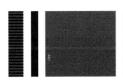

262 Bradley BARNES

Born: 12/12/1988, Manchester
Debut: No.4 v Stockport County (A, NLN), 04/08/2018

Midfielder

Season	LEAGUE			FA NATIONAL CUPS			OTHER CUPS / PLAY-OFFS			TOTALS		
	Starts	(+Sub)	Goals	Starts	(+Sub)	Goals	Starts	(+Sub)	Goals	Starts	(+Sub)	Goals
2018/19	1	(+0)	0	0	(+0)	0	0	(+0)	0	1	(+0)	0
Totals	1	(+0)	0	0	(+0)	0	0	(+0)	0	1	(+0)	0

A former Bolton Wanderers trainee, Brad entered non-league with Flixton, and first played against FC United in August 2006. In 2008 he switched to local rivals Trafford after their promotion to the Northern Premier League, then moved up to the Conference North with Southport in 2009. The following year he joined the newly-formed Chester FC and helped them to win the league in their first season, before signing for AFC Fylde in 2011 after a short loan at Colwyn Bay. He was sent off against FC when the clubs first met in 2012, but was an integral part of Fylde's team as they won two promotions through the Northern Premier League divisions. He was named in the Conference North team of the season in 2015, before moving to Salford City a year later and facing United again. He moved back into the Northern Premier League with Warrington Town in 2017, before joining the Reds on a contract in May 2018. He scored the first goal of pre-season at Irlam in July and was expected to be one of the team's key players. However, those hopes were ruined within two seconds of the campaign kicking off at Stockport County when he twisted a knee challenging for the ball. An attempt to continue proved futile and he limped off five minutes later. A later scan showed that he had ruptured his Anterior Cruciate Ligament, which ruled him out of contention for the remainder of the season and halted his semi-professional career.

263 Chris LYNCH

Born: 29/12/1984, Salford
Debut: No.6 v Stockport County (A, NLN), 04/08/2018

Centre-back/Right-back

Season	LEAGUE			FA NATIONAL CUPS			OTHER CUPS / PLAY-OFFS			TOTALS		
	Starts	(+Sub)	Goals	Starts	(+Sub)	Goals	Starts	(+Sub)	Goals	Starts	(+Sub)	Goals
2018/19	31	(+1)	1	3	(+0)	0	1	(+0)	0	35	(+1)	1
Totals	31	(+1)	1	3	(+0)	0	1	(+0)	0	35	(+1)	1

Chris came through the ranks at Wigan Athletic to sign as a professional, and was an unused substitute for the final three games of the 2002/03 season as the first team won the Division Two title. The versatile defender from Little Hulton was released in 2004 without playing a senior game, and began a long stay at Hyde United. He helped them to the Northern Premier League title in his first season and played a total of 287 games before a 2011 switch to Conference North rivals Altrincham. He moved back to the Northern Premier League in 2012 with Ashton United, and faced FC United four times as captain, and also had a summer in Western Australia at Perth club Sorrento. He linked up with Salford City in 2014, and led them to successive promotions to reach the Conference North in 2016, before returning to Australia for a spell with Murray United in Victoria. He rejoined Altrincham, via a brief return to Salford, in February 2017, then joined Atherton Collieries after their promotion to the Northern Premier League. He signed for FC in May 2018, and in his first game at Broadhurst equalised with a neat header in the friendly with Winterthur. His no-nonsense defending made him a firm favourite as he continuously put his body on the line, a symbol of which was a month out with two cracked ribs in January 2019. He won more man of the match awards than anyone else, particularly during a mid-season partnership with Steve O'Halloran, and was delighted with his first competitive goal for the club against Chorley on Boxing Day. He also showed his versatility by filling in at right-back, and was deservedly named as both Supporters' and Manager's Player Of The Season. He later returned to Atherton Collieries as player-coach.

264 Jack BANISTER

Born: 28/08/1995, Crystal Palace
Debut: No.7 v Stockport County (A, NLN), 04/08/2018

Winger

Season	LEAGUE			FA NATIONAL CUPS			OTHER CUPS / PLAY-OFFS			TOTALS		
	Starts	(+Sub)	Goals	Starts	(+Sub)	Goals	Starts	(+Sub)	Goals	Starts	(+Sub)	Goals
2018/19	19	(+14)	5	3	(+0)	2	2	(+0)	0	24	(+14)	7
Totals	19	(+14)	5	3	(+0)	2	2	(+0)	0	24	(+14)	7

After playing in the Cheshire League for AFC Macclesfield, Jack had spells at North West Counties League sides New Mills and Winsford United, and Northern Premier League clubs Skelmersdale United and Prescot Cables. He made his name at Widnes, whom he helped to promotion from the North West Counties in 2017/18. At the end of that term he alerted FC United to his talents by scoring twice for his development agency team in a behind closed doors friendly at Broadhust Park, and he was invited to join the Reds' pre-season programme. On his first outing for United he hit two late goals in the opening friendly at Irlam in July 2018, and he earned a place in the starting line-up as the campaign began. He claimed his first competitive strike on his home debut against Ashton United in August, but usually featured from the bench over the first two months. Jack began a run of five consecutive starts in October with an FA Cup goal against Witton Albion, and he also scored both FC's goals in the impressive win at promotion-chasing Kidderminster Harriers. New manager Neil Reynolds initially used him as a trusted substitute, but on a rare start Jack put the Reds ahead at Hereford in the FA Trophy. He reclaimed a starting spot in January 2019, and hit a superb long-range strike in the terrific win at high-flying Bradford Park Avenue. He was again key to the win at AFC Telford United in March, when he set up all three of FC's goals and hit the bar himself. His late equaliser in the last home game with Blyth Spartans briefly gave United hope of staying up, only for the visitors to regain the lead and condemn the Reds to relegation from National League North. He stayed at that level when joining Curzon Ashton in June, but spent much of the term on loan at Northern Premier League side Warrington Town before later spells at Atherton Collieries, Widnes and Mossley.

266 Kurt WILLOUGHBY

Born: 18/08/1996, Blackpool
Debut: No.10 v Stockport County (A, NLN), 04/08/2018 (scored)

Forward

Season	LEAGUE Starts	(+Sub)	Goals	FA NATIONAL CUPS Starts	(+Sub)	Goals	OTHER CUPS / PLAY-OFFS Starts	(+Sub)	Goals	TOTALS Starts	(+Sub)	Goals
2018/19	38	(+1)	18	3	(+0)	1	1	(+0)	1	42	(+1)	20
Totals	38	(+1)	18	3	(+0)	1	1	(+0)	1	42	(+1)	20

After spending a year in the Preston North End academy, Kurt completed a two-year scholarship with Fleetwood Town after leaving school. Following a loan spell at Radcliffe Borough, he returned permanently to the Northern Premier League with Padiham in 2014. Later that year he joined his local North West Counties League side AFC Blackpool, where he developed into a prolific striker capable of scoring a variety of goals. He moved back up to the Northern Premier League with Clitheroe in December 2015, and in a successful spell hit 54 goals and was named in the league's Division One North team of the season. He signed for FC in May 2018, and hit the ground running with six goals in pre-season. He carried this into the league campaign, netting in his first two appearances and then producing a wonderful solo winner at Altrincham to claim the team's first points of the season. Capable of playing as a lone striker or in a slightly deeper role, executing difficult strikes proved to be somewhat of a speciality, with long-range stunners against Hereford, Mossley and Leamington particularly memorable. He was also reliable in dead-ball situations under pressure, earning late points with penalties against Bradford Park Avenue and Guiseley and an injury-time free-kick against Hereford. He was missing from the starting line-up on just five occasions throughout the term, and on one of those it was a virus that restricted him to an appearance from the bench. A red card in the FA Cup against Witton Albion led to a three-match suspension, while his other absence was due to him becoming the first FC United player to be called up to the England C squad whilst at the club. He made his international debut as a substitute against Estonia under-23s in October at Leyton Orient, and he scored a free-kick on his first start against Wales at Salford in March. A month earlier he had been given the captain's armband by boss Neil Reynolds, and hit six goals in the seven games that he led the team until the return of regular skipper Michael Potts. After United's relegation he represented England again in the return fixture against Estonia in Tallinn, before signing a full-time contract with National League side AFC Fylde in June 2019. He scored his first goals at the higher level in September, but shortly afterwards an injury that required an operation kept him sidelined for three months. In a bid to regain match fitness he returned to National League North in January 2020 on loan at York City, where he bagged three goals in four games before returning to his parent club after a month. He rejoined York on a permanent deal in June 2021, and helped them to win the National League North promotion play-offs at the end of the 2021/22 season.

267 Matthew DEMPSEY

Born: 06/02/1990, Bradford
Debut: Sub v Stockport County (A, NLN), 04/08/2018

Defender/Midfielder

Season	LEAGUE Starts	(+Sub)	Goals	FA NATIONAL CUPS Starts	(+Sub)	Goals	OTHER CUPS / PLAY-OFFS Starts	(+Sub)	Goals	TOTALS Starts	(+Sub)	Goals
2018/19	0	(+1)	0	0	(+0)	0	0	(+0)	0	0	(+1)	0
Totals	0	(+1)	0	0	(+0)	0	0	(+0)	0	0	(+1)	0

A skilful and versatile defender or midfielder, Matt picked up plenty of non-league experience mainly in and around his native West Yorkshire. He played in the Northern Counties East League with Eccleshill United and Thackley, in the Northern Premier League with Garforth Town, Farsley Celtic, Scarborough Athletic and Ossett Albion, and also in the Conference North with Guiseley and Bradford Park Avenue. During a spell at Shaw Lane AFC he even saved a penalty when he took over the gloves from the team's regular goalkeeper, before first crossing the Pennines to join Hyde United in 2016. He linked up with FC United in May 2018, and filled various positions in the pre-season friendlies. He started the first game of the season on the bench, but was thrust into action in just the sixth minute to replace the injured Brad Barnes in central midfield at Stockport County. After the heavy defeat, he failed to reappear on the teamsheet and he signed for Northern Counties East club Yorkshire Amateur later in August.

268 Brodie LITCHFIELD

Born: 17/10/1997, Rotherham
Debut: Sub v Ashton United (H, NLN), 07/08/2018

Winger/Forward

Season	LEAGUE Starts	(+Sub)	Goals	FA NATIONAL CUPS Starts	(+Sub)	Goals	OTHER CUPS / PLAY-OFFS Starts	(+Sub)	Goals	TOTALS Starts	(+Sub)	Goals
2018/19	3	(+4)	1	0	(+1)	0	0	(+0)	0	3	(+5)	1
Totals	3	(+4)	1	0	(+1)	0	0	(+0)	0	3	(+5)	1

Brodie came through the youth ranks at his local club Stocksbridge Park Steels, and was just 16 when he made his senior debut in the Northern Premier League. He attracted the attention of Sheffield United, who signed him on a development contract in July 2015. After a short loan spell at his first club, he returned to non-league with Mickleover Sports in the summer of 2016, before rejoining Stocksbridge for a club record fee later that year. He joined FC United in May 2018, and bagged the first goal of the pre-season friendly at SV Austria Salzburg in July. He appeared just once in the first four league matches, but struck the bar with a long-range curling effort on his debut. He started the comeback with his first competitive goal as the Reds fought back from two down to draw with Bradford Park Avenue in caretaker boss David Chadwick's first game in charge. However, he was unable to claim a regular place and he signed again for Stocksbridge in early October. He went on to have later spells with Ilkeston Town, Gainsborough Trinity, Ossett United and Belper Town, and helped the latter to promotion to the Northern Premier League's top level in 2022.

269 Michael DONOHUE

Born: 12/11/1997, Warrington   Right-back/Midfielder/Forward
Debut: No.11 v Bradford Park Avenue (H, NLN), 02/09/2018

Season	LEAGUE			FA NATIONAL CUPS			OTHER CUPS / PLAY-OFFS			TOTALS		
	Starts	(+Sub)	Goals	Starts	(+Sub)	Goals	Starts	(+Sub)	Goals	Starts	(+Sub)	Goals
2018/19	24	(+9)	0	2	(+0)	1	2	(+0)	0	28	(+9)	1
2019/20	7	(+11)	1	6	(+2)	1	4	(+0)	1	17	(+13)	3
2020/21	5	(+1)	0	4	(+0)	1	0	(+0)	0	9	(+1)	1
2021/22	30	(+2)	4	2	(+3)	0	4	(+0)	0	36	(+5)	4
Totals	66	(+23)	5	14	(+5)	3	10	(+0)	1	90	(+28)	9

As a lively attacker, Michael progressed through the academy at Everton to sign as a professional in July 2015. In February 2016 he joined Barrow on a month's loan, playing six unbeaten games for the National League side. He joined League One side Fleetwood Town on a free transfer in July 2017, and played against FC United in a pre-season friendly at Broadhurst Park a month later. He made his competitive debut as a substitute in Fleetwood's EFL Trophy win at Carlisle United in November, before ending the season on loan in the National League North at Tamworth. Michael was the first player signed by caretaker-manager David Chadwick when he joined the Reds on loan in September 2018, and he started 15 consecutive matches as either a winger or a support striker. He scored his first goal with a perfectly placed header in the second minute against Colne in the FA Cup, but he was more of a provider of chances for others, with dangerous crosses and corners gratefully despatched by team-mates over the course of the campaign. His contract with Fleetwood was cancelled in January 2019 and he became a permanent FC United player. He also lined up in central midfield during a selection crisis during the run-in, and he agreed to stay with the club for the following campaign. He showed terrific form during the pre-season schedule, only for a training injury to rule him out of the opening four league matches. He returned against Morpeth Town to help the side to their first win of the campaign and kept his place for the next four matches. Thereafter he was mainly used as a substitute in league encounters during the autumn and winter, but he still made telling contributions, most notably when his effort from out wide nestled in the back of the net for a dramatic injury-time winner at Ashton United. He excelled in the cup competitions, grabbing his first goal of the season at Radcliffe in the Manchester Premier Cup, and also later netting in the shoot-out. He was particularly effective at home to Basford United in the FA Trophy, when he opened the scoring with a wonderful long-range header before playing in Tunde Owolabi for FC's third. Early in the New Year he also demonstrated his versatility and commitment by filling in at right-back, and after another brief injury interruption he returned to set up the final two goals in the win at Mickleover Sports in March. In the next curtailed season of 2020/21 he again filled three different positions, which included scoring in a forward role as the FA Cup run got underway against Pontefract Collieries, and lining up at right-back for the 1st round tie against Doncaster Rovers. Injury sidelined him for the first six games of 2021/22, but thereafter he was rarely absent as he recorded his best season for the Reds. He was more often deployed at right-back, from where he ran to chip a superb winner over Ashton United, and also bagged a brace in the home win over Basford United. When featuring in midfield or further forward, his highlight was grabbing the late winner at Grantham Town in January. He picked up his first silverware at FC as part of the team that lifted the FENIX Trophy in Rimini in June.

271 Lewis MANSELL

Born: 20/09/1997, Burnley   Forward
Debut: No.9 v Southport (H, NLN), 08/09/2018

Season	LEAGUE			FA NATIONAL CUPS			OTHER CUPS / PLAY-OFFS			TOTALS		
	Starts	(+Sub)	Goals	Starts	(+Sub)	Goals	Starts	(+Sub)	Goals	Starts	(+Sub)	Goals
2018/19	5	(+2)	1	0	(+1)	0	1	(+0)	0	6	(+3)	1
Totals	5	(+2)	1	0	(+1)	0	1	(+0)	0	6	(+3)	1

A tall and mobile forward, Lewis signed as a scholar at Blackburn Rovers in 2014, and as professional a year later as he scored regularly in the youth and under-21 sides. He started two EFL Trophy games for Blackburn in 2016, before he joined FC United on loan in September 2018. Despite impressing with his movement and control, he was often left cursing his luck. After a short injury lay-off, he thought he'd equalised against Darlington only for the referee to bizarrely send him off. His loan was extended, but when in the side he was again denied by the woodwork and inspired goalkeeping. He finally scored with a great finish to seal the win at Blyth Spartans, before Blackburn recalled him in November. After an initial loan, he signed for Scottish Championship side Partick Thistle in 2019. He moved to Accrington Stanley in November 2020 and played in League One either side of loans at National League side FC Halifax Town and National League North club Southport, before being released in the summer of 2022.

270 Lewis THOMPSON

Born: 10/10/1999, Ashton-under-Lyne
Debut: No.3 v Southport (H, NLN), 08/09/2018

Left-back

Season	LEAGUE Starts	(+Sub)	Goals	FA NATIONAL CUPS Starts	(+Sub)	Goals	OTHER CUPS / PLAY-OFFS Starts	(+Sub)	Goals	TOTALS Starts	(+Sub)	Goals
2018/19	11	(+0)	0	2	(+0)	0	1	(+0)	0	14	(+0)	0
Totals	11	(+0)	0	2	(+0)	0	1	(+0)	0	14	(+0)	0

Lewis spent seven years in Manchester United's academy prior to joining Blackburn Rovers as a scholar in 2016. He advanced quickly to feature at under-23 level, and turned professional in March 2018. The Stalybridge lad also won youth international caps for both England and Northern Ireland, for whom he qualifies through his Belfast-born father. He joined FC United on loan alongside club-mate Lewis Mansell in September 2018, and his instincts to attack from the left-back position instantly impressed. He played a part in Kurt Willoughby's goal on his debut, and was also willing to have a strike on goal with either foot. His loan was extended twice, and he continued to progress, particularly after the appointment of Neil Reynolds in October. His pinpoint centre was nodded home by Tom Peers at Blyth Spartans, before another great cross was turned in by a Hereford defender to extend FC's lead a week later. However, he was recalled by his parent club due to an injury in their ranks in November, and they extended his contract in March 2019. He made his debut for Northern Ireland under-21s against Malta in September 2019, and scored against Finland a few days later. After a brief loan at National League side AFC Fylde, he joined League Two side Scunthorpe United in July 2021. He made 17 senior appearances, but the club suffered a disastrous season with relegation from the Football League and Lewis was released at the end of the term.

272 Billy PRIESTLEY

Born: 30/05/1989, Burnley
Debut: No.5 v Chester (A, NLN), 11/09/2018

Centre-back

Season	LEAGUE Starts	(+Sub)	Goals	FA NATIONAL CUPS Starts	(+Sub)	Goals	OTHER CUPS / PLAY-OFFS Starts	(+Sub)	Goals	TOTALS Starts	(+Sub)	Goals
2018/19	4	(+0)	0	1	(+0)	0	0	(+0)	0	5	(+0)	0
Totals	4	(+0)	0	1	(+0)	0	0	(+0)	0	5	(+0)	0

Billy was a trainee at Accrington Stanley for two years, before joining local North West Counties League side Colne in 2007. After five years the tough left-footed defender switched to Barnoldswick Town, before moving up to the Northern Premier League with Ramsbottom United in 2013. He scored against FC United in a cup tie that November, before helping his side to promotion to the league's Premier Division at the end of the season. His performances earned a move to Conference North side Bradford Park Avenue in August 2014, and after a short loan at Ashton United a year later, he once again scored against FC in February 2016. The following month he was purchased by Salford City, and he helped them to promotion to National League North where he faced FC again, as he also did in subsequent spells with Alfreton Town and Southport. Just days after being an unused substitute against FC at Broadhurst Park in September 2018, he joined the Reds on a loan deal that was intended to last until January. His debut at Chester produced the team's first clean sheet of the season, and he also went close with a header at the other end. A first half injury sustained at Nuneaton Borough sidelined him for a month, but he was immense on his return in the first game under Neil Reynolds against Brackley Town in October. However, he was immediately recalled by Southport and played twice more for them before leaving on a further loan in November. He linked up again with Colne, and helped them to the Northern Premier League Division One West play-offs, before signing for Buxton in the summer of 2019. He made a return to Bradford Park Avenue during the early stages of the following season before signing for Clitheroe in May 2020. A year later he became their joint player-manager, alongside another former FC player, Gary Stopforth, before later assuming sole control. A trained lifeguard and swimming instructor, Billy made local headlines when he rushed to the aid of an unresponsive toddler in Colne in 2017.

273 Leighton EGAN

Born: 19/04/2000, Salford
Debut: Sub v Guiseley (A, NLN), 15/09/2018

Midfielder

Season	LEAGUE Starts	(+Sub)	Goals	FA NATIONAL CUPS Starts	(+Sub)	Goals	OTHER CUPS / PLAY-OFFS Starts	(+Sub)	Goals	TOTALS Starts	(+Sub)	Goals
2018/19	0	(+2)	0	0	(+0)	0	0	(+1)	0	0	(+3)	0
Totals	0	(+2)	0	0	(+0)	0	0	(+1)	0	0	(+3)	0

A former Manchester United academy player, Leighton switched to Burnley in his mid-teens, and signed as a full-time scholar upon leaving school in 2016. Able to play as an attacking full-back or in a more advanced role, the Eccles lad became a regular in the under-18 side and was also called up to the under-23s before beginning a spell on loan at Northern Premier League club Clitheroe in November 2017. He was released by Burnley in the summer of 2018 and made his way to FC United, first appearing in a friendly at Thackley in July. His performances in the new under-21 side prompted a senior call from caretaker boss David Chadwick, who introduced him as a substitute at Guiseley in September. The following month he also appeared from the bench to help the team achieve much needed wins at Glossop North End in the Manchester Premier Cup and Kidderminster Harriers in the National League North. Along with team-mate Liam Healey, he joined North West Counties side Prestwich Heys on a dual registration basis in November, before later featuring at the same level for Cheadle Town, Abbey Hey and Stockport Town.

PLAYER PROFILES

274 Theo BRIERLEY

Born: 06/11/1997, Manchester
Debut: No.11 v Nuneaton Borough (A, NLN), 29/09/2018

Midfielder

Season	LEAGUE			FA NATIONAL CUPS			OTHER CUPS / PLAY-OFFS			TOTALS		
	Starts	(+Sub)	Goals	Starts	(+Sub)	Goals	Starts	(+Sub)	Goals	Starts	(+Sub)	Goals
2018/19	3	(+3)	1	0	(+1)	0	1	(+0)	0	4	(+3)	1
Totals	3	(+3)	1	0	(+1)	0	1	(+0)	0	4	(+3)	1

Theo trained at the academies of Manchester United and Manchester City before joining Stoke City, signing as a scholar in 2014. He helped them to win the prestigious Dallas Cup by beating Real Salt Lake in the final, before leaving in 2017 to begin a scholarship at Missouri State University. He returned to England later that year and had spells in the Northern Premier League at Radcliffe Borough, Kidsgrove Athletic, Glossop North End and Buxton, and with Northwich Victoria in the North West Counties League. He was signed by David Chadwick for FC United in September 2018, and made his debut on the left of midfield at Nuneaton Borough. He was awarded three consecutive starts in a central position the following month, during which he opened the scoring with a rasping volley against Darlington at Broadhurst Park. Either side of that match he was prominent in the Manchester Premier Cup win at former club Glossop and the terrific league win at promotion-chasing Kidderminster Harriers. He appeared three times from the bench after the appointment of Neil Reynolds, before joining the new boss's previous club Bamber Bridge on a dual registration basis in January 2019. He moved on to Droylsden during the summer, and also returned to former club Stoke to work as an academy coach.

275 Jordan PERRIN

Born: 18/09/1999, Medway
Debut: Sub v Witton Albion (H, FAC:Q3), 06/10/2018

Goalkeeper

Season	LEAGUE			FA NATIONAL CUPS			OTHER CUPS / PLAY-OFFS			TOTALS		
	Starts	(+Sub)	Goals	Starts	(+Sub)	Goals	Starts	(+Sub)	Goals	Starts	(+Sub)	Goals
2018/19	1	(+0)	0	0	(+1)	0	1	(+0)	0	2	(+1)	0
Totals	1	(+0)	0	0	(+1)	0	1	(+0)	0	2	(+1)	0

A former academy goalkeeper at Charlton Athletic and Arsenal, Jordan joined Wigan Athletic after leaving school in 2016 and became a professional in 2018. He embarked on three separate loan stints during the next campaign, beginning the term with North West Counties League side Stockport Town. He joined FC United for a month in early October 2018, and played in three consecutive games in different competitions. He made his bow as a half-time substitute for the injured Dave Carnell in the FA Cup against Witton Albion, before starting the Manchester Premier Cup win at Glossop North End and the National League North encounter with Darlington. He returned to the bench for the next two league matches before going back to his parent club. After a further loan at Runcorn Linnets in the Northern Premier League Division One West, he was released by Wigan at the end of the term. He returned to Kent to join Sittingbourne of the Isthmian League South East Division, and switched to rivals Herne Bay in 2021.

276 Cole LONSDALE

Born: 16/06/1999, Bolton
Debut: No.3 v Glossop North End (A, MPC:1), 09/10/2018

Left-back/Centre-back

Season	LEAGUE			FA NATIONAL CUPS			OTHER CUPS / PLAY-OFFS			TOTALS		
	Starts	(+Sub)	Goals	Starts	(+Sub)	Goals	Starts	(+Sub)	Goals	Starts	(+Sub)	Goals
2018/19	1	(+0)	0	0	(+0)	0	1	(+0)	0	2	(+0)	0
Totals	1	(+0)	0	0	(+0)	0	1	(+0)	0	2	(+0)	0

Cole developed through the academy at local club Bolton Wanderers, where he became a scholar upon leaving school in 2015. He spent a short time gaining experience on loan at Northern Premier League side Glossop North End before returning to help Bolton's under-23 side to the 2018 Professional Development League title. He was released that summer and began training with FC United in September 2018, before signing for the club later that month. He was named on the bench for the trip to Nuneaton Borough and the FA Cup tie with Witton Albion, before making his debut at left-back in the Manchester Premier Cup win at former club Glossop in October. In the midst of an injury crisis, he featured as one of three centre-backs in a young selection at high-flying Kidderminster Harriers, where he was named as man of the match as United emerged with an impressive victory. He was named as a substitute just once under new boss Neil Reynolds, before joining Northern Premier League side Lancaster City on a dual registration basis in November. He was under consideration for a recall later in the month, but became sidelined by an off-field injury before making a switch to Clitheroe in February 2019. He also featured in the North West Counties League for Ashton Athletic before linking up with Workington in January 2020, but returned to Clitheroe in the summer. He moved on to Ashton United in February 2022, and was in their line-up that won the club's sixteenth Manchester Premier Cup when they defeated Hyde United at Broadhurst Park two months later.

277 Jan PALINKAS

Born: 21/01/2001, Rumburk (Czech Republic) **Centre-back**
Debut: No.5 v Glossop North End (A, MPC:1), 09/10/2018

Season	LEAGUE			FA NATIONAL CUPS			OTHER CUPS / PLAY-OFFS			TOTALS		
	Starts	(+Sub)	Goals	Starts	(+Sub)	Goals	Starts	(+Sub)	Goals	Starts	(+Sub)	Goals
2018/19	3	(+2)	0	0	(+0)	0	2	(+0)	0	5	(+2)	0
Totals	3	(+2)	0	0	(+0)	0	2	(+0)	0	5	(+2)	0

Born in the Czech Republic but raised in Salford, Jan joined FC United's academy upon leaving school and made rapid progress to sign first team forms near the end of his first season in March 2018. He first appeared on the senior teamsheet amongst the substitutes for the win at Altrincham in August 2018, before making an assured debut in the Manchester Premier Cup win at Glossop North End in October. The following weekend he emerged from the bench in the first half to replace the injured Mike Jones against Darlington at Broadhurst Park, and again performed very well in a defensive midfield role. He also started in the cup at Mossley before becoming a regular in the squad throughout the winter. Along with youth colleague Sam Harding, he also had trials at Wigan Athletic and the England Schools under-18 squad. His first league start came at right-back at Chorley on New Year's Day, but he was withdrawn shortly after the Reds were reduced to ten men and conceded the first goal of the eventual 0-4 defeat. He returned to the bench for the next month, before going on loan to Northern Premier League side Runcorn Linnets. After just a single outing he returned to FC, continuing in the academy and under-21 sides before earning a first team recall in April. To continue his development he joined North West Counties League side Wythenshawe Town ahead of the 2019/20 season, and became one of their star performers in a successful three-year stay. His progress was continually monitored by FC United, and he made a welcome return to rejoin the Reds in June 2022.

278 Henry LIMPITSHI Bongwanga

Born: 03/09/1997, Kinshasa (DR Congo) **Forward**
Debut: Sub v Darlington (H, NLN), 13/10/2018

Season	LEAGUE			FA NATIONAL CUPS			OTHER CUPS / PLAY-OFFS			TOTALS		
	Starts	(+Sub)	Goals	Starts	(+Sub)	Goals	Starts	(+Sub)	Goals	Starts	(+Sub)	Goals
2018/19	0	(+3)	0	0	(+0)	0	0	(+0)	0	0	(+3)	0
Totals	0	(+3)	0	0	(+0)	0	0	(+0)	0	0	(+3)	0

After playing in the Midland League for Coventry Sphinx and Kettering Town reserves, Henry moved north to study at UCFB in Manchester, through which he joined FC United's new under-21 squad in 2018. In October he was one of the students selected to represent Great Britain in the under-21 Mini-Football World Cup in Prague, where he ended up as the tournament's top scorer with 12 goals from just four games. The following week he was handed a first team debut by caretaker boss David Chadwick as a substitute at home to Darlington in October, and also came off the bench in the next two senior matches, before joining Northern Premier League side Clitheroe on a dual registration in November. He continued to turn out for FC's second string, for whom he struck 12 goals from 13 games, and returned to the senior bench for the win at Alfreton Town in April 2019. He later linked up with Glossop North End, Cheadle Town, Northwich Victoria, Stockport Town, 1874 Northwich and Winsford United.

279 Liam HEALEY

Born: 11/10/1999, Rochdale **Midfielder**
Debut: No.7 v Kidderminster Harriers (A, NLN), 20/10/2018

Season	LEAGUE			FA NATIONAL CUPS			OTHER CUPS / PLAY-OFFS			TOTALS		
	Starts	(+Sub)	Goals	Starts	(+Sub)	Goals	Starts	(+Sub)	Goals	Starts	(+Sub)	Goals
2018/19	1	(+0)	0	0	(+0)	0	0	(+0)	0	1	(+0)	0
Totals	1	(+0)	0	0	(+0)	0	0	(+0)	0	1	(+0)	0

Liam appeared for Oldham Athletic in the FA Youth Cup whilst still at school, before joining FC Halifax Town on a scholarship in 2016. He was promoted to train with the National League side's first team squad in 2018, but was surprisingly released that summer. He first appeared for FC United in a friendly at Shelley in July 2018, before playing in the club's new under-21 side. With the first team short of midfield options, he was called up to make his senior debut in October at high-flying Kidderminster Harriers. He was one of FC's outstanding performers in the unlikely win, and had a hand in Jack Banister's winning goal. A month later he joined North West Counties League side Prestwich Heys on a dual registration, along with team-mate Leighton Egan, before he ventured to the USA in 2019 to begin a scholarship at the University Of The Cumberlands in Williamsburg, Kentucky.

280 Michael POTTS

Born: 26/11/1991, Preston
Debut: No.6 v Brackley Town (H, NLN), 27/10/2018 (scored)

Midfielder

Season	LEAGUE			FA NATIONAL CUPS			OTHER CUPS / PLAY-OFFS			TOTALS		
	Starts	(+Sub)	Goals	Starts	(+Sub)	Goals	Starts	(+Sub)	Goals	Starts	(+Sub)	Goals
2018/19	16	(+1)	2	1	(+0)	0	0	(+0)	0	17	(+1)	2
2019/20	31	(+1)	4	8	(+0)	0	0	(+2)	0	39	(+3)	4
2020/21	6	(+0)	0	4	(+0)	0	0	(+0)	0	10	(+0)	0
2021/22	29	(+7)	1	6	(+0)	0	4	(+1)	0	39	(+8)	1
Totals	82	(+9)	7	19	(+0)	0	4	(+3)	0	105	(+12)	7

Michael spent the majority of his schoolboy years as an attacking player in the Manchester United academy, but he was released at the age of 16 and signed as a trainee with Blackburn Rovers. He signed a professional contract in 2010 and was eventually converted into an energetic midfielder before moving to Conference side York City in June 2011. He helped his new club back into the Football League via the play-offs in his first season, and was also on the bench when they won the 2012 FA Trophy at Wembley. He made 14 appearances in League Two in 2012/13, which included scoring twice in a 3-2 win at Rochdale, before being released at the end of the season. He then dropped down into the Conference North with Guiseley, and stayed at that level for three years with spells at AFC Fylde, Stalybridge Celtic, Curzon Ashton and Bradford Park Avenue, for whom he played against FC United in January 2016. In the summer of that year he joined Bamber Bridge, and he skippered them to success in the 2018 Northern Premier League Division One North play-offs. When Neil Reynolds was appointed FC United manager in October 2018, he made Michael his first signing and immediately installed him as captain. He made a fantastic start by putting the Reds ahead with a sweet long-range strike on his debut against Brackley Town. He led by example during the initial good run of results in the autumn, and was leading the way in man-of-the-match awards until he suffered a groin injury in January. He eventually required a hernia operation that threatened to end his season, but courageously returned before regaining full fitness to lead the team in the last five games of the campaign. After agreeing to stay with the club, he continued to lead by example in 2019/20 when he was missing from the teamsheet just once, a Manchester Premier Cup tie. In the Northern Premier League, FA Cup and FA Trophy he started all but one game, and in that he was introduced as a half-time substitute.

He got back amongst the goals, netting a spectacular screamer in the league win at Atherton Collieries and blasting home a volley in the draw at Witton Albion. At Broadhurst Park, he scored against Grantham Town and grabbed the crucial equaliser in the vital New Year's Day win over Radcliffe. He was also adept as a provider, with searching long passes picking out Tunde Owolabi for his first goal for the club against Morpeth Town as well as Curtis Jones for the dramatic injury-time equaliser against Warrington Town. He was missing just twice in 2020/21, and had led his team to the FA Cup 1st round to face Doncaster Rovers before that season was also curtailed. He played the first 25 games of 2021/22, during which he scored the winner at Basford United with another stunning strike, before a niggling injury began to restrict his minutes on the pitch. Despite that, he remained an inspiring presence during the second half of the term before announcing that he would be taking a break from football at the end of the season. He bowed out in perfect style by lifting the FENIX Trophy after his last game, against Prague Raptors in Rimini in June 2022.

281 Joshua WALLEN

Born: 05/09/1996, Sydney (Australia)
Debut: No.6 v Brackley Town (H, NLN), 27/10/2018

Midfielder

Season	LEAGUE			FA NATIONAL CUPS			OTHER CUPS / PLAY-OFFS			TOTALS		
	Starts	(+Sub)	Goals	Starts	(+Sub)	Goals	Starts	(+Sub)	Goals	Starts	(+Sub)	Goals
2018/19	20	(+4)	3	1	(+0)	0	1	(+0)	0	22	(+4)	3
Totals	20	(+4)	3	1	(+0)	0	1	(+0)	0	22	(+4)	3

Josh first came to England to join Watford, but returned to Australia in 2015 with Palm Beach SC in Queensland. He returned to sign a professional deal with Queens Park Rangers in January 2016, but suffered an ACL injury just weeks after his arrival. After his recovery, he captained the under-23 side before joining Chelmsford City on loan in March 2018, and helping them to the National League South play-offs. He was released by QPR that summer and had a trial with New Zealand's A-League representatives, Wellington Phoenix. He joined FC United as Neil Reynolds' second recruit in October 2018 and made his debut in a new-look central midfield pairing with Michael Potts against Brackley Town. He scored his first goal three days later when he headed home a corner against Alfreton Town, and also buried similar efforts in the home win over Curzon Ashton and the draw at Leamington in December. After signing he started the next 12 games, and had featured in every match before losing his place at the end of March. He announced his departure from the club in April 2019, and joined National League South side Hemel Hempstead Town that summer. He moved back north to Buxton in September, before later returning to Australia to play for Bentleigh Greens and South Melbourne.

282 Tom PEERS

Born: 23/10/1995, Warrington
Debut: No.9 v Blyth Spartans (A, NLN), 03/11/2018 (scored)

Forward

Season	LEAGUE			FA NATIONAL CUPS			OTHER CUPS / PLAY-OFFS			TOTALS		
	Starts	(+Sub)	Goals	Starts	(+Sub)	Goals	Starts	(+Sub)	Goals	Starts	(+Sub)	Goals
2018/19	14	(+7)	5	1	(+0)	0	0	(+0)	0	15	(+7)	5
Totals	14	(+7)	5	1	(+0)	0	0	(+0)	0	15	(+7)	5

Tom made his Conference North debut for Chester aged 17 in 2012/13 and also featured after promotion to the Conference. He was loaned to North West Counties side 1874 Northwich and Northern Premier League clubs Salford City and Marine, for whom he scored twice as they lost 5-2 to FC United in February 2015. After a spell at Hednesford Town he faced FC again, for AFC Telford United in 2016, before returning to the NPL with Droylsden, Nantwich Town and local side Warrington Town. He switched to Altrincham in 2017, and helped them to the title and promotion to the Conference North a year later, before signing for FC United in November 2018. He made an immediate impact by burying a header just 21 minutes into his debut at Blyth Spartans, and also found the net in the next two matches, at Hereford and at home to former club Telford. This made him the first Reds player to register in his first three outings since Adie Orr in the club's very first competitive games. However, the goals dried up after this initial run and he was mainly selected in a wider role. A reckless tackle against Spennymoor Town in December brought a red card and three-match ban, which coincided with a hamstring injury. Returning in February, he was instrumental in a four-match unbeaten run. He came on to coolly equalise late on against Guiseley, had a hand in both goals in the draw with Hereford, and completed the terrific win at Telford in March. In April he lined up in an unfamiliar role at right-wing-back in the memorable win at Alfreton Town, but soon after FC's demotion was confirmed he rejoined Altrincham. He helped them to another promotion, to the National League in 2020, before moving on to Curzon Ashton after an initial loan in 2021/22.

283 Jamie MILLIGAN

Born: 03/01/1980, Blackpool
Debut: No.6 v Mossley (A, MPC:QF), 13/11/2018

Midfielder

Season	LEAGUE			FA NATIONAL CUPS			OTHER CUPS / PLAY-OFFS			TOTALS		
	Starts	(+Sub)	Goals	Starts	(+Sub)	Goals	Starts	(+Sub)	Goals	Starts	(+Sub)	Goals
2018/19	0	(+1)	0	0	(+1)	0	1	(+0)	0	1	(+2)	0
Totals	0	(+1)	0	0	(+1)	0	1	(+0)	0	1	(+2)	0

Jamie began his career at Everton, and earned England under-18 caps as he progressed to make his Premiership debut at Arsenal in November 1998. After three more senior outings the cultured midfielder joined hometown club Blackpool in March 2001, but a fractured foot in training stalled his career and he was released in 2003. He signed for Division Two side Macclesfield Town, but stayed just a month without playing before going into non-league with Leigh RMI, followed by a two-year spell with Hyde United. After suffering a cruciate injury, he began a long association with Fleetwood Town, where he enjoyed five promotions to move from the North West Counties League to the Football League. During this time he scored two penalties to inflict FC United's first ever FA Cup defeat in September 2007. After featuring in Fleetwood's first League Two season in 2012/13, he returned to Hyde in the Conference, followed by spells at Southport and Conference North sides Stockport County and Harrogate Town. Jamie became player-coach at Northern Premier League side Bamber Bridge, and followed boss Neil Reynolds to FC United as assistant manager in October 2018. Also registered as a player, he featured in three consecutive games in different competitions. He became the oldest outfield player to start on his debut for the club when captaining the side in the Manchester Premier Cup win at Mossley in November, and played for over an hour before being replaced by the even older David Chadwick. He also appeared as a substitute in the following league game against AFC Telford United and in the FA Trophy at Hereford. He remained on the bench in December, before Reynolds took the difficult decision to release him in early January 2019 in order to increase the budget for playing staff. Later that month he joined his local North West Counties side AFC Blackpool, before returning to Bamber Bridge as manager in December 2019 and leading them to a well-earned win over FC in February 2020.

284 Ryan WHITE

Born: 09/11/1998, Blackpool
Debut: No.11 v Mossley (A, MPC:QF), 13/11/2018 (scored)

Left-winger/Left-back

Season	LEAGUE			FA NATIONAL CUPS			OTHER CUPS / PLAY-OFFS			TOTALS		
	Starts	(+Sub)	Goals	Starts	(+Sub)	Goals	Starts	(+Sub)	Goals	Starts	(+Sub)	Goals
2018/19	1	(+5)	0	1	(+0)	0	1	(+0)	1	3	(+5)	1
Totals	1	(+5)	0	1	(+0)	0	1	(+0)	1	3	(+5)	1

Whilst on a scholarship at Bolton Wanderers, Ryan was loaned to Northern Premier League side Hyde United in 2016/17, before aiding Bolton's under-23s to win the Professional Development League in 2018. He was released that summer and returned to non-league as a goalscoring left-winger at Bamber Bridge. He followed boss Neil Reynolds to FC United in November 2018, and became the third new recruit to score on his debut when he netted within 15 minutes at Mossley in the Manchester Premier Cup. He kept his place for the league match at home to AFC Telford United, before covering at left-back in the FA Trophy defeat at Hereford. He appeared as a substitute in each of December's five league fixtures, although he started the friendly win over Chadderton mid-way through the month and scored with a terrific curling effort. With limited opportunities in the New Year, he joined North West Counties side AFC Blackpool in January, and also played for Northern Premier League outfit Lancaster City before the season's end. He rejoined Bamber Bridge in June 2019 and came off the bench to face FC twice in the subsequent seasons.

285 Rowan ROACHE

Born: 09/02/2000, Manchester
Debut: Sub v Hereford (A, FAT:Q3), 24/11/2018

Forward

	LEAGUE			FA NATIONAL CUPS			OTHER CUPS / PLAY-OFFS			TOTALS		
Season	Starts	(+Sub)	Goals	Starts	(+Sub)	Goals	Starts	(+Sub)	Goals	Starts	(+Sub)	Goals
2018/19	1	(+0)	0	0	(+1)	0	0	(+0)	0	1	(+1)	0
Totals	1	(+0)	0	0	(+1)	0	0	(+0)	0	1	(+1)	0

Formerly in Manchester United's academy, Rowan switched to Blackpool, where he progressed rapidly to make his senior debut as a substitute at Doncaster Rovers in the EFL Trophy in December 2016, and also represented Ireland in the 2017 under-17 European Championship. The versatile attacker turned professional that summer, before a loan spell at National League North Southport was cut short due to injury. He was a star performer as Blackpool's youth team won a league and cup double, and reached the 2018 FA Youth Cup semi-final, where they drew at home with Arsenal before losing at the Emirates Stadium. Back on first team duty, he made his Football League bow at home to Bristol Rovers in January 2018, but suffered a metatarsal injury later in the year. Returning to fitness, he joined FC on loan in November 2018, and made his debut as a second-half substitute at Hereford in the FA Trophy. He started the next league game at York City, where he had a good effort well saved, and the Broadhurst Park friendly with Chadderton, but his time with the Reds was curtailed by injury in December. With his club not running a reserve team, he joined Derby County in January 2019 on a youth loan to feature for their under-23 side. He was released from his Blackpool contract in January 2020 after further loans at Lancaster City and Bamber Bridge, and later had spells at Altrincham, Workington, Atherton Collieries and Chester.

286 Caleb RICHARDS

Born: 08/09/1998, Salford
Debut: No.3 v York City (A, NLN), 01/12/2018

Left-back

	LEAGUE			FA NATIONAL CUPS			OTHER CUPS / PLAY-OFFS			TOTALS		
Season	Starts	(+Sub)	Goals	Starts	(+Sub)	Goals	Starts	(+Sub)	Goals	Starts	(+Sub)	Goals
2018/19	7	(+0)	0	0	(+0)	0	0	(+0)	0	7	(+0)	0
Totals	7	(+0)	0	0	(+0)	0	0	(+0)	0	7	(+0)	0

Caleb captained the youth team at Blackpool, where he became a professional in May 2017, and gained non-league experience on loan at Marine and Warrington Town. The attack-minded left-back made his senior debut as a substitute against Wigan Athletic in the EFL Cup in August 2017, before starting a 4-1 EFL Trophy victory over Middlesbrough, when he was nominated for player of the round. After further loans at Leek Town and Southport, for whom he faced FC United in January 2018, he joined Norwich City in the summer to play in their under-23 side. He joined FC on loan in November 2018, and made his debut at York City. A week later he helped the Reds to a great start against Curzon Ashton, when his second minute cross was headed home by Josh Wallen in what would be the only league win at home all season. He started seven consecutive National League North games before his parent club recalled him in January 2019. The next month he signed a new contract before moving to the USA to play on loan for Tampa Bay Rowdies during their 2019 USL Championship season. After further loans at Yeovil Town and Kidderminster Harriers in 2020, he joined the latter club permanently in 2021 and played for them against West Ham United the FA Cup 4th round in February 2022.

287 Chris SHARP

Born: 19/06/1986, Liverpool
Debut: Sub v Curzon Ashton (H, NLN), 08/12/2018

Forward

	LEAGUE			FA NATIONAL CUPS			OTHER CUPS / PLAY-OFFS			TOTALS		
Season	Starts	(+Sub)	Goals	Starts	(+Sub)	Goals	Starts	(+Sub)	Goals	Starts	(+Sub)	Goals
2018/19	12	(+6)	3	0	(+0)	0	0	(+0)	0	12	(+6)	3
2019/20	1	(+5)	0	0	(+1)	0	0	(+0)	0	1	(+6)	0
Totals	13	(+11)	3	0	(+1)	0	0	(+0)	0	13	(+12)	3

The son of Everton legend Graeme Sharp, Chris was born just days after his dad played for Scotland in the Mexico World Cup. Also a striker, he made his senior debut for Welsh Premier League side Rhyl in 2005. He won the Welsh Cup in 2006, but missed a whole season due to a horrific leg break in a UEFA Cup tie against Lithuanian side Sūduva. After recovering he joined Bangor City in 2008, where his goalscoring form prompted a transfer to The New Saints for an undisclosed fee in 2010. He won a championship medal and scored against Anderlecht in the Champions League qualifiers, before joining English Conference side AFC Telford United in 2011. He stayed in that division with a move to Hereford United in 2012, plus a loan spell at Lincoln City, before linking up with Conference North side Stockport County in 2014. He earned a call-up to the England C squad before dropping into the Northern Premier League in 2015 with spells at Colwyn Bay, Salford City and Marine. He returned to the National League North in 2016 and faced FC United with Bradford Park Avenue and Alfreton Town before short spells with Curzon Ashton and Stalybridge Celtic. He signed for FC in December 2018, making his debut as a substitute shortly after half-time against former club Curzon. The following week he hit a tremendous hat-trick during the first half of the Broadhurst Park friendly win over Chadderton, before scoring three goals in five starts in the New Year. Wearing a protective face mask, he rifled home a superb equaliser at former club Bradford PA in January as FC fought back to claim a terrific win, and then gave the Reds an early lead with an acrobatic volley at Boston United in February. A calm, opportunistic finish put FC ahead in the home draw with Hereford, before he returned to help the side for the final three games of the season in an unfamiliar wide role. His attitude on and off the pitch had impressed the manager and he was happy to remain at the club following relegation. He started just once as injury disrupted his 2019/20 campaign, before moving on to Hyde United in October. He lined up for them twice against FC before retiring at the end of the season.

288 Danny MORTON

Born: 09/11/1992, Burnley
Debut: No.2 v Chester (H, NLN), 05/01/2019

Right-back

Season	LEAGUE			FA NATIONAL CUPS			OTHER CUPS / PLAY-OFFS			TOTALS		
	Starts	(+Sub)	Goals	Starts	(+Sub)	Goals	Starts	(+Sub)	Goals	Starts	(+Sub)	Goals
2018/19	12	(+0)	0	0	(+0)	0	0	(+0)	0	12	(+0)	0
Totals	12	(+0)	0	0	(+0)	0	0	(+0)	0	12	(+0)	0

A former player in the academies of Burnley and Blackburn Rovers, Danny first played non-league football with North West Counties League sides Nelson and Barnoldswick Town. Normally a right-back, but also capable of playing at centre-back and midfield, he moved into the Northern Premier League with Clitheroe in 2013, eventually captaining the side. He moved up to National League North in 2015 with Stockport County, for whom he played in FC United's first competitive game at Broadhurst Park. After a short spell at Colne, he joined Stalybridge Celtic in October 2016 and skippered them against FC in the Manchester Premier Cup Final in May 2017. He was named in the Northern Premier League's team of the season a year later, before switching to Curzon Ashton shortly afterwards. He signed for FC United in January 2019, a month after facing the Reds in Moston, and performed admirably on his debut despite defeat to Chester. He helped the team to a tremendous win at high-flying Bradford Park Avenue the following week, before suffering three narrow losses. He then had a spell playing slightly further forward in a wing-back role as United picked up some valuable points, but as the side's confidence began to drain he was substituted at half-time in the home defeat to Nuneaton Borough in late March. The following week he was one of four players that left the club as the manager attempted to rally the troops in the ultimately unsuccessful fight to avoid relegation. He signed for North West Counties League side Padiham in the summer.

289 Salou McDowell-JALLOW

Born: 03/07/1998, Tabokoto (The Gambia)
Debut: Sub v Chester (H, NLN), 05/01/2019

Winger

Season	LEAGUE			FA NATIONAL CUPS			OTHER CUPS / PLAY-OFFS			TOTALS		
	Starts	(+Sub)	Goals	Starts	(+Sub)	Goals	Starts	(+Sub)	Goals	Starts	(+Sub)	Goals
2018/19	1	(+4)	0	0	(+0)	0	0	(+0)	0	1	(+4)	0
Totals	1	(+4)	0	0	(+0)	0	0	(+0)	0	1	(+4)	0

Salou's family moved from The Gambia to Belfast, and he went on to represent Northern Ireland at schoolboy and youth level. A pacy attacker or wing-back, he developed in the academy at Crusaders, who gave him a senior debut in November 2016. With his club entering the Scottish Challenge Cup, he was man of the match against Livingston in the cross-border tie. He switched to rivals Glentoran in January 2017, and featured in their first team before coming over to Manchester to study at UCFB that summer. When FC United and the university partnered ahead of his second year, he became part of the club's new under-21 side. In October 2018 he was one of the students that helped Great Britain to the quarter-final of the under-21 Mini-Football World Cup in Prague, where he scored the team's first goal of the tournament against India. His displays brought him into the first team set-up shortly after the appointment of Neil Reynolds, and he thrilled the watching crowd when coming off the bench during the Broadhust Park friendly with Chadderton in December. He made his competitive debut as a substitute against Chester in January 2019 as the Reds chased a late equaliser, and returned to contention in April for the run-in. Particularly impressive as a half-time replacement at home to Kiddermister Harriers, he was also thrown on just minutes before United grabbed a late winner at Alfreton Town. He played in most of FC's pre-season games, but was allowed to join Ramsbottom United in August 2019 for more experience. However he did not feature before returning to Glentoran in September. He scored in his first game back in East Belfast, before moving on to NIFL Championship side Ards in January 2020.

290 Zehn MOHAMMED

Born: 28/02/2000, Blackburn
Debut: No.4 v Bradford Park Avenue (A, NLN), 12/01/2019

Centre-back

Season	LEAGUE			FA NATIONAL CUPS			OTHER CUPS / PLAY-OFFS			TOTALS		
	Starts	(+Sub)	Goals	Starts	(+Sub)	Goals	Starts	(+Sub)	Goals	Starts	(+Sub)	Goals
2018/19	15	(+0)	0	0	(+0)	0	0	(+0)	0	15	(+0)	0
Totals	15	(+0)	0	0	(+0)	0	0	(+0)	0	15	(+0)	0

After a spell in the schoolboy academy at local club Blackburn Rovers, Zehn joined Accrington Stanley as a scholar and was given a professional contract at the age of 17. The confident centre-back was an unused substitute for the senior side's EFL Trophy tie at Lincoln City in December 2017, before embarking on a loan spell with Northern Premier League side Ramsbottom United later that month. The following season he had further loan spells at Clitheroe and Southport, for whom he played once in the FA Trophy, before making his first team debut for Accrington in the EFL Trophy against Bury in January 2019. He joined FC United on loan a few days later, and lined up alongside fellow 18-year-old loanee Billy Sass-Davies in central defence to help the Reds to an unlikely win at promotion-chasing Bradford Park Avenue on his debut. Three consecutive man-of-the-match performances followed before he was the victim of two cruel deflections that left FC empty-handed against Altrincham in February. Shortly after he spent a couple of games on the bench during a defensive reshuffle, but he reclaimed his place for the great win at high-flying AFC Telford United in March. He was once again imperious and played every single minute for the remainder of the season, picking up another three star man awards in the process. His performances were duly noted by his parent club as he was offered a new deal by Accrington in May 2019, before spending the next campaign on loan back in National League North with Southport. He was released by Accrington in the summer of 2021.

291 Billy SASS-DAVIES

Born: 17/02/2000, Abergele

Debut: No.5 v Bradford Park Avenue (A, NLN), 12/01/2019

Centre-back

Season	LEAGUE			FA NATIONAL CUPS			OTHER CUPS / PLAY-OFFS			TOTALS		
	Starts	(+Sub)	Goals	Starts	(+Sub)	Goals	Starts	(+Sub)	Goals	Starts	(+Sub)	Goals
2018/19	8	(+0)	0	0	(+0)	0	0	(+0)	0	8	(+0)	0
Totals	8	(+0)	0	0	(+0)	0	0	(+0)	0	8	(+0)	0

A big central defender, Billy joined Crewe Alexandra upon leaving school and turned professional in July 2017. Due to injuries and suspensions, he was named on the bench for the senior side's first five league matches of 2017/18, before making his debut from the start in the EFL Trophy against Newcastle United in August 2017. His progress was rewarded with caps for the Wales under-19 side, before he joined his local side Colwyn Bay on loan in February 2018. The following season he returned to the Northern Premier League on a similar arrangement with Leek Town, before he signed for FC United on another loan in January 2019. He produced a man-of-the-match performance on his debut alongside fellow 18-year-old loanee Zehn Mohammed in central defence as the Reds claimed an impressive win at Bradford Park Avenue. Before returning to Crewe in March, he started eight consecutive matches. In one of those he gave another star man display against Altrincham, for whom he subsequently signed on a further loan deal. He was recalled by Crewe in April, and made his League Two debut against Yeovil Town before signing a new two-year contract in May. He spent further time on loan at AFC Telford United, Ashton United, Altrincham again, and Yeovil Town, before returning to claim a regular place at Crewe in 2021/22. His side suffered relegation to League Two at the end of the season, but Billy enhanced his reputation by becoming a regular in the Wales under-21 team.

292 Dale WHITHAM

Born: 28/02/1992, Manchester

Debut: No.7 v Ashton United (A, NLN), 19/01/2019

Midfielder

Season	LEAGUE			FA NATIONAL CUPS			OTHER CUPS / PLAY-OFFS			TOTALS		
	Starts	(+Sub)	Goals	Starts	(+Sub)	Goals	Starts	(+Sub)	Goals	Starts	(+Sub)	Goals
2018/19	9	(+1)	3	0	(+0)	0	0	(+0)	0	9	(+1)	3
Totals	9	(+1)	3	0	(+0)	0	0	(+0)	0	9	(+1)	3

Formerly in Manchester United's academy, Dale also played for Maine Road's junior sides before making his senior non-league debut in the Northern Premier League for Leigh Genesis in 2008. He was still 16-years-old when he twice faced FC United early in 2009, and the following season he represented the England Schools under-18 team. A versatile and energetic midfielder, the Sale lad was snapped up by Chorley in May 2010, and helped them to three promotions during a long association. Along the way he became a thorn in FC United's side, scoring in both league fixtures in 2012/13 and grabbing the winner to knock the Reds out of the FA Cup in September 2013. After a spell on the sidelines due to injury, he joined FC in January 2019 on an initial month's loan, and made his debut in the disappointing defeat at Ashton United. He saw powerful headers saved on the line in the next two matches, before superbly nodding home an equaliser at home to Altrincham. His loan was extended, and after helping the team to three crucial draws, he was United's star performer at home to York City when he bagged a brace. Another strong header from a corner gave the Reds an early lead, before a well-struck volley restored the advantage. Unfortunately, the team were unable to hold on for the win, and after an embarrassing loss to basement side Nuneaton Borough, Dale returned to Chorley in April to provide cover for their promotion push. His club went up, but after nine years and 364 games he chose to leave Chorley in June and remain in the National League North with Alfreton Town. In 2019/20 he also spent a short time on loan with Northern Premier League side Buxton, and was in their side when FC won 7-0 at Broadhurst Park in October, playing an hour before being replaced by Ashley Young. He went on to link up with Curzon Ashton and Lancaster City.

293 Josh HMAMI

Born: 22/03/2000, Oldham

Debut: Sub v Ashton United (A, NLN), 19/01/2019

Midfielder

Season	LEAGUE			FA NATIONAL CUPS			OTHER CUPS / PLAY-OFFS			TOTALS		
	Starts	(+Sub)	Goals	Starts	(+Sub)	Goals	Starts	(+Sub)	Goals	Starts	(+Sub)	Goals
2018/19	0	(+3)	0	0	(+0)	0	0	(+0)	0	0	(+3)	0
Totals	0	(+3)	0	0	(+0)	0	0	(+0)	0	0	(+3)	0

After time in the academies at Bolton Wanderers and Barnsley, Josh joined Accrington Stanley on a scholarship. He was appointed captain of the youth team that also featured future FC United team-mate Zehn Mohammed, and was named on the first-team bench for an EFL Trophy tie against Middlesbrough in September 2017. He was given his senior debut as a late substitute in a League Two win at Grimsby Town in December, but was released to join Welsh Premier League side TNS on a free transfer in May 2018. He joined FC on loan in January 2019, and after training with the club awaiting international clearance he made his debut as a second-half substitute in the disappointing defeat at fellow strugglers Ashton United. Further appearances from the bench in the narrow losses to Stockport County and Boston United followed before he returned to his parent club at the end of his loan. In September 2019, he began another temporary stint with Northern Premier League side Ramsbottom United, and he returned to that level when he signed for Marine in June 2020. He was instrumental in helping his new club to reach the FA Cup 3rd round, when he was in the team that hosted Tottenham Hotspur in January 2021. He moved back up to National League North with Southport in June 2021.

294 Dominic McGIVERON

Born: 07/03/1996, Liverpool
Debut: Sub v Ashton United (A, NLN), 19/01/2019

Forward

Season	LEAGUE			FA NATIONAL CUPS			OTHER CUPS / PLAY-OFFS			TOTALS		
	Starts	(+Sub)	Goals	Starts	(+Sub)	Goals	Starts	(+Sub)	Goals	Starts	(+Sub)	Goals
2018/19	0	(+3)	0	0	(+0)	0	0	(+0)	0	0	(+3)	0
Totals	0	(+3)	0	0	(+0)	0	0	(+0)	0	0	(+3)	0

Once in the Liverpool academy, Dominic began in semi-professional football with North West Counties League sides Formby and Bootle, whilst also earning international honours with the England schools under-18 team. He went to the USA to join Kitsap Pumas in 2016, and also played in Finland for SJK07 and Norway for Valdres. He linked up with FC United in January 2019, and after training with the club while awaiting international clearance, he made his debut as a late replacement in the disappointing defeat at Ashton United. He was also sent on to chase an equaliser in the next two games against Stockport County and Boston United before moving on to join Bamber Bridge in February. He scored on his debut for his new club, and helped them to secure their Northern Premier League status. He returned to Scandinavia in March 2020 to sign for Swedish side Piteå IF.

295 Andy FISHER

Born: 12/02/1998, Wigan
Debut: No.1 v Altrincham (H, NLN), 09/02/2019

Goalkeeper

Season	LEAGUE			FA NATIONAL CUPS			OTHER CUPS / PLAY-OFFS			TOTALS		
	Starts	(+Sub)	Goals	Starts	(+Sub)	Goals	Starts	(+Sub)	Goals	Starts	(+Sub)	Goals
2018/19	13	(+0)	0	0	(+0)	0	0	(+0)	0	13	(+0)	0
Totals	13	(+0)	0	0	(+0)	0	0	(+0)	0	13	(+0)	0

Andy came through the Blackburn Rovers academy to sign a professional contract in January 2016, and became the regular reserve team goalkeeper the following season. He was an unused substitute for the club's EFL trophy matches in 2016/17, before making his senior debut in the same competition against Stoke City in August 2017. He signed an improved deal in November and was named on the bench for several matches in the Football League and FA Cup. He joined FC United on an initial month's loan in February 2019, and was only beaten by two cruel deflections in a good debut display against Altrincham. His commanding presence helped the Reds to a subsequent unbeaten run, notably in keeping a clean sheet at Southport, and his loan was extended until the end of the season. He continued to perform well, helping the Reds to gain vital points against AFC Telford United, York City and Alfreton Town, and was one of the few bright lights as the team slipped towards relegation. He ended the season alongside fellow former FC loanee Lewis Thompson in the Blackburn under-23 side that defeated Burnley in the Lancashire Senior Cup final. In August 2019 he joined Northampton Town on loan, and featured three times in the EFL Trophy. He was the hero on his debut against Arsenal when he saved two penalties in a shoot-out victory. After remaining an unused substitute in League Two fixtures, he later performed the same role after beginning another loan in League One at Milton Keynes in January 2020. After appearing for Blackburn in an EFL Cup victory over Doncaster Rovers in August 2020, he joined Milton Keynes permanently in October. His performances led to a move to Championship side Swansea City in January 2022, for a fee reportedly in the region of £400,000, and he established himself as the Swans' first-choice custodian.

296 Bob HARRIS

Born: 28/08/1987, Glasgow
Debut: No.3 v Altrincham (H, NLN), 09/02/2019

Left-back/Centre-back

Season	LEAGUE			FA NATIONAL CUPS			OTHER CUPS / PLAY-OFFS			TOTALS		
	Starts	(+Sub)	Goals	Starts	(+Sub)	Goals	Starts	(+Sub)	Goals	Starts	(+Sub)	Goals
2018/19	4	(+0)	0	0	(+0)	0	0	(+0)	0	4	(+0)	0
Totals	4	(+0)	0	0	(+0)	0	0	(+0)	0	4	(+0)	0

After a spell as a schoolboy at Rangers, Bob began his career as a youth at Scottish First Division club Clyde, for whom he made his senior debut at Ross County in May 2005. He began to emerge as a regular over the next two seasons, and was on the bench for their Challenge Cup final appearance in November 2006. He switched to Queen Of The South in July 2007, and helped the club to reach their first ever Scottish Cup final at the end of his first season. He lined up at left-back at Hampden Park, where his free-kick set up the equaliser after the underdogs had been two goals down, only for favourites Rangers to eventually prevail 3-2. The cup run meant that Queens entered the UEFA Cup 2nd qualification round, where they were eliminated by Danish side Nordsjælland, although Bob became the club's only player to score in a European away leg. After four years with the Dumfries club, he moved further south to join Blackpool in July 2011, but he struggled to claim a regular place with the Championship side. He joined League Two side Rotherham United on a month's loan in September 2012, before making a permanent switch to League One club Sheffield United in January 2014. He established himself in a progressive side that reached the FA Cup semi-final later that season, as well as both the League Cup and League One play-off semi-finals in 2015. He was subsequently restricted by injuries, and after short spells at Fleetwood Town and Bristol Rovers he dropped into the National League North with AFC Telford United in 2017/18. After a spell unattached, he signed for FC United in February 2019 and made his debut at home to Altrincham. Long throws into attacking areas were a notable feature of his game until he picked up an injury in the second half. He was back to help keep a clean sheet at Southport, playing as one of three centre-backs, but suffered another knock in that role during the draw with Hereford a week later. He returned to left-back against bottom side Nuneaton Borough, but after the humiliating home defeat he was one of four players that left the club as the manager attempted to refresh his squad for the run-in.

297 Louis MYERS

Born: 21/12/1997, Manchester   **Forward**
Debut: No.10 v Altrincham (H, NLN), 09/02/2019

Season	LEAGUE Starts	(+Sub)	Goals	FA NATIONAL CUPS Starts	(+Sub)	Goals	OTHER CUPS / PLAY-OFFS Starts	(+Sub)	Goals	TOTALS Starts	(+Sub)	Goals
2018/19	7	(+3)	1	0	(+0)	0	0	(+0)	0	7	(+3)	1
2019/20	0	(+2)	0	0	(+1)	0	0	(+1)	1	0	(+4)	1
Totals	7	(+5)	1	0	(+1)	0	0	(+1)	1	7	(+7)	2

Raised in Moston, Louis developed as a player with Moston Juniors, FC United's partners at Broadhurst Park. After time in the academies at Blackburn Rovers and Rochdale, he joined Fleetwood Town as a scholar in 2014. He was named as youth team player of the season in his first term, but was released in 2016 and linked up with Chorley. After a successful loan at Northern Premier League Ramsbottom United, he made his National League North debut in October 2016, but a cruciate injury left him sidelined for several months. After a further loan at Clitheroe, he moved to Scottish Highland League side Turriff United in 2017. He returned south to join Radcliffe in 2018, but after a decent start he suffered another serious knee injury. He recovered later in the year and was back amongst the goals prior to joining FC United in February 2019. He went straight into the side for the home game with Altrincham, when he had two decent chances in a lively first half, but was unfortunately withdrawn due to injury at the break. He was introduced for the closing stages of the great win at AFC Telford United, where his solo run and shot was denied by the woodwork. He was involved in each of the last nine games of the season, and grew in confidence with every outing. He scored his first goal in the terrific win at Alfreton Town in April, putting United ahead with a thumping back post header, and also hitting the bar with a free-kick. In May he accepted the offer to remain with the club for the following term. He began the pre-season campaign superbly with three goals in four games, before he was sidelined by a knee injury. Despite appearing as a substitute in the opening day defeat at Grantham Town he was still not fully fit and soon aggravated the injury. Whilst working back to fitness he played a game on loan for North West Counties League side Barnton, before returning to United's bench in late October. He rounded off the Manchester Premier Cup win at Hyde United with a fine solo effort before spending a month on loan at Prescot Cables. In December he began a similar deal at Premier Division rivals Atherton Collieries, where he was soon back amongst the goals as the arrangement was extended until the end of the campaign. He moved on to Hyde on a permanent basis in the summer of 2020, but returned to Atherton Collieries in December.

298 Dominic McHALE

Born: 18/02/1996, Manchester   **Midfielder**
Debut: No.11 v AFC Telford United (A, NLN), 09/03/2019 (scored)

Season	LEAGUE Starts	(+Sub)	Goals	FA NATIONAL CUPS Starts	(+Sub)	Goals	OTHER CUPS / PLAY-OFFS Starts	(+Sub)	Goals	TOTALS Starts	(+Sub)	Goals
2018/19	4	(+0)	1	0	(+0)	0	0	(+0)	0	4	(+0)	1
Totals	4	(+0)	1	0	(+0)	0	0	(+0)	0	4	(+0)	1

A product of Manchester City's academy, Dominic cancelled his contract by mutual consent and joined Barnsley in 2014. The energetic wideman made his professional debut as a substitute against Crewe Alexandra in the Football League Cup, but was released in 2015. He moved into non-league with spells at Northern Premier League sides Ramsbottom United and Northwich Victoria, plus North West Counties League outfit Northwich Flixton Villa, before playing for Cypriot Third Division club Achyronas Liopetriou. He later featured for Salford City, Trafford and Hyde United, before joining Ashton United in August 2018 and scoring the winner against FC United at Broadhurst Park a few days later. He moved on to play one FA Trophy game for Southport in December before training for several weeks with FC. He signed for the Reds in March 2019 and made a great start by opening the scoring in the fantastic win at AFC Telford United. He also looked very lively in the defeat at Curzon Ashton and the home draw with York City as he worked his way back to fitness. However, after an early booking at home to bottom side Nuneaton Borough, he was substituted before half-time as FC fell to a humiliating defeat, and he left the club three days later. After a successful pre-season trial he signed for Oldham Athletic in August 2019, and came off the bench at Plymouth Argyle in League Two the following month. However, his contract was terminated in November and he resumed in non-league with spells at Romford, Stockport Town, South Shields, Ashton United, Telford and Darlington.

299 Jack GRIMSHAW

Born: 22/12/1999, Stafford   **Midfielder**
Debut: Sub v AFC Telford United (A, NLN), 09/03/2019

Season	LEAGUE Starts	(+Sub)	Goals	FA NATIONAL CUPS Starts	(+Sub)	Goals	OTHER CUPS / PLAY-OFFS Starts	(+Sub)	Goals	TOTALS Starts	(+Sub)	Goals
2018/19	2	(+2)	0	0	(+0)	0	0	(+0)	0	2	(+2)	0
Totals	2	(+2)	0	0	(+0)	0	0	(+0)	0	2	(+2)	0

Jack signed as a trainee with Port Vale in 2016, and was a consistent member of the youth team's midfield during his two-year scholarship. In the summer of 2018, he moved to Manchester to study at UCFB, where FC United's newly-formed under-21 side was based. He was installed as the team's captain by manager David Chadwick, and was almost ever-present as the young Reds dropped just five points in their first 19 matches. During Chadwick's spell as first team caretaker-manager, Jack was an unused substitute for the home game with Darlington in October 2018. He received a further call-up by new boss Neil Reynolds in March 2019, and made his debut as a late replacement during the fantastic win at AFC Telford United. He was named on the teamsheet for the final six games of the term, starting against both Darlington and Kidderminster Harriers before helping to see out the memorable win at Alfreton Town. He linked up with Prescot Cables ahead of the 2019/20 season, and had later spells at Skelmersdale United, Macclesfield, Rocester, Newcastle Town and Ramsbottom United.

300 Will OZONO

Born: 19/03/2000, Southwark
Debut: No.7 v Darlington (A, NLN), 06/04/2019

Winger

Season	LEAGUE Starts	(+Sub)	Goals	FA NATIONAL CUPS Starts	(+Sub)	Goals	OTHER CUPS / PLAY-OFFS Starts	(+Sub)	Goals	TOTALS Starts	(+Sub)	Goals
2018/19	1	(+1)	0	0	(+0)	0	0	(+0)	0	1	(+1)	0
Totals	1	(+1)	0	0	(+0)	0	0	(+0)	0	1	(+1)	0

Will rose through Crystal Palace's academy to sign as a scholar in 2016. The speedy attacker recovered from a serious injury to help the youth team to win the Professional Development Southern Premier League in 2018, before the Premier League club released him that summer. He enrolled at UCFB in Manchester, where he became a star of FC United's new under-21 team based at the university. His form earned two player of the year awards and led to a first-team debut on the right wing at Darlington in April 2019. He was FC's most dangerous player before coming off after an hour, and he also featured a week later at home to Kidderminster Harriers. In agreement with the Reds, he joined Mossley ahead of the 2019/20 season, before spells at Ramsbottom United and under FC United legends Mike Norton and Dave Birch for North West Counties League side New Mills.

301 Mark WEST

Born: 20/01/1997, Bulawayo (Zimbabwe)
Debut: No.10 v Darlington (A, NLN), 06/04/2019

Midfielder

Season	LEAGUE Starts	(+Sub)	Goals	FA NATIONAL CUPS Starts	(+Sub)	Goals	OTHER CUPS / PLAY-OFFS Starts	(+Sub)	Goals	TOTALS Starts	(+Sub)	Goals
2018/19	2	(+0)	0	0	(+0)	0	0	(+0)	0	2	(+0)	0
Totals	2	(+0)	0	0	(+0)	0	0	(+0)	0	2	(+0)	0

Able to play in midfield or further forward, Mark had been in Southampton's academy before featuring in the Western League for Keynsham Town, Welton Rovers and Bitton. He began studying at UFCB in Manchester in 2016, and when the university partnered with FC United to run an under-21 team in 2018 he became a regular in the side. In October he was selected to represent Great Britain in the under-21 Mini-Football World Cup in Prague, where he scored in a win over India. He earned a first team call-up in April 2019, and started at Darlington and at home to Kidderminster Harriers. He briefly featured in the pre-season campaign before spells at Prescot Cables and Glossop North End, for whom he played against FC at Broadhurst in the Northern Premier League Challenge Cup in November. He moved on to North West Counties League side Cheadle Town in 2020.

302 Paddy WHARTON

Born: 27/05/2000, Liverpool
Debut: No.1 v Grantham Town (A, NPLP), 17/08/2019

Goalkeeper

Season	LEAGUE Starts	(+Sub)	Goals	FA NATIONAL CUPS Starts	(+Sub)	Goals	OTHER CUPS / PLAY-OFFS Starts	(+Sub)	Goals	TOTALS Starts	(+Sub)	Goals
2019/20	11	(+0)	0	3	(+0)	0	0	(+0)	0	14	(+0)	0
Totals	11	(+0)	0	3	(+0)	0	0	(+0)	0	14	(+0)	0

Previously in the academies of both Everton and Liverpool, Paddy became a professional with Tranmere Rovers in May 2017, a few weeks after he had been an unused substitute for the first team in the National League. He made his senior debut in the EFL Trophy at Shrewsbury Town in October 2018, but spent most of the campaign on loan in the Northern Premier League with Colwyn Bay, Marine and Stalybridge Celtic. He was released by Tranmere and signed for FC United in May 2019. Despite the team losing the first three league games, the young stopper performed heroically, particularly when pulling off a miraculous double save from a penalty at home to Hyde United. He kept five clean sheets in seven matches in September, but was struck down by a knee ligament injury early the following month. During his recuperation he witnessed the good form of Cameron Belford behind a settled backline, and so once fit again he joined Atherton Collieries on a loan agreement in December to gain playing time. After just three games he decided to make the move permanent, before later spells at Warrington Town, Runcorn Linnets and Lower Breck.

304 James JOYCE

Born: 03/11/1994, Liverpool
Debut: No.3 v Grantham Town (A, NPLP), 17/08/2019

Left-back

Season	LEAGUE Starts	(+Sub)	Goals	FA NATIONAL CUPS Starts	(+Sub)	Goals	OTHER CUPS / PLAY-OFFS Starts	(+Sub)	Goals	TOTALS Starts	(+Sub)	Goals
2019/20	3	(+2)	0	1	(+0)	0	1	(+0)	0	5	(+2)	0
Totals	3	(+2)	0	1	(+0)	0	1	(+0)	0	5	(+2)	0

A mobile left-back, James joined Tranmere Rovers as a scholar, but was released in 2013. After a short spell in Sweden with Kiruna FF, he joined Llandudno, where in a five-year spell he helped the side to promotion to the Welsh Premier League and played against IFK Göteborg in the Europa League qualifiers. After a trial at Crewe Alexandra, he signed for Northern Premier League side Marine in 2018, before joining FC United in July 2019. He started three of the first four games of the season, featuring both at left-back and further forward, but the form of Adam Dodd combined with work patterns restricted his outings. He moved back to Marine in October, a switch initially announced as a month's loan, to gain regular first team football. He was in their team that faced Tottenham Hotspur in the FA Cup 3rd round in January 2021, but emigrated to work in Dubai later in the year.

303 Aaron MORRIS

Born: 10/06/1995, Billinge   **Right-back/Centre-back**
Debut: No.2 v Grantham Town (A, NPLP), 17/08/2019

Season	LEAGUE			FA NATIONAL CUPS			OTHER CUPS / PLAY-OFFS			TOTALS		
	Starts	(+Sub)	Goals	Starts	(+Sub)	Goals	Starts	(+Sub)	Goals	Starts	(+Sub)	Goals
2019/20	29	(+0)	2	7	(+0)	1	2	(+0)	0	38	(+0)	3
2020/21	6	(+0)	0	4	(+1)	1	0	(+0)	0	10	(+1)	1
2021/22	41	(+0)	5	6	(+0)	0	4	(+0)	0	51	(+0)	5
Totals	76	(+0)	7	17	(+1)	2	6	(+0)	0	99	(+1)	9

Aaron began his semi-professional career in the North West Counties League with St Helens Town in 2014. The lad from Adlington was a regular name on the scoresheet in his early outings when he was utilised in several positions, before settling as a ball-playing centre-back. He moved on to ambitious Runcorn Linnets in 2016, and was ever-present in his first campaign when he picked up several Player Of The Season awards. The following term he helped the side to the North West Counties League title, and made a seamless step up to the next level, being named in the Northern Premier League Division One West Team Of The Year for 2018/19. He linked up with FC United in May 2019, but with four other central defenders on the books, he was asked to occupy an unfamiliar position as right-back in pre-season. He eventually settled into the role once the campaign was underway, and his name was missing from the teamsheet just once during the entire term, that being a Manchester Premier Cup tie. He never looked back after putting in a man-of-the-match performance in the hard-fought draw at Lancaster City in early September, and further grew in confidence when he headed the late winner in the FA Cup replay at Atherton Collieries a week later. He became more comfortable going forward, and notably provided crosses converted by Tunde Owolabi against Kettering Town in the FA Trophy and Michael Potts in the home league win over Radcliffe. He added further goals himself, rounding off the scoring with a volley against Grantham Town at Broadhurst and heading the only goal of the vital win at promotion rivals Nantwich Town in February 2020. He registered again when rounding off the scoring against Pontefract Collieries in his first outing of 2020/21, when he helped the Reds on their way to the FA Cup 1st round. He began 2021/22 at right-back, but the majority of his games came in his preferred position in the centre of defence as he had another excellent campaign. His standards remained high throughout, and he was trusted to captain the side on occasion. He continued to be a goal threat too, scoring five times which included breaking the deadlock at vital times at home to Buxton, Mickleover and Witton Albion. He helped FC to reach the FENIX Trophy final before moving on to join Warrington Rylands in June 2022.

305 Curtis JONES

Born: 27/07/1993, Manchester   **Centre-back/Right-back/Midfielder**
Debut: No.4 v Grantham Town (A, NPLP), 17/08/2019

Season	LEAGUE			FA NATIONAL CUPS			OTHER CUPS / PLAY-OFFS			TOTALS		
	Starts	(+Sub)	Goals	Starts	(+Sub)	Goals	Starts	(+Sub)	Goals	Starts	(+Sub)	Goals
2019/20	28	(+0)	2	8	(+0)	0	2	(+0)	0	38	(+0)	2
2020/21	7	(+0)	1	4	(+0)	1	0	(+0)	0	11	(+0)	2
2021/22	26	(+0)	2	4	(+0)	0	3	(+2)	0	33	(+2)	2
Totals	61	(+0)	5	16	(+0)	1	5	(+2)	0	82	(+2)	6

A former academy player at Stockport County, Curtis joined Scottish giants Celtic as a scholar after leaving school at Wright Robinson in 2009. After winning trophies in their youth and under-21 teams and appearing for the senior side in a friendly against Athletic Bilbao, he was released in 2012. The tall and mobile defender from Clayton spent a year with Bristol City before a short spell back in Scotland with Livingston in 2013. His next stop was at TNS in the Welsh Premier League in 2014 before returning to Manchester with local North West Counties side Abbey Hey in 2015. He moved to Northern Premier League side Nantwich Town the following year, before signing a contract with Southport in 2017 and facing FC United in the National League North. He later played for Ashton United and Trafford, with whom he won the Northern Premier League Challenge Cup at Broadhurst Park in April 2019. He returned to the scene of that triumph to sign for FC the following month. In the early weeks of the season he was used at centre-back and right-back, and also had a spell as a holding midfielder. When he returned to the centre of defence he developed a terrific understanding with Chris Doyle as part of a stable backline which remained largely unchanged for the rest of the term. He had been on duty for every game until a groin injury in January kept him out for four weeks. Before that he had headed his first goal for the club in the win at Hyde United early in the New Year. At the end of February his first goal at Broadhurst Park raised the roof when his deft header equalised in stoppage time of the thrilling 4-4 draw with promotion rivals Warrington Town. Although the season came to a premature end, Curtis was deservedly awarded the Manager's Player Of The Season accolade by Neil Reynolds. He missed just one game in 2020/21, and was in great form as the Reds reached the FA Cup 1st round. He also scored against Marske United in the FA Trophy, and again past Warrington in FC's league win before that season was also abandoned. He suffered with niggling injuries in the early stages of 2021/22, when he was mostly deployed in midfield until returning to centre-back in October. He scored the equaliser in FC's win at eventual champions Buxton in December, and also volleyed home in the draw at Mickleover shortly after returning from a month on the sidelines. He ended the campaign as part of the victorious team that brought home the FENIX Trophy from Rimini in June 2022.

306 Chris DOYLE

Born: 17/02/1995, Liverpool
Debut: No.5 v Grantham Town (A, NPLP), 17/08/2019

Centre-back

	LEAGUE			FA NATIONAL CUPS			OTHER CUPS / PLAY-OFFS			TOTALS		
Season	Starts	(+Sub)	Goals	Starts	(+Sub)	Goals	Starts	(+Sub)	Goals	Starts	(+Sub)	Goals
2019/20	28	(+0)	2	8	(+0)	0	3	(+0)	0	39	(+0)	2
2020/21	6	(+0)	0	4	(+0)	0	0	(+0)	0	10	(+0)	0
Totals	34	(+0)	0	12	(+0)	0	3	(+0)	0	49	(+0)	2

A former academy player at Everton, Chris moved to Morecambe where he signed a professional contract in 2012. The imposing central defender made his senior debut as a late substitute in a League Two win over Rochdale in March 2013, and remained a regular squad member throughout the following campaign. In September 2014 he began the first of four separate loan spells with Chorley, during which he featured in the 2015 Conference North play-off final. Back at Morecambe he was given a run in the side during the final stages of 2015/16, before surprisingly being released at the end of the season. He joined National League side Southport but soon suffered a serious knee injury that prevented him from appearing in their colours. He was sidelined for well over a year, and returned to train again with Chorley before moving into the Northern Premier League with his local side Marine in the summer of 2018. He trained with Chorley again in 2019, before playing in a friendly against the Magpies for FC United in July. A few days later he scored with a powerful header in a win over Chester at Broadhurst Park, and he subsequently signed for the Reds. Once the campaign began he was absent from the squad on just three occasions, partnering Tom Dean before developing a solid association with Curtis Jones in a settled defence. He was the victim of a brutal elbow in the FA Trophy at Radcliffe in October that saw him require stitches to a nasty facial injury, but shrugged it off to play four days later. His best moment in a red shirt arrived at the end of November, when he headed a dramatic injury-time winner against promotion rivals Lancaster City to send Broadhurst Park wild. He also netted with a neat volleyed finish a week later at home to Matlock Town. He received a red card for instinctively handling on the line in the FA Trophy defeat at National League leaders Barrow, but after serving his one-match ban was back to his imperious best as the Reds maintained a promotion push. He continued his tremendous partnership with Jones during the shortened 2020/21 season, missing just two games with injury as he helped United to the FA Cup 1st round. Just before the 2021 pre-season commenced he signed a contract to return to Southport to play for them in National League North.

307 Paul ENNIS

Born: 01/02/1990, Manchester
Debut: No.7 v Grantham Town (A, NPLP), 17/08/2019

Midfielder/Forward

	LEAGUE			FA NATIONAL CUPS			OTHER CUPS / PLAY-OFFS			TOTALS		
Season	Starts	(+Sub)	Goals	Starts	(+Sub)	Goals	Starts	(+Sub)	Goals	Starts	(+Sub)	Goals
2019/20	18	(+10)	10	4	(+3)	1	4	(+1)	2	26	(+14)	13
2020/21	3	(+3)	1	5	(+0)	4	0	(+0)	0	8	(+3)	5
2021/22	30	(+8)	5	2	(+2)	2	5	(+0)	3	37	(+10)	10
Totals	51	(+21)	16	11	(+5)	7	9	(+1)	5	71	(+27)	28

Commonly known by his nickname of 'Charlie', Paul grew up in Cheadle Hulme and began his career with local club Stockport County. After playing in the youth team he was initially released in 2008, but returned to sign a professional contract a few weeks later. The attacking midfielder progressed to make his Football League debut as a substitute at Northampton Town in March 2009, and also came off the bench at home to Walsall a month later. He was released that summer and became a much-travelled player on the non-league circuit, featuring in the Conference North, Northern Premier League and North West Counties League for a multitude of clubs, as well as for Bala Town in the Welsh Premier League. His longest association was with Stalybridge Celtic, where he had three spells and first played against FC United. He also faced the Reds in the colours of Hednesford Town, Curzon Ashton and Ashton United, before moving to Broadhurst Park in May 2019. He scored seven times to end the pre-season campaign as the team's top marksman, and bagged his first competitive goals with a brace at home to Morpeth Town as United claimed their maiden win of the term. After a spell out injured in September, he made a spectacular return from the bench to change the game at Stalybridge Celtic in October. He was thrown on with FC trailing, but within a minute set up Tunde Owolabi to equalise before twice putting the Reds in front, with his second goal a dramatic last minute winner. He came on again to net in the 7-0 thrashing of Buxton a week later, and was terrific in both scoring and assisting in the memorable FA Trophy win over Basford United in November. His early brace put FC in charge at home to Lancaster City later in the month, and he hit a purple patch with four goals in five games in the New Year. They included a spectacular injury time leveller at Buxton, and a great finish to put the Reds ahead in the clash at promotion rivals Basford. He also converted his fourth successful penalty of the campaign in February's 4-4 draw with fellow contenders Warrington Town. He grabbed United's first goal of 2020/21 and also struck four times in the team's run to the FA Cup 1st round before the season was abandoned. He was missing from the teamsheet just five times in 2021/22, three of those due to a suspension for a harsh red card at Hyde United in August. He often captained the side when Michael Potts was absent, and again hit double figures in the goalscoring stakes. He rounded off the first win of the season by burying a free-kick against Morpeth, and continued to prove his ability from set pieces by despatching six penalties. He was in the side that won the FENIX Trophy in June, having previously scored three times in the competition.

308 Luke GRIFFITHS

Born: 10/08/1998, Liverpool
Debut: No.8 v Grantham Town (A, NPLP), 17/08/2019

Midfielder

Season	LEAGUE Starts	(+Sub)	Goals	FA NATIONAL CUPS Starts	(+Sub)	Goals	OTHER CUPS / PLAY-OFFS Starts	(+Sub)	Goals	TOTALS Starts	(+Sub)	Goals
2019/20	26	(+4)	1	5	(+0)	0	4	(+1)	0	35	(+5)	1
2020/21	4	(+0)	0	4	(+0)	0	0	(+0)	0	8	(+0)	0
2021/22	21	(+4)	2	2	(+0)	0	1	(+2)	0	24	(+6)	2
Totals	51	(+8)	3	11	(+0)	0	5	(+3)	0	67	(+11)	3

Luke spent two years as a Bolton Wanderers scholar until his release in 2016. The creative midfielder joined North West Counties League side Runcorn Linnets in January 2017, before spells at Northern Premier League sides Warrington Town, Marine and Prescot Cables. He signed for FC United in July 2019, and began the league campaign in the engine room before his progress was stalled by a three-match ban for a red card in the hard-fought draw at Lancaster City in September. He returned with three appearances from the bench, before continuing his blossoming central partnership with Michael Potts. He missed just two further matches, and his performances were rewarded with a contract that he gladly signed in November. He was seen as the man who made the Reds tick, and his eye for a pass created numerous opportunities, such as his long crossfield ball for Regan Linney to finish at Hyde United. He came close himself with several free-kicks, before finally scoring his first goal for the club when his set-piece set FC on the way to victory against Stafford Rangers in February. Later that month he was immense as a composed playmaker in the vital win at Nantwich Town that created more distance between United and their rivals for promotion. He helped the Reds to the 1st round of the FA Cup in 2020/21, but had received two red cards even during the short campaign. He left FC in the summer of 2021 and underwent a trial at Port Vale before eventually rejoining Warrington in August. However, he was unable to settle and returned to United in October to reclaim his place in midfield. His first goal in two years gave the Reds an early lead at Scarborough Athletic in February, and he also claimed the equaliser as FC beat Basford United at home a month later.

309 Nialle RODNEY

Born: 28/02/1991, Nottingham
Debut: No.9 v Grantham Town (A, NPLP), 17/08/2019 (scored)

Forward/Right-winger

Season	LEAGUE Starts	(+Sub)	Goals	FA NATIONAL CUPS Starts	(+Sub)	Goals	OTHER CUPS / PLAY-OFFS Starts	(+Sub)	Goals	TOTALS Starts	(+Sub)	Goals
2019/20	3	(+2)	1	1	(+1)	0	1	(+0)	1	5	(+3)	2
Totals	3	(+2)	1	1	(+1)	0	1	(+0)	1	5	(+3)	2

A tall striker able to play in central or wide roles, Niall began his career at local club Nottingham Forest, where he turned professional in 2009. After a loan spell at Conference North side Ilkeston Town in 2009/10, he made his Championship debut for Forest as a substitute at Cardiff City in November 2010. Following a loan at Burton Albion, he moved on to fellow League Two side Bradford City in 2011, before further loans at Conference sides Darlington and Mansfield Town later that year. He remained at that level with spells at Lincoln City and AFC Telford United. He returned to the Football League with Hartlepool United in 2013, and scored his first senior goal in an EFL Trophy win over former club Bradford in September. Despite several outings from the bench, he was released in 2014 and began playing at amateur level due to his business interests. He returned to the semi-professional ranks in 2015, and had spells with Spalding United, Coalville Town and Long Eaton United, before he moved to Manchester. In July 2017 he played a friendly for FC United at Stalybridge Celtic, but featured for Wythenshawe Amateurs in the Manchester League during the subsequent term. He moved up to the Northern Premier League with Ramsbottom United in 2018, before linking up again with FC in May 2019. He scored the team's first goal of the 2019/20 campaign on his debut at Grantham Town, but after starting the first three league games his opportunities were limited following the arrival of Tunde Owolabi. Shortly after scoring on his final appearance, at Radcliffe in the Manchester Premier Cup in October, he left the club and later linked up with Lancaster City. Ironically he scored his only goal for them at Broadhurst Park in November before moving to Ashton United. He later rejoined both Ramsbottom and Wythenshawe Amateurs before signing for Runcorn Linnets.

310 Craig CARNEY

Born: 24/01/1993, Wigan
Debut: No.10 v Grantham Town (A, NPLP), 17/08/2019

Midfielder/Right-back

Season	LEAGUE Starts	(+Sub)	Goals	FA NATIONAL CUPS Starts	(+Sub)	Goals	OTHER CUPS / PLAY-OFFS Starts	(+Sub)	Goals	TOTALS Starts	(+Sub)	Goals
2019/20	5	(+3)	0	1	(+2)	0	0	(+0)	0	6	(+5)	0
Totals	5	(+3)	0	1	(+2)	0	0	(+0)	0	6	(+5)	0

Craig made his senior non-league debut for Southport in a County Cup tie just a week after his 17th birthday. The Appley Bridge lad ended that season with Chorley before switching to Leigh Genesis, where he earned a run in the Northern Premier League. He was at Lancaster City when he suffered a broken leg in November 2011, but recovered to later play for Bamber Bridge, Northwich Victoria, Squires Gate and Kendal Town. He had two further stints at Lancaster either side of a spell at Stockport County, for whom he faced FC United at Broadhurst Park in the National League North in August 2016. He spent 2018/19 with Marine before signing for FC in May 2019. After scoring three times in pre-season he started five of the first six league games, and created United's first goal of the campaign for Nialle Rodney at Grantham Town. He showed his versatility by featuring as a creative, central or wide midfielder as well as at right-back, but spent most of September appearing as a substitute. In early October he moved on to join Clitheroe to enjoy regular action. He later linked up with Warrington Town and Matlock Town, rejoined Bamber Bridge, and then signed for Colne.

311 Regan LINNEY

Born: 12/05/1997, Preston — Winger/Forward
Debut: No.11 v Grantham Town (A, NPLP), 17/08/2019 (scored)

Season	LEAGUE			FA NATIONAL CUPS			OTHER CUPS / PLAY-OFFS			TOTALS		
	Starts	(+Sub)	Goals	Starts	(+Sub)	Goals	Starts	(+Sub)	Goals	Starts	(+Sub)	Goals
2019/20	24	(+5)	9	8	(+0)	2	2	(+3)	1	34	(+8)	12
2020/21	5	(+0)	1	4	(+0)	3	0	(+0)	0	9	(+0)	4
2021/22	37	(+3)	14	4	(+2)	2	2	(+1)	4	43	(+6)	20
Totals	66	(+8)	24	16	(+2)	7	4	(+4)	5	86	(+14)	36

A former schoolboy in Preston North End's Centre of Excellence, Regan later played in the FA Youth Cup for AFC Fylde and also helped Lancashire to win the FA County Youth Cup in 2014. The exciting wide or central attacker made his senior debut aged 17 for Bamber Bridge in the Northern Premier League, and blossomed under manager Neil Reynolds. He scored in the League Challenge Cup final win over Grantham Town in 2017, and helped his side to promotion to the Premier Division a year later. In May 2019 he followed Reynolds to FC United, and in his first four outings scored three of the side's first four goals of the term. He netted with a wonderful curling shot on his debut at Grantham, and added further spectacular efforts during the campaign. He scored a similar goal to win the game at Atherton Collieries in October, and pulled off an acrobatic volley against Glossop North End in the League Challenge Cup a month later. He finished off a great run into the box against Matlock Town, and celebrated signing a contract with the Reds with a stunning brace at Hyde United in January. He was also reliable from the penalty spot, particularly when winning and converting the spot-kick that broke the deadlock in the hard-fought win at Ashton United. An unfortunate red card for alleged simulation at promotion rivals Basford United in February halted his momentum, but he had already scored 12 goals and when the campaign was suspended he was United's third-highest scorer. He struck four times in the even shorter 2020/21 campaign, which included a wonderful run and cool finish at home to Doncaster Rovers in the televised FA Cup 1st round tie. He made a slow start to 2021/22, with the winner deep into injury time at home to Bootle in the FA Cup his highlight of the first half of the campaign. However, he became transformed when moved into a central striking role in December, and struck 16 goals in a 20-game spell in the New Year. This included doubles at Radcliffe and Gainsborough Trinity, and hat-tricks at Ashton United and at home to AKS Zły in the FENIX Trophy. Undoubtedly his best strike was a wonderful solo effort when he beat five defenders to settle a tight encounter against Lancaster City. His form was rewarded with another contract, and he won all three Player of the Season awards as well as being named in the Northern Premier League's Team of the Season. His four goals in the FENIX Trophy helped the side to win the inaugural tournament.

313 Rhain HELLAWELL

Born: 17/12/1999, Ashton-under-Lyne — Winger
Debut: Sub v Grantham Town (A, NPLP), 17/08/2019

Season	LEAGUE			FA NATIONAL CUPS			OTHER CUPS / PLAY-OFFS			TOTALS		
	Starts	(+Sub)	Goals	Starts	(+Sub)	Goals	Starts	(+Sub)	Goals	Starts	(+Sub)	Goals
2019/20	0	(+4)	0	0	(+1)	0	0	(+0)	0	0	(+5)	0
Totals	0	(+4)	0	0	(+1)	0	0	(+0)	0	0	(+5)	0

Rhain began his semi-professional career with local side Stockport Town, and had made his senior debut in the North West Counties League when he was snapped up by Chester in January 2017. The exciting and pacy winger was called up to the first team a year later, and came off the bench in the National League against Maidstone United in April 2018. After signing professional terms he had loan spells in the North West Counties League with Barnoldswick Town and the Northern Premier League with Widnes, but a knee operation in January 2019 kept him sidelined for the rest of the term. He was released in May 2019 and was delighted to sign for FC United a few days later. He featured in every pre-season game, and impressed with his energetic running as well as a terrific long throw that created several openings. In competitive action he appeared five times from the bench in the first month of the season, but his chances became fewer as further attacking options arrived. He joined Widnes on loan in October, but continued to train with FC when possible before joining Radcliffe in January 2020. He was loaned to City Of Liverpool FC in 2020/21, before moving to Runcorn Linnets, for whom he faced FC in the FA Trophy in October 2021. He also had a spell on dual registration at Prestwich Heys.

314 Tom DEAN

Born: 18/03/1992, Macclesfield — Centre-back
Debut: No.5 v Hyde United (H, NPLP), 20/08/2019

Season	LEAGUE			FA NATIONAL CUPS			OTHER CUPS / PLAY-OFFS			TOTALS		
	Starts	(+Sub)	Goals	Starts	(+Sub)	Goals	Starts	(+Sub)	Goals	Starts	(+Sub)	Goals
2019/20	7	(+0)	0	2	(+0)	2	1	(+0)	0	10	(+0)	2
Totals	7	(+0)	0	2	(+0)	2	1	(+0)	0	10	(+0)	2

Tom is a former youth player with his local club Macclesfield Town, where he also became a junior coach. The tall central defender had drifted into Sunday football in his home town when he was spotted by Mossley in 2013. In a successful five-year spell with the Northern Premier League side he won several Player Of The Year awards, and was such a threat at set-pieces that he was even the team's top scorer in 2017/18. He switched to Buxton in 2018, before signing for FC United in May 2019. His personal highlight was grabbing both United's goals in the draw with Atherton Collieries in the FA Cup at Broadhurst Park in September. However, despite starting 10 of the first 15 games, the thriving partnership between Chris Doyle and Curtis Jones saw Tom move to Clitheroe in October to play more regularly. He returned to the Premier Division with Hyde United, for whom he came up against a rampant FC in January 2020. He joined Colne in the summer of 2020, and returned there after a brief spell at Macclesfield in 2021/22.

312 Jack LENEHAN

Born: 29/11/1998, Liverpool
Debut: Sub v Grantham Town (A, NPLP), 17/08/2019

Midfielder

Season	LEAGUE			FA NATIONAL CUPS			OTHER CUPS / PLAY-OFFS			TOTALS		
	Starts	(+Sub)	Goals	Starts	(+Sub)	Goals	Starts	(+Sub)	Goals	Starts	(+Sub)	Goals
2019/20	5	(+17)	0	1	(+6)	0	5	(+0)	0	11	(+23)	0
2020/21	1	(+2)	0	0	(+1)	0	0	(+0)	0	1	(+3)	0
Totals	6	(+19)	0	1	(+7)	0	5	(+0)	0	12	(+26)	0

A successful schoolboy track athlete, Jack then focused on football and became a Rochdale scholar in 2015. He was released two years later and entered non-league with Chorley's development squad, then managed by David Chadwick. Elevated to the senior side, he started at right-back in the 2018 Lancashire Challenge Trophy Final win over Clitheroe. After loan spells with Northern Premier League sides Skelmersdale United and Prescot Cables, he followed the latter's former boss Brian Richardson to FC United in May 2019. An attack-minded midfielder but also deceptively strong in the tackle, he scored against Runcorn Linnets in the final home pre-season friendly, and went on to start four of the first nine games when the competitive action began. As Michael Potts and Luke Griffiths developed a solid central partnership, his appearances thereafter were mainly from the bench. He carved a niche deputising for Potts in the minor cups, and scored vital penalties in the shoot-out wins over Radcliffe in the Manchester Premier Cup and Glossop North End in the League Challenge Cup. On league duty his most memorable contribution was the inviting cross that was headed home by Chris Doyle for the dramatic injury-time winner against Lancaster City in November. He was the only player to have appeared on every matchday teamsheet until March, when he was allowed to join Runcorn Linnets on a four-game loan. However, after his first outing the season was abruptly halted and then abandoned. After a strong pre-season in 2020 he began the league campaign in the starting line-up at right-back, but after coming off the bench in the next three games he moved on to Atherton Collieries in October, and faced FC twice for them the following term.

315 Adam DODD

Born: 14/05/1993, Preston
Debut: No.3 v Scarborough Athletic (H, NPLP), 24/08/2019

Left-back

Season	LEAGUE			FA NATIONAL CUPS			OTHER CUPS / PLAY-OFFS			TOTALS		
	Starts	(+Sub)	Goals	Starts	(+Sub)	Goals	Starts	(+Sub)	Goals	Starts	(+Sub)	Goals
2019/20	29	(+0)	3	8	(+0)	1	4	(+0)	2	41	(+0)	6
2020/21	7	(+0)	0	5	(+0)	0	0	(+0)	0	12	(+0)	0
2021/22	36	(+1)	2	5	(+0)	0	3	(+1)	1	44	(+2)	3
Totals	72	(+1)	5	18	(+0)	1	7	(+1)	3	97	(+2)	9

Raised in Kirkham, Adam came through the academy at local club Blackpool to sign as a scholar in 2009. During Blackpool's season in the Premier League in 2010/11, the versatile left sider was called up to the first team bench for an FA Cup tie at Southampton, before he signed a professional deal in May 2011. He joined Conference North side Altrincham on loan in November 2011, before embarking on another temporary spell, with Ayr United, in January 2012. He scored a stunning 30-yard free-kick on his home debut, and appeared 19 times in total for the Scottish Division One outfit, which included a League Cup semi-final at Hampden Park. Despite being on the bench several times for Blackpool in the Championship, he was never called onto the field before his release in 2014. He joined Conference North side Chorley that summer, but a serious shoulder injury restricted his progress and he moved on to Bamber Bridge in November 2015. He helped his new club to win the Northern Premier League Challenge Cup and promotion to the Premier Division under Neil Reynolds, and he eventually followed his old boss to sign for FC United in May 2019. He missed the first two league games through suspension, but from making his debut against Scarborough Athletic he was absent from duty on just one further occasion for the rest of the campaign, making more starts and playing more minutes than any other squad member. He was part of what became a very settled back four, but it was his attacking prowess that arguably made him stand out. He combined exceptionally well with Regan Linney down the left side, and got amongst the goals himself, particularly during a purple patch in November when he scored five times in four games. He opened his account by netting a free-kick at Hyde United in the Manchester Premier Cup before bagging a brace at Witton Albion, the first of which was a goal of the season contender. Next came his first goal at Broadhurst Park in the League Challenge Cup against Glossop North End, when he also smashed home a spot-kick in the shoot-out victory. In the FA Trophy at Runcorn Linnets he shrugged off the disappointment of having a penalty saved to later bomb forward and grab FC's third goal. He also hammered home in the win at Mickleover Sports in March as FC moved up to second in the table before the season halted a week later. Adam was later proudly voted by his team-mates as the Players' Player Of The Season. He started every game as he helped the Reds to the FA Cup 1st round before the 2020/21 season was also curtailed. His remarkable run also continued for the first 24 games of 2021/22, during which he also added another three glorious strikes to his tally. A 30-yard thunderbolt at home to Radcliffe was undoubtedly the goal of the season, and a tight finish in the FENIX Trophy at AKS Zły was also unstoppable. He then despatched a lovely free-kick against Gainsborough Trinity before suffering an injury in November that caused his first prolonged lay-off since joining the club. He returned to the starting line-up in January, and thereafter played in every game as he helped FC to the FENIX Trophy final, before being asked by the manager to become United's captain for the 2022/23 season. However, he sadly missed the match in Rimini after suffering a cardiac arrest the previous week, but thankfully he was saved by the prompt actions of his girlfriend Kat.

316 Tunde OWOLABI

Born: 26/07/1995, Ikorodu (Nigeria)
Debut: No.9 v Morpeth Town (H, NPLP), 31/08/2019 (scored 2)

Forward

Season	LEAGUE			FA NATIONAL CUPS			OTHER CUPS / PLAY-OFFS			TOTALS		
	Starts	(+Sub)	Goals	Starts	(+Sub)	Goals	Starts	(+Sub)	Goals	Starts	(+Sub)	Goals
2019/20	28	(+0)	27	8	(+0)	6	2	(+3)	1	38	(+3)	34
Totals	28	(+0)	27	8	(+0)	6	2	(+3)	1	38	(+3)	34

Tunde was born in Nigeria, but spent most of his childhood in Belgium after his father Ganiyu was signed by the country's oldest football club, Royal Antwerp. After moving to the UK and settling in Cheetham Hill, Tunde spent a year with FC United's reserve team, helping them to a Lancashire League and cup double in 2014. After a short loan at Clitheroe, the strong and pacy forward moved on to hone his finishing skills in the North West Counties League and Northern Premier League with spells at New Mills and Widnes. He signed for Hyde United in February 2017, shortly after scoring four goals in a reserve fixture against FC's second string at Broadhurst Park. He went on to assist Prescot Cables, Glossop North End and Skelmersdale United before a successful 2018/19 season with Radcliffe. In a team containing a number of former FC players, Tunde hit 26 goals, including one in the Northern Premier League Division One West play-off final to secure his team's promotion to the Premier Division. He moved to Malta in the summer of 2019 to sign for Victoria Hotspurs on the island of Gozo, but upon his return to Manchester he was quickly snapped up by Neil Reynolds in late August. He made his long-awaited Reds debut the following day against Morpeth Town and celebrated his return in spectacular fashion. Within five minutes he had opened the scoring with a powerful finish, and he added a second with an accurate low curling shot before the break. After four blank weeks he was back on the scoresheet with the only goal of the game against Bamber Bridge, which began a remarkable three-month streak during which he struck 24 times in just 21 matches. He equalised in the win at Stalybridge Celtic in early October, before helping himself to four goals in the 7-0 thrashing of Buxton a week later. After netting a stunner at home to Gainsborough Trinity in November he became the first player to be signed a contract in 2019/20, with a number of clubs higher up the pyramid unsurprisingly showing interest. The following week his Manchester Premier Cup goal at Hyde United broke a club record as he had **scored in seven consecutive matches**. Two doubles in the FA Trophy, at Runcorn Linnets and home to National League North Kettering Town, took him to six in that competition, whilst on league duty he bagged a tremendous treble against Matlock Town and a brace against Grantham Town. Arguably his most satisfying strike was on New Year's Day against former side Radcliffe, when he kept his cool under some provocation to seal a tense win for the Reds. After notching a superb brace at Hyde he then scored just once in his next ten outings, although that was also a screamer at home to Mickleover Sports. He was back amongst the goals in the thrilling 4-4 draw with Warrington Town at the end of February, then hit hat-tricks in each of the next two matches at Mickleover and South Shields before the term prematurely ended. In a little over six months he had already leapt to ninth in the list of FC United's highest ever goalscorers, and was unsurprisingly voted by supporters as the Russell Delaney Player Of The Season. His exploits inevitably attracted professional clubs and he signed a full-time contract with Scottish Premiership side Hamilton Academical for an undisclosed fee in July 2020. However, he started just one league game and was released from his contract in February 2021. He signed for League Of Ireland side Finn Harps a month later, before switching to their Premier Division rivals St Patrick's Athletic in December 2021.

317 Alex CURRAN

Born: 31/10/1998, Blackburn
Debut: No.11 v Stafford Rangers (A, NPLP), 14/09/2019

Midfielder/Forward

Season	LEAGUE			FA NATIONAL CUPS			OTHER CUPS / PLAY-OFFS			TOTALS		
	Starts	(+Sub)	Goals	Starts	(+Sub)	Goals	Starts	(+Sub)	Goals	Starts	(+Sub)	Goals
2019/20	16	(+1)	2	3	(+0)	0	3	(+1)	0	22	(+2)	2
Totals	16	(+1)	2	3	(+0)	0	3	(+1)	0	22	(+2)	2

An attacking midfielder or forward, Alex came through the academy at local side Blackburn Rovers to sign as a scholar in 2015. He entered non-league with Colne in 2017, and in an superb two-year spell he scored 43 goals and was named Northern Premier League Division One West Young Player Of The Year in both 2018 and 2019. He joined National League side Stockport County on a two-year full-time deal in May 2019, but after just two substitute outings he was allowed to join FC United on an initial month's loan in September. In his second game his corner was nodded home by Jordan Buckley for the only goal of a great win at Warrington Town, and he went on to settle as the central of the three attackers supporting Tunde Owolabi as the Reds began to click. He scored his first goal for the club when he ran from inside his own half to finish in the rout of Buxton in October, but later limped off after a heavy challenge from the visitors. His loan was repeatedly extended as he became an integral part of the team, and Stockport also gave him permission to play for FC in the FA Trophy. During a majestic performance at home to Grantham Town in December he had a hand in United's first three goals, and in a terrific display he headed the opener in the hard-earned win at Whitby Town in January. Unfortunately a week later he was the victim of a challenge at Buxton that broke his leg and damaged his ankle ligaments. After recovering he joined Curzon Ashton on loan in September 2020, and made that move permanent in July 2021 before a transfer to Macclesfield in 2022.

PLAYER PROFILES

318 Alex BABOS

Born: 22/08/1998, Stoke-on-Trent
Debut: No.7 v Warrington Town (A, NPLP), 24/09/2019

Midfielder

Season	LEAGUE			FA NATIONAL CUPS			OTHER CUPS / PLAY-OFFS			TOTALS		
	Starts	(+Sub)	Goals	Starts	(+Sub)	Goals	Starts	(+Sub)	Goals	Starts	(+Sub)	Goals
2019/20	6	(+0)	0	0	(+0)	0	0	(+0)	0	6	(+0)	0
Totals	6	(+0)	0	0	(+0)	0	0	(+0)	0	6	(+0)	0

A technically gifted attacking midfielder, Alex emerged in Derby County's academy to turn professional in 2016. The following term he started a Football League Trophy tie at Port Vale, and went on to regularly skipper the under-23 team. He qualifies to play international football for Wales, and received his first under-21 cap against Liechtenstein in 2018. He spent the first half of 2018/19 on loan with Real Unión, playing five games in Spain's Segunda División B. He began a second loan spell when he joined FC United in September 2019, and the Reds won four of the six matches in which he played during his month-long stay at Broadhurst. He was particularly impressive in the home wins over Bamber Bridge and Buxton, before returning to Derby. He was released in June 2020 and resumed in non-league with spells at Alfreton Town, King's Lynn Town and Banbury United.

319 Jordan BUCKLEY

Born: 01/05/1996, Manchester
Debut: No.10 v Warrington Town (A, NPLP), 24/09/2019 (scored)

Forward

Season	LEAGUE			FA NATIONAL CUPS			OTHER CUPS / PLAY-OFFS			TOTALS		
	Starts	(+Sub)	Goals	Starts	(+Sub)	Goals	Starts	(+Sub)	Goals	Starts	(+Sub)	Goals
2019/20	7	(+5)	3	1	(+2)	0	2	(+1)	0	10	(+8)	3
Totals	7	(+5)	3	1	(+2)	0	2	(+1)	0	10	(+8)	3

A lean and tall front man, Jordan became an exciting and prolific goalscorer in the North West Counties League with Irlam. In terrific form in the early weeks of the 2019/20 season, he netted eight goals in nine games as his team reached the FA Cup 2nd Qualifying Round. Shortly after leading the line aganst National League North side York City in September, he was signed by FC United. He made a great start when leaping high to head home the winning goal on his debut at Warrington Town, and followed that by opening the scoring in October's 7-0 rout of Buxton. He bagged again against Gainsborough Trinity in November, but that proved to be his last league start as the team went on a good run of form. He regularly emerged from the bench until January, when he switched to rivals Warrington. He was credited with two goals in the thrilling 4-4 draw when he returned to Broadhurst with his new side in February, the second a speculative long-range cross that caught the wind before deceiving Cameron Belford and nestling in the net. He played at Broadhurst again in FC's 3-1 win in November 2020, before signing for Cymru Premier side Flint Town United in February 2021. Back at Warrington, he haunted the Reds once more with both goals in our 0-2 defeat on the opening day of the 2021/22 season.

320 Cameron BELFORD

Born: 16/10/1988, Nuneaton
Debut: No.1 v Radcliffe (A, MPC:1), 08/10/2019

Goalkeeper

Season	LEAGUE			FA NATIONAL CUPS			OTHER CUPS / PLAY-OFFS			TOTALS		
	Starts	(+Sub)	Goals	Starts	(+Sub)	Goals	Starts	(+Sub)	Goals	Starts	(+Sub)	Goals
2019/20	21	(+0)	0	5	(+0)	0	5	(+0)	0	31	(+0)	0
Totals	21	(+0)	0	5	(+0)	0	5	(+0)	0	31	(+0)	0

Raised in a dedicated football family, Cameron signed as a Coventry City trainee in 2005. In December 2006 he played a game on loan for Conference side Tamworth, where grandfather Buster was the long-serving kitman, with father Dale on the bench as substitute goalkeeper. In 2007 he signed for Bury in League Two, but spent most of the season on loan at Conference North side Worcester City before returning to make his senior debut as a late substitute at Accrington Stanley in May 2008. He became first choice at Gigg Lane in 2010, and bounced back from a fractured cheekbone to help his side to promotion. After spells on loan at Southend United and Accrington, he rejoined Tamworth, where his dad was managing the side. After a short stint at Mansfield Town, Cam joined Rushall Olympic, and first enjoyed a rapport with FC fans in a Northern Premier League game in October 2014. He ended the season in League One at Swindon Town, where his sole outing provided another family quirk when he came on to replace red-carded younger brother Tyrell against Leyton Orient in May 2015. He moved on to National League side Wrexham, before joining Scottish League One club Stranraer in January 2016, where he was virtually ever-present for two years before returning south with League Two side Forest Green Rovers in January 2018. He began the following season in the Conference North with Chorley, but soon joined hometown club Nuneaton Borough and captained them twice to wins over FC United as both clubs were eventually relegated. He joined the Reds on loan in September 2019 and sat on the bench for five games before making his debut at Radcliffe in the Manchester Premier Cup in October. He saved a penalty in the shoot-out victory, and with Paddy Wharton's injury he kept his place for the remaining 31 matches as his deal was extended thanks to the support of his parent club. Despite the odd hair-raising moment, such as the freak header that beat him at home to Basford United, the popular character's experience proved vital as part of a settled defence. He was again a shoot-out hero against Glossop North End in the League Challenge Cup in November, saving a remarkable four spot-kicks as the Reds progressed, and also stopped a penalty in the FA Trophy defeat at Barrow when his display prevented an even worse scoreline. In the league the excellent shot-stopper was particularly impressive in vital away wins at Ashton United and Nantwich Town as FC rose to second in the table before the season was abruptly halted in March 2020. That brought his loan stay at the club to an end, and when his contract with Nuneaton expired he signed for Radcliffe in June 2020. He faced FC twice in the 2021/22 season, and once again pulled off a penalty save to deny Paul Ennis at Broadhurst Park in August. He joined Stafford Rangers in 2022.

321 Jack BARTHRAM

Born: 13/10/1993, Newham
Debut: No.2 v Radcliffe (A, MPC:1), 08/10/2019

Right-back

Season	LEAGUE			FA NATIONAL CUPS			OTHER CUPS / PLAY-OFFS			TOTALS		
	Starts	(+Sub)	Goals	Starts	(+Sub)	Goals	Starts	(+Sub)	Goals	Starts	(+Sub)	Goals
2019/20	0	(+0)	0	0	(+0)	0	1	(+0)	0	1	(+0)	0
Totals	0	(+0)	0	0	(+0)	0	1	(+0)	0	1	(+0)	0

Jack progressed through the academy at Premier League club Tottenham Hotspur, where he was awarded a professional contract in July 2012. Capable of appearing in both full-back positions as well as in midfield, he featured in the reserve side before joining League One side Swindon Town on a free transfer in June 2013. He made his senior debut in a League Cup tie against Torquay United that August, and scored his first goal against Plymouth Argyle in the Football League Trophy in October. Despite signing a contract extension in 2014, he was unable to establish himself and was released the following year. He joined Cheltenham Town, who had just been relegated to the National League, and became their regular right-back as they won the title to return to League Two at the first attempt. He started half the games for a struggling team back at the higher level before being released in June 2017. He returned to the National League with Barrow, playing 60 times in two seasons, but had been without a club when he linked up with FC United in October 2019. Short of match fitness, he started at right-back in the Manchester Premier Cup tie at Radcliffe, but was substituted just after the hour mark and left the club later that month. He later had a spell at Isthmian League club Haringey Borough.

322 Ashley YOUNG

Born: 14/07/1990, Ashton-under-Lyne
Debut: Sub v Radcliffe (A, FAT:Q1), 29/10/2019

Midfielder/Right-back

Season	LEAGUE			FA NATIONAL CUPS			OTHER CUPS / PLAY-OFFS			TOTALS		
	Starts	(+Sub)	Goals	Starts	(+Sub)	Goals	Starts	(+Sub)	Goals	Starts	(+Sub)	Goals
2019/20	0	(+2)	0	0	(+3)	0	2	(+0)	0	2	(+5)	0
Totals	0	(+2)	0	0	(+3)	0	2	(+0)	0	2	(+5)	0

Ashley was in the academy at local club Curzon Ashton when he was spotted by Burnley, who signed him as an apprentice. He switched to Bury in 2007, and was an unused substitute for their Football League Trophy tie at Rochdale in October that year. Alongside him on the bench that night was Cameron Belford, with other future Reds Glynn Hurst and Richie Baker in the starting line-up. The following summer he joined Scottish Premiership club Falkirk, where he was a regular in their reserve side, before venturing to the USA on a scholarship to play for Erie Admirals in Pennsylvania. He returned home to sign for Conference North outfit Hyde in November 2010, before moving abroad again for a season with Western Australia State League side Bunbury Force. He linked up with Mossley in the summer of 2012, and scored against FC United in the FA Trophy at Gigg Lane in October. After a short spell at Nantwich Town he faced FC several times during two seasons with Ashton United, where he was nominated for a midfield spot in the Northern Premier League's team of the season in 2015. That summer he began a three-year stint in the League Of Wales, where he featured for Bangor City, Rhyl and Aberystwyth Town, before signing for Buxton in 2018. Just over a week after appearing as a substitute at Broadhurst Park in October 2019, he signed for the Reds to provide midfield and defensive cover. With a settled team in good form, he started just two games for the club, at right-back in cup games, before returning to former club Hyde United the day after FC won there in January 2020.

323 Finlay SINCLAIR-SMITH

Born: 20/07/2000, Liverpool
Debut: Sub v Grantham Town (H, NPLP), 21/12/2019

Winger

Season	LEAGUE			FA NATIONAL CUPS			OTHER CUPS / PLAY-OFFS			TOTALS		
	Starts	(+Sub)	Goals	Starts	(+Sub)	Goals	Starts	(+Sub)	Goals	Starts	(+Sub)	Goals
2019/20	4	(+8)	0	0	(+1)	0	2	(+0)	1	6	(+9)	2
2020/21	5	(+0)	2	2	(+2)	1	0	(+0)	0	7	(+2)	3
2021/22	5	(+3)	1	3	(+1)	1	0	(+0)	0	8	(+4)	2
Totals	14	(+11)	4	5	(+4)	2	2	(+0)	1	21	(+15)	7

Finlay graduated through the academy at Blackpool to be rewarded with a professional contract in May 2018. Earlier that season he was one of eleven young apprentices at Football League clubs to be recognised with an annual award for sporting and academic achievements. The fast, exciting winger had already made his senior debut, which he marked by grabbing a late equaliser at home to Wigan Athletic in the EFL Trophy the previous August. After two further outings in the same competition he spent time on loan at Northern Premier League outfits Marine and Widnes in 2018/19, before being released by Blackpool at the end of the campaign. He linked up with North West Counties League side Longridge Town ahead of the following term, but with his performances earning rave reviews he was destined to move back up the football pyramid before long. He joined FC United in December, and made a terrific start. He struck the post with virtually his first touch on his debut against Grantham Town, before a foul on him produced the free-kick that led to the dramatic injury-time winner at Ashton United a week later. He was named man-of-the-match on his first start in the terrific win over Radcliffe, when he helped to set up the equaliser for Michael Potts, and was equally impressive in the comprehensive win at Hyde United. He was delighted to grab his first goal with a calm finish to equalize against Mickleover Sports, and also netted in the next game as the Reds beat Irlam in the Manchester Premier Cup semi-final. After a quiet start to 2020/21, his season burst into life when he came off the bench to hammer home a dramatic injury-time winner over Guiseley to propel FC into the FA Cup 1st round. He ensured his place for the visit of Doncaster Rovers when he also hit a brace in the great win over Warrington Town. In 2021/22, he had played in every game before surprisingly leaving for rivals Bamber Bridge in September.

324 Jorge SIKORA

Born: 29/03/2002, Bradford
Debut: No.3 v Ashton United (A, NPLP), 28/12/2019

Centre-back/Full-back

	LEAGUE			FA NATIONAL CUPS			OTHER CUPS / PLAY-OFFS			TOTALS		
Season	Starts	(+Sub)	Goals	Starts	(+Sub)	Goals	Starts	(+Sub)	Goals	Starts	(+Sub)	Goals
2019/20	1	(+0)	0	0	(+0)	0	0	(+0)	0	1	(+0)	0
2021/22	3	(+0)	0	0	(+0)	0	1	(+0)	0	4	(+0)	0
Totals	4	(+0)	0	0	(+0)	0	1	(+0)	0	5	(+0)	0

A strong, versatile defender, Jorge came through the academy at local club Bradford City to sign as a scholar. Eligible due to ancestry, he was contacted by the Poland FA with a view to playing for their international youth sides. He joined Northern Counties East League club Thackley on loan in March 2019, and gained further senior experience in a spell at Ossett United in the early weeks of the next term. He made his Bradford first team debut against Manchester City in the EFL Trophy, before starting his third loan spell when he linked up with FC United in December 2019. He contributed well to a hard-fought win as a deputy left-back for the trip to Ashton United, but was recalled by Bradford a week later to prepare for their FA Youth Cup trip to Chelsea. He continued to train with the senior squad, and made his League Two debut in May 2021. After a loan spell at National League North side Spennymoor United in 2021/22, he was released by Bradford and rejoined FC in February 2022. He added to his Reds appearance tally with four outings at centre-back.

325 Kyle HAWLEY

Born: 11/05/2000, Oldham
Debut: Sub v Whitby Town (A, NPLP), 18/01/2020 (scored)

Forward

	LEAGUE			FA NATIONAL CUPS			OTHER CUPS / PLAY-OFFS			TOTALS		
Season	Starts	(+Sub)	Goals	Starts	(+Sub)	Goals	Starts	(+Sub)	Goals	Starts	(+Sub)	Goals
2019/20	1	(+3)	1	0	(+0)	0	1	(+1)	0	2	(+4)	1
Totals	1	(+3)	1	0	(+0)	0	1	(+1)	0	2	(+4)	1

A tall and strong centre-forward, Kyle emerged through Morecambe's academy, and was just 16 when he made his Football League debut as a substitute against Cheltenham Town in April 2017. At the end of his scholarship he signed a professional contract, which was extended in 2019. After loan spells in the Northern Premier League with Skelmersdale United, Witton Albion and Lancaster City, he joined FC United on a similar deal in January 2020. He made an instant impact by grabbing the late winner on his debut at Whitby Town within five minutes of coming off the bench. He helped the Reds to three further league draws as well as a Manchester Premier Cup semi-final victory, but was injured during his only start in the win over Stafford Rangers in February. Released by Morecambe, he later played for Stalybridge Celtic, Glossop North End, Mossley and Wythenshawe Amateurs.

326 Ben KERR

Born: 08/03/2001, Birkenhead
Debut: No.2 v Sheffield (H, NPLCC:2), 21/01/2020

Right-back

	LEAGUE			FA NATIONAL CUPS			OTHER CUPS / PLAY-OFFS			TOTALS		
Season	Starts	(+Sub)	Goals	Starts	(+Sub)	Goals	Starts	(+Sub)	Goals	Starts	(+Sub)	Goals
2019/20	1	(+0)	0	0	(+0)	0	1	(+0)	0	2	(+0)	0
Totals	1	(+0)	0	0	(+0)	0	1	(+0)	0	2	(+0)	0

After captaining Wirral schoolboys, Ben signed a scholarship at local club Tranmere Rovers in 2017. A tenacious defender or midfielder, he was a regular in the under-18s but was released in 2019. After a spell at Gottne IF in Sweden's fourth tier, he joined FC United in November 2019. He waited patiently as an unused substitute before starting at right-back in the League Challenge Cup tie with Sheffield at Broadhurst Park in January 2020. Despite a last-gasp defeat, his display was one positive of the evening. He also started the crucial away win at promotion rivals Nantwich Town in February, before joining Runcorn Linnets on loan in March. He was released by FC in August, and went on to spells at North West Counties League sides Vauxhall Motors and Cammell Laird.

327 Matthew ELSDON

Born: 24/06/1997, Durham
Debut: No.6 v Mickleover Sports (H, NPLP), 01/02/2020

Centre-back

	LEAGUE			FA NATIONAL CUPS			OTHER CUPS / PLAY-OFFS			TOTALS		
Season	Starts	(+Sub)	Goals	Starts	(+Sub)	Goals	Starts	(+Sub)	Goals	Starts	(+Sub)	Goals
2019/20	5	(+1)	0	0	(+0)	0	1	(+0)	0	6	(+1)	0
Totals	5	(+1)	0	0	(+0)	0	1	(+0)	0	6	(+1)	0

Once a forward in Sunderland's academy, Matty became a ball-playing centre-back at Middlesbrough, where he turned professional and won England under-17 caps. He was ever-present in the 2015/16 UEFA Youth League campaign, and played three times in the next term's EFL Trophy before a loan at Scottish Championship side Inverness Caledonian Thistle in 2017/18. He signed a two-year deal with National League side Barrow in 2018, but his outings there were restricted by injuries. In August 2019 he joined Northern Premier League side Whitby Town on loan, before coming to FC United for another temporary spell in January 2020. He appeared in all seven February fixtures as he helped FC to nine league points and a Manchester Premier Cup semi-final victory. He started six of those games and also came off the bench to help United preserve a clean sheet in the tough away win at promotion rivals Nantwich Town. He went on to join Blyth Spartans before playing for Scottish League One side Clyde in 2021/22.

328 Morgan HOMSON-SMITH

Born: 26/01/1998, Preston   **Midfielder/Forward**
Debut: No.10 v Mickleover Sports (H, NPLP), 01/02/2020 (scored)

	LEAGUE			FA NATIONAL CUPS			OTHER CUPS / PLAY-OFFS			TOTALS		
Season	Starts	(+Sub)	Goals	Starts	(+Sub)	Goals	Starts	(+Sub)	Goals	Starts	(+Sub)	Goals
2019/20	4	(+3)	3	0	(+0)	0	1	(+0)	0	5	(+3)	3
2020/21	3	(+3)	0	0	(+2)	0	0	(+0)	0	3	(+5)	0
2021/22	0	(+1)	0	0	(+2)	0	0	(+0)	0	0	(+3)	0
Totals	7	(+7)	3	0	(+4)	0	1	(+0)	0	8	(+11)	3

A mobile attacker, Morgan was in the Blackburn Rovers academy, before joining Morecambe on a scholarship. After a work experience loan spell at Northern Premier League side Kendal Town, he left full-time football to study at university. Following stints at AFC Fylde, Harrogate Town and Prescot Cables, he signed a contract at Southport in September 2018, and faced FC United in National League North later that term. He began a loan at Northern Premier League First Division side Colne in October 2019, before joining FC on a similar deal in January 2020. He made an instant impact at Broadhurst Park, scoring on his debut against Mickleover Sports and producing a wonderful finish for the winner against Stafford Rangers in his next league outing. His free-kick opened the scoring in the 4-4 draw with Warrington Town, and he was also instrumental in terrific away victories at Nantwich Town and Mickleover before joining the Reds permanently in August. He had featured in every matchday squad in 2020/21 and helped United to the FA Cup 1st round, but surprisingly left for City Of Liverpool FC in early November just before the season was suspended. He rejoined FC in August 2021, but appeared just three times off the bench before joining North West Counties League side Longridge Town dual registration ahead of a permanent move to Bootle in November.

329 Daniel TRICKETT-SMITH

Born: 08/09/1995, Newcastle-under-Lyme   **Midfielder/Forward**
Debut: No.10 v Bamber Bridge (A, NPLP), 22/02/2020

	LEAGUE			FA NATIONAL CUPS			OTHER CUPS / PLAY-OFFS			TOTALS		
Season	Starts	(+Sub)	Goals	Starts	(+Sub)	Goals	Starts	(+Sub)	Goals	Starts	(+Sub)	Goals
2019/20	2	(+3)	0	0	(+0)	0	0	(+0)	0	2	(+3)	0
Totals	2	(+3)	0	0	(+0)	0	0	(+0)	0	2	(+3)	0

Dan won England under-16 caps at Crewe Alexandra before Liverpool signed him for an initial fee of £300,000 in 2012. The attacking midfielder turned professional a year later but suffered a series of injuries. Released in 2016, he played two summer seasons in California for United Soccer League side Sacramento Republic, before returning to his native Staffordshire in September 2017 to join Leek Town. His displays earned a return to the professional ranks in January 2019 with Port Vale, who loaned him back to Leek until the end of the term. He helped them to the Northern Premier League Division One West promotion play-off final, and was named in the division's team of the season. In September 2019 he joined National League North side Curzon Ashton on loan, before returning to make his Vale debut in a 2-1 victory over Newcastle United in the EFL Trophy. He joined FC United on a further loan deal in February 2020, and made his debut in the loss at Bamber Bridge before helping the Reds to seven crucial points in the next three games. Still on the Port Vale fringes, he was again loaned to Leek in October 2020 before a permanent return there in 2021.

330 Larnell COLE

Born: 09/03/1993, Manchester   **Midfielder/Forward**
Debut: Sub v Bamber Bridge (A, NPLP), 22/02/2020

	LEAGUE			FA NATIONAL CUPS			OTHER CUPS / PLAY-OFFS			TOTALS		
Season	Starts	(+Sub)	Goals	Starts	(+Sub)	Goals	Starts	(+Sub)	Goals	Starts	(+Sub)	Goals
2019/20	0	(+1)	0	0	(+0)	0	0	(+0)	0	0	(+1)	0
Totals	0	(+1)	0	0	(+0)	0	0	(+0)	0	0	(+1)	0

Regarded as one of the most technically accomplished players as he progressed through the Manchester United academy, Larnell signed as a full-time scholar in 2009. The pacy right-sided attacker was an integral part of a talented group that lifted the FA Youth Cup in 2011, during which he kept his nerve to score a penalty in the quarter-final at Liverpool to begin his team's tremendous comeback. In September 2011 he made his first team debut as a substitute in a League Cup win at Leeds United, and was named on the bench for four further senior matches which included fixtures in the Premier League and Champions League. Back in the reserve side, he experienced a glorious end to 2012/13 when he hit a hat-trick against Liverpool in the semi-final, then a brace to complete a comeback against Tottenham Hotspur as United won the Premier League under-21 Final. He was in the England squad for the 2013 FIFA under-20 World Cup in Turkey, to add to his earlier under-19 international caps. With further senior opportunities not forthcoming, Larnell joined Fulham in January 2014, and ironically made his only appearance for them just over a week later as a substitute in a Premier League draw at Old Trafford. After loans at Milton Keynes, Shrewsbury Town and Scottish Premiership side Inverness Caledonian Thistle, he was released in 2017. He linked up with National League club Tranmere Rovers, and helped his side to promotion back to the Football League in 2018. He scored a spectacular effort to conclude an extra-time triumph over Ebbsfleet United in the play-off semi-final, before starting the Wembley win over Boreham Wood. Despite beginning 2018/19 with a League Cup goal against Walsall, he lost his regular place and was released in January 2019. Larnell had been playing amateur football with Lancashire & Cheshire League side Whalley Range when he joined FC United in February 2020. He followed Phil Marsh and Nick Culkin to become only the **third player to play a senior game for both Uniteds** when he came on in the disappointing loss at Bamber Bridge. He remained on the bench for the win at Nantwich Town, before the suspension of the season put paid to any chance of a further outing. He later linked up with Radcliffe and Cymru Premier club Flint Town United.

331 Dan LAVERCOMBE

Born: 21/10/1996, Torquay
Debut: No.1 v Nantwich Town (H, NPLP), 19/09/2020

Goalkeeper

Season	LEAGUE Starts	(+Sub)	Goals	FA NATIONAL CUPS Starts	(+Sub)	Goals	OTHER CUPS / PLAY-OFFS Starts	(+Sub)	Goals	TOTALS Starts	(+Sub)	Goals
2020/21	7	(+0)	0	5	(+0)	0	0	(+0)	0	12	(+0)	0
2021/22	39	(+0)	0	6	(+0)	0	4	(+0)	0	49	(+0)	0
Totals	46	(+0)	0	11	(+0)	0	4	(+0)	0	61	(+0)	0

A former schoolboy with Exeter City, Dan came through a scholarship at Devon rivals Torquay United to make his National League debut in April 2015 as an 18-year-old. The following January he was snapped up by League One side Wigan Athletic, and after their promotion was named on the bench for several matches in the Championship the following season. After loan spells back at Torquay and with Welsh Premier League side Rhyl, he reverted to semi-professional status in 2019 with AFC Fylde in the National League. He linked up with FC United during the summer of 2020, and after some impressive friendly performances was installed as number one for the campaign, when he played the entirety of all twelve competitive matches. He was a model of consistency, and carried that form all the way through the 2021/22 season when he was absent for just three matches, all through illness. A number of outstanding performances were key to the Reds picking up points, most notably in the win at eventual champions Buxton and the home victory over Basford United that kept FC's play-off hopes alive. He was rewarded with a contract that he signed in March 2022, before keeping a clean sheet in the victorious FENIX Trophy final in Rimini in June.

332 Michael FOWLER

Born: 13/05/2001, Lincoln
Debut: No.9 v Nantwich Town (H, NPLP), 19/09/2020

Forward

Season	LEAGUE Starts	(+Sub)	Goals	FA NATIONAL CUPS Starts	(+Sub)	Goals	OTHER CUPS / PLAY-OFFS Starts	(+Sub)	Goals	TOTALS Starts	(+Sub)	Goals
2020/21	5	(+2)	2	2	(+3)	1	0	(+0)	0	7	(+5)	3
Totals	5	(+2)	2	2	(+3)	1	0	(+0)	0	7	(+5)	3

Once in Sunderland's academy, Michael joined Burnley as a scholar in 2017 and became a prolific scorer in the Premier League club's youth side before signing a professional deal with Fleetwood Town in March 2019. The strong centre-forward had sampled non-league on loan at Padiham, Radcliffe, Guiseley and Bamber Bridge, for whom he played against FC United in September 2019, before he arrived at Broadhurst Park on a season-long loan in August 2020. His first goal was a fierce volley to earn a draw at Hyde United, and he also struck late to earn a vital league win over Stafford Rangers and to equalise against Marske United in the FA Trophy. After the suspension of FC's season, he was released by Fleetwood in June 2021. He ventured to the USA to play at Coastal Carolina University before returning home to join Dunston UTS later in the year.

333 Dan COCKERLINE

Born: 15/11/1996, Warrington
Debut: Sub v Nantwich Town (H, NPLP), 19/09/2020

Forward

Season	LEAGUE Starts	(+Sub)	Goals	FA NATIONAL CUPS Starts	(+Sub)	Goals	OTHER CUPS / PLAY-OFFS Starts	(+Sub)	Goals	TOTALS Starts	(+Sub)	Goals
2020/21	5	(+2)	2	2	(+3)	1	0	(+0)	0	7	(+5)	3
Totals	5	(+2)	2	2	(+3)	1	0	(+0)	0	7	(+5)	3

Dan emerged through Sheffield United's academy to turn professional in 2015, but was released a year later. The tall and mobile striker had experienced non-league in loans at Grantham Town, Marine, Matlock Town and Curzon Ashton, and went on to have stints at Northwich Victoria, Barrow, Stalybridge Celtic, Southport, Farsley and Hednesford Town before playing for Adelaide Blue Eagles in the South Australian Super League in 2019. He returned later that year and joined North West Counties League side AFC Liverpool, where his prolific scoring record prompted FC United to sign him in June 2020. In his first four starts he struck three well-taken goals against Pontefract Collieries, Stafford Rangers and Lancaster City, but with the season suspended he joined Aberystwyth Town in January 2021 ahead of the restart of their Cymru Premier campaign. After a brief return to AFC Liverpool he came back to haunt FC when he scored for Nantwich Town in their win at Broadhurst Park in October 2021.

334 Tom STEAD

Born: 23/03/2000, Wigan
Debut: No.6 v Pontefract Collieries (H, FAC:Q1), 22/09/2020

Centre-back

Season	LEAGUE Starts	(+Sub)	Goals	FA NATIONAL CUPS Starts	(+Sub)	Goals	OTHER CUPS / PLAY-OFFS Starts	(+Sub)	Goals	TOTALS Starts	(+Sub)	Goals
2020/21	0	(+0)	0	1	(+0)	0	0	(+0)	0	1	(+0)	0
Totals	**0**	**(+0)**	**0**	**1**	**(+0)**	**0**	**0**	**(+0)**	**0**	**1**	**(+0)**	**0**

A centre-back from Golborne, Tom joined Preston North End as a scholar in 2016, but after time on loan at Ramsbottom United his progress was disrupted by a cruciate injury in his second year. He signed as a professional for the 2018/19 campaign, during which he spent time on loan in non-league with Ashton United and Kendal Town. Released in the summer of 2019, he had spells with Chorley, Clitheroe and Kendal again before joining FC United in August 2020. He played the whole of the FA Cup win over Pontefract Collieries, but this was his only action of the shortened season. He signed up for the newly-formed Macclesfield in the summer of 2021, before later switching to fellow North West Counties League side Longridge Town.

335 Kain DEAN

Born: 21/08/2002, Oldham
Debut: Sub v Pontefract Collieries (H, FAC:Q1), 22/09/2020

Left-back

Season	LEAGUE Starts	(+Sub)	Goals	FA NATIONAL CUPS Starts	(+Sub)	Goals	OTHER CUPS / PLAY-OFFS Starts	(+Sub)	Goals	TOTALS Starts	(+Sub)	Goals
2021/21	0	(+0)	0	0	(+1)	0	0	(+0)	0	0	(+1)	0
Totals	**0**	**(+0)**	**0**	**0**	**(+1)**	**0**	**0**	**(+0)**	**0**	**0**	**(+1)**	**0**

Kain completed a two-year scholarship with Mansfield Town, which included a loan at United Counties League side Anstey Nomads, but was released in 2020. The Crompton lad soon linked up with FC United, and impressed as an attacking full-back in the pre-season friendlies. He was in the matchday squad for six of the first seven competitive fixtures of the 2020/21 campaign, and enjoyed his debut as a substitute early in the second half of the FA Cup win over Pontefract Collieries. He also joined local North West Counties League side Chadderton on a dual registration basis, where he lined up alongside his twin brother Harry. He played for FC in the pre-season campaign in 2021 before signing for Mossley in July. He later joined Runcorn Linnets and Ramsbottom United.

336 Morgan PENFOLD

Born: 03/12/1998, Peterborough
Debut: No.7 v Curzon Ashton (A, FAC:Q2), 03/10/2020

Midfielder/Forward

Season	LEAGUE Starts	(+Sub)	Goals	FA NATIONAL CUPS Starts	(+Sub)	Goals	OTHER CUPS / PLAY-OFFS Starts	(+Sub)	Goals	TOTALS Starts	(+Sub)	Goals
2020/21	0	(+3)	0	1	(+1)	0	0	(+0)	0	1	(+4)	0
Totals	**0**	**(+3)**	**0**	**1**	**(+1)**	**0**	**0**	**(+0)**	**0**	**1**	**(+4)**	**0**

Morgan came through the academy at his local club Peterborough United, and was awarded a senior debut aged just 17 against Norwich City in the EFL Trophy in August 2016. After loan spells in non-league with St. Ives Town, Biggleswade Town, Boston United, Grantham Town, Bedford Town and Hitchin Town, he signed a two-year contract with National League side Barrow in May 2019. The versatile attacker was part of the squad that earned promotion to the Football League, before joining FC United on loan in October 2020. He looked sharp on his debut in the FA Cup victory at Curzon Ashton, but that was his only start as his subsequent outings were from the bench. He returned to his parent club at the end of the month, but was released by Barrow in June 2021.

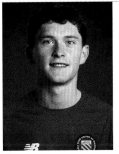

337 Joe WHITE

Born: 18/01/2002, Liverpool
Debut: Sub v Lancaster City (H, NPLP), 20/10/2020

Left-back/Midfielder

Season	LEAGUE Starts	(+Sub)	Goals	FA NATIONAL CUPS Starts	(+Sub)	Goals	OTHER CUPS / PLAY-OFFS Starts	(+Sub)	Goals	TOTALS Starts	(+Sub)	Goals
2020/21	0	(+2)	0	0	(+0)	0	0	(+0)	0	0	(+2)	0
2021/22	4	(+7)	0	1	(+1)	0	0	(+0)	0	5	(+8)	0
Totals	**4**	**(+9)**	**0**	**1**	**(+1)**	**0**	**0**	**(+0)**	**0**	**5**	**(+10)**	**0**

Joe joined Bolton Wanderers upon leaving school, and was aged just 17 when he made his debut as a substitute at Wycombe Wanderers in August 2019 as the crisis club were forced to field several academy players. He earned rave reviews on his first start at left-back a week later in a draw with Coventry City, and featured five times in total before the club were able to recruit more senior players. He was released at the end of the term and later joined North West Counties League side Lower Breck. He scored twice on his debut in October 2020 and was soon signed up by FC United, going on to appear twice from the bench before the season was halted. He missed two months with injury early in 2021/22, but earned a run covering at left-back in late autumn. With Adam Dodd fit again, Joe moved on to Marine in January 2022 and helped them to win the Northern Premier League Division One West play-offs.

338 Jordan SIMPSON

Born: 28/11/1998, Swindon
Debut: No.10 v Guiseley (H, FAC:Q4), 24/10/2020

Midfielder

Season	LEAGUE			FA NATIONAL CUPS			OTHER CUPS / PLAY-OFFS			TOTALS		
	Starts	(+Sub)	Goals	Starts	(+Sub)	Goals	Starts	(+Sub)	Goals	Starts	(+Sub)	Goals
2020/21	2	(+0)	0	2	(+0)	0	0	(+0)	0	4	(+0)	0
2021/22	5	(+6)	1	1	(+0)	0	0	(+0)	0	6	(+6)	1
Totals	7	(+6)	1	3	(+0)	0	0	(+0)	0	10	(+6)	1

Jordan emulated his father Fitzroy Simpson, the former Premier League midfielder who played for Jamaica in the World Cup, by turning professional at local club Swindon Town in March 2017. He was named in their League One matchday squad, but his Football League debut came with Forest Green Rovers later that year. After non-league loans at Hungerford Town, Havant & Waterlooville and Hampton & Richmond Borough, he returned to National League South with Bath City in 2019. The tall and energetic midfielder relocated to Manchester and signed for FC United in October 2020, starting four times before the season stopped. He scored in the win over Morpeth Town in the first home game of 2021/22, but his progress was disrupted by injuries, plus a red card just two minutes after coming off the bench against Radcliffe. He moved on to North West Counties League side Macclesfield in October, but returned to the Northern Premier League in December 2021 with Ashton United, with whom he won the Manchester Premier Cup in 2022.

339 Tre PEMBERTON

Born: 03/01/1999, Manchester
Debut: No.7 v South Shields (A, NPLP), 27/10/2020

Winger

Season	LEAGUE			FA NATIONAL CUPS			OTHER CUPS / PLAY-OFFS			TOTALS		
	Starts	(+Sub)	Goals	Starts	(+Sub)	Goals	Starts	(+Sub)	Goals	Starts	(+Sub)	Goals
2020/21	2	(+0)	0	1	(+0)	0	0	(+0)	0	3	(+0)	0
2021/22	0	(+0)	0	1	(+0)	0	0	(+0)	0	1	(+0)	0
Totals	2	(+0)	0	2	(+0)	0	0	(+0)	0	4	(+0)	0

After completing a two-year scholarship at Blackburn Rovers, Tre signed as a professional for Stoke City in July 2017. He made his senior debut against his former club in the EFL Trophy the following month, and played seven times in that competition whilst remaining a regular in the under-23 side, until he was released in 2020. A native of Moston, he joined his local club FC United in October, and impressed with his speed and trickery in three outings on the right wing before the campaign paused. He featured prominently during the 2021 pre-season, when he got amongst the goals, but was allowed to sign for North West Counties League side Longridge Town on a dual registration basis as the competitive campaign got underway. He earned a recall to Broadhurst Park to start the FA Cup replay with Bootle in early September, but moved on to Northern Premier League rivals Stafford Rangers the following month. In May 2022 he signed a one-year deal with the ambitious Northern Premier League Division One outfit Macclesfield.

340 Calum WOODS

Born: 05/02/1987, Liverpool
Debut: No.5 v Marske United (H, FAT:Q3), 31/10/2020

Defender

Season	LEAGUE			FA NATIONAL CUPS			OTHER CUPS / PLAY-OFFS			TOTALS		
	Starts	(+Sub)	Goals	Starts	(+Sub)	Goals	Starts	(+Sub)	Goals	Starts	(+Sub)	Goals
2020/21	0	(+0)	0	1	(+0)	0	0	(+0)	0	1	(+0)	0
Totals	0	(+0)	0	1	(+0)	0	0	(+0)	0	1	(+0)	0

A versatile defender, Calum came through the Liverpool Academy before joining Scottish Premier League side Dunfermline Athletic in July 2006. He played over 150 games for the Fife club before returning south in June 2011 to join Huddersfield Town, with whom he won the League One play-offs in 2012. He repeated that feat with Preston North End in 2015, but suffered relegation from that division with both Bradford City in 2019, and Tranmere Rovers a year later. He was a free agent when he joined FC United in October 2020, but only featured in the FA Trophy defeat to Marske United before the season was curtailed. In December it was announced that he had signed for Indian Super League club East Bengal. He then joined Cymru Premier side Bala Town in 2021.

fc-utd.co.uk

FC UNITED OF MANCHESTER

341 Jonathan SMITH

Born: 17/10/1986, Preston **Midfielder/Defender**
Debut: No.4 v Warrington Town (A, NPLP), 14/08/2021

Season	LEAGUE Starts	(+Sub)	Goals	FA NATIONAL CUPS Starts	(+Sub)	Goals	OTHER CUPS / PLAY-OFFS Starts	(+Sub)	Goals	TOTALS Starts	(+Sub)	Goals
2021/22	27	(+3)	2	0	(+0)	0	2	(+1)	1	29	(+4)	3
Totals	**27**	**(+3)**	**2**	**0**	**(+0)**	**0**	**2**	**(+1)**	**1**	**29**	**(+4)**	**3**

Jonathan is a product of the academy at Morecambe, where his highlight was scoring the winning penalty in a shoot-out victory in the EFL Trophy at Grimsby Town in October 2005. After loan spells at Northern Premier League clubs Fleetwood Town and Bamber Bridge, he was released to join Conference side Forest Green Rovers in 2007. After 148 appearances he switched to York City in 2010, before joining League Two club Swindon Town a year later. He rejoined York in 2012 ahead of their return to League Two, but returned to the Conference with Luton Town later that year on a loan deal that was soon made permanent. His time in Bedfordshire was the most productive of his career, as he helped them to promotion back into the Football League in 2014 and won a Player of the Year award in 2015. He moved on to local rivals Stevenage in 2017 before dropping back down to the National League in 2018 with Chesterfield, where he became club captain. He linked up with FC United in the summer of 2021, and his experience proved vital during the campaign. He scored the team's first goal of the season in the win over Morpeth Town, which was the first of a run of games that he was asked to play at right-back. He also filled in at centre-back, but it was in central midfield that he featured most, cementing a regular place there after shaking off an injury in November. He added to his goalscoring account with strikes against Whitby Town and the FENIX Trophy victory over AKS Zły at Broadhurst Park, before playing in the triumphant final in Rimini in June.

342 Drew BAKER

Born: 08/10/2002, Macclesfield **Centre-back**
Debut: No.5 v Warrington Town (A, NPLP), 14/08/2021

Season	LEAGUE Starts	(+Sub)	Goals	FA NATIONAL CUPS Starts	(+Sub)	Goals	OTHER CUPS / PLAY-OFFS Starts	(+Sub)	Goals	TOTALS Starts	(+Sub)	Goals
2021/22	20	(+0)	1	6	(+0)	0	1	(+0)	1	27	(+0)	1
Totals	**20**	**(+0)**	**1**	**6**	**(+0)**	**0**	**1**	**(+0)**	**1**	**27**	**(+0)**	**1**

As a Manchester Grammar School pupil, Drew earned international honours for the England Independent Schools FA and played in the academies at Manchester City, Crewe Alexandra and Bury. Able to play in midfield or as a ball-playing defender, he joined Oldham Athletic as a scholar and scored in their win over FC United's under-18s in the FA Youth Cup in October 2020. He was released the following summer and signed for the Reds after some impressive pre-season outings. He was virtually ever-present in the centre of defence for the first half of the campaign, and opened the scoring in October's win at Witton Albion. His performances attracted scouts from professional clubs, with League One side Fleetwood Town swooping to sign him in January 2022 on a full-time deal to initially feature for their Development Squad.

343 Alistair WADDECAR

Born: 07/06/1990, Preston **Forward/Winger/Right-back**
Debut: No.9 v Warrington Town (A, NPLP), 14/08/2021

Season	LEAGUE Starts	(+Sub)	Goals	FA NATIONAL CUPS Starts	(+Sub)	Goals	OTHER CUPS / PLAY-OFFS Starts	(+Sub)	Goals	TOTALS Starts	(+Sub)	Goals
2021/22	23	(+12)	3	5	(+1)	0	3	(+2)	2	31	(+15)	5
Totals	**23**	**(+12)**	**3**	**5**	**(+1)**	**0**	**3**	**(+2)**	**2**	**31**	**(+15)**	**5**

Once in Preston North End's academy, Ali had been playing in the West Lancashire League when he began a long and successful association with Bamber Bridge in 2010. He helped them to the Northern Premier League Division One play-offs twice, before succeeding at the third attempt with promotion in 2018. That summer he was voted 11th in the NPL's Top 50 Players OF All Time, and his 25 goals won the Premier Division's Golden Boot in 2018/19. His 448th game broke his club's appearance record in October 2019, before he opened the scoring against FC in a chastening defeat in February 2020. After 11 years he was finally enticed to join former boss Neil Reynolds at Broadhurst Park in May 2021. His energetic endeavours made him an instant crowd favourite, as did his willingness to occupy various positions without complaint. Naturally a central or right-sided forward, he also lined up at right-back when the need arose. He waited longer than anticipated to score his first goal, which arrived at Stafford Rangers in December, but within three minutes he had struck again to earn the Reds a 2-0 win. He grabbed his first goal at Broadhurst against title challengers Matlock Town in February, and also registered with a superb solo effort in Milan against Brera in the FENIX Trophy in April. He announced his impending retirement from football at the end of the season, and bowed out in style by opening the scoring against Prague Raptors to help FC to win the FENIX Trophy final in Rimini in June.

344 Cedric MAIN

Born: 15/07/1997, Paramaribo (Suriname) **Forward**
Debut: No.10 v Warrington Town (A, NPLP), 14/08/2021

Season	LEAGUE			FA NATIONAL CUPS			OTHER CUPS / PLAY-OFFS			TOTALS		
	Starts	(+Sub)	Goals	Starts	(+Sub)	Goals	Starts	(+Sub)	Goals	Starts	(+Sub)	Goals
2021/22	15	(+0)	3	4	(+0)	3	0	(+0)	0	19	(+0)	6
Totals	15	(+0)	3	4	(+0)	3	0	(+0)	0	19	(+0)	6

Raised in the Netherlands, Cedric played in his country for the youth and amateur sides at Groningen and Ajax. He moved to Spain in 2019 to join Segunda División B club La Nucía, before switching to Tercera División side Almagro a year later. He initially signed for FC United in January 2021, but the season did not restart and due to travel restrictions he only arrived in Manchester in July. He made a great start by scoring eight times in his first four pre-season games, which included a five-goal haul at AFC Darwen. However, possibly due to his preference for a slightly withdrawn role, he was not quite as prolific when the competitive action got underway. He opened his account to earn FC a deserved point at South Shields and hit two lovely finishes in the FA Cup draw at Bootle. He also equalised in the next round at Blyth Spartans before scoring his first home goals with another brace past Scarborough Athletic. He left the club in October and joined South Shields, for whom he set up the late winner at Broadhurst Park in April 2022.

345 Matthew RAIN

Born: 11/10/2001, Chester **Left-back/Midfielder**
Debut: Sub v Warrington Town (A, NPLP), 14/08/2021

Season	LEAGUE			FA NATIONAL CUPS			OTHER CUPS / PLAY-OFFS			TOTALS		
	Starts	(+Sub)	Goals	Starts	(+Sub)	Goals	Starts	(+Sub)	Goals	Starts	(+Sub)	Goals
2021/22	1	(+8)	2	3	(+1)	1	0	(+1)	0	4	(+10)	3
Totals	1	(+8)	2	3	(+1)	1	0	(+1)	0	4	(+10)	3

Previously in Liverpool's academy, Matty signed as a scholar with Burnley in 2018 and progressed to line up for their under-23 side. The attacking left-back in was released in 2021 and linked up with FC United during the summer. After three substitute outings he scored on his first start in the home victory over Radcliffe in August, and then struck a last minute equaliser in the dramatic FA Cup comeback win against Bootle. He also registered in the 6-0 triumph over Scarborough Athletic, but despite a terrific scoring record he was unable to dislodge Adam Dodd in his preferred position. He left the Reds in November and registered with rivals Warrington Town before featuring in National League North for Curzon Ashton. He moved on to Bootle in the summer of 2022.

346 Jack BENNETT

Born: 03/08/2004, Manchester **Midfielder**
Debut: Sub v Morpeth Town (H, NPLP), 17/08/2021

Season	LEAGUE			FA NATIONAL CUPS			OTHER CUPS / PLAY-OFFS			TOTALS		
	Starts	(+Sub)	Goals	Starts	(+Sub)	Goals	Starts	(+Sub)	Goals	Starts	(+Sub)	Goals
2021/22	0	(+3)	0	0	(+1)	0	1	(+0)	0	1	(+4)	0
Totals	0	(+3)	0	0	(+1)	0	1	(+0)	0	1	(+4)	0

Jack joined FC United's academy in 2020, and helped the under-18s to the 1st round of the FA Youth Cup in his first term. The tenacious midfielder impressed enough in the senior side's 2021 pre-season friendlies to be a regular squad member when the campaign began. When he made his competitive debut as a substitute in the win over Morpeth Town in the first home game in August, he became the **youngest player to represent FC United in a competitive first-team game**, aged just 17 years and 14 days. He also came on in the draw with eventual champions Buxton, in the FA Cup at Bootle and in the home thrashing of Scarborough Athletic. His progress was rewarded with a start in the club's first fixture in the inaugural FENIX Trophy, and he played the entirety of the 6-1 triumph over AKS Zły in Warsaw in October. He had featured in the matchday squad for over half of the first team's fixtures when he sadly picked up a serious injury in a youth game in November that ruled him out for the rest of the season.

347 Jamie COOKE

Born: 28/01/2002, Liverpool **Midfielder/Forward**
Debut: No.9 v Buxton (H, NPLP), 21/08/2021

Season	LEAGUE			FA NATIONAL CUPS			OTHER CUPS / PLAY-OFFS			TOTALS		
	Starts	(+Sub)	Goals	Starts	(+Sub)	Goals	Starts	(+Sub)	Goals	Starts	(+Sub)	Goals
2021/22	5	(+1)	1	0	(+0)	0	0	(+0)	0	5	(+1)	1
Totals	5	(+1)	1	0	(+0)	0	0	(+0)	0	5	(+1)	1

After a two-year scholarship at Fleetwood Town, Jamie joined Northern Premier League Division One side Colne in 2020, where his displays as an attacking midfielder or forward earned a two-year deal at National League outfit FC Halifax Town in 2021. He joined FC United on loan in August and contributed finely to two well-earned draws against title challengers Buxton and South Shields. He opened the scoring after just two minutes in the win over Radcliffe, but his progress was interrupted as he was unable to play in the FA Cup. He was recalled by his parent club in September, and almost immediately loaned out again to Matlock Town. He joined National League North side Curzon Ashton for another temporary spell in December until the end of the season.

348 Jacob HANSON

Born: 30/11/1997, Lancaster
Debut: Sub v Buxton (H, NPLP), 21/08/2021

Right-back

	LEAGUE			FA NATIONAL CUPS			OTHER CUPS / PLAY-OFFS			TOTALS		
Season	Starts	(+Sub)	Goals	Starts	(+Sub)	Goals	Starts	(+Sub)	Goals	Starts	(+Sub)	Goals
2021/22	0	(+1)	0	0	(+0)	0	0	(+0)	0	0	(+1)	0
Totals	0	(+1)	0	0	(+0)	0	0	(+0)	0	0	(+1)	0

Jacob came through Huddersfield Town's academy to turn professional at his local Championship club in 2015. The speedy, attack-minded full-back switched to rivals Bradford City in January 2017, and scored on his senior debut against Chesterfield in the EFL Trophy in August that year. He also started games in League One and the FA Cup before two loan spells at National League side FC Halifax Town led to a permanent transfer in January 2019. When his contract was cancelled he dropped down to National League North with Curzon Ashton in November 2020. He linked up with FC United in August 2021, and made his debut as a substitute in the home draw with Buxton. This was his only outing before he signed for Macclesfield on a dual registration basis later that month. He went on to help the newly-formed club to lift the 2022 North West Counties League title.

349 Keaton MULVEY

Born: 03/10/2001, Ashton-under-Lyne
Debut: Sub v Bootle (H, FAC:Q1R), 07/09/2021

Forward

	LEAGUE			FA NATIONAL CUPS			OTHER CUPS / PLAY-OFFS			TOTALS		
Season	Starts	(+Sub)	Goals	Starts	(+Sub)	Goals	Starts	(+Sub)	Goals	Starts	(+Sub)	Goals
2021/22	0	(+1)	0	0	(+1)	0	0	(+1)	0	0	(+3)	0
Totals	0	(+1)	0	0	(+1)	0	0	(+1)	0	0	(+3)	0

A striker from Hattersley, Keaton scored seven goals in seven games for Curzon Ashton's under-18 team as they reached the FA Youth Cup 3rd round in 2019. His exploits attracted Rochdale, who signed him on a professional contract in January 2020. He had loan spells in the Northern Premier League Division One with Runcorn Linnets and Mossley before being released in June 2021. He joined FC United and impressed with a couple of goals during the pre-season campaign. In August he joined North West Counties League side Longridge Town on a dual registration basis, before returning to make his Reds debut as a substitute against Bootle in the FA Cup replay win in September. He also came off the bench in the league defeat at Lancaster City and the FENIX Trophy win over AKS Zły in Warsaw in October, before joining Glossop North End on an initial loan in November.

350 Bradley HOLMES

Born: 16/12/2002, Blackpool
Debut: No.9 v Bamber Bridge (H, NPLP), 14/09/2021 (scored)

Forward

	LEAGUE			FA NATIONAL CUPS			OTHER CUPS / PLAY-OFFS			TOTALS		
Season	Starts	(+Sub)	Goals	Starts	(+Sub)	Goals	Starts	(+Sub)	Goals	Starts	(+Sub)	Goals
2021/22	11	(+1)	5	3	(+0)	0	1	(+0)	3	15	(+1)	8
Totals	11	(+1)	5	3	(+0)	0	1	(+0)	3	15	(+1)	8

A tall and mobile forward, Brad was previously in the youth system at Bolton Wanderers before switching to his hometown club, Blackpool. He signed a professional contract in 2020, and made five appearances in League One at the end of the 2020/21 season. He joined FC United on a three-month loan deal in September 2021, and scored the only goal on his debut in the home win over Bamber Bridge. In the next league game he hit a superb strike for the first of a brace in a defeat at Stalybridge Celtic, before also bagging in the thrashing of Scarborough Athletic. In October he scored FC's first ever goal in the FENIX Trophy, and went on to complete a hat-trick in the triumph over AKS Zły in Warsaw. He also struck in the defeat at Atherton Collieries in November, before returning to Blackpool in December. He then began another loan, at National League North side Chorley.

351 Hayden CAMPBELL

Born: 03/06/2002, Stafford
Debut: No.7 v Stalybridge Celtic (A, NPLP), 25/09/2021

Winger/Forward

	LEAGUE			FA NATIONAL CUPS			OTHER CUPS / PLAY-OFFS			TOTALS		
Season	Starts	(+Sub)	Goals	Starts	(+Sub)	Goals	Starts	(+Sub)	Goals	Starts	(+Sub)	Goals
2021/22	2	(+1)	0	0	(+0)	0	0	(+0)	0	2	(+1)	0
Totals	2	(+1)	0	0	(+0)	0	0	(+0)	0	2	(+1)	0

An attack-minded midfielder or forward, Hayden was a scholar at Port Vale when he first played in non-league on loan to Northern Premier League Divison One side Kidsgrove Athletic. In September 2020 he signed for Salford City, for whom he made three substitute appearances in the EFL Trophy. After a loan spell at Marine in December 2020, he began another temporary stint at FC United in September 2021. He looked lively in the early stages of his debut in the defeat at Stalybridge Celtic, and also when he came off the bench at Matlock Town. However he was disappointingly withdrawn in the first half in the home loss to Grantham Town and returned to his parent club. He had further loans at Stalybridge and in the National League with Altrincham, before his release by Salford in June 2022.

352 Sam BURNS

Born: 09/08/2002, Liverpool
Debut: Sub v Grantham Town (H, NPLP), 16/10/2021

Forward

Season	LEAGUE			FA NATIONAL CUPS			OTHER CUPS / PLAY-OFFS			TOTALS		
	Starts	(+Sub)	Goals	Starts	(+Sub)	Goals	Starts	(+Sub)	Goals	Starts	(+Sub)	Goals
2021/22	3	(+1)	1	1	(+1)	1	1	(+0)	1	5	(+2)	3
Totals	3	(+1)	1	1	(+1)	1	1	(+0)	1	5	(+2)	3

Sam became a prolific scorer as he advanced through the Blackburn Rovers academy to turn professional. He had been in good form for the under-23 side when he joined FC United on loan in October 2021. He performed well on his debut as a first half substitute in the disappointing home defeat to Grantham Town, and also in the win at Witton Albion a week later, before scoring in each of the next three games in different competitions. He struck in the FENIX Trophy against AKS Zły in Warsaw, put United ahead in the FA Trophy at Runcorn Linnets, then hit a great goal in the home league win over Gainsborough Trinity. He returned to his parent club in November, before starting another loan in January 2022 at Scunthorpe United. He made 15 League Two appearances, but the club lost their Football League status at the end of the term. He signed a new contract with Blackburn in May.

353 Omar SANYANG

Born: 18/11/1999, Brikama (The Gambia)
Debut: Sub v Grantham Town (H, NPLP), 16/10/2021

Winger

Season	LEAGUE			FA NATIONAL CUPS			OTHER CUPS / PLAY-OFFS			TOTALS		
	Starts	(+Sub)	Goals	Starts	(+Sub)	Goals	Starts	(+Sub)	Goals	Starts	(+Sub)	Goals
2021/22	0	(+2)	0	0	(+0)	0	0	(+0)	0	0	(+2)	0
Totals	0	(+2)	0	0	(+0)	0	0	(+0)	0	0	(+2)	0

Omar played in the academies of Leeds United, Bradford City and Huddersfield Town before a spell in the youth team at Doncaster Rovers. He signed a professional deal with League Two side Scunthorpe United in 2019 and featured for their under-23 squad as a pacy winger who could also operate at full-back. He joined Northern Premier League Division One side Tadcaster Albion in 2020 before spells in National League North with Bradford Park Avenue and Darlington. He joined FC United from the latter on a month's loan in October 2021 and came off the bench in the narrow defeats to Grantham Town and Atherton Collieries. He embarked on another loan with Pickering Town in December, and had scored five goals in ten games before his season was sadly ended by a broken leg in February 2022.

354 Cian HAYES

Born: 21/06/2003, Preston
Debut: No.7 v Witton Albion (A, NPLP), 23/10/2021 (scored)

Winger

Season	LEAGUE			FA NATIONAL CUPS			OTHER CUPS / PLAY-OFFS			TOTALS		
	Starts	(+Sub)	Goals	Starts	(+Sub)	Goals	Starts	(+Sub)	Goals	Starts	(+Sub)	Goals
2021/22	4	(+0)	2	0	(+0)	0	0	(+0)	0	4	(+0)	2
Totals	4	(+0)	2	0	(+0)	0	0	(+0)	0	4	(+0)	2

Cian became Fleetwood Town's youngest ever first team player when he made his debut at the age of 16 as a substitute in the EFL Trophy against Oldham Athletic in November 2019. The skilful attacker turned professional in January 2021, and joined FC United on a month's loan in October that year. He scored on his debut in the 3-2 win at Witton Albion, and was tremendous in the home win over Gainsborough Trinity. After a spell away earning further international caps for Ireland under-19s, he returned to top another outstanding display by hammering the second goal in the win over Mickleover. When his loan ended in November, he signed a new contract at Fleetwood and immediately claimed a regular place in their senior squad. He was on the teamsheet for every game until the end of the term, featuring 24 times as his side maintained their League One status.

355 Joshua BROOKS

Born: 03/02/2003, Bury
Debut: Sub v AKS Zły (A, EFT), 27/10/2021

Goalkeeper

Season	LEAGUE			FA NATIONAL CUPS			OTHER CUPS / PLAY-OFFS			TOTALS		
	Starts	(+Sub)	Goals	Starts	(+Sub)	Goals	Starts	(+Sub)	Goals	Starts	(+Sub)	Goals
2021/22	0	(+0)	0	0	(+0)	0	0	(+1)	0	0	(+1)	0
Totals	0	(+0)	0	0	(+0)	0	0	(+1)	0	0	(+1)	0

A tall and agile goalkeeper from Heywood, Josh joined the FC United academy in 2019, and first appeared on first team duty when he played the first two friendlies of the pre-season campaign in the summer of 2020. He remained part of the senior squad when the competitive action began, sitting on the bench for seven games as cover for Dan Lavercombe. One of those was the FA Cup 1st round visit of League One side Doncaster Rovers to Broadhurst Park in November before the season was suspended again. In October 2021 he travelled with the squad to Warsaw for the club's first fixture in the inaugural FENIX Trophy, and came on as a second half substitute to make his senior debut in the win over AKS Zły.

356 James DEADMAN

Born: 09/05/1991, Bury
Debut: Sub v AKS Zły (A, EFT), 27/10/2021

Right-back

Season	LEAGUE			FA NATIONAL CUPS			OTHER CUPS / PLAY-OFFS			TOTALS		
	Starts	(+Sub)	Goals	Starts	(+Sub)	Goals	Starts	(+Sub)	Goals	Starts	(+Sub)	Goals
2021/22	0	(+0)	0	0	(+0)	0	0	(+1)	0	0	(+1)	0
Totals	0	(+0)	0	0	(+0)	0	0	(+1)	0	0	(+1)	0

A popular figure around the club, Jimmy has been an FC United fan since the club's formation and made his way from the terraces to be an important member of the Broadhurst Park staff. The Heywood lad held roles as assistant facilities manager and kitman, before taking over as head groundsman in 2021. He had an eventful October that year, beginning with running the London Marathon to raise money for FC's Development Fund. Later in the month he travelled with the squad to Warsaw for United's first game in the FENIX Trophy, and was named on the bench for the game against AKS Zły. Jimmy's big moment came in the 79th minute when he was called on to replace Paul Ennis. He filled in at right-back and showed plenty of willingness to plough forward as he helped the Reds to begin their first European campaign with a 6-1 victory.

357 Jayden MAJOR

Born: 29/08/2002, Preston
Debut: No.11 v Runcorn Linnets (A, FAT:Q3), 30/10/2021

Winger

Season	LEAGUE			FA NATIONAL CUPS			OTHER CUPS / PLAY-OFFS			TOTALS		
	Starts	(+Sub)	Goals	Starts	(+Sub)	Goals	Starts	(+Sub)	Goals	Starts	(+Sub)	Goals
2021/22	0	(+3)	0	1	(+0)	0	0	(+0)	0	1	(+3)	0
Totals	0	(+3)	0	1	(+0)	0	0	(+0)	0	1	(+3)	0

A fast and tricky winger, Jayden was in the academy at Liverpool before joining Burnley as a scholar in 2018. After loan spells in the North West Counties League with Steeton and the Northern Premier League at Clitheroe, he was released in 2020 and had a short spell in Spain with fifth-level club UP Plasencia. He returned to join North West Counties League side Stockport Town, where his performances prompted FC United to sign him in October 2021. He started on the wing in the FA Trophy win at Runcorn Linnets, but was substituted at half-time. After a couple of games as an unused substitute, he came off the bench in the December wins over Stafford Rangers and Ashton United, as well as the New Year's Day draw at Radcliffe. He returned to play for Stockport Town in January, before switching to divisional rivals Alsager Town in March 2022.

358 Toby HUMPHRIES

Born: 14/06/2004, Stockport
Debut: Sub v Marske United (A, FAT:1), 13/11/2021

Midfielder

Season	LEAGUE			FA NATIONAL CUPS			OTHER CUPS / PLAY-OFFS			TOTALS		
	Starts	(+Sub)	Goals	Starts	(+Sub)	Goals	Starts	(+Sub)	Goals	Starts	(+Sub)	Goals
2021/22	0	(+0)	0	0	(+1)	0	0	(+3)	0	0	(+4)	0
Totals	0	(+0)	0	0	(+1)	0	0	(+3)	0	0	(+4)	0

Toby joined FC United's academy in 2020, and became a driving force in the centre of midfield in the youth team's National League under-19 Alliance fixtures. He was first called up to the senior squad in November 2021 following a season-ending injury to his youth colleague Jack Bennett. He was trusted enough to be handed a debut as a substitute for captain Michael Potts early in the second half of the FA Trophy tie at Marske United, and almost helped the Reds to an unlikely comeback. He became a regular member of the matchday squad during the second half of the season, and added to his appearances with further outings off the bench in the FENIX Trophy wins over AKS Zły and Brera at Broadhurst Park, plus the final victory over Prague Raptors in Rimini.

359 Vani DA SILVA

Born: 30/03/2003, Lisbon (Portugal)
Debut: Sub v Atherton Collieries (A, NPLP), 20/11/2021

Forward

Season	LEAGUE			FA NATIONAL CUPS			OTHER CUPS / PLAY-OFFS			TOTALS		
	Starts	(+Sub)	Goals	Starts	(+Sub)	Goals	Starts	(+Sub)	Goals	Starts	(+Sub)	Goals
2021/22	0	(+3)	0	0	(+0)	0	0	(+0)	0	0	(+3)	0
Totals	0	(+3)	0	0	(+0)	0	0	(+0)	0	0	(+3)	0

A former Bury academy player, Vani signed for Oldham Athletic as a scholar in 2019, and made his senior debut as a substitute in an EFL Cup win over Carlisle United in September 2020. The following month he scored for his club's under-18s in their win over FC United in the FA Youth Cup 1st round. After a loan spell in National League North at Curzon Ashton, the versatile and pacy attacker turned professional in May 2021. He made six senior appearances in the early stages of 2021/22, which included outings in League Two, before he joined FC United on loan in November. He made his debut as a late substitute in the agonising defeat at Atherton Collieries, and also made brief cameos in the wins at Stafford Rangers and Buxton in December. The following week he was back at Broadhurst Park, sitting on Ashton United's bench during FC's 4-3 win as he began another loan stint.

360 Joe DUCKWORTH

Born: 08/06/2001, Crewe
Debut: Sub v Mickleover (H, NPLP), 27/11/2021

Forward

Season	LEAGUE Starts	(+Sub)	Goals	FA NATIONAL CUPS Starts	(+0)	Goals	OTHER CUPS / PLAY-OFFS Starts	(+0)	Goals	TOTALS Starts	(+Sub)	Goals
2021/22	4	(+9)	4	0	(+0)	0	3	(+0)	3	7	(+9)	7
Totals	4	(+9)	4	0	(+0)	0	3	(+0)	3	7	(+9)	7

A pacy and mobile forward, Joe had spells at 1874 Northwich and Barnton in his native Mid-Cheshire, but became known for his scoring exploits at hometown club Winsford United. After a prolific start to 2021/22 for the North West Counties League side, he was snapped up by FC United in November 2021. His arrival coincided with a great run of results, to which he contributed massively. He came off the bench to nab the winner with a composed finish at eventual champions Buxton in December, before scoring twice in the home win over Ashton United. Another goal in the New Year draw at Radcliffe made it four in three games, but an ankle injury was affecting his match fitness. From January he combined bench duties for the Reds with outings for Winsford, with his only FC starts coming in the FENIX Trophy. He scored twice in the 10-0 victory over AKS Zły at Broadhurst Park in March, and played the whole of the 3-1 win against Brera in Milan a month later. He was back for the final trip to Rimini in June, and was named man of the match as he sealed United's win with the second goal against Prague Raptors. He signed for Witton Albion the following week.

361 Andy WHITE

Born: 08/10/1992, Chester
Debut: No.2 v Stafford Rangers (A, NPLP), 11/12/2021

Full-back

Season	LEAGUE Starts	(+Sub)	Goals	FA NATIONAL CUPS Starts	(+Sub)	Goals	OTHER CUPS / PLAY-OFFS Starts	(+Sub)	Goals	TOTALS Starts	(+Sub)	Goals
2021/22	4	(+0)	0	0	(+0)	0	0	(+0)	0	4	(+0)	0
Totals	4	(+0)	0	0	(+0)	0	0	(+0)	0	4	(+0)	0

A versatile defender able to play across the back four, Andy came through Crewe Alexandra's academy to turn professional in 2011. He was released in 2013 and joined neighbours Nantwich Town, where in a successful spell he won the club's Player of the Year award three seasons running and was also twice named in the Northern Premier League's Team of the Season. He switched to National League North side Southport in July 2017, but moved on to Altrincham in December that year. He helped them to two promotions from the Northern Premier League through to the National League, before his outings were restricted by a series of injuries. He had faced FC United for each of his three non-league clubs, and linked up with the Reds on a month's loan in December 2021. He occupied both full-back positions in four appearances, which yielded three wins and a draw, before a recall by his parent club in January. After Altrincham decided to operate a full-time squad, he moved to Warrington Town in the summer of 2022.

362 Harry WILSON

Born: 02/04/2004, Belfast
Debut: No.10 v Buxton (A, NPLP), 18/12/2021

Midfielder

Season	LEAGUE Starts	(+Sub)	Goals	FA NATIONAL CUPS Starts	(+0)	Goals	OTHER CUPS / PLAY-OFFS Starts	(+0)	Goals	TOTALS Starts	(+Sub)	Goals
2021/22	4	(+2)	0	0	(+0)	0	0	(+0)	0	4	(+2)	0
Totals	4	(+2)	0	0	(+0)	0	0	(+0)	0	4	(+2)	0

A tall and lively midfielder, Harry played in Glentoran's academy in his native Northern Ireland before joining Fleetwood Town as a scholar in 2020. He was awarded a three-year professional deal in March 2021, and was also called up to his country's under-19 squad. He joined FC United in December 2021 on an intial month's loan, and helped the Reds to a terrific win at Buxton on his debut. He also assisted victories over Stalybridge Celtic and Witton Albion, plus two hard-fought away draws. His only defeat was at home to Whitby Town, although it was his header that was diverted home by a visiting defender for FC's second goal. His stay was extended until the end of the season, but then sadly cut short when an injury in February prematurely ended his campaign.

363 George McMAHON

Born: 16/06/2000, Manchester
Debut: No.1 v Ashton United (H, NPLP), 27/12/2021

Goalkeeper

Season	LEAGUE Starts	(+Sub)	Goals	FA NATIONAL CUPS Starts	(+Sub)	Goals	OTHER CUPS / PLAY-OFFS Starts	(+Sub)	Goals	TOTALS Starts	(+Sub)	Goals
2021/22	1	(+0)	0	0	(+0)	0	0	(+0)	0	1	(+0)	0
Totals	1	(+0)	0	0	(+0)	0	0	(+0)	0	1	(+0)	0

George was born in Manchester before moving to Hull with his family, and played in the academies at Hull City and York City before becoming a scholar at Rotherham United in 2016. The Ireland youth international stopper moved to Burnley on a two-year professional deal in 2018, and was soon sat on the senior bench for a friendly with Espanyol. He had a loan spell at Ashton United, and kept goal for them against FC United in a National League North fixture in January 2019. He was a free agent when he came to FC's aid in an emergency when Dan Lavercombe was ill in December 2021. He was coincidentally pitched in to face Ashton United at Broadhurst Park, and took great delight in playing his part in a 4-3 win over his former club. That was his only action for the Reds, and he signed for Northern Premier League Division One East side Pontefract Collieries in January 2022.

364 Jack GOODEN

Born: 15/06/2003, Blackburn
Debut: Sub v Ashton United (H, NPLP), 27/12/2021

Winger

Season	LEAGUE			FA NATIONAL CUPS			OTHER CUPS / PLAY-OFFS			TOTALS		
	Starts	(+Sub)	Goals	Starts	(+Sub)	Goals	Starts	(+Sub)	Goals	Starts	(+Sub)	Goals
2021/22	0	(+1)	0	0	(+0)	0	0	(+0)	0	0	(+1)	0
Totals	0	(+1)	0	0	(+0)	0	0	(+0)	0	0	(+1)	0

A former academy player at Accrington Stanley, Jack moved on to play for AFC Fylde's youth team, and also had a spell in the Northern Premier League with Colne. He joined North West Counties League side Charnock Richard in 2021, and established himself as a goalscoring winger also capable of playing at left-back. He was signed by FC United in December 2021, and made his debut as an injury-time substitute to help see out the 4-3 home win over Ashton United. After five further matches as an unused substitute he returned to Charnock Richard to further his experience of senior football.

365 Andy HALLS

Born: 20/04/1992, Manchester
Debut: No.6 v Radcliffe (A, NPLP), 01/01/2022

Right-back/Centre-back

Season	LEAGUE			FA NATIONAL CUPS			OTHER CUPS / PLAY-OFFS			TOTALS		
	Starts	(+Sub)	Goals	Starts	(+Sub)	Goals	Starts	(+Sub)	Goals	Starts	(+Sub)	Goals
2021/22	10	(+0)	0	0	(+0)	0	0	(+0)	0	10	(+0)	0
Totals	10	(+0)	0	0	(+0)	0	0	(+0)	0	10	(+0)	0

A versatile defender from Urmston, Andy came through the ranks to sign professional at Stockport County. He made his senior debut as a substitute in League One at Leeds United in April 2009, and earned a long run during 2010/11. After successive relegations, he remained a regular during the next two terms in the Conference Premier, and stayed at that level when he switched to Macclesfield Town in 2013. He hardly missed a game in a consistent four-year spell, during which he also earned four caps for the England C team. He spent 2017/18 with Chester before joining Guiseley, whom he captained against FC United in National League North in September 2018. He moved on to Curzon Ashton the following year, and then to Chorley in 2020. After an injury lay-off, he joined FC on loan in December 2021 and made his debut at centre-back in the New Year's Day draw at Radcliffe. After six games at right-back he reverted to the centre as the loan was extended, and had performed well before his recall by his parent club at the end of February. He was released by Chorley at the end of the season, and made a welcome return to United in June 2022.

366 Ewan BANGE

Born: 15/12/2001, Manchester
Debut: No.11 v Stalybridge Celtic (H, NPLP), 22/01/2022 (scored)

Forward

Season	LEAGUE			FA NATIONAL CUPS			OTHER CUPS / PLAY-OFFS			TOTALS		
	Starts	(+Sub)	Goals	Starts	(+Sub)	Goals	Starts	(+Sub)	Goals	Starts	(+Sub)	Goals
2021/22	6	(+5)	1	0	(+0)	0	1	(+1)	2	7	(+6)	3
Totals	6	(+5)	1	0	(+0)	0	1	(+1)	2	7	(+6)	3

A tall cenre forward, Ewan became a scholar at Blackpool in 2018. He was still 17 when he was first called up to the senior squad, madking his debut in an EFL Trophy tie at Carlisle United in October 2019. After turning professional, he spent the majority of 2021/22 on loan at non-league clubs. He began a fruitful spell at Bamber Bridge in August 2021, which included a Northern Pemier League outing at Broadhurst Park against FC United the following month. In November he joined National League North side AFC Telford United, before linking up with the Reds in January 2022. He made a great start by burying a towering header after just 18 minutes of his debut at home to Stalybridge Celtic, but limped off with a hamstring injury shortly afterwards. He spent a month on the sidelines, and found goals more difficult to come by after his return. His brace in the 10-0 win over AKS Zły at home in the FENIX Trophy in March were his only other strikes before he returned to sign a new contract with Blackpool in May.

367 Josh GALLOWAY

Born: 21/01/2002, Glasgow
Debut: Sub v Whitby Town (H, NPLP), 25/01/2022

Winger/Forward

Season	LEAGUE			FA NATIONAL CUPS			OTHER CUPS / PLAY-OFFS			TOTALS		
	Starts	(+Sub)	Goals	Starts	(+Sub)	Goals	Starts	(+Sub)	Goals	Starts	(+Sub)	Goals
2021/22	7	(+8)	1	0	(+0)	0	3	(+0)	2	10	(+8)	3
Totals	7	(+8)	1	0	(+0)	0	3	(+0)	2	10	(+8)	3

An exciting and pacy attacker, Josh came through Carlisle United's academy to sign as a scholar in 2018. Shortly after representing the first team in pre-season friendlies, he was signed by Leeds United for an undisclosed fee in August 2019. He played in the Yorkshire outfit's under-18 and under-23 sides, and made two appearances when they entered the EFL Trophy in 2020/21. After a short trial at League Two side Barrow in November 2021, he joined FC United on a loan deal in January 2022 until the end of the season. He shone on his debut as a half-time substitute at home to Whitby Town, and marked his first start with a lovely finish to seal the Broadhurst Park win over Witton Albion. He added to his goals tally with further strikes in the home victories over AKS Zły and Brera to help FC top their FENIX Trophy group. He signed for Scottish League Two side Annan Athletic in June.

368 Chris TAYLOR

Born: 20/12/1986, Oldham
Debut: Sub v Gainsborough Trinity (A, NPLP), 12/02/2022

Midfielder/Defender

Season	LEAGUE			FA NATIONAL CUPS			OTHER CUPS / PLAY-OFFS			TOTALS		
	Starts	(+Sub)	Goals	Starts	(+Sub)	Goals	Starts	(+Sub)	Goals	Starts	(+Sub)	Goals
2021/22	1	(+1)	0	0	(+0)	0	3	(+1)	0	4	(+2)	0
Totals	1	(+1)	0	0	(+0)	0	3	(+1)	0	4	(+2)	0

A very versatile player, Chris came through the system at his local club Oldham Athletic to sign as a professional in 2005. He made his debut against Nottingham Forest in February 2006, and became a regular in midfield at Boundary Park over the next six years, during which he helped his side to the play-offs and was named in League One's Team of the Year. He moved up to the Championship with Millwall in May 2012, but returned to Lancashire a year later to join Blackburn Rovers, where his highlight was playing a prominent part in their run to the FA Cup 6th round in 2015. After a brief return on loan to Millwall, he joined Bolton Wanderers in 2016 before also returning to Oldham for a loan stint in January 2017. He moved on to League One rivals Blackpool for the 2018/19 season, before spending the next two terms in League Two with first Bradford City and then newly-promoted Barrow. In October 2021 he entered non-league football for the first time when he joined Radcliffe, for whom he sat on the bench against FC United on New Year's Day. However, he had already joined the Reds as an academy coach and so he switched his playing registration to United in February 2022. He featured just twice in the Northern Premier League as he mainly provided experienced cover on the bench, with the majority of his action coming in the FENIX Trophy. He lined up in both midfield and defence in the wins over AKS Zły and Brera at Broadhurst Park, and also against the Italian side in Milan, before coming on to help FC win the final against Prague Raptors in Rimini in June.

369 Harry McGEE

Born: 07/10/2002, Liverpool
Debut: Sub v Basford United (H, NPLP), 19/03/2022

Midfielder

Season	LEAGUE			FA NATIONAL CUPS			OTHER CUPS / PLAY-OFFS			TOTALS		
	Starts	(+Sub)	Goals	Starts	(+Sub)	Goals	Starts	(+Sub)	Goals	Starts	(+Sub)	Goals
2021/22	2	(+1)	0	0	(+0)	0	2	(+1)	0	4	(+2)	0
Totals	2	(+1)	0	0	(+0)	0	2	(+1)	0	4	(+2)	0

A former schoolboy in the Tranmere Rovers academy, Harry switched to Wigan Athletic to sign as a scholar in 2019. The combative and versatile midfielder turned professional in 2021, and was named on the bench for two EFL Trophy ties in the 2021/22 campaign. He joined FC United on loan in March 2022, and helped the Reds to a victory on his debut as a substitute at home to Basford United. He started the FENIX Trophy win over Brera in Milan in April, as well as two Northern Premier League games later in the month. He was released by Wigan at the end of the campaign and agreed to return to FC, before starting the FENIX Trophy final win over Prague Raptors in Rimini in June.

370 Josh ASKEW

Born: 20/02/1998, Ashton-under-Lyne
Debut: Sub v Mickleover (A, NPLP), 26/03/2022

Winger/Left-back

Season	LEAGUE			FA NATIONAL CUPS			OTHER CUPS / PLAY-OFFS			TOTALS		
	Starts	(+Sub)	Goals	Starts	(+Sub)	Goals	Starts	(+Sub)	Goals	Starts	(+Sub)	Goals
2021/22	4	(+2)	1	0	(+0)	0	2	(+1)	1	6	(+3)	2
Totals	4	(+2)	1	0	(+0)	0	2	(+1)	1	6	(+3)	2

Josh trained with the academies at both Manchester United and Manchester City before switching to Blackburn Rovers, where he progressed to turn professional in 2016. The Denton lad featured principally at left-back, but with a natural attacking instinct was also often deployed further upfield. He first played in non-league during loan spells at Ramsbottom United and Warrington Town in Northern Premier League Division One before being released to join National League North side Salford City in July 2017. He faced FC United three times during the next season, before further loans in that divison at Stockport County, Ashton United and Curzon Ashton preceded permanent moves to Boston United and then Chester in 2020. After a short spell at Clitheroe he returned to Chester in August 2021, before leaving again for Alfreton Town in February 2022. His stay there was brief too, as he signed for FC the following month and made his debut as a substitute at Mickleover. A week later he marked his first start by putting the Reds ahead in the home win over Atherton Collieries, and he also capped a terrific display with the opening goal of the FENIX Trophy win over Brera at Broadhurst Park in May. He ended the season playing at left-back as United won the inaugural FENIX Trophy final against Prague Raptors in Rimini in June.

371 Ryan HAMER

Born: 04/04/1999, Blackburn
Debut: No.1 v Brera (A, EFT), 06/04/2022

Goalkeeper

Season	LEAGUE			FA NATIONAL CUPS			OTHER CUPS / PLAY-OFFS			TOTALS		
	Starts	(+Sub)	Goals	Starts	(+Sub)	Goals	Starts	(+Sub)	Goals	Starts	(+Sub)	Goals
2021/22	0	(+0)	0	0	(+0)	0	1	(+2)	0	1	(+2)	0
Totals	0	(+0)	0	0	(+0)	0	1	(+2)	0	1	(+2)	0

A tall goalkeeper, Ryan was playing amateur football for Turton in the West Lancashire League when he signed for Atherton Laburnum Rovers in 2019. He returned to the North West Counties League in 2021 with Winsford United, where he was voted the supporters' Player of the Season. His displays had alerted FC United, who signed him on a dual registration basis as cover for Dan Lavercombe in January 2022. He made his debut in the FENIX Trophy win over Brera in Milan in April, and also came on as a second half substitute for Lavercombe in the return fixture with Brera at Broadhurst Park in May and the final win over Prague Raptors in Rimini in June.

372 Jack ANDERTON

Born: 29/08/2001, Preston
Debut: Sub v Prague Raptors (N, EFT:F), 11/06/2022

Winger

Season	LEAGUE			FA NATIONAL CUPS			OTHER CUPS / PLAY-OFFS			TOTALS		
	Starts	(+Sub)	Goals	Starts	(+Sub)	Goals	Starts	(+Sub)	Goals	Starts	(+Sub)	Goals
2021/22	0	(+0)	0	0	(+0)	0	0	(+1)	0	0	(+1)	0
Totals	0	(+0)	0	0	(+0)	0	0	(+1)	0	0	(+1)	0

A versatile winger also able to feature in a central forward position, Jack came through the reserve side at Longridge Town to make a senior debut in the North West Counties League in 2020. He became a regular starter in the 2020/21 campaign, and his progress was rewarded with a contract in August 2021. He had a terrific season in 2021/22, hitting 19 goals from 38 games which prompted FC United to swoop for his signature in June 2022. He was installed in the squad for the trip to Rimini for the FENIX Trophy final, and made his debut as a second half substitute to help the Reds to win the inaugural version of the competition.

373 James VINCENT

Born: 27/09/1989, Manchester
Debut: Sub v Prague Raptors (N, EFT:F), 11/06/2022

Midfielder

Season	LEAGUE			FA NATIONAL CUPS			OTHER CUPS / PLAY-OFFS			TOTALS		
	Starts	(+Sub)	Goals	Starts	(+Sub)	Goals	Starts	(+Sub)	Goals	Starts	(+Sub)	Goals
2021/22	0	(+0)	0	0	(+0)	0	0	(+1)	0	0	(+1)	0
Totals	0	(+0)	0	0	(+0)	0	0	(+1)	0	0	(+1)	0

A dynamic midfielder from Glossop, James came through Stockport County's academy to turn professional shortly after making his senior debut in League Two against Brentford in May 2008. He won a regular spot during the next three seasons in Leagues One and Two, before joining Conference Premier side Kidderminster Harriers in 2011. In a productive spell he was capped by the England C team, before signing for Scottish Premiership club Inverness Caledonian Thistle in June 2013. He helped his side to qualify for Europe in his first season, and also played in the League Cup Final against Aberdeen. The highlight of his career came in May 2015 when he came off the bench to score the winning goal in the Scottish Cup Final against Falkirk at Hampden Park. In March 2016 he signed a pre-contract agreement to play the following season for Dundee, alongside Inverness team-mate and former FC winger Danny Williams, and he helped them to retain their Premiership place. He joined Scottish Championship side Dunfermline Athletic on loan in January 2018, an arrangement that was extended for the 2018/19 season. He rejoined Inverness on a two-year deal in June 2019, before returning south to join National League North outfit Hereford in July 2021. He linked up with FC United in June 2022, and made his debut as a second half substitute against Prague Raptors as the Reds won the FENIX Trophy final in Rimini.

Unused Substitutes: A further 25 players have also been named on the bench for competitive FC United first-team fixtures, but were not called onto the field of play during a match.

Player	Born	Birthplace	Position	Season(s)	Player	Born	Birthplace	Position	Season(s)
Dylan Blackledge	30/05/2002	Manchester	Midfielder	2019/20 - 2 games	Ryan Howley	14/02/1994	Rochdale	Goalkeeper	2012/13 - 1 game
Daniel Cooke	14/12/1996	Manchester	Defender	2013/14 - 1 game	William Jones	01/04/1991	Grantham	Goalkeeper	2009/10 - 2 games
Sandro Da Costa	14/12/2003	Ballinasloe	Winger	2020/21 - 1 game	Scott Metcalfe	28/03/1988	Manchester	Winger	2011/12 - 1 game
Charlie Doyle	05/05/1996	Salford	Defender	2013/14 - 1 game	Taylor McDowell	20/09/2003	Manchester	Forward	2021/22 - 1 game
Jake Edwards	19/09/1990	Oldham	Goalkeeper	2008/09 - 7 games	Dylan Moloney	26/08/1993	Rhuddlan	Forward	2010/11 - 2 games
Steeve Eddy	01/11/1998	Cameroon	Defender	2016/17 - 1 game	Sam O'Donnell	01/02/2000	Manchester	Defender	2017/18 - 2 games
Andrew Farrimond	15/02/1994	Warrington	Goalkeeper	2011/12 - 2 games	Tyler Owen	16/12/2003	Oldham	Defender	2021/22 - 2 games
Lenny Fieldhouse	28/11/2002	Ashton-u-Lyne	Goalkeeper	2020/21 - 1 game	Joseph Power	28/11/1993	Manchester	Midfielder	2011/12 - 1 game
				2021/22 - 10 games	Mark Reeves	12/09/1990	Oldham	Midfielder	2008/09 - 1 game
Jason Fowles	12/06/1996	Manchester	Midfielder	2013/14 - 2 games	Sulaiman Sajjad	29/05/2000	Oldham	Goalkeeper	2018/19 - 1 game
Matt Haley	02/11/1985	Stockport	Winger	2005/06 - 1 game	Will Unsworth	04/04/2004	Stockport	Midfielder	2021/22 - 1 game
Silas Itotayagbon	16/04/2004	Dublin	Defender	2021/22 - 1 game	Mason Walker	19/08/2002	Manchester	Goalkeeper	2019/20 - 19 games
Dean Hope	22/08/1996	Manchester	Midfielder	2014/15 - 1 game	Keaton Ward	04/05/2000	Mansfield	Midfielder	2019/20 - 1 game

FC United Honours

Northern Premier League Premier Division
Champions: 2014/15   *Runners-up: 2013/14*   *Promotion play-off finalists: 2010/11, 2011/12, 2012/13*

Northern Premier League Division One North
Runners-up: 2007/08   Promotion play-off winners: 2007/08

North West Counties League Division One
Champions: 2006/07

Northern Premier League President's Cup
Winners: 2007/08

North West Counties League Division Two
Champions: 2005/06

North West Counties League Challenge Cup
Winners: 2006/07

FENIX Trophy
Winners: 2021/22

Manchester FA Premier Cup
Winners: 2016/17, 2017/18

Furthest progress in other competitions:
FA Cup
2nd round: 2010/11

Northern Premier League Challenge Cup
Quarter-final: 2011/12, 2013/14

FA Trophy
Quarter-final: 2014/15

FA Vase
3rd round: 2006/07

North West Counties Division Two Trophy
Quarter-final: 2005/06

FC United Records

Largest victories:
(All matches)   10-0 v AKS Zły   (H, FENIX), 05/03/2022
(League only) 10-2 v Castleton Gabriels (H, NWCFL2), 10/12/2005
                8-0 v Squires Gate   (H, NWCFL1), 14/10/2006
                8-0 v Glossop North End (H, NWCFL1), 28/10/2006
                8-0 v Nelson   (A, NWCFL1), 04/04/2007

Heaviest defeats:
(All matches) 0-7 v Barrow   (A, FAT:2), 11/01/2020
(League only) 0-6 v Harrogate Town   (A, NLN), 10/03/2018

Highest scoring draw:
(All matches) 5-5 v Cammell Laird   (H, NPLP), 12/11/2008

Most league points in a season:
112 in 2006/07, North West Counties League Division One

Most goals in a season:
(League only) 157 in 2006/07, North West Counties League Division One
(All matches) 186 in 2006/07

Highest Home Attendances:
6,731 v Brighton & Hove Albion (FAC:2R)   08/12/2010 at Gigg Lane, Bury
6,023 v Great Harwood Town   (NWCFL2)   22/04/2006 at Gigg Lane, Bury
4,328 v Winsford United   (NWCFL2)   02/01/2006 at Gigg Lane, Bury
4,158 v Salford City   (NLN)   28/01/2017 at Broadhurst Park, Manchester

Highest Away Attendances:
7,048 v Rochdale   (FAC:1)   05/11/2010 at Spotland, Rochdale
5,630 v Stockport County   (NLN)   18/02/2017 at Edgeley Park, Stockport

Complete playing record in all competitions:

Competition	Level	Pld	W	D	L	F	A	GD	Pts
National League North	6	168	51	38	79	236	297	-61	191
Northern Premier League Premier Division	7	379	195	81	103	723	479	+244	666
Northern Premier League Division One North	8	42	24	9	9	91	49	+42	81
North West Counties League Division One	9	42	36	4	2	157	36	+121	112
North West Counties League Division Two	10	36	27	6	3	111	35	+76	87
FA Cup	1-10	52	26	11	15	108	80	+28	
FA Trophy	5-8	43	21	7	15	82	67	+15	
FA Vase	9-10	4	3	0	1	11	6	+5	
Northern Premier League Premier Division Promotion Play-Offs	7	7	3	0	4	9	7	+2	
Northern Premier League Division One North Promotion Play-Offs	8	2	2	0	0	7	3	+4	
Northern Premier League Challenge Cup	7-8	16	6	2	8	23	27	-4	
Northern Premier League President's Cup	8	5	4	0	1	13	7	+6	
North West Counties League Challenge Cup	9-10	8	6	1	1	24	9	+15	
North West Counties League Division Two Trophy	10	2	1	0	1	5	1	+4	
Manchester FA Premier Cup	5-10	21	12	5	4	54	28	+26	
FENIX Trophy		5	5	0	0	23	3	+20	
TOTALS		832	422	164	246	1,677	1,134	+543	

League record by season:

Season	League	Position	Level	Pld	W	D	L	F	A	GD	Pts
2005/06	North West Counties League Division Two	1st ↑	10	36	27	6	3	111	35	+76	87
2006/07	North West Counties League Division One	1st ↑	9	42	36	4	2	157	36	+121	112
2007/08	Northern Premier League Division One North	2nd ↑	8	42	24	9	9	91	49	+42	81
2008/09	Northern Premier League Premier Division	6th	7	42	21	9	12	82	58	+24	72
2009/10	Northern Premier League Premier Division	13th	7	38	13	8	17	62	65	-3	47
2010/11	Northern Premier League Premier Division	4th	7	42	24	4	14	76	53	+23	76
2011/12	Northern Premier League Premier Division	6th	7	42	21	9	12	83	51	+32	72
2012/13	Northern Premier League Premier Division	3rd	7	42	25	8	9	86	48	+38	83
2013/14	Northern Premier League Premier Division	2nd	7	46	29	9	8	108	52	+56	96
2014/15	Northern Premier League Premier Division	1st ↑	7	46	26	14	6	78	37	+41	92
2015/16	National League North	13th	6	42	15	8	19	60	75	-15	53
2016/17	National League North	13th	6	42	14	12	16	69	68	+1	54
2017/18	National League North	16th	6	42	14	8	20	58	72	-14	50
2018/19	National League North	21st ↓	6	42	8	10	24	49	82	-33	34
2019/20	Northern Premier League Premier Division*	2nd	7	32	16	9	7	73	51	+22	57
2020/21	Northern Premier League Premier Division*	13th	7	7	2	4	1	9	7	+2	10
2021/22	Northern Premier League Premier Division	9th	7	42	18	7	17	66	57	+9	61
TOTALS				667	333	138	196	1,318	896	+422	1,137

*The 2019/20 season was formally abandoned on 26/03/2020 due to the coronavirus pandemic, and the 2020/21 season was curtailed on 24/02/2021 for the same reason.

Results summary by venue:

Ground		Seasons Played	LEAGUE				FA NATIONAL CUPS				OTHER CUPS / PLAY-OFFS				TOTALS			
			P	W	D	L	P	W	D	L	P	W	D	L	P	W	D	L
Broadhurst Park		2015/16 - 2021/22	125	49	29	47	20	9	3	8	8	4	2	2	153	62	34	57
Gigg Lane	(Bury FC)	2005/06 - 2013/14	167	106	25	36	23	11	3	9	7	5	0	2	197	122	28	47
Moss Lane	(Altrincham FC)	2005/06	1	1	0	0	0	0	0	0	0	0	0	0	1	1	0	0
Stainton Park	(Radcliffe Borough FC)	2007/08	1	1	0	0	1	0	0	1	2	1	0	1	4	2	0	2
Valley Road	(Flixton FC)	2007/08	0	0	0	0	0	0	0	0	1	1	0	0	1	1	0	0
Ewen Fields	(Hyde United FC)	2009/10	1	1	0	0	0	0	0	0	0	0	0	0	1	1	0	0
Bower Fold	(Stalybridge Celtic FC)	2010/11 - 2014/15	28	17	7	4	6	5	0	1	1	1	0	0	35	23	7	5
Tameside Stadium	(Curzon Ashton FC)	2011/12 - 2014/15	11	9	2	0	2	2	0	0	0	0	0	0	13	11	2	0
Wincham Park	(Witton Albion FC)	2013/14	0	0	0	0	1	0	0	1	0	0	0	0	1	0	0	1
		Home Total	334	184	63	87	53	27	6	20	19	12	2	5	406	223	71	112
Away Grounds	(135 different venues)	2005/06 - 2021/22	333	149	75	109	46	23	12	11	42	23	5	14	421	195	92	134
Neutral Grounds	(4 different venues)	2006/07 - 2021/22	0	0	0	0	0	0	0	0	5	4	1	0	5	4	1	0
		Overall Total	667	333	138	196	99	50	18	31	66	39	8	19	832	422	164	246

Most appearances:

Rank	Player	Seasons Played	LEAGUE Starts	(+Sub)	Total	FA NATIONAL CUPS Starts	(+Sub)	Total	OTHER CUPS / PLAY-OFFS Starts	(+Sub)	Total	TOTALS Starts	(+Sub)	Total
1	Jerome **Wright**	2006/07 - 2016/17 (10)	310	(+18)	328	48	(+1)	49	18	(+5)	23	376	(+24)	400
2	Matthew **Wolfenden**	2010/11 - 2016/17 (7)	213	(+38)	251	22	(+11)	33	17	(+4)	21	252	(+53)	305
3	Tom **Greaves**	2012/13 - 2018/19 (7)	156	(+74)	230	23	(+7)	30	7	(+7)	14	186	(+88)	274
4	Simon **Carden**	2005/06 - 2010/11 (6)	161	(+38)	199	16	(+8)	24	13	(+7)	20	190	(+53)	243
5	Sam **Ashton**	2006/07 - 2010/11 (5)	184	(+0)	184	30	(+0)	30	17	(+0)	17	231	(+0)	231
=6	Dean **Stott**	2011/12 - 2015/16 (5)	169	(+5)	174	26	(+5)	31	15	(+1)	16	210	(+11)	221
=6	Mike **Norton**	2010/11 - 2015/16 (6)	151	(+21)	172	26	(+6)	32	13	(+4)	17	190	(+31)	221
8	David **Chadwick**	2005/06 - 2018/19 (8)	156	(+19)	175	16	(+2)	18	16	(+1)	16	188	(+22)	210
9	Carlos **Roca**	2008/09 - 2012/13 (5)	118	(+44)	162	29	(+6)	35	7	(+0)	7	154	(+50)	204
10	Nicky **Platt**	2006/07 - 2012/13 (6)	105	(+45)	150	22	(+5)	27	14	(+6)	20	141	(+56)	197
11	Lee **Neville**	2010/11 - 2014/15 (5)	131	(+14)	145	23	(+1)	24	13	(+2)	15	167	(+17)	184
12	Jake **Cottrell**	2009/10 - 2012/13 (4)	125	(+16)	141	26	(+3)	29	9	(+3)	12	160	(+22)	182
13	Rob **Nugent**	2005/06 - 2009/10 (5)	136	(+7)	143	10	(+7)	17	13	(+3)	16	159	(+17)	176
14	Greg **Daniels**	2012/13 - 2015/16 (5)	73	(+64)	137	14	(+6)	20	9	(+2)	11	96	(+72)	168
15	Dave **Carnell**	2013/14 - 2018/19 (5)	128	(+0)	128	22	(+0)	22	7	(+0)	7	157	(+0)	157
16	Kyle **Jacobs**	2009/10 - 2012/13 (4)	105	(+7)	112	22	(+0)	22	10	(+0)	10	137	(+7)	144
17	Luke **Ashworth**	2014/15 - 2018/19 (4)	114	(+1)	115	21	(+0)	21	6	(+0)	6	141	(+1)	142
18	Rory **Patterson**	2005/06 - 2015/16 (4)	97	(+14)	111	6	(+2)	8	17	(+1)	18	120	(+17)	137
19	Liam **Brownhill**	2013/14 - 2015/16 (3)	107	(+2)	109	17	(+0)	17	4	(+3)	7	128	(+5)	133
20	Dave **Birch**	2012/13 - 2015/16 (4)	78	(+11)	89	14	(+6)	20	9	(+1)	10	101	(+18)	119
=21	Scott **Kay**	2015/16 - 2018/19 (4)	103	(+0)	103	10	(+0)	10	5	(+0)	5	118	(+0)	118
=21	Michael **Donohue**	2018/19 - 2021/22 (4)	66	(+23)	89	14	(+5)	19	10	(+0)	10	90	(+28)	118
23	Michael **Potts**	2018/19 - 2021/22 (4)	82	(+9)	91	19	(+0)	19	4	(+3)	7	105	(+12)	117
24	Adam **Jones**	2011/12 - 2013/14 (3)	84	(+1)	85	15	(+0)	15	7	(+0)	7	106	(+1)	107
25	Craig **Lindfield**	2014/15 - 2017/18 (3)	61	(+20)	81	15	(+3)	18	3	(+1)	4	79	(+24)	103
26	Ben **Deegan**	2009/10 - 2011/12 (3)	40	(+34)	74	16	(+7)	23	3	(+2)	5	59	(+43)	102
27	James **Spencer**	2011/12 - 2013/14 (3)	82	(+0)	82	14	(+0)	14	5	(+0)	5	101	(+0)	101
=28	Regan **Linney**	2019/20 - 2021/22 (3)	66	(+8)	74	16	(+2)	18	4	(+4)	8	86	(+14)	100
=28	Aaron **Morris**	2019/20 - 2021/22 (3)	76	(+0)	76	17	(+1)	18	6	(+0)	6	99	(+1)	100

Most appearances in each starting shirt number:

No.	Games	Player	Games	Player
1	231	Sam **Ashton**	157	Dave **Carnell**
2	132	Kyle **Jacobs**	107	Liam **Brownhill**
3	156	Lee **Neville**	95	Adam **Dodd**
4	95	Scott **Kay**	84	Nicky **Platt**
5	185	David **Chadwick**	97	Adam **Jones**
6	130	Rob **Nugent**	130	Luke **Ashworth**
7	187	Matthew **Wolfenden**	128	Carlos **Roca**
8	186	Simon **Carden**	79	Michael **Potts**
9	190	Mike **Norton**	144	Tom **Greaves**
10	369	Jerome **Wright**	35	Steve **Torpey**
11	111	Rory **Patterson**	69	Craig **Lindfield**
Sub	88	Tom **Greaves**	72	Greg **Daniels**
U/S	48	Tom **Brown**	42	Scott **Cheetham**

Most starting shirt numbers worn by individuals:

Player	Total	Shirts Worn
Nicky **Platt**	8	3 4 5 7 8 9 10 11
Richard **Battersby**	8	2 3 4 7 8 9 10 11
Greg **Daniels**	8	3 4 5 7 8 9 10 11
Tom **Brown**	7	3 4 5 6 7 8 10
Michael **Donohue**	7	2 4 7 8 9 10 11
Jamie **Baguley**	6	3 4 7 8 9 11
Jake **Cottrell**	6	3 4 7 8 9 11
Daniel **Grimshaw**	6	3 4 8 9 10 11
Dean **Stott**	6	2 3 4 5 6 10
Rory **Fallon**	6	3 7 8 9 10 11
Harry **Winter**	6	3 4 6 8 10 11
Paul **Ennis**	6	4 7 8 9 10 11

Higher numbers such as 13, 18, 19, 20 and 31 have also been worn when starting games. These are recorded as the 1-11 shirt that would typically have been worn.

Oldest players:

David Chadwick	43 years 47 days	Sub v Warrington Town (H, NPLP)	03/11/2020	
Darren Lyons	42 years 23 days	No.2 v Woodley Sports (A, NPLCC:3)	02/12/2008	(oldest in a starting line-up)
Adriano Basso	41 years 343 days	No.1 v Curzon Ashton (A, NLN)	27/03/2017	(oldest to start a league game)

Youngest players:

Jack Bennett	17 years 14 days	Sub v Morpeth Town (H, NPLP)	17/08/2021	
Sam Howell	17 years 37 days	Sub v Woodley Sports (H, FAC:Q1)	17/09/2011	
Scott Cheetham	17 years 101 days	Sub v Burscough (A, NPLP)	10/04/2010	
Sam Freakes	17 years 103 days	No.11 v Woodley Sports (A, NPLCC:3)	02/12/2008	(youngest in a starting line-up)
Ryan Schofield	17 years 118 days	No.1 v Bradford Park Avenue (A, NLN)	08/04/2017	(youngest to start a league game)

Highest goalscorers:

Rank	Player	League	FAC/FAT/FAV	Other Cups	Total	Seasons	Levels
1	Tom **Greaves**	87	10	6	103	2012/13 - 2018/19	6-7
2	Rory **Patterson**	84	4	11	99	2005/06 - 2015/16	8-10
3	Matthew **Wolfenden**	83	5	6	94	2010/11 - 2016/17	6-7
4	Mike **Norton**	70	15	8	93	2010/11 - 2015/16	7
5	Jerome **Wright**	70	7	5	82	2006/07 - 2016/17	6-9
6	Simon **Carden**	57	7	3	67	2005/06 - 2010/11	7-10
7	Stuart **Rudd**	44	3	7	54	2006/07 - 2007/08	8-9
8	Carlos **Roca**	33	9	0	42	2008/09 - 2012/13	7
9	Regan **Linney**	24	7	5	36	2019/20 - 2021/22	7
10	Tunde **Owolabi**	27	6	1	34	2019/20	7
11	George **Thomson**	26	3	3	32	2015/16 - 2016/17	6
12	Jason **Gilchrist**	21	3	5	29	2016/17 - 2017/18	6
=13	Kyle **Wilson**	25	3	0	28	2008/09 - 2009/10	7
=13	Greg **Daniels**	23	3	2	28	2012/13 - 2015/16	6-7
=13	Craig **Lindfield**	21	5	2	28	2014/15 - 2017/18	6-7
=13	Paul **Ennis**	16	7	5	28	2019/20 - 2021/22	7
17	Nicky **Platt**	15	8	3	26	2006/07 - 2013/14	7-9
18	Chris **Baguley**	17	0	8	25	2007/08 - 2008/09	7-8
19	David **Chadwick**	19	3	1	24	2005/06 - 2011/12	7-10
20	Ben **Deegan**	15	8	0	23	2009/10 - 2011/12	7
21	Dean **Stott**	14	4	4	22	2011/12 - 2015/16	7
22	Steve **Torpey**	16	0	5	21	2005/06 - 2011/12	7,10
=23	Kurt **Willoughby**	18	1	1	20	2018/19	6
=23	Adam **Jones**	16	3	1	20	2011/12 - 2013/14	7

Leading goalscorers per competition:

Level	Competition	Top Goalscorer
6	National League North	26 George **Thomson**
7	Northern Premier League Premier Division	70 Mike **Norton**
8	Northern Premier League Division One North	33 Rory **Patterson**
9	North West Counties League Division One	37 Stuart **Rudd**
10	North West Counties League Division Two	18 Rory **Patterson**
1-10	FA Cup	9 Mike **Norton**
5-8	FA Trophy	6 Mike **Norton** / Tunde **Owolabi**
9-10	FA Vase	3 Stuart **Rudd** / Simon **Carden**
7-8	Northern Premier League Promotion Play-Offs	3 Jerome **Wright**
7-8	Northern Premier League Challenge Cup	5 Mike **Norton**
8	Northern Premier League President's Cup	5 Chris **Baguley**
9-10	North West Counties League Challenge Cup	5 Rory **Patterson**
10	North West Counties League Division Two Trophy	3 Steve **Torpey**
5-10	Manchester FA Premier Cup	5 Tom **Greaves** / Jason **Gilchrist**
	FENIX Trophy	4 Regan **Linney**

Most goals in each shirt:

No.	Player	Goals
1	Sam **Ashton**	1
2	Dean **Stott**	7
3	Greg **Daniels**	10
4	Nicky **Platt**	11
5	David **Chadwick**	20
6	Rob **Nugent**	18
7	Matthew **Wolfenden**	57
8	Simon **Carden**	63
9	Mike **Norton**	91
10	Jerome **Wright**	78
11	Rory **Patterson**	89
Sub	Tom **Greaves**	16

Most hat-tricks:
7 Rory Patterson
4 Tom Greaves
4 Tunde Owolabi
4 Stuart Rudd
3 Matthew Wolfenden
2 Simon Carden
2 Regan Linney
2 Kyle Wilson

Most consecutive scoring appearances:
7 matches: **Tunde Owolabi** from 12/10/2019 to 12/11/2019

Fastest goal:
Kyle Wilson, 14 seconds v Witton Albion (H, NPLP), 04/10/2008

Oldest goalscorer:
Phil Power   40 years 263 days   Sub v Colne (A, NWCFL1)   14/04/2017

Youngest goalscorers:
Matthew Tierney   18 years 40 days   No.4 v Ashton United (A, NPLCC:3)   22/11/2010
Cian Hayes   18 years 124 days   No.11 v Witton Albion (A, NPLP)   23/10/2021   (youngest league goalscorer)